Learning and Teaching

Research-Based Methods

SIXTH EDITION

Don Kauchak

University of Utah

Paul Eggen

University of North Florida

PEARSON

Boston   Columbus   Indianapolis   New York   San Francisco   Upper Saddle River
Amsterdam   Cape Town   Dubai   London   Madrid   Milan   Munich   Paris   Montreal   Toronto
Delhi   Mexico City   Sao Paulo   Sydney   Hong Kong   Seoul   Singapore   Taipei   Tokyo

Senior Acquisition Editor: Kelly Villella Canton
Editorial Assistant: Annalea Manalili
Senior Marketing Manager: Darcy Betts
Production Editor: Renata Butera
Editorial Production Service: Integra Software Services Pvt. Ltd.
Manufacturing Buyer: Renata Butera
Electronic Composition: Integra Software Services Pvt. Ltd.
Interior Design: SD Graphics/Debbie Schneck
Photo Researcher: Annie Pickert
Cover Designer: Suzanne Duda

Library of Congress Cataloging-in-Publication Data
Kauchak, Donald P.
    Learning and teaching : research-based methods / Don Kauchak, Paul Eggen.
— 6th ed.
      p. cm.
    ISBN-13: 978-0-13-217934-8 (alk. paper)
    ISBN-10: 0-13-217934-2 (alk. paper)
    1. Teaching. 2. Effective teaching. I. Eggen, Paul D., 1940- II. Title.
LB1025.3.K38 2012
371.102—dc22

                                                2010043486

10 9 8 7 6 5 4 3 2 1 [EB] 14 13 12 11

Photo Credits:
Page 1, Bob Daemmrich Photography; p. 31, iStockPhoto; p. 71, Bob Daemmrich Photography; p. 105, Bob Daemmrich Photography; p. 142, Shutterstock; p. 175, Annie Pickert/Pearson Education; p. 206, iStockPhoto; p. 245, Pearson Scott Foresman; p. 279, Annie Pickert/Pearson Education; p. 306, Annie Pickert/Pearson Education; p. 336, Shutterstock; p. 378, Annie Pickert/Pearson Education; p. 407, Annie Pickert/Pearson Education.

www.pearsonhighered.com

ISBN-10:   0-13-217934-2
ISBN-13: 978-0-13-217934-8

About the Authors

DON KAUCHAK
Don has taught and worked in schools and in higher education in nine different states for 35 years. He has published in a number of scholarly journals, including the *Journal of Educational Research, Journal of Teacher Education, Teaching and Teacher Education, Phi Delta Kappan,* and *Educational Leadership.* In addition to this text he has co-authored or co-edited six other books on education. He has also been a principal investigator on federal and state grants examining teacher development and evaluation practices and presents regularly at the American Educational Research Association. He currently volunteers as a tutor for first, second, and third graders in a local elementary school.

Don strongly believes in the contribution that public schools make to our democracy, and his two children benefited greatly from their experiences in state-supported K–12 schools and public institutions of higher education.

PAUL EGGEN
Paul has worked in higher education for 38 years. He is a consultant for public schools and colleges in his university service area and has provided support to teachers in 12 states. Paul has also worked with teachers in international schools in 23 countries in Africa, South Asia, the Middle East, Central America, South America, and Europe. He has published several articles in national journals, is the co-author or co-editor of six other books, and presents regularly at national and international conferences.

Paul is strongly committed to public education. His wife is a middle school teacher in a public school, and his two children are graduates of public schools and state universities.

Contents

Chapter 4
Planning for Learning   105

Chapter 5
Effective Teaching   142

Preface

Teachers make an enormous difference in classrooms, and this book is designed to help you become a better teacher. The knowledge base for teaching continues to expand, confirming the powerful influence that teachers have on students and the importance of knowledge for effective teaching (Alexander, 2006). Research also continues to highlight the central role teachers play in determining the quality of learning in classrooms (Darling-Hammond & Bransford, 2005). Teachers *do* make a difference in how much students learn, and this difference depends on how they teach (Bransford, Darling-Hammond, & LePage, 2005). Teachers' powerful influence on learning is even more convincingly documented in the research literature today than it was in 1989, when the first edition of this text was published. Translating this research into teaching strategies that teachers can use to increase learning in their classrooms continues to be the central goal of this text.

New to This Edition

- New Chapter: Chapter 12, Differentiating Instruction
- New Feature: **Exploring Diversity**, found in every chapter including the following topics ition:
    - The Diversity of Our Learners (Chapter 1)
    - Urban Schools and At-risk Students (Chapter 2)
    - Personalizing Content to Increase Motivation in Students from Diverse Backgrounds (Chapter 4)
    - Direct Instruction with Culturally and Linguistically Diverse Students (Chapter 8)
    - Differences in Background Knowledge (Chapter 9)
    - Using Guided Discovery with Cultural Minorities (Chapter 10)
    - Problem-Based Instruction with Developmentally Different Learners (Chapter 11)
    - Effective Assessment with Learners from Diverse Backgrounds (Chapter 13)
- New Feature: **Technology and Teaching**, found in every chapter, including the following topics:
    - Using Technology to Increase Student Learning (Chapter 1)
    - Using Technology to Communicate with Parents (Chapter 3)
    - Using Technology to Plan (Chapter 4)
    - Using Technology to Create Lesson Focus (Chapter 5)
    - Using Technology to Increase Student Involvement (Chapter 6)

- Capitalizing on Technology in Direct Instruction (Chapter 8)
- Using Technology to Structure and Organize Content (Chapter 9)
- Using Databases in Guided Discovery Lessons (Chapter 10)

This book connects two areas in education. One is the research on how teaching influences learning, which includes a wide range of studies conducted since the early 1970s. Originally grounded in the research on effective teaching, this literature has expanded to include topics such as teacher and student thinking, constructivist views of learning, teaching for understanding, and the importance of social interaction in learning.

Teaching methodology is the second area addressed in this book. To be usable research findings need to be translated into teaching strategies that teachers can readily apply in their classrooms. This edition combines the best of these two areas. We apply the research on teaching to strategies that are theoretically sound, yet practical and usable.

Goals of This Text

We have two goals in combining these areas:

- To influence how teachers think about teaching
- To expand and improve their instructional strategies

The way teachers think and what they know are two major factors that influence how they actually teach. And, the way teachers think depends on what they know; in other words teacher thinking and teacher knowledge are interdependent. To meet our goals, this book helps teachers acquire the professional knowledge that influences both their thinking and the way they actually teach in their classrooms.

Without the research to provide a conceptual foundation methods become mechanical applications of rules implemented without understanding. Without practical suggestions for teaching practice the research literature remains abstract and irrelevant. In this sixth edition we again try to avoid both pitfalls by emphasizing the theoretical and conceptual underpinnings of the research and the implications of this research for classroom practice.

Text Themes

Today's schools are changing and these changes present both opportunities and challenges. To address these changes we have organized the sixth edition around three powerful and pervasive forces in education. These forces are translated into three themes that are integrated and applied throughout the text:

- *Standards and accountability*
- The *diversity* of our learners
- The use of *technology* to increase student learning

Standards and accountability are reshaping the ways teachers teach and students learn. Every state has created standards to guide student learning, and there is a movement to create national standards in areas such as reading and math. To respond to this movement, we have made standards and accountability a major theme for this text. We introduce the theme in Chapter 1 and relate the process of teacher planning to it in Chapter 4. In addition, we discuss how standards influence assessment as well as the implementation of specific teaching strategies in later chapters. The diversity of our learners, the second theme for this text, reflects the growing diversity of our classrooms. This diversity has important implications for the way we teach. In addition to an entire chapter on diversity (Chapter 2) and a new chapter on differentiating instruction (Chapter 12), we also address the topic of diversity in a feature, **Exploring Diversity,** found in every chapter.

Chapter 1: The Diversity of our Learners

Chapter 2: Urban Schools and At-risk Students

Chapter 3: Challenges to Home-School Communication

Chapter 4: Personalizing Content to Increase Motivation in Students from Diverse Backgrounds

Chapter 5: Teacher Attitudes and Learner Diversity

Chapter 6: Involving Students from Diverse Backgrounds

Chapter 7: Using Cooperative Learning to Capitalize on Diversity

Chapter 8: Direct Instruction with Culturally and Linguistically Diverse Students

Chapter 9: Differences in Background Knowledge

Chapter 10: Using Guided Discovery with Cultural Minorities

Chapter 11: Problem-Based Instruction with Developmentally Different Learners

Chapter 12: Entire chapter focuses on differentiating instruction

Chapter 13: Effective Assessment with Learners from Diverse Backgrounds

Technology is the third theme of this edition. Technology is changing the way we live, as well as the way we learn and teach. Various forms of technology, including white boards, document cameras, computers, and the Internet are all changing our classrooms. Tomorrow's teachers need to know how to integrate technology into their teaching. We address applications of technology in the feature, **Technology and Teaching,** found in every chapter.

Chapter 1: Using Technology to Increase Student Learning

Chapter 2: Employing Technology to Support Learners with Disabilities

Chapter 3: Using Technology to Communicate with Parents

Chapter 4: Using Technology to Plan

Chapter 5: Using Technology to Create Lesson Focus

Chapter 6: Using Technology to Increase Student Involvement

Chapter 7: Using Computer-Mediated Communication to Facilitate Cooperative Learning

Chapter 8: Capitalizing on Technology in Direct Instruction

Chapter 9: Using Technology to Structure and Organize Content

Chapter 10: Using Databases in Guided Discovery Lessons

Chapter 11: Using Technology as a Tool to Teach Problem Solving

Chapter 12: Technology as a Tool for Differentiating Instruction

Chapter 13: Using Technology in Assessment

We also added new sections on *Standards in Today's Schools, Professional Organizations' Standards, and National Standards* to help teachers understand how this reform will affect their teaching. These changes reflect the evolving realities of modern classrooms, as well as the new responsibilities today's teachers are being asked to undertake. In addition we have added feedback for our Preparing for Your Licensure Exam feature to help students master each chapter's content. We hope these changes in the sixth edition prepare you for the challenges of teaching in the twenty-first century.

Supplements

Instructor Manual/Test Bank

We've designed this manual to help you use *Learning and Teaching*, 6th edition, as effectively as possible. Many of the ideas contained in this manual come from years of using this text in our own classes as well as our continued work in the public schools. Others are the result of feedback and discussions we've had with teachers, students and our colleagues. We hope you find the suggestions useful.

The manual is organized by chapters. Each chapter contains chapter overview, objectives, chapter outlines, presentation outlines, multiple choice and short answer test items and an answer key. The presentation outline is organized in terms of the major topics in each chapter. Under these topics you will find teaching suggestions including ways to use large- and small-group activities, as well as ways to integrate the discussion questions and portfolio activities into your instruction. Following the presentation outline you'll find *Feedback for Preparing for Your Licensure Exam: Questions for Analysis* prior to the test items and answer key.

The power of classroom practice:

> Teacher educators who are developing pedagogies for the analysis of teaching and learning contend that analyzing teaching artifacts has three advantages: it enables new teachers time for reflection while still using the real materials of practice; it provides new teachers with experience thinking about and approaching the complexity of the classroom; and in some cases, it can help new teachers and teacher educators develop a shared understanding and common language about teaching. (Darling-Hammond & Bransford, 2005)

As Linda Darling-Hammond and her colleagues point out, grounding teacher education in real classrooms—among real teachers and students and among actual examples of students' and teachers' work—is an important, and perhaps even an essential, part of training teachers for the complexities of teaching in today's classrooms. For this reason we have created a valuable, timesaving website—MyEducationLab—that provides you with the context of real classrooms and artifacts that research on teacher education tells us are so important. The authentic in-class video footage, interactive skill-building exercises, and other resources available on MyEducationLab offer you a unique valuable teacher education tool.

MyEducationLab is easy to use and integrate into both your assignments and your courses. Wherever you see the MyEducationLab logo in the margins or elsewhere in the text, follow the simple instructions to access the videos, strategies, cases, and artifacts associated with these assignments, activities, and learning units. MyEducationLab is organized topically to enhance the coverage of the core concepts discussed in the chapters of your book. For each topic in the course you will find most or all of the following resources:

Connection to National Standards   Now it is easier than ever to see how your coursework is connected to national standards. In each topic of MyEducationLab you will find intended learning outcomes connected to the Interstate New Teacher Assessment and Support Consortium (INTASC) standards. All of the Assignments and Activities and all of the Building Teaching Skills and Dispositions in MyEducationLab are mapped to the appropriate national standards and learning outcomes as well.

Assignments and Activities   Designed to save instructors preparation time, these assignable exercises show concepts in action (through video, cases, or student and teacher artifacts) and then offer thought-provoking questions that probe your understanding of theses concepts or strategies. (Feedback for these assignments is available to the instructor.)

Building Teaching Skills and Dispositions   These learning units help you practice and strengthen skills that are essential to quality teaching. First you are presented with the core skill or concept and then given an opportunity to practice your understanding of it multiple times by watching video footage (or interacting with other media) and then critically analyzing the strategy or skill presented.

Video Examples   Intended to enhance coverage in your book with visual examples of real educators and students, these video clips (a number of which are referenced explicitly in this text) include segments from classroom lessons as well as interviews with teachers, administrators, students, and parents.

General Resources on Your MyEducationLab Course   The *Resources* section on your MyEducationLab course is designed to help you pass your licensure exam; put together an effective portfolio and lesson plan; prepare for and navigate the first year of your teaching career; and understand key educational standards, policies, and laws. This section includes the following:

- **Licensure Exams.** Access guidelines for passing the Praxis exam. The *Practice Test Exam* includes practice questions, *Case Histories*, and *Video Case Studies.*
- **Portfolio Builder and Lesson Plan Builder.** Create, update, and share portfolios and lesson plans.
- **Preparing a Portfolio.** Access guidelines for creating a high-quality teaching portfolio that will allow you to practice effective lesson planning.
- **Licensure and Standards.** Link to state licensure standards and national s tandards.
- **Beginning Your Career.** Educate yourself—access tips, advice, and valuable information on
    - **Resume Writing and Interviewing.** Expert advice on how to write impressive resumes and prepare for job interviews.

- **Your First Year of Teaching.** Practical tips to set up your classroom, manage student behavior, and learn to more easily organize for instruction and assessment.

- **Law and Public Policies.** Specific directives and requirements you need to understand under the No Child Left Behind Act and the Individuals with Disabilities Education Improvement Act of 2004.

Visit **www.myeducationlab.com** *for a demonstration of this exciting new online teaching resource and to download a MyEdLab guide correlating MEL course assets to this text.*

Acknowledgments

In preparing this edition of *Learning and Teaching*, we want to sincerely thank the people who have supported its development. We want to particularly thank our editor, Kelly Villella Canton, for her guidance, support, and cooperation as we attempted to implement a number of new ideas for this edition. She epitomizes what authors look for in an editor. We also want to thank Annalea Manalili and Paula Carroll for their help in bringing the project to fruition, as well as our reviewers: Norbet O. Aneke, City University of New York; Christine K. Lemley, Northern Arizona University; Janet Schiavone, George Washington University; and Alice M. Waddell, Mary Baldwin College.

Finally, we again want to thank the many teachers in whose classrooms we've worked and visited, and on whose instruction the case studies in the book are based. They helped make this text more real and true to the realities of classroom life.

P.E.

D.K.

Learning to Teach

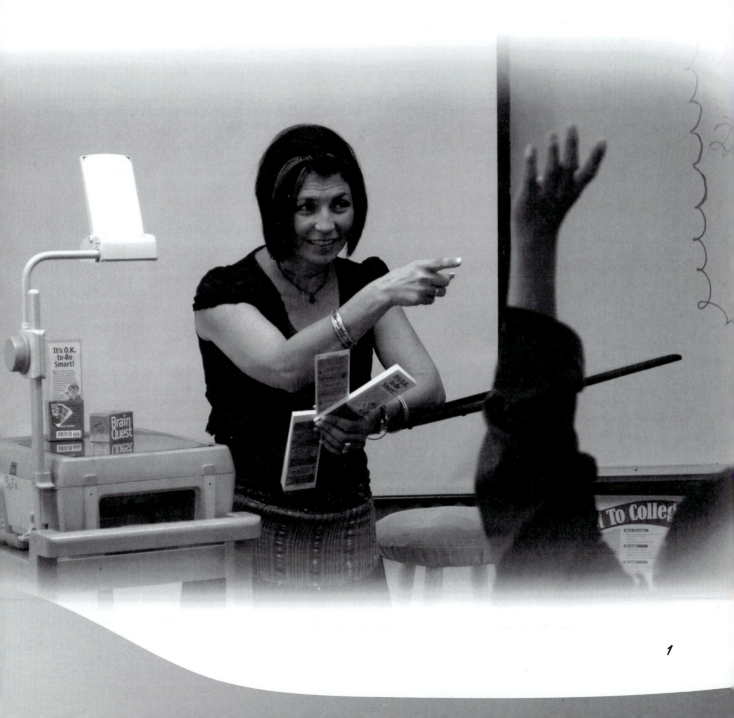

Chapter Outline	Learning Objectives
	When you've completed your study of this chapter, you should be able to
Defining good teaching	1. Define effective teaching and explain how it influences learning.
The search for effective teaching ■ Teacher characteristics and the search for the right method ■ Teacher effectiveness research: Teacher *do* make a difference? ■ Understanding effective teaching: A focus on student learning	2. Describe the search for a definition of good teaching.
Contemporary views of teaching and learning ■ From behaviorist to cognitive perspectives ■ Constructivism: Students as creators of understanding	3. Describe different views of learning and explain how they influence teaching.
Text themes ■ Standards and accountability ■ Exploring Diversity: The diversity of our learners ■ Technology and Teaching: Using technology to increase learning	4. Describe different ways that teachers can help students with exceptionalities succeed in their classrooms.
Learning to teach ■ The importance of knowledge in teaching ■ Teacher decision making ■ Educational reform ■ Learning to teach in an era of reform ■ Standards-based professional development ■ Developing a professional portfolio	5. Explain how the text themes–standards and accountability, diversity, and technology–influence classroom teaching and learning.
Using this book to learn to teach	6. Describe how to use this book to learn to teach.

This book focuses on effective teaching and the different ways teachers help students learn. Next to the students themselves, teachers are the most important influence on student success (Marzano, 2007). This chapter begins by examining effective teaching, and what you can do to help your students learn. In this chapter we also describe the different components of learning to teach, including the different forms of professional knowledge that contribute to teacher expertise. In addition, we describe how decision making integrates this knowledge into purposeful teacher actions.

Finally, in this chapter we introduce three themes that run through this text: standards and accountability, diversity, and technology. Standards and accountability are reshaping classrooms and influencing teacher decision making in myriad ways, ranging from planning to instruction to assessment. We describe how standards influence each of these dimensions of teaching in later chapters.

Exploring diversity, the second text theme and a feature in every chapter, examines how different forms of diversity influence classroom teaching. *Technology and Teaching*, a third text theme and an additional feature found in chapters, describes how teachers can use technology to increase student learning.

To begin our discussion, let's look in on a group of teachers talking about their students. As you read the vignette, think about your own definition of effective teaching and how you plan to help your students learn.

Three middle school teachers are eating lunch together on their 40-minute break between classes. After weather and local politics, the conversation turns to teaching, or, more specifically, to students.

"How are your seventh graders this year?" Paul Escobar asks. "I can't seem to get them motivated."

Stan Williams replies with a frown. "I've got three basic math classes, and I've spent the first two months reviewing stuff they're supposed to know already. They don't seem to want to think," he concludes, turning to the others with an exasperated look.

"Mine aren't so bad," Leona Foster replies. "In fact, the other day we had a great discussion on individual rights. We were discussing the Bill of Rights, and I got them to think about their rights and responsibilities in our school. Some of them actually got excited about it. And it was even one of my slower classes. I was impressed with some of their comments."

"But how am I going to get them to think if they don't even know how to multiply or divide?" Stan answers in frustration.

"I know what you're talking about, Stan," Paul interjects. "I'm supposed to teach them to write, but they don't even know basic grammar. How am I supposed to teach them subject-verb agreement when they don't know what a noun or verb is?"

"Exactly!" Stan answers. "We've got to teach them basics before we can teach them all the other stuff, like problem solving and thinking skills."

"Hmmm. . . . It might be more complicated than that," Paul replies. "I had a real eye-opener the other day. . . . Let me tell you about it. I've been going to workshops on using writing teams to teach composition. I tried it out, putting high- and low-ability students on the same team. They were supposed to write a critical review of a short story we had read, using television movie critics as a model. We talked a little about basic concepts like *plot* and *action* and watched a short clip of two movie critics arguing about a movie. Then I turned them loose. I couldn't believe it—some of the kids who never participate actually got excited."

"That's all fine and good for English classes, but I'm a math teacher. What am I supposed to do, have them critique math problems? Oh, I give this math problem two thumbs up! Besides, these are supposed to be middle school students. I shouldn't have to sugarcoat the content. They should come ready to learn. My job is to teach; theirs is to learn. It's as simple as that."

Defining Good Teaching

"It's as simple as that," . . .or is it? Teaching has always been a challenging profession, but changes both within and outside classrooms have made it even more challenging. Teachers are being asked to teach thinking and problem-solving skills at the same time that students come from increasingly diverse backgrounds. Both students and teachers are being held accountable by standards and high-stakes testing. Your personal definition of good or effective teaching is becoming not only more crucial but also more complex.

But, what is effective teaching? How does effective teaching relate to learning? What responsibilities do teachers have to motivate their students? What are the implications of student diversity on the teaching/learning process? And, how can you use new technologies to promote learning?

These are important questions for teachers because they center on the question "What is good teaching?" These concerns are particularly important to developing teachers because your answers to these questions will influence the kind of teacher you become. As you ponder these questions, thinking about yourself and the classrooms you've experienced, each of you will construct a personal definition of effective teaching. This individual response is as it should be: each teacher is as unique as each student. But beyond this individual uniqueness, some strands exist that pull these questions together.

Let's consider these commonalities a bit further. Does your definition of effective teaching apply to all levels? For example, are there similarities in the ways effective kindergarten and high school teachers instruct? What about students? Would your definition of good teaching apply equally well to low- and high-ability learners? And, how about subject matter? Does an effective history teacher teach the same way as an effective English or art teacher? Finally, how does time influence your definition? Do effective teachers teach the same way at the beginning of the school year as at its close, at the beginning of a unit as at the end, or even at the beginning of a lesson and at its completion?

Each of you will wrestle with these questions, either implicitly or explicitly, as you begin and continue your teaching career. The purpose of this book is to help you resolve these questions based on the best information available to the profession.

The field of teaching is at a particularly exciting time in its history. Education has always been one of the most rewarding professions, but at the same time, it continues to be one of the most challenging. An effective teacher combines the best of human relations, intuition, sound judgment, knowledge of subject matter, and knowledge of how people learn—all in one simultaneous act. This task is extremely complex, and one of the factors making it particularly difficult has been the lack of a clear and documented body of knowledge on which to base professional decisions.

The situation has changed. Education now has a significant and rapidly expanding body of research that can guide your teaching practice. That's what this text is all about; it is a book about teaching practice that is based on research. As you study the chapters, you will be exposed to this detailed body of research, and you will learn how this research can be applied in your classroom to increase student learning.

We developed this text around a series of themes that will be introduced in this chapter. As your study continues, you will see how research helps teachers as they make their professional decisions. This research, as with all research, is not perfect, but having it as a foundation is a giant step forward (Richardson, 2001). This research marks a major advance in education and is already finding its way into tests used to certify teachers (Educational Testing Service, 2008), and into both preservice and inservice programs for teachers. Your study of this text will provide you with the best information available to the profession at this time.

*T*he Search for Effective Teaching

Historically, teaching has been a profession in search of a body of knowledge that could inform classroom practice. In the past, educators often looked to teacher characteristics to guide them, as we'll see in the next section.

Teacher Characteristics and the Search for the Right Method

As researchers began to seek connections between teaching and learning, they initially focused on teacher characteristics, such as neatness, sense of humor, or cognitive flexibility (Rosenshine, 1979). Initial research asked whether teachers having these desirable traits resulted in increased learning. For example, do students taught by a teacher with a good sense of humor learn more and/or have better attitudes than those taught by a more serious teacher? Unfortunately the question was oversimplified; magnificent teachers of many different personalities can be found.

In hindsight, the research on teacher characteristics was not completely misguided. Two teacher characteristics—teacher experience and understanding of subject matter— have proved to be powerful variables influencing how teachers understand events in the classroom and explain content (Berliner, 1994; Shulman, 1987). Veteran teachers are able to use their experience to interpret the complex events that occur in classrooms and to make the many split-second professional decisions that are needed every day. Similarly, subject-matter expertise allows effective teachers to frame and explain ideas in ways that make sense to students. We will return to both of these ideas later in the chapter.

The next wave of research focused on global methods, attempting to link certain teaching strategies, such as inquiry instruction or discovery learning, with student outcomes, such as scores on standardized achievement tests (Dunkin & Biddle, 1974; Medley, 1979). This research was characterized by a belief that a particular type of teaching, such as discussion, was better than an alternative, such as lecture. To investigate this question, teachers were trained in a particular technique and then asked to teach their students by this method. The performance of their students was compared to the performance of students taught by an alternate method.

Like research on teacher characteristics, this line of research was also flawed. Researchers concluded that no one way of teaching was better than others and, instead, teachers required professional decision making to adjust their teaching methods to situational variables that included the students themselves as well as the content being taught.

Teacher Effectiveness Research: Teachers *Do* Make a Difference

As a consequence of the results or, more accurately, the *non*results of earlier efforts, research on teaching finally focused on teachers' actions in classrooms, attempting to find links between what teachers actually do in classrooms and student learning. These studies marked a new way of thinking about research in education. Unlike previous work, this research focused on the teacher and the kinds of interactions teachers had with students (Good & Brophy, 2008). Researchers identified teachers whose students scored higher than would be expected on standardized tests and other teachers whose students scored lower. They then went into classrooms, videotaped literally thousands of hours of instruction, and tried to determine what differences existed in the instruction of the teachers in the two samples. Because these efforts focused on *differences between less and more effective teachers, it became known as the* **teacher effectiveness research** (Good & Brophy, 2008). A number of significant differences were found, which we'll describe in later chapters.

Understanding Effective Teaching: A Focus on Student Learning

The effective teaching literature made an invaluable contribution to education because it both confirmed the critical role teachers like you play in student learning and provided teachers with a knowledge base to help them make their instructional decisions.

Despite impressive results, critics also identified a major shortcoming in the teacher effectiveness research—it identified strategies that effective teachers use in their classrooms but didn't explain why they worked. In essence, critics were reminding us that students and student learning should be our primary focus in teaching. These criticisms resulted in fundamental changes in our views of effective teaching methods, with a major shift from focusing solely on the teacher to also considering how students learn and how teachers could help.

Contemporary Views of Teaching and Learning

At the same time that perspectives on teaching were changing, similar changes were occurring in the way researchers viewed learners and learning (Bransford, Brown, & Cocking, 2000). Behaviorist views of learning, which emphasized external influences in the form of rewards and punishment, gradually gave way to more cognitive perspectives. These cognitive perspectives emphasized students' use of strategies to organize, store, and retrieve information (Bruning et al., 2004). More recently, research has emphasized the critical role that learners play in constructing new knowledge (Eggen & Kauchak, 2010). We analyze these changes in the sections that follow.

From Behaviorist to Cognitive Perspectives

For the first half of the twentieth century, behaviorist views of learning predominated in education. **Behaviorism** *emphasized the importance of observable, external events on learning and the role of reinforcers in influencing student learning.* The goal of behaviorism was to determine how external instructional manipulations effected changes in student behavior. The teacher's role was to control the environment through stimuli in the form of cues and reinforcement for appropriate student behavior. Students were viewed as empty receptacles, responding passively to stimuli from the teacher and the classroom environment.

Over time educators found this perspective on learning to be oversimplified and perhaps misdirected. Although learners do indeed react to stimuli from the environment,

Table 1.1 Comparison of Behaviorist and Cognitive Views of Learning

	View of Learning	View of Learner	View of Teacher
Behaviorist	Accumulation of responses through selective reinforcement	Passive recipient of stimuli from environment	Controller of stimuli and shaper of behaviors through reinforcement
Cognitive	Development of strategies to encode and retrieve information	Active meaning maker through strategy use	Partner in the process of meaning making; teacher of organizational and retrieval strategies

research revealed that students were not passive recipients, but instead actively changed and altered stimuli as they attempted to make sense of teacher lessons. Student characteristics such as background knowledge, motivation, and the use of learning strategies all influenced learning (Bruning et al., 2004). The role of the teacher also changed from dispenser of rewards and punishment to that of someone who helped students organize and make sense of information. These differences between behaviorism and **cognitive psychology,** *which focuses on thought processes within learners*, are summarized in Table 1.1.

Constructivism: Students as Creators of Understanding

Recently, constructivism—a recent development in cognitive psychology—has focused our attention on the central role that learners play in constructing new knowledge. Influenced by the work of Jean Piaget (1952, 1959) and Lev Vygotsky (1978, 1986), as well as the work of linguists and anthropologists, **constructivism** *is a view of learning that emphasizes four key components:*

1. *Learners construct their own understanding rather than having it delivered or transmitted to them.*
2. *New learning depends on prior understanding and knowledge.*
3. *Learning is enhanced by social interaction.*
4. *Authentic learning tasks promote meaningful learning.*

Constructivism has fundamentally changed the way we view teaching and learning. As opposed to passive recipients of information, learners become active meaning-makers, building upon their current knowledge. To facilitate the process, teachers design learning activities in which learners can work with others on meaningful learning tasks. Many of the teaching strategies that you'll learn about in this text are based upon constructivist views of learners and learning.

In addition to these broad, general changes in views about teaching and learning, content-specific ones have also arisen. The National Council for the Teaching of Mathematics (NCTM) has developed guidelines that stress student involvement in meaningful problem-solving activities (NCTM, 1991, 2000). Those in the field of science have also published guidelines that call for deeper, more thoughtful, and intensive study of science topics (American Association for the Advancement of Science, 1993).

Common to all of these is refocused attention on the learner and what teachers can do to help students learn.

These changes make this an exciting time to study education and become a teacher. Researchers are uncovering a number of links between teacher actions and student achievement. Because of this research, and other related research, our views of teacher expertise and professional development have changed. Our goal in preparing this text is to communicate these findings and their implications to prospective teachers and practicing teachers in the classroom.

*T*ext Themes

In response to recent developments in education, three themes appear throughout the text:

- *Standards* and *accountability*
- The *diversity* of our learners
- The use of *technology* for increasing learning

Because these topics influence so many different aspects of teaching, they are integrated throughout the text. Let's examine them briefly.

Standards and Accountability

Standards, *statements that describe what students should know or be able to do at the end of a period of study* (McCombs, 2005), have become a major influence on teachers' lives. Standards, together with **accountability,** *the process of requiring students to demonstrate mastery of the topics they study as well as holding teachers responsible for this learning,* have changed the ways teachers plan, instruct, and assess student learning.

The "standards movement" is commonly traced to the publication of *A Nation at Risk: The Imperative for Educational Reform,* published by the National Commission on Excellence in Education (1983). This document famously stated:

> If an unfriendly foreign power had attempted to impose on America the mediocre educational performance that exists today, we might well have viewed it as an act of war. As it stands, we have allowed this to happen to ourselves. We have even squandered the gains in student achievement made in the wake of the Sputnik challenge. Moreover, we have dismantled essential support systems which helped make those gains possible. We have, in effect, been committing an act of unthinking, unilateral educational disarmament. (p. 9)

This report came at a time when other countries, such as Germany and Japan, were outcompeting us both industrially and educationally, and it struck a chord with leaders in this country; if we were to compete internationally, we had to have better schools. Standards together with accountability were one way to accomplish this.

Since 1983, a number of reform efforts have attempted to address the concerns raised by *A Nation at Risk.* The revised federal *Elementary and Secondary Education Act* (ESEA), enacted by the George W. Bush administration in 2001 was one of the most significant. Renamed the *No Child Left Behind* (NCLB) *Act*, the law asked America's schools to document their success in terms of the extent to which students could meet specified standards. No Child Left Behind has been controversial, but it and the standards movement in general have left a lasting legacy.

Standards are here to stay; since the turn of this century, every state in the nation has developed standards in different content areas, and there is currently a movement to institute standards at the national level (Finn & Petrilli, 2009). In addition, reformers are advocating the use standards-based assessments to evaluate teachers and using the results for decisions about teacher pay and retention in their jobs (McNeil, 2010). Standards are having a major impact on education and will play a major role in your future professional life.

Standards in Today's Schools Standards at the state level have been written for content areas ranging from core curriculum areas, such as reading, writing, math, and science to others less prominent, such as

- Physical education
- Fine arts
- Economics
- Agricultural science
- Business education
- Technology applications
- Trade and industrial education
- Spanish language arts and English as a second language

Even this list is not exhaustive.

Let's look at several examples of state standards. Standards in different states are labeled in different ways, such as "Essential Knowledge and Skills" (Texas Education Agency, 2008a), "Learning Standards" (Illinois State Board of Education, 2008b), "Content Standards" (California State Board of Education, 2008a), or "Sunshine State Standards" (Florida Department of Education, 2007). Regardless of the labels, each state's standards describe what students should know or be able to do.

Since space doesn't allow us to list examples from every state, we're going to present representative samples for sake of illustration. For those of you reading this text who don't live in these states, you can easily access your own state's standards by clicking on the following link: http://www.education-world.com/standards/state/index.shtml. Then, click on the pull down menu and select your state.

How do standards from different states appear? The following is an example in fourth-grade math from the state of Texas (Texas Education Agency, 2008b).

(4.2) Number, operation, and quantitative reasoning. The student describes and compares fractional parts of whole objects or sets of objects
    The student is expected to:
    (A) use concrete objects and pictorial models to generate equivalent fractions.

The number (4.2) identifies this as the second standard in the list of fourth-grade standards in math, and the letter (A) describes what students should be able to do to meet this standard. Different states code their standards in different ways, but all are designed to describe learning and assessment targets for teachers and students.

As another example, the following standard comes from the state of Illinois in middle school science (Illinois State Board of Education, 2008a).

Illinois Science Assessment Framework
Standard 12F— Astronomy (Grade 7)
   12.7.91 Understanding that objects in the solar system are for the most part in regular and predictable motion. Know that those motions explain such phenomena as the day, the year, the phases of the moon, and eclipses.

Although the way the standard is coded is different from the coding used in Texas, both describe what students should know or be able to do.

Standards can also target important outcomes in secondary language arts. For example, consider the following example from the state of Florida (Florida Department of Education, 2009):

The student understands the common features of a variety of literary forms. (LA.E.1.4)

1. identifies the characteristics that distinguish literary forms.
2. understands why certain literary works are considered classics.

This standard is broader and more abstract, but it is still designed to guide both teachers and students in the classroom.

Professional organizations have also weighed in on the need for standards in education. Let's take a look.

Professional Organizations' Standards   Professional organizations are designed to provide leadership in different areas of education. Many professional organizations, such as the *National Council of Teachers of Mathematics* (NCTM, 2008), the *National Council of Teachers of English* (International Reading Association & National Council of Teachers of English, 2008), and others that focus on science, social studies, early childhood education, special education, the arts, health education, and bilingual education also have produced standards that shape teachers' lives. For example, the following are examples from the NCTM (2008). (These are only samples for pre-K–2 and grades 6–8; you can access standards for grades 3–5 and 9–12 together with complete lists online at www.nctm.org.)

Number and Operations Standard
Instructional programs from prekindergarten through grade 12 should enable all students to—

■ Compute fluently and make reasonable estimates.

Pre-K–2 Expectations
In prekindergarten through grade 2 all students should—

■ Develop and use strategies for whole-number computations, with a focus on addition and subtraction.
■ Develop fluency with basic number combinations for addition and subtraction.

Grades 6–8 Expectations
In grades 6–8 all students should—

■ Select appropriate methods and tools for computing with fractions and decimals from among mental computation, estimation, calculators or computers, and paper and pencil, depending on the situation, and apply the selected methods.

■ Develop and analyze algorithms for computing with fractions, decimals, and integers and develop fluency in their use.

A number of other professional organizations have also prepared standards to guide teachers' instructional efforts and these, plus their websites, are found in Table 1.2.

National Standards   In addition to state standards and standards from professional organizations, national standards are also being proposed (Gewertz, 2010). The Common Core State Standards Initiative, sponsored by the National Governors Association and the Council of Chief State School Officers, recently published a draft of national standards in language arts and math.

Table 1.2   Professional Organizations for Educators

Organization and Web Address	Organization Mission or Goal
American Council on the Teaching of Foreign Languages http://www.actfl.org	To promote and foster the study of languages and cultures as an integral component of American education and society
American Federation of Teachers http://www.aft.org	To improve the lives of our members and their families; to give voice to their legitimate professional, economic, and social aspirations
Association for Supervision and Curriculum Development http://www.ascd.org	To enhance all aspects of effective teaching and learning, including professional development, educational leadership, and capacity building
Council for Exceptional Children http://www.cec.sped.org	To improve educational outcomes for individuals with exceptionalities, students with disabilities, and/or the gifted
International Reading Association http://www.reading.org	To promote high levels of literacy for all by improving reading instruction, disseminating research and information about reading, and encouraging the lifetime reading habit
Music Teachers National Association http://www.mtna.org/flash.html	To advance the value of music study and music making to society and to support the professionalism of music teachers
National Art Education Association http://www.naea-reston.org	To promote art education through professional development, service, advancement of knowledge, and leadership
National Education Association http://www.nea.org	To fulfill the promise of a democratic society, NEA shall promote the cause of quality public education and advance the profession of education
National Science Teachers Association http://www.nsta.org	To promote excellence and innovation in science teaching and learning for all
National Council for the Social Studies http://www.ncss.org	To provide leadership, service, and support for all social studies educators
National Council of Teachers of English http://www.ncte.org	To promote the development of literacy, the use of language to construct personal and public worlds and to achieve full participation in society, through the learning and teaching of English and the related arts and sciences of language.
National Council of Teachers of Mathematics http://www.nctm.org	To provide broad national leadership in matters related to mathematics education
National Association for Bilingual Education http://www.nabe.org	To recognize, promote, and publicize bilingual education

(continued)

Table 1.2 Continued

Organization and Web Address	Organization Mission or Goal
Phi Delta Kappa http://www.pdkintl.org	To promote quality education as essential to the development and maintenance of a democratic way of life by providing innovative programs, relevant research, visionary leadership, and dedicated service
Teachers of English to Speakers of Other Languages http://www.tesol.org	To improve the teaching of English as a second language by promoting research, disseminating information, developing guidelines and promoting certification, and serving as a clearinghouse for the field

As you can see from Table 1.3, the format for these standards is not dramatically different from existing state standards. In addition, the content of these standards does not differ significantly from that found in state standards. This is not surprising, since drafters of the national standards, in an effort to gain widespread support, made a special effort to match their standards to existing state guidelines.

However, these standards are drafts, and their final form and whether they will be adopted at all will be determined by individual states. And critics abound (Cavanaugh, 2010; Gewertz, 2010). Foremost among these is the fear that national standards will result in a national curriculum and national accountability tests. This fear is especially prominent among advocates for state's rights, who are concerned about greater federal control over their lives. In addition, other critics question these standards' rigor and whether they emphasize critical thinking at the expense of subject matter content.

Table 1.3 Proposed National Standards

Grade 1

Language Arts
1. Ask and answer questions about key details and events in a text.
2. Identify who is speaking at various points in a story, myth, fable, or narrative poem.

Math
1. Read and write numbers to 100.
2. Understand that addition and subtraction apply to situations of adding to, taking from, putting together, taking apart, and comparing.

Grade 4

Language Arts
1. Determine the main idea of supporting details of a text; summarize the text.
2. Describe in detail a character, event, or setting, drawing on specific details in the text.

Math
1. Understand that a digit in one place represents ten times what it represents in the place to its right.
2. Solve multistep word problems involving the four operations with whole numbers.

Source: Common Core State Standards Initiative, 2010.

Exploring Diversity

The Diversity of Our Learners

A second theme appearing throughout the text is student diversity. The students attending our classrooms are becoming increasingly diverse. For example, teachers will encounter students with a wide range of learning abilities. Inclusion, which attempts to accommodate the learning needs of all students in as regular an educational setting as possible, results in more students with exceptionalities in regular classrooms (Hardman, Drew, & Egan, 2008; Heward, 2009). About 10 percent of the student population is included in this group, and exceptionalities range from mild learning disabilities to physical disabilities such as deafness and blindness (U.S. Department of Education, 2004).

Ethnicity and culture also contribute to classroom diversity. Cultural minorities make up a third of the U.S. population, and the 2000 census indicated that, for the first time, the Hispanic surnames Garcia and Rodriguez are among the 10 most common in our country, having replaced Moore and Taylor in that category (Roberts, 2007).

This trend is reflected in our classrooms, where more than 4 of 10 students are members of cultural minorities. Children of color currently make up the majority of public school enrollments in six states—California, Hawaii, Louisiana, Mississippi, New Mexico, and Texas, and more than 90 percent of the student population in six major cities: Baltimore, Chicago, Detroit, District of Columbia, Los Angeles, and New York (Padilla, 2006; Short & Echevarria, 2004/2005).

By the year 2020, the school-age population will experience many more changes. Experts predict considerable increases in the percentages of all groups of students except White, non-Hispanic. During this time the percentage of White students will decrease from more than 60 percent to a little more than half of the total school population (U.S. Census Bureau, 2003).

Whereas most immigrants during the early 1900s came from Europe, more recently they have come from Central America (nearly 40%), Asia (25%), and the Caribbean (10%), with only 14 percent with Europe as their point of origin (U.S. Census Bureau, 2004). This demographic shift has resulted in a dramatic increase in the proportion of students whose first language is not English (U.S. Department of Education, 2005).

One of five children in U.S. schools—out of approximately 14 million students—are children of immigrant parents, and they bring with them a variety of languages and dialects (Kober, 2006; Padilla, 2006). Experts estimate that the number of students who speak a native language other than English increased 72 percent between 1992 and 2002 (Padilla, 2006; Short & Echevarria, 2004/2005). Increasingly, our students are bringing different native languages to school, and their facility with English varies widely (Abedi, Hofstetter, & Lord, 2004).

English language learners (ELLs) *are students whose first or home language is not English.* As a result of immigration and high birth rates among immigrant families, the number of non-English-speaking students and those with limited English has increased dramatically over the past three decades (Gray & Fleishman, 2004/2005). Projections indicate that by 2015, more than half of all P–12 students in our country will not speak English as their first language (Gray & Fleischman, 2005). This language diversity is staggering; more than 450 languages are spoken in our schools, with Spanish being the most common after English (Abedi et al., 2004).

Technology and Teaching:

Using Technology to Increase Student Learning

The third theme for this text is technology. Technology has changed the way we live and has also changed the way we learn and teach. To say that technology is an integral part of our lives is an understatement. Technologies such as cell phones, *Facebook*, and *Twitter* have revolution-ized the way we communicate. Internet search engines, such as *Google, Dogpile*, or *Yahoo*, have revolutionized the way we find information. A print encyclopedia has become an anachro-nism and nearly the same is true for a dictionary. We don't look up places on a map anymore; we go to *www.mapquest.com* instead. Our vehicles are equipped with GPS systems that will send us straight to our desired destination. Technological literacy has become a basic skill, next in importance only to reading, writing, and math.

Currently, virtually all schools have access to the Internet, and 87 percent of classrooms can access the Internet (Ansell & Park, 2003). The ratio of students to computers has fallen dramati-cally, and experts now estimate it at four to one (Cuban, 2005). Most households with school-age children (83%) have a computer in the home (Corporation for Public Broadcasting, 2003).

Although the availability of televisions, DVDs, and CD-ROMs has also increased in class-rooms, probably the most dramatic growth has occurred in the area of computer technology. Initially, computer literacy, or the preparation of students for life in the age of computers, was the focus of most computer use in the schools. Over time, instructional uses of computers have expanded to include the following:

- Computer-assisted instruction, including simulations, multimedia instruction, drill and practice, and tutorials

- Information tools for students, including spreadsheets, databases, and other capabilities for information retrieval and processing and multimedia learning

- Computer-managed instruction, including student record keeping, diagnostic and prescriptive testing, and test scoring and analysis

- Design of instructional materials, including text and graphics (Roblyer & Doering, 2010)

Technology in general, and computers in particular, are viewed as essential elements of instruction to help students develop critical thinking skills (Forcier & Descy, 2005). Today's teachers need to know how to use these technologies to help students learn.

 ## *L*earning to Teach

Becoming an expert teacher is a complex, multifaceted process that continues throughout a person's professional lifetime. It requires intelligence, sensitivity, experience, and hard work. It also requires several different kinds of knowledge—knowledge of subject matter, such as history, literature, or algebra; knowledge of how to illustrate and represent abstract ideas in understandable ways; knowledge of learners and how they learn; and an understanding of how teachers can help in this process.

Let's turn now to a closer look at the different kinds of knowledge it takes to become an expert teacher.

The Importance of Knowledge in Teaching

Expertise in any field is built upon a knowledge base (Bruning et al., 2004). This knowledge comes from a variety of sources, including experience, research, and other professionals. One of the most important kinds of knowledge for teachers is knowledge of the content they are teaching.

Knowledge of Subject Matter   We can't teach what we don't understand ourselves. This simple statement is self-evident, and it is well documented by research examining the relationships between what teachers know and how they teach (Shulman, 1986; Wilson, Shulman, & Richert, 1987). To effectively teach about the American Revolution, for example, a social studies teacher must know not only basic facts about the event but also how it relates to other aspects of history, such as the French and Indian Wars, our relationship with England prior to the Revolution, and the characteristics of the individual colonies. The same is true for any topic in any other content area.

Pedagogical Content Knowledge   Knowledge of content—no matter how complete—is not enough, however; it is a necessary but not sufficient condition for effective instruction. An effective teacher also needs to know *how to represent that information in ways that learners will understand. The ability to do this is called* **pedagogical content knowledge** (Shulman, 1986). For example, consider the concept of *mammal*, which is typically taught in different ways to students at different levels. At the elementary level, the teacher might use pictures and concrete examples (e.g., a gerbil or guinea pig) to emphasize characteristics such as "covered with hair" and "warm blooded." At the junior high level, teachers build on this foundation by emphasizing additional characteristics such as "live birth" and "four-chambered heart." Finally, at the high school level, biology teachers discuss characteristics such as mammals' ability to adapt to their surroundings, different classes of mammals, and what it means to be a primitive (e.g., the duck-billed platypus that actually lays eggs) compared to an advanced mammal that gives birth to live offspring. The same concept is taught in different ways at each of these levels to accommodate the background, interests, and capabilities of students.

Teachers at these different levels undoubtedly had a thorough understanding of content, but it was not sufficient in helping their students understand the topics they were studying. Majoring in math, for example, doesn't ensure that a teacher will be able to create examples that will help students understand why multiplying two numbers sometimes results in a small number ($\frac{1}{4} \times \frac{1}{3} = \frac{1}{12}$, for instance), a counter-intuitive finding. The ability to create or choose effective examples requires both a clear understanding of content and pedagogical content knowledge. When either is lacking, teachers commonly paraphrase information in learners' textbooks or have students memorize steps that don't make sense to them.

Knowledge of Teaching and Learning   Learning to teach not only involves understanding content and how to translate that subject matter into an understandable form, but it also requires knowledge about the processes of teaching and learning themselves.

Knowledge of teaching and learning *involves a general understanding of learners and how instruction contributes to the process of learning* (Borko & Putnam, 1996). To understand how knowledge of teaching and learning is a central component of learning to teach, let's look at a teacher who has taught her students the process for adding fractions and is now reviewing with them.

"Class, look at this fraction on the board. What do we call the number on the bottom? Celena?"

"Uh. . .denominator."

"Good, Celena. And what do we call the number on the top, Carl?"

". . ."

"We talked about this yesterday, Carl. Remember, it tells us the number of parts in the fraction. Think about the term that it is derived from, number."

"Oh, yeah, numerator."

"Excellent, Carl. Now, look closely at this addition problem. It says to add $\frac{1}{2}$ and $\frac{1}{3}$.

What do we have to do first? Think for a moment, because this is important. Look up at the pies that I've drawn on the board to represent these different fractions."

This teacher was trying to help her students do several things in her review. First, she wanted them to remember the names for the top and bottom number in a fraction—two concepts that she had already taught. When Carl could not answer, the teacher provided a prompt that helped him respond correctly. After students recalled the terms *numerator* and *denominator*, the teacher referred them to a problem on the board. She illustrated the abstract problem with a concrete example (the pies) to promote their understanding of the process. Finally, she told them to pause for a moment—an idea called "wait-time"— encouraging them to take some time to think about why changing the denominator was important.

Review, concept, prompting, concrete example, and *wait-time* are all pedagogical concepts—concepts about teaching and learning. As such, they are part of a professional body of knowledge that helps us understand and analyze our teaching and student learning. Your teacher education program is designed to aid you in understanding these and many other pedagogical concepts, which will help you recognize and appreciate effective teaching when you observe it, and ultimately help you plan and implement effective lessons in your own classroom. Each of the chapters in this text describes connections between teaching and learning.

Teaching Strategies   As we've seen, research on effective teaching has established links between teacher actions and student learning (Good & Brophy, 2008; Marzano, 2007). Research on wait-time, for example, indicates that giving students time to think about a question increases the quality of both their immediate responses and their long-term achievement. Research also tells us that providing students with concrete examples to illustrate abstract ideas improves students' ability to understand those ideas. An expert teacher understands the relationships between teacher actions and student learning and can implement these actions with their students.

In our work with teachers, we have found that sharing research with them is not enough. Research results must be translated into teaching strategies that work in classrooms, and teachers must be given opportunities to practice the strategies and receive feedback about their efforts. Teaching strategies are a fourth component of learning to teach. A **teaching strategy** *is an interconnected set of teaching actions designed to accomplish specific goals.* Teaching strategies can be thought of as research translated into integrated teacher actions.

To illustrate the idea of a teaching strategy, let's visit a high school language arts teacher wrestling with the concept of *theme* in writing.

"Class, today we're going to learn about the idea of *theme*. It's an idea that will help us understand and appreciate the literature we read. Look up at the white board and read the definition there.

'A theme is an idea that reoccurs or repeats itself throughout a story.'"

"Let's see if we can understand how theme relates to a story, Hemingway's *The Old Man and the Sea*, which we've just finished. One of the major themes in that book was the struggle of man against nature. Hemingway introduced this theme at the beginning when he told us about the old man's struggles to make a living catching fish. He worked hard every day but went for weeks without catching a decent fish. That's one place where the theme—man struggling against nature—occurred. The fisherman represented man, and the sea that wouldn't let him catch fish was nature. Who can give me a second example of this theme where man struggled with nature? Deena?"

"Well, like when the old man hooked the fish and had to fight with it for a long time."

"Good, Deena. Go ahead and explain how that illustrates the idea of this theme."

"I. . .I'm not sure,. . .but I'll try. The theme . . .the theme is man's struggle against nature and the fish is nature, so he's struggling with it."

"Good thinking, Deena. Note, everyone, how the same idea—man against nature—is repeated in the story. That's why it's a theme. Who can think of another place where this theme reoccurred or repeated itself? Eddie?"

". . .How about the shark attack?"

"Go on."

". . .Well, after he caught the fish, he tried to bring it back to sell it, but the sharks wouldn't let him. So he. . ."

"What was he struggling with—besides the sharks?"

"Oh, okay, nature. He was struggling with nature."

How does this illustrate a teaching strategy? A teaching strategy consists of coordinated teacher actions designed to reach a particular goal—in this case, helping students understand the concept of *theme*. The teaching strategy used by this teacher involved three basic steps:

- Defining the concept
- Illustrating the abstract idea with specific examples taken from the story
- Questioning to promote students' active involvement in learning and to help them connect the examples to the concept

Research indicates that this is an effective strategy when we want students to understand abstract concepts (Eggen & Kauchak, 2010). Defining the idea provides a frame of reference for the rest of the lesson, the examples illustrate the concept and give it meaning, and questioning involves students in the learning process. In Chapters 6 through 12, we describe a number of teaching strategies ranging from learner-centered, constructivist strategies that

To view a video clip of teachers at different grade levels and in different content areas demonstrating these different forms of professional knowledge, go to the Book Specific Resources tab in MyEducationLab, select your text, select Video Examples under Chapter 1, and then click on *Demonstrating Knowledge in Classrooms.*

capitalize on social interaction to more teacher-centered approaches such as direct instruction and lecture-discussions. Each contains a specific set of research-based steps designed to accomplish specific goals.

Teacher Decision Making

Teachers need to know the content they teach and how to transform this content into a form students can understand. They also need to understand how to help students learn and how to translate this knowledge into teaching strategies. We call these four components of learning to teach knowledge of subject matter, pedagogical content knowledge, knowledge of teaching and learning, and teaching strategies. But learning to teach involves even more than a thorough understanding of these components. Expert teachers not only have a repertoire of knowledge and strategies, but also understand when specific teacher actions are effective and why. For example, the teacher-centered approach to teaching concepts described earlier, which results in increased understanding of concepts, may not be effective for teaching other important goals, such as social interaction skills that include active listening and building on others' ideas, or developing attitudes and values such as openness to alternate points of view. These goals need different approaches that require student-student interaction (Alexander, 2006). Understanding how to implement knowledge of teaching and learning and when and how different teacher strategies are effective is an important dimension of effective teaching, requiring a great deal of expertise. This dimension is called professional decision making, a process that governs and guides the other four components.

Decision making *involves the application of professional judgment in deciding when, where, how, and why to use the other components of teaching.* As shown in Figure 1.1, decision making is an executive function that governs the application of the other teaching components.

Professional decision making can be thought of as a filter that helps determine when and where research findings should be used. Educational research needs to be applied selectively and strategically, with students' well-being and with our goals for teaching continually in mind; this is the essence of professional decision making. Let's see how decision making influences teaching in the classroom.

A kindergarten teacher has just distributed materials for an art project and is now surveying the room to see if everyone has started. She notices that Jimmy is staring out the window with his thumb in his mouth and tears in his eyes. It is the beginning of the school year, and Jimmy still isn't used to the idea of being away from home.

Should the teacher wait a minute and see if the art materials will do the trick, or should she intervene?

A middle school teacher is getting more and more frustrated. Mary is obviously more interested in her friends than in English, and the teacher can't keep her from talking. He calls on her; she doesn't hear the question. Should he reprimand her, repeat the question, or go on to another student?

A high school teacher has just distributed an assignment. She goes over the work in some depth, explaining its importance and how it should be done. She concludes by reminding the class that the grade for the assignment counts as one-fourth of the semester grade. A barely audible "Who cares?" follows. Should the teacher ignore it and go on, or should she respond?

We all remember our educational psychology texts' admonitions about the effects of reinforcement and punishment on behavior. These are documented research findings. But what do the findings tell the classroom teachers in the preceding examples? In each case, direct interventions might cause as many problems as they solve. Ignoring the problem raises similar issues. To make the situation more complex, these decisions must be made immediately.

The number of decisions—conscious or otherwise—that teachers must make every day is staggering. One estimate suggested that teachers make more than 800 decisions per day in elementary classrooms (Jackson, 1968); another estimated the number at 1,500 (Murray, 1986). Even using the more conservative figure, that translates into more than 130 decisions per hour in a six-hour teaching day!

Before you get discouraged, remember that effective teachers not only make these decisions but also make them well. Expert teachers structure their classrooms to run efficiently, so more time and energy can be devoted to important decisions—decisions that affect learning (Emmer, Evertson, & Worsham, 2009; Evertson, Emmer, & Worsham, 2009).

Figure 1.1

Components of Learning to Teach

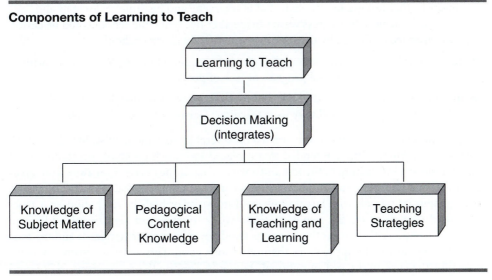

Educational Reform

You are becoming a teacher in one of the most tumultuous periods in the history of American education. Critics, both inside and outside the profession, are calling for **reforms,** *which are suggested changes in teaching and teacher preparation intended to increase the amount students learn*. To implement these reforms, teachers must be well prepared, and leaders in education are saying that we need to professionalize teaching (Blair, 2000). We examine the implications of these reform efforts for your professional development as a teacher in this section.

No Child Left Behind   By far the most far-reaching federal reform effort was the No Child Left Behind Act. This legislation, signed by President George W. Bush in 2002, was a reauthorization of the Elementary and Secondary School Act of 1965 and provided, among other things, guidelines for teacher and school accountability that included the following:

- **Annual testing.**   By the 2005–2006 school year, reading and math assessments from grades 3 to 8 were required, with each state deciding which test to use and what a passing or proficient grade would be. By 2007–2008, science assessment requirements were added in elementary, middle, and high schools. Schools were required to report not only test scores for the school, but also scores broken out by race, ethnicity, disability, social class, and limited English proficiency to ensure that no group is left behind—the reason for the legislation's name.

- **Academic improvement.**   Each state was required to define academic proficiency for their students, and all students were to be proficient in reading and mathematics by 2013–2014. The progress each state and each school made was measured annually, and schools that failed to make adequate yearly progress (AYP) for two consecutive years were labeled "underperforming." Although underperforming schools were entitled to special assistance, they also needed to give parents the option of sending their children to successful schools and to pay transportation costs. If a school did not achieve AYP for three years, additional supplemental services were to be provided to children, including private tutoring, also paid for by the school. After four years of unsatisfactory test grades, the state had to intervene and institute major staff and curricular changes. If progress wasn't made after five years, the school could be closed and either reconstituted by the state or reopened as a charter school.

- **Report cards.**   States and school districts were required to provide the public with reports of district and school progress or lack of progress.

- **Teacher qualifications.**   All teachers were to be highly qualified, licensed with an academic major in the field they were teaching (Hardy, 2002; Jennings, 2002).

No Child Left Behind was controversial on several levels (Allen, 2004; Marshak, 2003; Mathis, 2003). First, critics contended that it placed too much emphasis on standardized testing, resulting in teaching to the test and a narrowing of the curriculum away from areas such as art and literature that aren't tested. A second criticism was that it placed unreasonable demands on schools with large numbers of minority or high-poverty children. Critics contended that meeting the needs of these students required significant additional resources. A third criticism was that states watered down both their standards and the tests linked to them in an attempt to make themselves look good. This watering down is a major reason for the current interest in national standards. Despite these criticisms, NCLB and other reform efforts have caused major changes in teacher licensure, which will affect you as a beginning teacher.

Changes in Teacher Preparation   Reform in teacher education focuses on upgrading the knowledge and skills of teachers, including

- Raising standards for acceptance into teacher-training programs
- Requiring teachers to take more rigorous courses than they have in the past
- Requiring higher standards for licensure, including teacher tests
- Expanding teacher-preparation programs from four years to five
- Requiring experienced teachers to take more rigorous professional development courses (Wayne & Youngs, 2003)

Some of these suggestions are almost certainly going to affect you. We'll describe two as examples. First, you will likely be required to take more courses in English, math, science, history, and geography than have been required of teachers in the past. In addition, there is a movement to require all teachers, elementary and secondary, to major in a content area for their undergraduate degree. The rationale behind this push is related to both knowledge of content and pedagogical content knowledge—that teachers can't teach what they don't know themselves.

Second, you probably will be required to pass a test before you're awarded your teaching license. Currently, most states require some form of testing for prospective teachers, but the exact form that this testing takes varies from state to state (Swanson, 2008). Some states require tests of basic skills prior to admission to a teacher education program, whereas others test professional knowledge after program completion. In addition, some states require tests of your knowledge of the subjects you'll be teaching, especially if you're a middle or high school teacher. Virtually all of these tests are paper-and-pencil, although most new teachers will also be evaluated in terms of their classroom performance during their first year.

Testing teachers is not new; for example, teachers were tested all the way back in the 1840s using oral exams that focused primarily on candidates' moral qualifications (Wilson & Youngs, 2005). The current emphasis on testing teachers is part of a larger accountability movement in education in which students, teachers, and even principals are tested, and the results are used to evaluate the effectiveness of educational efforts.

The Praxis Series, published by the Educational Testing Service, is the most common form of teacher testing, although several large states such as Florida, New York, and Texas publish their own (Educational Testing Service, 2008). The Praxis Series (*praxis* means "putting theory into practice") is currently being used in more than 30 states and consists of three components (Educational Testing Service, 2008):

- Praxis I: Academic Skills Assessments—designed to measure basic or "enabling" skills in reading, writing, and math that all teachers need.
- Praxis II: Subject Assessments—designed to measure teachers' knowledge of the subjects they will teach. In addition to 70 content-specific tests, Praxis II also includes the Principles of Learning and Teaching (PLT) test and the Professional Knowledge test.
- Praxis III: Classroom Performance Assessments—use of classroom observations and work samples to assess teachers' ability to plan, instruct, manage, and understand

professional responsibilities. In addition, Praxis III assesses the teacher's sensitivity to learners' developmental and cultural differences.

You are most likely to encounter Praxis I during your teacher preparation, Praxis II after its completion, and Praxis III during your first year of teaching.

Standards-based Professional Development

One important outcome of the reform movement in education is the increased use of standards to focus curriculum and instruction on important learning goals. Standards-based education is changing K–12 education, as you read about earlier in the chapter. It is also changing the kinds of experiences you'll have in your teacher education programs.

Beginning Professional Development: INTASC Standards   In the past, learning to teach was easier and the demands on beginning teachers were not as great. This has changed (Berliner, 2000). A rapidly expanding body of literature consistently demonstrates that teaching now requires professionals who are highly knowledgeable and skilled (Darling-Hammond, 2000; Marzano, 2007).

The profession is responding. Created in 1987, the *Interstate New Teacher Assessment and Support Consortium* (INTASC, 1993) was designed to help states develop better teachers through coordinated efforts of support and assessment. INTASC's work is guided by the premise that effective teachers should possess the knowledge and abilities to assure that *all* students learn and perform at high levels. To make this happen INTASC has established rigorous standards that describe the knowledge and skills that all teachers should possess. The current standards, along with proposed revisions, are outlined in Table 1.4 (Interstate New Teacher Assessment and Support Consortium, 1993; Council of Chief State School Officers, 2010).

As you can see, both the current and proposed new principles describe broad areas of knowledge and expertise that all teachers, including new ones, should posses. In addition, the new, proposed principles are grouped into four main areas: The Learner and Learning, Content, Instructional Practice, and Professional Responsibility. Note that these new principles are currently under review and, will in all likelihood be revised with minor revisions and published in final form sometime in 2011. These principles provide broad goals for teachers as they enter into the profession and develop as competent and effective professionals.

Table 1.4   Current and Proposed New INTASC Principles

Current INTASC Principles

1. Knowledge of subject	**6.** Communication skills
2. Learning and human development	**7.** Planning
3. Adapting instruction	**8.** Assessment
4. Strategies	**9.** Commitment
5. Motivation and management	**10.** Partnership

Proposed New INTASC Principles

Principle	Description
The Learner and Learning Standard #1: Learner Development	The teacher understands how children learn and develop, recognizing that patterns of learning and development vary individually within and across the cognitive, linguistic, social, emotional, and physical areas, and designs and implements developmentally appropriate and challenging learning experiences.
Standard #2: Learning Differences	The teacher uses understanding of individual differences and diverse communities to ensure inclusive learning environments that allow each learner to reach his/her full potential.
Standard #3: Learning Environments	The teacher works with learners to create environments that support individual and collaborative learning, encouraging positive social interaction, active engagement in learning, and self motivation.
Content Standard #4: Content Knowledge	The teacher understands the central concepts, tools of inquiry, and structures of the discipline(s) he or she teaches and creates learning experiences that make these aspects of the discipline accessible and meaningful for learners.
Standard #5: Innovative Applications of Content	The teacher understands how to connect concepts and use differing perspectives to engage learners in critical/creative thinking and collaborative problem solving related to authentic local and global issues.
Instructional Practice Standard #6: Assessment	The teacher understands and uses multiple methods of assessment to engage learners in their own growth, to document learner progress, and to inform the teacher's ongoing planning and instruction.
Standard #7: Planning for Instruction	The teacher draws upon knowledge of content areas, cross-disciplinary skills, learners, the community, and pedagogy to plan instruction that supports every student in meeting rigorous learning goals.
Standard #8: Instructional Strategies	The teacher understands and uses a variety of instructional strategies to encourage learners to develop deep understanding of content areas and their connections, and to build skills to access and appropriately apply information.
Professional Responsibility Standard #9: Reflection and Continuous Growth	The teacher is a reflective practitioner who uses evidence to continually evaluate his/her practice, particularly the effects of his/her choices and actions on others (students, families, and other professionals in the learning community), and adapts practice to meet the needs of each learner.
Standard #10: Collaboration	The teacher collaborates with students, families, colleagues, other professionals, and community members to share responsibility for student growth and development, learning, and well-being.

The INTASC standards are demanding, but this is as it should be. If you expect to be treated as a professional, you should have the knowledge and skills that allow you to make the decisions required of a professional. Being able to meet the INTASC standards is a good beginning and developing a professional portfolio is one of the most effective ways to demonstrate your mastery of these standards. We discuss how in the next section.

Developing a Professional Portfolio

The interview was going okay, but I was uneasy. The principal I was interviewing with was cordial, but she certainly wasn't enthusiastic. "I've had it," I thought to myself. She even quit asking me questions after about 20 minutes. I really wanted the job too.

As I was about to leave, I happened to mention, "Would you like to see my portfolio?" She looked at it for a couple of minutes, and then she started asking some probing questions. When she stuck my CD-ROM in her computer and saw me teaching, she really lit up. I got the job! (Shannon, a recent graduate and new teacher)

As you begin this section, you might wonder, "Why are they talking about interviews and portfolios now in the middle of my teacher education program? Jobs and interviews may be months, even years, away." The answer is simple. The sooner you start on your professional portfolio, the better, and professional portfolios are one of the best ways to document and reflect on your growth as a teacher. A **professional portfolio** *is a collection of work produced by a prospective teacher* (Devlin-Scherer, Burroughs, Daly, & McCarten, 2007). Just as artists use portfolios of produced work to illustrate their talents and accomplishments, teachers use portfolios to document their knowledge and skills.

The reason to think about your portfolio now is that you may want to include products that you complete throughout your program, including assignments for the course you're in now. For instance, you might teach a particularly good lesson for one of your methods classes. You may want to include a copy of the lesson plan, a videotape of you teaching the lesson, and student work samples to document the lesson's effectiveness and your growth as a developing teacher. Although this experience will have occurred long before you actively seek a job, it can be a valuable entry nevertheless. The sooner you start thinking about what to include in your portfolio, the less likely you are to omit valuable or important entries.

Portfolios also provide tangible benchmarks that you can use for reflection, and **reflection,** or *thinking about and analyzing your actions and beliefs,* can accelerate your growth as a professional. For instance, you have videotaped yourself teaching a lesson for one of your teaching methods courses. The videotape is a concrete indicator of your skills at that point and provides a tangible basis for your reflection. Later, you may complete another videotaped lesson during an internship experience or student teaching. A comparison of your performance in the two lessons provides a concrete measure of your progress.

Possible Portfolio Entries   The contents of a professional portfolio can take many forms. Some possible suggestions are included in Table 1.5.

These different types of portfolio entries provide different perspectives on your growth as a professional.

Table 1.5 Potential Professional Portfolio Entries

Lesson plans	Community involvement
Unit plans	Grading policies
Videotapes of lessons taught	Transcripts
Student work samples	Volunteer work
Student projects	Technology competence
Action research projects	As a teacher:
	Principal evaluations
	Supervisor evaluations
Classroom management plan	
Communications with parents	

Source: Adapted from Bullock and Hawk (2001).

Preparing a Portfolio   Preparing a portfolio involves five steps (Kilbane & Millman, 2003):

1. Specify a goal. For example, you're probably taking this course because you've either decided that you want to teach or you're at least considering teaching. Finding a satisfying job would be a likely goal.

2. Determine how both past and future experiences relate to the goal. You might choose to tutor a student with a reading problem, for example, to get professional experience that will make you more marketable.

3. Strategically collect items that provide evidence of your developing knowledge and skill. A video clip of you working with the student would be an excellent entry, for instance.

4. Decide which items among your collection best illustrate your knowledge and skills. Since a prospective employer is unlikely to view a bulky collection or series of video-tapes, you'll need to be selective about the items you choose to insert in your portfolio.

5. Determine how to best present the items to the person or people connected to your goal, such as the personnel director of a school district in which you want to teach.

All professional portfolios have four components:

- **Purpose:**   To document a particular aspect of your growth as a teacher, such as your ability to plan or implement a specific type of lesson

- **Audience:**   Can vary from a professor or instructor to a prospective employer

- **Evidence:**   Consists of work samples that document accomplishments and growth

- **Reflections:**   Thoughts about the evidence and how it documents professional growth (Bullock & Hawk, 2001)

As you begin your portfolio, we offer three suggestions:

- Initially, err on the side of including too much in the portfolio. If you think you might use it, include it now. You can always remove an item, but retrieving an item you've discarded is difficult if not impossible.

- Always date the entry. If you want to organize your portfolio chronologically, the dated items will make organizing the information simpler.

- Make all entries and supporting information with clear communication in mind. You're trying to convince a potential employer that you're knowledgeable and skilled, and you want to make his or her decision as easy as possible. A well-organized portfolio creates a positive impression; the opposite occurs with a disorganized one.

Electronic Portfolios.   As we move further into the information age, the development of electronic portfolios is becoming more commonplace. They include everything a paper-based product includes, but they do it more efficiently. For example, one CD-ROM disk can hold the equivalent of 300,000 text pages. Typed documents can be scanned into word processing files and stored on floppy disks or CD-ROMs, and video can be digitized and also stored on CD-ROMs. This saves both time and energy. People who want to view a video episode in a paper-based portfolio must find a VCR, review the tape, and put it back into the correct portfolio container. In contrast, video footage in an electronic portfolio can be augmented with text and graphics and accessed with the click of a mouse. This is what got Shannon her job. The principal was impressed with both her teaching and the fact that the information in her portfolio was so easy to access.

Because of these advantages, it is likely that paper-based portfolios will become obsolete, so the sooner you develop your technology skills in these areas, the more effective your portfolio will be.

Using This Book to Learn to Teach

This book can help you become an expert teacher in several ways. Perhaps most important, it includes research findings that describe how teachers can increase student learning. Much of this research is described as concepts that are highlighted in **boldface** type and *defined in italics* to identify them as important ideas. These "Important Concepts," with page numbers, are also found at the end of each chapter to aid you in your study. Other research findings appear as teaching strategies designed to accomplish specific goals. Our goal in presenting this information is to provide you with the conceptual tools you need to analyze your own and others' teaching and to plan and implement effective lessons in your own classroom.

Case studies are used throughout this book in an attempt to connect theory with classroom practice. We begin each chapter with a case that frames important concepts and major issues in the chapter, and we end each chapter with an additional case for you to analyze called "Preparing for Your Licensure Exam."

These case studies serve several functions. First, they illustrate important educational concepts, helping you understand what these ideas look like in classrooms. For example, we used brief case studies in the previous section to illustrate *teacher decision making*—an abstract and potentially difficult to understand concept. In addition to being useful illustrations, case studies show how important ideas can be applied in classrooms. Also, the Praxis II series, as well as many state teacher exams, use case studies to test beginning teachers' knowledge. Your familiarity with the use of cases to illustrate complex ideas will assist you on these tests. The cases in this text are based on our experiences in classrooms and schools and are an attempt to provide you with a realistic slice of classroom life.

Discussion questions are also found at the end of each chapter. They invite you to go beyond the content, to look for relationships between ideas, and to integrate the material in a personal way. The answers to some of these questions can be found within the text, whereas others are more open-ended, asking you to use your own experience and judgment. We hope that they will stimulate your growth in professional decision making.

The third set of exercises, "Portfolio Activities," is designed to assist you in developing your own professional portfolio by applying research findings in actual classrooms through assignments that demonstrate the implications of research findings for classroom practice. These portfolio activities appear in three forms. Some ask you to interview teachers to discover how expert teachers think about and solve real-world problems. Talking to expert teachers and analyzing their teaching are productive way to learn about teaching, and reflecting on the thoughts and actions of others provides you with a concrete frame of reference to construct your own developing personal philosophy of good teaching. A second kind of activity asks you to observe teachers in action, based on information you've studied in this book. You'll watch teachers teach, analyze the strategies they use to help students learn, and reflect on their effectiveness, not only for these students, but also for the students you'll be teaching. The third kind of activity invites you to try these ideas for yourself. It involves structured teaching experiences designed to help you apply concepts and strategies in real classrooms with real students and to reflect on their effectiveness. If at all possible, we recommend that you use all of these to make the content of this text personally meaningful and to document your growth as a teacher.

Summary

Defining Good Teaching

The central role of research in informing teaching practice has changed the way we think about teaching and learning. Research now provides us with tools to analyze teaching to maximize learning.

The Search for Effective Teaching

Initially, research on teaching focused on teacher characteristics and later moved to a search for one effective method. Both lines of research failed to link teacher actions to student learning. The teacher effectiveness research established that teachers do indeed make a difference in students' learning and identified a number of productive strategies to increase student learning.

Contemporary Views of Teaching and Learning

As research has shifted from behaviorist to cognitive views of learning, teaching has focused on active ways to involve students in learning. Constructivist approaches to instruction stress the central importance of student's active involvement in learning.

Text Themes

Recent developments in education shaped the three major content themes for this text—standards and accountability, diversity, and technology. Standards and accountability influence how teachers plan, instruct, and assess. A focus on diversity explores ways to capitalize on student differences in the classroom. Technology provides us with electronic tools to enhance student learning.

Learning to Teach

Learning to teach is a complex process involving many components. Teachers need to know their subject matter but also need pedagogical content knowledge—an understanding of how to translate this content into forms that are understandable by students. Knowledge of teaching and learning, which addresses the relationship between teachers' actions and students' learning, needs to be combined with teaching strategies aimed at specific goals. Teacher decision making combines all of these components in effective teaching. Learning to teach in an era of reform will require teachers to demonstrate their competence to teach throughout their professional careers.

Using This Book to Learn to Teach

A number of features in this book are designed to help you learn to teach. Important concepts are highlighted in bold and listed at the end of each chapter. Cases provide access to classrooms, encourage you to connect important ideas to students and learning, and provide practice for Praxis and state-specific exams. Discussion questions invite you to go beyond the content in the book and link this content to your own experiences. Finally, portfolio activities suggest ways that you can use chapter concepts to observe, analyze, and implement ideas in classrooms.

Important Concepts

Accountability (p. 7)

Behaviorism (p. 6)

Cognitive psychology (p. 6)

Constructivism (p. 6)

Decision making (p. 17)

English language learners (p. 12)

Knowledge of teaching and learning (p. 15)

Pedagogical content knowledge (p. 14)

Professional portfolio (p. 22)

Reflection (p. 23)

Reforms (p. 19)

Teacher effectiveness research (p. 5)

Teaching strategy (p. 16)

Discussion Questions

1. Rank order the following teaching strategies on a continuum in terms of students' active involvement. Explain how each can involve students in the learning processes.

   Cooperative learning groups

   Discussion

   Drill and practice

   Homework

   Lecturing

   Student projects

2. Reexamine the information in Table 1.1, comparing behaviorist and cognitive views of learning. Which view do you think is more motivating for students? Why? Which view is more demanding for teachers? Why?

3. In terms of effective teaching, research suggests that content mastery is an essential component. Is this component equally important at all grade levels? In all subject-matter areas?

4. How does your definition of good teaching vary in terms of high- and low-ability students? Are there more similarities or differences between the two groups? What would you do with one group that would be different from the other?

5. What kinds of diversity did you encounter in the schools that you attended? What types of diversity do you anticipate encountering in the classrooms you'll teach in? How can student diversity be both an asset and a challenge to your teaching?

6. Reread the case study at the beginning of this chapter. What *is* the teacher's responsibility in terms of motivation? Do you agree with Stan Williams? What about the question regarding basic skills versus thinking strategies? Do basic skills need to precede thinking skills? What are the advantages and disadvantages of this approach?

7. What forms of technology did you encounter in the schools that you attended? How were they used to promote learning? What types of technology are you encountering in your teacher education program? What is the biggest challenge involved in using technology in your teaching?

8. One of the problems in learning to teach is that good teaching often appears effortless. Think back to some of the good teachers that you've had. What specific things did they do that made them effective? Compare these behaviors with those of other, less effective teachers.

Portfolio Activities

1. *Effective Teaching: The Teacher's Perspective.* How do experienced teachers think about effective teaching? Interview two teachers and ask the following questions:

   What is effective teaching?

   How do they know when it is occurring in their classroom?

   What are some ways to measure effective teaching?

   Which factors (e.g., students, content area) influence the definition of good teaching?

   Compare the responses of the two teachers with your own ideas about effective teaching.

2. *Effective Teaching: The District's Perspective.* How does the district evaluate its teachers? In your interview with the teachers in Exercise 1, find out how they are evaluated. If a form or instrument is used, ask to see it. Consider the following questions:

   What criteria are used? Are these based upon research findings?

   How is the form used? That is, how many times is the teacher observed with it?

   What does the teacher think of the process?

   How will the process of being evaluated as a teacher influence your professional development?

3. *Effective Teaching: The Student's Perspective.* The bottom line in our teaching is its effect on students. This exercise is designed to make you more sensitive to the learning process from a student's perspective.

   Identify six students to observe; three should be male and three female. Also, two should be high achievers in the class, two medium, and two low or struggling learners. If you are using another teacher's classroom, an ideal way to do this is to have the teacher select the students but not identify their status. This provides you with an opportunity to infer classifications from students' behavior and responses.

   Position yourself at the side of the classroom and toward the front so you can see the students' faces. Observe the six students as they enter the class, at the beginning of the lesson, during the major part of the lesson, and during any seatwork. Answer these questions:

   Which students are most attentive?

   Which students take notes?

   Which students participate the most in the lesson?

   Is there any relationship between teacher actions (e.g., questioning) and student engagement rates?

   If possible, interview the students and ask them the kinds of things the teacher does to help them learn.

   What implications do the students' perspectives have for your instruction as a teacher?

4. *Diversity.* Observe a classroom and note the kinds of diversity you find there. How do students in the class differ in terms of

    a. gender
    b. ability
    c. culture and ethnicity
    d. English language facility

   Do all students participate equally in the class? Interview the teacher and ask how diversity influences his or her teaching. What opportunities and challenges will student diversity provide you as a developing teacher?

5. *Motivation.* Observe a classroom and try to determine the following:

    a. Students' level of motivation during the lesson. (How can you tell?) Does it seem to vary during the lesson?
    b. Different students' level of motivation. Is there any pattern? How does location in the room influence this?
    c. The teacher's strategies to influence student motivation.

   If possible, discuss your observations with the teacher afterward. How do you plan to motivate students in your own classroom?

6. *Technology.* Which kinds of technologies are being used in the classroom you are observing? What other types of technologies are available in the school? Interview the teacher and ask

    a. How does technology enhance learning and teaching?
    b. What influence does it have on student motivation?
    c. What obstacles are there to the teacher's greater use of technology?
    d. How did the teacher learn to use this technology?

   How will you use technology in your classroom?

To check your comprehension of the content covered in Chapter 1, go to the Book Specific Resources in MyEducationLab, select your text, and complete the Study Plan quiz. In addition to receiving feedback on your answers, a study plan will be generated from the quiz that will direct you to access Review, Practice, and Enrichment materials to enhance your understanding of chapter content.

Student Diversity

Chapter Outline	Learning Objectives
	When you've completed your study of this chapter, you should be able to:
Capitalizing on cultural diversity ■ Multicultural education: The challenge ■ Theories of minority achievement ■ Culturally responsive teaching	1. Define the concept of *culture* and explain how it influences learning.
Language diversity ■ English dialects ■ English language development programs ■ Language diversity in the classroom	2. Explain how language influences learning.
Teaching students with different learning abilities ■ Intelligence: What does it mean? ■ Multiple intelligences: The work of Howard Gardner	3. Describe how teachers can adapt their instruction to meet the needs of students of different learning abilities.
Students with exceptionalities ■ Inclusion ■ Support for classroom teachers who work with students with exceptionalities ■ The exceptional student population ■ Teachers' roles in working with students with exceptionalities ■ Adapting instruction for students with exceptionalities **Technology and Teaching:** Employing technology to support learners with disabilities	4. Describe different ways that teachers can help students with exceptionalities succeed in their classrooms
At-risk students ■ At-risk students: Understanding the problem ■ Resiliency: Capitalizing on student strengths ■ Teaching at-risk students ■ Motivation: The need for challenge **Exploring Diversity:** Urban schools and at-risk students	5. Identify factors that influence at-risk students and describe effective teaching practices for these students.
Learning styles ■ Implications for teachers	6. Explain how students' learning styles affect classroom learning.

When we walk into classrooms across the country, one fact is obvious—the amazing diversity among our students. This diversity appears in a variety of forms, ranging from obvious differences in physical appearance to the ways different students respond to our instruction. In a single grade we have learners who are mature for their age and others who are slower in developing. Some will be poised and self-confident, while others will be shy and hesitant. A number will have traveled extensively, and still others will have spent most or all of their lives in one small neighborhood. Each of these differences influences our students' ability to benefit from our teaching.

In this chapter we examine different aspects of student diversity and discuss ways that teachers can adapt their instruction to best meet the needs of all their students. In the process we look at the influence that culture, language diversity, learning ability, socioeconomic status, and learning styles have on classroom learning. In addition we examine different ways that teachers help students with exceptionalities learn in their classrooms.

Shanda Jackson is a first-grade teacher in an urban elementary school. As you read the following vignette, think about her students' diversity and what she could do to accommodate that diversity.

Shanda watches as her first graders stream into the room on the first day of school. Though she has read the class rolls, she can't believe the different shapes, colors, and sizes before her eyes. Some are tall—looking almost like second graders—while others are tiny. A few are husky and well developed, while others are short and skinny.

"I wonder if all their parents know about the free breakfast program," she silently asks herself. And the names—she hopes she'll be able to remember them and pronounce them all correctly. There are Jones and Lees and Wongs and Hassads and Trangs and Jamals. This is going to be an interesting class.

As she learns about her students, she also notices differences in the way they act and learn. Some come to class bright and eager, while others look like they haven't gotten enough sleep. Several know how to print and read their names; others act as if they have never held a book before. A few use their fingers to count and even add, and others begin sucking on them when they become tired or discouraged.

"They're lovable," Shanda thinks as she smiles to herself, "but how am I ever going to help them all to learn?"

How indeed? One of the facts of modern teaching is the increasing diversity of our students. They not only come in different sizes and levels of maturity, as they always have, but now, more than ever, they come to our classes speaking different languages and bringing with them different cultural and background experiences.

Research can be a powerful tool to help us teach more effectively, and it can also help us capitalize on these differences in our students. Research can identify general teaching strategies that are effective with *all* learners and also suggest ways to modify our teaching to meet the needs of different learners. One of the most important dimensions of diversity that teachers deal with is culture, which we discuss in the next section.

Capitalizing on Cultural Diversity

To begin this section, let's look in on Shanda again as she works with her students.

Shanda sits back on the bus and breathes a sigh of relief—26 students there and 26 students back. Success! There were moments at the zoo when she wondered if she would get them all back on the bus, but now that the head counting is over she can relax.

Was it worth all the trouble, she wondered. It *was* a fun trip and many of her first graders had never been to the zoo. It also gave Shanda a chance to see her students in action in a different setting. She couldn't believe how different they were.

It wasn't just how different they looked. Shanda knew when she signed her contract to teach in this large inner-city school district that her students would be diverse, but she wasn't prepared for this—11 different cultures and six different languages. She jokingly refers to her class as her "Little United Nations." They not only respond differently in class but also on this field trip. Some were active and assertive and led the way in exploring the zoo, while others hung back, clinging to her for emotional and physical support. Some eagerly asked questions, while others listened shyly. She knows some of these differences are due to what they are used to at home, but she hasn't quite figured out how to capitalize on these differences in the classroom.

The varying cultural backgrounds of our students are an ever-increasing source of diversity. The United States has always been a nation of immigrants, and this immigration has produced a country of many cultures. More than 14 million people immigrated to the United States during the 1980s and 1990s. These changes can be seen in Table 2.1.

This trend is reflected in our classrooms, where more than 4 of 10 students in the P-12 population are members of cultural minorities. Children of color currently make up the majority of public school enrollments in six states—California, Hawaii, Louisiana, Mississippi, New Mexico, and Texas, and more than 90 percent of the student population in six major cities: Baltimore, Chicago, Detroit, District of Columbia, Los Angeles, and New York (Padilla, 2006; D. Short & Echevarria, 2005). Experts estimate that by the year 2020, two-thirds of the school population will be African American, Asian, Hispanic, or Native American (Meece & Hurtz-Costes, 2001; U.S. Department of Education, 2000). Each of these groups brings a distinct set of values and traditions that influences student learning. This diversity has been hailed as one of our country's strengths, bringing new ideas and energy to the country. But it also poses challenges to teachers as they attempt to teach children with different attitudes, values, and languages.

Table 2.1 **U.S. Census Bureau (2003) Ethnicity Comparisons**

Population Group	Percentage of Total		
	1980	**1990**	**2000**
Non-Hispanic	79.8	75.6	69.1
White	11.5	11.7	12.1
Black	6.4	9.0	12.5
Hispanic	1.6	2.8	3.7
Asian	0.6	0.7	0.7
American Indian	0.1	0.1	0.2
Some other race	na	na	1.6
Two or more races			

Multicultural Education: The Challenge

Culture *refers to the attitudes, values, beliefs, and ways of acting and interacting that characterize a social group* (Banks, 2008). It influences the foods we eat, the clothes we wear, how we play, the music we listen to, and the churches we attend. It also influences the attitudes and beliefs students have about learning and the beliefs they have about schools and classrooms.

Multicultural education *examines ways that culture influences learning and attempts to find ways that students' cultures can be used to complement and enhance learning.* It attempts to help teachers become more aware of and sensitive to the subtle and not so subtle ways that students' cultures can affect the way they approach learning.

Theories of Minority Achievement

The data on minority student achievement indicate that schools are not doing an effective job of educating minority students. Whether the measures are achievement test scores or dropout rates, statistics indicate that minority students underperform in schools (Macionis, 2009). Why is this so?

Cultural Deficit Theory   According to the **cultural deficit theory**, *the linguistic, social, and cultural backgrounds of minority children prevent them from performing well in the classroom* (Nieto, 2004; Villegas & Lucas, 2002). Minority children come to school lacking "cultural capital," which represents the accumulation of experiences in the early years that schools use and build upon. According to the cultural deficit theory, minority students do poorly in school because what they bring to school is inadequate compared to what children of the majority population bring.

There are two problems with this theory. The first is that it points the finger of blame at minority children, absolving the schools from responsibility for their success. In one sense it's as foolish as saying, "I taught them; they just didn't learn." If they don't learn, then we didn't teach them. In the same way it is our professional responsibility to take students, regardless of their backgrounds, and teach them.

The second problem with the deficit theory is that it proposes—theoretically—that once students get to school, the school should be able to "reduce" the deficit, filling in areas where the students are deficient. By spending increased periods of time in the schools, minority students should gradually "catch up." However, just the opposite occurs; as the number of years in school increases, the gap in achievement grows wider and wider.

Teacher Expectations   A second theory used to explain underachievement in minority students focuses on lowered teacher expectations. **Teacher expectations** *include the attitudes and beliefs that teachers hold about students' abilities to learn, which then influence student achievement* (Good & Brophy, 2008). Positive teacher expectations form a powerful foundation for learning, influencing how teachers instruct and how much students learn.

Negative expectations do the opposite, influencing learning in both explicit and implicit ways. Explicitly, they influence minorities through tracking and grouping practices that diminish learning. Implicitly, they influence how we interact with students, including the kinds of challenging questions we ask and on whom we call. Research indicates that a disproportionately higher percentage of minorities are found in lower groups and tracks (Good & Brophy, 2008). When cultural minorities find themselves in low-ability groups in the elementary grades, they are often headed down a one-way street to an inferior education throughout their school lives.

Teachers need to be aware of the expectations they have for students and should continually monitor their own actions to ensure that positive expectations are communicated to all students. But what else can teachers do to increase learning for students from different cultures?

Cultural Differences   A third theory used to explain differences in cultural minorities' achievement looks at differences between students' home cultures and the culture of schools. When students come to school, they bring with them patterns of behaviors sometimes at odds with those in our classrooms. Let's look at an example:

> Cynthia Edwards, a second-grade teacher in an elementary school in the Southwest is reading a story. "What do you think is going to happen next?... Tony?" Cynthia asks in response to his eagerly waving hand.
> "I think the boy is going to meet his friend."
> "How do you think the boy feels about meeting his friend?" she continues.
> After Tony responds, Cynthia calls on Sharon Nighthawk, one of the Native Americans in her class, even though Sharon has not raised her hand. When Sharon doesn't answer, Cynthia prompts her by rephrasing the question, but Sharon continues to look at her in silence.
> Slightly exasperated, Cynthia wonders if Sharon understands her questions, or if she is asking the right kind of questions, since Sharon seems to be enjoying the story and also understands it. Why won't she answer?
> Thinking about the lesson after school, Cynthia realizes that this has happened before, and that, in fact, her Native American students rarely answer questions in class. She can't get them to talk.

How might we explain this problem? Experts suggest that many Native American children are not used to the fast-paced, give-and-take patterns that characterize many American classrooms (Starnes, 2006). When involved in discussions, such as the one in Cynthia's class, they are uncomfortable and reluctant to participate (Banks, 2008). Similar issues can exist with students who are members of other cultures.

Why don't Native Americans eagerly respond to teacher questions? Aren't they interested in the same kinds of topics and issues as other students? Do they think that answering questions in class is important? Could the questions have been asked differently to encourage their participation? The cultural difference theory provides answers to these and other related questions about the influences of culture on learning.

The **cultural difference theory** *of learning attributes academic problems of minority students to cultural differences or discontinuities between home and school* (Nieto, 2004; Villegas & Lucas, 2002). Probably the most important of these is language. When home language patterns are congruent with school patterns, learning is enhanced; when they aren't, conflict occurs. Let's see how this works by analyzing the language patterns in two different "cultures"—school and Native American families.

Language use patterns in classrooms are amazingly homogeneous, not only over time but across grade levels and different parts of the country (Cazden, 1986; Cuban, 1984):

> [T]he dominant form of interaction is the teacher-directed lesson in which the instructor is in control, determining the topics of discussion, allocating turns at speaking, and deciding what qualifies as a correct response. Verbal participation is

required of students. Implicitly, teaching and learning are equated with talking, and silence is interpreted as the absence of knowledge. Students are questioned in public and bid for the floor by raising their hands. They are expected to wait until the teacher awards the floor to one of them before answering. Speaking in turn is the rule, unless the teacher specifically asks for choral responses. Display questions prevail. Individual competition is preferred to group cooperation. Topics are normally introduced in small and carefully sequenced steps, with the overall picture emerging only at the end of the teaching sequence. (Villegas, 1991, p. 20)

Contrast this pattern with one uncovered by researchers working with Native American children. They found that Native American children grew up being supervised by older children rather than adults (Philips, 1972). Learning from adults occurred more through observation rather than direct verbal instruction. Question-and-answer sessions between adults and children seldom, if ever, occurred. Children would observe adults and then try things out on their own, receiving praise and feedback not from adults but from other children.

When we contrast the "culture" of their classroom with that of their home, we can see why these students were reluctant to ask and answer questions in front of the whole class. Over time they became less and less involved in classroom activities and fell further and further behind in achievement. Sensitized to these differences, teachers found that when these students were placed in peer learning situations, such as group projects or peer tutoring, they spoke freely with their peers and participated in classroom activities; this was something they were used to doing.

A similar problem of cultural language discontinuity was discovered with African American students (Heath, 1989). Like Native American students, these children also struggled with the teacher-centered question-and-answer format found in most classrooms. Both teachers and parents were perplexed and frustrated about these students' failure to participate in school. As these researchers studied the language patterns found in African American homes, they discovered why.

Researchers found that these parents did not regard children as legitimate conversational partners until they were older, instead tending to give directives rather than ask questions. When questions were used, they were "real" questions asking for "real" information (e.g., "Where you been?") rather than questions designed to test the child's knowledge. Or they were more of the "open-ended story-starter" type (e.g., "What you been doin' today?") that did not have a single, convergent answer. These patterns contrasted with those found in schools where teachers asked many convergent questions, testing students' knowledge and providing specific practice and feedback. When these students entered school, they were unprepared to participate in the active give-and-take of convergent question-and-answer sessions.

When teachers were made aware of these differences, they incorporated more open-ended question in their lessons. For example, in an elementary social studies unit on "our community," teachers would show the class photographs of different aspects of local communities and ask questions such as, "What's happening here?" "Have you ever been here?" and "Tell me what you did when you were here." This not only fit African American students' home language patterns more closely but also provided safe, nonrestrictive opportunities for students to tell what they knew about a topic. Teachers also helped these children become more comfortable and competent with answering factual questions. Effective bridges were built between students' natural, culturally learned interaction styles and those of the schools.

Culturally Responsive Teaching

What does this suggest to us about our teaching? Should minority students from various cultures be made to fit in with schools as they exist today? It hasn't happened to this point, and it isn't likely to occur in the near future. Should schools be completely overhauled to match the learning patterns of a particular cultural group? Probably an impractical idea, since most classrooms contain several different cultural groups. Logistics alone preclude the use of any *one* particular strategy or adaptation.

What *is* required is a general approach of acceptance and valuing, which can create a positive classroom climate that invites all students to learn. In addition, teachers in multicultural classrooms need to implement **culturally responsive teaching**, which includes *understanding the cultures of the students they teach, communicating positive attitudes about cultural diversity, and employing a variety of instructional approaches that build upon students' cultural diversity* (Gay, 2005; Leonard, 2008). These strategies are listed in Table 2.2 and discussed below.

Learning About the Cultures of Our Students   Culture affects learning, and one of the most effective ways of capitalizing on this is to find out about the cultures our students bring to school. One principal did this by attending a special ceremony at a local church to honor Pacific Islander students, a significant minority population in her school. She arrived a few minutes early and was seated on the stage as a guest of honor. She settled down and waited for the ceremony to begin—and waited and waited—until it finally began nearly an hour late. She didn't quite know what to make of this.

The ceremony itself was warm and loving, showcasing each child, who was applauded by the group. After the ceremony the kids returned to their seats for the remainder of the meeting, which involved adult concerns. For a while they were fine; then they got bored and started fidgeting. The principal describes the rest:

> Fidgeting and whispering turned into poking, prodding, and open chatting. I became a little anxious at the disruption, but none of the other adults appeared to even notice, so I ignored it, too. Pretty soon several of the children were up and out of

Table 2.2   **Strategies for Working in Multicultural Classrooms**

Strategy	Examples
Learn about the cultural resources in your classroom	■ Visit homes and talk to parents. ■ Observe students both in and out of school. ■ Read literature by writers who are members of other cultures. ■ Talk to teachers of other cultures.
Accept and value student diversity	■ Emphasize mutual respect for all types of diversity. ■ Encourage students to share cultural patterns and norms with each other.
Build on students' cultural backgrounds	■ Teach about different cultures. ■ Use different strategies (e.g., peer tutoring or cooperative learning) to accommodate different cultural styles. ■ Eliminate grading practices that emphasize competition and differences among students.

their seats, strolling about the back and sides of the auditorium. All adult faces continued looking serenely up at the speaker on the stage. Then the kids started playing tag, running circles around the seating area and yelling gleefully. No adult response—I was amazed and struggled to resist the urge to quiet the children. Then some of the kids got up onto the stage, running around the speaker, flicking the lights on and off, and opening and closing the curtain! Still nothing from the Islander parents! It was not my place, and I shouldn't have done it, but I was so beyond my comfort zone that with eye contact and a pantomimed shush, I got the kids to settle down.

I suddenly realized then that when these children, say, come to school late, it doesn't mean that they or their parents don't care about learning or that they're a little bit lazy—that's just how all the adults in their world operate. When they squirm under desks and run around the classroom, they aren't trying to be disrespectful or defiant, they're just doing what they do everywhere else. (Winitzky, 1998, p. 123)

Our students bring with them sets of attitudes, values, and ways of acting that may or may not be conducive to learning in traditional, unidimensional classrooms. We saw this in the examples of language conflict, and we can see it in the example with the Pacific Islander students. Teachers in multicultural classrooms need to make an active effort to enter into students' lives to understand their attitudes and values and how these affect the ways they act and behave.

Some effective ways to learn about your students include the following (Echevarria & Graves, 2007; Peregoy & Boyle, 2008):

■ Take time at the beginning of the school year to introduce yourself, and ask students to do the same.

■ Use dialogue journals to encourage students to share information about themselves. Set aside a given time every day and provide journal starters such as "favorite foods" or "favorite hobbies." Collect these periodically and respond to them.

■ Begin the school year with a unit on family origins, supplemented with a world map with string connecting each child's name and birthplace to your city and school.

■ Make yourself available before and after school to help students with assignments as well as to talk with them about their lives.

Activities such as these can redefine your classroom from a place where students come to learn content to one in which they are all part of a learning community.

Accepting and Valuing Student Diversity   Our students need to know that we understand their home cultures and that we value the diversity that they bring to our classrooms. We do this by openly discussing cultural differences, emphasizing their positive aspects both in classrooms and in society as a whole. We also communicate positive attitudes about diversity by encouraging students to bring their cultures into the classroom, including their music, dress, and foods. In addition, recognizing and celebrating different holidays, such as Martin Luther King Day, Muslim holy days, Mexican Independence Day, and the Jewish holidays, communicates that students' cultures are important and valued. We also teach positive attitudes by emphasizing mutual respect for all cultures and ensuring that all cultural groups are treated with respect.

Building on Students' Cultural Backgrounds

Maria Sanchez, a fifth-grade teacher in a large urban elementary school, walks around her classroom, helping her students with their social studies projects, which they are working on in small groups. Maria's class is preparing for Parents' Day, an afternoon in which parents and guardians join in the class's celebration of the different countries that students came from. Student projects, focusing on these different countries, were designed to provide information about the different countries' history, geography, and cultures. The class had been studying these countries in social studies all year long, and a large world map with pins and yarn on it mark different students' country of origin with a picture of the student. Although many of the pins are clustered in Mexico and Central and South America, there were also many students from all over the world. Each student was encouraged to invite someone from his or her family to come and share a part of their native culture. Some are bringing food, while others are bringing music or native dress from their different homelands.

Effective teachers learn about their students' cultures and use this information to promote personal pride and motivation, as we saw in Maria's class and as we see in the following example:

Jack Seltzer, a high school biology teacher on the Navajo Nation Reservation, uses his students' background experiences to illustrate hard-to-understand science concepts. He uses Churro sheep, a local breed that Navajos use for food and wool, to illustrate genetic principles. When they study plants, he focuses on local varieties of squash and corn that have been grown by students' ancestors for centuries. He uses geologic formations in nearby Monument Valley to illustrate igneous, sedimentary, and metamorphic rocks. (Baker, 2006)

Both students and their parents benefit from building on students' cultural backgrounds (Leonard, 2008). Student achievement increases, and parents become more positive about school, both of which enhance student motivation. Maria recognized this when she invited parents and other caregivers to share their cultural heritages with her class. Jack also capitalized on this idea by providing examples with which the students could personally identify. Students bring to school a wealth of experiences embedded in their home cultures. Sensitive teachers build on these experiences, and all students benefit.

To view a video clip of one teacher's attempt to address cultural diversity in her classroom, go to the Book Specific Resources tab in MyEducationLab, select your text, select Video Examples under Chapter 2, and then click on *Capitalizing on Diversity in Classrooms*.

Language Diversity

In addition to cultural differences, increased immigration has resulted in increasing numbers of students with limited backgrounds in English entering our classrooms. In the 2003–2004 school year, 5.5 million school-age children were English language learners (Leos, 2004)—up nearly 100 percent from a decade earlier.

Nationwide, the number of students whose primary language is not English is expected to triple during the next 30 years (Echevarria & Graves, 2007; Peregoy & Boyle, 2008). The most common language groups for these students are Spanish (73%), Vietnamese (4%), Hmong (1.8%), Cantonese (1.7%), and Cambodian (1.6%). This language diversity poses a challenge to teachers because most instruction is verbal. How should schools respond to this linguistic challenge? Let's examine this question, beginning with the topic of dialects.

English Dialects

Mrs. Caplow says, "Let's write a story about our school tour."

Andrea says, "I write no story."

"I no want to," Mike adds.

Mrs. Caplow responds, "I know you do not want to, but we must learn how to read and write."

Joe says, "I want to make horseshoe."

Mrs. Caplow says, "Not now, Joe."

She then writes on the top of the chalkboard, "Our School Tour," and continues, "Okay boys and girls, what did we do on our school tour?"

"Went outside," Laura responds.

"Did we take a tour?"

After hearing no response she continues, "What is a tour?"

Laura says, "A trip."

"Okay. Let's write, 'We took a trip and we met our school helpers.'" (Actually they met no one.)

She then says, "That is a short story."

Susan calls out, "I ain't got no paper."

Mrs. Caplow responds, "Oh no, Susan, let's not say 'ain't.' Let's say, I haven't any paper.'"

Susan says, "I haven't no paper."

(Rist, 1973, pp. 79–80)

Anyone who has traveled in the United States can confirm the fact that our country has many regional and ethnic dialects. A **dialect** is a *variation of Standard English that is distinct in vocabulary, grammar, or pronunciation.* Everyone in the United States speaks a dialect; people merely react to those different from their own (Banks, 2008). Some dialects are accepted more than others, however, and language plays a central role in what Delpit (1995) calls "codes of power," the cultural and linguistic conventions that control access to opportunity in our society. What does research say about these dialects?

Research indicates that students' use of non-Standard English can result in lowered teacher expectations for their performance and lowered assessments of students' work and of the students themselves (Gollnick & Chinn, 2009). Teachers often confuse non-Standard English with mistakes during oral reading, and some critics argue that dialects, such as Black English, are substandard. Linguists, however, argue that these variations are just as rich and semantically complex as Standard English (Bohn, 2003; Labov, 1972).

So, what should a teacher do when a student says, "I ain't got no pencil," bringing a nonstandard dialect into the classroom? Opinions vary from rejection and correction to complete acceptance. The approach most consistent with culturally responsive teaching is to accept the dialect and build on it. For example, when the student says, "I ain't got no pencil," the teacher might say, "Oh, you don't have a pencil. What should you do then?" Although results won't be apparent immediately, the long-range benefits make the effort worth it.

Language differences don't have to form barriers between home and school. **Bidialecticism**, *the ability to switch back and forth between a dialect and Standard English, allows access to both* (Gollnick & Chinn, 2009). For example, one first-grade teacher built upon her students' African American dialect to develop pride in them while also helping them learn Standard English (Bohn, 2003). A high school language arts teacher explicitly taught differences between Standard and Black English, analyzing the strengths of each and specifying respective places for their use. The teacher read a series of poems by Langston Hughes, the African American poet, focusing on the ability of Black English to create vivid images. The class discussed contrasts with Standard English and ways in which differences between the two languages could be used to accomplish different communication goals (Shields & Shaver, 1990). In this way students were made aware of differences in dialects, the strengths of each, and when different dialects should be used.

English Language Development Programs

In many instances our students come to us speaking a language other than English. Many terms are used to describe students whose first language isn't English: English learners, English language learners, nonnative English speakers, and second language learners are all used to refer to students learning English as a second language (Peregoy & Boyle, 2008). The term *limited English proficient* (LEP) is also used to refer to students who range from beginners to intermediates in learning English. There are also several terms given to educational programs for these students, with English as a second language (ESL) and English language development (ELD) the most common.

Numerous approaches are used to teach English as a second language. They differ in how fast English is introduced and to what extent the first language is used and maintained. True bilingual programs offer instruction to nonnative English speakers in two languages: English and their primary language. They attempt to maintain and enhance the native language while building on it to teach English. Other programs place more emphasis on English acquisition. We look at three of these English language development programs: bilingual maintenance programs, transitional bilingual programs, and English as a second language programs.

Bilingual Maintenance Programs   **Bilingual maintenance programs** *teach in both the native language and English, maintaining and building on the students' native language* (Peregoy & Boyle, 2008). These programs are found primarily at the elementary level and occur where large numbers of students speak the same language, such as the Southwest

United States. Their purpose is to develop students who are truly bilingual, that is, can speak, read, and write in two languages. Although maintenance programs help maintain and build students' language and culture, they are difficult to implement, because they require groups of students with the same native language and bilingual teachers who speak this language. They are also controversial, with critics claiming they fail to teach English quickly enough (U.S. English, 2008).

Transitional Bilingual Programs   **Transitional bilingual programs** *use the native language as an instructional aid until English is proficient.* In transitional programs, instruction begins in the native language, and English is gradually introduced. However, the transition period is sometimes too short, leaving some learners ill prepared for instruction in English.

English as a Second Language (ESL) Programs   **English as a second language (ESL) programs** *differ from the other programs in their emphasis on teaching students English and mainstreaming them into regular classrooms.* Often ESL programs place students in regular classes for most of the day and pull them out for separate instruction in ESL classrooms for the remainder. These ESL classes are often called **sheltered instruction** and are *designed to provide students with content instruction along with English language development.* ESL programs are common when classes contain students who speak a variety of languages, thus making maintenance or transitional programs difficult to implement. They are also common at the high school level, where the logistical problems of students going from one content classroom to the next make other alternatives impossible.

Language Diversity in the Classroom

How will language diversity affect you as a teacher? First, although bilingual programs have been reduced, the need for teachers with ESL expertise will only increase. Experts estimate that by 2015, U.S. schools will need an additional 56,000 teachers with ESL certification to meet the demands of these students, and 11 states have incentive policies to encourage teachers to pursue education in this area (Honawar, 2009). In addition more than 7 of 10 urban school districts identify bilingual teachers as a critical hiring need (Recruiting New Teachers, 2006). Teacher candidates who speak two languages, and especially Spanish, are in high demand across the country.

Second, the likelihood is high that you will have students whose first language is not English in your classroom. Your ability to make informed professional decisions will be essential to help them learn. In working with students from diverse cultural and language backgrounds, your professional knowledge will be tested, perhaps more than in any other area of your work.

Teachers can assist ELL students through sensitivity and awareness and by taking advantage of opportunities to facilitate language development. As you work with these students, it's easy to fall into a trap of tacitly assuming that all ELL students are similar with respect to their understanding of their native languages. This isn't true (Zehr, 2009). As with students in general, some come from homes where books, newspapers, and the Internet are a regular part of their lives, whereas others come from families that can barely read and write in their native language. Also, the ability to converse in English doesn't mean that students can learn effectively in English (Tong et al., 2008; Zwiers, 2007). ELL students usually pick up enough English to communicate with peers and teachers after three or four years, but it can take up to eight years to learn enough English to function effectively in academic content areas.

Research offers a number of general suggestions for working with students from varying language backgrounds (Echevarria & Graves, 2007; Peregoy & Boyle, 2008):

- Create a warm and supportive classroom environment by taking a personal interest in all students and involving everyone in learning activities. Get to know students, and attempt to personalize the content you're teaching.

- Mix whole-class instruction with group work and cooperative learning to allow students to interact informally and practice their developing language skills with the topics they study.

- Use question-and-answer sessions to involve all students in classroom activities and concrete examples to provide reference points for new ideas and vocabulary.

- Continually check for understanding through questions, assignments, and quizzes. Misunderstandings are a normal part of teaching, and even more common with students who are members of cultural minorities. Use these checks to adjust instruction.

- Avoid situations, such as making students read aloud in front of the whole class, that draw attention to students' lack of English skills.

These strategies represent good instructional practice for all students; for ELL students, they are essential.

A second way to help LEP students is through the use of instructional strategies that encourage student language use and development (Echevarria & Graves, 2007; Peregoy & Boyle, 2008). These are outlined in Table 2.3 and described below.

When teaching ELL students you need to provide concrete examples of the ideas you are presenting. For example, a lesson on ecosystems in science becomes much more meaningful when it begins with pictures of different ecosystems. In a similar way, a first-grade story on hats becomes more meaningful when the teacher brings in several hats to share during the lesson. These concrete examples and pictures can then serve as a frame of reference for key concepts and terms that the teacher writes on the board to provide both focus and information about how important words are spelled. Interactive questioning provides opportunities to actively involve students while assessing their understanding of new vocabulary. Group work provides further opportunities for students to practice their language skills of listening and speaking while also learning new content. All of these strategies have proven effective for learners in general (Eggen & Kauchak, 2010); for ESL students they are essential (Peregoy & Boyle, 2008).

Table 2.3 Effective Instruction for ELL Students

1. Use examples and learning activities to provide a concrete frame of reference.
2. Write key concepts and terms on the board and refer to them during discussions.
3. Use interactive questioning strategies.
4. Use groupwork to provide opportunities for linguistic and academic development.

Teaching Students with Different Learning Abilities

Emma Taylor, an intern from a nearby university, is ready to teach her first math lesson in Mrs. Jenkins's middle school math class. The topic is the decimal system, and she has preplanned with Mrs. Jenkins, who suggested a review of place value, such as identifying 3 tens and 2 ones in the number 32. Though Emma is nervous at the beginning, everything goes smoothly as she explains the concept and uses interlocking cubes to illustrate it. As she passes out practice worksheets, Mrs. Jenkins walks over to Emma and whispers, "You're doing great. I need to run down to the office. I'll be right back." The students quickly begin to work; since they are accustomed to having interns and pre-interns in the class, they don't react when Mrs. Jenkins leaves.

Emma's nervousness calms as she circulates among the students, periodically making comments. She notices that some are galloping through the assignment, others need minor help, and a few are totally confused. As she works with students, she notices that the quiet of the classroom is turning into a low buzz.

"Joel, why aren't you working?" Emma asks as she turns to a student near her.

"I'm done."

"Hmm?" she thinks as she looked around the room.

"Beth, finish your assignment and stop talking," Emma says, turning to another student visiting with her neighbor.

"I can't do this stuff!"

Emma looks at the clock and sees that there are still 10 minutes to the bell, and, from the fidgeting and talking, it appears that several of the students have completed their assignment, while others have barely begun. Panic! What to do?

Just then Mrs. Jenkins walks in the room, surveys the class, and looks at the clock as she walks over to Emma.

"How is it going?"

"Fine, but half of them are done and the other half need extra help."

Mrs. Jenkins then turns to the class and says in an authoritative voice. "Class if you're done with your work, put it away in your homework file for tomorrow. Then you can either do the math exercises on the computer in the back of the room or find a partner for one of the math games. Let's get busy now."

As Emma quickly learned, the students we teach differ in their ability to learn and how much assistance they need from the teacher. As one veteran teacher jokingly estimated, "In any lesson, probably a third already know it, another third are really learning it, and the rest don't know what you're talking about." Although probably overstated, there is some truth to what she said. The students in our classes vary considerably in their ability to learn, and this has important implications for instruction.

What does this variability look like in the classroom? In a typical second-grade classroom, students will typically range from below first grade to beyond the fourth grade in reading ability, meaning that some will still be working on beginning reading skills, such as sounding out words, whereas others will be ready to focus on complex comprehension skills. In higher grades the range of abilities is even greater.

The amount of time it takes students to master new content is another way of thinking about the variability in student learning ability. Emma's experience illustrates this idea;

some students understood the topic quickly, while others struggled to understand it at all. In many classes it can take slower students more than five times longer than their faster peers to master a topic (Bloom, 1981).

Although reading grade levels and time required for learning are alternate ways of describing variations in learning ability, it is still most commonly expressed in terms of *intelligence* or intellectual ability. For example, experts suggest that you're likely to have students with intelligence test scores (I.Q.) ranging from 60 or 70 to 130 or 140 in an average, heterogeneously grouped classroom (Hardman et al., 2008). This range is so great that students at the lower end would be classified as mildly handicapped and would be eligible for special help, whereas students at the upper end might be considered gifted and/or talented. In the next section we examine the concept of *intelligence* and discuss how it influences teaching.

Intelligence: What Does It Mean?

We all have an intuitive idea about intelligence. In everyday language it's how "smart" or "sharp" people are, how quickly they learn, the insights they have, or even the wide range of—sometimes trivial—knowledge they possess. More formally, intelligence is measured by standardized tests that produce the well-known I.Q. or intelligence test score (Salvia & Ysseldyke, 2004). The two most popular intelligence tests used today are the Weschler Intelligence Scale for Children (WISC) and the Stanford-Binet.

What do these tests actually measure, or, perhaps more appropriately, what is intelligence? Although experts disagree about some of the specifics, most define **intelligence** *as having three dimensions:*

- *Abstract thinking and reasoning*
- *Problem-solving ability*
- *Capacity to acquire knowledge (aptitude)* (Sattler, 2001)

When we think about these dimensions, we can see why intelligence is important for teachers, and why scores on intelligence tests correlate moderately well (.50 to .70) with school performance (Sattler, 2001). Students who do well on intelligence tests usually do well in school.

The concept of *intelligence* is controversial, with disagreements focusing on three issues. First is the "nature-nurture" controversy, with some authorities arguing that intelligence is genetically determined and essentially fixed at birth (Jensen, 1998)—the nature position. Others take the nurture position, contending that intelligence can be influenced both indirectly (e.g., through diet and access to medical care) and directly through educational interventions (Sternberg, 2004). This issue has important implications for how we view our students. Do they come to us with their intellectual abilities fixed and unchangeable or are there things that we can do to improve our students' intelligence? An optimistic view of education, called the *interactionist* position, holds that students come to our classrooms with genetic potential and that we as teachers can do much to help learners reach that potential (Coll et al., 2004; Shepard, 2001).

A second controversy focuses on the issue of cultural bias. Some experts argue that intelligence tests *are* culturally embedded and influenced by both language and a learner's past experiences (Valencia & Suzuki, 2001). This issue has important implications for the use of these tests with minority populations. Research has found that an over-reliance on intelligence tests with non-English-speaking populations results in a disproportionate number of these students being classified as intellectually disabled (Fine, 2001).

Multiple Intelligences: The Work of Howard Gardner

The third controversy relates to the concept of single versus multiple dimensions of intelligence. Historically, intelligence tests produced a single score producing a general measure of intellectual functioning; later, tests such as the WISC provided two scores, one verbal and the other performance. Currently there is considerable interest in the concept of *multiple intelligences* (Gardner & Moran, 2006; Sternberg, 2003). Theories of multiple intelligences suggest that there are several kinds of "smarts" rather than just one. For example, **Gardner's theory of multiple intelligences** *breaks intelligence into eight areas: linguistic, logical-mathematical, musical, spatial, bodily-kinesthetic, interpersonal, intrapersonal, and naturalist.*

Gardner's work is intuitively sensible. We all know people, for example, who don't seem particularly "sharp" at school tasks but have a special ability to get along well with others, or they appear to have insights into their own strengths and weaknesses. Gardner would describe these people as being high in interpersonal and intrapersonal intelligence respectively. In other cases we see people who excel in English but do less well in math—linguistic versus logical-mathematical intelligence—and we've all seen examples of gifted musicians and gifted athletes who don't excel in other areas. These different dimensions are summarized in Table 2.4.

Viewing intelligence as multidimensional suggests that teachers should create learning environments in which different kinds of students can excel (Denig, 2003; Shearer, 2002). Giving learners choices is consistent with this view. For example, a middle school English teacher breaks down assignments into required and optional. Seventy percent of the

---

Table 2.4 **Gardner's Dimensions of Intelligence**

Dimension	Example	Application
Linguistic intelligence and effectiveness: Sensitivity to the varied uses of language	Poet, journalist	How can I get students to talk or write about an idea?
Logical–mathematical intelligence: The ability to reason and to recognize patterns in the world	Scientist, mathematician	How can I bring in number, logic, and classification to encourage students to quantify or clarify the idea?
Musical intelligence: Sensitivity to pitch, melody, and tone	Composer, violinist	How can I help students use environmental sounds, or set ideas into rhythm or melody?
Spatial intelligence: The ability to perceive the visual world accurately, and creatively modify the world perceptively	Sculptor, navigator	What can I do to help students visualize, draw, or conceptualize the idea spatially?
Bodily-kinesthetic intelligence: A fine-tuned ability to use the body effectively and creatively	Dancer, athlete	What can I do to help students involve the whole body or to use hands-on experience?
Interpersonal intelligence: A sensitivity to others' thoughts and feelings	Therapist, salesperson	How can peer, cross-age, or cooperative learning be used to help students develop their interactive skills?
Intrapersonal intelligence: An understanding of self	Self-aware individual	How can I get students to think about their capacities and feelings to make them more aware of themselves as persons and learners?
Naturalist intelligence: Recognizing similarities and differences in the physical world	Naturalist, biologist, anthropologist	How can I encourage students to observe and think about the world around them?

Source: Adapted from Armstrong (1994), Chekles (1997), Gardner and Hatch (1989).

assignments are required for everyone; the other 30 percent provide students with choices about what to read and do, and they negotiate with the teacher on the specific assignments.

Sometimes, however, the differences in learning ability are so great that both teachers and students need extra help. We call these learners *students with exceptionalities* and describe how to help them learn in the next section.

Students with Exceptionalities

Jim Kessler circulates around the room while his sixth-grade students work on their unit test. Most are working smoothly, writing an answer and then looking up to think. Others are obviously struggling, and Jim can only shake his head in both under-standing and frustration. It was like this during regular class time.

There is quiet Samantha—barely says a word in class—shy, slow, she seems to struggle in every subject. She is a sweet girl, never complains, tries her hardest. Next to her is Jake. Even now his feet are shuffling, and his pencil beats a rhythm on the desk. He is energy looking for a destination. Although he does all right in math, he struggles in any subject in which he has to read. Jim has to cajole and coerce him just to pick up a book. Next to Jake is Steven, the playground terror. Steven does all right in the classroom, when other students leave him alone, but he has a temper with a short fuse that seems to ignite at just the slightest provocation. Once Jim gets him settled down again, he does fine, but it takes some doing.

What a collection! If he didn't have the resource teacher to help him, he didn't know what he'd do.

Samantha, Jake, and Steven are students with exceptionalities. **Students with exceptionalities** *are those who require special help to reach their full potential*, and you will almost certainly have some of them in your classes (Heward, 2009). This is the result of Public Law 94-142, the *Individuals With Disabilities in Education Act* (IDEA), which was passed in 1975 with the goal of ensuring a high-quality, free public education for all students with exceptionalities.

Inclusion

In the past students with exceptionalities were often placed in separate classrooms and facilities. As educators realized that segregated classes and services were not meeting the needs of students with exceptionalities, they wrestled with alternatives (Karten, 2005; Smith et al., 2004). One of the first was **mainstreaming**, *the practice of moving students with exceptionalities from segregated settings into regular classrooms*. Popular in the 1970s, main-streaming had advantages and disadvantages (Hardman et al., 2008). Mainstreaming began the move away from segregated services and allowed students with exceptionalities and other students to interact. However, students with exceptionalities were often placed into classrooms without the necessary support to help them succeed.

As educators grappled with these problems, they developed the concept of the **least restrictive environment (LRE)**, *one that places students in as normal an educational setting as possible while still meeting their special academic, social, and physical needs*. Broader than the concept of *mainstreaming*, the LRE can consist of a continuum of services ranging from mainstreaming to placement in separate facilities. Mainstreaming into a regular classroom occurs only if parents and educators decide it best meets the child's needs.

Central to the LRE is the concept of **adaptive fit**, *which is the degree to which a student is able to cope with the requirements of a school setting and the extent to which the school accommodates the student's special needs* (Hardman et al., 2008). Adaptive fit implies an individualized approach to dealing with students having exceptionalities; it can be determined only after an analysis of a student's specific learning needs. As educators considered mainstreaming, the LRE, and adaptive fit, they gradually developed the concept of *inclusion*.

Inclusion *is a comprehensive approach to educating students with exceptionalities that advocates a total, systematic, and coordinated web of services* (Heward, 2009; Turnbull et al., 2010). Inclusion has three components:

1. Including students with special needs in a regular school campus

2. Creating appropriate support and services to guarantee an adaptive fit

3. Coordinating general and special education services

Inclusion is both proactive and comprehensive; it makes all educators responsible for creating supportive learning environments and leaves open the possibility of services being delivered in places other than the regular classroom. Its basic thrust is to include students with exceptionalities in regular classrooms whenever possible, but it also allows for delivering services in other places (Heward, 2009).

Support for Classroom Teachers Who Work with Students with Exceptionalities

The practice of inclusion often places students with exceptionalities in regular classrooms, and teachers are expected to help in meeting the needs of these students. They are not alone, however; support systems such as the following can assist the regular classroom teacher in adapting instruction to meet the learning needs of students with exceptionalities:

1. Specially trained special educators and school psychologists meet with the classroom teachers to help adapt instruction.

2. If warranted, students with exceptionalities receive extra assistance in pullout resource rooms.

3. Assistance or collaborative consultation teams (Heward, 2009) bring special educators into the regular classroom to help the classroom teacher in the following ways:
   - Meet with the classroom teacher to identify and define any learning problems.
   - Observe a student's classroom behavior.
   - Collect work samples from the classroom.
   - Cooperatively design specific instructional changes with the teacher.
   - Team-teach with the regular teacher.

A major outcome of these meetings is the construction of an individualized education program (IEP). Mandated by law, the **IEP** *outlines an individualized plan of action for each exceptional student.* Each IEP must contain the following components:

   - The child's present levels of educational performance
   - Annual goals and short-term instructional objectives

- Specific educational services to be provided

- The extent to which the child will participate in regular education

- Projected date for initiation of services

- Expected duration of those services

- Objective criteria and evaluation procedures (Smith et al., 2004)

The classroom teacher's input during both planning and implementation is essential to the program's success.

The Exceptional Student Population

How common are students with exceptionalities in the classroom? Approximately 11 percent of the school-age population is classified as exceptional, and the majority of these (about 70%) are taught either in the regular classroom or in a regular classroom with assistance from a resource room (U.S. Department of Education, 2002). If your class is typical, you will have several students with exceptionalities needing extra help, and most of these will have mild to moderate disabilities.

Students with Mild to Moderate Disabilities   The vast majority of students with exceptionalities have mild to moderate disabilities (Hardman et al., 2008; Heward, 2009). **Students with mild to moderate disabilities** *learn well enough to remain in the regular classroom but have enough problems with learning to warrant special help*. The three major subcategories of mild to moderate disabilities are *mental retardation, learning disabled, and behaviorally disordered*. Let's look at them.

Students with an intellectual disability *have limited intellectual ability resulting in problems in adapting to classroom tasks*. The majority of these students are mildly or educable mentally retarded and have I.Q.s ranging from 50 to 70 (an average I.Q. is around 100) (Luckasson et al., 2002). This lower level of intellectual functioning requires that classrooms need to be adapted to match the learner's capabilities.

In contrast, **students with learning disabilities** *have normal intellectual capabilities but have problems with specific classroom tasks such as listening, reading, writing, spelling, or math operations*. This category is the largest group of handicapped students, constituting more than 45 percent of the total exceptional student population (Hardman et al., 2008; Heward, 2009). Behavior patterns include hyperactivity and fidgeting, problems with attention, disorganization, lack of follow-through, and uneven performance in different school subjects.

Students who are behaviorally disordered, emotionally disturbed, or emotionally handicapped *display persistent behaviors that interfere with their classroom work and interpersonal relations*. Students with behavioral disorders fall into two general categories—the acting out child (externalizing) and the quiet, withdrawn child (internalizing) (Hallahan & Kauffman, 2009). The acting out child can be physically aggressive and display uncooperative, defiant, and even cruel behaviors. The quiet, withdrawn child is much less visible and is often timid, shy, and depressed and lacks self-confidence. Experts warn that virtually all students act like behaviorally disordered students sometime in their school years; the key characteristic is that the behavior pattern is chronic and persistent.

In addition to the students we have just discussed, you may have learners in your classes with impaired sight, hearing, or speech. If you see indicators of these disabilities in any of your students, immediately bring them to the attention of your principal, school nurse, school psychologist, or guidance counselor, who can have the student tested.

Students Who Are Gifted and Talented   As a classroom teacher you'll also encounter students who are gifted and talented. What is it like to be gifted or talented in a regular classroom? Here are the thoughts of one 9-year-old:

> *Oh what a bore to sit and listen,*
> *To stuff we already know.*
> *Do everything we've done and done again,*
> *But we still must sit and listen.*
> *Over and over read one more page*
> *Oh bore, oh bore, oh bore.*
> *Sometimes I feel if we do one more page*
> *My head will explode with boreness rage*
> *I wish I could get up right there and march right out the door.*

(Delisle, 1984, p. 72)

Although we don't typically think of gifted and talented students as having exceptionalities, they often have learning needs not met by the regular education curriculum. **Students who are gifted and talented** *are at the upper end of the ability continuum and need special services to reach their full potential.* The National Center for Education Statistics (2005a) reports a total of approximately 3 million students who are gifted and talented, slightly more than 6 percent of the total student population. At one time the term *gifted* was used to identify these students, but the category has been enlarged to include both students who do well on intelligence tests and those who demonstrate above-average talents in a variety of areas such as math, creative writing, and music (Davis & Rimm, 2004).

Meeting the needs of students who are gifted and talented requires both early identification and instructional modifications. Conventional procedures often miss students who are gifted and talented because they rely heavily on standardized test scores and teacher nominations As a result females, low-SES students, and students from cultural minorities are typically underrepresented in these programs (Gootman & Gebelof, 2008; Lewis, DeCamp-Fritson, Ramage, McFarland, & Archwamety, 2007). To address this problem experts recommend more flexible and less culturally dependent methods, such as creativity measures, tests of spatial ability, and peer and parent nominations in addition to teacher recommendations (Davis & Rimm, 2004).

As a regular classroom teacher you may be responsible for adapting instruction for students who are gifted and talented, or students may attend special programs. These programs are typically based on either **acceleration**, *which keeps the curriculum the same but allows students to move through it more quickly,* or **enrichment**, *which provides richer and varied content through strategies that supplement usual grade-level work* (Schiever & Maker, 2003). Table 2.5 lists different acceleration and enrichment options. Failure to address the needs of these students can result in gifted underachievers, with social and emotional problems linked to boredom and lack of motivation (Cross, 2005).

Table 2.5 Acceleration and Enrichment Options for Student Who Are Gifted and Talented

Enrichment Options	Acceleration Options
■ Independent study and independent projects	■ Early admission to kindergarten and first grade
■ Learning centers	■ Grade skipping
■ Field trips	■ Subject skipping
■ Saturday programs	■ Credit by exam
■ Summer programs	■ College courses in high school
■ Mentors and mentorships	■ Correspondence courses
■ Simulations and games	■ Early admission to college
■ Small group investigations	
■ Academic competitions	

Teachers' Roles in Working with Students with Exceptionalities

In working with students with exceptionalities, teachers have three major roles—*identification, fostering acceptance,* and *modifying instruction.* As you read the following case, see if you can identify each of these roles.

Toni Morris has been working with her class of second graders for a week trying to get them into reading and math groups that matched their abilities. Marisse, a transfer student, is hard to place. She seems to understand the material but loses attention during different parts of lessons. When Toni works with her one-on-one, she does fine, but Toni often notices her staring out the window.

One day as Toni watches the class work in small groups, she notices that Marisse holds her head to one side when she talks to someone on the opposite side of the group. Toni wonders…She speaks to the principal, who recommends that Marisse be referred to the school psychologist for possible testing.

Two weeks later the school psychologist came by to discuss her findings. Marisse had a hearing problem in one ear that would require a hearing aid as well as special help from Toni.

In a few days Marisse came to school with her hearing aid. She obviously felt funny about it and wasn't sure if this was a good idea. Toni moved her to the front of the room so she could hear better, made sure to give directions while standing in front of Marisse's desk, and double-checked after an assignment was given to ensure that the directions were clear to her.

Toni also took Marisse aside to talk about her new hearing aid. Marisse *could* hear better, but she still felt a little strange with it. Some of the kids looked at her funny, and that made her uneasy. Toni had an inspiration: Why not discuss the hearing aid in class and let the others try it? This was a risky strategy, but Marisse reluctantly agreed to it.

It worked. During show-and-tell, Marisse explained about her new hearing aid and gave the class a chance to try it out themselves. The strange and different became understandable, and Marisse's hearing aid became a normal part of the classroom.

The first step in working with students with exceptionalities is identification. Because teachers are able to observe students on a day-to-day basis, teachers are in a unique position to identify learning problems in their students.

In the past a discrepancy model was used, which targeted students when a difference existed between a students' potential and actual performance in the classroom. Many experts became dissatisfied with the discrepancy model, arguing that it identifies a disability only after a problem surfaces, sometimes after several years of failure and frustration (e.g., Brown-Chidsey, 2007). Instead, they argue, educators need early screening measures, so that teachers can prevent failure before it occurs. Critics also contend that the discrepancy model does not provide specific information about the nature of the learning problem and what should be done to correct it (Lose, 2008).

The **response to intervention (RTI) model of identification** *addresses both of these problems through early diagnosis and remediation.* RTI typically begins at the beginning of the school year with pretesting designed to identify any potential learning problems early (Samuels, 2008, 2009). As soon as a learning problem surfaces, the classroom teacher attempts to adapt instruction to meet the student's needs. Common adaptations include small-group work, working with students while other students do seatwork, or one-on-one tutoring outside of regular school hours. Developing skills, such as highlighting important vocabulary and developing study strategies, such as using a dictionary, reading assignments aloud, and finding a quiet place to study that is free of distractions, is also emphasized. If the adaptations are unsuccessful, a learning exceptionality is possible. As teachers adapt their instruction, they also specify what works and what doesn't. This provides valuable information for later interventions. If instructional modifications aren't proving successful, the teacher can then refer the student to a special educator or school psychologist for formal evaluation.

A second role that teachers perform in working with exceptional children is fostering acceptance (Cook, 2004; Turnbull et al., 2010). Perhaps the most difficult obstacles students with exceptionalities face are the negative attitudes of other students and the impact these attitudes have on their own confidence and self-esteem (Hallahan & Kaufman, 2009). Having a disability and being different are often not well understood or accepted by other students, and just placing students together in inclusive classrooms is often not sufficient to bring about attitude change and acceptance. The teacher's active efforts are necessary to change attitudes and bring about acceptance.

Teachers can help by modeling acceptance, by actively teaching about diversity, and by making every possible effort to ensure that these students experience success and feel needed and wanted. Toni Morris did this by adapting her classroom to meet Marisse's special learning needs and by emphasizing that Marisse was a valued and integral part of the classroom learning community. This may be the most important contribution a classroom teacher makes for these students. Teachers also help by helping other students understand the nature of the learning problem. Toni did this when she had Marisse explain her hearing aid to other students.

Adapting Instruction for Students with Exceptionalities

Many classroom teachers are apprehensive when faced with adapting instruction for students with exceptionalities. They are not sure about what exactly to do to help these students learn in their classrooms. This is unfortunate because research shows that many of the basic approaches that work with non-mainstreamed students also work with mainstreamed students (Hardman et al., 2008; Heward, 2009). These include

- Warm academic climate
- Effective use of time
- Effective classroom management
- High success rates
- Effective feedback

The biggest challenge teachers face in working with students with exceptionalities is adapting instruction to ensure success. Teaching topics at a slower pace, providing more opportunities for practice and feedback, giving shorter assignments (e.g., 10 versus 15 problems), and breaking assignments into smaller parts (e.g., 20 problems into 4 groups of 5) all can help in this process (Bos & Vaughn, 2006; Vaughn et al., 2006).

Reading assignments pose special problems for mainstreamed students because available texts are often inappropriate for their reading level. Some ways of adapting regular reading materials include

- Setting goals at the beginning of an assignment
- Using advance organizers that structure or summarize the passage
- Introducing key concepts and terms before students read the text
- Creating study guides with questions that focus attention on important information
- Asking students to summarize information in the text (Bos & Vaughn, 2006; Vaughn et al., 2006)

These adaptations also work with non-mainstreamed students; their use with students with exceptionalities provides extra structure and support to help ensure success (Barr, 2001).

At-risk Students

Today's students are different in yet another way. Never before have schools attempted to teach so many students who are physically and mentally ill prepared to learn. A combination of economic and social forces threatens the ability of many students to profit from their educational opportunities.

At-risk students *are those in danger of failing to complete their education with the skills necessary to survive in modern society*. The term is borrowed from medicine, where it refers to individuals who don't have a specific disease but are likely to develop it, such as an overweight person with high blood pressure being at-risk for a heart attack. The term became widely used after 1983 when the National Commission on Excellence in Education proclaimed the United States a "nation at risk," emphasizing the growing link between education and economic well-being in today's technological world (National Commission on Excellence in Education, 1983). For example, between 1979 and 1996

Technology and Teaching

Employing Technology to Support Learners with Disabilities

Jaleena is partially sighted, with a visual acuity of less than 20/80, even with corrective lenses. Despite this disability, she is doing well in her fourth-grade class. Tara Banks, her teacher, has placed her in the front of the room so that she can better see the chalkboard and overhead and has assigned students to work with her on her projects. Using a magnifying device, she can read most written material, but the computer is giving her special problems. The small letters and punctuation on website addresses and other information make it difficult for her to use the computer as an information source. Tara works with the special education consultant in her district to get a monitor that magnifies the display. She knows it is working when she sees Jaleena quietly working alone at her computer on the report due next Friday.

Julio is partially deaf, barely able to use a hearing aid to understand speech. Kerry Tanner, his seventh-grade science teacher, works closely with the special education instructor assigned to her classroom to help Julio. Seated near the front of the room to facilitate lip-reading, Julio takes notes on a laptop computer during teacher presentations. Other students take turns sharing their notes with him so he can compare and fill in gaps. He especially likes to communicate with other students on the Internet, as this levels the communication playing field. When he views video clips on his computer, he uses a special device with earphones to increase the volume.

Assistive technology, *a set of adaptive tools that support students with disabilities in learning activities and daily life tasks,* can be a powerful tool to assist students with exceptionalities. These assistive tools are required by federal law under the Individuals with Disabilities in Education Act and include motorized chairs, remote control devices that turn machines on and off with the nod of the head or other muscle action, and machines that amplify sights and sounds (Heward, 2009; Hopkins, 2006).

Probably the most widespread use of assistive technology is in the area of computer adaptations. Let's look at them.

Adaptations to Computer Input Devices

To use computers, students must be able to input their words and ideas. This can be difficult for those with visual or other physical disabilities that don't allow standard keyboarding. Devices that enhance the keyboard, such as making it larger and easier to see, arranging the letters alphabetically to make them easier to find, or using pictures for nonreaders are adaptations that accommodate these disabilities. AlphaSmart, one widely used program, helps developing writers by providing spell-check and word-prediction scaffolding (Fine, 2002). When a student hesitates to finish a word, the computer, based on the first few letters, then either completes the word or offers a menu of suggestions, freeing students to concentrate on ideas and text organization.

Additional adaptations bypass the keyboard altogether. For example, speech/voice-recognition software translates speech into text on the computer screen (Silver-Pacuilla & Fleischman, 2006). These systems can be invaluable for students with physical disabilities that affect hand and finger movement. Other adaptations use switches activated by a body movement, such as a head nod, to interact with the computer. Touch screens also allow students to go directly to the monitor to indicate responses.

Research also indicates that students with learning disabilities encounter difficulties translating ideas into written words (Hasselbring & Bausch, 2005/2006; Quinlan, 2004). Speech-recognition technology eases this cognitive bottleneck by bypassing the keyboard, helping to produce initial drafts that are longer, with fewer errors.

Adaptations to Output Devices

Adaptations to computer output devices also exist. For example, the size of the visual display can be increased by using a special large-screen monitor, such as the one Jaleena used, or by using a magnification device that increases the size of the print. For students who are blind, speech synthesizers read words and translate them into sounds. In addition, special printers can convert words into Braille and Braille into words.

These technologies are important because they prevent disabilities from becoming obstacles to learning. Their importance to students with exceptionalities is likely to increase as technology becomes a more integral part of classroom instruction.

Students will be naturally curious when introducing any of these new technologies into your classroom. Use this as an opportunity to discuss the whole topic of exceptionalities, how everyone is different, with unique strengths and abilities, and knowing these allows us to make the most out of what each of us possesses.

the real earnings of 25- to 34-year-old male high school dropouts actually fell by 28 percent (Murnane & Tyler, 2000). Compounding the problem is the fact that the percentage of 18- to 24-year-olds who left school without a diploma increased from 21.2 percent in 1994 to 25.3 percent in 1998.

The following factors are often associated with students being at risk:

- **Poverty and low SES.**   Poverty creates a number of stress factors that adversely affect students' physical and mental health (Barton, 2004; Lee & Burkam, 2002, 2003).

- **Cultural minority.**   Being a member of a cultural minority can pose problems when schools are not responsive to cultural differences (Borman & Overman, 2004; Noguera, 2003a, 2003b).

- **Nonnative English speaker.**   Learning is hard enough when students can understand the language of instruction. Struggling with both language and content can be an overwhelming task (Bielenberg & Fillmore, 2004/2005; Zwiers, 2004/2005).

- **Mobility.**   High rates of student mobility often result from low-paying jobs that require parents to move. When this occurs, learning suffers (Garza et al., 2004; Ream, 2003).

- **Substandard schools.**   Unfortunately, the students who need quality educational experiences the most are often provided with substandard buildings and equipment as well as less qualified teachers (Perkins-Gough, 2004; Thirunarayanan, 2004).

- ■ **Motivational and self-esteem problems.** Learning problems often result in motivational and self-esteem problems. When students struggle to learn, they feel worse about themselves and are less excited about learning (Brophy, 2004).

- ■ **Disengagement from schools.** Many students feel like they don't belong. Tardiness, poor attendance, and dropping out often result (R. Brown & Evans, 2002).

- ■ **Management problems.** Boredom, frustration, and apathy often result in management problems. Alcohol and drug use is a persistent problem (Barr & Parrett, 2001).

At-risk children often come to school underfed and without proper care. They may not be eager to learn because their emotional needs for safety and security have not been met. At-risk students can be difficult to teach and can pose serious educational problems for teachers. To deal with these challenges we need to understand how economic and social factors interact to impact learning.

At-risk Students: Understanding the Problem

How does poverty, and the myriad ills that go with it, result in decreased learning and motivation? To understand the connection sociologists use **socioeconomic status (SES),** *the combination of parents' income, occupation, and level of education.* SES consistently predicts not only performance on intelligence tests but also classroom performance, achievement test scores, grades, truancy, and dropout and suspension rates (Byrnes, 2003; Macionis, 2009). Children of wealthier parents, parents who have white-collar jobs, and parents with higher levels of education generally perform better on all of these school-related measures. Of the three, the best predictor of a student's academic performance is the level of schooling attained by the parents. We'll see why shortly.

SES influences learning in a number of ways. First, it impacts learning at a basic needs level; students who don't receive adequate nutrition and medical and dental care, for example, come to school physically unprepared to learn (Rothstein, 2004). Free breakfast and school lunch programs for low-income families are one government response to this problem. Many teachers in low-income neighborhoods keep a box of crackers in their desks for students who come to school without breakfast.

SES also influences the kind of experiences students bring with them to school (Orr, 2003; Wenner, 2003). High-SES students are more likely to travel extensively, to visit museums and zoos, and to talk about these experiences with their parents. When they come to school, they are more likely to know concepts such as *big and small, up and down,* and *left and right.* Why are these concepts important? Think for a moment about teaching the differences between "d" and "b," "p" and "q," and a capital "C" and a small "c" without these concepts. All learning builds on prior experiences. Low-SES students' early years often fail to provide the experiences needed to help them succeed in school.

The impact of SES is also transmitted through parental attitudes and values (Brown et al., 2004). Is learning important? Are schools essential for learning? How do hard work and effort contribute to learning? Why is homework important? These attitudes and values are learned in subtle and not-so-subtle ways.

Learning to read is a classic example. High-SES homes have books, magazines, and newspapers around the house, and parents model the importance of reading by reading themselves and reading to their children (Neuman & Celano, 2001). They develop "print awareness" in their young children by holding up cereal boxes, pointing to stop signs, and putting the child's name on the door to his or her bedroom. When their children enter school, they not only know about the power of the printed word, they are eager to read.

The opposite is also true. Poor homes are less likely to have books and magazines lying around. The television set plays continually, competing with quiet reading and homework time. The parents are less likely to read, and when the young child comes to school, reading is more a mystery than an exciting challenge.

Resiliency: Capitalizing on Student Strengths

Research on at-risk students has focused on the concept of *resilience*. **Resilience** *is a learner characteristic that results in a heightened likelihood of success in school and in other aspects of life despite environmental adversities* (Borman & Overman, 2004). Resilient young people thrive in spite of the obstacles they encounter as at-risk students. Resilient children set and meet goals, they expect to succeed, they feel as if they're in control of their own lives, and they have well-developed interpersonal skills (Downey, 2003).

Resilient children come from families that are caring and hold high moral and academic expectations for their children. Schools that are both demanding and supportive also help promote resilience; in many instances, these schools serve as a home away from home (Wilson & Corbett, 2001; Parish, Parish, & Batt, 2001). Let's look more closely at what you can do in your classroom to help these students succeed.

Teaching At-risk Students

Research offers some suggestions for helping at-risk students, who need greater structure and support in our classrooms (Brophy, 2004). They need to experience success and to understand that effort results in achievement. To examine instruction that is effective with at-risk students, let's return to Shanda Jackson's classroom and see how she helps her at-risk first graders succeed.

Shanda begins her math lesson by having students from each row come up to distribute baggies of beans. When all the students have these, she begins.

"Class, I need to have everyone's eyes up here. Good. Today we're going to learn a new idea in math. It's called subtraction. Can everyone say subtraction? Good! Subtraction is when you take away. Let's look up here at the overhead and the felt board.

"*Kareem had four cookies in his lunch. He sat down next to his friend Jared. Jared didn't have any, so Kareem gave him two of his. How many are left?*

"Let's do that up here on the felt board. Hmm, four cookies—see how they're round—take away two cookies, leaves how many cookies? Let's count them. Four minus two equals two. That's subtraction."

"Now I want each of you to take out four beans from your bag and do the same."

As the students work at their desks, Shanda moves around the room to make sure they are doing it correctly.

"Excellent, everyone. Now I have another problem for you. Let's pretend the beans are pieces of candy. Who likes candy? (All hands go up.) Cassie had three pieces of candy. Everyone take out the right number of beans to show how much candy she had."

Shanda circulates again to make sure every student has three beans out.

"Now Cassie's two friends came along and each of them wanted a piece, so Cassie gave one to each. Can you take away two beans, one for each of her friends? Now who can tell me how many pieces of candy Cassie had left?"

Teaching at-risk students is not fundamentally different from teaching students in general. It utilizes basic principles of effective teaching and refines them to provide high structure and strong support for learning. The increased structure and support appear in several forms, as we see in Table 2.6.

Let's look again at Shanda's lesson in the context of these elements. **Active teaching** *means that the teacher assumes responsibility for explaining and modeling the idea to be learned.* Shanda did this when she called the class together and told the children that they were learning a new skill and then explained the skill at the felt board.

She then used manipulatives and questioning to help her first graders learn the process of subtraction. Note that she didn't just write numbers on the board, such as $4 - 2 = 2$. Instead, she illustrated the process with real-life examples using cookies and candy—examples that 6-year-olds could understand and identify with. In addition, she actively involved students, having all students do the physical operation at their own desks.

Interactive teaching also involves all students through questioning. This not only allows all students to participate but also provides the teacher with opportunities to informally check students' developing understanding. Shanda used interactive teaching in three ways:

■ She asked students to say "subtraction."

■ She asked who liked candy.

■ She asked how many pieces of candy Cassie had left.

These questions both encouraged student involvement and helped Shanda monitor their attention and developing understanding.

Interactive teaching methods are essential. In a comparison of more and less effective urban elementary teachers, researchers found that less effective teachers interacted with students only 47 percent of the time versus 70 percent of the time for their more effective counterparts (Waxman et al., 1997). Interactive teaching is characteristic of good instruction in general; its importance with at-risk students is crucial (Barr & Parrett, 2001; Wilson & Corbett, 2001).

Table 2.6 **Effective Instruction for At-risk Students**

Strategy	Description
Active teaching	The teacher explains concepts and skills through interactive teaching.
Use of concrete examples	Abstract ideas are illustrated with examples and concrete manipulatives.
Interactive teaching	Teachers use questioning to actively involve students in learning activities.
Practice and feedback	Students have opportunities to practice the concept or skill they're learning.
High success rates	Students are successful as they practice skills and concepts.

Effective teaching also allows students opportunities to actively try out their developing ideas. To be effective, opportunities for practice and feedback should be available to all students. For example, all of Shanda's students had beans to add and subtract with, and she moved around the room to make sure all students were involved and on task.

Student success is critical in the process (Brophy, 2004). Because at-risk students often don't have a history of successful school experiences, lack of success can result in frustration and can further detract from motivation that may already be low. Shanda ensured high success rates by taking small instructional steps and monitoring learning progress as the lesson proceeded.

By now you might be saying to yourself, "Wait a minute. Aren't these procedures for at-risk students just good teaching?" If you did, you're absolutely correct. Effective instructional practices for at-risk students are not qualitatively different from those for "regular" students (Good & Brophy, 2008). The same principles of good teaching that work in the regular classroom also work with at-risk students. It is, however, all the more critical that they be applied conscientiously and thoroughly with students placed at risk. Collectively, these practices provide an instructional safety net that minimizes the possibility for frustration and failure, two factors that are especially damaging for at-risk students.

Motivation: The Need for Challenge

Although increased structure and support are important when teaching at-risk students, additional research highlights the importance of challenge (Brophy, 2004). All too often teachers provide increased structure and support without creating classrooms that have challenge and excitement.

What does this suggest for teachers? First, it reminds us that high expectations and emphasis on higher-order thinking are as important for at-risk students as they are for other students (Downey, 2003). Second, it makes teachers' ability to use challenging teaching strategies all the more important.

To view a video clip of a teacher using challenging instruction to motivate her students, go to the Book Specific Resources tab in MyEducationLab, select your text, select Video Examples under Chapter 2, and then click on *Studying Learning and Motivation: Writing Paragraphs in Fifth Grade.*

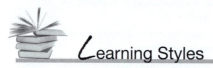

Learning Styles

In order to understand something do you need to "see" it? Or hear it described? Or touch it? People often describe themselves as *visual, verbal,* or *tactile* learners. These descriptions reflect your unique **learning style**, *your preferred way of learning and studying* (Denig, 2003).

Learning styles also influence classroom teaching, as Chris Burnette discovers.

Exploring Diversity

Urban Schools and At-risk Students

At-risk students face special challenges in urban schools, which tend to be large and located in high-poverty areas. As a result they are not as well funded as their suburban counterparts. Because they are large, they can become impersonal (Kincheloe, 2004). Urban high schools can be "tough, confusing places where students can easily get lost" (Ilg & Massucci, 2003, p. 69).

The diversity of urban neighborhoods, the distances students often must travel over public transportation, and the fact that teachers in urban schools typically don't live in the same neighborhood make it difficult for teachers to connect with students and empathize with their lives outside school (Charner-Laird et al., 2004). Extracurricular activities, which can serve as a meeting point for students, are often inaccessible (R. Brown & Evans, 2002). This compounds the problem of establishing supportive interpersonal relationships with students (Kincheloe, 2004). One study found that only 20 percent of urban African American males and less than 30 percent of African American females thought that their teachers supported them and cared about their success (Noguera, 2003b). It is difficult for teachers to influence their students' development when mutual trust and caring are absent.

Poverty often has an adverse effect on student achievement, and research indicates that urban environments have higher rates of poverty (nearly 20%) than areas outside central cities (less than 10%) (Macionis, 2011; Macionis & Parillo, 2010). In addition incomes in urban areas are about two-thirds of those in the suburbs.

Lower incomes and the lower residential property values that go with them mean less money for schools. Less money often means that class sizes are larger and schools have fewer resources, such as computers and science lab equipment (Archer, 2003; Blair, 2003).

Finally, because working in urban areas is viewed as very challenging with few rewards, veteran teachers often choose jobs in the suburbs instead of urban settings. As a result, urban students, who most need experienced professionals, are unlikely to get them. This can present opportunities for you; if you're willing to work in an urban environment, the likelihood of getting a job is high. In addition, schools are increasingly offering incentive pay for teachers willing to work in urban schools, and working in them can be rewarding as you help their students develop, both personally and intellectually.

The challenge for urban educators is to create contexts in which students can interact in meaningful ways with both teachers and other students. One proposed solution is to create smaller schools, or schools within a school, that allow for the creation of more personal learning communities. Students in smaller schools "behave better, are more likely to be involved in extra-curricular activities, . . . fight less, feel safe, and feel more attached to their schools" (Ilg & Massucci, 2003, p. 69).

Although teachers alone can't create smaller schools, urban teachers can make a special effort to create learning communities within their classrooms that nurture both the social and cognitive development of their students. Let's see what an urban seventh grader has to say about one of her teachers.

She's probably the strictest teacher I've ever had because she doesn't let you slide by if you've made a mistake. . . . If you've made a mistake she's going to let you know it. And if you're getting bad marks, she's going to let you know it. She's one of my strictest teachers and that's what makes me think she cares about us the most. (Alder, 2002, pp. 251–252)

Effective urban teachers combine high expectations for academic success with clear messages about the need for student effort and responsibility.

One thing Chris remembers from his methods classes is the need for variety. He has been primarily using large-group discussions in his middle school social studies classes, and most of the students seem to respond okay. But others seem disinterested, and their attention often drifts.

Today, Chris decides to try a small-group activity involving problem solving. The class has been studying the growth of American cities, and he wants the students to think about solutions to some of the problems of big cities. As he watches the groups interact, he is surprised at what he sees. Some of the students who are most withdrawn in whole-class discussions are leaders in the groups.

"Great!" he thinks. But at the same time, he notes that some of his more active students are sitting back and not getting involved.

There is no doubt that each student approaches learning differently, but which of these differences are important? One approach to studying learning styles distinguishes between deep and surface approaches to processing information (Evans, Kirby, & Fabrigar, 2003). For instance, when you study a new idea, do you ask yourself how it relates to other ideas, what examples of the idea exist, and how it might apply in a different context? If so, you were using a deep-processing approach. On the other hand, if you simply memorized the definition, you were using a surface approach. As you might expect, deep-processing approaches result in higher achievement if subsequent tests focus on understanding and application, but surface approaches can be successful if tests emphasize fact learning and memorization.

An alternate approach to applying learning styles in classrooms was created by Rita and Kenneth Dunn (1978, 1987). They identified a number of preferred learning style dimensions, including the following:

- **Modality**—does the student learn better through listening or reading?

- **Structure/support**—does the learner need high structure or is he or she an independent learner?

- **Individual/group**—does the learner work best independently or in groups?

- **Motivation**—is the student self-motivated or does he or she require external rewards?

- **Environment**—how do light, temperature, noise, and time of day influence learning? (Dunn & Dunn, 1978)

These preferences or "styles" make intuitive sense. We've all heard people say, "I'm a morning person" or "Don't try to talk to me until I've had my cup of coffee." And, as you saw earlier, many people describe themselves as visual, verbal, or tactile learners.

The work of Dunn and Dunn was popular with teachers in the 1970s and 1980s, and many consultants conducted inservice workshops for teachers on both the Dunns' and others' approaches to learning styles. These approaches are controversial, however. Advocates claim matching learning environments to learner preferences results in increased achievement and improved attitudes (Farkas, 2003; Lovelace, 2005). Critics counter by questioning the validity of the tests used to identify learning styles (Stahl, 2002), and they also cite research indicating that attempts to match learning environments to learning preferences have resulted in no increases and, in some cases, even decreases in learning (Brophy, 2004; Kratzig & Arbuthnott, 2006). In fact, the vast majority of the research examining learning styles supports critics (Brophy & Good, 2008). The following quote summarizes critics' position:

> We also do not see much validity in the claims made by those who urge teachers to assess their students with learning style inventories and follow with differentiated curriculum and instruction. First, the research bases supporting these urgings tend be thin to nonexistent. Second, a single teacher working with twenty or more students does not have time to plan and implement much individualized instruction. With respect to student motivation, much more is to be gained by focusing on students' learning goals, values, and expectancies than on the variable emphasized in learning style inventories. (Good & Brophy, 2008, p. 268)

Implications for Teachers

The idea of learning styles has three implications for teachers. First, as Chris Burnette discovered when he tried to use a one-size-fits-all approach to his teaching, no single instructional approach works with all students, so you should vary the way you teach. This notion is both intuitively sensible and corroborated by research (Brophy, 2004).

Second, knowledge of learning styles can increase your sensitivity to differences in your students, making it more likely that you will respond to them as individuals. You should try to represent the topics you teach as concretely as possible. And, you should always represent them both visually and verbally, and even tactilely if possible, which helps meet the needs of visual, verbal, and tactile learners.

Third, it suggests that teachers should encourage students to think about their own learning, that is, to develop their metacognition.

Metacognition refers to *students' awareness of the ways they learn most effectively and their ability to control these factors.* For example, a student who realizes that studying with music reduces her ability to concentrate, and then turns the radio off, is demonstrating metacognition. Students who are metacognitive can adjust strategies to match learning tasks better than their less metacognitive peers can and, as a result, they learn more (Eggen & Kauchak, 2010). By encouraging students to think about how they learn best, teachers provide students with a powerful learning tool they can use throughout their lives.

Summary

Capitalizing on Cultural Diversity

Students in today's classrooms are more diverse than ever, and this diversity poses special challenges and opportunities for teachers. Diversity appears as differences in cultural and language backgrounds, socioeconomic status, and learning abilities and learning styles.

The cultural backgrounds of our students influence their ability to profit from instruction. Cultural deficit, teacher expectations, and cultural differences are three prominent theories that attempt to explain differences in achievement among cultural groups. Teachers can capitalize on cultural diversity by using the cultural resources of their students, communicating positive attitudes about diversity, and employing teaching strategies that build upon diversity.

Language Diversity

Language diversity results from large numbers of students immigrating to this country and from dialect differences in different sections of the United States. In dealing with dialects the most effective strategy is to accept and build on them.

Different language development programs emphasize retaining native languages to differing degrees. Maintenance bilingual programs attempt to nurture and retain the native language; transitional bilingual programs use the native language as an instructional aid until English is proficient. ESL programs focus primarily on the mastery of English.

Teaching Students with Different Learning Abilities

Current views hold that intelligence is alterable, culture embedded and multifaceted. Flexible time frames, grouping, strategy instruction, and peer tutoring and cooperative learning activities are all ways teachers adapt their instruction for students of different abilities.

Students with Exceptionalities

Students with exceptionalities require special help to reach their full potential. Teachers help these students through identification, fostering acceptance, and modifying instruction to meet their special needs.

At-risk Students

At-risk students are in danger of failing to complete their education with the skills necessary to survive in a modern technological society. Economic and social problems combine to produce conditions that detract from learning. These include nutrition and health problems and experiential differences that fail to provide a firm foundation for learning. Effective teaching for at-risk students is not fundamentally different from good teaching in general. Teachers are also becoming increasingly aware of the need for high expectations and challenge.

Learning Styles

Learning styles emphasize differences in the ways students prefer to learn in the classroom. The concept of learning styles reminds us that all students learn differently. Effective teachers are sensitive to these differences, adapt their teaching accordingly, and help students become metacognitively aware of their own learning styles.

*I*mportant Concepts

Acceleration (p. 51)

Active teaching (p. 59)

Adaptive fit (p. 49)

Assistive technology (p. 55)

At-risk students (p. 54)

Bidialecticism (p. 42)

Bilingual maintenance programs (p. 42)

Cultural deficit theory (p. 35)

Cultural difference theory (p. 36)

Culturally responsive teaching (p. 38)

Culture (p. 35)

Dialect (p. 41)

English as a second language (ESL) programs (p. 43)

Enrichment (p. 51)

Gardner's theory of multiple intelligences (p. 47)

Inclusion (p. 49)

Individualized education program (IEP) (p. 49)

Intelligence (p. 46)

Learning styles (p. 60)

Least restrictive environment (p. 48)

Mainstreaming (p. 48)

Metacognition (p. 63)

Multicultural education (p. 35)

Resiliency (p. 58)

Response to intervention (RTI) (p. 53)

Sheltered instruction (p. 43)

Socioeconomic status (p. 57)

Students who are behaviorally disordered, disturbed, or emotionally handicapped (p. 50)

Students who are gifted and talented (p. 51)

Students with exceptionalities (p. 48)

Students with intellectual disabilities (p. 50)

Students with learning disabilities (p. 50)

Students with mild to moderate disabilities (p. 50)

Teacher expectations (p. 35)

Transitional bilingual programs (p. 43)

*P*reparing for Your Licensure Exam

As you've studied this chapter, you've seen how our students are different in several important ways. As you read the following case study of a teacher attempting to teach her students about indirect objects, analyze her success in adapting her instruction to the learning needs of her students.

The Power of Classroom Practice
www.myeducationlab.com

Having read this case, go to the Book Specific Resources tab in MyEducationLab, select your text, select *Preparing for Your Licensure Exam* under

Chapter 2 to complete the questions that accompany the case and receive feedback on your responses.

Diane Henderson, a fifth-grade teacher at Martin Luther King Elementary School, begins her language arts class by saying, "Class, look up at the overhead. What do you notice about the two sentences?"

He gave the gift to her.
John sent him the letter.

She calls on Naitia.

"The second one has a proper noun."

"Okay. What else?" Diane says, smiling. "Sheila?"

"Both verbs are past tense."

"Indeed they are!" Diane nods and smiles again. "What else, Kelvin?" she asks quickly.

"The first has a pronoun for the subject."

"That's true," Diane confirms. "Does everyone see that?" she asks energetically.

"Now, let's look more closely at the first sentence. What is the direct object in that sentence? . . . Kwan?" Diane asks as she walks down the aisle.

"*Her*?" Kwan responds.

"Hmm. What do you think, Luciano?"

"*Gift*?" answers Luciano, hesitating.

"Class, what do you think? Is the direct object in sentence one *her* or *gift*? I want everyone to think about this in your head. Okay, Todd, do you want to try?"

"Uh, I think it's *gift*."

"That's correct. But why is *gift* the direct object, Theresa?"

"Because that's what he gave," Theresa replies.

"Good answer, Theresa. The direct object takes the action from the verb. But now, what about *her*? What is *her*?" Diane asks, looking around the room. "Well, that's what we are going to learn about today. *Her* is an indirect object. An indirect object receives the action. So, in the first sentence, *gift* is the direct object and *her* is the indirect object. Every language has direct and indirect objects, so what we are learning today will help you with both English and all other languages.

"Now let's look at the second sentence. It has both a direct object and an indirect object. Who can tell us which is which? Mireya?"

"The direct object in the second sentence is *letter*," Mireya responds hesitantly.

"Yes, good," Diane says and smiles reassuringly.

"So what is the indirect object? Rashad?" Diane continues.

"It must be *him*."

"Very good, Rashad! And why is *letter* the direct object? Laura?"

"Because that's what John sent."

"And how about *him*? Why is it the indirect object? . . . Jacinta?"

"'Cause that's who received the letter."

"Good! Now look at this sentence, and tell me which is the direct and indirect object."

The batter hit the shortstop a line drive.

"Katya?"

"Umm."

"Oh, I know," Tom blurts out.

"That's great, Tom, but remember what we said about giving everyone in the class a chance to answer? Go ahead, Katya."

"I think *line drive* is the direct object."

"Good, Katya. That's right. Now who can tell us why it's the direct object? Angie?"

"Because that's what the batter hit."

"And what's the indirect object, Kareem, and why?"

"I think it's *shortstop* because that's who the batter hit the line drive to."

"Yes, good answer." Diane nods and then continues.

"I think we're starting to understand the difference between direct and indirect objects. Now we need to practice to make sure. I want you to get into your learning groups, and I want each of you to complete the exercise that asks you to label the direct and indirect objects in the sentences BEFORE you discuss it as a group. Then, I want you to take turns explaining your answers to each other. Quickly now, into your groups, and today's group leaders should come up and pick up the exercise sheets."

Diane watches as her students quickly get into their groups and start working. A list on the bulletin board ensures that everyone in the group will have an opportunity to be a "Group Leader." In addition, she has strategically composed the groups so they are heterogeneous in terms of ability, gender, and culture. She also has paired students with limited English proficiency with other students with similar language backgrounds to provide assistance.

As the students begin working on their sentences, Diane walks up and down the rows, monitoring each student's progress. After 15 minutes, Diane discusses the exercises with the whole class, focusing on sentences students had difficulties with.

Then, Diane continues, "That's excellent. Now I want each of you to write a sentence that has in it one example of an indirect and a direct object. Underline them in each case and label them. If you are having problems getting started, raise your hand and I'll be by in a minute."

While the students write their sentences, Diane circulates among them, periodically stopping to comment on students' work and to offer suggestions. Mario, a student who receives extra help from a resource teacher, sits with his head on his desk.

"What's the problem, Mario?"

"I don't understand this," Mario replies with a shrug.

"Well, getting started is often the hardest part. Why don't you write down a sentence and then raise your hand, and I'll help you with the next step."

After 5 minutes, Diane announces, "All right, everyone. Please switch your paper with the person in the next row, and let's see how you did."

Questions for Analysis

1. To what extent did Diane display culturally responsive teaching in her lesson?
2. To what extent did Diane's teaching reflect sensitivity to differences in language ability?
3. What did Diane do to accommodate differences in learning styles?

Discussion Questions

1. What cultural groups live in the area where you will be teaching? What do you know about these cultures? How do their cultural beliefs and attitudes influence learning?
2. What important differences exist between the cultural difference theory and the other two theories (cultural deficit and teacher expectations)? Why are these differences important for teachers and students?
3. How were the interaction patterns of the Native American students similar to those of African American students? How were they different? What implications do these similarities and differences have for instruction?

4. How are the different instructional approaches to teaching English similar? How are they different? What are the advantages and disadvantages of each?

5. Think about the dimensions of intelligence identified by experts: (a) abstract thinking and reasoning, (b) problem-solving ability, and (c) capacity to acquire knowledge. Which do you think is most important in today's world? Which is least important? Why?

6. Which of Gardner's multiple intelligences is most emphasized in schools today? Which is least emphasized? Which do you think should be emphasized more? Why?

7. What are the pros and cons of teachers attempting to modify instruction to match students' learning styles? Which learning style difference is most important to you? Why?

8. How do learning styles relate to Gardner's multiple intelligences? Do you think these differences are genetically or environmentally influenced? Explain.

9. How are at-risk students similar to students from different cultural groups? How are they different? What implications does this have for instruction?

10. At-risk students used to be called *underachievers* or *potential dropouts*. Why is *at-risk* a more appropriate term and how does the use of this term signal changes in society?

Portfolio Activities

1. *Student Diversity.* Interview a teacher about the diversity in that teacher's classroom. How do students differ in terms of the following?

   a. culture
   b. home language
   c. socioeconomic status (SES)
   d. learning styles

   What does the teacher do to accommodate these differences?

2. *Diversity and Classroom Interaction.* Observe a classroom and focus on several minority students.

   a. Where do they sit?
   b. With whomWWW do they talk to and make friends?
   c. Do they attend to the class and are they involved?
   d. Do they participate in classroom interaction?

   Ask the teacher what she or he does to build on differences in these students.

3. *Cultural Minorities: The Students' Perspective.* Ask the teacher to identify several minority students. Interview these students and ask the following:

   a. How long have they been at this school?
   b. What do they like most about school?
   c. What do they like lWhat do teast?
   d. What can teachers do to help them learn better?

4. *Teaching in Diverse Classrooms.* Observe a class using interactive teaching. In observing this classroom, analyze the class for any differential participation rates by minority students. To do this identify a comparable number of minority and

nonminority students to observe (three or four of each is optimal). Observe them during the lesson, noting the following:

    a. How do their attending rates compare; that is, are they participating in the lesson and listening to the interaction?

    b. How often do students from each group raise their hands to answer a teacher question?

    c. How often do students from each group get called on?

What implications do your results have for your teaching?

5. *Differences in Learning Ability: Student Perspectives.* Observe a class working on an in-class assignment. As you do this, circulate around the room so you can observe the work progress of different students. As you do so, note the following:

    a. Beginning Times—Do all students get immediately to work or do some take more time starting?

    b. On-task Behaviors—What percentage of the class stays on task throughout the assignment?

    c. Completion Times—When do the first students complete the assignment? When do the last students finish?

    d. Teacher Monitoring—What does the teacher do during the seatwork? How do students signal that they need help?

    e. Options—What options are there for students who complete their assignments early?

What strategies can teachers use to accommodate students with different learning abilities?

6. *Students with Exceptionalities.* Interview a teacher about students with exceptionalities in the classroom. Ask the following questions:

    a. Which students are classified as exceptional?
       What behaviors led to this classification?
       What role did the teacher play in identification?

    b. In working with students with exceptionalities, what assistance does the classroom teacher receive from the following people?

       (1) Special education teacher
       (2) School psychologist or school counselor
       (3) Principal

    c. What does an IEP. look like? How helpful is it in working with exceptional students in the classroom?

    d. What strategies does the teacher use to help these students in the classroom?

What implications do the teacher's responses have for you as a teacher?

7. *Inclusion.* Interview a teacher about inclusion and ask the following questions:

    a. How many students with exceptionalities are included in the classroom?

    b. How has the teacher adapted instruction to meet the needs of these students?

    c. What assistance does the teacher have in working with these students?

    d. What suggestions does the teacher have to make the process more effective?

8. *Teaching At-risk Students.* Identify a class with considerable numbers of at-risk students. Observe a lesson in that class and analyze it in terms of the following strategies:

   a. Active teaching
   b. Use of manipulatives and examples
   c. Active student involvement
   d. Interactive teaching
   e. Practice and feedback
   f. High success rates

What else does the teacher do to effectively teach these students? What implications do your findings have for you as a teacher?

PEARSON
myeducationlab
The Power of Classroom Practice
www.myeducationlab.com

To check your comprehension of the content covered in Chapter 2, go to the Book Specific Resources in MyEducationLab, select your text, and complete the Study Plan quiz. In addition to receiving feedback on your answers, a study plan will be generated from the quiz that will direct you to access Review, Practice, and Enrichment materials to enhance your understanding of chapter content.

Creating Productive Learning Environments: Classroom Management

Chapter Outline	Learning Objectives
	When you've completed your study of this chapter, you should be able to:
The importance of classroom management	1. Explain why classroom management is important to classroom teachers.
Classroom management: A definition	
■ Goals for classroom management: Learning and self-regulation	2. Explain how classroom management can develop student responsibility and self-regulation.
■ Creating responsibility-oriented classrooms	
■ Classroom management: A historical perspective	
Planning for classroom management	3. Describe factors that influence planning for classroom management.
■ Student characteristics	
■ The physical environment	
■ Classroom rules: Establishing standards for behavior	
■ Procedures: Creating an efficient learning environment	
Implementing management plans	4. Describe strategies for implementing management plans.
■ Implementing plans: The first 10 days	
Technology and Teaching:	
Using technology to communicate with parents	
Exploring Diversity:	
Challenges to home-school communication	
■ The relationship between management and instruction	
Management interventions	5. Explain how effective teachers use interventions to deal with misbehavior.
■ An intervention continuum	
■ Dealing with persistent individual problems	
■ Serious management problems: Violence and aggression	

If you are uneasy about being in front of a classroom of students for the first time, you're not alone. This apprehension is common among interns, first-year teachers, and even some veterans. Often the concern results from uncertainty about their ability to prevent disruptions or deal effectively with them when they occur. In this chapter we describe how you can design a classroom management system that will help you retain your own sanity while also creating a productive learning environment for your students. As you read the following vignettes, think about the management challenges you'll face in your own classroom.

Maria Perez looks around her empty classroom and tries to imagine what it will be like with 27 live first graders. This is preplanning, the few days teachers have to do their final preparation for the year ahead.

Maria had completed her student teaching internship in a school not far from this one, and she had worked all summer on unit and lesson plans until she was comfortable with what she wanted to teach.

But she still isn't sure about classroom management. "How in the world will I get all those rambunctious kids to sit quietly and pay attention to the important ideas they need to learn?" she wonders. She had watched veteran teachers and saw that they were able to "keep the lid on," but she wants to do more; she wants to help her children grow-in every sense of the word.

Jeff Thompson, a third-year middle school teacher, walks around his classroom, trying to burn off some nervous energy.

"The room looks great," he thinks to himself. Having survived two years of up-and-down teaching, Jeff wants this year to be different. Students like his social studies classes, but they were noisier and more frenetic than he wanted. He realized that some noise was inevitable, but his students seem to be constantly testing him. If only he could get them to willingly cooperate and do their work without his having to get after them all the time. If only. . . .

The Importance of Classroom Management

Historically, both teachers and the public at large have believed that creating an orderly classroom is essential for learning. For example, national Gallup polls continually identify classroom management as one of the most important and challenging problems facing teachers (Bushaw & Gallup, 2008).

Classroom management is a topic of enduring concern for teachers, administrators, and the public. Beginning teachers consistently perceive student discipline as their most serious challenge, management problems continue to be a major cause of teacher burnout and job dissatisfaction, and the public repeatedly ranks discipline as the first or second most serious problem facing the schools (Evertson & Weinstein, 2006, p. 3).

It has also historically been the primary concern of beginning teachers. Disruptive students are an important source of stress for beginners and veterans alike (Bohn, Roehrig, & Pressley, 2004; Public Agenda 2004). It also is a major reason teachers leave the profession during their first years of teaching.

Commonly overlooked in discussions of management and discipline is the role of effective instruction. Research indicates that it is virtually impossible to maintain an orderly classroom in the absence of good teaching and vice versa (Rimm-Kaufman, La Paro, Downer, & Pianta, 2005; Good & Brophy, 2008). The relationship between classroom management and learning is well documented (Good & Brophy, 2008; Marzano, 2003). Effective classroom management increases student engagement, decreases disruptive behaviors, and provides increased opportunities for instructional time, all of which are related to improved student achievement (Emmer et al., 2009; Evertson et al., 2009). Clearly, students learn more in well-managed classrooms.

To underscore this important relationship, in this chapter we'll emphasize teachers' ability to create a **productive learning environment**, *which is a classroom that is orderly and focuses on learning.* In it students feel safe, both physically and emotionally, and the day-to-day routines are all designed to help students learn.

Classroom Management: A Definition

Classroom management *consists of all the teacher thoughts, plans, and actions that create a productive learning environment.* As examples of the broad array of teacher actions that fall under this umbrella, consider the following:

> Maria Perez has her first graders practice the routines of finishing seatwork and putting it in folders in front of the room. She has them finish a short assignment and then "walks them through" the process of taking the paper, filing it efficiently, and returning to their desks.
>
> Jeff Thompson has a list of rules written on a piece of poster paper in the front of the room that describes what students are to do when they work in groups. Jeff has found that his middle school students like to work in groups, but they often get sidetracked by socializing. Each time he breaks students into groups, he goes over the rules and reminds them that he expects a written product from each group. As they work in their groups, Jeff circulates around the class providing both structure and support.
>
> Rosa Chacon carefully prepares each morning for her high school American history classes. "These kids are sharp, and their disagreements are animated," she comments to a colleague in the faculty workroom. "If I'm not prepared, they know it, and their discussions get a little out of hand. They're good kids though, so all I have to do is tell them to tone it down a little, and they're fine."

Each of these situations is unique, but they're all part of the management process. Maria teaches small children who need to learn classroom routines; Jeff's focus is on rules for helping his middle school students work in groups; Rosa spends much of her effort in planning for instruction. Planning, organization, creating routines, and developing ways to handle disruptions are all part of effective classroom management.

Goals for Classroom Management: Learning and Self-Regulation

We have two goals when we create productive learning environments. The first is to maximize learning, and you should continually ask yourself if your management system contributes to student learning. Our second goal is to develop in students the ability to manage and direct their own learning (Jones, 2005). The classroom environment should become a vehicle for promoting student self-understanding, self-evaluation, and the internalization of self-control.

To accomplish both of these goals effective teachers communicate a *responsibility* rather than an *obedience* orientation (Jones, 2005). An **obedience model of management** *teaches students to follow rules and obey authority, using rewards and punishment.* The goal is conformity. By contrast, a **responsibility model of management** *helps students make appropriate choices and learn from their actions and decisions.*

Creating Responsibility-Oriented Classrooms

Teachers' interactions with students are central to the development of responsibility. Research on parenting styles and their effects on children provide us with some guidelines.

Three distinct parental interaction styles were identified, and these patterns had clear effects on children (Baumrind, 1991). *Authoritarian* parents valued conformity, were emotionally detached, didn't explain their reasons for rules, and discouraged discussions about issues related to behavior. Their children tended to be withdrawn, and they worried more about pleasing their parents than solving problems (Maughan & Cicchetti, 2002).

Permissive parents, by contrast, had few expectations for their children and gave them total freedom. This freedom didn't result in happiness or growth, however. Children of permissive parents were immature, lacked self-control, and were anxious and uncertain.

Authoritative parents were firm but caring. They had high expectations, were consistent in their expectations, and explained the reasons for rules. Their children were more confident and secure, had higher self-esteem, and were more willing to take risks (Christenson & Havsy, 2004).

Similar styles have been identified in teachers (Gill et al., 2003); effective teachers tend to be more authoritative than authoritarian or permissive. They establish rules and procedures and take the time to explain why they're necessary. They have high expectations for their students, and they're supportive as students attempt to meet their expectations. When disruptions occur, they quickly intervene, solve the problem, and return just as quickly to the learning activity. Like authoritative parents, they are firm but caring, they establish rules and limits, and they expect students to demonstrate self-control. In time students in their classrooms become self-regulated learners.

Classroom Management: A Historical Perspective

Before continuing, let's put classroom management into historical perspective. Researchers in the area haven't always focused on the teacher as a manager of classroom activities and creator of productive learning environments. Early research viewed the teacher as either a clinical practitioner who was both a counselor and therapist or an effective disciplinarian (Doyle, 1986; Jones & Jones, 2010).

The problem with the clinical practitioner view was that it was both unrealistic and impractical. Although every teacher needs to be sensitive and responsive to students, and teachers should be caring listeners, counseling is not their primary role. Rather, they are expected to promote learning and responsibility in their students. A second reason was logistical; it's impossible for teachers, with their many students and widely varying responsibilities, to spend the time needed to work on each student's problems. That's what school counselors and psychologists are hired to do. This doesn't suggest that teachers never deal with students' personal problems on a one-to-one basis. As a general approach, however, it's impractical.

A second perspective viewed classroom managers as disciplinarians. An effective manager, for example, would be one who could quickly quiet a class when students get too noisy or could get them back in their seats quickly after a disturbance. Research, however, didn't support this view, and the story behind this research is interesting.

Jacob Kounin (1970) is primarily responsible for turning our attention away from discipline or intervention strategies to more preventive approaches. But he didn't do so without some fitful starts. In short, he found that successful classroom managers were good at preventing problems in the first place, rather than putting out fires after they occurred.

One of the challenges researchers encountered was the near invisibility of an effective teacher's actions in a productive learning environment; they were so efficient that it was difficult to pinpoint specific actions that made a difference. In hindsight we see that this was one of the most important findings of this research.

Planning for Classroom Management

Few veteran teachers would think of getting up in front of a group of students without planning for what they were trying to accomplish. Although they might not write down everything on paper, they are very clear about what they want to accomplish and how they will go about it.

As with effective instruction, creating a productive learning environment begins with planning, and beginning teachers often underestimate the amount of time and energy this takes. The cornerstone of effective classroom management is a clearly understood and consistently monitored set of rules and procedures, which accommodate both the characteristics of students and the physical environment of the classroom (Emmer et al., 2009; Evertson et al., 2009). Let's look at how the students you teach influence your management planning.

Student Characteristics

Jeff Thompson just completed a semester of clinical experiences in a high school and had a very positive experience. His lessons went generally well, and the students were quite mature, responsive, and well behaved.

For his second semester Jeff was placed in a middle school. The students seemed hyperactive, and admonishments to sit quietly and wait to be called on worked for a few minutes at the most. He prepared as he had for his lessons at the high school, but his first one here was a disaster.

Learner diversity is a fact of teaching life. In addition to cultural diversity, students at different ages think, act, and respond differently to rules and procedures. You need to anticipate these differences as you plan for classroom management. Descriptions of developmental differences that influence management and their implications for classroom management are outlined in Table 3.1.

Although differences between developmental stages suggest different emphases and approaches, the same basic principles apply to all students. All students—younger or older—respond well to understandable sets of rules and procedures that are clearly explained and consistently enforced. Research examining learners with exceptionalities who are included in regular classrooms suggests that they respond to the same supportive and structured approach (Hardman et al., 2008).

The Physical Environment

"I can't see the board."

"I didn't get a worksheet. Kevin didn't pass them back."

"What did she say? I couldn't hear her!"

The physical environment of your classroom is a second planning consideration, and the question you're trying to answer is, "How can I arrange the room to minimize distractions and maximize learning?"

Several guidelines aid your decisions. First, all students must be able to see the board, projector screen, maps, and other instructional aids. Surprisingly, some teachers don't consider this factor. For example, they sometimes display material on the board or screen

Table 3.1 **Developmental Differences in Learners**

Stage	Description
Stage 1: Lower primary	Students in the lower primary grades are generally compliant and oriented toward pleasing their teacher; their attention spans are short, and they tend to break rules more from simply forgetting or not fully understanding them than for other reasons. Rules must be carefully and explicitly taught, modeled, practiced, and frequently reviewed with students at this age. Role-playing and positive reinforcement for compliance can help solidify the rules in students' minds.
Stage 2: Middle elementary	This level is characterized by children who understand the game of schooling and generally are still interested in pleasing the teacher. Many elementary teachers believe this age group is the easiest to teach and manage because of these characteristics. Rules are easier to (re)teach at this level, and the teacher's central management task becomes one of maintenance and monitoring.
Stage 3: Middle and junior high	This stage spans grades seven through about nine and includes the tempestuous period of adolescence. As students become more oriented toward their peers, authority is questioned more often, and more disruptions result from attention seeking, humorous remarks, horseplay, and testing of limits. Classroom management can be demanding at this stage. Motivating students and maintaining compliance with the rules are the teacher's major tasks.
Stage 4: High school	In the later high school years, students mature, becoming more personally adjusted and more oriented toward academic learning. Management becomes easier, and more time and energy can be devoted to instructional tasks.

that is too small to be seen clearly by all students, which can lead to inattention and possible management problems.

The room should also be arranged so you can move easily from one aid, such as the board or map, to another, without students having to turn their desks or, if possible, even shift their bodies. Something as simple as turning in a desk can disrupt the flow of an activity for a group of rambunctious students.

Materials, such as paper and scissors, should be easily accessible, and procedures for routine activities, such as using the drinking fountain, sink, and pencil sharpener, should be specified. Many teachers make their desks and storage areas off limits without permission.

When arranging desks, consider the types of learning activities students will be involved in (e.g., cooperative learning groups, whole-class instruction, individual assignments). For instance, many teachers combine groupwork with whole-class presentations, so students need to be able to make the transition from small-group to large-group activities quickly and easily. As you begin teaching, try different arrangements and select the one that works the best for you. The following is one middle school teacher's experience:

Jeff Thompson has 33 seventh graders in a room designed for a maximum of 27, and as a result, the students are close together. He tries arranging the desks in his room in a two-ring semicircle with the outer row behind the inner.

He soon moves the desks back to their original positions, explaining the move in this way, "They weren't trying to be disruptive. . . . But as they faced each other across the front of the room, they would inaudibly mouth questions like 'What are you doing tonight?' or they were pinching each other on the rear ends. They couldn't handle it, so I went back to a standard arrangement of rows."

This example illustrates the need to consider both the physical arrangement of the room and the characteristics of students in developing a management system. Jeff experimented with different arrangements and found the one that was most effective for his students.

Where individual students should sit is another issue. Several factors affect this decision. First, for students in the fourth or fifth through the eighth or ninth grades, the social aspects of schooling increase, and who sits next to whom becomes important. An "action zone" exists in classrooms; students seated in the center or front of the classroom tend to interact more frequently with the teacher, and the number of behavioral problems increases as students sit farther away. Students in the back and corners of the room are more likely to be off task than are those close to the front or the teacher's desk.

In response to these factors, some teachers change their room arrangement and student seating charts on a regular schedule, both for the sake of variety and to put different students at the front of the room. They use seat assignments as a management tool to help students become involved and to maintain that involvement throughout the day. Many effective teachers begin the school year with arbitrary seat assignments, planning to make changes after they've had several weeks to observe the patterns of behavior that evolve.

Should students be allowed to sit where they want? If you are a new teacher, a bit anxious about management, or have had management problems in the past, this isn't a good idea. Later, it can be used as a reward for good classroom behavior with the condition that the desirable behavior continues. Student choice is a privilege, not a right, and it may not be possible in the lower elementary grades or even middle school where self-control hasn't yet developed.

Allowing students to choose their own seats also creates another potential problem— segregation of students by race, ethnicity, or culture. Cliques are a fact of life in schools, and students tend to form friendships based upon similarities. A potentially negative by-product of allowing students to choose their own seats is that classrooms can become segregated into seating blocks, with White students in one area and minorities in another (Lee, 2007). This runs counter to our overall goal of helping students learn about and form friendships with a variety of students. So, if you do decide to allow students to choose their own seats, be aware of this potential problem and deal with it if it occurs.

Classroom Rules: Establishing Standards for Behavior

As we said earlier in the chapter, effective managers prevent misbehavior rather than eliminate problems after they occur; a clear set of rules, consistently enforced, is essential in this process.

Classroom rules *are descriptions of standards for acceptable student behavior.* Examples include the following:

- Treat the teacher and your classmates with respect.
- Keep hands and materials to yourself.
- Speak only when given permission by the teacher.
- Remain in your seat until given permission to leave.
- Bring all materials to every class.

Research confirms the value of rules such as these; reasonable rules, clearly explained and fairly and consistently enforced, not only reduce behavior problems that interfere with learning but also can promote a feeling of pride and responsibility in the classroom (Good & Brophy, 2008; Marzano & Marzano, 2003). Perhaps surprisingly, students also see setting clear standards of behavior as evidence that the teacher cares about them (Brophy, 2004).

The rules just presented pertain to most classrooms. For example, researchers have found that up to 80 percent of classroom management problems involve students talking inappropriately, and much of the remaining 20 percent are related to students' being out of their seats without permission or failing to bring books, pencils, or notebook paper to class (Jones, 2005). In addition, teachers, particularly at the middle and junior high levels, also complain about students' tendencies to hit, poke, shove, and grab at one another and at others' belongings. If the rules listed were consistently enforced, many management problems could be prevented before they occur.

Certain ways of establishing rules are better than others. Guidelines are outlined in Figure 3.1 and discussed in the paragraphs that follow.

We see "Solicit student input" at the top of Figure 3.1. Involving students in the process is consistent with a responsibility model of management and has three important benefits:

- It promotes a sense of student ownership in the rules and increases the likelihood they will follow them.

- It emphasizes student self-regulation and personal responsibility.

- It treats students as moral thinkers and helps them learn the values, such as respect for others, behind rules.

"State rules positively" and "Minimize the number" are two other important guidelines for establishing rules. Stating rules positively specifies desired behavior; those stated negatively identify only what students are not to do. To behave responsibly, students must be aware of and remember the rules, and the more they have to remember, the more difficult this is. One of the most common reasons students break rules is that they simply forget them. This tendency is particularly true with young children, but it is often the case with older students as well. For example, middle school and high school students are sometimes given legal-size sheets of paper with long lists of single-spaced rules, the rules are discussed on the first day of class, and they aren't referred to again until they're broken. Under these conditions, we all would forget. The solution is to identify a short list that you intend to enforce consistently.

Figure 3.1

Guidelines for Developing Rules

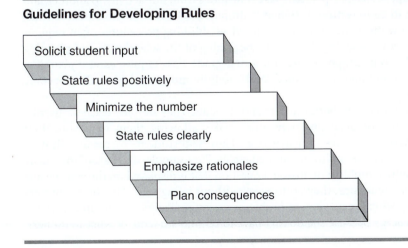

- Solicit student input
- State rules positively
- Minimize the number
- State rules clearly
- Emphasize rationales
- Plan consequences

Rules should also be stated clearly and as specifically as possible. For example, compare the following:

1. Bring your book, notebook, paper, and pencil to every class.

2. Always come to school prepared.

The first rule specifically describes the desired behavior; its meaning is clear. In contrast, the second requires interpretation; interpretation adds to uncertainty and, in extreme cases, can lead to misunderstanding and controversy. When rules are stated in general terms, such as "Treat the teacher and your classmates with respect," explaining and providing examples of following the rule and other examples that illustrate breaking the rule help students understand the rule and its intent.

Emphasizing the reasons or rationales for rules is one of the most important aspects of creating and teaching them. It demonstrates that they aren't arbitrary and communicates that the world is a sensible and orderly place. This might be as simple as explaining why one person talking at a time is necessary for learning, or it could involve a longer discussion about the need to respect the rights of others. It's virtually impossible to implement a "responsibility model" of management without providing reasons for rules, and we want to strongly emphasize its importance.

Planning consequences is the final suggestion in developing rules. Teachers sometimes struggle with management because they haven't made specific decisions about how to respond when students break a rule. Planning for consequences in advance helps eliminate much of this uncertainty.

In considering consequences, the student characteristics we discussed earlier are important. High school students may need only a simple reminder, and specific consequences may be unnecessary. With younger students you may have to consistently enforce rules with specific consequences until they understand the rules and have learned to follow them essentially automatically.

Procedures: Creating an Efficient Learning Environment

Procedures are *guidelines for accomplishing daily routines that recur frequently in classrooms.* Effective classrooms have well-established procedures for all routine activities, such as how students turn in papers, sharpen pencils, make transitions from one activity to another, and obtain permission to go to restrooms (Good & Brophy, 2008). With high school students, who understand how the game of school is played, establishing procedures often requires little more than briefly discussing them at the beginning of the school year, and planning for them is easy. In contrast, procedures for a first-grade class require careful planning; procedures need to be taught, explained, and carefully monitored until they become automatic routines.

Routines are invaluable to both teachers and students. They simplify teachers' lives by reducing the number of decisions they must make, allowing them to devote their emotional and physical energies to instruction. They help students by communicating expectations and making the environment predictable. For example, if as part of their daily routine, students solve a problem or answer a question that is displayed on the board while the teacher checks attendance, they go to work without being told. This both prevents "dead time" during which management problems are more likely to occur and saves the teacher time and energy because she doesn't have to remind students of what to do next.

Table 3.2 Areas for Considering Classroom Procedures

Procedural Area	Concerns
1. Entering classroom/beginning of period	What should students do when they enter the classroom?
2. Large-group instruction	What are the rules for participation (e.g., should students raise their hands to respond)?
3. Individual/small-group instruction	What should students do when they need help? When they're done?
4. Materials and equipment	How are papers handed in and back? What about tape and scissors?
5. End of period	How do students leave the classroom (e.g., does the bell or the teacher signal permission to leave)?
6. Out-of-room policies	How do children receive permission to use the bathroom or go to the main office?

Some general areas in which procedures are important are outlined in Table 3.2; since establishing procedures for the beginning of class is particularly important, some additional suggestions for this crucial time are included in Table 3.3. Planning, both for procedures in general and for the beginning of class in particular, is essential for the smooth functioning of your classroom.

PEARSON
myeducationlab
The Power of Classroom Practice
www.myeducationlab.com

To view a video clip of a teacher implementing rules and procedures in her classroom, go to the Book Specific Resources tab in MyEducationLab, select your text, select Video Examples under Chapter 3, and then click on *Establishing Rules and Procedures at the Beginning of the School Year.*

Table 3.3 Sample Beginning-of-Class Procedures

Area	Questions
1. Entering class	Should students go directly to their seats when they enter the class? Can they talk? Can they walk around the room? Is there an assignment on the board?
2. Attendance	How will the teacher take attendance? What about tardies (e.g., do they go to the office to remove their names from the absentee list)?
3. Previous absences	Is a note from parents required? What about missed work (e.g., homework and quizzes)?
4. Logistics	What about lunch count? Milk money? Special schedule for the day (e.g., assemblies and PE)?

*I*mplementing Management Plans

It is August 29, Yolanda's first day of kindergarten. She has been to the school to see her brother in a play and to attend the Fall Carnival. She knows about school from her brother and parents, but still she is not sure what to expect. Her dad walks her to school, and she is excited. As she gets closer, she notices all the people and cars. Her dad helps her thread her way through the crowds to her classroom. She sees some familiar faces of neighborhood playmates, but most of the people are strangers. Mrs. Davis, her teacher, approaches, smiles, welcomes her, and takes her to her desk just as the bell rings. She apprehensively sits down, not sure what to do next.

Jim, too, is excited about his first day of school. He is in fifth grade and is looking forward to playing on the playground before school and seeing all of his friends. When he arrives, the playground is just as he expects—chaotic. He goes over to the baseball diamond where some of his friends are playing catch and half-heartedly trying to get a game going.

Soon the bell rings, and the students funnel into the school. Jim knows that his teacher will be Mr. Wood, who has the reputation of being strict, but fair. His teacher stands at the door and tells each student to find the desk with his or her name on it. As Mr. Wood moves to the front of the room, Jim thinks, "I wonder what this year will be like."

Delia is beginning her junior year of high school. In addition to the rest of her schedule, she is taking Advanced Placement American history, even though she was in standard world history as a tenth grader. She is excited to be in school this first morning but somewhat anxious about the AP class. The bell sends her to first period, where Mrs. Perez, her teacher, waits. As she enters the class, she notes a sign on the board: "Seat yourself and fill out the card on your desk." For better or for worse, she is in AP American history.

These examples have two things in common. First, each involves students beginning the first day of school, and second, all students are experiencing some apprehension. Uneasiness in response to uncertainty is natural and essentially universal. We all feel more comfortable when we know what is expected of us. Teachers' responses to students during this crucial period set the stage for the remainder of the year.

Implementing Plans: The First 10 Days

Research consistently confirms that patterns of behavior for the entire year are established in the first few days of school (Gettinger & Kohler, 2006). Let's see how two teachers handle the first day.

Donnell Alexander is waiting at the door for her eighth graders with prepared handouts as students come in the room. As she distributes them, she says, "Take your seats quickly, please. You'll find your name on the desk. The bell is going to ring in less than a minute, and everyone needs to be at his or her desk and quiet when it does. Please read the handout while you're waiting." She is standing at the front of the room, surveying the class as the bell rings. When it stops, she begins, "Good morning, everyone."

Vicki Williams, who also teaches eighth graders across the hall from Donnell, is organizing her handouts as the students come in the room. Some take their seats while others mill around, talking in small groups. As the bell rings, she looks up and says over the hum of the students, "Everyone take your seats, please. We'll begin in a couple minutes," and she turns back to organizing her materials.

In these first few minutes, Donnell's students learned that they were expected to be in their seats and ready to start at the beginning of class, whereas Vicki's learned just the opposite. Students quickly understand these differences, and unless Vicki changes this pattern, she will soon have problems, perhaps not dramatic, but chronic and low grade, like nagging sniffles that won't go away. Problems such as these cause more teacher stress and fatigue than any other (Friedman, 2006; Weiner, 2002).

Guidelines for starting the year off right are illustrated in Figure 3.2 and discussed in the paragraphs that follow.

Plan for Maximum Contact and Control   Plan instructional activities during the first two weeks of class with management concerns as a high priority. Use whole-class instruction rather than small-group work, minimize work with individual students, and keep the number of transitions from one activity to another low. Stay in the classroom and don't allow yourself to become distracted by parents or new students (Evertson et al., 2009).

Actively Teach Rules and Procedures   Just as any idea needs to be explained and illustrated, rules and procedures should be explicitly taught. Teachers often simply "present" their rules, which is much like teaching a concept in the abstract. Students construct understanding of rules and procedures, just as they construct understanding of any idea. So, just as you would provide examples to teach the concepts *arthropod, metaphor,* or *culture,* for example, you need to provide concrete examples to help your students understand how your rules and procedures operate.

Let's see how one fourth-grade teacher does this.

Steve Matheson begins his first day of class by creating a seating chart that will allow him to call on each student by name. He also writes his rules on a poster board and places these up at the front of the class so all can see. He begins his first class with:

Steve: Now, everyone, when I teach I have some rules that will help make our class a better place to learn. My first rule is that when we're having a discussion, it is important that you wait until I call on you. I will call on each of you as we go along, so you must wait your turn. Now, what is the first rule, Sidney (motioning to the rules on the poster)?

Sidney: . . . We don't talk until you call on us.

Figure 3.2

Guidelines for the First Day of Class

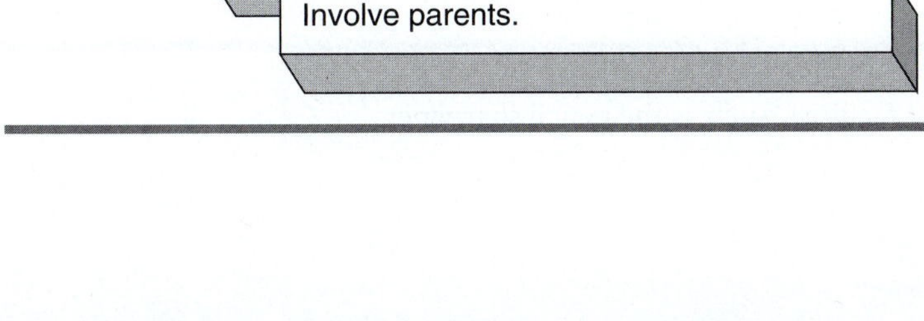

Plan for maximum contact and control.

Teach rules and procedures.

Enforce rules with complete consistency.

Communicate openly and congruently.

Involve parents.

Steve:	Yes, exactly, Sidney. So, if I call on Sharon and she is having a hard time answering the question, what do you do? . . . Carlos?
Carlos:	I . . . wait. I don't say anything.
Steve:	Yes, excellent, Carlos. And why do you suppose this rule is so important? . . . Kim?
Kim:	If, . . . if we shout out answers, other kids can't hear.
Steve:	That's right, Kim. That's very important. And it's also important that we all get a chance to think about and practice the ideas we're learning. So, we must wait our turn.

Steve "taught" students his rule, much in the same way he would teach any concept. He presented and explained it, followed with an example, and explained why the rule was important. Time and effort spent on this process, beginning with the first day pay dividends in the long run. They eliminate problems before they begin and result in a more smoothly functioning classroom throughout the year.

Some teachers display their rules on a front bulletin board, a portion of the chalkboard, or some other prominent place, as Steve did. Others prefer to hand rules out on a sheet of paper, discuss them at the beginning of the school year, and send them home so parents know what they are. How the rules are displayed isn't crucial; it is essential, however, that they are carefully taught, reviewed, and reinforced. Our goal is for all students to be aware of the rules at all times.

Teaching procedures is similar. Effective teachers in the lower elementary grades have young children practice "dry runs" on procedures such as putting papers in folders at the front of the room and using and returning materials, such as scissors. Let's see how Maria Perez, the first-grade teacher introduced at the beginning of the chapter, attempts to get her students to understand how to put away worksheets.

I put each of their names, as well as my own, on cubbyholes on the wall of my room. To demonstrate the process, I did a short worksheet myself and literally walked it over and put it in my storage spot, talking aloud as I went: "I'm finished with my worksheet. . . . What do I do now? . . . I need to put it in my cubbyhole. If I don't put it there, my teacher can't check it, so it's very important. . . . Now, I start on the next assignment."

Then I gave my students the worksheet, directing them to take it to their cubbies, quietly and individually, as soon as they were finished. After they had done that, we spent a few minutes discussing the reasons for taking the finished work to the cubbies immediately, not touching or talking to anyone as they move to the cubbies and back to their desks, and starting right back to work. Then I gave them another worksheet, asked them what they were going to do and why, and had them do it. We then spent a few more minutes talking about what might happen if we didn't put papers where they belong. I asked them whether they had ever lost anything and how this was similar.

Now we have a class meeting nearly every day just before we leave for the day. We discuss classroom life and offer suggestions for improvement. Some people might be skeptical about whether or not first graders can handle meetings like this, but they can. This is also one way I help them keep our procedures fresh in their minds.

With practice such as Maria provided for her first graders, procedures then become essentially automatic routines.

Some necessary procedures that should be considered the first few days include the following:

- Entering and leaving the classroom
- Using materials and facilities, such as the pencil sharpener

- Using the bathroom
- Turning in assignments

Enforce Rules Consistently   Rule and procedures need to be enforced with complete consistency during this beginning period. Your goal is to make your classroom environment safe and predictable. However, despite your best efforts to carefully teach rules and procedures in the first few days, students will still break them, usually because they simply "slip up." Each time this happens, successful teachers take the time to stop and immediately remind students of the rule and why it is important. For example,

---

The second day of class, Jeff Thompson begins reviewing problems for finding the area of irregular plane figures with his seventh graders. He knows that they covered the topic in fifth grade, but he isn't sure how much they remember. He displays a problem and begins, "What's the first step in the solution? . . . Toni?"

". . ."

"We multiply," Susan jumps in.

Jeff turns directly to Susan and asks firmly but evenly, "Susan, what was the first rule we discussed?"

"We . . . don't talk until you call on us."

"Yes, exactly. Very good. Thanks, Susan. Now, what are we asked for in the problem, Toni?"

Although most students comply with our rules when they are carefully taught and reviewed, some students "test" us; in these cases, it is even more important that rules are monitored thoroughly and consistently. We "pass the test" by dealing with the infraction before continuing instruction.

Instruction may be disrupted by these interventions during the first few days of the year. However, it is essential that the patterns you expect for the remainder of the year are established during this period. Unfortunately, some teachers reach the end of the first or even second grading period still trying to teach while students are chatting, inattentive, or even sitting facing away from the teacher. As with spending time teaching rules and procedures, time spent enforcing them and establishing desired patterns during the first two weeks will pay enormous dividends during the rest of the year.

Communicate Openly and Congruently   Clear, open, and congruent communication is essential during this period. Jeff, for example, intervened directly and firmly when Susan broke the rule. Verbal and nonverbal behavior should be congruent, meaning your words and body language are consistent with each other. This congruence is particularly important during the first few days of school when you're trying to establish patterns for the year. Telling students to be quiet as we glance at them over our shoulders communicates a very different message than moving toward them, facing them directly, making eye contact, and then telling them to stop talking.

Threats and ultimatums, however, should be avoided. They detract from a positive emotional climate and reduce a teacher's credibility. Open and honest communication makes the teacher accessible and human without reducing authority and enhances the dignity of both students and the teacher.

Involve Parents   Involve parents as you implement your management system. Students benefit from home-school cooperation in five ways:

- More positive attitudes and behaviors
- Greater willingness to do homework

- Higher long-term academic achievement
- Better attendance and graduation rates
- Greater enrollment in post-secondary education (Garcia, 2004; Hong & Ho, 2005)

These outcomes result from parents' increased participation in school activities, their higher expectations for their children's achievement, and teachers' increased understanding of learners' home environments.

One teacher's efforts to involve parents from the beginning of the year are illustrated in Figure 3.3.

Figure 3.3

Letter to Parents

September 30, 2010

Dear Parents and Students,

It was a pleasure meeting so many of you during our open house. Thank you for your cooperation and help in making this year the best one ever for your youngster.

I am looking forward to an exciting year in geography, and I hope you are too! In order for us to work together more effectively, some guidelines are necessary. They are listed below. Please read through the information carefully and sign the bottom of the page. If you have any questions or comments, please feel free to call Lakeside Junior High School (272–8160). I will return your call promptly. This sheet must be kept in your studentís notebook and/or folder all year.

Sincerely,

Survival Guidelines
1. Treat your classmates and the teacher with respect.
2. Be in class, seated, and quiet when the bell rings.
3. Bring covered textbooks, notebook, folder, paper, pens, and pencils to class every day.
4. Raise your hand for permission to speak or to leave your seat.
5. Keep hands, feet, and objects to yourself.

Homework Guidelines
1. Motto: I will always TRY, and I will NEVER give up!
2. I will complete all assignments. If the assignment is not finished or is not ready when called for, a zero will be given.
3. Head your paper properly—directions were given in class. Use pen or pencil—no red, orange, or pink ink. If you have questions, see Mrs. Barnhard.
4. Whenever you are absent, it is your responsibility to come in early in the morning (8:15–8:50) and make arrangements for makeup work. Class time will not be used for this activity. Tests are always assigned three to five days in advance. If you are absent the day before the test, you should come prepared to take the test as announced.
5. No extra credit work will be given. If you do all of the required work and study for the tests, there should be no need for extra credit.

_____(student)_____(parent)

Technology and Teaching:

Using Technology to Communicate with Parents

Communication is an essential step in home-school cooperation, but parents' and teachers' busy schedules are often obstacles. Technology can help make home-school links more effective (Bitter & Legacy, 2008). Voice mail and e-mail can help overcome these obstacles by creating communication channels between parents who work and teachers who are busy with students all day.

A growing number of teachers use websites that describe current class topics and assignments. In addition, students and parents are now able to monitor missing assignments, performance on tests, and current grades via e-mail (Gronke, 2009). Schools also use electronic hotlines to keep parents informed about current events, schedule changes, lunch menus, and bus schedules. However, many parents still prefer traditional information sources such as newsletters and open houses. This may be because some households don't have e-mail, as well as the instinctive desire for the face-to-face contact that exists during open houses.

One innovation uses the Internet to provide parents with real-time images of their children (Kleiman, 2001). Increasing numbers of preschool and daycare programs are installing cameras and Internet systems that provide parents with secure access websites that can be used to monitor their children during the day.

This communication serves three functions. First, parents are made aware of important rules and procedures. As a result, when students leave for school in the morning, parents will be more likely to ask, "Do you have your homework with you?" or "Do you have your books?" Unfortunately, not all parents will be helpful, but if the letter increases the support in only a few, you are ahead of where you would have been.

Second, the letter communicates that you're accessible, and it sets the tone for further communication if you should need to call parents about some issue later in the year.

Finally, the signature at the bottom symbolizes a form of commitment to the rules and procedures by students and parents; it's a type of contract. As a result, serious infractions are less likely to take place.

Communication can be enhanced in other ways. A simple handwritten note sent home with a child who has been doing particularly well takes only a minute and can do much to promote a positive home-school partnership. Periodic phone calls and e-mails can be helpful in establishing home-school cooperation. This pattern can also be established in the first two weeks. Getting a phone call during the first week of school communicates that the teacher is "on top of things" and that he or she cares about the student. "Why weren't we told he was misbehaving?" and "We never knew he was having trouble in history" are common complaints from parents. You are much more likely to have problems with parents by not communicating than you are by being overzealous at the beginning of the school year.

Exploring Diversity

Challenges to Home–School Communication

Classrooms with large numbers of students from diverse backgrounds present unique communication challenges. Lower parent participation in school activities often is associated with families that are members of cultural minorities, of lower-socioeconomic status, or have a child enrolled in either special education or the English as a second language program. Each of these makes communication between home and school more challenging, both for parents and teachers.

Barriers to home-school communication include the following:

- Economics
- Culture
- Language

Economic Barriers

Communication and the development of links between home and school take time. Parents working two jobs and struggling to make ends meet, for example, may not have the time or energy to become fully involved in their child's schooling (Barton et al., 2004). Child care and lack of transportation are other potential obstacles. Research indicates that parents do care about their children's education but that schools need to be flexible in working with them (Kaplan, Liu, & Kaplan, 2001).

Cultural Barriers

Many parents experienced a very different educational system than the one their children are in, and they may not understand our goals, rules, and procedures in the way we intend. For example, one study found that Puerto Rican parents believed schools in the United States were too impersonal and that teachers didn't demonstrate that they cared for children enough (Harry, 1992).

Misinterpretation can occur in both directions. Asian and Latino parents often defer to the school and a teacher's authority in matters of discipline, believing schools are the proper place for handling management problems. Teachers sometimes view this deference as apathy, not realizing that parents care but believe that the school's authority shouldn't be questioned (Gollnick & Chinn, 2009). This again illustrates the need for open communication.

Language Barriers

Language can be another obstacle to home–school cooperation. Some parents speak only halting English, making communication through letters and phone calls difficult, and making it hard for parents to help their children with homework. Strategies for overcoming language barriers include the following:

- Ask other teachers or parents to translate letters into parents' native languages.
- Use older students in the school to help translate letters.
- Involve students in three-way parent–student–teacher conferences. (Epstein, 2001)

Research consistently indicates that parents want to help and become involved (Barton et al., 2004). Teachers need to capitalize on this desire by making every effort to open and maintain communication with parents.

The Relationship Between Management and Instruction

Earlier we emphasized that productive learning environments are orderly and focus on learning. It is virtually impossible to maintain an orderly classroom in the absence of good teaching and vice versa. We want to revisit this relationship now.

By establishing expectations, rules, and procedures early in the school year, we can devote more time to instruction and to monitoring the rules and procedures we've created. When instruction is effective, the need for management interventions sharply decreases.

We focus now on four instructional factors that help minimize the likelihood of management problems: *momentum, smoothness, orchestration,* and *overlapping.*

Momentum *is a characteristic of lessons that provides them with strength and direction.* Momentum can be thought of as a vector, a line indicating the strength and direction of a force. Just as forces have direction and strength, so do lessons. Some lesson vectors are weak, barely maintaining students' interest. Successful lessons have strong lesson vectors, actively involving students who are swept along by the lesson's momentum. Lessons with momentum move at a brisk pace, fast enough to keep learners involved, but not so fast that they get lost.

Let's see how one teacher created and maintained lesson momentum with a potentially dry topic.

I was starting a lesson on the Crusades in my world history class, and I knew that it was deadly last year. The students could have cared less about that old stuff.

So, I decided that I would try something different. I went into the room and said, "I have an announcement. The school administration has just decided that all extracurricular activities will be eliminated in the school. They decided that the benefits didn't warrant the cost, and the purpose of school is for learning, not extracurricular activities."

The students, of course, were outraged. I let them talk for a few minutes and then I asked what we might do about it. Well, one thing led to another, and we finally decided that we would be on a "crusade" to have extracurricular activities reinstated. I used it as a framework and we kept referring back to it as an analogy as we studied the real Crusades.

By involving students in the lesson and relating the content to students' own backgrounds and concerns, the teacher created a powerful lesson vector that carried through the whole unit.

Events that drain energy away from the thrust of a lesson detract from momentum. Some teacher-related obstacles to momentum are found in Table 3.4.`

Table 3.4 Obstacles to Momentum

Behavior	Example
Behavior overdwelling	Nagging or preaching. Continuing to talk about a misbehavior after it stopped. For example, "How many times do I have to tell you to stop that talking?" or "This is the third time today that I've told you to stop playing with your pencils."
Content overdwelling	Staying on task well after students have mastered it. For example, teaching the concept of odd numbers by having the class name *all* odd numbers up to 100.
Fragmentation	Having single students or small groups do work that the whole group could do. (If this is the case, why not do the activity as a whole and save time and effort?)

Source: Adapted from Kounin, 1970.

Certain types of learning activities are harder to manage than others, and knowing this can help you plan for contingencies that might arise. For example, as you might expect, students are most engaged in teacher-led activities and tend to be less engaged during seatwork and student presentations (Kounin & Sherman, 1979; Rosenshine, 1980). Further, the more often seatwork is used, the greater the likelihood that students will be off task.

Lesson momentum helps us understand this research. Brisk question-and-answer sessions, which are typical of whole-group activities, help maintain momentum, whereas students must regulate their own pace and momentum during individual assignments and seatwork. These are reasons we suggested using whole-group instruction at the beginning of the school year. Then, when your rules and procedures are well established, you can begin varying your instruction.

A second instructional factor that influences management is smoothness. **Smoothness** *describes a lesson's continuity.* When teachers allow lessons to wander, or they spend too much time interrupting lessons to reprimand students, problems with smoothness occur. Some obstacles to smoothness are shown in Table 3.5.

The keys to maintaining smoothness are well-planned lessons with aligned instruction, together with a well-established system of rules and procedures that maintain order.

Classrooms are busy places where teachers juggle many balls at one time. **Orchestration** *refers to the teacher's ability to keep a lesson flowing smoothly and comfortably while simultaneously maintaining order.* A student blurting out, "Can I go the bathroom?" or having to say, "Sarah, please turn around," can be disruptive. Effective teachers accommodate these potential disruptions without losing the flow of the lesson.

Table 3.5 Obstacles to Smoothness

Behavior	Examples
Distractions	Calling attention to a piece of paper on the floor in the middle of explaining a math problem. (This *may* be important, but should it occur now?)
Intrusions	In the middle of a reading lesson, the teacher says, "I just noticed that Sally isn't here. Does anybody know why she's absent?" (The teacher should write a note to himself or herself and find out later.)
Flip-flops	Returning to an activity after it is done. After science books are put away and social studies has begun, the teacher says, "Oh, yeah, I just remembered one more thing about arthropods."

Source: Adapted from Kounin, 1977.

Well-established procedures make orchestrating a lesson easier. If a procedure for going to the bathroom has been taught and practiced, for example, a quick nod of the head to the one student and a quiet "Sarah, please turn around," can be smoothly integrated into the overall lesson.

Overlapping, *or the ability to attend to two events at the same time*, is closely related to orchestration (Kounin, 1970). It is especially important in elementary classrooms, in which it is common for most of the students to be working at their desks while the teacher conducts a small reading group. At the middle or secondary level, asking a question while moving near a student who is whispering is another example of overlapping.

Dealing with individual problems, such as students who were late or absent the day before can also detract from the flow of a lesson. Effective teachers have procedures for dealing with these situations, and when emergencies arise they give the class a short task, such as solving a problem or answering a question, quickly deal with the incident, and just as quickly return to the lesson. With practice and effort, you will learn to attend to two or more events at the same time. Effective rules and procedures help reduce the demands these interruptions place on you.

Management Interventions

The best laid plans of mice and men often go awry. Robert Burns

In spite of carefully planning and explaining your rules and procedures, incidents of disruptive behavior will inevitably occur. **Management interventions** *are teacher actions designed to eliminate undesirable student behavior*. In our discussion of management during the first 10 days of school, we briefly described the need for interventions when students break rules. Interventions are essential during the first few days of school and will periodically be necessary throughout the year as well.

A prerequisite for effective interventions is **withitness**, *a teacher's awareness of what is going on in all parts of the classroom at all times and communicating this awareness to students* (Kounin, 1970). Expert teachers describe withitness as "having eyes in the back of your head." Let's compare the withitness of two teachers.

Jeff Thompson is explaining the process for finding percentages to his seventh graders. While Jeff illustrates the procedure, Steve, in the second desk from the front of the room, is periodically poking Katilya, who sits across from him. She retaliates by kicking him in the leg. Bill, sitting behind Katilya, pokes her in the arm with his pencil. Jeff doesn't respond to the students' actions. After a second poke, Katilya swings her arm back and catches Bill on the shoulder. "Katilyna!" Jeff says sternly. "We keep our hands to ourselves! . . . Now, where were we?"

Karl Wickes has the same group of students in life science. He puts a transparency displaying a flowering plant on the overhead. As the class discusses the information, he notices Barry whispering something to Julie, and he sees Steve poke Katilya, who kicks him and loudly whispers, "Stop it." As Karl asks, "What is the part of the plant that produces fruit?" he moves to Steve's desk, leans over, and says quietly but firmly, "We keep our hands to ourselves in here." He then moves to the front of the room, watches Steve out of the corner of his eye, and says, "Barry, what other plant part do you see in the diagram?"

Karl, in contrast with Jeff, demonstrated withitness in three ways:

- He identified the misbehavior immediately and quickly responded by moving near Steve. Jeff did nothing until the mischief had spread to other students.

- He correctly identified Steve as the original cause of the incident. In contrast, Jeff reprimanded Katilya, leaving students with a sense that he didn't know what was going on.

- He responded to the more serious infraction first. Steve's poking was more disruptive than Barry's whispering, so Karl first responded to Steve and then called on Barry, which drew him back into the activity, making further intervention unnecessary.

Withitness involves more than dealing with misbehavior after it happens (Hogan et al., 2003). Teachers who are with it also watch for evidence of inattention or confusion; they approach, or call on, inattentive students to bring them back into lessons; and they respond to signs of confusion with questions such as "Some of you look puzzled. Do you want me to rephrase that question?" They are sensitive to students and make adjustments to ensure that they are as involved and successful as possible.

Withit teachers still have to exercise judgment when intervening because not all misbehaviors are equal, and the context in which they occur is an additional factor complicating interventions. For example, two students briefly whispering at the back of the room is very different from someone repeatedly poking and kicking other students, or even fighting. And, talking during a transition takes place in a different context than talking during a learning activity.

Because infractions vary, your reactions should also vary (Jones & Jones, 2010). To maintain lesson momentum and maximize instructional time, interventions should be as unobtrusive as possible. A continuum of interventions designed to respond to varying infractions is shown in Figure 3.4 and described in the following sections.

An Intervention Continuum

The intervention continuum is designed to minimize classroom interruptions by initially focusing on positive behaviors and gradually moving to more overt and obtrusive forms of intervention as the seriousness of the misbehavior increases. Let's examine it.

Praising Desired Behavior   Teachers are commonly encouraged to "catch 'em being good," and since our goal in any classroom is to promote positive actions, "praising desired

Figure 3.4

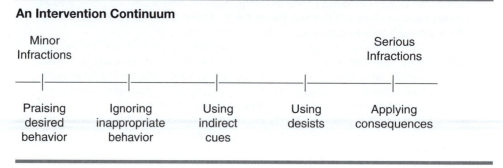

An Intervention Continuum

behavior" is a sensible beginning point, particularly as a method of preventing misbehavior (Jones & Jones, 2010). Elementary teachers praise openly and freely, and middle and secondary teachers often quietly make comments to students, such as, "I'm extremely pleased with your work this last week. You're getting better and better at this stuff. Keep it up."

It is interesting that praise for desirable behavior occurs less often than we might expect, probably because desired behavior is taken for granted, whereas misbehavior attracts attention. Making an effort to change these patterns and acknowledge desired behavior and good work can significantly contribute to a productive learning environment.

Ignoring Inappropriate Behavior If an incident of misbehavior is brief, it is often most effective to simply ignore it. The attention students receive when they're admonished for minor misbehaviors can be reinforcing, so ignoring the behavior can eliminate the reinforcers you might inadvertently provide (Alberto & Troutman, 2009). Ignoring misbehavior is effective, for example, if two students whisper to each other, but soon stop. Combining praise for positive actions with ignoring misbehavior can be very effective with minor disruptions (Charles & Senter, 2008).

Using Indirect Cues You can use **indirect cues**, which *signal intentions without disrupting the flow of the classroom and are used when students are displaying behaviors that can't be ignored but can be stopped or diverted without addressing them directly.* These include proximity, redirecting attention, and praising other students. For example, Chris has just poked Tanya, and you hear her mutter, "Stop it, Chris." You move near Chris and call on him, which is likely to bring him back into the lesson and eliminate his poking. Your proximity and question are indirect cues that redirect his attention.

Praising other students can also be effective. Teachers, especially in the lower grades, use statements, such as, "I really like the way Armondo is working so quietly," which uses Armondo as an example for the rest of the students.

Using Desists A **desist** *occurs when a teacher tells a student to stop a behavior* (Kounin, 1970). "Glenys, we don't leave our seat without permission," "Glenys!," a finger to the lips, or a stern facial expression are all desists, and they're the most common teacher reaction to misbehavior (Jones & Jones, 2010).

Clarity and tone are important in desists. For example, "Randy, what is the rule about touching other students in this class?" or, "Randy, how do you think that makes Willy feel?" are clearer than "Randy, stop that," because they link the behavior to a rule or the consequences of the behavior. Students react to these subtle differences, preferring rule and consequence reminders to teacher commands (Charles & Senter, 2008).

The tone of desists should be firm but not angry. Research indicates that kindergarten students handled with rough desists actually became more disruptive, and older students felt uncomfortable in classes in which rough desists were used (Kounin, 1970). In contrast, gentle reprimands and the suggestion of alternative behaviors, combined with effective questioning techniques, reduced time off task in elementary classrooms (Borg & Ascione, 1982). Here again we see the interdependence of management and instruction.

Clear communication (including congruence between verbal and nonverbal behavior), an awareness of what's happening in the classroom (withitness), and effective instruction are essential in effectively using desists to stop misbehavior. However, even when these important elements are used, desists alone sometimes don't work.

Applying Consequences   Careful planning and effective instruction will eliminate much misbehavior before it starts. Some minor incidents can be ignored, and simple desists will stop others. When these strategies don't stop disruptions, consequences are needed.

Logical consequences is a classroom management strategy that *treats misbehaviors as problems and demonstrates a link between the behavior and the consequence.* Teachers help students learn to be responsible by explaining the reasons for rules and applying logical consequences, which help students see the results of their actions. Let's look at an example.

> Jason, a high-energy sixth grader, for some unknown reason, decided to knock Dave's books out of his hands as they were changing classes in the hallways. Sharon Phelps, monitoring the hall, saw what Jason had done and quickly called him over. "Jason, how do you think that makes Dave feel when you do that?" When Jason didn't answer immediately, she continued, "Go on right over right now and help Dave pick up his papers and think about my question while you're doing it. When you're done, I want an answer to 67ytmy question."

Helping Dave pick up his papers is a logical consequence. Jason caused the problem; he fixes it. The act and the consequence are conceptually linked. Sharon helped Jason see the link between his actions and their effects on others and hopefully taught Jason that he's accountable for his actions.

Logical consequences communicate to students that the world is a sensible and orderly place, that actions have consequences, and that we are responsible for our actions. Let's look at another classroom example.

> The kindergarten boys found a lovely mud puddle in the playground during recess. They had much fun running and splashing and then came back into the room wet and dripping and proceeded to leave muddy footprints all over the room. Their teacher, using logical consequences rather than punishment, called them aside for a conference.
>
> "Boys, we have two problems here. One is that you have made our classroom very dirty, and it needs to be fixed so that the other children don't get wet and dirty. What can you do to fix it?" One little boy suggested that they could mop the floor.
>
> "Good idea!" said the teacher. "Let's find our custodian, Mrs. Smith, and you can get a mop from her and mop the floor. Now, what about our other problem, your dirty clothes?"
>
> "We could call our mothers and ask them to bring use clean clothes!" suggested one boy. "
>
> "Another good idea," said the teacher. "But what if your mothers are not home?" This was a tougher problem.
>
> "I know," one boy finally said, "we could borrow some clean clothes from the lost and found box!"
>
> "Good thinking," said the teacher. "And what can we do so that you don't lose so much time from class again?"
>
> "Stay out of mud puddles!" was the reply in unison. (McCarthy, 1991, p. 19)

By helping students see the relationship between their actions and the problem, the teacher was not only solving the immediate problem but also teaching students how to take responsibility for their actions. Research indicates that children who are helped to understand the consequences of their actions on other people become more altruistic and are more likely to take actions to make up for their misbehavior (Berk, 2008).

Classrooms are busy places, however, and it isn't always possible to solve problems with logical consequences. In these instances, behavioral consequences can work:

Damon is an active sixth grader. He loves to talk and seems to know just how far he can go before Maria Ortiz gets exasperated with him. He understands the class rules and the reasons for them, but his interest in talking takes precedence. Ignoring him isn't working. A call to his parents helps for a while, but soon he is back to his usual behavior–never quite enough to require a drastic response, but always a thorn in Maria's side.

Finally, she decides that she will give him one warning. At a second disruption, he is placed in timeout from regular instructional activities. She meets with Damon and explains the new rules. The next day, he begins to misbehave almost immediately.

"Damon," she warns, "you can't work while you're talking, and you're keeping others from finishing their work. Please get busy."

He stops, but five minutes later, he's at it again. "Damon," she says quietly as she moves back to his desk, "I've warned you. Now please go back to the time-out area."

A week later, Damon is working quietly and comfortably with the rest of the class. (Adapted from Eggen & Kauchak, 2007)

Damon's behavior is common, particularly in elementary and middle schools, and this type of behavior is the source of more teacher stress than any other cause (Bohn, Roehrig, & Pressley, 2004). Damon is disruptive, so his behavior can't be ignored; praise for good work helps to a certain extent, but much of his reinforcement comes from his buddies. Desists work briefly, but teachers burn out constantly monitoring him. Maria had little choice but to apply consequences.

Consistency is essential in handling students like Damon. He understands what he is doing, and he is capable of controlling himself. When he can—with certainty—predict the consequences of his behavior, he'll quit. He knew that his second infraction would result in timeout and, when it did, he quickly changed his behavior. There was no argument, little time was used, and the class wasn't disrupted.

Dealing with Persistent Individual Problems

So far, we have approached classroom management primarily from a group perspective. Periodically, however, we will have one or more students who don't respond like the rest of the class and who need concentrated individual action that focuses on both the causes of behavior as well as productive alternatives.

One approach to this problem is both humanistic and informational, based on the works of Gordon (1974) and Glasser (1969, 1977). These experts stress the importance of clear and open communication between teacher and students. Gordon emphasized active listening in which both teachers and students acknowledge each another's messages by restating them to communicate understanding. Glasser (1977) emphasized helping students understand the roles and obligations of everyone in the classroom and outlined 10 sequential steps for dealing with behavior problems. The steps range from simple intervention to contact with an outside agency. The process stops as soon as the behavior improves. The procedure is labor intensive, so you won't be able to implement it with many students. However, with one or two students, and as a last resort, it may be useful.

Glasser's steps, which reflect progressively increased effort on the teacher's part, are outlined as follows:

1. Identify problem students and list typical interventions in response to their past behavior.

2. Look at the list, discard ineffective interventions and focus on those that are more productive.

3. Talk to the students, give them special responsibilities, and use extra encouragement in an effort to make them feel accepted.

4. If progress isn't made, discuss the problem with the students, and require them to describe the behaviors in their own words. When you're satisfied that the students understands why the behaviors present problems, ask that they stop.

5. Again, confer with the students, have them describe the behaviors and state whether they are against the rules. Ask them what they should be doing instead.

6. Repeat step five but call attention to the fact that previous attempts haven't been successful. Require that a plan of action be drawn up that will solve the problems. This plan must include the students' commitment to the plan.

7. If students don't follow the plan, take action. Isolate the students, using a procedure such as timeout. During this time, the students are responsible for devising a reinstatement plan intended to solve the problems. You must approve the plan.

8. Place the students in in-school suspension. Because they have not been able to behave acceptably, the principal is called in. Their return to the classroom is contingent upon following the rules.

9. If a student cannot be integrated back into the classroom, the parents are called in to discuss the problem and made aware that the students will be sent home. One-day home suspensions are used when students continue to ignore the rules.

10. If the students still don't respond, it may be necessary to refer them to another agency.

To be effective, a plan such as this must be carried through as far as necessary, so the approval and cooperation of your principal is essential. If he or she disapproves, you have little chance of succeeding.

Parental support and cooperation are also important. A conference with parents designed to explain the plan and solicit their support can do much in contributing to its success.

Serious Management Problems: Violence and Aggression

Class is disrupted by a scuffle. You look up to see that Ron has left his seat and gone to Phil's desk, where he is punching and shouting at Phil. Phil is not so much fighting back as trying to protect himself. You don't know how this started, but you do know that Phil gets along well with other students and that Ron often starts fights and arguments without provocation. (Brophy & Rohrkemper, 1987, p. 60)

This morning several students excitedly tell you that on the way to school they saw Tom beating up Sam and taking his lunch money. Tom is the class bully and has done things like this many times. (Brophy & Rohrkemper, 1987, p. 53)

What would you do in these situations? What would be your immediate reaction? How would you follow through? What long-term strategies would you employ to try and prevent these problems from recurring? These questions were asked of teachers identified by their principals as effective in dealing with serious management problems (Brophy & McCaslin, 1992). In this section we consider their responses, together with other research examining violence and aggression in schools.

Problems of violence and aggression require both immediate actions and long-term solutions. Let's look at both of these, beginning with immediate actions.

Immediate Actions   Immediate actions involve three steps: (a) stop the incident (if possible), (b) protect the victim, and (c) get help. For instance, in the case of the classroom scuffle, a loud noise, such as shouting, clapping, or slamming a chair against the floor will often surprise the students enough so they'll stop (Evertson et al., 2009). At that point, you can begin to talk to them, check to see if Phil is all right, and then take them to the administration where you can get help.

If your interventions don't stop the fight, immediately rush a student to the main office for help. Unless you're sure that you can separate the students without danger to yourself, or them, attempting to do so is unwise.

You are legally required to intervene in the case of a fight (Fischer, Schimmel, & Stellman, 2006). If you ignore a fight, even on the playground, parents can sue for negligence, on the grounds that you are failing to protect a student from injury. However, the law doesn't require you to physically break up the fight; immediately reporting it to the administration is an acceptable form of intervention.

Responding to Bullying   Bullying, a more subtle form of school violence, is receiving increased attention, as educators are realizing its damaging effects on students, as well as possible links to suicide and other forms of school violence (Fast, 2008). In most school shootings, the perpetrators had been victims of bullying (Aspy et al., 2004).

Teachers should respond to bullying in the same way they react to other aggressive acts (Raskauskas & Stoltz, 2007). Those committing the acts should be stopped, and victims should be protected. Attempts can then be made to help the bullies understand the consequences of their actions, both for the victims and for themselves. (We examine long-term efforts later in this section.)

Responding to Defiant Students

Damien, one of your students, has difficulty maintaining attention in learning activities and staying on task during seatwork. He often disrupts the class with loud and inappropriate comments. You warn him, reminding him that his behavior is unacceptable, and another disruption will result in timeout.

In a few moments, Damien again disrupts the class. "Please go to the timeout area," you say evenly.

"I'm not going," he says defiantly, remaining seated at his desk.

The possibility of dealing with a student like Damien is frightening, particularly for a beginning teacher. What do you do when he says, "I'm not going"? Experts offer two suggestions (Good & Brophy, 2008; Henricsson & Rydell, 2004). First, remain calm and avoid a power struggle. A teacher's natural tendency is to become angry and display a show of force to demonstrate to students that they "can't get away with it." Remaining calm gives you time to get your temper under control, and the student's mood when facing a calm teacher is likely to change from anger and bravado to fear and contrition (Good & Brophy, 2008).

Second, if possible, give the rest of the class an assignment, and then tell the student calmly but decisively to please step outside the classroom so you can talk. Communicate a serious and concerned, but not threatening, tone.

Defiance is often the result of a negative student-teacher relationship (Gregory & Weinstein, 2004). These negative relationships occur most often with students who display aggressive behavior toward other students, temper tantrums, and impulsive and hyperactive behavior (Henricsson & Rydell, 2004). When overt problems occur, it is important to let the student express everything that is on his or her mind in a private conference before responding. Finally, arrange to meet with the student outside of class, treat the defiance as a serious problem, and attempt to generate solutions that are acceptable to both of you.

When a student refuses to step outside the classroom or becomes physically threatening, immediately send someone to the front office for help. Defiance at this level likely requires help from a mental health professional.

Long-Term Solutions   Long-term, students must first be helped to understand the severity of their actions, that aggression will not be allowed, and that they're accountable for their behavior (Brophy, 1996). In the incident with the lunch money, for example, Tom must understand that his behavior was reported and that it's unacceptable and won't be tolerated.

As a preventive strategy, students must learn how to control their tempers, cope with frustrations, and negotiate and talk, rather than fight. One approach uses problem-solving simulations to help aggressive youth understand the motives and intentions of other people. Research indicates that these youngsters often respond aggressively because they misperceive others' intentions as being hostile (Berk, 2008). Following problem-solving sessions, aggressive students become less hostile in their interpretation of ambiguous situations and less aggressive.

Other approaches to preventing aggression include teaching students to express anger verbally instead of physically and to solve conflicts through communication and negotiation rather than fighting (Johnson & Johnson, 2006). One form of communication and negotiation is learning to state and defend a position—to argue effectively. Students taught to make effective arguments—emphasizing that arguing and verbal aggression are very different—become less combative when encountering others with whom they disagree. Learning to argue also has incidental benefits: people skilled at arguing are seen by their peers as intelligent and credible.

Experts also suggest the involvement of parents and other school personnel (Christenson & Havsy, 2004). Parents want to be notified immediately if school problems occur and their assistance can play a central role in preventing problems in the future. In addition, school counselors, school psychologists, social workers, and principals have all been trained to deal with these problems and can provide advice and assistance. Experienced teachers can also provide a wealth of information about how they've handled similar problems. No teacher should face persistent or serious problems of violence or aggression alone.

In conclusion, we want to put problems of school violence and aggression into perspective. Although they are possibilities, and you should understand options for dealing with them, the majority of your management problems will involve issues of cooperation and motivation. Most can be prevented, many others can be dealt with quickly, and some will require individual attention. We all hear about news reports describing students carrying guns to school and incidents of assaults on teachers. Statistically, however, considering the huge numbers of students who pass through schools each day, these incidents remain extremely rare.

Summary

The Importance of Classroom Management

Classroom management is an essential component of a productive learning environment. It is the primary concern of beginning teachers, and disruptive students are an important source of teacher stress. It has historically been a major concern of school policy makers, parents, and the public at large.

Effective management is strongly linked to student achievement; students learn more in environments that are orderly and safe.

Classroom Management: A Definition

Classroom management includes all the teacher plans and actions that contribute to a productive learning environment. It is dependent upon three factors. First, classroom management and effective instruction are interdependent; one cannot exist without the other. Second, effective teachers prevent, rather than solve, most classroom management problems, and third, effective teachers intervene quickly and consistently in incidents of disruptive behavior and just as quickly return to instruction.

Planning for Classroom Management

Planning for management is as essential as planning for instruction. Both developmental differences in students and the physical environment influence the ways teachers plan their management systems.

A well-designed system of rules and procedures is the cornerstone of an effective management system. Rules describe standards for acceptable behavior; procedures specify ways of completing a myriad of routine classroom tasks. As procedures become established, they develop into routines that make the classroom operate smoothly.

Implementing Management Plans

The beginning of the school year is crucial for classroom management. The patterns for the remainder of the school year are established during this time.

Effective managers orchestrate their classrooms so that routines and procedures complement instruction. Lesson momentum creates a positive vector that pulls students into lessons and involves them in learning. Smoothness maintains the direction of the lesson while minimizing internal and external distractions.

Management Interventions

Misbehaviors vary. Teachers need to help students understand what constitutes misbehavior and to understand that they're responsible for behaving appropriately.

In responding to misbehavior, the match between the misbehavior and the intervention is important. Interventions should be kept as brief and unobtrusive as possible.

More serious or persistent breaches of conduct need to be dealt with firmly and directly. In dealing with problem students, expectations should be clearly defined and enforced in agreed-upon contracts. If this approach doesn't work, other adults, including principals and parents, need to be called in to provide support.

Important Concepts

Classroom management (p. 74)

Classroom rules (p. 78)

Desists (p. 93)

Indirect cues (p. 93)

Logical consequences (p. 94)

Management interventions (p. 91)

Momentum (p. 89)

Obedience model of management (p. 74)

Orchestration (p. 90)

Overlapping (p. 91)

Procedures (p. 80)

Productive learning environment (p. 73)

Responsibility model of management (p. 74)

Smoothness (p. 90)

Withitness (p. 91)

Preparing for Your Licensure Exam

As you studied this chapter, you saw that planning for classroom management and systematically implementing these plans are essential for creating a productive learning environment. As you read the following case study, think about how effectively the teacher applies these ideas. Read the case study and answer the questions that follow.

After reading this case, go to the Book Specific Resources tab in MyEducationLab, select your text, select *Preparing for Your Licensure Exam* under Chapter 3 to complete the questions that accompany the case and receive feedback on your responses.

Selina Moreno sits at her desk during planning week, the time before students return from summer vacation, and looks out the window.

"This year has got to be better than last year," she thinks, and then with a half smile she mumbles audibly, "How could it be any worse?"

Selina had been hired in the middle of the school year to replace a fifth-grade teacher who left for "health reasons." Some of Selina's colleagues implied that the other teacher had quit out of frustration, and Selina soon found out why. The classroom was a mess, the previous teacher seemed to have no rules, and the students couldn't describe any routines that they were used to following. In addition to the lack of structure, the class had more than its share of "problem students," whom the other teachers nicknamed "The Wild Bunch." It didn't take Selina long to figure out who these students were, but it took her the rest of the school year to try to figure out what to do with them. This year was going to be different, she vowed, and she started making plans to ensure that it happened.

On the first day of class, she greets her fifth graders with a stern, but pleasant face. She tells them that their names are on their assigned seats and directs them to quickly find the seats and sit down quietly.

When they are settled, she begins, "Good morning, class. My name is Miss Moreno and I'm glad to have you in my class this year. Every class needs rules and I've written some up here on this bulletin board. I'd like to go over them briefly. Who can read the first one? . . . Andrea?"

". . . Talk only when called on by the teacher," Andrea reads hesitantly.

"Good, Andrea. You need to be quiet unless you raise your hand and I call your name. Who can read the second one? . . . Javier?"

"Don't leave your seat without permission."

"Good, Javier. We can't just wander around the classroom. You need to stay in your seat unless I tell you that you can leave it."

The discussion of rules continues until Selina summarizes by saying, "Class, these rules are important. If you follow them we'll get along fine. If not, you're going to have trouble in here and you don't want that, do you?"

Selina then spends about five minutes on procedures. After that she outlines the schedule for the day and the week and launches into her first lesson of the year. Initially, the class was a little disorganized but after a couple of weeks the students were doing what Selina wanted.

About a month later Selina was sitting in the faculty lunchroom when her friend, Freddie, another second-year teacher came by.

"How's it going?" Freddie asks as she looks into her lunch bag. "Ugh, not yogurt and fruit again. This diet is getting real old."

"I know what you mean. My class is kind of like that."

"What do you mean?" replies Freddie with a puzzled look.

"Well, it's a lot better than last year. At least the kids aren't driving me nuts, but the kids don't seem very excited about coming to class."

"Why not?" prompts Freddie, between spoonfuls of yogurt.

"Well, we're doing whole-class instruction, just like the management books say to do at the beginning of the year, but the kids seemed bored. I tried to do some small-group work, but Tony, the class clown, spoiled it for everybody, so I told them we couldn't do small-group work anymore. That went over like a lead balloon."

Freddie nods sympathetically.

"Then I tried a structured reward system for the class. Between you and me, the class didn't need it. It was designed to rein in Tony. So, I told them that any day that we got through with any of the three tokens left over, we'd do tech learning centers at the back of the room for the last half hour of the day. They really like to play the math and word games. So, true to form, Tony messes it up just about every other day and the class gets mad at him. I thought peer pressure would work but Tony seems oblivious. Sometimes I think he even likes the negative attention. Needless to say, I'm a little bummed. Any suggestions?"

Questions for Analysis

Let's examine Selina's lesson now based on the information in this chapter. In your analysis, consider the following questions. In each case, be specific and take information directly from the case study in doing your analysis.

1. Was Selina's class more obedience or responsibility oriented? Provide evidence from the case study to support your conclusion.

2. Assess the way Selina established rules and procedures in her classroom. How could the process have been improved?

3. Assess the effectiveness of Selina's strategies for teaching procedures. How might they be improved?

4. Describe the relationship between Selina's instruction and her approach to classroom management. How could this relationship be improved?

5. Analyze the effectiveness of Selina's structured reward system. How could it be improved?

Discussion Questions

1. How can a teacher tell if students have developed personal responsibility? How might the definition of responsibility change with grade level? What types of instructional and managerial strategies promote responsibility? What types discourage the development of responsibility?

2. How do the following factors influence the optimal number of procedures in a classroom?

   a. Grade level
   b. Subject matter
   c. Type of student (e.g., high versus low achiever)
   d. Type of instruction (e.g., large group versus small group)

3. What advantages are there to seeking student input on rules? What are the disadvantages? Is this practice more important with younger or older students? Why?

4. If you were a substitute teacher taking over a class mid-year for the rest of the year or a student teacher getting ready to assume complete responsibility for the class, what would you need to know and do in terms of classroom management?

5. Explain the statement "Misbehavior is contextual." Give a concrete example. Why might this idea be difficult to understand for some students? Why is it important that students understand it? What can teachers do to help students understand this idea?

6. What are the advantages and disadvantages of the following interventions?

   a. Praising desired behavior
   b. Ignoring inappropriate behavior
   c. Using indirect cues
   d. Using desists
   e. Applying consequences

*P*ortfolio Activities

1. *Management: The Teacher's Perspective.* Interview a teacher to find out his or her views about management. The following questions could serve as a framework:

    a. What are your goals for classroom management?
    b. How have these changed over the years?
    c. How does the particular class that you teach right now influence either your management goals or how you implement your management plans?
    d. How do your management strategies change over the school year?
    e. What is the most difficult or challenging aspect of classroom management?

    Analyze these responses in terms of the contents of this chapter.

2. *Classroom Rules and Procedures.* Interview a teacher about the rules and procedures in his or her classroom.

    a. What are they?
    b. How are they communicated to students?
    c. What are the biggest problem areas?
    d. How have these changed over the years?
    e. What management advice does the teacher have for a beginning teacher?

    Analyze the teacher's responses in terms of the contents of this chapter.

3. *School Rules.* Observe students as they move and interact in the halls. Infer what the rules are in regard to dress, appropriate hall behavior, and tardiness and the bell. Discuss these topics with a teacher and compare your conclusions. What role will you play in enforcing school rules?

4. *Classroom Rules.* Interview two high- and two low-ability students in a class and record their answers to the following questions:

    a. What rules do you have in your class?
    b. Which ones are most important?
    c. Why do you have them?
    d. What happens if they are not followed?

    Compare the responses of the two groups of students. What do their responses suggest about working with different types of students?

5. *Classroom Procedures.* Observe a class for several sessions and try to identify the procedural rules that are functioning for the following activities:

    a. Entering the class
    b. Handing in papers
    c. Sharpening pencils and accessing materials
    d. Volunteering to answer a question
    e. Exiting class

Discuss your findings with a student (or teacher) to check their accuracy. Which of these procedures would you use in your classroom?

6. *Interactive Management.* Tape and observe a classroom lesson. Identify places in the lesson at which the teacher either verbally or nonverbally exhibited the following behaviors/characteristics:

   a. Withitness
   b. Overlapping
   c. Accountability
   d. Momentum
   e. Smoothness

How did these contribute to the lesson's effectiveness?

To check your comprehension of the content covered in Chapter 3, go to the Book Specific Resources in MyEducationLab, select your text, and complete the Study Plan quiz. In addition to receiving feedback on your answers, a study plan will be generated from the quiz that will direct you to access Review, Practice, and Enrichment materials to enhance your understanding of chapter content.

Planning for Learning

Chapter Outline	Learning Objectives
	When you've completed your study of this chapter, you should be able to

Why do teachers plan?	1. Explain why teachers plan.
Factors influencing instructional planning	2. Identify factors that influence instructional planning.
■ The teacher	
■ Learner development	
■ Learner motivation	
Exploring Diversity:	
Personalizing content to increase motivation in students from diverse backgrounds	
■ Teaching context	
■ Accountability and standards-based education	
■ Materials and resources	
■ Time	

A planning model	3. Describe how the planning model can assist teachers as they plan.
■ Selecting topics	
■ Specifying learning objectives	
■ Preparing and organizing learning activities	
■ Preparing assessments	
■ Instructional alignment	
■ Backward design	

Lesson, long-term, and unit planning	4. Explain how teachers integrate long-term, unit, and lesson planning.
■ Daily lesson planning	
■ Long-term planning	
■ Unit planning	
Technology and Teaching:	
Using technology to plan	

Integrating the curriculum: Interdisciplinary and thematic units	5. Identify advantages and disadvantages of integrated and thematic units.
■ An integrated curriculum	
■ Research on integrated planning	
■ Designing and implementing integrated units	
■ Does integrated planning work?	

Planning is an essential element of teaching and affects not only student learning, but also teachers' peace of mind. Effective teachers plan for what they do in their classrooms, and this planning will do much to increase your confidence as you face your first classroom. In this chapter we discuss how you can plan for student learning in your classroom. To see how planning can affect both teachers and students, let's look at two teachers involved in planning.

Peggy Stone, a first-year teacher in a large middle school, is scheduled to be observed by her principal. Although a bit apprehensive at the prospect of being evaluated, she feels like she's ready, because she carefully planned her lesson the night before.

As the students file in the room, she hands her principal the following copy of her lesson plan.

Unit Title: Mathematical Operations

Learning Objective: Students will understand the order of arithmetic operations, so when given a series of problems involving the four operations, they will solve each correctly.

Rationale: Students need to understand the order of operations so they can accurately simplify and solve algebraic expressions.

Content: Arithmetic operations are completed in the following sequence:

1. Multiply and divide (left to right).
2. Add and subtract (left to right).

Procedures:

1. Show the students the following problem:

$$14/7 \times 2 + 5 - 6$$

   Ask what the right answer is. Encourage multiple answers.

2. Explain to students that we're beginning the topic "Order of Operations."

3. Ask students to explain what operation means. Clarify if necessary.

4. Present the rules for order of operations. Write on board.

5. Demonstrate a solution to the problem, referring students to rules for order of operations as the demonstration proceeds.

6. Show students the following problem:

$$6 + 9 \times 4/3 - 7$$

7. Solve the problem with the help of students, calling on individuals to verbally describe each step.

8. Present several other problems and solve them as a group.

9. Present students with the attached worksheet and guide them through the first two problems.

10. Have students work the remaining problems on the sheet as I monitor the class.

11. Give homework assignment, p. 194; all odd-numbered problems.

Assessment: Present students with problems involving order of operations. Have them solve the problems.

Materials and Aids: Sample problems, worksheet, text.

Now, let's look at a second teacher.

Jim Hartley, a veteran of 10 years teaching high school American history, walks into his room early, as he always does, and pulls out his plan book. He looks to see what he has written in anticipation of the day's work, nods to himself, and heads off to the media center. His plan appears as follows:

British Exploration

Religious freedom, secular, nongovernment sponsored

Spanish Exploration

3 Gs—gold, God, glory

More integration with natives, slave labor

(Film on Spanish and Mexican fiesta)

Were Peggy's and Jim's lessons well planned? Since Peggy's was more detailed, was it better planned than Jim's? What does "planning" mean, and how important is it for effective teaching? We answer these questions in the paragraphs that follow.

Let's look at the last question first. Definitions of instructional planning range from the simple products that appear on paper or in a planning book, such as Peggy's and Jim's, to complex thought processes involving both short- and long-term goals and the means necessary to reach them.

In all cases, your planning decisions will attempt to answer one essential question: "What can I do to help my students learn as much as possible?" In making these decisions you will consider the content, learning objectives, materials, and activities that will maximize student learning. With year-long planning, your thinking will be general and somewhat abstract, whereas your daily lesson planning will be more specific and concrete.

For beginning education students, "planning" often simply amounts to writing a lesson plan. It's much more than that, however, and it's also much more than the information in Peggy's and Jim's plans. For example, Jim wanted his students to compare Spanish and Mexican cultures, so he showed them a video of their fiestas to encourage a comparison and ultimately lead to questions about cultural similarities and differences. He wanted his students to think about differences between them, in spite of the fact that the two groups' origins were similar in many ways. He also wanted his students to compare the way Spanish and English settlers interacted with the Native Americans. Typical of veteran teachers, his thinking was much more complex than was suggested by his written plan. In contrast, Peggy's plan was more detailed. This is typical of beginning teachers; because of inexperience and anxiety they structure their lessons in greater detail and write down more steps (So & Watkins, 2005).

In this book we define **planning** as *all the instructional decisions teachers make prior to actually teaching.* Decisions about content, learning objectives, activities, student motivation, the way students will be grouped, grading practices, and classroom management are all part of this process.

Why Do Teachers Plan?

Why do teachers plan? In this section we focus on the answers to this question. Since no two teachers teach in exactly the same way, they won't plan in exactly the same way. Teaching is like life in many ways, and just as we approach life's experiences in personal and idiosyncratic ways, we do the same with teaching. Planning allows you to personalize the curriculum—in a sense, to make it your own. In this regard it serves four important functions:

- It helps you clarify your learning objectives, so you know exactly what you're trying to accomplish when you work with your students.
- It helps you anticipate instructional needs in advance so you can gather and organize needed materials.
- It provides a "script" that guides your interactions with students.
- It provides a form of emotional or psychological security, which will bolster your confidence and help reduce the normal anxiety associated with teaching. (Ediger, 2004)

To see these functions in practice, let's return again to Peggy's work.

Because Peggy's transcript indicates that she has taken some computer courses, she has been assigned to teach a computer-programming course for which she has little background. Not surprisingly, she is experiencing considerable anxiety, both because she is new and because she lacks confidence in her understanding of the content. She spends hours every day studying but is quite dissatisfied with her plans as she enters the classroom each day.

One day she enters the teachers' lounge with an extra bounce in her step; her conversation is more animated, and she is more enthusiastic.

"You're in a good mood today," remarks another rookie who has become her confidant.

"I've found the secret," she replies. "It's PowerPoints. When I have to present new material, I just type my outline on a PowerPoint slide with questions or problems for students. I use them to remind me where I am, and then I can keep the flow of my presentation going."

She adds with a grin, "It takes seven PowerPoints to make it through a whole class."

Now, let's look at another example.

Trina Arnold is an elementary teacher planning a lesson on invertebrates.

"The kids don't like science," she thinks to herself. "I even heard two of them saying how boring it is. What am I going to do?"

As she tries to think of ways to make her unit more motivating, she seizes on the idea of bringing in some real animals to class. On her way home from school, she stops at a fish market and buys a crab, a clam, and a small fish. The next day she takes all three, plus her daughter's hamster, into class. During the lesson, students examine and compare the four animals, analyzing their similarities and differences and, using the chart shown in Figure 4.1, comparing vertebrates and invertebrates. As they work, she noticed a level of energy and excitement that she hadn't seen in them before.

"That's the best science lesson I've ever had," she concludes to herself afterward. After that experience, Trina tries to bring something interesting to class and involve students actively in each science lesson.

Let's see how each of the planning functions was illustrated in these two scenarios. We said that planning organizes instruction and helps teachers feel more confident and secure.

Figure 4.1

Matrix Comparing Vertebrates and Invertebrates

	Examples	Similarities	Differences
Vertebrates			
Invertebrates			

Peggy's experience illustrates these functions. By structuring content on her PowerPoint slides, she was able to organize and personalize it, emphasizing some topics and deleting others. In addition, the PowerPoints provided a script for her interactions with students; she no longer had to keep all the information in her head. Finally, the transparencies bolstered her confidence and helped ease her anxiety because she felt well prepared.

We have all felt uncertain about a lesson we're teaching. The content may be unfamiliar, we are unsure of our audience, or we've had a bad experience in the past. The tendency in these cases is to plan in more detail and to write more information on paper. This also helps explain why Peggy, in our vignette at the beginning of the chapter, has more extensive written plans than does Jim; she's a first-year teacher, whereas he has 10 years of experience.

Trina's experience was quite different from Peggy's. Although Peggy used her planning time to identify and organize topics that helped her feel more secure, Trina used hers to consider the motivation and involvement of her students.

Does planning actually influence the way teachers teach? Researchers have found a link between teacher's planning and their tendency to remain focused on the topic they were teaching (e.g., Ediger, 2004). They further found that written suggestions about teaching procedures were related to the way teachers actually interacted with their students.

What factors influence the shape teacher plans take? We focus on this question in the next section.

Factors Influencing Instructional Planning

A number of factors—teachers and their personalities, students, content, the instructional context, resources, and available time—all affect the planning process. These are illustrated in Figure 4.2 and discussed in the sections that follow.

The Teacher

You, the teacher, are the most significant factor in planning. Your beliefs about the role of schools and what children should learn, your capacity to help students, and your philosophical approach to teaching and learning all affect the planning decisions you will make (Wiles & Bondi, 2007). Your philosophical position, although seemingly remote and abstract, is important. If you feel a sense of mission and believe all students can and will

Figure 4.2

Factors Influencing Teacher Planning

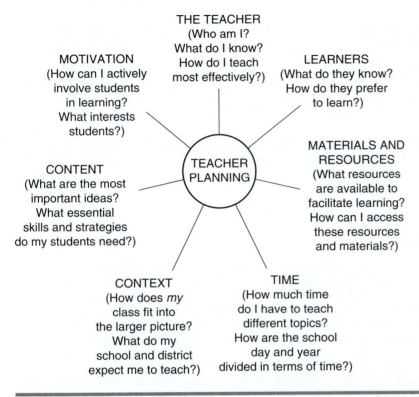

learn, you will be more active in your role, have higher expectations, and work harder to help your students achieve (Good & Brophy, 2008).

So, we encourage you to commit yourself to excellence, take personal responsibility when your students don't do well, and increase your efforts to help underachieving students. This is what professionals do. Less committed teachers are more likely to attribute lack of achievement to student shortcomings, lack of parental involvement, or weaknesses in the school administration (Schunk, Pintrich, & Meece, 2008).

Your understanding of the content you teach also affects they way you will plan. You can't teach what you don't know, and teachers who are unfamiliar with lesson content ask lower-level questions, stick closer to the text, and discourage students from asking questions (Dykstra, 1996). The implications for you are clear and simple: When teaching unfamiliar content, you need to spend extra time studying to ensure that you thoroughly understand the topic you're teaching, and this study is an integral part of your planning.

Learner Development

Karen Passey, a kindergarten teacher, sits down to plan her next week's lessons. "Hmm, let's see, figures and shapes. I better plan on something active for my afternoon group, or they'll go bonkers after five minutes of sitting quietly."

Pam Shepard looks at her planning book to refresh her memory about the topics for her next semester. "Hmm. Shakespeare. My honors classes should be able to handle it without any problems, but I'll have to really plan carefully with my third period class."

Learner development plays a powerful role in planning because development affects attention span, which determines, at least in part, how long an activity within an individual lesson can go (Berk, 2010). One teaching adage recommends, "Don't plan any single learning activity longer than the age of your students." Karen, in planning for her kindergartners, made sure that any quiet listening time wouldn't exceed five minutes. A middle school teacher might be able to stretch this to 12 or 15 minutes, but even that is probably overly optimistic.

Since all new learning depends on current understanding, students' prior knowledge also strongly influences their learning (Eggen & Kauchak, 2010). For example, a lesson on writing paragraphs depends on skills such as writing grammatically correct sentences, organizing ideas, and presenting information succinctly and accurately. Later in the chapter we describe how task analysis can be used to determine prerequisite knowledge.

Learner Motivation

Student interest is a major interest to me in planning sessions. I don't think kids have to love everything I'm teaching, but if they are "sleeping" before I even get into the lesson, they don't get a chance to see where the lesson is going. (Elementary teacher)

Student interest is the major concern after the mandated curriculum. I try to take each thing I have to do and find some way to relate it to the students, or find an aspect of it [that] will really grab their attention. (Secondary history teacher) (Zahorik, 1996, p. 559)

As you see from these quotes, experienced teachers in the classroom take student motivation into account when they plan. If you are just beginning your teaching career, and are like other beginning teachers, student motivation will be one of your biggest concerns—exceeded only by classroom management. If you're an experienced teacher, motivation will continue to be a major concern, and you'll continue to struggle with it long after you've resolved your management issues (Zahorik, 1996).

In a general sense student motivation reflects the cumulative effects of their learning history. If successful, students come to learning experiences confident, alert, and eager for new learning. Unfortunately, the opposite is also true.

Lesson-specific motivation is more malleable and you can take several steps to increase it as you plan. First, you can make specific plans to capitalize on students' interests. Effective teachers use student interest as a springboard to pull them into your lessons. For example, if you're an elementary teacher, you can use children's fascination with Halloween to teach writing, poetry, art, and music. In a similar way, if you're a middle or high school teacher, you can capitalize on teenagers' fascination with their changing bodies to teach biology and health concepts. Strategic planning integrates motivation into every lesson.

A second way to plan for student motivation is to design activities that arouse students' curiosity, drawing them into lessons, and keeping them there (Eggen & Kauchak, 2010). Beginning lessons with questions or problems is one way to arouse curiosity. With awareness and some practice, it can be accomplished quite easily. For example, a lesson on dinosaurs might begin with, "Consider the dinosaur—the largest and most fearsome of all land animals, some as big as a house. Suddenly they became extinct. Why?"

Increasing student motivation can even be accomplished with routine topics. For instance, if you're a math teacher, you might start a lesson by saying, "When we divide 6 by 2, we get 3, which is half of 6. But if we divide 6 by 1/2, we get 12, which is twice as much as 6. How can that be when we're dividing in both cases?" Or, a language arts teacher might write on the board,

Carlos and I went to the movie.
Stephanie went to the movie with Carlos and me.

and then say, "In the first sentence we use the pronoun *I* but in the second we had to use *me*. Why should that be the case?"

Actively involving students in your lessons is a third strategy that you can use to increase student interest and motivation (Schraw & Lehman, 2001). Hands-on manipulatives, games, simulations, role-playing and drama, projects, problems, and puzzles all increase involvement and motivation. In planning motivating lessons, effective teachers consciously avoid activities that place students in passive roles.

Exploring Diversity

Personalizing Content to Increase Motivation in Students from Diverse Backgrounds

Capitalizing on student interest is an effective way to plan for student motivation, but this strategy can be challenging when we have students from diverse backgrounds. However, getting to know our students plus a little creativity can solve this problem. Let's see how one teacher did this.

Dan Shaeffer heard some of his 6th graders talking on the playground about the upcoming Cinco de Mayo celebration in their community. When he asked them about it they didn't seem to know about the festival except that it was coming up and their families were going to celebrate it. After doing a little research on the topic himself, Dan taught a lesson on the holiday, relating the Mexican victory over French forces to the American Revolution and our victory over England. Through prompting he was able to help his class see that both struggles were against a larger and stronger European country and both were important to each country's independence. Dan and his class had learned something, and his Mexican American students realized that history was something that could help them understand their own culteral heritage.

Minority students' disengagement with school is often exacerbated by the curriculum, much of which is oriented toward mainstream, middle-class, nonminority students (Anderson & Summerfield, 2004). Since students who are members of cultural minorities don't personally identify with the topics being taught, their interest and motivation suffer.

Research suggests that gender differences in interest also exist (Buck, Kostin, & Morgan, 2002). For instance, males tend to be more interested in topics such as war, politics, hard science, and business, whereas females are more interested in human relationships, arts, and literature.

To see how teachers can capitalize on students' interests, let's turn back to Jack Seltzer and his work with his Navajo students. He attempted to create a sense of interest in his lesson by capitalizing on the motivating effects of personalization. This variable is important for all students, but it can be particularly effective with members of cultural minorities, who commonly say they don't belong or don't feel welcome in school (Rubinson, 2004). When these students are presented with examples and experiences that directly relate to their lives, as Jack did, their interest and sense of belonging can significantly increase.

Planning for student interest can be as simple as continually asking, "How can I help my students understand how this topic relates to their own lives?" Lessons that connect to students' lives can have a powerful effect on students' motivation.

Teaching Context

Another powerful factor influencing your planning is the context in which you'll teach. Teaching context includes school and district policies, as well as state and district guidelines, standards, and tests. For example, even though all the principals in one study required written plans, their definition of plans varied greatly in detail, format, and length of time (McCutcheon, 1982). Some principals inspected plans every week, others monthly, and still others at random intervals. Clearly, the plans written for principals would be quite different from those in a school where planning was considered to be an individual and personal professional activity. When you land your first job, you'll need to find out what is required of you in terms of written plans.

Accountability and Standards-based Education

Planning is also influenced by national, state, and district standards and standards-based tests that hold teachers accountable for their students' achievement (Wiggins & McTighe, 2006). When teachers feel pressured to cover certain content and topics because the information will appear on a standardized test, their planning and teaching are affected. **Standards-based education**, *which is the process of focusing curriculum and instruction on predetermined standards*, is currently exerting a powerful influence on teacher planning, through both the learning objectives they choose and the tests that follow from them.

Sometimes these standards originate at the national level. The following are examples of national standards for middle school math students created by the National Council of Teachers of Mathematics.

Number and Operations Standard for Grades 6–8

Instructional programs from pre-kindergarten through grade 12 should enable all students to compute fluently and make reasonable estimates:

In grades 6–8 all students should:

- select appropriate methods and tools for computing with fractions and decimals from among mental computation, estimation, calculators, or computers, and paper and pencil, depending on the situation, and apply the selected methods;
- develop and analyze algorithms for computing with fractions, decimals, and integers and develop fluency in their use;
- develop and use strategies to estimate the results of rational-number computations and judge the reasonableness of the results;
- develop, analyze, and explain methods for solving problems involving proportions, such as scaling and finding equivalent ratios. (National Council of Teachers of Mathematics, 2000, p. 214)

What do standards from different states look like? The following is an example in fourth-grade math from the state of Texas (Texas Education Agency, 2008b).

(4.2) Number, operation, and quantitative reasoning. The student describes and compares fractional parts of whole objects or sets of objects

The student is expected to:

(A) use concrete objects and pictorial models to generate equivalent fractions.

The number (4.2) identifies this as the second standard in the list of fourth-grade standards in math, and the letter (A) represents the first in a list of student expectations. Different states code their standards in different ways, but all are designed to describe learning and assessment targets for teachers and students.

As another example, the following standard is from the state of Illinois in middle school science (Illinois State Board of Education, 2008a).

Illinois Science Assessment Framework

Standard 12F - Astronomy (Grade 7)

12.7.91 Understanding that objects in the solar system are for the most part in regular and predictable motion. Know that those motions explain such phenomena as the day, the year, the phases of the moon, and eclipses.

Although the way the standard is coded is different from the code used in Texas, both describe essential knowledge to be learned and assessed on tests.

As you can see, these standards are often general and vague. Not until they are translated into specific learning activities or test items do teachers or students have a clear idea of what should be learned or how it will be measured. This is another reason why teacher planning is so important.

Testing   As you begin reading this section, you might wonder, "What does testing have to do with teacher planning?" A great deal. One way that states and districts attempt to influence what is taught is through the tests they give. One elementary teacher, reassigned to a different grade level, found out about her new curriculum in this way:

> When I came up to fifth grade, I really didn't know everything that would be covered in the fifth grade, so one of the teachers said, "Well, this skill will be on the achievement test, and you'll find this on the achievement test, and you'll find this on the test." And I know to teach my children survival skills that I had to teach those. Let's just face it, that's just the way it is. You know, I tell them, "This may be on the achievement test and this is something that I really want to stick" (Brown, 1991, pp. 102–103).

Tests provide concrete guidelines about what should be taught, and principals and other teachers often pressure teachers to "cover" all of the knowledge and skills that will be tested sometime during the year.

As enthusiasm for accountability has increased around the country, all states have adopted statewide testing systems, especially in the areas of reading, math, and sciences. It is virtually certain that the curriculum in your school will be influenced by a standardized test developed or adopted at the state or local level. As a beginning teacher, you need to be aware of the different kinds of tests your students will be required to take. Armed with this information you can make wise professional planning decisions about what curriculum is best for your students.

Materials and Resources

Materials and other resources also have a major impact on teacher planning. Textbooks are first among them. Beginning teachers depend heavily on text materials to help them decide the topics to be taught, sequencing, depth, and even the test items they give their students (Blumenfeld, Hicks, & Krajcik, 1996). As teachers acquire experience, they become more independent, adding and deleting topics and generally personalizing their curriculum. However, even veterans rely heavily on available materials and often voice frustration when topics covered by district or state objectives do not appear in their textbooks (Reys, Reys, & Chavéz, 2004).

Although textbooks will strongly influence your planning decisions, you shouldn't depend on them completely. The following are some reasons why:

- **Student needs.** The topics presented in textbooks may not be consistent with the specific needs of your students, school, or district. Following a textbook too closely then fails to meet these needs as effectively as possible.

- **Scope.** To appeal to a wide market, textbook publishers include a huge number of topics, more than you can possibly teach in the time available. So, you will need to be selective in the topics you teach. Experts advise teachers to pick out the most important concepts and skills to emphasize so they can concentrate on the quality of understanding rather than on the quantity of information presented (Patton & Roschelle, 2008).

- **Quality.** Textbooks are sometimes poorly written, lack adequate examples, or even contain errors of fact (Hecht, 2006; Oakes & Saunders, 2004). Following a textbook too closely can then lead to shallow understanding or even faulty ideas that detract from learning.

What does this information suggest for you as a teacher? Nowhere in teaching is professionalism more important than in teacher planning. This is particularly true regarding textbooks. It's easy to allow textbooks to make professional decisions for you, such as teaching the next chapter because it's there, and this is what many teachers unfortunately do.

Textbooks can be a valuable resource, and they will certainly influence your planning and teaching decisions. However, don't be afraid to de-emphasize, or even eliminate, topics and chapters in the text and include other topics that aren't in it. Curriculum decision making such as this requires professional understanding, effort, and energy.

Time

Finally, time will also exert a powerful effect on your planning. Planning can consume a great deal of teacher time, and beginning teachers, who are learning to survive, spend considerable time wrestling with topics for the first time.

Time also serves as a frame of reference, helping teachers structure their planning. The school year is divided into grading periods, the grading periods into weeks, and courses and units are framed in terms of these time periods. Breaking time down into manageable chunks makes the task of planning manageable. We discuss this process in the next section of the chapter.

A Planning Model

Planning is a logical, sequential process in which teachers make conscious decisions about the learning activities they'll use to help students learn. It begins with the selection of topics, proceeds with the formulation of learning objectives and activities, and culminates with the selection of assessments to determine if learning has occurred (Figure 4.3). Within this framework, teacher knowledge, thinking, and professionalism are important (Darling-Hammond, 2000).

Planning has been strongly influenced by Ralph Tyler and his book, *Basic Principles of Curriculum and Instruction*, first published in 1950. This book has become a classic and has served as a basis for guiding teachers' thinking since that time. The model in Figure 4.3 is grounded in Tyler's work, as well as research examining teachers' planning strategies. The model provides a framework for planning regardless of whether the plans are for the entire year, units, or single lessons. We discuss the model in the sections that follow.

Selecting Topics

"What is important for students to learn?" is one of the most fundamental questions that you'll face as you plan. For example, in the vignettes that introduced the chapter, Peggy's topic was *order of mathematical operations,* and Jim's was *British and Spanish exploration.* Based on their plans we would conclude that they believed these topics were important to study. Textbooks, curriculum guides, and standards, such as those we discussed in the last section, are all sources teachers use to help answer this important question (Reys et al., 2004). Their personal philosophies as well as students' background knowledge and interests in the topic are other sources.

Figure 4.3

A Planning Model

Selecting Topics

↓

Specifying Learning Objectives

↓

Preparing and Organizing Learning Activities

↓

Preparing Assessments

Specifying Learning Objectives

Learning objectives *are statements that specify what students should know, understand, or be able to do with respect to a topic or course of study.* They're called "learning" objectives because they focus on learners and learner outcomes. "To put students into cooperative groups," or "to demonstrate how to add two-digit numbers," for instance, are *not* learning objectives; they describe teacher actions, not learner outcomes.

We saw that Peggy wanted her students to be able to solve order-of-operation problems. This is a learning objective because it specified what students should be able to do after the lesson. We also saw that a learning objective wasn't stated in Jim's plan. Even though it isn't stated, if Jim is an effective teacher, he has a clear and specific learning objective in mind. Unfortunately, teachers often conduct learning activities without clear objectives (Eggen & Austin, 2004), and, as we would expect, learning suffers.

Tyler (1950) suggested that the most useful form for stating objectives is "to express them in terms which identify both the kind of behavior to be developed in the student and the content or area of life in which this behavior is to operate" (p. 46). Other planning experts, in an attempt to further clarify the specific intent of an objective, included the conditions under which learners would demonstrate the behavior and the criteria for acceptable performance (Mager, 1962, 1998). The following are examples of objectives written according to Mager's format:

1. Given a ruler and compass, geometry students will construct the bisector of an angle within one degree of error.

2. From a list of sentences, language arts students will identify 90 percent of the prepositional phrases in the sentences.

3. Based on a written argument, the advanced composition student will outline the logic of the presentation, identifying all assumption and conclusions.

In the examples, the conditions respectively are (1) given a rule and compass, (2) from a list of sentences, and (3) based on a written argument. The observable performances are (1) will construct, (2) will identify, and (3) will outline; the respective criteria are (1) within one degree of error, (2) 90 percent, and (3) all assumptions and conclusions.

A popular alternative to Mager's approach was offered by Norman Gronlund (2004), who suggested that teachers state a general objective, such as *know, understand,* or *apply,* followed by specific learning outcomes that operationally define these terms. Using the same content as illustrated in the previous examples, Gronlund's objectives would appear as follows:

General Objective:	Applies rules of geometric constructions
Specific Behavior:	1. Constructs bisectors 2. Constructs prescribed shapes
General Objective:	Understands prepositional phrases
Specific Behavior:	1. Provides examples of prepositions 2. Identifies prepositional phrases in sentences 3. Writes sentences including prepositional phrases

General Objective: Assesses persuasive communications

Specific Behavior: 1. Outlines logic
                                     2. Identifies assumptions
                                     3. Identifies conclusions

We use *learning objectives* throughout this book to model this important starting point in teacher planning.

Learning Objectives in Different Domains

Three physical education teachers are comparing their goals for a unit on exercise. Carol comments, "I'm trying to develop muscle tone, strength, and flexibility so that no matter how they use their bodies in other activities, they'll have a good foundation." "I'm interested in that, too," adds Sharon, a second-year teacher, "but I'm more concerned that they know about the different kinds of exercise. They need to know the difference between aerobic and anaerobic exercise and how each affects their bodies." "Both of those are important," Tanya acknowledges, "but I'm more concerned about what happens after they leave school. We've got too many couch potatoes out there already. I'm trying to get them turned on to exercise for the rest of their lives."

Which of these objectives is most important? What kinds of learning should schools focus on? How will your class contribute to the overall growth of your students? These questions don't have easy answers. Part of the reason for this difficulty is that schools have a broad spectrum of objectives for students, and individual teachers must select from this broad array in selecting objectives for their classrooms and students.

Taxonomies, or classification systems, help teachers think about their goals during the planning process. These taxonomies first divide objectives into three areas or domains—cognitive, affective, and psychomotor—which correspond to the different kinds of learning in classrooms. These domains apply to physical education teachers, such as Carol, Sharon, and Tanya, as well as to other content areas area teachers. Let's look at them.

Objectives in the Cognitive Domain.   The **cognitive domain** *deals with the acquisition of knowledge, understanding, and skills.* Sharon's unit focused on the cognitive domain because it dealt with students' understanding of aerobic and anaerobic exercise. Most of the emphasis in schools is in this domain.

Not all cognitive learning objectives are the same, however. For instance, consider the following:

- To be able to define the concepts *simile* and *metaphor*
- To be able to identify examples of similes and metaphors in a written passage
- To be able to use similes and metaphors to make writing more attractive

Each of these is a cognitive objective and all are in language arts. But the student outcomes are different, and from a teacher perspective, so are your planning decisions. To respond to these differences, researchers developed a system that classified these objectives by the kind of thinking required of students. This system became the famous "Blooms Taxonomy" that

Table 4.1 Bloom's Taxonomy	
Level	**Description**
Knowledge	At the knowledge level, the student can recognize, define, or recall specific information. This might include remembering important names, dates, capitals, or even the equation for a formula.
Comprehension	This level targets whether students understand content. Ways of demonstrating comprehension include summarizing, translating, or providing examples of a concept.
Application	The application level focuses on whether students can use information to solve problems. Examples of application-level goals include having students solve math word problems and using punctuation properly in written communication.
Analysis	This level involves asking students to break something down to reveal its organization and structure. Students perform analysis when they discuss why a short story "works" or when they identify the component parts of a science experiment.
Synthesis	Students employ synthesis when they create a unique (for them) product. This might include writing a poem, painting a picture, or creating a computer program.
Evaluation	In the highest level of the taxonomy, students judge the value or worth of something by comparing it to predetermined criteria. We ask students to evaluate when they critique a plan to solve a pollu tion problem or when we ask students to assess a writing sample.

has been used since the middle of the twentieth century (Bloom, Englehart, Furst, Hill, & Krathwohl, 1956). The levels of the taxonomy and a description of each level are outlined in Table 4.1.

In looking at the descriptions of the levels in Table 4.1, we see that our three objectives would be classified as being at the knowledge, comprehension, and application levels respectively.

To reflect the dramatic increase in understanding of learning and teaching since the middle of the twentieth century, Bloom's original taxonomy has been revised (Anderson & Krathwohl, 2001). The revised taxonomy is a matrix containing 24 cells that represent the intersection of four types of knowledge with six cognitive processes. It appears in Figure 4.4.

Using the revised taxonomy, we would classify the first objective into the cell where *conceptual knowledge* intersects with *remember*, since *simile* and *metaphor* are concepts and students are remembering a definition; the second would be classified into the conceptual *knowledge/understand* cell, since being able to identify examples reflects understanding; and the third would be in the *procedural knowledge/create* cell, because being able to write requires knowledge of writing conventions and procedures, and using similes and metaphors to making writing more attractive is a creative process.

Both of these taxonomies remind us that specifying learning objectives requires careful decision making, and it reinforces the idea that thinking about learning objectives requires much more that simply identifying topics. We must also answer the question "What do we want students to know or understand about this topic?" or "What should they be able to do with it?"

The Affective Domain.   As Tanya suggested, schools exist for more than just making students smarter. We also want them to develop into individuals with healthy views about themselves and others. Her objective was in the **affective domain**, *which focuses on the development of attitude and values* and divides this process into five levels that correspond

Figure 4.4

A Taxonomy for Learning, Teaching, and Assessing

The Knowledge Dimension	The Cognitive Process Dimension					
	1. Remember	2. Understand	3. Apply	4. Analyze	5. Evaluate	6. Create
A. Factual knowledge						
B. Conceptual knowledge						
C. Procedural knowledge						
D. Metacognitive knowledge						

Table 4.2 **The Affective Taxonomy**

Level	Description
Receiving	At this level, the student is willing to listen passively to or attend to some message. Students who listen to a speaker talking about drugs without tuning him or her out are acting at this level.
Responding	Beyond simply receiving a message, students must also react to it. Students react by obeying, discussing, or responding to the attitude or value.
Valuing	When students respond at this level, they show their preference for an idea by voluntarily displaying it. For example, a health class has been talking about nutrition. A student turns to his friend in the cafeteria and says, "Those french fries aren't good for you. They've got too much fat."
Organization	Organization occurs when students take an attitude or value and incorporate it into a larger value system. In the health example, this would occur when the student looks at his or her own diet and examines implications for himself or herself.
Characterization	At the highest level of the affective domain, students not only reorganize their own thinking but also act consistently with their beliefs. A student who actually changes the way he or she eats over a long period of time would be operating at this level.

to the degree to which attitudes and values are internalized by the individual (Krathwohl, Bloom & Masia, 1964). A taxonomy for affective goals is outlined in Table 4.2.

Like the cognitive taxonomy, the affective taxonomy helps guide teachers' thinking as they plan. If respect for the rights of others is one of our objectives, do we just want students to nod when we talk about the importance of respect or do we want students to respect one another, helping create a classroom in which all students feel secure in responding, knowing they won't be interrupted or laughed at? In a larger sense, the affective taxonomy provides some interesting answers to the question "What are schools for?" (Noddings, 2003).

The Psychomotor Domain. A third area that serves as a source of objectives for our teaching is the **psychomotor domain,** *which involves the development of coordination and physical skills.* Carol's objective of wanting her students to develop their muscle tone, strength, and flexibility would fall into this domain. Although we typically associate the psychomotor domain with physical education, other areas such as word processing, music, art, and home economics are also involved. In addition, preschool, kindergarten, and the lower elementary grades focus on psychomotor goals through activities such as cutting and pasting, coloring, printing, and writing. Like the other areas, the psychomotor taxonomy (Harrow, 1972) shown in Table 4.3, proceeds from simple to complex and from externally to internally controlled actions.

Preparing and Organizing Learning Activities

After you specify your learning objectives, your next task is to prepare and organize learning activities. This stage of the planning process answers the question "What will I have students do that will help them reach the learning objective?" This question reminds us of why clear learning objectives are so important. If the objective isn't clear, it is difficult to design learning activities to help students reach it.

To gain insights into Peggy's thinking about learning activities, look again at her list of procedures in her lesson plan at the beginning of the chapter. This list provided guidance to her as she actually implemented her plan.

Because of the brevity of Jim's plan, we don't know how he answered the question. Again, if he is an effective teacher, he has a clear and ready answer, which links learning activities to objectives.

Task Analysis: A Planning Tool to Organize Activities   **Task analysis** *is the process of breaking down content into component parts and making decisions about sequencing the parts* (Alberto & Troutman, 2009). For example, a task analysis for the skill of changing a tire

Table 4.3 **The Psychomotor Taxonomy**

Level	Description
Reflex movements	Behaviors outside the conscious control of the learner
Basic fundamental movements	Behaviors learned at an early age (e.g., grasping, walking) that form the foundation for later growth
Perceptual abilities	Coordination of muscular movements with the outside world through feedback with the sense organs
Physical abilities	The development of strength, endurance, flexibility, and agility
Skilled movements	Complex physical skills (e.g., skipping rope, shooting a basket) that use the first four levels
Nondiscursive communication	The use of our bodies to express feelings or ideas

could be broken down into subskills, such as jacking up the car, loosening the wheel nuts, taking off the flat, replacing it with the spare, replacing the wheel nuts, and lowering the car.

Task analysis helps answer these questions: "How should different parts of the learning activity be sequenced?" and "What will students need to move from one part of the learning activity to the next?" It involves the following four steps:

- Specify the terminal or target behavior.
- Identify prerequisite skills.
- Sequence subskills.
- Diagnose students.

Task analysis begins by specifying a learning objective. By identifying prerequisite skills, you are attempting to specify the subskills that lead to the learning objective. Sequencing helps you by providing an order for teaching and provides learners with a structure for learning. In the final phase you attempt to find out which of these subskills your students have already mastered. Let's see how one teacher uses these steps during planning.

Jerilyn McIntire stares at the stack of writing assignments on her desk and doesn't know where to begin. Her seventh-grade English students aren't afraid to write, but it seems as if half of them have never heard of punctuation. There are sentence fragments, run-on sentences, and sentences without periods, and commas and semicolons were virtually nonexistent. Where should she start?

In considering the problem, Jerilyn decides to start with punctuating simple sentences with the following learning objective:

Students will be able to write a simple sentence with correct end-of-sentence punctuation.

Using this objective as a guide, Jerilyn writes down the skills she feels are prerequisite to meeting the objective:

- Being able to differentiate between complete sentences and sentence fragments
- Knowing the difference between declarative, interrogatory, and imperative sentences
- Knowing whether periods, question marks, or exclamation marks go with each type of sentence
- Correctly using these marks to punctuate different kinds of sentences

As she wrestles with the problem of ordering these prerequisites, Jerilyn decides that the sequence of subskills as written made sense. First students have to understand what sentences were. Then she could work on helping them understand the different kinds of sentences and how they were punctuated. Finally, she wants them to write and punctuate their own sentences.

Jerilyn faced a final problem: How many (and which) students had already mastered the prerequisites? To diagnose her students Jerilyn designs a simple quiz to administer the next day. In the first part students would have to differentiate between sentences and sentence fragments. In the second, they'd have to punctuate different kinds of sentences, and in the third they'd have to write their own sentences and punctuate them.

Outlining content can also be a useful part of task analysis. For instance one teacher used the following outline to organize a unit on the causes of the Civil War:

Causes of the Civil War

I. Historical antecedents
   A. Westward expansion
   B. Missouri Compromise
   C. Dred Scott decision
   D. John Brown's raid on Harper's Ferry

II. Conflicting philosophies
   A. Industrial versus agrarian
   B. States' rights versus federal rights
   C. Slavery

III. Events
   A. Election of 1860
   B. Fort Sumter

The outline supports a task analysis by helping the teacher decide which of the components of the outline should be taught first, which should come second, and so on.

Task analysis can be an effective planning tool for three reasons. First, it encourages us to clarify our thinking by carefully specifying learning objectives. Second, it encourages us to break complex skills into smaller subskills that are easier for students to master. And third, task analysis shifts our attention from abstract concepts and skills to our students and encourages us to ask "What do they already know and where should I begin teaching them?"

Preparing Assessments

Formal assessments such as tests, quizzes, or performance assessments are typically given after students complete learning activities, so we might assume that thinking about assessment also occurs after learning activities are conducted. This isn't true; effective teachers think about assessment while preparing objectives and learning activities. Effective assessments not only answer the question "How can I determine if my students have reached the learning objectives?" but also "How can I use assessment to facilitate learning?" Assessment decisions are essential during planning because they help teachers align their instruction, the topic of the next section.

Instructional Alignment

Thinking about assessment during planning serves an additional function. It helps teachers answer the question "How do I know that my instruction and assessments are logically connected to my learning objectives?"

Instructional alignment *is the match among learning objectives, learning activities, and assessments and is essential for promoting learning.*

> Without this alignment, it is difficult to know what is being learned. Students may be learning valuable information, but one cannot tell unless there is alignment between what they are learning and the assessment of that learning. Similarly, students may be

learning things that others don't value unless curricula and assessments are aligned with . . . learning goals. (Bransford et al., 2000, pp. 51–52)

Instructional alignment helps students understand what is important to learn and helps teachers match instructional strategies and assessments to learning objectives (Miller et al., 2009).

Maintaining alignment isn't as easy as it appears. For instance, if a teacher's objective is for students to be able to write effectively, yet learning activities focus on isolated grammar skills, the instruction is out of alignment. It is similarly out of alignment if the objective is for students to apply math concepts to real-world problems, but learning activities have students practicing computation problems. Instructional alignment encourages you to ask "What does my objective (e.g., "apply math concepts") actually mean, and do my learning and assessment activities actually lead to the objective?"

To view a video clip of a lesson in which you can analyze the instructional alignment, go to the Book Specific Resources tab in MyEducationLab, select your text, select Video Examples under Chapter 4, and then click on *Analyzing Instructional Alignment*.

Backward Design

Using specific learning objectives to frame planning decisions and making decisions about learning activities assessments during planning is a process called **backward design** (Wiggins & McTighe, 2006). Backward design first identifies desired learning outcomes or objectives, then specifies ways to determine or assess whether these objectives are met, and finally establishes learning experiences to reach the objective. The notion of "backward" derives from the fact that thinking about learning experiences comes *after* thinking about assessments, which is different from traditional teacher thinking. Backward design is really nothing more than good instructional planning that ensures alignment among learning objectives, learning activities, and assessments.

The concept of backward design has evolved from the emphasis on standards and accountability. A standard, in essence, is a learning objective. Unfortunately, standards are stated in widely varying ways, so they often must be interpreted so that a learning objective can be specified based on them. However, once interpreted, decisions about learning activities and assessments are then based on the learning objective. This is the essence of backward design.

*L*esson, Long-Term, and Unit Planning

The planning model we just described can be used to guide teachers' thinking regardless of whether long-term, unit, or daily lesson plans are being prepared. However, different aspects of the model are emphasized with lesson planning compared to long-term or unit

Figure 4.5

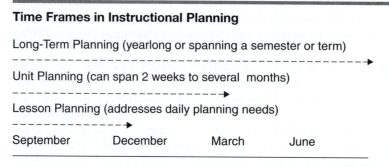

Time Frames in Instructional Planning

Long-Term Planning (yearlong or spanning a semester or term)

Unit Planning (can span 2 weeks to several months)

Lesson Planning (addresses daily planning needs)

September   December   March   June

planning, and the amount of specificity is one of the factors involved. These different time frames are illustrated in Figure 4.5. We begin our discussion of instructional planning in the next section by analyzing lesson planning.

Daily Lesson Planning

When teachers plan, they typically think about the specific steps they will take to help students learn. **Daily lesson plans** *focus teachers' efforts on a specific day and class and provide enough specificity to guide them when they actually teach the lesson.* At the middle and high school levels a lesson plan typically corresponds to a given period, whereas at the elementary levels, in self-contained classrooms, lesson length may vary from 15 minutes to an hour or more, depending on the topic, activities, and maturity of students.

As with other dimensions of planning, each teacher approaches lesson planning in a personal way. In addition, the process varies with the topic; if you are familiar with and confident about a subject, you will plan differently than if you are hesitant about it. Experience also makes a difference, in general terms (i.e., if you're experienced, you'll plan differently than if you're a beginning teacher) but also in relation to whether you have taught the specific topic before. We saw this in the beginning of the chapter in the different ways that Peggy and Jim planned for their teaching.

With these ideas in mind we examine two different models of lesson planning. As you think about them, we encourage you to adapt selectively from them to fit your individual needs.

A Basic Lesson Plan Model   A lesson plan needs to be specific enough to provide structure for the lesson, but general enough to provide flexibility when the situation warrants. Few lessons proceed exactly as planned. This fact makes teaching both challenging and potentially bewildering at times.

The lesson plan in Table 4.4 contains basic elements that all effective teachers think about as they plan for instruction. As you can see, this lesson plan begins by linking the individual lesson to the unit in which it is embedded. Goals and learning objectives are then stated, and a rationale is considered. This is followed by the content, instructional procedures, and the assessment procedures for the lesson. Finally, materials and aids are noted to serve as last-minute logistical reminders for the teacher. We saw an example of this model at the beginning of this chapter with Peggy and her math lesson.

Table 4.4 **Elements of a Basic Lesson Plan**

Component	Function
Unit title	Helps identify the relationship between this lesson and others in the unit
Instructional goal	Identifies the broad goal for the lesson
Objective(s)	Identifies specifically what the students should learn
Rationale	Explains why the lesson is important
Content	Identifies and organizes the major ideas/skills in the lesson
Learning activities	Describes the learning experiences that will be used to help the students reach the objective(s)
Assessment procedures	Specifies how student learning will be measured
Materials and aids	Identifies the equipment and supplies that will be needed

A shorter variation of the basic lesson plan model is outlined in Table 4.5. This model eliminates the unit component, the goal statement, and the rationale, on the assumption that a teacher will keep these in mind during the planning process.

Weekly Plan Books The teacher plan book, a mainstay of classrooms throughout the country, provides teachers with a handy way to summarize planning decisions they have made. An example appears in Figure 4.6.

The boxes are small; typically, they average one by two inches. There is a room only for brief comments, such as

Homework
Review place value
(Text, pp. 217–222)
Do problems 9–14 on board (p. 228)
Fri. Quiz, Chpt. 9
Homework, p. 228, #s 15–30

Table 4.5 **An Abbreviated Lesson Plan Model**

Component	Function
Objective(s)	Identifies specifically what the students should learn
Content	Identifies and organizes the major ideas/skills in the lesson
Learning activities	Describes the learning experiences that will be used to help students reach the objective(s)
Assessment procedures	Specifies how student learning will be measured
Materials and aids	Identifies the equipment and supplies that will be needed

Figure 4.6

Weekly Lesson Plan Book

Day	Period 1	Period 2	Period 3	Period 4	Period 5
Monday					
Tuesday					
Wednesday					
Thursday					
Friday					

This abbreviated format raises two questions: "Why is this planning form so popular?" and "How does it relate to the other formats we have discussed?" The answer to the first question is simple; the format takes little time and effort, and it's functional. Teachers are very busy; when not actually working with students, they plan, grade papers, and do a myriad of other professionally related activities. A plan book provides them with a quick and efficient way of recording and keeping track of their planning thoughts. A teacher can plan on Friday, go home and enjoy the weekend, and return on Monday feeling as if the week is "under control."

The answer to the second question isn't as clear. The brief notes that we see in planning books such as this belie the complexity of teachers' thinking when they plan. We see that this plan format is similar to Jim's, shown at the beginning of the chapter. With his 10 years of experience, he could leave many of the components of a more detailed lesson plans implicit and unstated. For example, he—and all effective teachers—could quickly state what his specific learning objectives for the lesson were, why they were important, and how he planned to help his students reach them. Because these components were unstated doesn't means that they didn't exist or weren't considered.

As teachers plan and record their planning efforts and products, they often do so in a shorthand, cryptic fashion in plan books much as Jim did. The brevity of these directions belies the thought and energy that go into the plans.

Lesson plans are like shopping lists; the items on a grocery list represent considerable implicit planning and coordination for different menus. Such planning and coordination are not evident from a brief inspection of the shopping list. In a similar way, the brief description of activities in a plan book does not do justice to the considerable amount of mental planning that precedes them.

However, not all veteran teachers are effective, and part of the problem might relate to planning. Would more detailed planning with more specific written information help? This is an interesting question.

Long-Term Planning

Daily lesson plans don't exist in isolation; the learning experiences we plan for our students should be connected in some meaningful way. To do this and organize the school year into manageable chunks, teachers use long-term planning. **Long-term planning** *involves preparing for a year or semester and serves primarily as a framework for later planning efforts.* Long-term planning serves the following purposes:

- It adapts the curriculum to fit the teacher's knowledge and priorities.
- It helps the teacher focus on the structure and content of new curricula.
- It develops a practical schedule for instruction.

In addition to framing content issues, long-term planning also serves to establish routines for how the school year will run. The structure provided by routines plays a major role in teachers' planning and reflects decision making about how they want their classrooms to run. One elementary classroom routine that was effective in producing high math achievement looked like this:

> Monday starts with a longer than usual review to compensate for the weekend. Each subsequent day begins with homework checking and then proceeds to presentation of new material, and then group and individual practice. Friday's session wraps up the week with further review and a quiz. Students know what to expect each day as math begins, and there is a natural rhythm to the tempo of the classroom during the week. (Good, Grouws, & Ebmeier, 1983, p. 44)

Establishing routines during long-term planning provides a superstructure that helps guide both teacher and student actions for the entire school year.

Much of the initial effort during long-term planning involves covert mental activity, which is often continual, occurring at strange times and places, such as late evening or while driving to school or watching a program on television. As one teacher described it, "The subconscious does a lot of sorting for you. You can think of many things simultaneously. The sorting is rapid, not logical or sequenced, and is different for different reasons" (McCutcheon, 1982, p. 265).

A primary focus during long-term planning is selection of content. To aid in this process, teachers turn to a number of sources including state standards, curriculum guides, textbooks, teachers' guides, and other teachers' experiences. They often take notes, list and sequence topics, and then adjust the sequence. Secondary teachers focus primarily on state standards and content when they plan, and content decisions are typically made first; elementary teachers are more likely to begin with standards and use these to frame student activities.

As teachers proceed with long-term planning, they produce lists that are framed in terms of time. These lists are refinements of the notes and thinking that occur in the beginning of the long-term planning process. For example, the products of a seventh-grade geography teacher's long-term planning might appear as follows:

World Geography (First Semester)

1. Basic concepts (September/October)
2. Maps, landforms, water and waterways, elements of climate, population patterns
3. Cultural change and development (November 1–15)

4. Anglo-America (Canada and United States) (November 15–December 15)

5. Latin America (Mexico, Central America, South America) (December 15–January 15)

As we can see from this example, long-term planning is concrete enough only to provide a framework for more specific unit planning. Day-to-day learning activities usually are not considered at this point, nor is extensive study to refresh content background. Too much specificity can be counterproductive, as one teacher observed:

> If I plan too far ahead, the curriculum isn't flexible enough to incorporate children's interests and the needs I see while teaching. Also, if students are absent or gone for band or something I have to do so much reteaching that too much specificity gets in the way of long-range planning because it interrupts the flow of my thinking.

A brief outline simplifies planning efforts by reducing the number of decisions that must be made later. At this point you'll think of content, possible learning objectives, and resources, such as finding materials on the Internet, that require extra time and effort. Otherwise, you will typically wait until the topic approaches before unit planning. Later, you'll refer to these outlines and say, for example, "Ah, yes. I'll be starting Anglo-America next week, so I need to get ready." The specifics are a function of unit planning.

Unit Planning

Once a general framework is established in long-term planning, teachers find it useful to convert this framework into specific units. A **unit** *is a series of interconnected lessons focusing on a general topic.* It can last anywhere from a week or two to a month or more depending on the topic and age of the students. Unit planning essentially amounts to planning daily lessons that all relate to a general topic and all point to a broad goal. Some examples of unit topics and broad goals are outlined in Table 4.6.

Having identified the unit topic and general goal, the next task is to plan a series of daily lessons that are connected and all point to the broad goal. For instance, the science teacher would then plan one or more lessons on the skeletal system, nervous system, muscular system, and so on, with emphasis on how each of the systems contributes to the overall functioning of the body. Similar decisions would be made for each of the other topics.

Table 4.6 Unit Topics and Goals

Content Area	Topic	Goal
Science	Systems of the body	To understand the parts and functions of our body's systems
Literature	Twentieth-century American authors	To understand the styles and significance of a series of twentieth-century American authors
American history	The Civil War	To understand the causes, events, and outcomes of the Civil War
Algebra	Quadratic equations	To understand different methods for solving quadratic equations
Writing	Figurative language	To understand and be able to use different forms of figurative language in writing

Technology and Teaching

Using Technology to Plan

Planning can be a time- and labor-intensive activity. This is especially true for beginning teachers who don't have previous lessons and experiences to build upon. Fortunately, technology can make your planning efforts more effective and efficient.

Technology can assist your planning efforts in three ways. First, it can provide access to resources, for both you and your students. Second, technology can also assist you directly during the planning process. Third, it can serve as an efficient storage and retrieval system to make planning efforts in the future more efficient. We examine each of these in the sections that follow.

Technology as a Planning Resource

All effective planning includes a clear goal, and technology via the Internet can help us shape and clarify our goals. One way to do this is to consult the content standards that exist in different content areas in all 50 states. These can be found on the following website and can provide some sense of direction for your planning: http://www.education-world.com/standards/state/index.shtml. In addition to these state-specific standards, professional organizations such as the International Reading Association and the National Council of Teachers of Mathematics also publish content standards for different subject matter areas. Website addresses for these professional organizations can be found in Table 1.2 in Chapter 1 and can serve as alternate beginning points for your planning.

A word of caution, however; experts recommend that considerable teacher decision making is required before broad, general standards can be translated into specific learning objectives to guide instruction in your classes (Wiggins & McTighe, 2006). However, standards, whether from state or national sources, can be a productive starting point for your planning.

A second way that technology can serve as a planning resource is as an information source, for both you and your students. In previous times teachers often referred back to old college textbooks and alternate student texts to find information for their lessons. Although these resources are still valuable and available, a much broader and deeper source of information exists on the Internet. Major search engines such as Google and Yahoo provide a wealth of information, both for background information for you and for insertion into lessons.

The Internet can also serve as an information source for your students as they write papers and work on projects. Experts caution, however, that the wealth of information found on the Internet can often be overwhelming, and students frequently need direction and assistance to wade through all the information that's there (Roblyer & Doerring, 2010). In addition you'll need to work with students to help them identify sites that contain unreliable or inaccurate information.

Technology as an Aid During Planning

Once you've examined standards and feel confident about your understanding of lesson content, technology can also assist you in putting your thoughts down in words. A number of websites offer lesson makers or lesson planners that provide on-screen prompts to remind you of critical components of an effective lesson plan, such as objectives, learning activities, and assessment. In addition, **IEP Generator Software** *provides teachers with templates that can assist teachers in constructing individualized education programs (IEPs) for* their students. Finally, a number of websites contain constructed lesson plans for a myriad of areas and levels, but teachers need to examine these carefully for their fit with their own students and classrooms.

Technology as a Planning Time-Saver

The amount of energy involved in planning can be overwhelming for beginning teachers and also is a major time drain for experienced teachers. Technology can make the process more efficient for both groups of teachers through computers' storage and retrieval capabilities. Veteran teachers attest to the amount of time that can be saved by modifying and using previous plans. In essence, experienced teachers use what worked, delete what didn't, and modify aspects that need changes. For this timesaving strategy to work, teachers need an effective way to store and retrieve previous lessons. There are few tried and true suggestions that work for all teachers, but we believe this is one of them: save and store all planning materials for future reference! It might take a little extra time at the moment, but the pay-off down the line will be considerable.

In addition to actual lesson plans and planning notes, teachers also find that saving exercises, assignments, and quiz and test items can save enormous amounts of time later. Teachers used to use file cabinets to store their plans; today teachers have personal computers that can save and store planning information almost effortlessly. This dimension of technology will save you countless hours in your future as a professional.

*I*ntegrating the Curriculum: Interdisciplinary and Thematic Units

So far our discussion of planning has focused on specific, individual topics. Sometimes, however, teachers want to help their students make connections between topics or even different content areas. This is when interdisciplinary or thematic planning is useful. To illustrate this process, let's look at the thinking of Janine Henderson, a fourth-grade teacher, as she attempts to connect topics across different content areas.

One weekend Janine was planning for the remainder of the school year. Looking at her long-range plan, she saw that her unit on "plants" was coming up in science. The timing was right, spring was on the horizon, and her students often brought her plants and flowers to identify and talk about.

As she looked at standards in other areas of her curriculum, she noticed that graphing was an upcoming topic in math. "Hmm," she thought, "I wonder if I could combine the two and have students graph something on plants. She recalled some of the experiments she'd done with bean seeds, investigating the effects of different amounts of water, sun, and fertilizer. She jotted down, "Graph plant growth."

She also noticed that "Knowledge of state economy" was a standard in her state's fourth-grade social studies curriculum. She got out a piece of paper and drew the information shown in Figure 4.7.

Figure 4.7

Planning for Integration of Content Areas

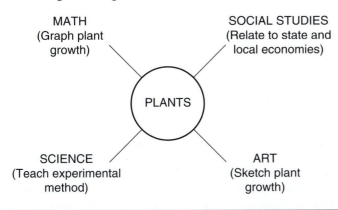

Much of the school curriculum is divided into separate content areas. At the elementary level teachers divide the school day into time frames allocated to different areas such as math and reading, and these content divisions are reflected on report cards. At the secondary level subject matter divisions become even more pronounced, with students taking different classes from experts in different content areas.

This division of the curriculum into discrete content areas has both advantages and disadvantages. Advantages include the following:

- The simplicity of disciplinary boundaries, which makes them understandable and acceptable to parents

- Being able to make efficient use of subject matter "experts"

- Use of content areas to help students understand how different disciplines are structured in terms of major concepts

- Understanding of the processes of inquiry unique to different disciplines (Donovan & Bransford, 2005; Stevens, Wineburg, Herrenkohl, & Bell, 2005)

Despite these advantages dividing the curriculum into discrete and isolated subject matter areas also has two major disadvantages. First, artificial distinctions between disciplines encourage students to see knowledge as fragmented and disconnected, and second, opportunities for interdisciplinary problem solving are lost.

An Integrated Continuum

Several options exist for teachers to organize their curriculum to address these problems. These vary from truly separated disciplined-oriented units on the left to fully integrated ones on the right. These are illustrated in Figure 4.8 and discussed next.

At the far left end of the continuum, we have discipline-based organization. Much of the instruction in schools is based on disciplines, or separate subject areas (Donovan & Bransford, 2005). Janine's initial planning was discipline based as she thought about it in terms of separate content areas.

Figure 4.8

Options for Integrating the Curriculum

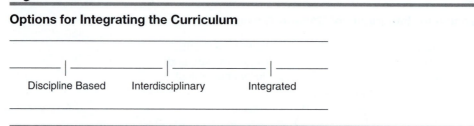

Discipline Based   Interdisciplinary   Integrated

Interdisciplinary planning *involves creating units in which several subject areas focus their content around a theme.* Janine moved to an interdisciplinary approach when she used plants as a focal point and investigated the topic from math, science, and social studies perspectives. Middle school teachers often do this when subject matter teachers maintain their separate disciplines but agree to focus them on a common topic. This is quite common in project-based instruction and other forms of problem-based learning.

In a truly **integrated approach**, *subject matter lines blur and even disappear.* Students are encouraged to pursue topics holistically, drawing from different subject matter areas when they prove useful. Here, real-life problems or topics that are meaningful and interesting to students become most prominent, and disciplines are called upon only as tools to understand or solve the problem.

Designing and Implementing Integrated Units

In designing thematic or integrated units your first task is to identify a focal point for student investigations. Themes or topics often serve as starting points for interdisciplinary or integrated units. Janine Henderson used plants as the theme to structure and organize her planning. Some additional examples of themes follow:

Inventors and inventions

Space exploration

Discovery and exploration

Seasons

These broad topics provide a cognitive menu for students, giving them specific options to pursue under the theme's broad umbrella.

Problems can also serve as focal points for thematic units, such as the following:

What can we do about pollution?

What could be done to increase voter participation and turnout?

How could school lunches be made more appealing and nutritious?

Where did present-day popular music come from? What are its origins?

In planning for thematic units an organizing web or network is useful. Teachers typically start in the center with a topic or problem and then branch out from there with additional topics or questions. These topics or questions provide students with options to pursue in their studies. An example of one network can be seen in Figure 4.9.

Figure 4.9

Sample Network for Integration

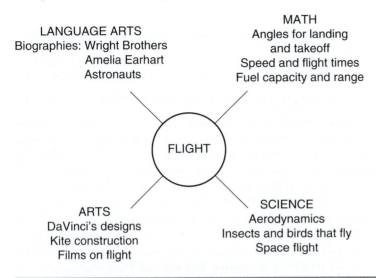

In using interdisciplinary and thematic units your role changes dramatically. Instead of being an information provider, you become a facilitator, helping students investigate topics of interest. Instruction becomes much less teacher centered.

Student roles also change. Interdisciplinary and thematic units provide opportunities to pursue areas of interest in a coherent and integrated way. Instead of listening, taking notes, and answering questions, students are actively engaged in researching topics. The products that they produce will appear in various forms, including

- Written research reports
- Posters
- Bulletin boards
- Models
- Dioramas
- Videotapes
- Oral presentations

Research on Integrated Planning

Integrating the curriculum, although intuitively sensible, is controversial. Proponents make the following arguments (Brown, 2006; Wood, 2005):

- Integrating curriculum increases the relevance of content by making connections among ideas explicit.

- Integrating curriculum improves achievement. Integrating the curriculum results in fewer transitions, leaving more time available for instruction.

- Integrating curriculum promotes collaborative planning, which increases communication among teachers.

Critics of curriculum integration counter with the following arguments (Nikitina, 2006):

- Integrating curriculum results in a de-emphasis on important concepts, since teachers don't have a deep understanding of all the content areas that are to be integrated.

- Planning and instruction for integrating curriculum are inordinately time consuming.

Integrated curriculum is most popular at the elementary level, where a single teacher can relate several topics, and at the middle school level, where teams of teachers periodically meet to interconnect content areas. It is least common at the high school level where a disciplinary approach to curriculum is entrenched. National standards driven by subject matter areas, as well as increased emphasis on testing, are likely to maintain this trend at the high school level.

The essential question with respect to this issue is "Does evidence indicating that integrating curriculum increases learning exist?" At present the answer is unclear. For example, one study found that elementary teachers who integrated reading with science or social studies produced greater reading comprehension in their students (Portner, 2000). Experts explained these results by suggesting that students were more motivated to read about interesting topics such as pirates and motorboats. However, other research is mixed, finding either no benefits or negative results (Senftleber & Eggen, 1999; Stevens et al., 2005). Advocates of curriculum integration counter this negative evidence by arguing that the measures presently available are inadequate, unable to assess the subtle and difficult-to-measure benefits to students. The debate is likely to continue.

 Summary

Why Do Teachers Plan?

Instructional planning involves decisions about content, students, learning activities, and evaluation procedures. Planning serves a number of functions, ranging from providing security and confidence to simplifying instructional decisions.

Factors Influencing Instructional Planning

A number of factors affect the planning process. Teachers' values and beliefs, learners' developmental and motivational needs, state and district standards, content, teaching context, materials and resources, and available time all frame planning decisions.

A Planning Model

Effective planning begins with selecting topics and continues with specifying learning objectives, preparing and organizing learning activities, and designing assessments. Specifying objectives and assessments during planning and ensuring that they are aligned are part of a process called backward design.

Lesson, Long-Term, and Unit Planning

Individual lesson plans prepare for a specific class period. The form that specific lesson plans take will vary with the teacher and the situation. Long-term planning represents teachers' first attempts to place planning decisions within a time frame, and it usually amounts to lists of topics together with notes and thoughts. Unit planning bridges the gap between long-term planning and lesson planning. A unit plan is essentially a series of individual lesson plans with a common general goal and theme.

Integrating the Curriculum: Interdisciplinary and Thematic Units

Interdisciplinary planning allows students to see how different disciplines can be focused on a common problem. An integrated approach to planning deemphasizes subject matter boundaries and instead focuses students' attention on a problem or theme.

*I*mportant Concepts

Affective domain (p. 120)

Backward design (p. 125)

Cognitive domain (p. 119)

Daily lesson plans (p. 126)

IEP Generator Software (p. 132)

Instructional alignment (p. 124)

Integrated approach (p. 134)

Interdisciplinary planning (p. 134)

Learning objectives (p. 118)

Long-term planning (p. 129)

Planning (p. 108)

Psychomotor domain (p. 122)

Standards-based education (p. 114)

Task analysis (p. 122)

Unit (p. 130)

*P*reparing for Your Licensure Exam

At the beginning of the chapter you saw how Peggy Stone and Jim Hartley planned for instruction. Let's look now at another teacher's thinking as she plans and then puts her plans into action. As you read about Angie's planning, compare it to the information you read in this chapter.

After reading this case, go to the Book Specific Resources tab in MyEducationLab, select your text, select *Preparing for Your Licensure Exam* under Chapter 4 to complete the questions that accompany the case and receive feedback on your responses.

Angie Becker, a fifth-grade teacher, was wrestling with a pile of books on her desk. "Maybe I shouldn't do a unit on nutrition," she thought to herself. "It's not something I'm an expert at and it's going to take a lot of work. But, the kids really need it—I can't believe the stuff they eat for lunch. Oh, well, here goes."

As Angie checked her notes in her planning folder she saw the following:

Food pyramids
Food groups
Analyze lunches
Change eating habits

"Well, this is a start," she continued. "What I need to do is grab their attention. Once I get them into the unit, they'll be okay. It's that first activity that makes or breaks a unit. And since I'm not real solid on this stuff, I'd better make it a good one."

"Hmm, what I really want them to do is eat healthier but first they need some basic concepts. I'd better write these down or I'll forget them." She continued by writing the following terms on the sheet of paper in front of her:

Calories
Food groups
Vitamins
Minerals
Carbohydrates
Protein
Fat
Cholesterol
Food pyramid

"I think I know where I want them to go but I'm not sure how to get there. They need to be able to analyze their own diets and come up with positive suggestions for improving it. But first things first. I need to teach them some basic concepts."

As Angie continued to sketch out ideas, her face brightened. "I've got it! I'll talk to the school dietitian and see if she has any ideas. I could look on the Internet to see what's out there. Also, Harvey, the science teacher, might still have that video on the digestive system. That might be fun."

On the first day of her unit Angie begins the class by writing "Nutrition" on the board and asking students what it meant. After several half-hearted student attempts at defining it, Angie brings out a cafeteria tray with the day's lunch on it. Her students respond immediately.

"Yuck."

"Gross."

"Cafeteria food."

"Smells good to me."

"Okay, class, settle down. Good . . . Now is this a nutritious meal?" she asks, pointing to the pizza, salad, milk and jello.

Students look at the tray and exchange puzzled looks. Finally, Rashad offers, "Yeah, it's nutritious—else they wouldn't feed it to us. But that doesn't mean it's any good."

"Interesting comment. . . . Do you all agree? Is this a nutritious meal? Most of you are nodding your heads 'yes' but how do you know? Well, that's what we're going to learn about in health for the next couple of weeks."

Angie then has each student write down all the things he or she had eaten in the past 24 hours and to write a short analysis of this diet. When they complete this task, she asks them to hand it in so she can read them that evening.

Angie spends the next couple of days talking about different food groups. At the end of the week she gives the class a quiz that measures basic nutritional concepts. She begins the next week's class with a diary assignment. Students are to write down everything they eat that week and turn their analyses in on the next Monday.

Questions for Analysis

Let's examine Angie's lesson now based on the information in this chapter. In your analysis, consider the following questions. In each case, be specific and take information directly from the case study in doing your analysis.

1. What evidence do we have that Angie did any long-term planning? Was her long-term planning consistent with the actions of other teachers described by research?
2. What factors discussed in this chapter influenced Angie's planning?
3. What learning objectives did Angie have for her unit? How were these written? How could they be rewritten using the format suggested by the taxonomy table developed by Anderson and Krathwohl (2001)?
4. In what ways was Angie's general planning consistent with the planning of other teachers described by research?
5. What evidence do we have that Angie considered motivation in her planning?
6. If Angie had terminated her unit after the quiz on Friday, would her unit have been aligned?

Discussion Questions

1. Some people believe that teacher planning is heavily influenced by a teacher's personality. Do you agree or disagree with this assertion? What evidence do you have for your belief?
2. Is including motivation in the planning process becoming more or less important now that we've moved into the twenty-first century?
3. The chapter discussed attempts to capitalize on student interest and arouse curiosity as strategies to increase learner motivation. What other ways can teachers plan for student motivation? How is planning for motivation influenced by grade level or content area?
4. Are learning objectives easier to write in some areas of the curriculum than others? What about grade levels? Within a curriculum area, is it easier to write objectives for some types of goals? What can be done in areas in which objectives are hard to write?
5. You are a substitute teacher who has been called at the last minute to take over a class. How will the following influence your teaching?
   a. The teacher's long-term plans
   b. The teacher's unit plan
   c. The teacher's lesson plan
6. Is interdisciplinary or thematic planning more effective at some grade levels than at others? Why? Is interdisciplinary or thematic planning more beneficial for high- or low-ability students? What do your responses to these questions tell you about your view of the relative importance of content in planning and teaching?

Portfolio Activities

1. *Teacher Planning.* How do experienced teachers plan? Interview a teacher to find out how he or she plans. Some possible questions might include the following:

   a. Where do you begin?
   b. What help are state and district curriculum guides and standards?
   c. Is there a teacher's edition, and, if so, how is it useful?
   d. Do you coordinate your planning activities with those of other teachers?
   e. What does your administrator expect of you in terms of lesson plans?
   f. What do the products of the planning process look like?

   How do the teacher's responses compare with the research described in this chapter? What implications do these responses have for you as a teacher?

2. *Teacher Planning: Contextual Factors.* Analyze a teacher's syllabus or outline for a course, or a unit within a course. In doing this, compare it with

   a. State guidelines
   b. District guidelines
   c. State standards
   d. The text being used
   e. Your college courses in this area (either subject matter text or special methods courses)

   What things are missing? What things are there that you wouldn't do? How would your syllabus look different?

3. *Curriculum Guides.* Analyze either a state or district curriculum guide in one area of the curriculum (or compare two levels).

   a. How recent is it?
   b. Who constructed it?
   c. How is it organized (e.g., chronologically, developmentally, topically)?
   d. How do the topics covered compare with a text for this area?
   e. How many objectives are listed for a particular course of study?
   f. How many objectives per week are implicitly suggested? Is it a realistic number?
   g. What types of learning (e.g., memory versus higher levels) are targeted?

   How could you use a guide like this in your instructional planning?

4. *Teacher's Editions.* Examine a teacher's edition of a text. Does it explain how the text is organized? Does it contain the following aids?

   a. Chapter overview or summary
   b. Objectives
   c. Suggested learning activities
   d. Ditto or overhead masters
   e. Test items
   f. Enrichment activities
   g. Supplementary readings

How helpful would these aids be to you as a teacher? How could you integrate them into your instructional planning?

5. *Objectives.* Write an objective for a lesson you might want to teach. Share it with a fellow student. Is it clear? (Could he or she construct a complete lesson plan based on it?) How could it be made clearer?

6. *Objectives and Assessment.* Take the objective you wrote in Exercise 5 and construct an assessment item for it. How else might you assess your goal?

7. *Task Analysis.* Using the objective you wrote for Exercise 5, do a task analysis on it. This should include the following:

   a. Prerequisite knowledge and skills
   b. A sequence for these prerequisites
   c. Some type of diagnostic instrument to let you find out what students already know

   How useful is task analysis for planning instructional activities?

8. *Lesson Planning.* Using one of the models discussed in this chapter, construct a complete lesson plan. Share it with a fellow student and ask him or her to critique it in terms of clarity. (Use the substitute teacher's test—if a sub had to come in for you, would he or she know what to do?) What did you learn from this planning exercise?

9. *Planning and Microteaching.* Microteaching is a teaching technique that allows prospective teachers to focus on one aspect of their teaching at a time. This exercise focuses on planning. Take the lesson you constructed in Exercise 8 and teach it to either a small group of your peers or a small group of actual students. Audio or videotape the lesson. Listen to or watch the tape and answer these questions:

   a. Were you over- or underprepared?
   b. How well did the planning model you chose fit your personal needs?
   c. In hindsight, what should you have done differently in the planning process to improve your teaching?

To check your comprehension of the content covered in Chapter 4, go to the Book Specific Resources in the MyEducationLab for your course, select your text, and complete the Study Plan. Here you will be able to take a chapter quiz, receive feedback on your answers, and then access review, practice, and enrichment activities to enhance your understanding of chapter content.

5

Effective Teaching

Chapter Outline	Learning Objectives
	When you've completed your study of this chapter, you should be able to
Classroom climate: A prerequisite to learning ■ Acceptance and caring: The human dimension of teaching ■ A safe and orderly learning environment ■ A learning-focused classroom	1. Explain how classroom climate factors such as caring, safety, and a learning focus contribute to a positive learning environment.

Characteristics of effective teachers
■ Teacher attitudes
  Exploring Diversity:
    Teacher attitudes and learner diversity
■ Effective communication
■ Effective communication: Implications for your teaching
	2. Describe teacher characteristics associated with increased learning and motivation.

Effective teaching and teachers' use of time ■ Allocated time: Priorities in the curriculum ■ Instructional time: Time from a teacher's perspective ■ Engaged time: Time from a learner's perspective ■ Academic learning time: The role of success	3. Identify ways effective teachers use time.

A general instructional model
■ Effective lesson beginnings
  Technology and Teaching:
    Using technology to create lesson focus
■ Developing the lesson
■ Ending lessons effectively
	4. Describe how effective teachers begin, guide learning during lessons, and bring them to closure.

What exactly is effective teaching? One way to answer that question is to look in classrooms. Imagine going into a number of classrooms, sitting at the back of the room, and watching different teachers at different grade levels and in different content areas work with their students. They could be at the first, fifth, eighth, tenth, or any other grade level, and the class could be working on any topic. In some, students learn more, whereas in others they learn less. What is the difference between these two kinds of classrooms?

Researchers have looked at teachers in these two kinds of classes, and they've found important differences (Good & Brophy, 2008; Shuell, 1996). *These differences in the actions of high-achieving students' teachers compared to low-achieving students' teachers make up the body of knowledge* called **teacher-effectiveness research**. The goal of this chapter is to help you understand how effective teachers make a difference in their classrooms and how you can apply this knowledge to your own classroom.

Let's turn now to an elementary teacher working with her class on a social studies lesson. As you read the case study, decide whether her teaching is effective and identify specific teacher actions that contributed to her students' learning.

Kathy Johnson is a sixthgrade teacher in an urban school in the Midwest. Half of her 27 students are considered to be "at risk," coming mostly from lower-income families. A veteran of six years, she is at her desk working on a unit on the Northern and Southern states prior to the Civil War.

"Hey, what's up?" her friend Marisse asks as she walks in Kathy's room.

"I'm working on this social studies stuff," Kathy responds. "I know a lot of these kids don't have a lot of background in some ways, but in others, they're actually sharp. I know that if I can get their thinking channeled a little, I can get them to understand a whole lot more than I'm getting out of them now."

"Such as . . ."

"Well, you know that I've been going to this series of workshops to upgrade my certificate, and they are emphasizing student thinking and involvement so much, . . . and, at first I was skeptical, you know, 'this won't work with my kids' stuff,' but I said I'd give it a shot, . . . and the kids actually are doing well. . . . That's what I mean when I say that they're actually sharper than we give them credit for."

"Anyway, I've got them working in teams and doing some research on different states in the North and South, and we've put the information in a big chart and we're going to start analyzing it tomorrow to see how it might have affected the Civil War. Some of them are a little uncertain, but most of them are doing really well. . . . Anyway, I'll let you know how it goes."

As Marisse waves goodbye, Kathy returns to her work.

We join Kathy the next morning near the end of her morning break. She typically schedules her day as follows:

8:15–9:15	Math
9:15–10:45	Language Arts
10:45–11:00	Break
11:00–11:30	Social Studies
11:30–12:00	Lunch
12:00–1:25	Reading
1:25–1:35	Break
1:35–2:00	Science
2:00–2:45	(Art, Music, P.E., Computers)

Kathy is standing at the door at 10:55 as students file in from recess. "Nice shirt, Jerome," she smiles. "I didn't notice it before."

"Come up here, Simon," she motions quietly, guiding him to her desk. "You've missed the last two math assignments. . . . I want you to come in tomorrow morning as soon as the bus gets here, and we'll work on them. . . . Okay? Don't forget now."

Kathy smiles as Simon nods shyly and watches him as he shuffles back to his desk. Simone has recently come to this country from Haiti, and English is still difficult for him.

The students are in their desk and settled at 11:01, and Kathy says, "I'm pleased to see that you're ready to go. We never have enough time, and I appreciate your help.

"Look over there," she says, referring students to a large chart taped to the sidewall of the room. It appears as follows:

	People	Land and Climate	Economy
Northern states	Small towns Religious Valued education Cooperative	Many trees Remains of glaciers Poor soil Short growing season Cold winters Mountains	Syrup Rum Lumber Shipbuilding Fishing Small farms
Southern states	Aristocratic Isolated Social class distinctions	Good soil Hot weather Large rivers Long growing season Coastal plain	Large farms Tobacco Cotton Unskilled workers Servants and slaves

"Today we're going to look at the chart we've been working on. This is an important topic, and it will help us understand why our country is the way it is today. This is one of my favorite topics and I think you'll find it fascinating too. Now, as we look at the chart, let's think about what we've been doing for the last week. Someone go ahead and describe what we've been doing . . . Latisha?"

". . . We looked up stuff about the different states, and . . . we worked together . . . and we wrote it down, and we turned it in."

"Good," Kathy smiles, "and what were some of the things you found? . . . Michael?"

". . . We found that in the South, like Mississippi and Georgia, they had big farms and grew cotton, and . . ."

"And in New Hampshire and up there, they had little farms," Jason jumps in, pointing to the map of the United States at the front of the room.

"That's good information, Jason," but remember that we don't interrupt our classmates when they're talking.

"What else? . . . Kristi?"

". . . They had servants and slaves in the South but not so much in the North."

"Good everyone," Kathy waves, ". . . Now, you heard what Latisha and Michael and Jason and Kristi have said. Keep that in mind as we look at our chart. The information you gathered is in the chart, and I added a little of my own. Now, looking at the chart brings up some questions. . . . How are these states different, and why, since all these states are part of the same country–our United States–why are they so different? . . . That's what we're going to try and figure out today. If we work hard, I bet we come up with some really important—and interesting—ideas. . . . Everybody ready? . . . Let's go."

Let's stop now and analyze Kathy's actions and see what she did to promote learning in her classroom.

Classroom Climate: A Prerequisite to Learning

Think back to some of your own school experiences, and consider classes in which you felt comfortable and looked forward to being there, compared to those in which you were uneasy or perhaps even thought were a waste of time. How were they different?

One important difference can be explained with the concept of **classroom climate,** *which describes the emotional and academic tone in classrooms* (Brown, 2004). Classrooms with a positive climate are emotionally safe, orderly, and focused on learning. In classrooms with a negative climate students are disruptive, they worry about being criticized or ridiculed, and learning isn't emphasized. Much of the differences between the two can be attributed to a positive classroom climate.

A positive climate is created in three ways, which are outlined in Figure 5.1. Let's look at them.

Acceptance and Caring: The Human Dimension of Teaching

Kathy Johnson surveys her sixth graders as she passes out a unit exam. The desks are spread apart and there is a feeling of anticipation in the air as they begin the test. As Kathy moves around the room, she notes with satisfaction that most of her students have plunged into the test and are working diligently. Tony, however, is sitting at his desk and staring out the window.

Kathy doesn't initially say anything, but when Tony still hasn't started the test after five minutes, she goes over to him, bends down, and quietly says, "Tony, you still haven't started the test. Is something wrong?" Tony turns away to avoid looking at Kathy and says nothing.

"Please come out in the hall," Kathy says to him. When they get there, she can see that Tony is close to crying–something for which rough and tough boys like Tony aren't noted. Tony hesitantly describes a fight between his parents the night before, which ended with Tony's dad storming out of the house. As Tony describes the incident, tears come to his eyes, and Kathy decides that the test won't do Tony any good at this time.

"Go wash your face," Kathy smiles as she pats Tony on the back. "Then, come back into the room until the period ends. We'll make the test up tomorrow before school. . . . You okay?"

Tony manages a weak smile and nod, as he heads to the boys' bathroom.

When classroom climate is positive, students know they are valued as human beings, regardless of their appearance, personality, or achievement. One of the most important ways that teachers communicate that students are valued is through acceptance and caring (Certo, Cauley, & Chafen, 2002; Davis, 2003). **Caring** *refers to teachers' ability to empathize with and invest in the protection and development of young people* (Noddings, 2001). Kathy

Figure 5.1

Creating a Positive Classroom Climate

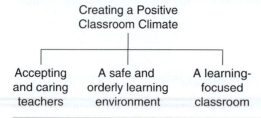

was empathetic when she understood Tony's feelings and invested time and energy in his protection.

Students quickly recognize differences between teachers who care and those who don't. A fourth grader commented, "If a teacher doesn't care about you, it affects your mind. You feel like you're a nobody, and it makes you want to drop out of school" (Noblit, Rogers, & McCadden, 1995, p. 683). Research supports this perception; students have lower motivation in classrooms when the teachers are perceived as cold and uncaring (Brophy, 2004; Schunk et al., 2008). In addition, students are more engaged in classrooms when they perceive their teachers as liking them and being responsive to their needs (Osterman, 2000).

How do teachers communicate that they care about their students? Here are some ways:

- Learning students' names quickly and calling on students by their first name
- Greeting them as they enter the classroom and taking the time to get to know them as individuals
- Making eye contact, smiling, using body language to communicate listening.
- Using "we" and "our" in reference to class activities and assignments
- Spending time with students
- Maintaining standards and positive expectations for all students (Alder, 2002; Perry, Turner, & Meyer, 2006)

The last two items on the list deserve special emphasis. We all have 24 hours in our days—no more, no less, and the way we choose to allocate our time is the truest measure of our priorities. Choosing to allocate some of our time to an individual student communicates caring better than any other single factor. Helping students who have problems with an assignment or calling a parent after school hours communicates that teachers care about student learning. Spending personal time to ask a question about a baby brother or compliment a new hairstyle communicates caring about a student as a human being.

Maintaining standards and having high expectations for all students' learning is a second powerful way that teachers demonstrate caring:

> One of the best ways to show respect for students is to hold them to high standards— by not accepting sloppy, thoughtless, or incomplete work, by pressing them to clarify vague comments, by encouraging them not to give up, and by not praising work that does not reflect genuine effort. Ironically, reactions that are often intended to protect students' self-esteem—such as accepting low-quality work—convey a lack of interest, patience, or caring. (Stipek, 2002, p. 157)

This view is corroborated by additional research. When junior high students were asked "How do you know when a teacher cares about you?" they responded that paying attention to them as human beings was important, but more striking was their belief that teachers who care are committed to their learning and hold them to high standards (Wilson & Corbett, 2001). Caring teachers who value all students regardless of academic ability or performance lay the foundation for a positive classroom climate, which is essential for both learning and motivation (Marzano, 2007).

A Safe and Orderly Learning Environment

The teacher says, "We have a DVD on weather," and quickly overviews the content on the video. As the teacher arranges the projector, she says, "Before we start this, we're going to turn out the lights, but you can finish your work afterwards when we're done." Greg says, "Miss, I can't see to take notes." The teacher says, "Yes, you can. Your eyes will adjust." Andrew yells, "Lights off " four times. Finally, the teacher starts the video and someone turns the lights off. Everyone starts yelling, "I can't see. It's dark in here." The teacher assures them that their eyes will adjust. As the video is running, the students talk and move around, two of them actually go outside to work. Some move desks; no one can hear the movie. Joe comes in from the hall and stands at the front of the room to watch. The class finally settles a little. About half are watching the film, and half are talking to each other in the dark. The teacher walks out of the room. When she returns, she says, "In a few minutes, you're going to see the part about the mud. That's my favorite part. They describe the ound of people walking in the mud." Greg says, "Turn on the lights." The teacher ignores him. During the video there is a steady exchange of students with restroom passes. Susan comes in; Joe goes not. The teacher goes out. Robert calls after her sarcastically, "You missed the mud."

These events actually occurred in one middle school classroom (Carter, 1986). How much learning is likely to occur in this kind of environment?

Positive classroom environments require teachers who care, but caring, although fundamental, isn't enough. Students can't learn if their classrooms are chaotic. A safe and orderly learning environment is the second component of a positive classroom climate.

The relationship between orderly learning environments and learning is well documented (Good & Brophy, 2008). In orderly classrooms, instructional time is maximized, students are more engaged, and achievement increases (Emmer et al., 2009; Evertson et al., 2009). This dimension is so essential for effective teaching that we devoted all of Chapter 3 to the topic of classroom management.

A Learning-Focused Classroom

Effective teachers believe that their most important role is to maximize learning for their students. Although extracurricular activities are important, they don't take precedent over learning (Feldman & Matjasko, 2005). Effective teachers, for example, don't allow students to use class time to discuss club events, and socializing is done out of class, not during time when students should be completing seatwork.

Teachers create a learning-focused classroom in several ways:

- Modeling a belief in the importance of study, effort, and learning
- Clearly communicating learning goals and reasons for the goals
- Preventing disruptions that interfere with learning
- Thoroughly and frequently measuring students' understanding with quizzes, assignments, and alternative assessments
- Providing timely (i.e., the day after they're given) feedback about performance on assessments
- Using time effectively (Marzano, 2007)

Kathy communicated a learning focus with her students in three ways. First, social studies was scheduled to begin at 11:00, and she began within a minute of that time. Second, she immediately reacted to Jason's disruption by saying, "That's good information, Jason, but remember that we don't interrupt our classmates when they're talking." Third, she began her lesson in this way, "Now, looking at the chart brings up some questions. How are these states different, and why, since all these states are part of the same country—our United States—are they so different? That's what we're going to try and figure out today. If we work hard, I bet we come up with some really important ideas." Her comment set an academic tone and provided a clear goal for the lesson.

The final item in our list-using time effectively-is so essential to effective teaching that we examine it more thoroughly later in the chapter.

Characteristics of Effective Teachers

Effective teachers are at the core of effective teaching. Their attitudes toward students and their beliefs about themselves as well as about their students influence how much their students will learn. Let's see how these components interact to increase student learning.

Teacher Attitudes

Your attitudes and beliefs will have a powerful influence on your students' learning (Good & Brophy, 2008; Marzano, 2007). These attitudes are often demonstrated subtly, but their influence on learning is clear. Let's see how.

> Lorna Davis, a veteran with 14 years of experience, teaches three sections of Advanced Placement biology and two sections with students of below average to average ability. We look in on one of her average classes.
>
> "We better get moving," Clarice says to Leroy as they approach the door of the classroom. "The bell is going to ring and you know how Davis is about this class."
>
> "Yeah," Leroy smiles wryly. "She thinks this all this genetic stuff is *sooo* important. She thinks she can make scientists out of all of us."
>
> "Did you finish your homework?"
>
> "Are you kidding," Clarice returns. "You miss a homework assignment in this class and you're a dead duck."
>
> "Right," Leroy confirms. "Nobody messes with Davis."
>
> "I didn't know what she wanted on that explanation about attached and detached earlobes, so I went to her help session after school yesterday, and she went over everything again," Clarice continues. "She really tries to help you get it."

From this short episode we can infer a great deal about Lorna and her attitudes about learners and learning. These attitudes and beliefs consist of the following three elements:

- Personal teaching efficacy
- Teacher modeling and enthusiasm
- Teacher expectations

Personal Teaching Efficacy If you really try, will you be able to make a difference in your students' learning? Teachers high in **personal teaching efficacy**, *the belief that teachers and schools can have an important positive effect on students*, actually teach differently and have a greater impact on students' lives (Woolfolk-Hoy, Davis, & Pape, 2006; Yeh, 2006). To see how, let's look again at Lorna's teaching. Leroy commented, "She thinks she can make scientists out of all of us." Although we can't be sure about her goals based on this short vignette, Leroy's reaction provides some information about Lorna's attitudes; she is high in personal teaching efficacy. High-efficacy teachers teach differently than those who are low in personal efficacy. They use praise rather than criticism, persevere with low achievers, use time efficiently, and praise students for their efforts. Low-efficacy teachers, in contrast, spend less time in learning activities, "write off" low achievers, and are more likely to criticize students.

Teacher Modeling and Enthusiasm How do teacher modeling and enthusiasm influence learning? Let's look at how two teachers begin their lessons on the antecedents of our Civil War.

> Today we are going to look at the differences between the North and South before the Civil War. It's not one of my favorite topics, but it will be on the test at the end of the year so we better learn it.
>
> This is a really interesting and important topic and will help us understand why our country is the way it is today. This is one of my favorite topics, and I think you'll find it fascinating too.

Teacher **modeling**, *the imitation of our actions by others* can have a powerful effect on student motivation and learning (Bandura, 1993; Schunk, Pintrich, & Meece, 2008). The two teachers in our examples modeled vastly different perspectives on the lessons they were teaching, and these differences influenced how their students approach the learning task at hand. In the second one, Kathy Johnson modeled both interest and enthusiasm for the lesson she was teaching. We also see the effects of modeling everyday in the world around us. People imitate the hairstyles of movie stars, the clothing of rock musicians, and the behaviors of professional athletes. This is often unfortunate, given the questionable lifestyles of many of these. Students pick up attitudes and expressions from the thousands of hours of TV they watch. Observing and imitating the behaviors of others are important ways that all people learn (Bandura, 1986, 1993).

You can also strongly influence students' attitudes toward learning through your modeling (Good & Brophy, 2008). Leroy's conclusion that Davis thinks "this stuff is *sooo* important" was the result of Lorna's modeling. It wasn't anything in particular that she said; it was the general way she approached her class. Students who see their teachers study and examine—or even struggle with—ideas are acquiring important information that they can apply to their own learning. They see that effort, struggle, and persistence are positive and desirable.

Enthusiasm is one of the most important qualities that teachers model (Brophy, 2004; Good & Brophy, 2008). Teachers who are enthusiastic increase learning, student confidence, and achievement, and teacher modeling is the most likely mechanism.

How do we demonstrate enthusiasm? Teacher enthusiasm doesn't require pep talks or unnecessary theatrics; rather, enthusiastic teachers clearly communicate why they find topics interesting and meaningful. Teachers communicate enthusiasm both verbally and nonverbally and their genuine interest in a topic is literally contagious.

Teacher Expectations   Teachers also influence attitudes by the way they treat students.

Mary Willis looks around the room as her fourth graders put away their math books and take out their language arts workbooks. When she sees that all books are out, she says, "Class can I have everyone's eyes up here. . . . Good. Today we're going to learn a new skill, how to alphabetize. This is an important skill that you will use again and again, not only this year, but every year of your life. If you don't know the meaning of a word, it will help you find it in the dictionary. I know that all of you will learn how to do this and we'll practice until we're all good at it. Now let's turn to p. 47 in our workbooks and see how we begin."

As the students open their books, Mary notices Will leaning forward to poke Steve with his pencil. She walks down the aisle, looks Will in the eye, and asks, "Will, have you found the page yet? Quickly now. This is too important for you to be wasting time monkeying around."

The lesson continues with Mary explaining and modeling the skill at the board and then asking students to come to practice with new lists of words. With each she asks for a show of hands to see who is performing the skill correctly. When she is confident that most students understand, she gives an assignment that all students are to complete before free reading. As they work on the lists, Mary moves around the room checking papers and answering questions.

Teacher expectations are *the inferences teachers make about students' future academic potential and achievement,* and they strongly influence teachers' actions, and ultimately student learning (Marzano, 2007). Effective teachers clearly communicate positive expectations for learning; they tell students that something is important, and they explain why. They also openly communicate that they expect all students to learn—for example, "I know that all of you will learn how to do this and we'll practice until we're all good at it."

Sometimes effective teachers' expectations are communicated more subtly. They monitor the class for misbehavior, communicating that it is unacceptable because it interferes with learning, as Mary did when she said, "Quickly now. This is too important for you to be wasting time monkeying around." They provide opportunities for all students to practice new skills and receive feedback. Finally, they communicate positive expectations by holding all students accountable for learning (Marzano, 2007).

Unfortunately, teachers often treat students they perceive as high achievers better than those perceived as lower in ability. This differential treatment occurs in providing emotional support, teacher effort and demands, questioning, and feedback. These differences are outlined in Table 5.1 (Eggen & Kauchak, 2010; Good & Brophy, 2008).

Table 5.1   **Dimensions of Differential Teacher Expectations**

Characteristic	Teacher Behaviors Favoring Perceived High Achievers
Emotional support	More interactions; interactions more positive; more smiles; more eye contact; stand closer; orient body more directly; seat students closer to teacher
Teacher effort and demands	Clearer and more thorough explanations; more enthusiastic instruction; more follow-up questions; require more complete and accurate student answers
Questioning	Call on more often; more time to answer; more encouragement; more prompting
Feedback and evaluation	More praise; less criticism; more complete and more lengthy feedback; more conceptual evaluations

Do students sense this differential treatment? One study concluded, "After 10 seconds of seeing and/or hearing a teacher, even very young students could detect whether the teacher talked about, or to, an excellent or a weak student, and could determine the extent to which that student was loved by the teacher" (Babad, Bernieri, & Rosenthal, 1991, p. 230). Think about the cumulative effects of different teacher expectations over the course of a school year!

Exploring Diversity

Teacher Attitudes and Learner Diversity

Our learners are becoming increasingly diverse, and many feel alienated from school and their teachers. Teachers' attitudes toward differences in learners are crucial in making all learners feel welcome and involved in all aspects of school.

The implications for learning and motivation are clear. We need to demonstrate that we care about and value all learners in our classrooms, regardless of gender, culture, ethnicity, socioeconomic status, or ability. Further, we want to communicate positive expectations for every student in our classroom.

We saw specific ways that teachers communicate caring earlier in the chapter. What else might we do? Research offers some suggestions. One program trained teachers to treat students as equally as possible. They learned to call on all students equally, give equivalent feedback, and maintain positive interactions with students. The results were dramatic. The study found that not only did students' achievement go up, but also the number of discipline referrals and absentees went down (Kerman, 1979)!

Teachers can make their classrooms more welcoming learning environments for all students in the following ways:

- Make an effort to call on all students equally. This means calling on boys and girls, cultural minorities and nonminorities, high and low achievers, and learners from high and low socioeconomic backgrounds as equally as possible. Calling on all learners communicates that you believe all students are capable learners and you expect them to participate and learn.

- When students are unable to respond, rather than redirecting questions to others, prompt them until they give an acceptable answer. This also communicates that you expect all learners to be able to answer.

- When girls, cultural minorities, or low achievers give incorrect answers, provide as much information about why answers are incorrect as you would for boys, nonminorities, or high achievers.

- Make eye contact with all students, and orient your body directly toward all individuals as you talk to them.

- Change seating arrangements of students in your classes so everyone is periodically near the front. Move around so you are physically near all students as much as possible.

- Take a minute or two to discuss something personal with students, such as a question about their family, special interest, or recent accomplishment. As people, all of us are pleased when someone pays individual attention to us, and students are no exception.

Effective Communication

In addition to positive attitudes, effective teachers also communicate clearly. The link between the clarity of teachers' language and student achievement is well documented (Good & Brophy, 2008; Weiss & Pasley, 2004). In addition, students perceive clearly communicated instruction more positively. Let's see how teacher language can influence learning:

> This mathematics lesson will enab . . ., will get you to understand number uh, number patterns. Before we get to the main idea of the, main idea of the lesson, you need to review four concepts . . . four prerequisite concepts. (Smith & Land, 1981, p. 38)

Although this example seems extreme, it is a quote from an actual lesson. False starts, halting speech, and redundant words and phrases that don't make sense all detract from learning.

Now, let's compare this example with the following:

> The purpose of this lesson is to help you understand number patterns. Before we begin the number patterns themselves, however, there are four concepts we want to review. They are . . .

Here the purpose of the lesson is stated clearly and precisely, increasing the likelihood that students will know what the lesson is about and where it's going.

What are the elements of clear communication? Researchers have identified four components:

- Precise terminology
- Connected discourse
- Transition signals
- Emphasis

Precise Terminology   **Precise terminology** *means that teachers eliminate vague and ambiguous words and phrases in their lessons.* Vague terms such as *might, a little more, some, usually,* and *probably* detract from learning (Smith & Cotten, 1980). In addition, teachers who use vague language are perceived by students as being more disorganized, unprepared, and nervous (Smith & Land, 1981).

Connected Discourse   **Connected discourse,** a second element of teacher clarity, *means that the teacher's presentation is logically connected and leads to a point.* By contrast, scrambled discourse includes loosely connected ideas that occur when a teacher rambles, interrupts the direction of the lesson by including irrelevant material, or sequences the presentation ineffectively.

Compare the following two examples:

> We've been studying the countries on the Arabian Peninsula as part of our unit on the Middle East. As we know, these countries make most of their money from oil; they also supply most of the oil that our country uses to run cars and heat homes. Oil producers from Venezuela and other non-Middle Eastern countries also meet many of our energy needs. This dependency is contributing to our inflation rate as well as a trade imbalance. These countries also have a problem with water. Most of the people live on the coast or near water, although the holy city of Mecca is inland. Three major religions, Islam, Judaism, and Christianity, have their roots there. The people tend to overextend their water supply, and often there isn't enough water to extract and refine the oil.

We've been studying the countries on the Arabian Peninsula as part of our unit on the Middle East and have continually stressed the importance of oil in this area of the world. As we know, these countries make most of their money from oil, which they use to buy goods and services from the Western economies. However, as precious as oil is, water looms as even a bigger problem. Most of the people live near water and overextend the available supplies, and, in some cases, even extracting and refining the oil has been hampered by the lack of water.

In the first example the point is uncertain; is the theme the water problem, religion, or our oil dependency? With the added information about Venezuela and the inflation rate, it isn't even clear whether the focus is on the Middle East. Although essentially free from vague terms, the presentation is still unclear. In the second example, the discourse is clear and logically connected and leads to a point, with increased learning resulting.

Transition Signals   Teachers also contribute to the clarity of their presentations through clear transition signals. A **transition signal** *communicates that one idea is ending and another is beginning and explains the link between the two.* Using our illustration of the countries on the Arabian Peninsula, a teacher might say, "We've been discussing the problems these countries have with water. Now let's talk about the countries of North Africa and see if the situation is similar," or "We're going to stop talking about the countries on the Arabian Peninsula for now, and turn to those in North Africa." In either case, the teacher clearly indicates that a shift in the topic is occurring. This signal allows students to mentally structure the content as the lesson develops. Our chapter headings serve the same purpose.

Emphasis

"When you're solving equations, remember that whatever you do to one side of the equation, you must do exactly the same thing to the other side."

"We said that one of the characteristics of the Jackson era was the rise of the common man."

These two statements are examples of **emphasis**, *which communicates that an idea or topic has special significance.* It is a form of effective communication that helps students determine the relative importance of the topics they're learning. If there is something in the lesson that is essential for students to learn, we ought to tell them it is important. Emphasis does that.

Emphasis can be accomplished in four different ways, which are illustrated in Table 5.2.

Table 5.2 **Forms of Emphasis in the Classroom**

Type	Example
Verbal statements	"Be sure to get this," "Now remember . . ."
Nonverbal behaviors	Raised or louder voice Gestures or pointing to specific information
Repetition	"What did Heather say about our first example?"
Written signals	"As you'll see on the board, the three functions of the circulatory system . . ."

Effective Communication: Implications for Your Teaching

The research on effective communication has two important implications for all of us. First, we need to thoroughly understand our content, and when our understanding is incomplete or uncertain, we need to spend extra time studying and preparing. If you fully understand the content you teach, you will use clearer language, and your discourse will be more connected than if your understanding is uncertain. This makes sense. Teachers with a deep understanding of their subject's content are more likely to use precise language, present ideas logically, and emphasize appropriate points. They model enthusiasm and confidence, and their students feel more confident as a result.

Second, we should try to monitor our own communication—literally listen to ourselves talk as we teach—to try to be as clear and concise as possible. Seeing ourselves on videotape can be eye opening. Even veteran teachers are often surprised when they see and hear themselves on tape. Other processes, such as peer coaching, in which a colleague observes a portion of a lesson and provides feedback, can also be very helpful. Whatever the method, the increase in clarity and student learning is worth the effort.

*E*ffective Teaching and Teachers' Use of Time

> Dost thou love life? Then do not squander time, for that is the stuff life is made of.
> Benjamin Franklin, *Poor Richard's Almanac*, 1775

Ben Franklin recognized the importance of time all the way back in 1775. It's important for effective teaching as well, because it's precious and, unfortunately, often used inefficiently.

In introducing this chapter we suggested that you ask yourself what you would expect to see if you observed effective teachers at any grade level. One feature they would have in common is that they use their available time efficiently.

That time is critical in learning is suggested by the fact that students in many other industrialized countries typically spend more time in school than do American students, and these students also score higher than their American counterparts on standardized tests. This has led to suggestions that the American school year and school day be lengthened (Associated Press, 2009).

These suggestions are simplistic, however, because the length of the school year or day is only one dimension of time. A more complete picture examines how teachers actually use their available time and how this influences learning (Weinstein & Mignano, 2007). In analyzing classroom time we'll focus on the four dimensions outlined in Table 5.3. Let's examine them.

Table 5.3   Dimensions of Classroom Time

Allocated time	The amount of time a teacher or school specifies for a content area or topic
Instructional time	The amount of time available for teaching time after routines and administrative tasks are completed
Engaged time	The amount of time students are attending and involved in learning activities
Academic learning time	The amount of time students are involved in learning activities during which they're successful

Allocated Time: Priorities in the Curriculum

Allocated time is *the amount of time teachers assign to different content areas or topics.* If we look back at Kathy's schedule, for instance, we see that she allocates an hour and a half for reading, almost as much for language arts, and an hour for math. By contrast, social studies gets only a half hour and science a mere 25 minutes. These allocations are typical and reflect the fact that elementary teachers emphasize reading, language arts, and math more strongly than social studies and science.

Although it appears that elementary teachers have more control over time allocations than do middle or secondary teachers because their school day isn't broken up by periods and bells, this isn't necessarily the case. For instance, a middle school English teacher could choose to emphasize writing, whereas another might devote that time to grammar instead.

There is a positive but weak correlation between allocated time and learning (Weinstein & Mignano, 2007). As a way of thinking about this correlation, imagine that we double the allocated time for a certain subject. Although we would expect students to learn more, they would not learn twice as much. In fact, they learn only slightly more than they did with the previous allocation.

Instructional Time: Time from a Teacher's Perspective

The bell has rung and Dennis Orr's eighth graders are filing into his class. Dennis is at the back of the room working on some equipment as students move to their seats.

In a few moments he moves to the front of the room and says, "Now, let's see who's here today." He glances at the top of his desk looking for his roll book, and not seeing it, looks in his desk drawer. "I let some of you look at your averages yesterday," he calls out to the class. "Did you return my book?"

"We put it in your file cabinet," one of the boys responds.

"Ah, yes, here it is," Dennis says quietly as he looks in the drawer and sees the book.

Having finished taking roll, he says to the class, "I'm going to show you a demonstration today. Get your books and notebooks out while I finish getting this set up."

The students, basically well behaved, do as he suggests as he begins to take equipment from a nearby shelf and assemble it. A few minutes later he signals the class.

"Okay, everyone, let's take a look at what we have here." He begins the demonstration, having students make observations of the equipment and the phenomenon taking place. Suddenly he says, "Oh, I almost forgot. All of you in the band will be released ten minutes early today so you can gather your instruments for the trip to Seaside Middle School."

Now, let's look at another eighth-grade teacher in essentially the same situation.

Steve Weiss, Dennis's colleague across the hall, is sitting at his desk as his students walk in. As they sit down, they get their books and notebooks out of their backpacks and place them on their desks. As they move toward their seats, Steve checks their names in his roll book.

"I see Jim isn't here. Has he been absent all day?" he asks as the last student was sitting down.

"He's sick," a classmate volunteers, and with that Steve signs the roll and hangs it on the clip on his door. As he walks, he points to an announcement on the board: "All band students go to the band room immediately after school to get your equipment ready for the trip to Seaside."

Walking back to the center of the room, Steve begins, "We studied the concept of pressure yesterday, and today we want to look at how pressure changes under different conditions. I have a demonstration for you. Everyone take a look at the cart."

With that, he rolls a cart to the center of the room with some equipment assembled on it. "What do you notice on the cart, Tony?" he asks as he begins the lesson.

In comparing the two teachers we see that Dennis spent several minutes taking roll, searching for his grade book, preparing his demonstration, and making an announcement, whereas Steve took roll as students came in the door, made his announcement as he hung up his roll slip, and had his demonstration prepared in advance. Dennis spent more time on noninstructional activities than did Steve.

Instructional time *is the amount of time available for learning activities.* As Dennis's case illustrates, significant portions of time are frequently lost to noninstructional activities, often more than a third of teachers' allocated time (Weinstein & Mignano, 2007). Further, some teachers seem to be unaware of the value of time as a resource, thinking of it as something to be filled, or even "killed," rather than an opportunity to increase learning (Eggen, 1998). With instructional time so important, teachers need to do everything they can to maximize the amount they have.

Organization   A major way that effective teachers maximize instructional time is through their organization. The term *organization*, as is *time*, is one that we use in discussing both teaching and our everyday lives: "I've got to get organized," "My new year's resolution is to be better organized this year," or "He would be good at the job, but he is so disorganized." These are familiar-sounding statements, and we all struggle to be better organized. We write lists; we arrange elaborate filing systems that we don't use; we pick up the same piece of paper several times before we do anything with it. Each example underscores the fact that organization seems quite simple, but in reality it can be a major stumbling block to efficiency. This is particularly true in classrooms.

Steve Weiss, our eighth-grade science teacher, used more of his available time for instruction than did his colleague Dennis Orr. This was primarily the result of more effective organization. When we compare the two, we find three important differences, which are outlined in Table 5.4. In examining these differences we see that each aspect of organization increases instructional time, which both increases learning and reduces classroom management problems (Emmer et al., 2009; Evertson et al., 2009).

Table 5.4 **Characteristics of Effective Organization**

Aspect of Organization	Example
Starting on time	Steve Weiss began class when the bell stopped ringing. Dennis Orr moved to the front of the room after several minutes.
Materials prepared in advance	Steve's demonstration was prepared in advance. Dennis finished preparing his demonstration while the students waited.
Established routines	Steve's students knew what to do when they came to class. Dennis had to tell his students how to get started.

Engaged Time: Time from a Learner's Perspective

Although increasing instructional time is important, **engaged time**, the *proportion of instructional time that students are focused and on task*, is even more important.

A comparison of high- and low-achieving students demonstrates the importance of engaged time, or "time on task." High-achieving students are typically engaged for 75 percent or more of the time, whereas low achievers often are engaged less than 50 percent of the time (Evertson, 1980). Further, researchers have found that effective teachers are much better than less effective teachers at actively engaging students (Bohn et al., 2004). Engaged time is a tangible measure of a teacher's impact on students, and, not surprisingly, when principals observe in classrooms, one of the first things they look for is student engagement rates, or the extent to which students are paying attention and involved in learning activities. In classrooms where students are engaged and successful, achievement is higher, learners feel a sense of competence and self-efficacy, and interest in topics increases (Bransford et al., 2000).

How can we tell if students are on task? Or, more specifically, what would you look for in determining if your students are with you? One of the best indicators is eye contact—are they watching you during a teacher-led discussion, and during individual work do their eye movements suggest that they are reading and actually responding to the materials they're studying?

So, we see that the issue is not as simple as merely allocating more time to a particular subject, nor does increasing efficiency so that instructional time is maximized solve the problem. If students aren't paying attention during learning activities, learning won't occur regardless of how well organized and efficient a teacher is. (Because involving students is so essential to learning, we devote all of Chapter 6 to the topic.)

Academic Learning Time: The Role of Success

Research indicates that part of the reason that low achievers go off task relates to frustration (Anderson, Hiebert, Scott, & Wilkinson, 1985). The work they're assigned is often beyond their present capabilities, making it nearly impossible to complete. As a result, they often give up and go off task. This leads us to the concept of **academic learning time**, which *is the amount of time students are successfully engaged*.

Student success is important for three reasons:

- It indicates that the new learning is building effectively on what students already know.

- Success is reinforcing; it is much more rewarding to get questions and problems right than wrong.

- Success builds confidence, preparing students for future learning. (Bransford et al., 2000; Marzano, 2007)

Success is important for the immediate learning task at hand, as well as for creating positive expectations for future student efforts.

How high should success rates be? The answer depends on the context. Research suggests that students in interactive question-and-answer sessions should be about 80 percent successful, but in homework assignments, where the potential for confusion and frustration is higher, teachers should plan so success rates are even higher (Good & Brophy, 2008).

Implementing high success rates is not as simple as it appears on the surface, and success rates vary with the type of student. Younger students, low achievers, and students from lower socioeconomic backgrounds typically need more success than do their older, higher achieving, or more advantaged counterparts. These students often lack a robust history of classroom success and tend to become easily frustrated or discouraged (Brophy, 2004).

As we move from allocated time to academic learning time, the correlation with learning becomes stronger and stronger. Our goal should be a well-organized classroom that has students successfully engaged in meaningful learning activities. Although this isn't easy, with effort it is attainable. We begin our discussion of ways to accomplish this goal in the next section.

A General Instructional Model

To make our discussion of effective teaching more meaningful, we have organized it around the general instructional model that you see in Figure 5.2. With the characteristics of effective teachers as an umbrella, we divide lessons into three segments, each requiring teacher actions to maximize learning. We discuss these segments in the sections that follow, relating them to effective teaching that enhances learning in all classrooms.

Effective Lesson Beginnings

An effective lesson introduction draws students into the lesson, focuses their attention on the topic, and relates the new material to content they already understand. Let's see how this occurs.

Review   When we learn new information, we interpret it based on what we already know (Eggen & Kauchak, 2010). **Review** *examines information that has been covered in earlier lessons, activates learners' background knowledge, and sets the stage for the new topic.* Review helps learners remember what they already know, which then provides an anchor for the new information to come.

Figure 5.2

A General Instructional Model

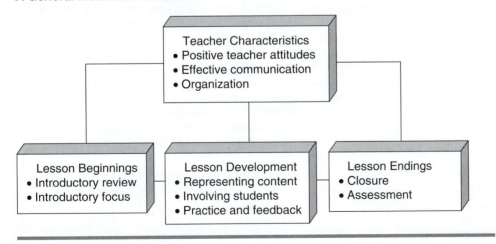

Let's see how two teachers use review to help their students learn:

> Ken Thomas has begun a unit on the Crusades and wants to examine their effects on the Western world. He begins his lesson by saying, "We've been discussing the Crusades. . . . Let's think for a moment now about what we learned yesterday. First, let's identify some reasons the Crusades occurred in the first place. . . . David?"

> Dorothy Williams's students have studied gerunds and participles, and she now wants to move to infinitives. She begins her lesson by saying, "We talked about gerunds and participles yesterday. Who can give me an example of each. . . . Jeff?"

In both cases the teachers used students' existing understanding as the framework for the day's lesson. Students can then connect the new learning to the old—Dorothy's students related infinitives to gerunds and participles, for example—which makes both more meaningful.

Focus   One of the biggest challenges facing teachers is attracting students' attention at the beginning of a lesson. **Focus** *is the process teachers use to attract and maintain students' attention during a learning activity.* For instance, rather than merely saying, "Today we're going to discuss the Northern and Southern states," Kathy introduced her lesson by referring to the chart and asking, "Now, that brings up some questions. . . . How are these states different, and why, since all these states are part of the same country—our United States—why are they so different? . . . That's what we're going to try and figure out today. If we work hard, I bet we can come up with some really important ideas. . . . Everybody ready? . . . Let's go."

By introducing her lesson with her chart and questions to be answered during the lesson, she provided an effective focus for her lesson.

Effective lesson focus provides students with something that attracts their attention and also something to think about during the lesson. Let's look at some additional examples.

> As an introduction to the topic of cities and where they are located, Jim Edwards, a fifth-grade teacher, passes out a map of a fictitious island. On it are physical features such as lakes, rivers, mountains, and bays. The map also includes the latitude, prevailing winds, ocean currents, and rainfall for the island. He begins, "We have been sent to this island to settle it. Based on the information we have here, we need to decide where would be the best place to start our first settlement."
>
> Susan Wood begins a unit on heat and atmospheric pressure with her science students by putting a cup of water in an empty duplicating fluid can, heating the can with a hot plate, and capping it. As the students watch, the can collapses, almost "magically." Susan then comments, "Now, keep what you saw in mind, and we'll be able to figure out why it happened as we study this unit."

> Jessie Andrews begins his math lesson on percentages by displaying the following question on an overhead: "Who's the best hitter in baseball today?" After a number of opinions are offered by students, Jessie continues, "Do you want to learn one way to find out? Let's look at percentages and see how they can tell us who the best hitter is."

In each of these examples the teachers provided students with something to see, which helped attract their attention. Although something to see is most powerful, something to hear, feel, smell, or even taste can also be used. The need for a sensory focus to attract attention is based on the idea that all learning begins with attention (Eggen & Kauchak, 2010).

A variety of techniques can be used to focus attention at the beginning of a lesson. For instance, a series of sentences on the chalkboard or equations on an overhead projector can work effectively in an English or algebra class. In addition, outlines, hierarchies, or objectives are also effective, giving students something to focus on as well as providing them with information about the lesson's direction.

When visual forms of sensory focus are used, writing the information on the board or displaying it on an overhead projector is more effective than the same information given to students on individual sheets. If students are looking down at their desks, the teacher can't tell if they're looking at the sheet or are looking down because they are not paying attention. When the focus is at the front of the room, the teacher can monitor students' attention through eye contact, which is one of the most effective ways to assess student engagement.

To view a video clip of teachers using effective focus to begin their lessons, go to the Book Specific Resources tab in MyEducationLab, select your text, select Video Examples under Chapter 5, and then click on *Attracting Students' Attention.*

Using Focus to Increase Student Motivation.   Curiosity can be a powerful source of motivation in learners (Schunk et al., 2008). Some of the best forms of focus capitalize on the effects of curiosity to grab and hold students' attention. Teachers can capitalize on the effects of curiosity in three ways:

- Presenting information or ideas that are discrepant from present understanding or beliefs and that appear surprising or incongruous
- Asking paradoxical questions
- Presenting ideas in concrete form

For example, a teacher might have students hold two pieces of paper parallel to each other and blow between them. Because of Bernoulli's principle (the principle that helps us understand how airplanes are able to fly), the papers come together instead of moving apart. This event is surprising and inconsistent with learners' expectations.

In another case a teacher might ask, "Why have most of the powerful civilizations throughout history eventually collapsed and declined in power?" or as Kathy asked, "Since all these states are part of the same country—our United States—why are they so different?" She purposely worded her question in a paradoxical way to increase her students' curiosity and motivation.

As another example, imagine the attention-getting power of bringing someone's pet snake, guinea pig, or hamster to class during a science lesson on vertebrates. Each would be much more effective than drawings or even colored pictures in arousing interest.

Planning for increasing learner motivation doesn't have to be difficult or labor intensive. Despite this simplicity, many problems with students' inattention and lack of motivation can be traced directly to lack of focus at the beginning of lessons (Brophy, 2004). Effective focus is not a panacea, of course, but it can make an important contribution to student motivation and, in turn, learning.

Technology and Teaching

Using Technology to Create Lesson Focus

Technology provides a powerful tool to focus students' attention on the topic at hand. In addition, it can also provide an effective tool to help students learn abstract and difficult ideas. Some of the topics we teach are difficult to represent, and this fact is what makes them hard to learn. For instance, it's easy to demonstrate that all objects fall at the same rate regardless of weight—simply drop two objects, such as a pencil and a book, to demonstrate that they hit the floor at the same time. It's much more difficult to illustrate the acceleration of an object as it falls, however. In these cases, technology can be a powerful tool. For example, Figure 5.3 illustrates the position of a falling object at uniform time intervals. We see that the distance between the images becomes greater and greater, which illustrates the fact that the object is falling faster and faster. This visual representation makes the concept of acceleration much more meaningful than it would be otherwise, and without technology it's virtually impossible to represent in a meaningful way.

Figure 5.3

Representation of a Falling Object

A similar program called *Ballistics* allows physics students to see how initial velocity, angle of projection, and drag medium (such as air) influence the flight of a projectile. Because the program is interactive, students can manipulate the different variables and observe their effect on a projectile's path illustrated on a computer monitor. The computer program is able to bring the complexities of the real world into the classroom and make them accessible to students.

Simulations provide another opportunity for students to see abstract ideas presented in realistic settings (Roblyer & Doering, 2010). For example, one biology program allows students to experiment with laws of genetics by pairing animals with different characteristics and showing the resulting offspring. You have also probably encountered videos of real classrooms in your teacher education program. These videos represent attempts by your instructors to bring the real world of teaching into your college classroom. They allow you to see how abstract teaching and learning concepts relate to the real world of classrooms.

Developing the Lesson

During effective lessons teachers present ideas in a systematic and organized way, actively involve students in the lesson, and provide opportunities for practice and feedback. To illustrate these ideas, let's return to Kathy's work with her students. She began the lesson by asking her students why the Northern and Southern states were so different, since they were all part of the United States. Let's see how she develops the lesson from there.

"Now, before we start trying to answer our questions, where are all these states compared to where we live? . . . Jo?"

". . . They're over here," Jo answers, motioning to the right with her hand.

"Yes, they're generally east of us," Kathy adds, as she walks quickly and points to the map at the side of the room, identifying the general location of the states relative to their location with a wave of her hand. "As we look at our chart, keep this map in mind to remind yourselves about where we are and where these states are.

"And about how long ago are we talking about, a few years or a long time? . . . Greg?" she continues.

"A long time. Like when our great, great grandfathers and grandmothers might have lived, I think," Greg responds hesitantly.

"At least," Kathy smiles. "We're talking about time during the early and middle 1800s."

"We also talked about some important ideas, like 'Economy,'" Kathy continues. "What do we mean by economy? . . . Carol?"

". . . It's . . . the way they make money, like when we said that the economy here is based on manufacturing, like making cars and stuff and stuff for cars," Carol responds haltingly.

"Good idea, Carol," Kathy waves. "You identified auto manufacturing as an important part of our economy, and that's a good example."

"Now, look here," Kathy directs, pointing to the column marked 'Economy.' I want you to work with your partner and I want you to write down at least three things that were different about the economy in the North compared to the economy in the South. . . . You have four minutes. Ready? . . . Go ahead."

The students, seated next to their partners, turn to each other and begin working. The classroom quickly becomes a buzz of voices and questions, such as, "How many differences?" "Three differences?" "Is like fishing in the North different from the South? There's no fishing there." "Big farms and small farms is a difference isn't it?" and others.

Kathy patiently answers their questions among comments of encouragement and admonitions to work quickly, since they don't have much time.

At the end of the four minutes, Kathy says, "All right everyone, look up here. . . . Let's see what we have. . . . Go ahead. Which group wants to go first? . . . Go ahead, Ann Marie."

". . . The farms were big in the South but they were little in the North."

"Okay, good observation," Kathy nods. "Now why might that have been the case? Jim?"

". . ."

". . . Would you like me to repeat the question?" Kathy asks, knowing that Jim hasn't heard her.

"Yes," Jim responds quickly, with a look of relief.

"Why might the farms have been so much bigger in the South than in the North?"

". . . They had good soil in the South, but poor soil in the North," Jim says slowly peering intently at the chart.

"Good, Jim," Kathy smiles. "Any other possible reason, anyone?"

". . . They had mountains in the North," Nataly volunteers after looking at the chart for a few seconds. . . . "You can't farm the mountains."

"Excellent," Kathy nods. "Let's look at another difference. . . . Go ahead, Stephanie."

Kathy continued guiding students' analysis of the information on the chart, in the process finding relationships among the geography, climate, and economy. When students were unable to answer, she rephrased her questions and provided cues to help them along. She then had them consider why the economy of their city might be the way it is.

Now, let's consider this part of Kathy's lesson and see what made it effective. There are three important aspects of lesson development:

■ The way content is organized and presented

■ The extent to which learners are involved

■ The kinds of practice and feedback learners are given

Organization of Content   Effective lessons organize and present information in a systematic, coherent way and make this organization clear to students. Kathy did this in her lesson with a chart comparing the Northern and Southern states in terms of people, land and climate, and economy. The following are other effective ways to organize content:

■ Outlines

■ Hierarchies

■ Networks

■ Schematic diagrams

Each of these makes links between ideas explicit and provides students with an effective way to learn and remember new content (Mayer, 2008).

Student Involvement   Active student involvement is a second essential element of effective lessons. As we develop our lessons, we want to actively involve students in them, and teacher questioning and groupwork are two effective ways to do this. Kathy used both of these to motivate students and encourage them to think about the new content they were learning.

Practice and Feedback   Practice and feedback are a third characteristic of effective lessons. Students need opportunities to play with ideas and explore connections; they also need to know if the ideas they are developing are accurate. This is why practice and feedback are essential.

Kathy provided practice and feedback by placing students in groups and asking them to think about three ways the economies of the North and South were different. This provided students with opportunities to think about the new ideas they were learning and put their developing understanding into their own words—processes that promote learning (Eggen & Kauchak, 2010). In addition, Kathy provided feedback to the different groups through the whole-class discussion in which they analyzed the differences in the economies they had found. Feedback provides students with information about the accuracy of their new ideas as well as providing teachers with a gauge of their students' learning progress.

We'll return to these essential elements of effective lessons in later chapters as we discuss planning and implementing different kinds of lessons.

Ending Lessons Effectively

How many times have you sat through a class and left wondering and not sure what the whole thing was about? Effective lessons end by bringing closure to the lesson, wrapping up loose threads and preparing students for future learning. To see how teachers do this, let's return once more to Kathy's work with her students.

"You have done very well, everyone," Kathy smiles, pointing her finger in the air for emphasis. "Now, everyone, get with your partner again, take two minutes and write three summary statements about what we've learned here today. . . . Quickly now, get started."

The classroom quickly becomes a buzz of voices as students start peering and pointing at the chart and begin writing. In some cases they stop, crumple their papers, and begin again. As they work, Kathy walks among them offering encouragement and periodic suggestions.

At the end of two minutes Kathy announces, "One more minute, and then we're going to look at what you've written."

"OK, let's see what you've got," she continues. "What did you and Linda conclude? . . . David?"

"…We said that the weather and the land had a lot to do with the way the different states made their money."

"Excellent! That's good. How about someone else? . . . Danielle, how about you and Tony?"

Kathy has several other pairs offer their summary statements, they examine each as a whole group, and then Kathy collects the papers.

At 11:28 she announces, "Almost lunch time. Please put away your papers."

Students quickly put their books, papers, and pencils away, glance around their desks for any waste paper, and are sitting quietly at 11:30.

Just as effective lessons begin by drawing students into the activity and providing a reference frame for new material, effective lessons end by tying the different parts of the lesson together and assessing students' understanding. Closure encourages students to summarize the major ideas in the lesson, and assessment tells both the teacher and students what has been learned and what needs further work. Let's look at these components of an effective lesson ending.

Review and Closure

"We're near the end of the period, so we'll stop here and pick it up tomorrow."
"That's all for now. Put your stuff away and get ready for lunch."

We have reviewed previous material, have provided an attention-getting lesson beginning, and have carefully developed the lesson with high levels of student involvement and feedback. The positive effects of these efforts are diminished, however, if we abruptly end the lesson as we see in the two examples just given.

Closure *is the process of summarizing a topic and preparing for future learning.* Closure allows students to leave the class with a clear sense of the day's content and what they were supposed to have derived from it. It also provides a springboard for their further study at home.

The need for closure is both pervasive and intuitively sensible. Perhaps you have even used the term in a conversation, saying something such as, "Let's try and get to 'closure' on this." Closure is important in lessons because it provides one more opportunity for students, who may have drifted off at some point during the lesson, to tie ideas together. If they leave a learning experience with uncertainties, the ideas they intuitively form may be invalid, and because new learning builds on old, these misconceptions can detract from future learning.

The best lesson endings actively involve students in summarizing the main points of the lesson. Kathy did this when she broke students into groups and asked each group to provide three summary statements about the lesson. Let's look at several additional examples.

Mary Eng has developed the process for factoring the difference of two squares in her Algebra I class. She notes, "It's near the end of the period, so let's go over what we've covered so far. First, give me an example that is the difference of two squares. . . . Katilya."

In finishing a lesson on "main idea," Harry Soo says, "Class, I want you now to tell me in your own words what the main idea of a story is. Define it for me."

Teresa Bon has finished a lesson relating the pitch of a sound to the length, thickness, and tension of the object producing the sound. She completes her lesson by saying, "Now let's write a statement that tells us in one sentence what we've found today."

Asking students for additional examples of the ideas they've studied or to form a definition or summary can be used to tie the different pieces of the lesson together.

Assessment and Effective Teaching

"They seem to be able to solve percent increase problems, but I wonder if they really understand how these are different from percent decrease problems."

"Most of them are getting some ideas down on paper, but they don't seem to elaborate very well. I wonder if I should work more on that, or if I should start having them work a little harder now on the mechanics of their grammar?"

"The homework looked good on solving density problems, but how many of them just put the numbers in the formula without knowing what they were doing?"

These are valid questions; teachers constantly ask themselves if their students really "get it." They are continually trying to determine how fast they can present content, deciding whether they should go on to the next topic, and finding out if students understand the new content clearly. Assessment helps teachers answer these questions.

Assessment *is the process of gathering information about learning progress and making instructional decisions based on the information.* Its purpose is to gauge learner progress and provide feedback for both the teacher and students. It can take several different forms:

- Seatwork and homework exercises
- Observations of student performance
- Answers to teachers' questions
- Samples of student work
- Quizzes and tests

Kathy used two forms of assessment in her teaching. First, she informally assessed her students with her questioning during the lesson. **Informal assessment** *is the process of gathering incidental information about students' understanding during learning activities.* Second, the homework that she might give is a form of **formal assessment**, *the process of systematically gathering information from all students.* Tests, quizzes, and performance assessments, such as observing science students as they design an experiment, are also formal assessments. Both formal and informal assessments are essential for determining how much students are learning.

Assessment is an integral component of the teaching-learning process: "Effectively designed learning environments must also be assessment centered. The key principles of assessment are that they should provide opportunities for feedback and revision and that what is assessed must be congruent with one's learning goals" (Bransford et al., 2000, pp. 139–140).

Without specific feedback, students' understanding may be incomplete or they may retain misconceptions. In addition to giving students feedback about their learning progress, assessment also provides teachers with information about the effectiveness of their lesson.

This completes our examination of the general instructional model. It is designed to serve as a framework for the content of Chapters 7 through 13. Our hope is that the information presented here will serve as a foundation for your study of those chapters.

To view a video clip of a lesson demonstrating essential teaching skills, go to the Book Specific Resources tab in MyEducationLab, select your text, select Video Examples under Chapter 5, and then click on *Essential Teaching Skills in an Urban Classroom.*

Summary

Classroom Climate: A Prerequisite to Learning

A positive climate invites students into your classroom, communicates that they are valued as individuals, and focuses on learning. Students need to know that they are accepted and that their teachers care for them as people.

Positive classroom environments are also safe and orderly; students' learning suffers when their classmates are disruptive.

Classrooms with a positive climate focus on learning. Teachers who focus on learning provide students with tasks that are interesting, meaningful, and challenging.

Characteristics of Effective Teachers

The key to effective classrooms are effective teachers, who influence students through their attitudes and beliefs. They care about their students, are high in personal teaching efficacy, have high expectations for learning, and are positive and enthusiastic models. Effective teachers communicate with clear language and logical presentations and use emphasis to highlight important ideas.

Effective Teaching and Teachers' Use of Time

A thrust of the chapter is captured in the question "If we watch effective teachers, regardless of grade level, content area, or topic, what would we expect to see?" One answer to the question lies in their use of time—they allocate their time wisely, they limit the time spent on noninstructional activities, and they design learning activities in which students are engaged and successful. Effective teachers are also well organized; they begin learning activities promptly, have materials prepared in advance, and have well-established, timesaving routines.

A General Instructional Model

The general instructional model includes teacher characteristics, together with the features of effective lesson beginnings, well-designed lesson development, and clear lesson endings.

Effective teachers begin their lessons with reviews of previous work, which activate students' prior knowledge and help them connect new topics to content they already know. They also plan for student motivation, hoping to capture and maintain student attention.

As their lessons are developed, effective teachers organize content and communicate this organization to students through visual aids while maintaining high levels of student involvement. They provide students with accurate feedback about their progress and provide practice to reinforce learning.

Effective teachers end their lessons with a thorough review to summarize the topics they've studied and use a well-developed assessment system to provide information about learning progress.

 $\mathcal{I}$mportant Concepts

Engaged time (p. 158)

Focus (p. 160)

Formal assessment (p. 167)

Informal assessment (p. 167)

Instructional time (p. 157)

Modeling (p. 150)

Personal teaching efficacy (p. 150)

Precise terminology (p. 153)

Review (p. 159)

Teacher expectations (p. 151)

Teacher-effectiveness research (p. 143)

Transition signal (p. 154)

Preparing for Your Licensure Exam

At the beginning of the chapter you saw how Kathy Johnson applied effective teaching research in her work with her students. Let's look now at another teacher, and analyze the extent to which he applies this research. Read the case study below and answer the questions that follow.

After reading this case, go to the Book Specific Resources tab in MyEducationLab, select your text, select *Preparing for Your Licensure Exam* under Chapter 5 to complete the questions that accompany the case and receive feedback on your responses.

Dan Kaiser, a veteran with 15 years of experience teaching social studies, is sitting over a cup of coffee in the teachers' lounge on a Thursday. He is moving into a unit on Ancient Greece and the Age of Pericles in his world history classes, and he is working on his planning.

"You look deep in thought," Ann Stoddard, one of his colleagues comments, seeing him hunched over his work.

"Yeah, right—I actually am," he nods. "I'm starting ancient Greece on Monday, and the kids hate it. I want them to understand how Greece has impacted us in modern Western civilization, but they think it's about funny old people wearing sheets. . . . I know it's tough for them, but I think this stuff is important. . . . They always have a hard time with it."

We rejoin Dan on the following Monday. The bell rings at 9:35 signaling the beginning of third period as the last of the students scurry through the door to beat the tardy bell.

"Get to your seats quickly, now," Dan calls over his shoulder. "Andrew, you're just about late. . . . Settle down, class, and we'll get started."

As students talk while getting settled, Dan shuffles through the materials on his desk, looking for those he prepared over the weekend.

"All right, settle down," Dan says again, to several students at the back of the room who are talking, as he adjusts his notes.

At 9:42 he displays the PowerPoint with an outline of the unit on it. "We're going to be studying ancient Greece during this week," he comments, pointing to the PowerPoint on the screen. "We'll look at some of the great thinkers and the great ideas of the age. We'll refer to this outline as we go along. Have paper and pencil ready, because you need to take careful notes on this information."

Dan then begins by identifying and describing some of the main historical figures of the period, such as Socrates, Plato, and Aristotle. As he begins, most of the students are looking at him, but as he continues, several start looking out the window or down at their desks. A few are busily writing notes.

"Did you know," Dan asks with a slight smile, moving over to sit on a stool at the front of the room, "that Socrates in some ways was sort of shiftless? He was often in trouble with his wife because he wouldn't work; he wanted to spend his time talking to his students about whatever."

As he proceeds with his description of Socrates' problems at home, some of the students who were looking away turn back to the front of the room.

Dan continues, telling the class that the Greeks have had a major influence on today's language, thinking, culture, and architecture. As he talks, he writes terms on the board, such as "Language influence," "Cultural influence," and "Influence on architecture." Some of the students continue taking notes, whereas others seem somewhat listless.

"Let's slow down for a second," Dan suggests, ". . . and see what you know about Greece. . . . Where is it located? . . . Juanita?"

". . . Sort of over there," she says, pointing toward the map of Europe Dan has hanging on the side of the room. "Over there, sort of by Italy."

"Okay," Dan responds, stepping down from the stool and moving over to point to the map to confirm the location. "What is its capital? . . . Calvin?"

"Got me," Calvin shrugs.

"Anyone?"

"Athens," Jerome calls out from the side of the room.

Dan continues for a few more minutes, asking additional questions such as, "What are some famous Greek plays?" "What is the geography of Greece like?" and "What is the name of a famous Greek landmark?"

Some of the students eagerly try to respond, whereas others appear disinterested. The answers to most of the questions come from a relatively small group of students.

Dan then continues presenting additional information about the geography of Greece, pointing out that Athens had a large navy and was a thriving commercial center, which allowed trade with other parts of the known world at the time, which helped it become a center of intellectual activity.

Again, after a few minutes, he notices the inattention of several of his students and comments, "You know, I've given you an awful lot of information. Let's slow down again. Based on what I've told you thus far, what do you personally find most interesting about the ancient Greeks?"

Several students offer comments, although they tend to be the same ones who had answered the earlier questions. Two of them get into a slight argument over whether the Greeks had slaves. Dan waves his hand to stop the argument and tells them that the Greeks did indeed have slaves.

Seeing that there are only 10 minutes left in the period, Dan says, "There are just 10 minutes left, so we'll stop here for today. . . . I have your papers here from last week. If you have any questions on the papers, see me."

He then returns papers the students had written for an earlier unit. Each has a letter grade on the front of it. The students quickly scan the papers and put them in their notebooks. He then tells the students to talk quietly among themselves until the bell rings.

Questions for Analysis

Let's analyze Dan's lesson now based on the information in the chapter. In responding to the following questions, be specific and use information directly from the case study to document your conclusions.

1. Instructional alignment describes the logical match between teachers' learning objectives and their instructional activities and assessments. Was Dan's instruction aligned? Explain why or why not.

2. Assess the effectiveness of Dan's organization. What could he have done to make it more effective?

3. Based on the discussion of instruction and motivation in the chapter, how effective were Dan's attempts to motivate his students? What could he have done to make the lesson more motivating?

4. Assess the beginning of Dan's lesson, its development and its ending. What could he have done to make each more effective?

5. Now, provide an overall assessment of Dan's lesson. If you believe the lesson could have been made more effective, offer specific suggestions for doing so.

 *D*iscussion Questions

1. Some authorities suggest lengthening the school day or school year, supporting their position by citing the relationship between allocated time and achievement. How would you respond to these people? What are some arguments for and against this approach to increasing learning?

2. In research studies, engagement is often inferred from the expressions and actions of students. What are some behaviors that suggest student engagement? Lack of engagement? What are some problems involved in inferring attention from student behavior?

3. The ideal engagement rate is, of course, 100 percent. What is a realistic engagement rate for students you work with? (Estimate a percentage.) How does this engagement rate vary with the type of students? Time of day? Different times within the same class period? What can be done to increase engagement rates? What factors outside the teacher's control will affect student engagement rates?

4. This chapter focused on enthusiasm from a teacher perspective. What are some indicators of students' enthusiasm? Lack of enthusiasm?

5. Are positive teacher attitudes more important at some grade levels than others? Why? In some curriculum areas and/or content areas? Why?

6. Review the findings on teacher expectations with respect to teacher effort and questioning. What might be an explanation for why teachers treat high achievers and low achievers differently in terms of effort and questioning?

Portfolio Activities

1. *Allocated Time.* Contact several teachers teaching at the same grade level or in the same content areas. If they are elementary teachers, ask them how much time they devote to different subject-matter areas, and if they are middle or secondary teachers, to topics within their content area. Ask them why they have decided on these allocations. Bring the information back to class. Compare the rationales these teachers offer to those uncovered by researchers (e.g., how much they like the area or topic, how much preparation it requires, and how difficult they perceive it to be for their students). Finally, describe what you personally believe to be an optimal time-allocation plan for the grade or subject, and justify your answer.

2. *Instructional Time.* Observe (or tape) a complete lesson and note the amount of time spent in each of the categories that follow.

Lesson Segment	Amount of Time Spent
a. Introduction to lesson	
b. Development (main part of lesson)	
c. Summary	
d. Seatwork or practice	
e. Total	

Analyze the use of instructional time in the lesson. In your analysis, discuss the following factors:

- Context (type of school, grade level, characteristics of the students)
- Pace (Did the lesson move too quickly or too slowly?)
- Student reactions to the lesson

3. *Student Engagement.* In this exercise, you will be measuring student engagement through a time-sampling technique. Select four students to observe, two high achieving and two low achieving (ask the teacher for help in selecting the students), and seat yourself so that you can observe their faces during the lesson. Focus on each student at 15-second intervals and decide whether the student was attending to the lesson. A "Y" indicates yes, an "N" indicates no, and a question mark indicates that you cannot tell. At the end of the 20-minute observation period, compute averages for each student and the group as a whole.

   a. Were the engagement rates similar for each student? If they varied, suggest a reason why.
   b. Did the engagement rates vary during the course of the presentation? If so, why?
   c. Were there any specific teacher actions that appeared to produce high or low engagement rates? Explain.
   d. Were the engagement rates for the high- and low-achieving students similar or different?
   e. Observe the same students for three days and see if any patterns emerge.

f. Observe several classes (or subjects) taught by the same teacher and see if engagement rates are similar.

g. Select students who are physically close to where the teacher spends most of his or her time during lessons and compare engagement rates with those of students farther away.

h. Does the type of activity influence student engagement rates? Find out when the teacher is going to be using two different types of lessons and observe students during each.

i. Compare your responses with those of your classmates. How can you use engagement rates to improve your effectiveness as a teacher?

Student A	**Student B**	**Student C**	**Student D**
Minute 1			
Minute 2			
Minute 3			
. . .			
Minute 20			

4. *Success Rates.* Observe (or tape) a lesson during an interactive teaching session and count the number of questions asked, the number answered correctly, the number answered correctly with prompting, and the number answered incorrectly or not at all. Comment on the success rate in terms of what you have learned in this chapter.

5. *Enthusiasm.* Identify one of your instructors whom you would describe as "enthusiastic." Describe specifically what the instructor does that makes you believe he or she is enthusiastic. Discuss your description with your classmates.

6. *Effective Communication.* Videotape yourself teaching a lesson. Then, watch the tape and note when vague, ambiguous terms and other distracting speech mannerisms occur. Is there any pattern to their occurrence? Do more of them occur at the beginning or end of a lesson? Do transitions or interruptions affect these speech mannerisms? If possible, teach another lesson to the same group and try to eliminate these distractors. What did you learn about yourself from analyzing the tape?

7. *Student Involvement.* This exercise examines patterns of interaction in a classroom. Observe a class during an interactive teaching session after sketching a seating chart with boxes large enough to allow you to put numbers in them. Code the teacher's first interaction with a student with a 1 in that student's square. The second student called on gets a 2, the third a 3, and so on. You now have a running tally of who got called on and in what order.

   Is there any pattern to the interactions? Do all students participate? Does location make a difference? Is there any pattern to the sequence of interactions? Discuss your analysis in terms of the teacher expectations research.

8. *Feedback.* Observe a class or videotape yourself teaching a lesson. Using the instrument that follows, note the kind of feedback given following students' responses to questions for a 10-minute segment of your lesson. Then, answer the questions that follow.

   a. What is the most common form of teacher response to a student answer?
   b. Does the teacher verbally acknowledge every response? If not, what effect does this appear to have on students?
   c. How does the teacher deal with either an incomplete or partial response?

   How could the use of feedback be modified to improve student learning?

Question	Student Answer	Teacher Response
1.		
2.		
3.		
4.		
5.		
6.		
7.		
8.		
9.		
10.		

To check your comprehension of the content covered in Chapter 5, go to the Book Specific Resources in MyEducationLab, select your text, and complete the Study Plan quiz. In addition to receiving feedback on your answers, a study plan will be generated from the quiz that will direct you to access Review, Practice, and Enrichment materials to enhance your understanding of chapter content.

Increasing Learning Through Student Involvement

Chapter Outline	Learning Objectives
	When you've completed your study of this chapter, you should be able to
Student involvement: A key to learning and motivation ■ Student involvement: The need for clear learning objectives ■ Student involvement: The role of content representations	1. Explain why involvement is essential for student motivation and learning.
Involving students through teacher questioning ■ Assessing current understanding ■ Increasing student motivation ■ Guiding new learning	2. Describe how teachers can use questioning to increase student involvement.
Elements of effective questioning ■ Questioning frequency ■ Equitable distribution ■ Open-ended questions ■ Prompting ■ Repetition for emphasis ■ Wait-time **Exploring Diversity:** Involving students from diverse backgrounds	3. Identify elements of effective teacher questioning.
Classroom questions: Additional issues ■ Low- and high-level questions ■ Selecting students ■ Call-outs ■ Choral responses **Technology and Teaching:** Using technology to increase student involvement	4. Explain how different elements of teachers' questioning affect their effectiveness.

In which do you learn more, classes in which you're asked questions and are actively involved in learning activities, or those in which the teacher gives long lectures as you sit passively? In the latter, many learners—including college students—become inattentive in a matter of minutes. The key to attracting and maintaining student attention is to actively involve them in the lessons. Because student involvement is so essential for learning, we devote this entire chapter to the topic.

To see how teachers can promote student involvement, let's turn to José Alvarez, a fourth-grade teacher working with his class on a science lesson. As you read the case study, think about the different ways he involves students in his lesson.

José has 30 students in his class. The class is described as average and is composed primarily of lower- to lower-middle-class students. Keith, Tyrone, Latisha, Jason, and Ginny are the five lowest achievers in his class.

José typically teaches science for 30 minutes each day. In this lesson he wants his students to understand that heat makes substances expand by increasing the movement of molecules and making the molecules move apart. The students have studied molecules in earlier lessons, so they have a basic understanding of them.

He begins his activity by displaying two soft drink bottles with balloons covering them, and a coffee pot two-thirds full of hot water, as shown Figure 6.1.

"Class, I want you to look at these bottles," he begins as he holds them up. "What can you tell us about them? . . . Keith?"

"You drink out of them."

"Fine, Keith. . . . Beverly?"

"They're sort of green."

"Yes, they are," José smiles. "What else? . . . Lavonia?"

". . . They look like they're the same size."

"Yes, indeed, they certainly do. Good, Lavonia.

"What's in the bottles? . . . Nikki?" he proceeds on.

"They're empty."

"Wave your hand in front of your face, Nikki," José prompts. "What do you feel?"

". . . I . . . feel the air on my face."

"Yes!" he smiles. "So what do you think might be in the bottles?"

". . . Air?"

"Yes indeed. Good, Nikki. And what was one of the characteristics of air that we've discussed?"

"It's all around us," Jason volunteers.

"That's right. Air is all around us. Good thinking, Jason.

"Now look at the balloons on these bottles," José continues, holding the bottles up again.

"How would you compare the balloons? . . . Amir?"

Figure 6.1

Bottles with Balloons on Top

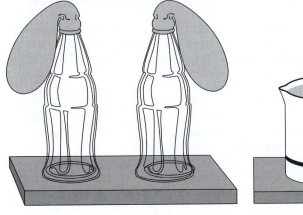

"One is red and the other is yellow."

"Yes. Good, Amir. What else? . . . Rachel?"

"They look like they're made out of rubber."

"Yes, they are rubber balloons. How would you compare their sizes? . . . Michael?"

"They look like they're the same size."

"Good, Michael. They actually *are* the same size.

"Now look at the balloons and bottles, everyone," he continues. "What did Lavonia say about the bottles themselves? . . . Cliff?"

"We drink out of them."

"Yes we do," José smiles. "How do the sizes compare? . . . Alfredo?"

"They're the same."

"Good, Alfredo. We said they were the same size. And how about the balloons? . . . Linda?"

"They were the same size, too?"

"And what is in the bottles? . . . Steve?"

"Air."

"So, now what do we know about the amount of air in each system? Kathy?"

" . . . "

"How did the two bottles compare?"

"They're the same size."

"So, what does that suggest about the amount of air in each?"

"It's the same."

"And how do we know, Tyrone?"

" . . . "

"What did we say about the sizes of the balloons and bottles? . . . Tyrone?"

" . . . They . . . were . . . equal."

"Good," José nods, "So, how do we know the amount of air in each is the same?"

" . . . The bottles and balloons . . . are the same size."

"Yes, Tyrone. Good thinking."

"Now watch what I do." José says, placing one of the bottles in the coffee pot. He then continues by asking, "And what did we say about the amount of air in each of the systems, everyone?"

"IT IS THE SAME," everyone shouts.

"Just watch now," he says with anticipation.

As students watch, the balloon begins to slowly rise above the bottle placed in the hot water as shown in Figure 6.2.

The students begin to giggle as the balloon pops up and José laughs with them.

"Now," he says, taking advantage of their interest, "work with your partner, and make as many comparisons as you can of the two bottles. As always, write them down. Work quickly now. You have three minutes."

The students, all of whom are sitting next to their partners, turn to each other and immediately go to work. In seconds, a hum of activity can be heard throughout the room as students begin talking, pointing at the two bottles and balloons, and writing their observations on their papers. José walks among them as they work, periodically stopping to make brief comments to individual pairs.

"OK everyone, all eyes up here," José directs at the end of the three minutes. He pauses a few seconds as the groups stop their writing and turn their attention to him.

"Good, everyone," he smiles. "Let's see what you came up with. Give us one of your comparisons. Judy?"

"The bottles are the same size."

Figure 6.2

Bottles with Expanded Balloon

"Yes, the size of the bottles hasn't changed," José responds, smiling. "And what else? . . . Jim and Latisha?"

"The red balloon is sticking up," Latisha answers for the pair.

"And what else? . . . Stacy and Albert?"

"We think that the amount of the air has increased in the first bottle," Stacy answers.

"Interesting idea," José smiles. "Now, when you mean amount of air, do you mean volume or do you mean mass? . . . Think about it for a moment everyone. . . . OK, what do you think?"

"We think volume."

"Good thinking," José nods. "Outstanding work. . . . Now, how do the masses compare? What did you and Amir come up with there? . . . Robin?"

". . . We think the masses are still the same."

"Excellent thinking again," José smiles and shakes his head. "Boy, you're sharp today.

"Now, let's look at some other things," he continues. "Jim and Latisha said the red balloon was sticking up. Why do you suppose it is sticking up? . . . Mike?"

"It was heated," Mike responds quickly.

"How do we know it was heated? . . . Ginny?"

". . . I, er, I didn't hear the question," she answers sheepishly.

"What did I do with this bottle, Ginny?" he asks, holding up the bottle with the red balloon.

"You put it in the coffee pot."

"Yes I did, Ginny. Good. And how do we know the coffee pot was hot? . . . Rosemary?"

"I saw steam coming off from it."

"Good observation, Rosemary," he smiles. "So, what can we say happened to the balloon? . . . Jill?"

"It stuck up."

"What else might we say?" he continues, forming semicircles with his hands and spreading them apart.

Hesitantly, Jill responds, "It got bigger."

"Yes, excellent, Jill. Now, everyone, I'm going to give you another word for gets bigger. It's called expand. Everyone say expand."

"EXPAND," they all shout in unison.

"So what happens when we heat something? . . . Deandra?"

"It expands," Deandra responds instantly.

"And what expanded in this case? . . . Toni?"

"The balloon."

"And what else?"

" . . ."

"What is in the bottles and balloons?"

"Air," Toni blurts out.

"Good. So, what is expanding in addition to the balloon?"

"The air!" Toni proclaims.

"Yes! The air is expanding. And what did we say made that happen? . . . Keith?"

"We heated the bottle?"

"So now let's make a statement about heat and expansion. Give it a try. . . . Gary?"

" . . ."

"What does heat do to things?"

" . . . It makes them expand," Gary answers finally.

"Good! Now let's write that down." With that, José writes the statement on the board as he has the class repeat it.

José then brings out two drawings (see Figure 6.3). He establishes with the students that the arrows in the drawings are there to help visualize the direction of movement of the air molecules, and the marks that look like small parentheses around the dots are there to help visualize the motion of the molecules (two sets of parentheses suggesting that the molecules were moving faster than one set of parentheses). He also leads students to conclude that the drawing on the left represents the bottle in the hot water.

José continues by asking students to work with a partner and compare the two drawings. Through additional questioning, José helps students understand that heat makes molecules move faster and farther apart and this resulted in the balloon expanding on the one bottle.

Looking at the clock, José sees it is 11:25, so he asks the class to tell him where in the room the air molecules would be moving the fastest. They conclude that over by the window would be the fastest, reasoning that it was the hottest over there. They further decide that the molecules would be farther apart at the ceiling than they would be at the floor. José praises them for their thinking and then finishes the lesson with a summary of the major ideas.

In this lesson we saw how José actively involved his students in his lesson. In this chapter we'll examine the different strategies José used to encourage his students to think about the ideas he was teaching.

Figure 6.3

Drawings with Molecules

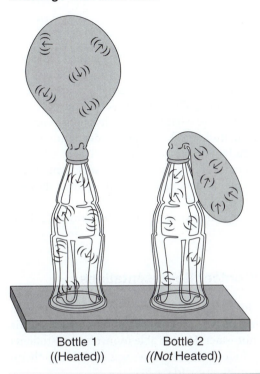

Bottle 1
((Heated))

Bottle 2
((*Not* Heated))

Student Involvement: A Key to Learning and Motivation

We know from our own experiences that we are more motivated and learn more when the instructor involves us in learning, and research into student learning supports this contention. Students learn more and retain information longer when they are put in active roles than they do when passively receiving information from others (Eggen & Kauchak, 2010).

When we actively involve students in lessons, we need to have a clear idea of what we want them to learn or take away from the lesson. In the next section we discuss the need for clear learning objectives.

Student Involvement: The Need for Clear Learning Objectives

The focus of this chapter is on the need for student involvement. However, this idea isn't as simple as it appears on the surface. To illustrate this point, let's look back at José's lesson. His students weren't involved merely for the sake of involvement. Instead, their involvement was directed toward a specific learning objective.

José's learning objectives were clear and precise; he wanted his students to understand that

- Heat makes substances expand.
- Heat makes molecules move faster.
- The concept *expand* means that molecules move apart.

The clarity and specificity of his objectives guided his thinking both as he planned the lesson and as he conducted it.

Effective teaching begins with clear learning objectives. This is particularly true as we work in standards-based learning environments. Clear and precise objectives are essential for three reasons. First, if teachers aren't sure what they want learners to understand or be able to do, how can they guide their students' developing understanding, and how will they be able to determine what students have accomplished? Second, clear learning objectives help teachers make decisions about ways to represent content for learners; the examples teachers use help students understand the abstract ideas they are trying to learn. José did this with the soft drink bottles and balloons he used. Third, clear learning objectives provide the conceptual framework for the interaction that is so essential for student learning.

Student Involvement: The Role of Content Representations

To begin this section let's think again about José's lesson. Students were involved, but this involvement didn't just happen. It occurred in large part because he represented his topic effectively, using bottles, balloons, and hot water. He was able to involve his students because the information students needed to understand the topics was available to them. They didn't have to recall essential information; they could see it.

The emphasis on "seeing" important information captures the essence of effective representations. The ideal that we strive for is this: *All the information students need to understand the topic and reach the learning objectives exists in the representations.* For instance, José first wanted his students to understand that heat makes substances expand. His students were able to see this relationship by observing the balloon expand when the bottle was put in the hot water. They didn't have to know or remember this relationship; they could see it. Then José used his drawings of the bottles, balloons, and molecules to help students visualize the movement of the molecules in the two bottles.

Effective representations exist in a variety of forms:

- Examples—the "real thing"
- Demonstrations
- Charts and matrixes
- Models
- Vignettes and case studies

The type of representation depends on the teacher's objective, which illustrates again why learning objectives are so essential. Teachers' can't decide what representation to find or create if they haven't thought about what they want students to know or understand.

Some sample objectives and illustrations of matching representation are outlined in Table 6.1.

Table 6.1 Different Ways to Represent Content

Type of Representation	Goal	Example
Example	To understand the characteristics of the concept *arthropod*	A real lobster
Demonstration	To understand that heat makes materials expand	José's demonstration with the expanding balloon in the hot water
Charts and matrixes	To understand the differences between the northern and southern states	Kathy Johnson's chart showing the differences between the states
Model	To understand that heat increases the movement of molecules	José's drawings of the bottles, balloons, and molecules
Vignette	To understand the characteristics of the social studies concept *mercantilism*	Vignettes illustrating *mercantilism*

Let's examine the information in Table 6.1 a bit more closely. For instance, pictures can be effective representations when getting the "real thing" is difficult or impossible. Many young children are interested in dinosaurs, for example, but using real dinosaurs is obviously impossible, so pictures are a reasonable compromise.

Models *are representations that allow us to visualize what we can't observe directly*, and they're particularly useful in science when topics such as the structure of the atom and combinations of atoms into molecules are being studied. José's drawings were models because they helped students visualize the idea that the molecules in the heated bottle were moving faster than the molecules in the unheated one.

Vignettes can effectively represent topics difficult to illustrate in other ways. For instance, consider the following vignettes that illustrate the concept of *mercantilism.*

In the mid-1600s the American colonists were encouraged to grow tobacco, since it wasn't grown in England. The colonists wanted to sell it to France and other countries but were told no. In return the colonists were allowed to import textiles from England but were forbidden from making their own. All the materials were carried on British ships.

Early French colonists in the New World were avid fur trappers and traders. They got in trouble with the French monarchy, however, when they attempted to make fur garments and sell them to Spain, England, and other countries. They were told that the produced garments would be sent to these countries from Paris instead. The monarchy also told them that traps and weapons would be made in France and sent to them as well. Jean Forjea complied with the monarchy's wishes but was fined when he hired a Dutch ship to carry some of the furs back to Nice.

In comparing these examples we see that in each case a relationship between a mother country and a colony existed, and the colony was required to produce raw materials, ship the raw materials to the mother country on the mother country's ships, and buy manufactured goods back from the mother country. These are the characteristics of the concept of *mercantilism.* Like José's demonstration for the relationships among heat, expansion, and the movement of molecules, the vignettes provided students with information they needed to construct new knowledge.

The importance of effective content representations is impossible to overstate, and once clear learning objectives have been established, much of the thinking of expert teachers focuses on ways to represent topics in ways that are understandable for students.

Representing content effectively also helps us accommodate differences in our students' background knowledge. You can best accommodate these differences by representing the topics you teach with examples. For instance, if you bring a real lobster to class, it doesn't matter if a student is African American, Asian American, Hispanic, bright, slow, a boy or a girl, or a student with an exceptionality. They can all feel the lobster's cold, hard shell; see the different body parts; and notice the jointed legs. When these are combined with other examples such as a crayfish, beetle, and grasshopper, students can form an accurate concept of *arthropod*, despite differences in prior knowledge.

Unquestionably, you'll still need to be sensitive to differences in students' attitudes, values, and motivations, many of which are culturally dependent. However, effectively representing the topics you teach is a powerful way to accommodate student diversity.

 # Involving Students Through Teacher Questioning

Teacher questioning is the single most effective and most generally applicable strategy teachers have for promoting student involvement. Regardless of grade level, content area, or topic, being able to guide your students' learning with questions is the most important teaching skill that you can develop (Leinhardt & Steele, 2005; Olson & Clough, 2004). Effective teachers ask more questions than their less effective colleagues and use these questions to guide learning and provide feedback (Good & Brophy, 2008).Because questioning is such a powerful tool for involving students, we devote the rest of the chapter to this topic.

The effectiveness of questioning can be explained by the functions they perform, including

- Assessing current understanding

- Increasing student motivation

- Guiding new learning

Let's look at them.

Assessing Current Understanding

A well-known maxim in teaching is "Start where they're at." One way to know where students are at in terms of their knowledge of a topic is through questioning. Questioning provides information that helps teachers make the many instantaneous decisions that they face as they interact with students during a lesson.It helps them decide whom to call on, how long to give the student to answer, and how quickly to move through a lesson.

The need for interaction to assess our audience's understanding is an intuitively sensible idea. Even in informal conversations we assess other people's understanding of a discussion topic by the way they respond to our questions and statements. In classrooms, questions provide teachers with continual feedback about the learning progress of their students.

Increasing Student Motivation

Effective questioning also increases student curiosity and interest–two important dimensions of motivation (Schunk et al., 2008). Effective questions engage students, challenge their thinking, and pose problems for consideration. José used questioning to capitalize on his students' curiosity and increase their interest in the lesson. For example he asked,

> "So, now what do we know about the amount of air in each system?"
> "How do we know that the amount of air is the same?"
> "How do the masses compare?"

and

> "How do we know the coffee pot was hot?"

Each of these questions required higher-order thinking; students had to go beyond just memorizing information. This kind of thinking promotes feelings of challenge and competence in students, both linked to increased motivation (Ryan & Deci, 2000).

Guiding New Learning

Guiding students' learning is the third important function of questioning. Effective questions help students relate ideas and integrate new learning with their existing understanding.

To illustrate these ideas, think back to José's lesson. The entire lesson was conducted with questioning. The process of constructing understanding requires the careful guidance of expert teachers, and questioning is the most powerful skill teachers have for providing this guidance.

To be an effective learning tool, your questions need to impact student thinking. The best planned and executed questioning sequence is ineffective if it doesn't cause students to think, relate ideas, and construct new knowledge.

In answering one of your questions, students engage in five separate mental operations, outlined in Figure 6.4 and discussed in the paragraphs that follow.

Learning begins with attention (Eggen & Kauchak, 2010); the most thoroughly planned and well-thought-out lesson is ineffective if students aren't paying attention. Effective questions draw students' attention away from distractions, such as the clock, what's outside the window, and each other and invite them into the lesson.

Once students are paying attention, they also need to interpret the meaning of the questionaccurately. This isn't always easy; the intent of the question may be clear to you, but it may be misperceived by students. This again illustrates the importance of questioning as a form of informal assessment. Teachers will know if a student misinterprets a question if the answer is incomplete or inaccurate. When this occurs, the teacher can intervene.

An effective question should also elicit a covert response from each student. Although you will typically call on one student to answer, your goal should be to have all students think about and mentally answer each question. We discuss strategies to promote covert responses from all students later in the chapter.

Covert responses are put into words when you call on a student to answer. Verbalizing an answer helps clarify the content in students' minds and make connections with other ideas. Verbalizing an answer takes time and effort, especially if the question is a complex or demanding one (Bruning et al., 2004). Effective teachers provide students with enough time to think about and produce an answer.

Figure 6.4

Student Mental Operations Elicited by an Effective Question

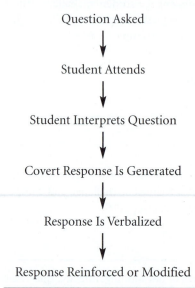

Question Asked

↓

Student Attends

↓

Student Interprets Question

↓

Covert Response Is Generated

↓

Response Is Verbalized

↓

Response Reinforced or Modified

Finally, based on your feedback, students judge whether the response was complete and accurate, and if there is a problem, they generate a revised response. A correct answer is recognized and reinforced; an incorrect answer is modified. This entire process occurs in a few seconds and is repeated hundreds of times a day in classrooms.

The sequence we just described is the ideal we strive for, but it doesn't always occur. Not all students attend, some misinterpret the question, others don't generate a covert response, students don't always listen to the answers of their classmates, and they may not revise their original thinking. When these alternatives occur, learning suffers. Understanding the mental operations questions are intended to elicit helps us see why the elements of effective questioning are so important. Let's look at them.

 ## Elements of Effective Questioning

As you we saw earlier, effective questioning depends on two essential factors. The first is clear and precise learning objectives;you should begin your lessons knowing what you want your students to learn. A second factor in effective questioning is the use of some type of representation of content, which provides a focal point for the lesson. Keep these ideas in mind as you study this section.

The essential questioning strategies that effective teachers use, regardless of grade level or topic, include the following:

- Questioning frequency
- Equitable distribution

- Open-ended questions
- Prompting
- Repetition for emphasis
- Wait time

These strategies are outlined in Figure 6.5 and discussed in the following sections.

Questioning Frequency

Questioning frequency *refers to the number of questions that teachers ask over a period of time,* and effective teachers ask more questions than their less effective counterparts (Leinhardt & Steele, 2005). Student involvement is essential for learning, and effective teachers ask a large number of questions to actively involve their students in the lesson.

We saw the effects of questioning frequency in José's lesson. He asked a large number of questions and guided his students to his learning objectives with his questions.

Equitable Distribution

Equitable distribution *describes a questioning pattern in which all the students in the class are called on as equally as possible* (Kerman, 1979). Equitable distribution runs counter to two common teaching patterns. First, in typical classrooms, most teacher questions are undirected, meaning that students who volunteer are allowed to answer, and those who don't are allowed to remain passive. This practice detracts from achievement, because the involvement of students who don't volunteer decreases (Good & Brophy, 2008).

Second, many teachers tend to treat students differently based on their expectations; they call on students they perceive as high ability more frequently than low-ability ones.

Figure 6.5

Essential Questioning Strategies

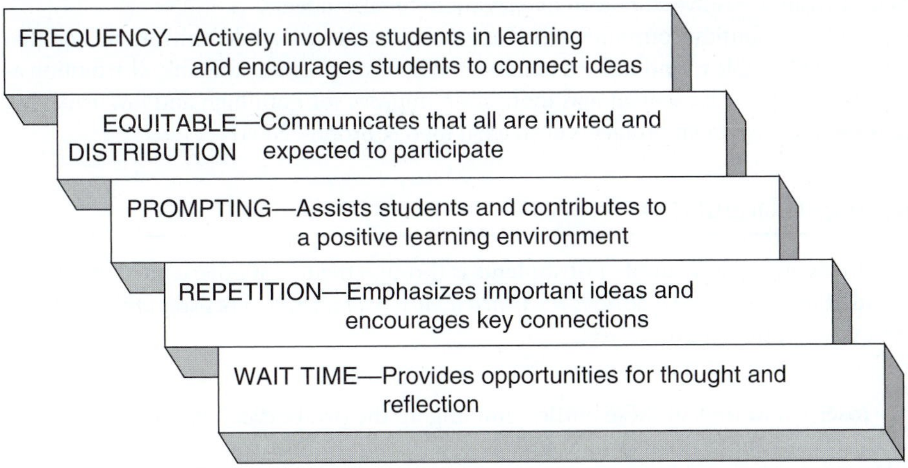

FREQUENCY—Actively involves students in learning and encourages students to connect ideas

EQUITABLE DISTRIBUTION—Communicates that all are invited and expected to participate

PROMPTING—Assists students and contributes to a positive learning environment

REPETITION—Emphasizes important ideas and encourages key connections

WAIT TIME—Provides opportunities for thought and reflection

This is easy to understand. They expect high-ability students to be able to answer, and getting correct answers is reinforcing for teachers, so they fall into patterns of calling primarily on high-ability students.

> Teachers should distribute questions widely rather than allow a few students to answer most of them. A few reticent students who rarely participate in discussions may still get excellent grades, but most students benefit from opportunities to practice oral communication skills, and distributing response opportunities helps keep them attentive and accountable. Also, teachers who restrict their questions primarily to a small group of active (and usually high-achieving) students are likely co communicate undesirable expectations . . . and generally [tend]to be less aware and less effective. (Good & Brophy, 2003, p. 384)

In contrast to these patterns, José called on all the students in his class *as equally as possible and by name.* He had 30 students in the class, and they all responded at least once. (In the actual lesson we observed, each student answered several questions.)

Although not apparent in a written case study, we want to emphasize that José called on his students whether or not they had their hands up. Students in José's class knew that all students were going to be called on and, as a result, their attention increased. When students "drifted off," José intervened immediately, as illustrated in the segment with Jason when he was momentarily inattentive.

> **José:** Excellent, Della. So now let's make a statement describing heat and the speed of molecules. Go ahead, Jason.
>
> **Jason:** . . .
>
> **José:** Do you want me to say that again?
>
> **Jason:** Yes (looking relieved).
>
> **José:** Let's try and make a statement relating heat and the speed of molecules.

This simple sequence took less than five seconds but served two important functions. First, it got Jason back into the lesson, and second, it contributed to a positive classroom climate. Jason knew that José had caught him not paying attention, but José didn't admonish or criticize him. Instead, José simply rephrased his original question and went on. This sequence communicated that José was "on Jason's side," wanting him to contribute and learn. This helped create a positive climate in his classroom for all students.

Equitable distribution communicates that you expect all your students to attend and that each student will be able to and assisted to answer. When you practice equitable distribution as a day-to-day pattern, achievement and motivation improve for both high and low achievers, and classroom management problems decrease (Good & Brophy, 2008).

Open-Ended Questions

One way to involve a large number of students is through the use of open-ended questions. **Open-ended questions** *are questions for which a variety of answers are acceptable,* and José used a number of these in his lesson.

Let's see how he did this.

> **José:** Now look at these bottles [holding up the two bottles]. What can you tell us about them? . . . Keith?
>
> **Keith:** You drink out of them.

José: Fine, Keith. . . . Beverly?

Beverly: They're sort of green.

José: Yes, they are. What else? . . . Lavonia?

Lavonia: They look like they're the same size.

José: Yes, indeed they certainly do. Very good, Lavonia.

In this case, José asked **description questions**, *which are open-ended questions that asks students to make an observation.*

In addition to descriptions, **comparison questions**, *open-ended questions that ask students to compare and contrast different items,* can also be used effectively to elicit responses from a number of students. Let's see how José used comparison questions to involve his students.

José: Now look at the balloons on these bottles [holding up the bottles]. How would you compare the balloons? . . . Leroy?

Leroy: One is red and the other is yellow.

José: Yes. Good, Leroy. What else? . . . Rachel?

Rachel: They look like they're made out of rubber.

Leroy: Yes, they are rubber balloons. How would you compare their sizes? . . . Michael?

Michael: They look like they're the same size.

Leroy: Good, Michael. They are the same size.

Open-ended questions are powerful tools for involving students because they invite participation in a nonthreatening way. For instance, we saw that José asked one simple question, "What can you tell us about them?" and he was able to elicit acceptable answers from three students in a matter of seconds. He did virtually the same thing when he asked students to compare the balloons. Because open-ended questions are easy to ask and also easy to answer, accomplishing equitable distribution is less demanding. It is very difficult to call on all students in a large class without asking some open-ended questions.

Asking questions that don't have specific answers may seem like a waste of time; why don't we just tell students or ask more direct questions? In addition to making equitable distribution easier, open-ended questions are useful for several other reasons:

- Open-ended questions provide an informal assessment of students' current understanding, which allows teachers to adjust their lessons to students' backgrounds.

- Because a variety of answers are acceptable, students are virtually assured of success, which in turn increases motivation. This is particularly important for students who are low achievers and who have a past history of failing to answer many of the questions teachers ask.

- Because students are assured of success, they learn to feel "safe" in question-and-answer sessions. A sense of safety also contributes to positive classroom climate and student motivation (Eggen & Kauchak, 2010).

- Open-ended questions are effective in working with cultural minorities, who sometimes lack confidence in fast-paced, convergent question-and-answer sessions.

Let's look at the first point in a bit more detail. In a class that has recently studied adjectives, the teacher displays the following sentence,

Teri moved quickly to remove the hot dish from the stove,

and asks, "What can you tell me about the different words in the sentence?" If students understand the concept, they will identify *hot* as an adjective in one of their first few responses. If they don't, it suggests that they are less sure of the concept than they should be, and the teacher needs to provide additional instruction.

The power of open-ended questioning as an instructional tool is confirmed by our experiences in schools. We have seen students who were nearly hostile and openly refused to respond at the beginning of a class period begin to volunteer responses to questions *by the end of the same class period*, all because they could see that other students were able to successfully respond. Open-ended questioning induced this change. This powerful and exciting change in students occurred very quickly. Imagine the impact of assured success on participation and motivation over an extended period of time!

Finally, open-ended questions address the objections of teachers who are reluctant to call on non-volunteers, because they are afraid to embarrass students who might be initially unable to answer. Because students are virtually assured of giving an acceptable response, they can be "put on the spot" without danger of embarrassment or anxiety. When students are put in a situation in which they know they will be called on, and are almost certain of being able to answer, their attention and motivation sharply increase.

Prompting

We know that all students should be called on as equally as possible, but we also know that targeting our lessons toward specific learning objectives is important, which means that students must supply "right answers" if the lesson is going to move toward these objectives. So you need a tool to help students when they're unable to answer successfully. **Prompting**—*cues teachers provide or other questions they ask when students are unable to correctly answer the original question*—is that tool.

When done effectively prompting can

- Create a climate of support in the classroom
- Communicate positive expectations for success
- Assist students in thinking through and answering a specific question

To see how, let's take another look at some additional dialogue from José's lesson.

José: What's in the bottles, Nikki?
Nikki: They're empty.
José: Wave your hand in front of your face, Nikki . . . What do you feel?
Nikki: . . . I . . . feel the air on my face.
José: Yes, so what do you think might be in the bottles?"
Nikki: . . . Air?

Here, José asked a question for which only one answer—air—was acceptable. However, Nikki initially said the bottles were empty. He then prompted her by asking her to wave her hand in front of her face, which led her to conclude that air was in the bottles.

In this example, José prompted with a cue. Now, let's look at another segment in which he prompted by asking additional questions.

José: So, what does that suggest about the amount of air in each? . . . Kathy?

Kathy: It's the same.

José: And how do we know, Tyrone?

Tyrone: . . .

José: What did we say about the sizes of the balloons and bottles, Tyrone?

Tyrone: They . . . were . . . equal.

José: Good. So, how do we know the amount of air in each is the same?

Tyrone: The bottles and balloons . . . are the same size.

When Tyrone was unable to answer his original question, José rephrased it by asking, "What did we say about the sizes of the balloons and bottles?" This prompt was efficient, since earlier in the lesson the class had concluded that the sizes were the same.

Prompting can also increasestudent motivation. Research indicates that *students' beliefs about their capability to accomplish learning tasks*—a concept called **self-efficacy**—is a powerful factor in increasing motivation (Schunk et al., 2008). In other words, if students believe they can succeed on challenging tasks, they develop a sense of self-efficacy, and their motivation is likely to increase.

In developing self-efficacy, student success is essential. The combination of effective representations of content, open-ended questions, and prompting is one of the most powerful tools you have for assuring success and increasing learner motivation.

Repetition for Emphasis

Some of the ideas we teach are more important than others, and effective teachersemphasize important contentto help students target essential information to learn. Repetition is one way to do this. A **repetition question** *asks students to reconsider a question or point that has been made earlier in the lesson* and is an effective way to emphasize key points. Repetition questions not only provide emphasis and focus, they also help maintain interaction between you and your students and give you a quick estimate of whether students "got it" earlier. We have all had the experience of periodically getting lost as a teacher develops a topic, and although impossible to completely avoid, this problem can be minimized with strategic repetition questions.

The following segment illustrates José's use of repetition:

José: Now, look at the balloons and bottles, everyone. What did Lavonia say about the bottles themselves? . . . Cliff?

Cliff: We drink out of them.

José: Yes, we do. . . . How do the sizes compare? Alfredo?

Alfredo: They're the same.

At this point José wanted to emphasize that the bottles were the same size and asked Cliff what Lavonia had said about them earlier. The need for repetition is illustrated by Cliff's response, "We drink out of them," suggesting that he had lost the direction of the lesson, which was to establish that the two bottles were identical except for their temperature and the air molecules inside them. Without the repetition Cliff, and probably others, would have been uncertain about where the lesson was headed.

José used repetition extensively, and some might even conclude that he used it excessively. This is a matter of professional judgment, but it is clearly better to refocus students too often than not often enough. Our experience in working with P-12 teachers suggests that repetition is often essential in helping students follow the direction of complex lessons.

Wait-Time

"What's the square root of 256? Quick!" Some of you probably answered the question immediately,whereas others fidgeted with a paper and pencil first. Still others may have seen the "Quick!" and given up immediately.

This problem is analogous to what occurs in classrooms. Many teachers, after asking a question, typically wait less than one second for a student to respond before interrupting, prompting, giving the answer themselves, or calling on another student (Rowe, 1986; Stahl, Demasi, Gehrke, Guy, &Scown, 2005). In addition some teachers tend to "cutoff" students' responses, rather than letting them think through and construct their answers fully. Both of these problems are more pronounced when students are perceived as low achievers or are members of cultural minorities.

In contrast, when you pause and give students time to think about their answers, the quality of student responses increases significantly. *The pause between a question or the pause after a student answer and a teacher interruption or response* is called **wait-time**.

A number of benefits result from lengthening wait-time. Extending wait-times to about three to five seconds improves both your effectiveness and students' performance in the following ways (Rowe, 1986; Stahl et al., 2005):

- Lessons are smoother and more focused.

- The length and quality of student responses increase, resulting in more higher-order and critical student thinking.

- Failures to respond are reduced, the variety of students participating voluntarily increases, and the number of disciplinary interruptions by the teacher decreases.

- Teachers become more responsive to students by matching the wait-time to the difficulty of the question, improving equitable distribution, and increasing participation from minority students.

- Finally, and perhaps most important, achievement increases.

Effective wait-times occur at two points in the questioning sequence, as illustrated in Figure 6.6.

Figure 6.6

Effective Use of Wait-Time

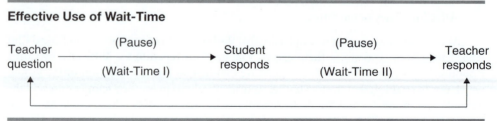

Exploring Diversity

Involving Students from Diverse Backgrounds

Questioning is one of the most effective tools youhave for communicating that you value all students and welcome them in their classrooms. Equitable distribution and prompting,when used effectively, communicate "I don't care if you're a boy or girl, minority or nonminority, or high or low achiever; I want you in my classroom. I believe you're capable of learning, and I will do whatever it takes to ensure that you're successful." In addition to conveying positive expectations, calling on all students and helping them respond successfully communicates caring and concern for student learning.

Students are sensitive to these practices. They quickly come to interpret your efforts to distribute questions to cultural minorities and nonminorities equally, for example, as an indication that both groups are expected to achieve, and the effect on classroom climate is very positive. Prompting all students as equally as possible reinforces this message.

The first wait-time pause in Figure 6.6 gives everyone in the class time to think about the question and generate the *covert responses* so important for learning. The second pause gives other students time to think about and react to the student's answer. Wait-time can be thought of as "think time," providing students with opportunities to think about the content they are learning.

As with any strategy, professional judgment is required when implementing wait-time. For example, with drill and practice, where overlearning and automaticity are desired (such as recall of multiplication facts), quick answers are desirable, and wait times should be short. On the other hand, when students are making comparisons, forming conclusions, providing evidence and demonstrating other higher-order abilities, wait times should be longer.

Classroom Questions: Additional Issues

Each of the essential questioning skills we've discussed in this chapter—frequency, equitable distribution, prompting, repetition, and wait-time—are well documented by research, as are links between effective questioning and motivation (Good & Brophy, 2008).

However there are several additional issues that often surface in classroom questioning, and we consider them in this section. They include the following:

- High-level versus low-level questions
- Questioning patterns: selecting students
- Call-outs
- Choral responses

Let's look at them.

Low- and High-Level Questions

When we discussed wait-time, we found that the kind of question influences the amount of time a teacher should wait for a response. But how does the level of your questions affect student learning? In this section we consider the benefits of low-level questions (e.g., "Who wrote *Hamlet*?) versus high-level questions ("Why is Shakespeare's *Hamlet* considered a tragedy, in the classical sense of the term?"). Let's see what research says about the issue.

Intuitively we might conclude that high-level questions are better than low-level ones because they stimulate more student thinking. However, research examining how the levels of teacher questions influence student learning, has produced mixed results(Good & Brophy, 2008). Some studies have found a positive correlation between higher-level questions and achievement, others found no relationship, and still others identified a negative correlation between the two(Good &Brophy, 2008). What explains these contradictory findings?

The answer can be found in the objectives for the lesson, the age of students, and their backgrounds. For instance, if the objective is for students to know facts such as $7 \times 9 = 63$, a high percentage of low-level questions is effective. For more complex objectives, such as understanding the impact of Columbus's discovery of the new world, higher-level questions are necessary. In addition, students with limited prior knowledge about a topic should initially be asked many low-level questions to establish a knowledge base, with the number of high-level questions increasing as their knowledge grows.

The only sensible approach to determining question levels to have a clear learning objective in mind prior to the lesson and to be alert, sensitive, and responsive to students as the lesson develops. The appropriate level of questions will then take care of itself.

This was illustrated in José's work with his students. His objective for the lesson was very clear; he knew exactly what he wanted his students to understand. The responses of the students and his objective, rather than preconceived decisions about level, guided his questioning. For example, he began his lesson with simple descriptions and then moved to higher-level questions as he asked the students to make comparisons. Then, knowing that he wanted to help students understand that the two systems were the same size, he asked a higher-level question when he asked Tyrone how they knew the amount of air was the same in each system. When he called on Tyrone, he was not thinking, "I will now ask a high-level question." Instead he was working toward his learning objective. This objective-driven flexibility is the essence of expert teacher questioning.

Selecting Students

Who should we call on when we ask a question? As you saw earlier, teachers typically call on students who volunteer, but this is less effective than calling on both volunteers and non-volunteers.

The most desirable alternative is to call on students randomly, and expert teachers manage this process by mentally monitoring whom they've called on as the lesson proceeds (Good & Brophy, 2008). As the activity develops, if you lose track of whom you've called on, you can simply ask "Who have I not called on yet?" When students are in an environment in which large numbers of questions are being asked, and you support students in their efforts to answer, being called on is desirable, and they will freely admit it if they haven't been called on (or one of their classmates will point it out). Further, a straightforward question, such as "Who haven't I called on," promotes a comfortable climate of support and open communication.

So, should you ask the question first and then call on a student, or call on a student first, before asking the question? Research suggests asking the question first is more effective, and this is the pattern we saw in José's questioning (Good & Brophy, 2008). Asking the question, pausing, and then calling on a specific student communicates that the question is meant for *all* students and everyone is expected to pay attention and think about the answer. If the teacher selects a student before asking the question, the rest of the students are less likely to generate a covert response, an essential mental operation for student learning.

However, exceptions to this rule can occur for management or motivational reasons. For example, "John, what did we say yesterday about the relationship of Hemingway's early life to his later writing?" can communicate that John ought to refrain from his conversation with a classmate or recognize that John made a comment yesterday that was especially pertinent to the topic. The fact that this sequence violates the teacher's regular one, as well as the inflection in the teacher's voice, communicates the intent of the message.

Call-Outs

A **call-out** *is an answer given by a student before the student is recognized by the teacher*. We have all been in classes in which teachers have said, sometimes pleadingly, "Now, don't shout out answers," or "Don't answer until you're called on." These are efforts to eliminate call-outs.

In general, call-outs should be prevented. This is most effectively accomplished by establishing and consistently enforcing a rule requiring students to be recognized before answering. Allowing students to respond without being called on is undesirable because call-outs usually come from higher achieving or more aggressive students in the class. These students can dominate the interaction, and slower or more reticent students learn that they won't be required to respond, their attention wanes, and learning is decreased. In addition call-outs also increase management problems and decrease the amount of time other students have to think about answers.

However, exceptions to these patterns have been found in studies with minority students and students from low socioeconomic backgrounds. With students who lack confidence and may be reluctant to respond, allowing at least some call-outs has been positively linked to increased learning (Good & Brophy, 2008).

We saw this illustrated in José's lesson. Let's take a look.

> **José:** So what do you think might be in the bottles?
>
> **Nikki:** . . . Air?
>
> **José:** Yes indeed. Good, Nikki. What was one of the characteristics of air that we've discussed?"
>
> **Jason:** It's all around us.
>
> **José:** That's right. Air is all around us. Well done, Jason. . . . Now look at the balloons on these bottles [holding the bottles up again]. How would you compare the balloons? . . . Leroy?

In this sequence José allowed Jason to interject a response without admonishing him, because Jason was a low achiever. With more confident and aggressive students, however, call-outs result in shorter thinking times and unequal opportunities to respond, both conditions that decrease achievement.

As with many instructional issues, professional judgment is essential in these situations. The ability and confidence of the student, the learning objectives for your lesson, and the general behavior of your students are all factors you should consider in deciding whether to allow a student to call out an answer.

Choral Responses

The entire class answering a question at the same time is termed **choral responding**. Choral responses are effective for practicing skills, terms, and facts that should be overlearned and available for immediate recall. It is commonly used in foreign language classes when students need to repeat words and phrases in the new language, and it's sometimes used in math classes when developing automaticity is important. José effectively used a choral response when he taught his students the term *expand.*

José:	Yes, excellent, Jill. Now, everyone, I'm going to give you another word for gets bigger. It's called expand. Everyone say expand."
Class:	EXPAND.

José was teaching a new term and wanted everyone in the class to know it.

In contrast, choral responses are inappropriate for open-ended or higher-level questions. Imagine a choral response to a question such as "Who do you think was our most effective president, and why do you think so?"

As you've seen in this chapter, skilled questioning is one of the most important abilities teachers possess. Questioning promotes student involvement, accommodates variations in students' prior knowledge, and increases motivation to learn. Becoming an expert requires practice, but if you persevere you will acquire this expertise. When you do, you will also experience the rewards that result from helping students understand ideas previously inaccessible to them.

Technology and Teaching:

Using Technology to Increase Student Involvement

When we use questioning in the classroom, our goal is to involve as many students as possible. In addition, for our questions to be effective, everyone in the class needs to attend, think about them, and formulate an answer or response. This ideal is often difficult to achieve in a classroom of 25 to 30 when students soon realize that their chances of actually being called on are slim. When we add to this the problem of calling only on volunteers, the likelihood of our questions influencing learning in *all* students diminishes. Fortunately, technology can help here.

One of the most effective, low-cost ways to encourage student involvement is also relatively low-tech: wooden popsicle sticks or tongue-depressors. Effective teachers write the names of their students on these and place them in a jar or container for easy access during question-and-answer sessions. Instead of calling only on students who have their hands up, you can use these to randomly call on students. The *random* is important; when students realize that they can be called out even if they don't have their hand up, attention (and learning) increases. The fact that everyone's name is in the jar also provides for equitable distribution, ensuring that everyone gets called on and becomes involved.

One major tactical decision is required when using this system. Should the names of students who have been called on be placed back in the jar or left out until everyone has been called? Leaving them out ensures that everyone will be called on; returning them signals that a student can be called on again, even though he or she already responded. Most teachers find that returning a students' name to the "possible" pile works best, because it encourages students to maintain involvement with the lesson and that, over time, the probability that everyone will be called increases. In addition, teachers sometimes "fudge,"silently returning a student's name to the pile without calling on them if that student has just been called on.

Student Response Systems

A second, and decidedly more high-tech, way to increase student involvement during questioning is through student response systems. Also called audience or educational response systems, or clickers, **student response systems** are forms of technology that *provide each student with a way to respond to a teacher's question so that the teacher has immediate access to students' answers through either a wired or wireless connection to each student's handheld remote responder* (Fies& Marshall, 2006). After teachers ask a question, they can immediately see whether everyone responded and what each student's response was. This not only encourages the active involvement of each student, but also provides the teacher with immediate feedback about the whole class's learning progress. No more wondering if the response of a single student (often with hand raised) is truly representative of the whole class. In addition to information about individual student's answers, these systems can also provide group data, showing, for example, how many students chose alternate responses on a multiple-choice item. This allows the teacher to respond immediately to misconceptions that have developed.

Both teachers and students like these systems (Dangel & Wang, 2008). Teachers find that students are more motivated and attentive, and the immediate feedback from *all* students provides invaluable information about a lesson's progress. Students like the system because it provides immediate feedback and helps them stay involved during lessons. These systems seem especially valuable in areas such as math and science, in which convergent answers predominate.

The systems do have drawbacks, however, with cost being a major factor. In addition they require extra work by the teacher to frame questions so that they fit into a fixed response mode, and there is a tendency when initially used to focus on lower-level fact questions (Dangel & Wang, 2008). With work, however, teachers can learn to construct questions that both challenge students and tap higher-level thinking. In addition, teachers have found that pairing these systems with opportunities to collaborate with a partner before responding combines the best of technology and the beneficial effects of social interaction.

Summary

Student Involvement: A Key to Learning and Motivation

Students must be actively involved to learn most effectively. Involving students depends on three factors: clear and precise learning objectives, high-quality representations of content, and skilled questioning by teachers.

Effective lessons begin with clear and precise learning objectives. The ways teachers choose to represent their content, and the kinds of questions they ask as they guide students through their lessons, depend on their objectives. Without clear objectives, effective lessons are virtually impossible.

High-quality representations of content are essential for involving students, because the information they need to answer teachers' questions and understand the topics is provided for them. Effective content representations contain all the information students need to understand the topic they're studying.

Effective representations exist in a variety of forms, including the actual object, pictures, demonstrations, charts and matrices, models, and vignettes and case studies. The type of representation depends on the teacher's objective.

Involving Students Through Teacher Questioning

The most effective tool teachers have for promoting involvement is questioning. Questions can be used to assess students' current understanding, increase motivation to learn, and guide students as their understanding develops. Expert teachers efficiently manage all three functions as they help students reach their learning objectives. In using questions it is essential to think about their effect on students' attention and thought processes.

Elements of Effective Questioning

Effective teachers ask many questions, use repetition to emphasize important points and make connections, direct questions equally to all students in the class, and give individuals adequate time to think about their answers. They first ask the question, pause briefly, and then call on an individual by name to answer. When students are unable to respond, or respond incorrectly, expert teachers provide cues or other questions that help students give acceptable answers.

Distributing questions equally to all students communicates that everyone, regardless of personal characteristics, background, or ability, is welcome in the classroom, should be involved, and is expected to learn. Questioning is also effective for accommodating student background differences. Open-ended questions are a particularly effective way of ensuring success, increasing student self-efficacy, and promoting student motivation.

Classroom Questions: Additional Issues

Theeffectiveness of high- versus low-level questions depends on the teacher's learning objectives. Call-outs generally detract from achievement, but in some cases a mix of choral and individual responses may be desirable. Effective use of each depends on the context of the lesson and the teacher's objective.

 *I*mportant Concepts

*P*reparing for Your Licensure Exam

We saw how José Alvarez encouraged learning by involving his students in his lesson. Let's look now at another teacher and assess the extent to which she demonstrates these same abilities. Read the following case study and answer the questions that follow.

The Power of Classroom Practice
www.myeducationlab.com

After reading this case, go to the Book Specific Resources tab in MyEducationLab, select your text, select *Preparing for Your Licensure Exam* under Chapter 6

to complete the questions that accompany the case and receive feedback on your responses.

Darren Anderson is an American history teacher discussing the events leading up to the American Revolutionary War. Pointing to a timeline above the white board, she begins, "About where are we now in our progress? . . . Anyone?"

". . . About . . . there," Adam responds uncertainly, pointing to about the middle of the 1700s on the timeline.

"Yes, good," Darren smiles. "That's about where we are. However, today I would like for us to understand what happened before that time, so we're going to back up a ways. . . . Actually, all the way to the early 1600s. When we're finished today, we'll understand that the Revolutionary War didn't just happen; there were events that led up to it that made it almost inevitable. . . . That's the most fun part of history. To see how something that happened at one time affected events at another time, . . . and even all the way to today. . . . Okay, let's go.

"We know that the Jamestown Colony was established in 1607," she continues, "and was founded by the British, but we haven't really looked that carefully at French expansion into the New World. Let's look again at the map," she says, pulling a map down in the front of the room.

"Here we see Jamestown, . . . but at nearly the same time, a French explorer named Champlain came down the St. Lawrence River and formed Quebec City here," again pointing to the map. "And, . . . over the years at least 35 of the 50 states were discovered or mapped by the French, and several of our big cities, such as Detroit, St. Louis, New Orleans, and Des Moines, Iowa, were founded by the French. It began with French fur traders and continued from there. A string of French forts were built along the Ohio and Mississippi Valleys," she continues pointing to a series of locations she has marked on the map.

"Now, what do you notice about the map, . . . or what does it suggest to us?"

After thinking a few seconds, Alfredo offers, "The French had a . . . lot of Canada, and . . . it looks like this country too . . . sort of all that," waving to the north and west on the map.

"It looks like the east was, . . . like British, and the west was like French," Troy adds.

"Yes, and remember, this was all happening at about the same time," Darren continues. "Also, the French were friendlierthan the British with the Native Americans, and the Iroquois nation, the biggest Native American group, was actually more powerful than either the French or the British at that time.

"Also, the French had what they called a seigniorial system, whereby the settlers were given land if they would serve in the military. . . . So . . . what does this tell us about the military power of the French?"

". . . Probably . . . good," Josh suggests. "The people got land if they did it,. . . I mean,. . . went in the army."

"And the Native Americans probably helped . . .'cuz the French,. . . they were friendly with the French," Tenisha adds.

"Now, what else do you notice here?" Darren asks moving her hand up and down the width of the map.

". . . Mountains?" Danielle answers uncertainly.

"Yeah, exactly," Darren smiles. "So, what doesn't that suggest? . . . Anyone?"

". . . The British were sort of fenced in . . . maybe . . . and the French were home free . . . I mean . . . they could do as they pleased. Then, the British started going . . . you know,. . . over the mountains, and they started fighting," Sarah offers haltingly.

"Anyone else . . . how do you respond to Sarah's idea?"

Amid nods, mumbles, and a few comments later, the class agrees that Sarah's suggestion makes sense.

"Now, when the French and British were fighting, why do you suppose the French were initially more successful than the British? . . . What do you think? . . . Dan?"

". . . Well . . . they had that signor . . . you know . . . system, so they were more motivated to fight, 'cuz of the land and stuff."

"Other thoughts? . . . Bette?"

". . . I think that the Native Americans were part of it. The French got along better with them, so they helped the French."

"Okay, good thinking everyone . . . now let's think about the British. . . . Let's look at some of their advantages.

"First," Darren continues, "there were more of them. There were more than a million British, and there were fewer than 100,000 French, so what ratio of British to French would there be? . . . Think about that," Darren smiles. "A million British and 100,000 French."

"That's like . . . mmm . . . 10 to one," Audrey muses.

"Good thinking, Audrey . . . yes, there were more than 10 British for every French.

"And . . . the British originally came because of religion. . . . What's an example of that? . . . Someone?"

"The Mayflower. . . . the Plymouth Colony," Yussra offers.

"Yes, good Yussra," Darren nods smiling. "So, the British came because of religion, and they brought their families. They were committed to living in this country and making new lives for themselves. The French had originally come as explorers and trappers and traders, and they weren't as committed, even though they had the seigniorial system.

"Now, what else have we found so far?" Darren asks. "Let's think about it for a minute. What was probably the biggest advantage for the British?"

". . . There were way more of them," Denisha adds.

"Good, anything else?"

". . . That stuff . . . about . . . the Mayflower,. . . like the British came 'cuz of religion, and . . . brought their families," Antonio offers.

"Okay, very good. . . . now, the British and French are fighting. Let me show you some additional information, and she then displays the following on an overhead.

"Now, look carefully at the chart. What is something you see in both these columns?" she asks, pointing to the two columns on the left.

After several seconds, Jason offers, "It says 'wars incredibly costly' in both of them."

French	British	Conflicts
Quebec 1608	Jamestown 1607	King Williams' War (1689–1697)
Fur traders	Expanded west (1689–1697)	Iroquois nation dominant
Hudson bay to Gulf of Mexico	New York center of trade and	Seven Years' War (1756–1763)
Forts on Ohio-Mississippi Valley	commerce	Washington taken prisoner in 1754
Influence waned after 1763	Wars very costly	Powerful British navy blockaded French
Population of 100,000	Colonialists taxed	Quebec falls—1759
Wars very costly	Administrative difficulty in colonies	Treaty of Paris—1763
Seigniorial system	Population of 1,000,000	

"Excellent, Jason," Darren waved enthusiastically, smiling. "Yes, it cost both of them, the British and the French, a ton of money.

"So, what do you suppose the British did about it? . . . Look at the information again."

". . . Taxed . . . the colonies?" Andrea offers uncertainly.

"Yes, that's exactly what they did. . . . Now, how do you suppose that made the colonists feel?"

"Not too good," Deon says quickly.

"Ticked 'em off," Charlie adds.

"Sure,. . . so, now let's go a little further and then think about another question. We know that the Revolutionary War happened a relatively short time after all of this. Now,. . . how might all of this have related to the Revolutionary War, or . . . if you want to think of it another way, how might the British fighting with the French and Native Americanshave contributed to the Revolutionary War? . . . I'm going to give you five minutes, and I want you to write down your best answer to that question. . . . Go ahead."

Darren watches as students begin trying to write their ideas. She sees that several of them struggle to get started and offers a brief suggestion in each case.

After about five minutes she calls again for the students' attention.

"Okay, pencils down everyone. . . . What did you come up with? . . . Devon?"

". . . Got me," Devon shrugs. ". . . I'm clueless."

"No you're not," Darren responds firmly. "You know a lot about this. . . . Let's think about it. . . . What's going on here?"

". . . They're fighting," Devon mumbles somewhat reluctantly.

"Yeah, good," Darren responds matter-of-factly. "Who are?"

". . . The British and French."

"Sure. . . . So, what do we know about the fight?"

"The Native Americans were on France's side," Belinda adds.

"Good, what else?"

"More British," Ray puts in.

"What else?"

"Cost a ton of money," Zariah offers.

"And, where did the British get the money?"

". . . Colonists," Tanyia adds.

"And how did that make the colonists feel?"

". . . Aggravated," Ricci adds.

"So, how might that have affected the Revolutionary War?"

". . ."

"Give it a try somebody. . . . Sheri, how about you?"

". . . Ahh,. . . well, if they,. . . like,. . . I mean, the colonists got sick of it,. . . you know,. . . being taxed like that,. . . maybe they would finally say,. . . like no, we ain't gonna take it any longer, so they decided to be independent,. . . or try to be."

"What do the rest of you think about that?"

Amid nods, murmurs, and comments like, "Makes sense," "I guess so," and "Looks like it," the class generally agrees with Sheri's analysis.

"The most important thing," Darren adds, "is that we're able to see how events at one time influence other events so strongly. Today, we've seen how the French and Indian Wars, as they're commonly called, influenced the American Revolutionary War.

"Now, for tomorrow, I want you to think about this. Suppose somehow, that the outcome of these wars had been different, and that the French had essentially 'won' them instead of the British. What would our lives be like today, if that had happened? I want you to write a one-page response to that question. . . . Again, the question is 'What would our lives be like today, if the French had won the French and Indian Wars?'. . . Turn that in at the beginning of class tomorrow."

Questions for Analysis

Let's examine Darren's lesson now based on the information in this chapter. In your analysis, consider the following questions. In each case, be specific and take information directly from the case study in doing your analysis.

1. Was Darren's learning objective clear? Why do you believe it was or was not?

2. What did Darren use to represent her topic for students? How effective were her representations? Explain.

3. Assess the effectiveness of Darren's questioning as a means of involving students in the lesson. Cite evidence from the case study to support your conclusion.

4. Assess Darren's activity with respect to student motivation. If you believe that the lesson might have been more motivating, offer specific suggestions for improvement.

5. How effective was Darren's lesson for students from diverse backgrounds? Be specific in your response.

 *D*iscussion Questions

1. How might the following factors influence the ideal number of questions asked in a class?
   a. Grade level
   b. Content area (e.g., math versus art)
   c. Subject-matter expertise of teacher
   d. Ability level of students
   e. Learning objectives of the lesson
   f. Place of the lesson in a unit (e.g., beginning or end)

2. With respect to using questions to informally assess student understanding, what are the advantages and disadvantages of teacher-centered questioning? What alternatives could you recommend?

3. How would the importance of questioning as a way of assessing student understanding vary with
    a. Time of school year (e.g., beginning or end)
    b. Place in a teaching unit (e.g., beginning or end)
    c. Diversity in terms of student ability
    d. Type of content (e.g., difficult or easy)

4. Why should the success rates for questions be relatively high? Are there times when this should vary?

5. Some people believe that higher-level questions encourage more learning than dolower-level ones. Why might higher-level questions be more effective than lower-level ones? In what circumstances wouldn't they be?

6. What would be the effects of the following questioning decisions with respect to lesson pace, or the tempo of a lesson?
    a. High level versus lowlevel
    b. Calling on volunteers versus calling on students randomly
    c. Wait-time
    d. Redirected questions

 *P*ortfolio Activities

1. *Questioning Frequency.* Observe or videotape two different interactive lessons. Record the number of questions asked in each minute of each lesson.
    a. How many questions were asked in each lesson (the total number of questions)?
    b. During which time in the lesson (beginning, middle, end) were the most questions asked in each lesson?
    c. In which lesson were students more attentive and involved?
    d. Which lesson was more briskly paced? How did the number of questions influence the pace of the lesson?
    e. What suggestions do you have for increasing the effectiveness of the questioning in each lesson?

2. *Success Rates.* Tape a class in which questioning plays a significant role (this might be your class or someone else's). Listen to the tape and count the number of times
    a. The original question was answered correctly.
    b. The original question was answered partially correctly.
    c. The original question was answered incorrectly.
    d. The original question elicited no response.
       Add the number of questions in *a* through *d*. Divide the number in *a* by this total. This gives you the average success rate of questions. Now respond to these questions:
    e. Was the difficulty level appropriate for this type of class?
    f. What do the numbers in *b, c,* and *d* tell you about the effectiveness of the questions? What could be done differently to make the questioning more effective?

3. *Questioning Level.* Tape a lesson in which questions play a major role. Play the tape and jot down the questions in the order they were asked. Now, classify these questions in terms of whether they are low level (knowledge and recall) or high level. What is the ratio of high to low? Is there any pattern in terms of the sequence (e.g., LLLH or LHLH)? How did the teacher use questioning level to reach his or her learning objectives? What might the teacher have done differently to use the level of questions to increase learning?

4. *Choosing a Student to Respond: Volunteers.* Tape a lesson in which volunteers are called upon to respond. Listen to the tape with a seating chart in front of you and mark the number of times different students are called on. Respond to the following questions:

   a. Were the volunteers evenly distributed in terms of ability level?
   b. Were the volunteers evenly distributed in terms of student gender?
   c. How did student location in the classroom affect participation rates?
   d. What suggestions do you have for increasing the effectiveness of the selection process?

5. *Choosing a Student to Respond: Random Selection.* Teach and tape a lesson with a questioning format, and randomly select students by using a deck of cards with the students' names to call on them. (Tell students beforehand what you are doing and why.) Analyze the tape in terms of these questions:

   a. Was this lesson harder or easier to teach than one in which you selected students in some other way?
   b. Did the pace of the lesson differ from the first? How?
   c. Comment on students' attentiveness. Was it higher or lower? How could you tell?
   d. What changes in your questioning style did you have to make to adapt to this modification?
   e. What are the advantages and disadvantages of using this method to select a student to respond?

6. *Wait-Time.* Tape yourself (or another teacher) as you use questions in a lesson and then listen to yourself and try to determine how long you wait after asking a question before calling on a student, how long you wait for a student to answer before intervening, and how long you wait for the student to complete his or her answer. Also, identify the student selected to respond and whether he or she was a high or low achiever. Then respond to the following questions:

   a. What was your longest wait-time? What type of question did it follow?
   b. What was your shortest wait-time? What type of question did it follow?
   c. What was your average wait-time?
   d. Did your wait-times differ for students of varying abilities?

   Teach and tape another lesson and consciously try to respond to any problems uncovered answering the previous questions. Were you able to do this? What difficulties did you encounter in trying to modify your wait times?

7. *Call-Outs.* Interview a teacher about the presence of or absence of call-outs in his or her room:

   a. How does the teacher feel about call-outs?
   b. What does the teacher do to encourage or discourage them?

    c. Are there ever any situations in which they allow or encourage call-outs? How will you deal with call-outs in your classroom?

8. *Choral response.* Interview a teacher about the use of choral response in his or her room.

    a. Does the teacher ever use choral response? When and why?

    b. What does he or she believe are the advantages and disadvantages of choral response?

    c. What suggestions does he or she have for maximizing the instructional benefits of choral responding? How will you use choral responding in your classroom?

To check your comprehension of the content covered in Chapter 6, go to the Book Specific Resources in MyEducationLab, select your text, and complete the Study Plan quiz. In addition to receiving feedback on your answers, a study plan will be generated from the quiz that will direct you to access Review, Practice, and Enrichment materials to enhance your understanding of chapter content.

7

Teaching and Learning in Groups

Chapter Outline	Learning Objectives
	When you've completed your study of this chapter, you should be able to
The need for social interaction in classrooms	1. Describe how social interaction facilitates learning.
■ Why social interaction works	
■ Components of effective small-group activities	
Using group work to facilitate learning	2. Explain how teachers can use the social interaction in group work to increase learning in other instructional strategies.
■ Organizing and conducting group work activities	
Cooperative learning	3. Describe how different forms of cooperative learning can be used in the classroom.
■ Cooperative learning: Getting started	
■ STAD: Student teams achievement division	
■ Jigsaw	
■ Group investigation	
Technology and Teaching:	
Using computer-mediated communication to facilitate cooperative learning	
Exploring Diversity:	
Using cooperative learning to capitalize on diversity	
Discussions	4. Describe how discussions can be used to attain both cognitive and affective goals.
■ Using discussions to promote student growth	
■ Planning for cognitive growth in discussions	
■ Promoting cognitive growth with discussions: Implementation	
■ The teacher's role	
■ Affective discussions: Promoting ethical and moral growth	
Assessing learning in social interaction strategies	5. Describe how to assess learning in different social interaction strategies.
■ Assessing cognitive achievement	
■ Assessing growth in social interaction skills	

Expert teachers know that student involvement is a critical part of classroom learning, and social interaction is one effective way to promote this involvement and increase learning. In this chapter we examine how you can use social interaction in the form of group work, cooperative learning, and discussions to increase learning in your classroom.

To begin our discussion read the following case and think about the problems that Maria Sanchez has, and how social interaction might address these problems.

Maria Sanchez, a sixth-grade teacher at Woodrow Wilson Elementary, is staring out the window of the teacher's lounge, when Terry Cummings, her friend and confidant, comes up behind her.

"Hey, what's wrong?" Terry asks. "You look like you lost your dog or something."

"Not really," Maria replies with a wry smile. "I'm just a little discouraged. I've been teaching my tail off, but I can't seem to get the kids into it. I'm putting my whole self into it, or at least I think I am, and half the class isn't even listening. They seem bored, and I hate to admit it, when they're that way, it drags me down. Any ideas?"

"Hmm . . . don't know . . . maybe . . . maybe you're trying too hard. Sounds like you're giving a hundred percent, but maybe it's in the wrong direction. I used to be 'Ringmaster Ned' too, but the rest of the circus wasn't with me," Terry replies with a sympathetic shrug.

"I'm not sure what you mean. . . . Say more. . . . I thought that's what good teaching was all about—being in front of them and giving it my all."

"Well, it is, . . . I mean, sure, we're giving our all, but, . . . and yes, . . . there are times when we need to stand up and explain and model things, but . . . if that's all you do, you know, I mean . . . if that's all *we* do, . . . no matter how enthusiastic we are, we'll lose 'em. My kids need to be doing stuff—talking, writing, working with each other. I've got some ideas if you're interested."

"Sure, can't hurt, . . . I'm sort of desperate. I'll try anything."

When people think about instruction, they often picture a teacher at the front of the room explaining, writing on the board, and asking questions. This approach can be effective for learning skills such as graphing equations in algebra; understanding concepts such as *simile, metaphor,* or *personification;* or acquiring organized bodies of knowledge, such as understanding comparisons of different authors' works.

Some goals, however, aren't met most effectively with teacher-centered, whole-group instruction. We've all heard teachers say, or perhaps even said it ourselves, "My class is capable. They just won't work." Often the problem is motivation, and motivation suffers when teachers talk too much and students listen passively. This is one reason we use teaching strategies that employ social interaction. They are motivating to students.

In other cases students won't listen to each other. They appear narrow minded and are even rude to their classmates. Their actions reflect their attitudes, values, and lack of interpersonal skills. Developing students' inclination and ability to listen, to work with their classmates on projects, and to cooperate in solving problems is an important educational goal. To reach these goals, alternatives to whole-group teacher-centered instruction are needed. This chapter describes instructional approaches designed to reach these goals.

The Need for Social Interaction in Classrooms

Both kids and adults prefer to talk than to listen—it's a natural human tendency. Many of the teaching strategies used in our classrooms, however, ask students to sit passively while teachers talk and explain. Why exactly is this kind of teaching so prevalent and how does social interaction both motivate students and increase learning? In this section we describe the role that social interaction plays in learning and—ultimately—in our teaching.

Why Social Interaction Works

The powerful role that social interaction plays in learning can be explained from three perspectives. The first of these are the developmental theories of Jean Piaget and Lev Vygotsky, who investigated how language influences development. The second explanation for the effectiveness of social interaction relates to the way people learn and the connections they make as they learn new things. The third perspective on the effectiveness of social interaction examines the motivational benefits of students working together. Let's examine each of these now.

Social Interaction and Development   From a developmental perspective social interaction promotes learning because it encourages students to re-evaluate their own views of the world.

Devon:	Look at the bugs. (*Holding a beetle between his fingers and pointing at a spider.*)
Gino:	Yech . . . Put that thing down. Besides, that's not a bug. It's a spider. (*Gesturing to the spider.*)
Devon:	What do you mean? A bug is a bug. They look the same.
Gino:	Nope. Bugs have six legs. See? (*Touching the legs of the beetle.*) He has eight legs. . . . Look. (*Pointing to the spider.*)
Devon:	So, . . . bugs . . . have . . . six legs, and spiders have eight. Hmmm?

From the perspective of Jean Piaget (1952, 1959, 1970), the Swiss developmental psychologist, Devon's equilibrium was disrupted by the discussion since he saw evidence that the beetle and spider were different, and he resolved the problem by reconstructing his thinking to accommodate the evidence. The same occurs when we share our political views with someone else and change our views in light of the conversation. In both instances, social interaction results in exposure to a different perspective, encouraging people to reevaluate and change their beliefs.

Lev Vygotsky (1978, 1986), another developmental psychologist, explains the importance of social interaction from a different perspective. He views development and learning as processes that begin on the outside and then are internalized. For example, let's see how social interaction helps a father teach his toddler how to get dressed.

"Okay, here we go. Let's get dressed so we can go visit Grandma. First, we take off your pajamas and put on your underwear. Wow, these pajamas are tight. Next we put on your shirt. There. Then your big boys, and now your pants. Look at those little doggies on the pants."

"Doggy?"

"Yes, those are doggies. Aren't they cute? Ruff, ruff! Grrr! Now we put on this sock. Then your shoe. Now you do the other one."

"Shoe?"

"Yes, that's a shoe. Wait a minute, though. What do we have to put on before the shoe? Look over here" (pointing to the sock). "That's right, first you put on your sock, then your shoe."

"Sock first?"

"Yeah, that's right. Put on your sock first, then your shoe. Atta boy!"

Through interactive dialogue embedded in activity, the father helped his son learn how to dress himself. Social interaction plays a similar role in the classroom. It provides a forum for the exchange of ideas that are first discussed externally or orally and then internalized in our minds.

As we use language to learn new concepts, our view of the world changes. For example, after we take an art or music history class, we see and hear things that we didn't know existed before. Language also allows us to share our thoughts with others, refining them in the process.

In both perspectives on social interaction—Piaget's and Vygotsky's—social interaction facilitates learning by encouraging people to listen to the views and perspectives of others. Piaget views this social interaction as a catalyst for students to reevaluate their own beliefs about the world; Vygotsky sees social interaction as a vehicle for more knowledgeable people to share their expertise with others. In both instances students learn by listening and talking.

Elaboration   When we learn, we form links between new content and ideas that are already there. **Elaboration** *makes information meaningful by forming additional links to existing knowledge*. Research on the way people learn suggests that one of the most effective ways to retain new information is to elaborate on it or restructure it and connect it to what we already know (Eggen & Kauchak, 2010). For example, note taking is most effective when we actively restructure the information in ways that are meaningful to us. In a similar way when we read, active note taking encourages us to elaborate on content and connect it to what we already know.

Social interaction facilitates elaboration in two ways. Putting our own ideas into words forces us to organize them, restructuring them so they make sense to us as well as to other people. Social interaction also encourages us to elaborate on the ideas of others, as we listen to them and connect new ideas to what we already know and believe.

Motivation   A third explanation for the effectiveness of social interaction in the classroom relates to motivation (Brophy, 2004; Schunk et al., 2008). In all-too-many classrooms, the primary mode of interaction is teacher-student, with students not only competing for the right to speak but also for the teacher's approval for a right answer. Since interaction is competitive, and one student's success decreases the chances that others will succeed, many drop out, fail to participate, or view participants as nerds or teacher's pets. Social interaction, when structured effectively, can encourage students to work together toward common learning goals.

A final thought—if social interaction is so good, why don't we just let students talk all the time? The answer is that what they talk about and how they talk about it influences learning; not all talk is equally effective for promoting learning We discuss ways of effectively structuring social interaction in the classroom through different social interaction strategies in the next sections.

To view a video clip of the effects of social interaction on learning, go to the Book Specific Resources tab in MyEducationLab, select your text, select Video Examples under Chapter 7, and then click on *Promoting Learning: The Role of Social Interaction.*

Components of Effective Small-Group Activities

Five essential elements undergird all small-group strategies (Johnson & Johnson, 2006):

- Student–student interaction
- Group goals
- Individual accountability
- Collaborative skills
- Group processing

Student-student interaction has several benefits. First, it encourages students to put their sometimes fuzzy thoughts into words. We have all said at one time or another, "I know what I'm trying to say; I just don't quite know how to say it," and the more practice students get in using language to express their ideas, the better off they are. Second, social interaction also allows for the sharing of alternate perspectives, helping students view ideas in different ways. Face-to-face interaction also allows students to co-construct knowledge, building upon the ideas of others (Eggen & Kauchak, 2010).

Group goals *refer to incentives that create a team spirit and encourage students to help one another.* This is similar to the reward that occurs on soccer or basketball teams when individuals of unequal ability work together to meet team goals. Although individual effort is important, the gauge of this effort is the team's performance.

Group goals also motivate students to help one another, which in turn gives them a stake in one another's success. Successful groups have extensive interactions focusing on content, and group goals encourage students to explain content to their teammates. Group goals also encourage students to ask for and give help. You can promote group goals by setting up incentive systems, such as free time, certificates of achievement, or even bonus points to reward students for the group's performance.

Individual accountability, another component of effective group interaction, means that *each individual in the group is held responsible for learning essential content as measured by quizzes, tests, or individual assignments.* Individual accountability can be combined with group goals when the group grade or reward is based on the average of individual members' quiz scores. Without individual accountability, the most able students in the group may do all the work, with teammates being ignored or given a "free ride."

Effective group interaction strategies also develop students' collaborative skills. *Collaborative skills* are interaction skills that students utilize in small group work, including

- Turn taking
- Listening
- Learning to disagree constructively
- Giving feedback
- Reaching consensus
- Involving every member in the group

These collaborative skills are some of the most important skills learned in group interaction activities and often have to be taught and developed (Berk, 2010).

Group processing encourages members to reflect on the effectiveness of their group. This not only makes the group more effective, it also helps individuals understand how their actions contribute to the workings of the group.

Having examined the characteristics of effective small-group activities, we turn now to a discussion of how teachers can use group work to increase learning in their classrooms.

Using Group Work to Facilitate Learning

Because of typical interaction patterns in crowded classrooms, quiet or less confident students often fail to stay involved. In large classrooms students soon learn that the odds of being called on are small, and less attentive ones often drift off. Group work is one strategy that you can use to promote the participation of all students.

A kindergarten teacher is teaching her students basic shapes. After explaining and illustrating each with cardboard shapes, she divides the class into groups of two and asks each group to find examples of circles, squares, and triangles in their own classroom. When the class comes back together, students share their examples.

A middle school math teacher is teaching how to solve word problems involving areas of different geometric shapes. She divides the class into teams of four students and asks each team to solve the next few problems. Students in each team take turns explaining their solutions to the problems. Later the teams take turns at the board explaining to the whole class how they solved the different problems.

A senior high English teacher is reviewing literary devices such as simile, metaphor, personification, and alliteration. He assigns a scene from Shakespeare's *Julius Caesar* and asks students in groups of two to identify as many of these devices as they can. The whole class compares the groups' findings after 15 minutes.

Group work *involves students working together in a group small enough so that every-one can participate on a clearly assigned task that typically supplements other instruction.* The purpose of group work is to provide opportunities for each student to become actively involved in the task at hand and increase his or her learning through social interaction.

To understand how student group work works, let's consider the teaching episodes at the beginning of this section. In each the teacher presented a cognitive task to students that built upon and reinforced lesson content. In each the teacher broke the class into manage-able groups and required that each member become actively involved in discussing the learning task at hand. Finally, the teacher provided feedback by discussing the products of the groups. The combination of these elements—focus on lesson content, active interactive involvement, and feedback—made group work effective.

Let's examine more closely how teachers can design effective lessons using group work.

Organizing and Conducting Group Work Activities

A major goal of group work is to provide opportunities for all students to become actively involved in the learning task. The assignment of the task by the teacher provides cognitive focus; the fact that the task is done within small groups of students provides opportunities for student interactions, which can be both instructionally and motivationally beneficial.

Effective use of group work requires careful planning and organization to ensure that the task and the interactions contribute to learning. If the process isn't well organized, a great deal of instructional time is lost in the transitions to and from group work. Goals and directions to students need to be very clear to prevent the activities from disintegrating into aimless "bull sessions."

Guidelines for planning and organizing effective group work activities include the following:

- Train students in group work with short, simple tasks. Have students practice moving into and out of the groups quickly.

- Seat group members together prior to the group work activity so the transition from the whole-class activity to student groups and back again can be accomplished with a minimum of disruption.

- Give students a clear and specific task to accomplish in the groups.

- Specify the amount of time students have to accomplish the task (and keep it short). Five minutes is usually the maximum, and teachers should monitor learner progress carefully.

- Require that students produce a product as a result of the group work.

Effective use of student groups requires that all of the elements are employed. For instance, seating students together prevents loss of instructional time in transitions. Clear directions, a specific and short time allotment, a required written product, and monitoring all help keep students on task and academically focused.

The process of repeatedly moving back and forth from group work to whole-class activities requires considerable logistical planning. One way to manage it is to provide a signal such as flipping the lights off and on or a clacker that makes a noise loud enough for all to hear. Another is to raise your hand as a signal to reconvene and teach your students to stop talking when they see the signal.

Working in Pairs: Introducing Group Work   The simplest form of group work involves organizing students in pairs and giving each pair a task. This strategy, also called **think-pair-share** encourages students to *think about content, compare their thoughts with those of their partner, and share their answer with the whole group* (Kagan, 1999). Both the elementary and the high school teachers in the episodes at the beginning of this section used this strategy in their lessons.

Simple collaboration in pairs has several positive features:

- It is easy to implement; students can learn to work with one other person more easily than with a larger group.

- Working in pairs encourages each member of the pair to contribute, and the likelihood of one or more members of a group being "left out" or dominating is less than it would be in larger groups.

- Involvement is high when pairs are working, and teachers have to call on only half as many students as they would during a whole-class discussion, since each is speaking for a pair.

Another strategy that employs working with groups of two is called *pairs check* (Kagan, 1999). With **pairs check**, *pairs of students are provided with handouts containing problems* *with specific right and wrong answers* (e.g., math, capitalization, or punctuation problems in English), *which one member of the pair solves and the second member checks.* After every two questions or problems each pair checks with another group to compare answers. The class can then discuss areas of disagreement or confusion after all the groups have had a chance to complete the assignment.

Working with Larger Groups   Collaboration in pairs is easiest to manage, and it is a good place to begin when you are first introducing your students to group work. There are times, however, when you may want students to work in groups of three, four, or five. Groups larger than five are unwieldy and are generally not recommended.

The primary advantage in having students work in groups of three or more is the opportunity to develop collaboration and social skills, in addition to the cognitive goals of the lesson. The middle school math teacher used teams of four for her group work activities. An important difference between learning in and out of school is that in-school learning is primarily individual, whereas out-of-school learning is usually collaborative. Giving students practice in collaborating while they work on cognitive tasks provides opportunities to practice social interaction skills in larger groups.

Combining Pairs   *Combining pairs is a group work strategy that begins with pairs and combines these into larger groups of four; it retains the simplicity of a single pair yet promotes the social skill development of larger groups.* Our middle school math teacher employed this strategy when she had students first solve each problem individually, then share and explain the answer with a partner, and then had partner teams compare their answers. Combining pairs is effective for group work on comprehension and application activities in either a seatwork or class discussion setting. Let's look at its implementation in a seatwork arrangement first.

Combining Pairs with Seatwork.   The strategy is organized and implemented in the following steps:

1. Student pairs are formed.

2. Pairs are combined into groups of four. The groups of four can be seated together, such as illustrated in Figure 7.1.

Figure 7.1

Seating Arrangement for Combined Pair Activity

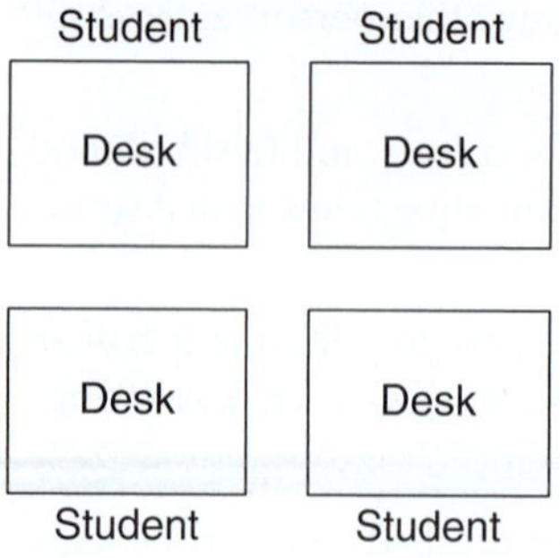

Seating pairs side-by-side facing the opposite pairs facilitates social interaction.

3. Students are given a series of exercises with convergent answers, such as solving math problems, identifying parts of speech in sentences, or applying a grammar or spelling rule.

4. Individuals respond to an exercise.

5. Partners compare their answers.

6. When the partners cannot agree on the correct answer, they confer with the other pair.

In classes not divisible by four, one or more groups of five can be arranged, and in those groups, a pair and a trio work together. As with all forms of group work, this arrangement requires careful monitoring to prevent individuals from deferring to their partners or "free-loading," by merely copying their partners' answers.

Combining Pairs in Interactive Questioning. Combining pairs in interactive question-and-answer sessions is a group work process that can effectively promote learning in teacher-centered lessons. It is similar to combining pairs with seatwork. The steps in organizing and implementing this instructional strategy are as follows:

1. Groups of four are formed.

2. Group members are assigned a number from one to four.

3. The teacher asks the class a question with a convergent answer, such as the solution to a problem, the longitude of a designated city, or the correct punctuation of a sentence.

4. Group members are responsible for seeing that all members of their group know the answer and are able to explain *why* that answer is correct, so that any member of the group can explain it to the whole class.

The teacher then calls a number from one to four, and the students in the groups with those numbers raise their hands. The teacher calls on an individual to answer and *explain* why their answer is correct.

A simple incentive system can also be implemented with this process. If the individual answers correctly, every student in his or her group gets a point. If the student provides an adequate explanation, each member gets an additional point.

The incentive system can be made more complex and competitive among groups if the teacher chooses to do so. For example, one group could be called on to answer the question, and a second could be asked to provide the explanation, which would allow two different groups to earn a point. If a group member is unable to answer or explain, a different group would have the opportunity to respond and earn the point.

This process is relatively simple and promotes high levels of student involvement, even in large classes. For example, a class of 33 would have seven groups of four and one group of five. In a typical question-and-answer session, each group would have several opportunities to respond and earn points. Students of all ability levels are motivated, because the whole group is rewarded if the individual called on is able to correctly respond. High achievers explain and even tutor others in their group who are struggling to understand, and the lower achievers experience success and the rewards of contributing to their group.

Group Work with Higher-Level Tasks Group work can also be used to involve students in higher-level learning tasks such as problem solving or inquiry. However, when this is done, the teacher needs to ensure that all members of the group participate; lower achievers or less aggressive members of the pairs often defer to the higher achievers or more aggressive partners, resulting in reduced involvement by less able students.

Although there is no simple answer to this problem, teachers can take several steps to encourage equal participation. First, require that students solve each problem individually before conferring with their partners, explaining the rationale for this action to students. Second, monitor the groups to be sure they are following your directions, encouraging equal participation as you circulate around the room. Third, strategically call on non-volunteers in groups, reminding the class that both members of the group need to understand how to solve the problems.

We next examine cooperative learning, a more structured and complex form of group work that can be effective for promoting students' learning and development.

Cooperative Learning

Cooperative learning *is a general term that describes a set of instructional strategies, all of which have specific structures and are designed to teach content and develop interpersonal skills.* Cooperative learning strategies typically last longer than the general group work strategy discussed in the previous section, and cooperative learning uses intact groups to accomplish teachers' goals. In the next section we describe some logistical issues that you'll face when first implementing cooperative learning.

Cooperative Learning: Getting Started

"I don't get it. What are we supposed to do?"

"I can't hear; it's too noisy."

"Teacher, Ken won't share the materials."

Successful cooperative learning activities don't just happen. Instead, they are the result of thoughtful planning and preparation. When students have had limited experience with cooperative learning, you need to make a special effort to introduce it to them.

Teachers implementing cooperative learning strategies in their classes identify the following potential problem areas:

1. Noise
2. Failure to get along
3. Misbehavior
4. Ineffective use of group time

Let's see how you can address each of these potential problem areas.

Noise   Noise is often a healthy by-product of productive student interaction. When implementing cooperative learning strategies, we should expect our classrooms to be slightly noisier, because students are working and talking in small groups. Excessive noise, however, can interfere with group functioning, frazzle the teacher, and bother other classrooms.

Student energy and enthusiasm are the most common causes of noise in cooperative learning activities. Students become so involved in their interactions with other team members that they don't realize that noise is becoming a problem.

Some teachers deal with the problem by discussing and modeling the social skill "using quiet voices," which encourages students to work together yet keep the noise level to a minimum. Other teachers use signals, such as flicking the light switch, as cues to remind students to lower the noise level.

Failure to Get Along   Learning to work together effectively doesn't automatically happen; it's a social skill that needs to be developed (Berk, 2010). Remember that in many of their learning activities students sit quietly, isolated from one another. Cooperative learning requires that students talk, listen, and help one another learn. The process is often made more complicated by the heterogeneous nature of groups.

Effective teachers use the following cooperative team-building exercises to develop students' interactive skills:

1. *Name learning.*   Allocate some time at the beginning of group formation for students to learn one another's names. Make this a game and give an oral "quiz" in quiz other team members have to name each of their partners.

2. *Interview.*   Extend the name-learning exercise to one in which students interview one another about interests, hobbies, favorite foods, or something that no one else knows about them. Have students present these in a short introduction to the rest of the class.

3. *Team name or logo.*   Encourage students to develop a name for their group. In doing this stress broad participation, consensus building, and respect for individual rights.

Students who are social isolates or who protest being assigned together can be particular problems. To protect quiet students, have a classroom rule that requires students to treat one another with courtesy and respect, and *enforce the rule consistently*. An important goal for cooperative learning in particular, and school in general, is for students to learn to treat one another fairly. Breaking this rule should be the one cardinal sin in your class. With effort and persistence you can enforce this rule, and many of the problems associated with students wanting to work only with their friends will disappear.

Misbehavior   Cooperative learning strategies are designed to be interactive and often the freedom and lack of structure results in increased student management problems (Emmer et al., 2009; Evertson et al., 2009). Solutions to this potential problem are specific task demands and agenda setting, accountability, and careful student monitoring.

Many management problems occur because of unclear student roles and expectations (e.g., "What are we supposed to do?"). Before you break students into groups, make sure that all students know what they are expected to do. Don't just describe student tasks; directly model them with the same learning materials students will be using. Student accountability also helps create structure and minimize management problems. When students know there is a product expected or a quiz that will be given, their efforts become more focused on the learning task at hand. Once students are in groups, monitor the groups by circulating around the room and assisting individual groups.

Ineffective Use of Group Time   Teacher monitoring, an effective tool against misbehavior, can also help combat wasted time. Stand back from time to time and observe the whole classroom. Which groups are working well? Which students are busy and which ones are dawdling or playing? Spend extra time with groups that need extra help. Make sure that groups that do work effectively are rewarded with group recognition and make a special effort to call the whole class's attention to the link between group work and group performance. This works on the individual level and should also work at the group level.

Let's look now at three types of cooperative learning instructional strategies.

STAD: Student Teams Achievement Divisions

One of the most well-known types of cooperative learning is called **Student Teams Achievement Divisions (STAD)**, which *uses four- or five-member, multi-ability teams to master basic skills.* Let's see how Maria Sanchez uses STAD to teach spelling and vocabulary and remedy her motivation problems.

Maria begins her Friday's language arts class by passing back the vocabulary and spelling quizzes from the previous day. As she circulates around the room, she overhears the following comments,

"Uh oh, another D."

"I can't do this."

"I hate spelling."

Several students don't say anything; instead they look at their papers, crumple them up, and throw them in their desks.

"I can't really blame them; over one-third failed the quiz," she acknowledges to herself. And, it seems it's the same third that has problems every week.

Recalling her conversations with Terry Cummings, she decides to try something different. She calls Terry on Saturday, and the two of them talk for an hour and a half. Based on Terry's suggestions, she goes to work. Although it takes most of her weekend, she feels she is ready on Monday.

With renewed enthusiasm, she begins Monday's class by saying, "I know we've been having problems with our spelling and vocabulary quizzes, and I've decided it's time to try something different. I know everyone can learn this information, so I've designed a different kind of activity to help you. We're going to help each other learn this information, and I'll show you how."

With that she breaks the class into groups of four, explains how each group is a team, and how they are to work as a team and help one another learn. She has the teams move their desks together and gives each team five minutes to decide on a team name.

She then explains another new feature by saying, "We're going to have some competition in here, and it's the best kind of competition there is. You all are going to be competing with yourselves. If your quiz score this week is above your average, you are going to earn 'improvement points' that contribute to your team score. If your whole team improves, you will be eligible for additional rewards. You'll all see how it works when we get started."

Next she goes over the spelling and vocabulary words as she normally does on Monday, explaining their definitions and helping students understand the structure of each word. Then she asks each student to take out a sheet of paper for a pretest, similar to the actual test they'll receive on Thursday. She explains that the pretest isn't for a grade but is designed to help each student find out what words he or she knows or doesn't know.

After they take the quiz, students exchange papers and grade each other's. Then Maria passes out an envelope and four sets of different-colored flash cards to each group. She explains how each set is for a different student in the group and that each student is to write the definition and correct spelling of each word that he or she missed to study in class on Tuesday.

She begins Tuesday's language arts class by reminding students of the new seating arrangement. Each student then chooses a partner from within the group for that day and the next. As Maria circulates around the room, students take turns helping each other either spell the word or provide the definition. Maria reminds them that they are finished only when *all* the members of their teams know the spellings and definitions perfectly. Some pairs do this very effectively, whereas others need extra guidance from Maria on helping each other.

On Thursday they take the quiz as usual. She is struck by their comments as they leave the class.

"Easy, Miss Sanchez. Piece of cake."

"Miss Sanchez, I think I got all of them right."

Even Randy, who pretends to dislike anything academic admits, "It was okay. I think I did all right."

At lunchtime, rather than joining the other teachers, she decides to score the papers to see how they did.

"Terrific?" she thinks as she records the last score in her grade book. "No, not quite. Some of the students are still struggling, but more than 90 percent of the class got a B or better and only two students failed."

STAD: An Overview STAD is a widely applicable teaching strategy that teachers use to teach a range of topics, some of which are described in Table 7.1. Common to each of these is content that is convergent and has a right and wrong answer.

When using STAD, teachers initially present the content or skill as they normally would. For example, if you're teaching the concepts *insect* and *arachnid*, you might introduce the topic using a direct instruction strategy as discussed in Chapter 8. Then, rather than work on the concept or skill individually, such as an assignment asking students to identify additional examples or the essential characteristics of insects, students collaborate on the assignments in a structured group setting. When they understand the content, an individual assessment is administered and scored by the teacher, and the scores are used to calculate improvement points (which we'll discuss shortly). These are averaged for each team, and teams earning a specified number of improvement points are offered group rewards or recognitions (e.g., free time, pictures on the bulletin board, or certificates).

Table 7.1 **Applications of STAD in Different Curriculum Areas**

Subject Area	Examples of Topics
Language arts	Capitalization rules Rules for using apostrophes Punctuation rules
Math	Adding fractions Solving word problems Simplifying expressions
Science	Facts about the solar system Balancing chemical equations Understanding concepts, such as *insect, crustacean*, or *arachnid*
Social studies	State and national capitals Longitude and latitude problems Climate regions throughout the world
Health	Parts of body systems Characteristics of different drugs

Table 7.2 Steps in Planning and Implementing STAD Activities

Planning

1. Identify content or skills to be mastered.
2. Plan large-group presentation and seatwork materials similar to planning for any topic.
3. Plan for assigning students to groups.
4. Plan for improvement points.
5. Plan for group rewards.

Implementation

1. Introduce and explain procedures.
2. Provide initial instruction on target skill or content.
3. Divide students into groups and distribute worksheet materials.
4. Assign students to pairs and use team study to ensure mastery of content.
5. Monitor groups for active involvement of all members.

Assessment

1. Administer quiz or test as you normally do.
2. Score and assign improvement points.
3. Recognize team achievement and provide feedback about different groups' performance.

Planning STAD Activities   The teacher's actions in planning and implementing STAD activities are summarized in Table 7.2 and discussed in the sections that follow. As we see in Table 7.2, planning for STAD activities is similar to planning for any instruction. In addition, however, STAD requires careful planning for the cooperative elements of the process, together with designing a system for improvement points and group rewards.

Assigning Students to Groups.   In organizing cooperative learning activities you should attempt to place students in groups of four that have an approximately equal mix of high, medium, and low achievers and are balanced in terms of gender and cultural backgrounds. This heterogeneity is important and *students should not be allowed to select the members of their groups.*

Assigning students to heterogeneous groups is important for several reasons. One is the ability imbalance that student self-selection creates; brighter students tend to select brighter students as members of their group, causing imbalances in the overall groups. Student self-selection also tends to create homogeneous groups in terms of gender and ethnicity, robbing students of valuable opportunities to learn about students different from themselves. Finally, allowing students to select group partners can also lead to management problems that result from students talking and playing with friends rather than working.

Team composition can be changed periodically, such as after four or five weeks, to allow students to work with other classmates and to give students on low-scoring teams a chance for increased success.

Implementing STAD Learning Activities   As you can see in Table 7.2, after introducing and explaining procedures, STAD activities begin with regular whole-class instruction designed to provide an informational base. However, in place of independent practice, students then become involved in *team study*, which allows students to interact and help one another.

Team study structures the interaction in the cooperative learning groups and requires you to

1. *Prepare work sheets.* Work sheets should require direct application of the concepts, principles, or skills taught in the lesson. Answers to the items on the work sheets must also be prepared to provide feedback to students.

2. *Arrange the room so groups can work together.* This can be done by having teammates move desks together or meeting at team tables. During the first session, let students select a team name. Teach students how to talk with one another in quiet voices just above a whisper.

3. *Identify pairs.* Within each team of four students, identify pairs who will work together on the new skill.

4. *Hand out two work sheets per team.* Only two are given to encourage students to work together. Each person individually works the problems or answers the questions and checks with his or her partner. If they disagree, they should present their arguments and resolve the problem themselves. If they can't settle the disagreement, they confer with the other pair on their team. If the entire team of four cannot resolve the disagreement, then—and only then—they can ask the teacher for help. (To emphasize that the work sheets are for studying and not merely to be filled out and handed in, Slavin [1995] recommends including answers with the work sheets. Teachers, however, report more success when the answers are not included.)

5. *Clarify assignment.* Emphasize that students are finished studying only when they are certain that everyone on their team understands and can explain each of the items on the work sheet.

6. *Teacher role.* Circulate among the teams, promoting cooperation and offering encouragement and praise.

Teachers have found it useful to place the following information on a poster, discuss it with the class, and leave it up for reference:

- Group memberships for different teams
- Location in the room for different teams
- Procedures for obtaining and turning in materials
- Time frames

Spending time on logistics at the beginning of cooperative learning lessons lays the foundation for smoothly functioning groups later on.

Assessment and Grading. After team study is completed, students are given a quiz that measures their understanding of the content. Students take the quiz individually, and the quiz is scored as it normally would be. The quiz should parallel the work sheet, but identical items should be avoided to prevent students from merely memorizing the information. Improvement points, which are based upon the extent a student improves from previous quizzes, are then calculated and team rewards are given.

Jigsaw

In addition to learning basic facts, skills, and concepts, cooperative learning strategies can also be adapted to help students learn organized bodies of knowledge. Jigsaw is a cooperative learning strategy that assigns students to groups and asks each student to become an "expert" on one aspect or part of an organized body of knowledge. These "experts" then are responsible for teaching other team members, all of whom are then held accountable for all the information covered by each member. Let's see how Jigsaw works in a middle school social studies class.

Tom Harris is passing back tests from a unit on Early Americans on the North American Continent. As he finishes, he notices that there are still five minutes of class time, so he calls the class together. "Excellent job on this test! You all worked hard and I could tell, because it showed up on your scores. Class, we have only a few minutes, but I'd like to say a few words about our next unit of study. The topic is early explorers and we'll be looking at the explorers from Europe who helped discover and explore not only our country, but other countries in North and South America. Who remembers one of these early explorers? Anyone? Think now, you've studied these before. . . . Sal?"

". . . How about Christopher Columbus?"

"Good, Sal. Any others? . . . Sal, did you have something else you wanted to say?"

"Yeah. Do we have to study this stuff again? We've done it so many times and it's boring."

"I know you've studied this before . . ."

Just then the bell rings and Tom concludes by saying, "Let's continue this on Monday. Everybody have a good weekend. No homework. See you then!"

As Tom thinks about this class during his planning period, he shakes his head, thinking, "The kids are right. . . . This chapter is a little dry. But they need to know this material. But how to get them involved and excited? . . . Hmmm?"

The next Monday Tom begins his American History class by saying, "I thought quite a bit about our new unit over the weekend. . . . Sal, you'll be interested to know that I listened to you on Friday. You probably *have* studied this information before, but I'm not sure you learned it in an organized way. That's important because we're going to use this information later on when we study other topics.

"To learn this material we're going to try something different. We're going to form into teams of four, and each team member is going to become an expert on one group of explorers. Then that student will teach the other team members to get them ready for the test. To help us organize the information I've constructed the following sheets."

With that he passes out the following chart.

Names	Reasons for Places	Dates	Exploring	Accomplishments
Spanish				
Portuguese				
English				
French				

"I've divided the class into eight different teams of four," he continues, "and each of you will be responsible for one of these groups of explorers. To help you put the information into the charts, I've gathered some other books that you can use. On Thursday the experts from each group will get together to check their information. That means all of the people studying the Spanish explorers will get together to review their findings. The same for the other groups. On Friday and Monday we'll go back to our groups and each of you will share your information with other team members—you'll be the expert and each of you will teach the other students. Then we'll take our quiz on Tuesday.... Questions?... Maria?"

"Who gets which topic in the group?"

"Good question. That's the first thing you need to decide when you get into groups. Now I'd like Group 1 to come up here and pull your seats together. That will be Xavier, Melissa, Brad, and Tanya. Group 2..."

Jigsaw *is a cooperative learning strategy that uses task specialization to make individual students "experts" on a particular area or topic.* It is similar to STAD in two respects. First, students work cooperatively and are held accountable for their learning with a test or quiz at the end of the unit of study. Second, students are mixed according to ability, gender, and cultural background, as they are with STAD.

Jigsaw differs from STAD in three ways, however. First, the goals of instruction are not specific facts, concepts, or skills, but rather students' understanding of the interconnections between ideas—organized bodies of knowledge. Second, the source of information is different. When using STAD the teacher presents new information, whereas with Jigsaw students rely primarily on texts, books, and the Internet.

A final difference relates to the idea of task specialization, from which the strategy gets its name. Each member of a Jigsaw learning group becomes an expert on a particular topic and uses this expertise to teach other members. When groups work together, the different parts of the "jigsaw" puzzle fit together to make a coherent picture. This task specialization is important because it promotes interdependence; each student must depend on his or her partners to learn the information. For teams to do well on the quiz, individual students must work and pull together as a group. When this occurs, students can see tangible evidence of their cooperative efforts.

The steps involved in using Jigsaw in the classroom are summarized in Table 7.3.

Table 7.3 Steps in Implementing Jigsaw II

Planning

1. Identify an area of study requiring students to understand interconnected or organized
2. bodies of information that can be broken down into subtopics.
3. Divide the content area into three or four roughly equal subtopics that will allow different students to specialize in their study.
4. Locate resources (e.g.,Websites, textbooks, reference books, encyclopedias) that students can use to study the topic.
5. Develop expert worksheets or charts that structure students' study efforts and ensure that students will learn essential information.
6. Divide students into heterogeneous groups.

Table 7.3 **Continued**

Implementation

1. Introduce and explain procedures and divide students into groups.
2. Hand out worksheets or charts and explain how they are to be used to guide individual study and group teaching.
3. Monitor study in the different groups.
4. Convene expert groups (use groups of six or smaller) to discuss and compare information.
5. Monitor students as they teach their topic to other members of the group.

Assessment

1. Administer quiz or test as you normally would. Make sure quiz covers all topics and encourages students to interrelate information across topics.
2. Score, using improvement points.
3. Recognize team achievements and provide feedback about group performance.

A key to the effectiveness of Jigsaw is the expert work sheets or charts that students use. Typically, students—on their own—won't be able to identify key points of information. It is essential that you organize and structure the content to guide students' study and work with their peers. If the expert study guides are disorganized and disjointed, student learning suffers.

Group Investigation

Karen Selway is enjoying a good year with her third graders. Virtually all have made major progress on their basic skills, and she feels good about the foundation she has laid in reading and math. But she still wants them to work on their writing and library skills and wants to give them experience in handling a large group project.

After their return from lunch on Monday afternoon, she begins by saying, "Class, today we're going to begin a new unit of study. And this time rather than everyone learning the same thing, each of you will have a chance to read and learn about something that you're specifically interested in. When I tried to think of a topic that we all could study, I asked myself, 'What's something that every third grader in my class likes?' Guess what I decided? Think for a minute while I put this word on the board."

PETS

She could tell from the wiggles and excited talking that she had guessed correctly. She then brainstorms with the group about different pet topics. After considerable discussion the class decides to pursue the following topics:

Dogs	Bunnies and Hamsters
Cats	Fish
Birds	Other Pets (Turtles, Hermit Crabs, Snakes)

Students individually decide which topic they want to investigate, and Karen asks them to list several kinds of pets they are interested in learning more about and uses this information to group them together into topic groups that night.

When the students come to class the next day, she has stacks of pet books from the public library on tables at the back of the room. She also has the names of different students divided into groups on the basis of their interest. There are two groups of four each for both dogs and cats because of the high interest in these topics; other groups have between three and five members. After a general overview of each group's responsibilities and procedures, she breaks the class into groups and has them begin researching their topics.

As she circulates around the room, a number of questions surface:

"What do we do first?"
"Where do we find out about the pets?"
"Who is supposed to do what?"

She has anticipated most of these questions and when they seem common to all the groups, she calls the class together and discusses them. Other questions such as "Do we want to report on all the different kinds of dogs?" are particular to an individual group; when Karen encounters these, she sits down with each group to help the members work through it.

For the next two weeks her students spend their time reading books, going to the school library, visiting pet stores, interviewing people who own pets, and compiling a report on the room's computers, complete with pictures and posters. They also consult the following alternate sources of information:

- The Internet

- Videotapes, videodiscs, and CD-ROMs

- Textbooks from other classes or levels

- Encyclopedias and other reference books

- Resource people (e.g., veterinarians, pet store owners).

On Pet Day they invite parents and the principal to come in and visit the different groups that are set up in different places around the room. Each member of the team is assigned responsibility to talk about one aspect of the report. On the next day Karen helps the class pull together all the information by using the following chart:

Pet	Care and Cost	Feeding	Advantages	Disadvantages
Dogs				
Cats				
Birds				
Fish				
Other Pets				

Analyzing Group Investigation   This was an example of **group investigation**, *a cooperative learning strategy that promotes group planning and inquiry.* Like STAD and Jigsaw, it places students into cooperative groups to learn about some topic, but it differs in that the focus is relatively less on content goals and more on inquiry skills.

Group investigation is less structured than the other strategies you've studied, and this lack of structure has advantages and disadvantages. Group investigations have the advantage of giving students the chance to wrestle with ill-structured tasks, which are the kinds of problems we face in real life. Seldom are we presented with

Table 7.4 Strategies for Teaching Learning Strategies in Group Investigation

Teaching Strategy	Example
Modeling	"Class, I've had several students ask about how to outline your reports. Let's look up on the board and I'll show you how you might do it with the topic of horses."
Think-alouds	"We're encountering some problems in finding our topics in the encyclopedia. Let's go over to the encyclopedia and brainstorm some words that might help us find our topics."
Examples	"There have been some questions about what kinds of pictures to put on your bulletin boards. Let me show you some examples of one's done last year. Remember, you don't have to do it just like these. They're simply designed to give you some ideas."

situations in which we are told what to learn and how to learn it. Instead, we're required to first clarify and then structure problems before we solve them (Eggen & Kauchak, 2010).

This can be challenging for students. Some get lost when first encountering this lack of structure. Karen dealt with this issue both individually and in whole-class discussions. Teachers using group investigation for the first time should anticipate these fits and starts.

One way to deal with these problems is to use teacher-directed strategies such as modeling, think-alouds, and the liberal use of examples. Examples of these strategies applied to Karen's class can be found in Table 7.4.

Implementing Group Investigation In implementing group investigation, the teacher's role changes from information disseminator to facilitator and resource person. As a facilitator the teacher circulates around the room helping students in different groups work together. As a resource person the teacher helps students understand and structure the learning task, as well as helping them access resources available to them. The specific steps involved in planning and implementing group investigations can be found in Table 7.5.

Table 7.5 Steps in Implementing Group Investigations

Planning

1. Identify a common topic that will serve as a focal point for the class as a whole.
2. Catalog or gather resources that students can use as they investigate the topic.

Implementation

1. Introduce the general topic to the class and have students identify specific subtopics that individual groups will investigate.
2. Divide students into study groups on the basis of student interest and heterogeneity.
3. Assist students in cooperative planning regarding goals, procedures, and products.
4. Monitor student progress, assisting students to work effectively in groups.

Assessment

1. Use group presentations to share information gained.
2. Provide individual and group feedback about projects, presentations, and group effectiveness.

Technology and Teaching

Using Computer-Mediated Communication to Facilitate Cooperative Learning

Technology is changing the way teachers teach and students learn. Perhaps nowhere is this change more dramatic than the Internet. The Internet, which has changed the way we communicate with others, is also an effective source of information on a variety of topics (Roblyer & Doering, 2010). Through the Internet students can not only access information from a vast array of sources, but can also interact with other students across the country and around the world.

Technology as an Information Source

One way that technology can support cooperative learning is as an information source. Through the Internet students can access millions of sites of information displayed in hypermedia format. Search engines, sites on the Internet that students can use to locate topics of interest, make the process of information access quick and efficient.

Technology can also be used to gather and share raw data. For example, in one project, NGS Kids Network, funded by the National Geographic Society, middle school students studied the problem of water pollution (Bradsher & Hagan, 1995). They gathered water samples from nearby reservoirs and tested them for acidity and other water pollutants. They then shared their data with other sites across the country, looking for patterns and asking questions about other sites' data: "In essence students and teachers explore science by doing what scientists do; they participate in a scientific community devoted to learning about the world" (Bradsher & Hagan, 1995, p. 41).

Technology Facilitates Student Interaction

When we think about student interaction, we typically envision learners talking face to face in cooperative learning or discussion groups. This face-to-face communication has definite advantages in terms of both ease of communication and motivation. However, computer-mediated communication through e-mail and the Internet provides opportunities for students to communicate and work with students thousands of miles away through electronic mail.

Students in one fifth-grade classroom are engaged in a research project on pets. As one source of data they interviewed their classmates about their pets. Then they put the information on a computer and shared this data with other students around the country. One class wrote back to another, "We would like to know more about your pet bear. . . . Where does the bear stay? How much food does the bear eat in a week?" (Julyan, 1989, p. 33)

In investigating the topic of pets through computer-mediated communication, students wrestled with the problem of definitions ("Is an ant a pet?") and tried to answer questions such as "Do dog owners in warm climates have more short-haired dogs?" and "Do cat owners tend to have more pets than dog owners?" Through a computer network, students were able to gather data from other locations and experience the process of doing real investigation in their own classrooms.

Through the Internet, students

■ Are provided access to remote data sources

■ Can collaborate on group projects with students at different locations

■ Can send their work to other students for evaluation or response

Teachers we've worked with who have used computer-mediated communication in their teaching have found it to be both motivating and challenging.

Exploring Diversity

Using Cooperative Learning to Capitalize on Diversity

In addition to learning content, cooperative learning can also help students learn about one another and develop their interpersonal skills. When groups are mixed by ethnicity, gender, and ability, the strategy can result in improved attitudes toward different ethnic groups and increased interethnic friendships (Johnson & Johnson, 2006). The same benefits can occur in using cooperative learning to help students with exceptionalities integrate into the regular classroom (Hardman et al., 2008).

One teacher reported this success:

A special education student in the sixth grade was transferred to our classroom, a fifth/sixth grade. The classroom she was in has several special education students. The first—I'll call her Sara—was having behavior difficulties in her first classroom and was about to be expelled because of her unacceptable behavior with her peers. We offered her the opportunity to try our room with no special education students and with cooperative learning techniques being applied in various subjects along with TAI (cooperative learning) math. Sara was welcomed by her new classmates. We added her to one of the TAI math learning teams, and the students taught her the program's routine. Sara worked very steadily and methodically trying to catch up academically and to fit in socially. She began to take more pride in her dress and grooming habits. I have been working with Sara on her basic facts in preparation for the weekly facts quizzes. Her attitude toward her schoolwork and her self-concept have blossomed within the length of time she has been in our classroom. (Nancy Chrest, Fifth/Sixth Grade Teacher, George C. Weimer Elementary School, St. Albans, WV, cited in Slavin, 1995, p. 58)

These are impressive results. Especially when you consider that they were achieved with little additional teacher effort and without outside help. They are a testimony to the power of students helping students in general, and cooperative learning in particular.

The positive effects of cooperative learning on interpersonal attitudes result from several factors:

■ Opportunities for different types of students to work together on joint projects

■ Equal status roles for participants

- Opportunities for different types of students to learn about one another as individuals
- The teacher's implicit but unequivocal support for diverse students working together (Slavin, 1995)

Cooperative learning's effects on intergroup relations result from opportunities for friendships and blurring of intergroup boundaries. As students work together, they develop friendships across racial and ability groups, which tend to soften and blur well-defined peer group boundaries and lead to other cross-group friendships.

However, developing improved relationships requires careful planning. The following strategies can be effective:

- Strategic grouping
- Specific tasks
- Training

To maximize cooperative learning's positive effects, groups should be strategically composed so that they have equal numbers of high- and low-ability students, boys and girls, and students from different ethnic and SES groups. Specifically planning for the appropriate mix of group members has been stressed throughout our discussion of cooperative learning.

Learning tasks also need to be structured so they require cooperation and communication (Johnson & Johnson, 2006). Teachers need to rotate student roles so everyone in the group has an opportunity to perform different tasks such as presenting information and checking answers.

Training is required to develop these important group interaction skills:

- **Listening.** Listening to each others' ideas and helping other students verbalize and express their ideas.
- **Checking for understanding.** Asking for clarification when answers are incomplete or unclear.
- **Emotional support.** Providing positive feedback for answers.
- **Staying on task.** Maintaining focus on the specific learning task at hand.

Teacher explanations, modeling, and reinforcement are effective ways to teach and maintain these skills.

This completes our examination of cooperative learning. We turn now to *discussions*, another strategy designed to capitalize on social interaction.

Discussions

Shannon Wilson's sixth-grade language arts class has been reading *Sounder*, the story of a poor, African American sharecropper family in the South during the Great Depression. The father, concerned about his family's diet and health, had taken to raiding rich people's smokehouses at night to put some meat on his family's table. Shannon's class is discussing the moral implications of his stealing.

"So where do you think the father goes at night when his wife can't find him?"

". . . He's going out to get food for his family," Tanesha replies.

"And where is he getting this food? . . . Ramon?"

". . . From other people's smokehouses."

"Which other people? . . . Tanya?"

"From the rich, white folks who have big farms."

"Okay, we've got the facts of the story down. Now let's focus on the stealing itself. Was the father wrong to steal?. . . . Let's think about it. . . . What do you think? . . . Kareem?"

". . . Well,. . . I . . . think maybe he was,. . . like . . . because he's bound to get caught . . . eventually . . . and thrown in jail or something."

"Francisco?" Shannon nods, seeing his raised hand.

". . . I . . . agree. He shouldn't done it,. . . cuz . . . it's against the law."

". . . I want to ask,...what's he s'pposed to do,. . . let his family starve?" Gabriela interjects.

"Gabriela asks a really good question, class. Anybody want to respond? . . . Kerry?"

". . . I kinda think so, too. Even though it's bad to steal, he can't just,. . . like . . . let his kids go hungry. It said right in the book that they weren't getting enough to eat."

"Hey,. . . You can't just break the law any old time you please,. . . even if you're hungry," Trang retorts.

"Now, everyone, let's think about what we've been saying . . .," Shannon interjects.

The lesson continues as the class continues to wrestle with the moral dilemma raised by the book they are reading.

Using Discussions to Promote Student Growth

Discussions *are instructional strategies that use teacher-student and student-student interactions as the primary vehicle for learning.* They are characterized by decreased focus on the teacher, increased student-to-student interactions, and high levels of student involvement. When effectively used, discussions can stimulate thinking, challenge attitudes and beliefs, and develop interpersonal skills (Burbules & Bruce, 2001; Meter & Stevens, 2000). However, if not organized and managed properly, they can be boring for students, frustrating for you, and a general waste of time.

In contrast with the strategies we've discussed earlier in this book—which focus primarily on cognitive goals—discussions are effective for dealing with both cognitive and affective topics. In addition they can help develop students' communication and interpersonal skills. Let's look at these different goals.

Cognitive Goals in Discussions   Discussions are useful when we want students to develop critical thinking abilities and investigate questions that don't have simple answers. Because they focus on areas in which there isn't a single best answer, students feel comfortable contributing, knowing that they won't be "right or wrong," and involvement increases. As students interact, their background knowledge increases, and social interaction helps students see problems and issues from different points of view.

Affective Goals in Discussions   As we saw in Shannon's class, discussions can also be used to help students examine their attitudes and values. By focusing on specific issues, discussions can provide the intellectual grist that allows students to examine their own beliefs. Through teacher questioning and listening to the different opinions of their classmates, students can evaluate the adequacy of their own beliefs while comparing them to the views of others. Research reveals that discussions can be an effective vehicle to clarify values and promote moral growth (Turiel, 2006).

Communication Skills   Because discussions provide extended opportunities for students to talk and listen to one another, they are a powerful tool for developing students' communication and social skills. Developing these communication skills should be an integral goal for all discussions. These social skills include

- Expressing ideas and opinions clearly

- Justifying assertions

- Acknowledging and paraphrasing others' ideas

- Asking for clarification and elaboration when others' ideas aren't clear

- Sharing ideas equally and avoiding monopolizing discussions

- Inviting silent group members to participate

How can teachers use discussions to accomplish these diverse goals? We begin answering this question by analyzing planning for cognitively oriented discussions in the next section.

Planning for Cognitive Growth in Discussions

Planning for discussions is similar to planning for the use of any strategy. Teachers first identify a *topic* and specify a clear *goal*. In addition, considering *students' background knowledge* and the *physical arrangement of the room* is also critical when discussions are used. Let's see why.

Identifying Discussion Topics   Discussions are effective strategies when topics are complex and open ended and don't have cut-and-dried answers. For example, topics such as solving word problems in math, identifying parts of speech in language arts, or describing characteristics of mammals in science would not be effective discussion topics. With them, there is little to discuss. Discussions are most effective in low-consensus areas such as social studies and the humanities, in which questions are likely to have multiple answers.

Specifying Goals   Merely identifying a topic isn't enough, however. Teachers also need to consider what they want students to take away from a discussion. Let's examine the importance of goals by comparing two lessons.

Paula Marsh had assigned the chapter on the beginnings of the Revolutionary War to be read as homework and begins her American history class by saying:

"Today we begin our discussion of the Revolutionary War. We've been talking about all of the events that led up to the war. What were some of these? Lanal?"
   "The Stamp Act."
   "Good. Angelo?"
   "The Tea Act and the Boston Tea Party."
   "Fine, Angelo. Any others? Miguel?"
   "The First Continental Congress."
   "And when was that held? Does anyone remember? Go ahead, Miguel."
   "1774 in Philadelphia."
   "And what was the major outcome from this meeting?"

We leave this room and walk across the hall where Jacinta Lopez's American history class is studying the same topic.

Jacinta begins, "We've been studying the Revolutionary War, and you all know a lot about it. But," she continued, "some historians, reviewing all the facts about the War suggest that, on paper the British `, should' have won. When they say this, they're not saying 'should' like 'ought' but rather that the British had important advantages but wasted them. I'd like for us to think about that idea today, and see if our conclusions agree with those of the historians. . . . What do you think? Take a little time to consider it while I put this statement on the board."

She then writes "The British advantages during the Revolutionary War should have ensured victory" on the chalkboard.

"Okay," she continues, "now that you've had time to think, does anyone want to take a stab at this? Sharese?"

". . . I basically agree with the statement," Sharese replies. "They had more soldiers, more guns, and better equipment and should have won."

". . . I think Sharese's right," Martina adds. "They not only had more soldiers but the soldiers they did have were better trained. Also . . ."

"If the British had treated the Colonists decent, there wouldn't have been a war in the first place," Ramon interjects.

"That's an interesting point, Ramon," Jacinta smiles. "But, given that there was a war, we're considering whether or not the British should have won. . . . Anything else, Martha?"

". . . No,. . . not really I was just going to say that they had a physical advantage."

"Okay, Martha," she nods. "Hank, you look like you were going to say something."

"Oh, I was just going to say that the British soldiers often weren't in the right place."

"I don't know what you mean, Hank," Jeff says.

"Well, even though they had more soldiers, this wasn't always important. Like at Saratoga. One big part of Burgoyne's army captured Philadelphia instead of going to Albany like he should've. So those troops were wasted. It would be interesting to know what might've happened if Burgoyne had gone to Albany. Maybe we'd still be British."

"That's a very interesting thought, Hank. Jeremy, do you have something to add?"

". . . Just that some of the troops the British had were mercenaries. They were just being paid to fight, so they didn't fight all that hard."

"So numbers might not be the only thing to think about when we talk about advantages and disadvantages. Is that what you're saying?"

". . . I . . . guess so."

"Okay! Very good, everyone. Now, let's return to our question on the board. What other advantages or disadvantages did the British have that influenced the outcome of the war?"

Now let's compare the two episodes. Although the *topic was the same* for both lessons, and both teachers focused students on the content through their questioning, their *goals were very different*. Paula was reviewing facts about events leading up to the Revolutionary War, whereas Jacinta was trying to get students to identify relationships between ideas and make applications. To meet these goals, questions from the upper levels of the cognitive taxonomy (Anderson & Krathwohl, 2001) served as a conceptual framework and guide. For example, the following questions served as guides in Jacinta's lesson.

Jacinta's goals did not stop there, however. In addition to understanding an organized body of knowledge that focused on the Revolutionary War and developing their thinking,

Analyze:	What were the relative strengths and weaknesses of the American and British forces? How did the French influence the outcome of the war?
Create:	Design a strategy or plan that would have used Britain's sea power to greater advantage.
Evaluate:	Was the American victory the result of a lucky chain of events or superior strategy? Take a position and defend it.

she also wanted them to develop other important skills, such as willingness to listen to others' points of view, cooperation, and the ability to take and defend a position. These are important goals for discussions. Because of these additional goals, discussions are much less driven by the content per se, instead providing opportunities for students to use this content as they develop discussion skills.

Students' Background Knowledge   When a teacher uses discussion as a strategy, student background knowledge is an essential factor in the decision. Unlike other strategies, in which content is taught as an integral part of the lesson, discussions require that students be thoroughly conversant with the information related to the topic *prior* to the lesson. This was clearly demonstrated in Jacinta Lopez's lesson. For instance, Sharese demonstrated her background knowledge by observing that the British had more soldiers, guns, and equipment. Martha's comment about the soldiers' training in response to Sharese reflected similar background knowledge. Hank's comment about the battle of Saratoga is perhaps more significant, because he demonstrated understanding of a cause-and-effect relationship in addition to a knowledge of facts.

Student background knowledge is essential to the quality of discussions. Students must have something meaningful to discuss if a discussion is going to work, and the teacher must be sure that their background knowledge is extensive before using discussion as a strategy. If students' background knowledge is inadequate or undeveloped, discussions can easily disintegrate into aimless "bull sessions."

Arranging the Room for Discussions   A final planning task is to arrange the room to promote communication and involvement among participants. Research indicates that students are more likely to interact if they sit facing one another (Gall, 1987).

To accomplish this, you might consider either circles or half-circles. These configurations allow everyone in the class to see everyone else, and they position the teacher within the group. This communicates that the teacher is an equal among other participants and encourages students to take a more active role in participating in and structuring the discussion.

Promoting Cognitive Growth in Discussions: Implementation

In beginning discussion activities we need to draw students into the lesson and help them understand the lesson's goal, refocusing them when necessary during the course of the lesson. Finally, teachers help students reach closure by encouraging them to summarize the discussion at the end. These goals are accomplished through the following three steps:

- Agenda setting
- Refocusing students during the lesson
- Summarization

Agenda Setting Jacinta began her lesson by saying, "Some historians, reviewing all the facts about the war suggest that, on paper, the British 'should' have won. . . . I'd like for us to think about that notion today, and see if our conclusions agree with those of the historians. . . . What do you think?" By introducing the topic in this way she both clarified the goal and presented a question that attracted students' interest. She then wrote the question on the board as a way of maintaining academic focus. Effective discussions begin with clear focusing questions or events.

Refocusing Students During the Lesson It's easy for students in a discussion to "drift off the subject" and begin dealing with issues that aren't relevant to the lesson's goal. For instance, Ramon's comment, "If the British had treated the Colonists decent, there wouldn't have been a war in the first place," although appropriate as a discussion issue in itself, was irrelevant to the issue of whether the British should have won the war. A less effective teacher might have allowed the discussion to drift in that direction, but Jacinta refocused the class by saying, "That's an interesting point, Ramon. . . . But, given that there was a war, we're considering whether or not the British should have won." The ability to recognize irrelevant information is an important thinking skill, and Jacinta's comment helped the class recognize Ramon's comment as irrelevant. At the same time her own social skills and positive manner refocused the class without "cutting Ramon off," or admonishing him in any way.

Summarization As with other lessons, discussions need to be brought to closure. Because discussions sometimes meander, this part is critically important. The most effective way to summarize a discussion is to ask students to recap the major points. For example you might ask, "What are the major points we've talked about today?" This not only actively involves students but also provides you with insights into what students took away from the lesson. As students respond, you should write their comments on the board to provide a visual summary of main points and organize these comments into a coherent outline.

The Teacher's Role

In most classrooms teacher talk is the dominant element, and the teacher uses this talk to steer a lesson in a clear direction (Cazden, 2001). This pattern of teacher control is effective when the goal is to learn specific facts, concepts, generalizations, or skills, such as Paula Marsh's lesson on facts about the Revolutionary War. However, this type of interaction is less effective when the goals are for students to learn discussion skills and productive ways of interacting with one another. In contrast with Paula's lesson, Jacinta's lesson involved more student-to-student talk, and her role changed from lecturer or knowledge source to facilitator of the discussion.

Because the teacher's role in a discussion is less direct and often less apparent, it appears to be easier. In fact, it is just the opposite. During discussions a teacher must listen carefully to each student's response, avoid commenting when students are interacting effectively, interject questions when ideas need to be stimulated, and refocus the discussion when students drift off as Ramon did during Jacinta Lopez's lesson.

Effectively guiding a discussion requires more sophisticated skills than teacher-centered lessons because the teacher is not in direct control of the activity and a great deal of subtle judgment is required. A skilled discussion leader must do all of the following:

- **Focus the discussion.** A primary role for the teacher is to keep the class on track, without removing ownership of the discussion from students, as Jacinta managed to do so skillfully. Periods of silence characterized by student thought are typical (and potentially unnerving).

- **Encourage thoughtfulness.**   In conducting discussions, the teacher needs to be skilled in using questions that solicit alternate points of view, relationships between ideas, and analysis of different points of view rather than convergent, focused answers.

- **Maintain momentum.**   Discussion must be monitored constantly to ensure that momentum is maintained, and the teacher must intervene when the discussion lags. This requires careful judgment. If teachers intervene too often, the discussion reverts back to a teacher-directed activity, but if they don't intervene when necessary, the discussion can meander and even disintegrate.

You will need to intervene under the following conditions:

- Lesson digressions
- Errors of fact or logical fallacies
- A small number of students dominating the discussion
- When the lesson should be summarized and brought to closure

As a rule of thumb, cut a discussion off too soon instead of letting it go too long. To prevent teacher domination, some have advocated teachers refrain from questioning completely (Dillon, 1987). This isn't realistic, however, and in doing so, teachers abdicate important opportunities to stimulate thought and encourage connections. Teacher guidance is critical, and, as teachers acquire expertise, they develop a feel for when intervention is and is not appropriate.

Affective Discussions: Promoting Ethical and Moral Growth

The proper place of values and moral education in the curriculum is controversial. The controversy is less about whether values should be taught in schools—most educators agree that they are needed—and more about the form that it should take. For moral or character education to work, some public consensus must exist about the values included in it, and polls suggest that this consensus does exist (Bushaw & Gallup, 2008; Rose & Gallup, 2000). When asked whether the following values should be taught in public schools, the indicated percentages of a national sample replied affirmatively: honesty (97%), democracy (93%), acceptance of people of different races and ethnic backgrounds (93%), and caring for friends and family members (90%). At the other end of the continuum were acceptance of people with different sexual orientations, that is, homosexuals or bisexuals (55%) and acceptance of the right of a woman to choose an abortion (48%). In considering which values to promote in their classrooms teachers should be aware of local attitudes toward these topics. This doesn't mean teachers should avoid discussing controversial topics or values; instead, it suggests being aware of students' current values and beliefs and building upon them.

This makes sense both pedagogically (Eggen & Kauchak, 2010) as well as politically. But integrating affective content into the curriculum without proselytizing or appearing heavy handed is a delicate balancing act.

This problem is important for all teachers, as value-related discussions are impossible to avoid. Sometimes affective concerns are explicit, such as when freedom of speech and individual rights are discussed in social studies classes. Health classes deal with sex education, and evolution versus creationism continues to be debated in science classes in different parts of the country (Fischer, Schimmel, & Stellman, 2006).

Other instances of affective issues are more subtle, however, and teachers often address affective issues without realizing it. For example, teachers who say,

> "Class, the Civil Rights movement was perhaps the most important event in twentieth-century America," or
>
> "The effect of pollutants on our planet is the biggest problem facing modern man," or
>
> "*Julius Caesar* wasn't just a play about ancient Rome. It was a play about politics and democracy and the potential for abuse by people in power."

are making value-laden statements that can lead to lively discussions.

Opportunities to examine values often occur as natural by-products of other lessons. For example, a discussion in biology might consider benefits of pesticides, such as increased productivity, with negative side effects, such as the impact on the environment. A lesson on ethnic groups in the United States might focus on the internment of Japanese Americans during the Second World War, resulting in a discussion of the importance of individual rights versus perceived risks to national security. A literature class reading *Lord of the Flies* might consider individual responsibility versus peer pressure. A class focusing on career choices might list different occupations and use this as a springboard for a discussion of the values underlying different occupational choices. In each of these topics a conflict of values exists, with potential as a springboard for subsequent discussion.

Beginning Discussions with Moral Dilemmas   Value-oriented discussions can also be started through moral dilemmas (Cohen, 2006). A **moral dilemma** *presents students with an everyday problem, the solution to which involves the resolution of a value conflict.* Shannon Wilson, in the teaching episode at the beginning of this section, used a moral dilemma as the focus for her lesson. Was it right for the father to steal to feed his children? This dilemma was embedded in the book the class was reading, which provided both background knowledge and motivation for her students.

Teachers can also construct their own moral dilemmas to stimulate moral thought. Consider the following:

> John was working as a teacher's aide and ran across a copy of the final exam sitting on the teacher's desk. The exam was for a course that his best friend, Gary, was repeating for graduation. At lunch, Gary expressed concern that he wouldn't pass the course because his boss had made him work every night for the last two weeks, and the heavy schedule had prevented him from studying. Gary asked John to get him a copy of the test. If John didn't, Gary might not be able to graduate. John's refusal would almost certainly end their friendship. What should John do?

The conflicts here are honesty versus friendship. Questions to encourage thinking about this conflict might include:

> Which is more important, honesty or friendship?
>
> What would happen if John steals a copy of the exam?
>
> What if he doesn't?
>
> What circumstances in the problem make a difference?
>
> What other alternatives are there?

In leading a discussion involving a conflict of values, there are several guidelines to follow. Students should be encouraged to take a personal position in terms of the dilemma (e.g., What would *you* do?). This encourages involvement and causes students to reflect on their own values. In doing this an atmosphere of acceptance for different value positions should be established. Students should be encouraged to listen and respond to the views of others. One of the major advantages of discussing different value positions is each student's consideration of alternative views.

In dealing with any of these value-laden topics, the teacher's role is to help students understand the issues involved through strategic questions. These should establish what the problem is, what value positions are involved, and what alternatives exist. In addition, students should be encouraged to clarify and voice their own thoughts on the issues involved. Teachers should refrain from imposing their views on students, and students should not feel pressured to respond.

This concludes our examination of discussion strategies. In the next section we look at how peer tutoring can be used to facilitate learning in the classroom.

To view a video clip of a teacher using discussion strategies in the classroom, go to the Book Specific Resources tab in MyEducationLab, select your text, select Video Examples under Chapter 7, and then click on *The Discussion Model in High School English*.

Assessing Learning in Social Interaction Strategies

When we use social interaction strategies in the classroom, we have two goals. One is for students to learn content; the other is for students to learn how to function within groups. In this section we discuss assessment issues for these two types of learning outcomes.

Assessing Cognitive Achievement

Different social interaction strategies have different learning goals. For example, group work, STAD, and peer tutoring are designed to teach convergent content such as facts, concepts, and skills. Typical forms of assessment such as short answer, completion, and multiple choice are effective here. By contrast other strategies such as Jigsaw, group investigation, and discussions are designed to teach organized bodies of knowledge.

When we teach organized bodies of information, we want our students to leave with a deep understanding of the content involved and an increased ability to analyze and evaluate ideas. Essay and short-answer items are often effective for measuring this outcome.

Essay items *require students to make extended written responses to questions or problems.* Essay questions are valuable for two reasons. First, organizing, expressing, and defending ideas require higher-order critical thinking. Second, the essay format is often the only way these goals can be measured (Stiggins, 2008). Also, when students study for an essay versus short-answer or multiple-choice exam, they are more likely to organize information in a meaningful way. For example, Paula Marsh might ask her students,

> What advantages and disadvantages did the colonies and the British have during the Revolutionary War, and how did these influence the outcome?

In scoring this item, Paula would construct a scoring rubric that contained essential components (i.e., advantages and disadvantages as well as an evaluation of these) and the point total to be assigned to each. A scoring rubric such as this increases both validity and reliability and can be shared with students to help them become better essay writers (Stiggins, 2008).

A different type of assessment item measures how well students have learned the cognitive processes involved in these strategies. For example, in Jigsaw we want to assess the extent to which students are growing as expert presenters. This involves sophisticated learning skills such as note taking and organization, as well as the ability to communicate ideas to others. In a similar way in group investigation, we want to assess the extent to which students can conduct inquiry activities on their own.

In both of these instances a rubric can be constructed to assess student performance and provide detailed feedback about learning progress. For example, Figure 7.2 contains a

Figure 7.2

Rating Scale for Assessing the Process Skills during Group Investigations

	Needs Work	Fair	Good	Very Good	Excellent
Clearly stated problem	1	2	3	4	5
Clearly stated hypothesis(es)	1	2	3	4	5
Hypothesis connected to problem	1	2	3	4	5
Variables controlled	1	2	3	4	5
Data gathering appropriate to hypothesis	1	2	3	4	5
Data analyzed clearly	1	2	3	4	5
Conclusions logically connected to hypotheses and data	1	2	3	4	5
Inquiry evaluation instrument	1	2	3	4	5

rating scale to assess students' ability to conduct inquiry investigations on their own. A similar one could be constructed for assessing outcomes in Jigsaw.

Assessing Growth in Social Skills

When we use social interaction strategies, we also want students to become better at working together in groups. Basically we want to know whether students are getting better at learning to work together as a team.

The best source of information here comes from observing students as they work together in groups. Some questions to ask as you do this include

- Are all members contributing?
- Are some members dominating?
- Is the group interaction positive and supportive?
- Do boys and girls contribute equally?
- Are members from different racial and ethnic groups involved and being included?

A rubric similar to the one in Figure 7.2 can be constructed to assess each of these dimensions. By attending to these questions teachers can help individuals and groups learn to cooperate and work together more effectively.

Summary

The Need for Social Interaction in Classrooms

Constructivist theories support the use of social interaction in the classroom by emphasizing the central role that dialogue and verbalization play in learning. Piaget, a Swiss psychologist, emphasized the role of social interaction in precipitating conceptual change. Vygotsky, a Russian psychologist, viewed language as an important medium for both learning and development. Language provides a medium for students to conceptualize their own thoughts and refine these by comparing them to the thoughts of others.

Using Group work to Facilitate Learning

Group work provides an effective strategy for promoting and maintaining high levels of student involvement by engaging students in tasks to be solved in a group. It can also help students develop social skills and promote the development of higher-order thinking skills.

Cooperative Learning

Cooperative learning strategies place students on learning teams and reward group performance. Cooperative learning strategies can be used to teach both basic skills and other, higher-level skills. Effective cooperative learning strategies stress group goals and individual accountability and provide equal opportunities for success.

Student Teams Achievement Divisions (STAD) is an effective way to teach facts, concepts, and skills. Jigsaw techniques assign different students on a team to investigate different aspects of an organized body of knowledge. Subsequent sharing and quizzes or group projects make all students accountable for the information gained by the group. Group investigation places students in teams to attack a common problem from different perspectives. In all of these strategies, the development of social interaction skills and inquiry can be as important as content acquisition.

Discussions

Discussions are interactive instructional strategies that teach higher-level thinking skills, affective goals, and interpersonal communication skills. Content-oriented discussions invite students to use higher-level and critical thinking skills to refine and integrate previous information they have learned. Student content background is essential here. During discussions, the teacher's role is less directive and obtrusive, first framing the discussion with a question or problem and then monitoring its progress through questions and clarifying statements.

Affective discussions are designed to help students clarify their own values and beliefs through the dual processes of articulating their own views and listening to those of others. As with content-oriented discussions the teacher acts as facilitator and clarifier rather than position taker.

Assessing Learning in Social Interaction Strategies

Social interaction strategies have two goals: the learning of content and the development of social interaction skills. Assessing content acquisition depends upon the specific content goals. Traditional items such a completion and multiple choice can be used to assess convergent information. Essay items are needed to assess more complex outcomes such as organizing, analyzing, and evaluating ideas. Rubrics are helpful in grading essays and in providing feedback to learners. Rubrics can also be used to assess learners' ability to perform complex processes such as conducting an investigation.

A second important learning outcome is students' ability to function effectively in groups. Rubrics can also be used to assess this dimension of learning.

 *I*mportant Concepts

Combining pairs (p. 214)

Cooperative learning (p. 216)

Discussions (p. 229)

Elaboration (p. 210)

Essay item (p. 237)

Group goals (p. 211)

Group investigation (p. 223)

Group work (p. 239)

Individual accountability (p. 211)

Jigsaw (p. 222)

Moral dilemma (p. 236)

Pairs check (p. 213)

Student Teams Achievement Divisions (STAD) (p. 218)

Think-pair-share (p. 213)

$\mathcal{P}$reparing for Your Licensure Exam

This chapter examined different types of cooperative learning and the factors that influence the effectiveness of cooperative learning activities. As you read the following case study, think about the teacher's attempt to implement cooperative learning with his students and what he could have done to make it more effective.

After reading this case, go to the Book Specific Resources tab in MyEducationLab, select your text, select *Preparing for Your Licensure Exam* under Chapter 7 to complete the questions that accompany the case and receive feedback on your responses.

Ken Johnson has been reading and hearing about cooperative learning. A number of his colleagues at Franklin Middle School have experienced some success with it, so Ken has been wanting to try it. As he looks over his language arts curriculum for the next few months, he sees that "end-of-sentence punctuation" is one of the standards he needs to teach. "Hmm, I wonder if cooperative learning would work here," he thinks to himself.

As the day to begin the unit draws nearer, he makes specific plans for the cooperative learning unit. He knows that students should be involved in helping each other out on teams but isn't quite sure how to do this. He brings the topic up in the faculty lounge, but the explanations he receives aren't really clear. He can't quite understand the differences among STAD, Jigsaw, and group investigation. "Oh well, probably the best way to learn is by trying it out," he thinks as he looks through his teacher's edition of the language arts text that he is using.

On the first day of the unit he begins by saying, "Class, we're going to try something different. Instead of me teaching you everything, you're going to learn how to help each other. So the first thing we need to do is get into groups of three or four, and these will be our cooperative learning teams. I thought of assigning you to teams but thought you might learn better with someone you know, so go ahead and find two or three other student that you want to work with and decide on a group name. I'll give you five minutes to do this."

As Ken circulates around the room, he works at smoothing over group disputes. In some instances, teams of five arise and Ken is faced with the choice of breaking them up into smaller units or letting them go. He decides to let them go. He also encounters the problem of isolated students and students who can't find partners. He helps each of them find a potential partner.

When most of the students have found a group, he continues, "Here's how the activity will work. We're going to be learning about end-of-sentence punctuation. I know most of you know something about the topic, but I've been noticing on some of the writing that you've been handing in that we could use a little more work.

"So, first I'd like everyone in the team to read pages 170 to 175 in your language arts text. Then I'd like each of you to write three sentences that are declarative, interrogatory, and imperative. Don't worry if you don't know what that means. You'll find out. Then share these with your partners and see if they can figure out which is which.

We'll continue on with this tomorrow and I'll give each group a group quiz. Because we're using cooperative learning, I'll let you help each other and the grade you get for this assignment will be the same for everyone in the group. Any questions? Ryan?"

"What are we supposed to do in the groups? I'm not sure I understand."

"You're supposed to read pages 170 to 175 in your text. Here, I'll write them on the board. Then you make up one of each of the three kinds of sentences and share these with the other members of the team. Any other questions? Then let's get into our groups and start working."

As Ken circulates around the room, he helps students from different groups get going. He notices that some groups, mostly his A and B students, get right to work while other groups are slow to start. As Ken works with different groups, he repeats his directions and finally after about 10 minutes most of the groups are working productively. "Hmm," he thinks, "maybe this is going to work."

The next day he begins class by saying, "Class, we did a good job yesterday learning about different kinds of sentences and how periods, question marks, and exclamation points can help the reader understand what we're trying to say. To help you practice for the quiz today I've got an exercise that asks you to punctuate different kinds of sentences. This is exactly what you'll be doing on the group quiz at the end of our hour. So work hard and I'll be circulating around the room if you have any questions."

After Ken distributes the practice sheets to the different groups, he circulates around the room. He finds that a number of groups have trouble deciding whether a sentence really warrants an exclamation point or just needs a period. Students believe that they don't have enough background information to make a decision. Although Ken half-heartedly agrees, he urges them to make a decision anyway.

Toward the end of the class Ken asks all groups to look to the front of the room.

"Class, I've got your group quiz here. I'm only going to give one to each group, and you have to work cooperatively at deciding the right answer. That's why this is called cooperative learning. When you're done, hand the quiz in with all of the members of your group's names on it and I'll grade them for tomorrow. Good luck."

As Ken passes out the quiz he wanders around the room answering questions and making sure each of the groups is working okay. Some are and some aren't. He also notices that in most groups the brightest student is given the job of secretary and tends to do most of the work.

"I wonder if this is working like it should. They don't seem to be cooperating as I hoped," he thinks.

Questions for Analysis

Let's examine Ken's lesson now based on the information in this chapter. In your analysis consider the following questions. In each case be specific and take information directly from the case study in doing your analysis.

1. Which type of cooperative learning strategy should Ken Johnson have used? Why?
2. How effective was Ken in forming cooperative learning groups? What alternative might you suggest?
3. How effective was Ken's instruction in structuring the cooperative learning activity? What else might he have done?
4. Analyze Ken's cooperative learning activity in terms of the essential components identified by research. How could he adjust his activity to be more effective?
5. Analyze the effectiveness of the learning materials Ken used. How could their effectiveness have been increased?

Discussion Questions

1. Which of the three cooperative learning strategies—STAD, Jigsaw, or group investigation—is most appropriate for the lower grades? Upper grades? Why?

2. Are the three cooperative learning strategies more effective in some content areas than in others? Which and why?

3. Which of the three cooperative learning strategies would be most effective for fostering improved relations between different groups of students? Why?

4. What is the place of values in the curriculum? How would you respond to objections from people who contend that values don't belong in the curriculum? What advantages and disadvantages are there to character and moral education approaches to teaching values?

5. Which values should the schools try to develop? Examine the following values and rank order the five most important values from an educational perspective. Compare these with other people in the class.

Broad-minded	Logical
Forgiving	Loving
Honest	Obedient
Imaginative	Polite
Independent	Responsible
Intellectual	Self-controlled

6. Are discussions more valuable in some areas of the curriculum than others? Which and why? How does the value of discussion vary with grade level? What is the lowest grade level that can still benefit from discussions?

Portfolio Activities

1. *Group work.* Plan and teach a lesson incorporating student group work.
   a. Which kind of group work did you use? Was it appropriate for your goal?
   b. How well did you plan for logistical concerns such as transitions into and out of group work? What would you do differently next time?
   c. How did group work influence student motivation?
   d. How effective was the group work activity in promoting learning? How can you tell?

2. *Cooperative Learning.* Identify a classroom that is using cooperative learning. Observe the classroom and answer the following:
   a. Which kind of cooperative learning strategy was being used?
   b. Which content goals were targeted?
   c. How were the groups composed (teacher interview)?
   d. How did the teacher promote (1) group goals, (2) individual accountability, and (3) equal opportunity for success?

e. Which special management strategies did the teacher use?

f. How could the lesson be changed to improve learning?

3. *Affective Goals.* Examine a blank report card. What do the categories in the report card say about the affective goals in that school at that level? What areas are emphasized? What areas are missing? How could the report card be modified to help students develop in these areas?

4. *Discussions: Interaction Patterns.* The purpose of this exercise is to analyze the interaction patterns in a discussion. To do this, sketch out a seating chart of the participants before observing a class discussion. Mark the first person who talks with a 1, the second with a 2, and so on. After the session, analyze your data in terms of the following questions:

a. How did the discussion begin?

b. Was the prevalent interaction pattern T-S-T or S-S?

c. What percentage of the students participated? What did the teacher do to influence this?

d. What role did the teacher play?

e. How did the teacher's questions guide the discussion?

f. How did the discussion end?

g. What suggestions do you have to make the discussion more effective?

5. *Discussions.* Identify an instructor at the elementary, secondary, or college level who is good at leading discussions and ask to sit in on one of his or her discussions.

a. What instructional activities (e.g., readings or lecture) preceded the discussion?

b. What kinds of interaction patterns developed?

c. What kinds of questions seemed most effective in provoking thoughtful interaction?

d. How was silence used?

e. How appropriate would this discussion style be in your content area or level?

To check your comprehension of the content covered in Chapter 7, go to the Book Specific Resources in MyEducationLab, select your text, and complete the Study Plan quiz. In addition to receiving feedback on your answers, a study plan will be generated from the quiz that will direct you to access Review, Practice, and Enrichment materials to enhance your understanding of chapter content.

Direct Instruction

Problem 1: $2\frac{1}{4}$

Problem 2: 2 with one left over or 3 for one person, 2 for the others

Problem 3: 2 dollars and a quarter or $2.25

Problem 4: 2.25

In earlier chapters we focused on general teaching strategies, such as questioning, that are effective for all forms of learning. We now turn to specific teaching strategies and how teachers can use them to increase student learning. Because it is applicable in all grade levels with a wide variety of topics, we begin with *direct instruction*, a strategy with a long history in education (Cuban, 1984).

The teachers in the following case studies are using direct instruction in their classrooms. In the first, Sean Barnett, a second-grade teacher, is using the strategy to teach a skill, and in the second, Al Lombana, a middle school Spanish teacher, is using it to teach a concept. As you read the case studies, try to identify the features that the two lessons have in common.

Sean is working with his students on a unit on addition. With his plan on his desk, Sean begins math by saying, "Okay, class, today we are going to go a step further with our work in addition so that we'll be able to solve problems like this," displaying the following on the document camera.

Jana and Patti are friends. They were saving special soda cans to get a free CD. They can get the CD if they save 35 cans. Jana had 15 cans and Patti had 12. How many did they have together?

After pausing briefly to give students a chance to read the problem, Sean continues. "Now, why do you think it's important to know how many Jana and Patti have together?"

". . . So, they can know how much they got, like . . . so they can get their CD," Devon answers haltingly.

"Sure," Sean smiles. "If they know how many they have, they'll know how close they are to getting their CD. If they don't, they're stuck. That's why it's important.

"We'll come back to this problem in a minute," Sean continues, "but before we do, let's review. Everyone take out your counter sticks and beans and do this problem."

Sean then puts the following on the chalkboard and watches as students use their sticks and beans to demonstrate their answer.

$$\begin{array}{r} 8 \\ +7 \\ \hline \end{array}$$

"Very good," Sean smiles as most of the students lay a stick with 10 beans glued on it and 5 more beans on the centers of their desks. Others lay out 15 beans, and Sean shows them how they could exchange 10 of them for a stick with 10 glued on it.

Sean has the students do two more problems with their counters and then continues, "Let's return to our problem again."

Turning on the overhead again he says, "Everyone look up here. Good. Now what does the problem ask us? . . . Shalinda?"

"How many . . . they have together?" Shalinda responds hesitantly.

"And how many does Jana have? . . . Abdul?"

". . . Fifteen?"

"Good, Abdul. And how many does Patti have? Celinda?"

"Twelve."

"Okay, so let's put the problem on the board like this," Sean continues, writing the following:

$$\begin{array}{r} 15 \\ +12 \\ \hline \end{array}$$

"Now, I'd like everyone to show me how to make a 15 at your desk by using your sticks and beans."

Sean pauses as the students work at their desks.

"Does everyone's look like this?" Sean asks as he demonstrates at the flannel board.

They do the same with the 12, and Sean continues, "Now, watch what I do here. . . . When I add 5 and 2, what do I get? Hmm, let me think about that . . . 5 and 2 are 7. Let's put a 7 up on the chalkboard," Sean says as he walks to the chalkboard and adds a 7.

$$\begin{array}{r} 15 \\ +12 \\ \hline 7 \end{array}$$

"Now show me that with your beans," and he watches as the students combine seven beans on their desks.

"Now, we still have to add the 10s. What do we get when we add two 10s? Hmm, that should be easy. One 10 and one 10 is two 10s. Now, look where I have to put the 2 up here. It is under the 10s column because the 2 means two 10s." With that, he writes the following on the chalkboard.

$$15$$
$$\underline{+12}$$
$$27$$

"So, how many cans did Jana and Patti have together? . . . Alesha?"

". . . 27?"

"Good, Alesha. They had 27 all together. Now, with your beans, what is this 7?" he asks, pointing to the 7 on the chalkboard. . . . Carol?"

". . . It's this," she says, motioning to the seven beans on her desk.

"Good, yes it is. It's the seven individual beans. . . . Now, . . . what is this 2? . . . Jeremy?" Sean continues on, pointing to the numeral on the chalkboard.

"It's . . . these," Jeremy answers, holding up the two sticks with the beans glued on them.

"Good. Now, we saw that I added the 5 and the 2 before I added the two 1s. Why do you suppose I did that? . . . Anyone?"

"Maybe . . . you have to find out how many . . . ones you have to see if we can make a 10 . . . or something," Callie offers.

"That's excellent thinking, Callie. That's exactly right. We'll see why again tomorrow when we have some problems in which we'll have to regroup, and that will be just a little tougher, but for now let's remember what Callie said.

"Now, who can describe in words for us one more time what the 2 means? . . . Leroy?"

"It's . . . two, ah, two . . . bunches or something like that of 10 beans."

"Yes, that's correct, Leroy. It's two groups of 10 beans or, in the case of Jana and Patti, it's two groups of 10 soda cans.

Let's leave Sean's classroom now and look in on Al Lombana's work with his students.

Al is working with his students on parts of speech, and in this lesson he wants to help his students understand indirect objects.

As the bell rings, he begins by saying, "Class, in Spanish just like in English it's important to know how words work in a sentence so we know where to place them. For example, look up here at the board.

Mis padres me mandaron el libro.

It says, 'My parents sent me the book,' explains Al, writing that under the Spanish. "Who remembers what part of the sentence is 'parents'? . . . Ajar?"

"I think it's the subject."

"Good, Ajar. And how about 'book'? What part of the sentence is book? . . . Jacinta?"

"Umm, direct object?"

"Yes, Jacinta, 'book' is the direct object because that's what the parents sent. Now we've got this other funny word–'me.' 'Me' is an indirect object. It's important to know about indirect objects because in Spanish they go before the verb. Today we're going to learn about indirect objects. I've written a definition on the board."

He continues, "Read that definition for me, Karen."

Karen reads aloud, "An indirect object is the part of a sentence that tells who or what received the direct object from the subject of the sentence."

"Okay," Al smiles. "Let's look at the definition. First, we've been studying different parts of sentences all year. What is a subject of a sentence? . . . Gabriella?"

"It's a word in the sentence that does the action or a state of being."

"Good, Gabriella. Give me an example of a subject in a sentence. Steve?"

"He hit me. He is the subject."

"Fine, Steve. Now what do we mean when we say direct object? . . . Octavio?"

"I think they are words that receive the action of the verb," Octavio responds. "Like, 'Bill hit the ball.' Ball is the direct object."

"Real fine, Octavio," Al praises. "Now remember indirect objects tell who or what received the direct object from the subject of the sentence. Let's change Octavio's sentence to read, 'He hit Ted the ball.' Ball is still the direct object, but Ted is the indirect object. It tells who Bill hit the ball to. Let's look at another example. See if you can identify the indirect object in this one (writing it on the board): 'Mom bought Jim the jacket.' Which is the indirect object and why? . . . Mario?"

"I think it's Jim, because it tells who Mom bought the jacket for."

"Excellent, Mario. Now let's try this one," writing the following sentence on the board: 'He told the policeman the details of the accident.' Which is the indirect object? . . . Sally?"

"Policeman," Sally responds, "because it describes who received the details."

"Good! That's exactly correct. You've identified precisely why the policeman is the indirect object. Now how about this one? 'The student gave the teacher the homework.'

"What do you think? . . . Jacinta? Which is the indirect object?"

"Hmm, I think it's homework."

"Look again, Jacinta. What did the student give?"

"The homework."

"Okay," Al smiles. "So that's the direct object. Now, whom did he give it to?"

"The teacher."

"Good, Jacinta. So what is 'teacher'?"

"An indirect object."

"Good thinking, Jacinta!"

Al then gives the students the example "Santa Claus brought the kids presents," has them analyze it, and asks individual students to provide additional examples for analysis. After four different students give an example, Al passes out a worksheet with a series of sentences. As he does this, he says, "Now, we're going to see if you can find the indirect object in Spanish sentences."

Direct Instruction in the Classroom

Direct instruction is *a teaching strategy in which the teacher presents well-defined knowledge and skills and explicitly guides the learning process* (Kuhn, 2007; Rosenshine & Stevens, 1986). Its use in the classroom has increased with the growing emphasis on standards and accountability because of its effectiveness in teaching basic knowledge and skills. Direct instruction has the following characteristics:

- **Goal oriented.** During planning, both Sean and Al identified specific learning objectives for their lessons and designed learning activities to help students meet the objectives.

- **Focused and aligned.** Their lessons remained focused on their objectives.

- **Teacher scaffolding.**   Sean took primary responsibility for guiding the learning by modeling and explaining the skill. In a similar way, Al used examples and questioning to help his students understand the concept of indirect object.

- **Opportunities for practice and feedback.**   Sean's students practiced the skill with the goal of developing automaticity; Al's students had multiple opportunities to see and discuss examples of indirect objects. (Kroesbergen, van Luit, & Maas, 2004)

Direct instruction is effective when lesson content has one or more of the following characteristics (Carnine, Silbert, Kame'enui, Tarver, & Jungjohann, 2006):

- It is something that all students need to master, either because it is a basic skill or content needed for future learning. Sean's goal was for all his students to master the process of addition, a basic skill; Al's goal was for his students to understand and be able to use indirect objects, something they would use throughout their study of Spanish.

- It is content students have difficulty learning on their own.

- It is specific and well defined. Adding one- and two-digit numbers, as Sean's students were doing, is an example; learning about indirect objects is another.

Why Direct Instruction Works

The effectiveness of direct instruction is well documented (Kroesbergen et al., 2004). This research comes from three primary sources:

- The teacher effectiveness literature

- Observational learning

- The work of Lev Vygotsky

Teacher Effectiveness Research   Direct instruction is supported by research that attempted to explain why some teachers are more effective than others. One of the major findings of this research was that teachers who produced more learning in their students than would be expected based on the students' backgrounds used direct instruction extensively in their classrooms. A review by Weinert and Helmke (1995) summarizes these findings:

> Many studies–both in the classroom and in the laboratory under experimental conditions–have shown that instruction in which the teacher actively presents information to students and supports individual learning processes is more effective than instruction in which the teacher's only role is to provide those external conditions that make individual or social learning success possible. (1995, p. 138)

Observational Learning   The second source of support for direct instruction comes from a body of research on observational learning (e.g., Bandura, 2001). **Observational learning** *occurs when people acquire new attitudes, skills, and behaviors by watching and imitating the actions of others.* Modeling is one of the most important aspects of observational learning. **Modeling** occurs when *people imitate behaviors they observe in others*, and everyday examples are common. Teenagers imitate the fashion and hairstyles of athletes and celebrities, and young people imitate the behaviors of their parents. (For instance, children are 10 times more likely to exercise if both their parents exercise than if neither exercises.)

Students also imitate the behaviors of their teachers, and teachers take advantage of this when they demonstrate positive attitudes such as tolerance and respect for people. Teachers also use modeling to demonstrate complex skills such as writing and solving algebraic equations. Research indicates that teacher modeling is one of the most powerful vehicles available for teaching both attitudes and skills (Bandura, 2001).

Social Interaction and Learning: The Work of Lev Vygotsky   Research on the social aspects of learning documents the importance of verbal interaction in helping students understand new content (Bruning et al., 2004; Horn, 2003). Much of the effectiveness of direct instruction results from the verbal interaction between teachers and students.

Lev Vygotsky (1978, 1986), the famous Russian developmental psychologist, uses the concept of *scaffolding* to describe the way we can capitalize on this interaction with our students. **Scaffolding** *is the instructional support teachers provide as students master new content* (Puntambekar & Hübscher, 2005). You can provide instructional scaffolding in a variety of ways, including breaking complex skills into subskills, asking questions that guide students' developing understanding, presenting and explaining examples, modeling the steps in solving problems, and providing prompts and cues.

For example, when Sean first introduced adding with two-digit numbers, many of his students were not able to perform this skill by themselves. Because of the scaffolding, in the form of questions, problems, and the bean counter sticks, that he provided, most of his students could perform the skill on their own by the end of the lesson.

Content Taught by Direct Instruction

Direct instruction is designed to teach two types of content that are central to the school curriculum: skills and concepts. In this section we analyze these different forms of content, emphasizing how their characteristics influence learning.

Skills   Skills are a major form of content that we teach with direct instruction. **Skills** have three essential characteristics:

- *They have a specific set of identifiable operations or procedures* (which is why they're sometimes called *procedural skills*).
- *They can be illustrated with a large and varied number of examples.*
- *They are developed through practice.* (Eggen & Kauchak, 2010)

Adding two-digit numbers, which we saw in Sean's lesson, is a skill. The four basic operations—adding, subtracting, multiplying, and dividing—are skills, as are simplifying expressions such as $9 + 3 \times 8 - 10/5$ or solving equations such as $3(2 \times 8 + 6) = 24$ in algebra. Solving algebraic equations is obviously more complex and challenging than simple subtraction problems, but they are skills nevertheless.

Skills are not limited to math. Applying academic rules in any content area involves skills. For instance,

get	getting
jump	jumping
play	playing

The academic rule we follow for adding *-ing* to words is "Double the ending consonant if it is preceded by a short vowel sound, but do not if it is preceded by another consonant or a long vowel sound." Applying this rule is a skill, as is applying the rules for capitalization, punctuation, subject-verb agreement, and many others in the language arts curriculum.

Examples of skills can also be found in other areas of the curriculum. When geography students use longitude and latitude to pinpoint locations or chemistry students balance equations, they are practicing skills. They can be very basic, as in Sean's lesson, or very sophisticated, such as verifying identities in trigonometry; applying study skills, such as summarizing, in English; or using thinking skills, such as recognizing irrelevant information, in all curriculum areas.

Skills are useful because they apply in a variety of contexts. As a simple example, addition allows us to combine apples as well as dollars and cents. What we are adding doesn't matter; addition is an essential skill because it can be applied in a variety of situations. In a similar way, the ability to punctuate a sentence properly allows us to communicate in both school essays and love letters. When students have learned a skill, they have an ability that will be useful in later learning.

It is interesting that the importance of skills has increased at the same time that technology has become a central component of American life and work. The need for people who can think and use technology in an intelligent manner has replaced the need for those who can simply remember large amounts of information (Jonassen, 2000).

Concepts   **Concepts**, a second form of content taught by direct instruction, *are mental categories, or classes, of objects, events, or ideas, illustrated by examples and defined by common characteristics.* For example, if students understood the concept of *square* and encountered the polygons in Figure 8.1, they would describe them all as squares, even though the shapes vary in size and orientation. *Square* is a concept, a mental category or class into which all examples of squares can be placed.

Concepts help simplify the world. The concept of *square*, for example, allows people to think and talk about the examples in Figure 8.1 as a group, instead of as specific objects. Having to remember each separately would make learning impossibly complex and

Figure 8.1

Squares as Concepts

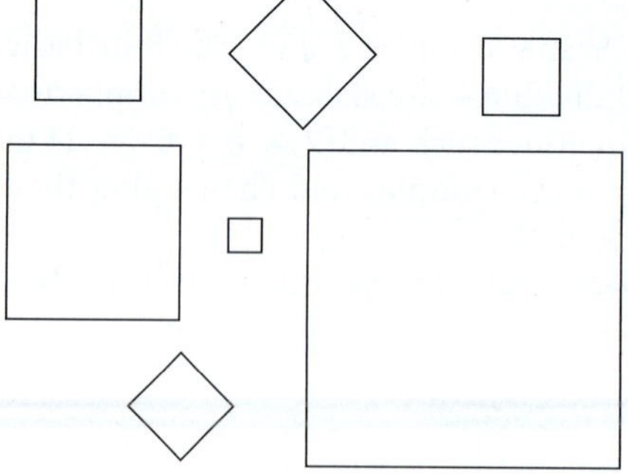

unwieldy. In a similar way, understanding the concept of *indirect object* allows Al Lombana's students to use them correctly in their Spanish sentences.

Additional examples of concepts in language arts, social studies, science, and math are listed in Table 8.1. This is only a brief list, and you can probably think of many more for each area. For example, students also study *major scale* and *tempo* in music, *perspective* and *balance* in art, and *aerobic exercise* and *isotonic exercise* in physical education. In addition we teach many other concepts in school that don't neatly fit into a particular content area, such as *honesty, justice, love, internal conflict,* and *bias.*

People learn concepts by focusing on the essential **characteristics** (sometimes called *attributes* or *features*), which are *a concept's defining elements. Square,* for instance, has four characteristics—*closed, plane, equal sides,* and *equal angles*, and students can identify examples of squares from a rule based on these characteristics. Other characteristics, such as size, color, or orientation aren't essential, so students disregard them in deciding whether something is a square.

Teaching Concepts: Examples and Non-Examples. Examples are essential for learning and understanding concepts. Specific **examples**—*typical members of the class*—and **non-examples**—*nonmembers of the class*—help learners understand what the concept is, as well as its essential characteristics. Regardless of a concept's complexity, the key to concept learning is a carefully selected set of examples and non-examples (Schunk, 2004).

To illustrate the importance of examples, let's look at a simple illustration of learning a concept such as *dog*, as it occurs naturally. Children learn about dogs by encountering collies, terriers, poodles, Chihuahuas, and other examples. Parents and other adults help with directive statements, such as "Look, Anya, there's a dog!" As with the illustration of the concept of *square*, the collies, terriers, and other dogs are dissimilar in many ways, but having been told that all are dogs, children identify similarities among them, and they begin to construct the concept.

The process is also aided by non-examples such as cats and bears, and later, more closely related non-examples such as coyotes, wolves, and foxes. In these instances learners are told, "No, Matt, that's not a dog. It's a kitty. Listen to him meow," or "No. It looks like a dog, but it's a wolf. It lives in the wild and not with people."

The examples tell us what a concept *is* by illustrating its essential characteristics, and the nonexamples help us discriminate the concept from closely related concepts. Consider the following examples:

Sammy, the running back, was a freight train moving down the field.
As a running back, Sammy was like a freight train moving down the field.

Table 8.1 **Concepts in different content areas**

Language Arts	Social Studies	Science	Math
Gerund	Culture	Acid	Composite number
Noun	Republican	Conifer	Equivalent fraction
Plot	Conservative	Compound	Square
Simile	Mercantilism	Force	Multiplication
Direct object	Gross national product	Momentum	Ellipse

Obviously, the two statements are closely related. However, they illustrate two different concepts from the language arts curriculum. The first is a metaphor, which involves a nonliteral comparison, and the second is a simile, which also makes a nonliteral comparison but includes the words *like* or *as* in it. The essential characteristics of metaphors are illustrated in the first example, and a key discriminating characteristic is shown in the non-example. As students learn the concept of *metaphor*, non-examples such as *similes* are crucial to prevent them from overgeneralizing and including inappropriate examples in the category. The same process occurs when we tell young children that foxes and wolves are not dogs.

Concept learning as it occurs naturally and concept learning in formal school settings are similar in that they both depend on examples. Learners encounter examples and non-examples in either day-to-day experience—as in the case with dogs—or are systematically presented examples and non-examples—as demonstrated with Al's lesson on indirect objects. In both cases the concept is learned by identifying its essential characteristics and discriminating them from those of closely related concepts.

Different Types of Examples. We know examples are the key to effectively representing concepts, but finding effective examples for our instruction can be difficult. For instance, how would you illustrate concepts such as *atom* or *culture*? When teachers have difficulty finding or creating good examples, they often revert back to definitions alone, which students then memorize. The memorized definitions then exist in isolation, unconnected to other ideas they've learned or the real world in which they live. Table 8.2 contains various forms of examples that can be used to teach concepts.

The ideal in illustrating any concept is the real thing; teachers should try to use actual objects and demonstrations whenever possible. Sometimes this is impractical, however, and alternatives are required. **Models**, *concrete representations that help us visualize what we cannot observe directly*, are one of these alternatives. They are especially useful in science for a variety of topics ranging from molecules to atomic structure.

Just as models are useful in science, simulations are commonly used in social studies to illustrate concepts impossible to illustrate in other ways. Several social simulations are now available on DVDs to help students understand complex processes. One, *Oregon Trail*, designed to illustrate the difficulties and complex decisions faced by pioneers, places students in the role of pioneers traveling across the plains, making decisions about supplies, trails, and mode of travel. Another, *SimCity*, allows students to construct a city, in the process investigating factors such as transportation and the placement of utilities.

Table 8.2 **Types and Illustrations of Examples**

Realia (the real thing)	A real heart from the butcher shop to be cut open and shown to students Paragraphs in which parts of speech are embedded
Models	A plastic model of the solar system with the order and sizes of planets represented A plastic heart illustrating the heart's structure
Pictures	Pictures of the Rockies and Appalachians to illustrate young and mature mountains Pictures of firefighters and postal workers to illustrate community helpers
Simulations	A mock trial to illustrate the judicial system at work A debate in which students are asked to take conservative and liberal positions on issues
Case studies	Written dialogue between two people, illustrating opinion versus fact The case studies that introduce the chapters of this book The case study illustrating *mercantilism* in Chapter 5

The use of case studies is another powerful instructional tool that can be used to illustrate difficult concepts. We introduce each of the chapters of this text with a case study to illustrate the concepts that help you understand learning and teaching. Without them the content would be much less meaningful to you as developing professionals. Case studies form the backbone of much of the instruction in many teacher education programs, as well as courses in business and law (Putnam & Borko, 2000; Siegel, 2002).

What Makes Concepts Easy or Hard to Learn?   The ease of learning a concept is directly related to the number of characteristics it has and how concrete they are. *Square* is easy to learn because it has few characteristics and they're concrete. *Liberal* and *conservative*, in contrast, are much harder. Their characteristics are more abstract, and there are many more of them. This helps us understand why many people have difficulty precisely describing what makes a conservative a conservative and a liberal a liberal and how liberals and conservatives are different.

These differences are reflected in where concepts are placed in the school curriculum. Simple, concrete concepts, such as squares and other shapes are taught in kindergarten or before, whereas many abstract concepts don't appear until the middle school years or later.

Making Concepts Meaningful: Superordinate, Coordinate, and Subordinate Concepts. We have two goals when we teach concepts. The first is to have our students understand what the concept is, which we do by providing examples that illustrate the essential characteristics that define the concept. Al, for example, used examples (indirect objectives embedded in sentences) to teach his students the concept of *indirect objects*.

The second is to help students understand how the concept relates to other concepts. This prevents them from being remembered as isolated categories. For example, when students learn that indirect objects are parts of a sentence, we also want them to know that other parts of a sentence also exist, such as subject, verb, and direct objects, and what indirect objects' relationship is to them.

Al did this when he related indirect objects to subjects and direct objects, other concepts that were parts of a sentence that students already knew. We want concepts to be connected to students' background knowledge and to be differentiated from closely related concepts. When we accomplish these two goals, meaningful concept learning occurs.

We can describe these connective links by using the idea of superordinate, coordinate, and subordinate concepts. **Superordinate concepts** *are larger categories into which the concept fits*, **coordinate concepts** *are "parallel" concepts that fit into the same superordinate category*, and **subordinate concepts** *are subsets of the concept we're focusing on*. These relationships are illustrated in Table 8.3.

Superordinate concepts serve two important functions. First, they provide a link to the concept being learned by relating it to a broader, more inclusive category. What is a dog? A dog is a mammal. What is an indirect object? An indirect object is a part of a sentence. *Mammal* and *parts of a sentence* are superordinate to *dog* and *indirect object*. If we understand the superordinate concept, it provides a mental "hook" to which the concept can be attached. Superordinate concepts help make a concept meaningful by providing associations between it and related concepts.

Second, superordinate concepts allow us to make inferences about examples that we have not yet encountered. For instance, if we learn that kayaks and yawls are both boats, we can make some conclusions about their characteristics, even if we have no direct experience with them. We know, for example, that they are designed for travel on water, they're probably large enough to carry people, and they are watertight.

Table 8.3	The Relationship Between Superordinate, Coordinate, and Subordinate Concepts		
Concept	**Superordinate Concept**	**Coordinate Concept**	**Subordinate Concept**
Dog	Mammal	Dog, horse, cat	Beagle, collie
Verb	Part of speech	Noun, adjective	Action verb, linking verb
Square	Plane figure	Rectangle, triangle, circle	Large square, colored square
Conservative	Political philosophy	Liberal	Economic conservative, social conservative
Metaphor	Figure of speech	Simile, alliteration, personification	Types of metaphors

Understanding coordinate concepts is useful because they provide links to closely related concepts and can also be used as non-examples. In looking at the coordinate concepts in Table 8.3 we see that metaphor, simile, personification, and alliteration are all coordinate to one another. They are all different kinds of figures of speech, making that concept richer or deeper for students. Examples of similes, alliteration, and personification can also be used as non-examples for the concept of *metaphor*.

Similarly, subordinate concepts provide more detailed information about the concept we are teaching and can also help determine additional examples. For instance, *action verbs* and *linking verbs* are both subordinate to the concept of *verb* and the examples we choose when teaching should include cases of each.

Defining Concepts.   An efficient way of making a concept meaningful is to summarize it in a **concept definition**, which is *a statement relating the concept, a superordinate concept, and characteristics.* Al defined *indirect object* as follows: "An indirect object is the part of the sentence that tells who or what received the direct object from the subject of the sentence." *Indirect object* (the concept) is linked to *part of a sentence* (a superordinate concept), and *that tells who or what received the direct object from the sentence* (characteristics).

Concept Name.   As we introduced this section, we provided a list of concepts in Table 8.1. Technically, we provided a list of labels or terms we use to name concepts. This distinction is important, because teachers sometimes tacitly assume that they're teaching a concept by simply using the name in a definition. For instance, how much do we learn about the concept of *oxymoron* from the following description?

> An oxymoron is a statement that uses contradictory language or terms juxtaposed in the same sentence.

The answer is, typically, not much. Names are simply labels used for communication. When one person uses the term *metaphor*, for example, it communicates meaning to another person if they both understand the concept.

This is the key idea—*understanding* the concept—and this is the reason we emphasize the difference between the concept itself and the name of the concept. Understanding is best achieved by studying examples and non-examples. When learners see examples such as "The cruel kindness of an insincere kiss," or "The sweet pain of a remembered love," the concept of *oxymoron* begins to become meaningful. This meaningfulness is impossible to achieve using a name and definition alone. This same emphasis on understanding is also important in skill learning, the topic of the next section.

Goals of Direct Instruction

We have three goals when we use direct instruction to teach skills and concepts—*understanding, automaticity,* and *transfer.* They are illustrated in Figure 8.2 and discussed in the sections that follow.

Understanding   Our most fundamental goal when using direst instruction is student understanding, and, interestingly, this represents a change in thinking about teaching both concepts and skills (Bransford et al., 2000). Historically, teaching skills typically consisted of three steps: (1) the teacher would describe the skill, (2) students memorized a series of steps and practiced the skill, and (3) teachers assessed students' abilities to perform the skill. Student understanding was not a major goal of instruction; the teacher's goal was to teach students to follow the steps, *not* understand why the steps were necessary.

In a similar way, concepts were often taught as terms to be memorized. Instruction consisted of lectures in which concepts were mentioned but seldom discussed or analyzed in terms of examples, characteristics, or related concepts.

This has completely changed, and understanding is now a major goal of direct instruction. Sean's lesson illustrates this change of emphasis in skill learning. Let's look at some of his attempts to promote understanding. First, he presented the skill in the context of a real-world problem:

> Jana and Patti are friends. They were saving special soda cans to get a free CD. They can get the CD if they save 35 cans. Jana had 15 cans and Patti had 12. How many did they have together?

Using a real-world problem helped connect the new knowledge to students' existing cognitive structures and helped ensure transfer to new learning situations (Van Merriënboer, Kirschner, & Kester, 2003). Then, after reviewing to activate students' prior knowledge, he analyzed the problem to make sure students understood the logic behind the procedures they were learning. Let's see how he promoted understanding.

> **Sean:**   Everyone look up here. Good. Now what does the problem ask us? . . . Shalinda?
>
> **Shalinda:**   How many . . . they have together?

Figure 8.2

Goals of Direct Instruction

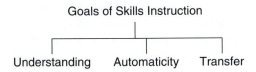

Goals of Skills Instruction

Understanding   Automaticity   Transfer

Sean:	And how many does Jana have? . . . Abdul?
Abdul:	Fifteen.
Sean:	Good, Abdul. And how many does Patti have? Celinda?
Celinda:	Twelve.
Sean:	Okay, so let's put the problem on the chalkboard like this (writing the 15 plus 12 on the board).

Sean then demonstrated the addition, using instructional scaffolding in the form of questioning to walk students through the logic of the process.

Sean:	Now show me that with your beans (he watches as students combine seven beans on their desks).
Sean:	So, how many cans did Jana and Patti have together? . . . Alesha?
Alesha:	Twenty-seven.
Sean:	Good, Alesha. They had 27 altogether. Now, with your beans, what is this 7 (pointing to the 7 on the chalkboard)? . . . Carol?"
Carol:	It's this (motioning to the seven beans on her desk).
Sean:	Good, yes it is. It's the seven individual beans. Now, what is this 2? . . . Jeremy (again pointing to the numeral on the board)?
Jeremy:	It's . . . these (holding up the two sticks with the beans glued on them).

Two aspects of Sean's teaching are important. First, he did very little lecturing; he helped students understand the skill primarily through an instructional dialogue based on questioning (Leinhardt & Steele, 2005). This not only placed them in active roles but also allowed him to monitor their developing understanding. Second, he had his students demonstrate the meaning of the numbers with concrete examples (such as having Jeremy demonstrate with the sticks and beans that the 2 in 27 was two groups of 10). In all this he strongly stressed understanding and de-emphasized memorization.

Automaticity   When we teach concepts and skills, we want students to "overlearn" them to the point that they can use the content effortlessly and virtually without conscious thought. We call this the point of automaticity. **Automaticity** *occurs when concepts and skills are overlearned so that they can be used with little conscious effort* (Bruning et al., 2004). Learning to drive a car is one example of the facilitative effects of automaticity. Initially when we learn to drive, we clutch both hands to the wheel, devoting all of our attention to the process of driving. As automaticity develops we can listen to the radio, engage in conversation, and monitor road signs and traffic signals while driving. We can do this because the skill of driving has become automatized.

Automatized skills are done (1) quickly, (2) effortlessly, (3) consistently, and (4) free of the need for conscious control (Eggen & Kauchak, 2010). These characteristics allow us to "plug in" the skills while we perform other cognitive operations.

Although we don't often think about automaticity in terms of concepts, the same ideas apply. Understanding concepts clearly allows students to use them in other cognitive endeavors. For example, understanding the concept of *place value* to the point of automaticity allows students to perform complex operations with understanding and without having to continually think about, "Now why are these numbers arranged in different columns?"

Automaticity pays off when students overlearn content (Feldon, 2007). Our available working memory is limited, and automatized content frees memory space that can be devoted to more complex tasks. For example, in writing a paper, if we have learned word-processing skills to the point of automaticity, we can use them effortlessly, allowing us to concentrate on organization and development of the paper. Similarly, if students have overlearned basic math operations, they can focus their mental energy on the solutions to word problems rather than on basic skills such as addition or subtraction. A major reason poor math students have difficulties with word problems is that performing the necessary skills requires so much available memory that they have too little left to think about or solve the problem (Bruning et al., 2004).

Transfer   When we teach skills and concepts, we want them to be used in a wide variety of settings and situations. **Transfer** *occurs when a skill learned in one context can later be applied in a different context* (Schunk, 2004). Transfer occurs, for example, when writing skills learned in English are successfully applied in writing assignments in science and social studies. Transfer also occurs when a student learns map-reading skills in geography and uses those skills to help plan a family trip. Al Lombana's goal was for his students to know what indirect objects were and to be able to use them in both English and Spanish. Our ultimate goal in teaching concepts and skills is to have them transfer both to other subject matter areas and into the real world.

Direct Instruction and Standards and Accountability

Many people equate direct instruction with standards and accountability. The reason for this is simple—many of the standards focus on skills, and direct instruction is an effective and efficient way to teach skills (Carnine et al., 2006). Consider the following elementary language arts standards from California:

Concepts About Print
1.2   Identify the title and author of a reading.
1.4   Distinguish initial, medial, and final sounds in single-syllable words.

Comprehension & Analysis of Grade-level Appropriate Text
2.3   Follow one-step written instructions.
2.7   Retell the central idea of simple expository or narrative passages.

(California Department of Education, 2010)

Each of these standards describes a skill, and direct instruction would be an effective strategy to help students learn these skills.

Although we believe that direct instruction should exist in every teacher's instructional repertoire, and that it will play a major role in teachers' efforts to help their students reach skill-based standards, we also want to voice several cautions. First, direct instruction can be overdone, resulting in what some critics call "drill and kill" teaching, and if direct instruction is the only or predominant strategy used in classrooms, the criticism is valid. Although we want our students to learn standards-based skills, we also need to remember that a total education consists of more than just skills. We also want our students to learn to think critically; appreciate topics such as art and literature; and grow up to be happy, healthy, socially competent individuals. Other teaching strategies such as guided discovery, problem solving, and cooperative learning not only help reach these other goals, but also provide much-needed motivational variety in our classrooms.

In addition, direct instruction doesn't mean that students have to work in isolation as they practice new skills to develop automaticity and learn to transfer skills to new contexts. Cooperative learning and group work provide effective alternatives to students working alone in seatwork. These social interaction strategies not only provide opportunities to practice skills, but also help develop social interaction skills in the process.

Planning for Direct Instruction

Planning for direct instruction lessons involves three steps:

- Specifying a clear learning objective
- Identifying prerequisite knowledge
- Preparing examples or problems

Specifying Clear Learning Objectives

As with all effective teaching, having precise learning objectives in mind when using direct instruction is essential. Sean, for example, had two objectives for his lesson:

- For students to be able to add two-column numbers when regrouping wasn't required
- For students to explain the difference between the ones place and the 10s place in a two-column number

As we saw during his lesson, both received instructional time and effort. This dual emphasis was a result of his clear thinking about what he wanted students to learn. Al also had a clear objective in mind—for students to understand indirect objects—and he pursued it strategically throughout his lesson.

Identifying Prerequisite Knowledge

Direct instruction focuses on teaching and learning specific concepts or skills. However, research indicates that all new learning depends on what students already know—their prior knowledge. Prior knowledge provides hooks for new learning (Schunk, 2004). In planning for direct instruction teachers need to consider how the concept or skill will be introduced and connected to what students already know.

Planning for prerequisite knowledge is slightly different for teaching a concept compared to a skill. For concepts, the task involves identifying a superordinate concept to which the concept can be linked. Although one objective when using direct instruction is to understand a specific concept (or concepts), a broader one is for students to understand how the concept relates to other, related ideas. Al did this when he related indirect objects to other parts of a sentence, such as subject and direct object.

Identifying prerequisites for a skills lesson is slightly more complicated, because it involves finding the subskills that lay the foundation for the new skill. **Task analysis**, *or the process of breaking a skill into its subparts*, can be helpful here (Morrison, Ross, & Kemp, 2004). Sean, for example, taught—and reviewed—one-column addition before he moved to two-column addition. And, his students had to know basic math facts-additional prerequisites-—before they could solve two-column addition problems.

Preparing Examples or Problems

The final task in planning for direct instruction is preparing examples or problems. A strength of direct instruction is the opportunities it provides for practice, but this practice takes different forms with different kinds of content. When learning a concept, practice involves relating the definition to concrete examples and categorizing additional examples. In learning a skill, sample problems provide practice by helping students understand the procedures within the skill and by giving them a chance to practice the skill on their own. In both, selecting concrete examples and problems is essential to the success of the lesson.

Selecting Examples in Concept Learning   When teaching concepts with direct instruction the teacher has two tasks: (1) selecting examples and (2) sequencing the examples. Examples are selected based on the extent to which they illustrate the concept's essential characteristics.

When sequencing examples, the clearest and most obvious ones are usually presented first; this simplifies the initial learning task and minimizes errors. For example, when teaching the concept of *mammal*, we would first use obvious examples such as dog, cat, cow, or horse rather than less obvious ones such as whale, seal, or bat. Once student understanding of the concept develops, additional examples such as kangaroo and duck-billed platypus can be used to enrich their understanding and broaden the concept.

The extent to which examples illustrate the essential characteristics is a second way to think about sequencing. Again in a lesson on mammals, *dog* and *cat* are good examples because they clearly illustrate characteristics such as being furry and warm blooded and nursing their young. Since most students have had direct experiences with these mammals, this makes the examples more meaningful.

Selecting Problems in Skills Instruction   In selecting and sequencing examples and problems for skill learning, student understanding and success are also important. One reason for using direct instruction is to help students acquire proficiency with the skill as efficiently and with as little student confusion and frustration as possible. This suggests that problems should be selected and sequenced so that students can develop both the skill and confidence through successful practice.

Sean accomplished this goal by providing easier problems first. He initially used problems that involved single-digit addition and then moved to two-column addition. As his students' skills develop, he will move to two-column problems that require regrouping and then to three-column or more. By sequencing from simple to complex, Sean provided instructional scaffolding that ensured high success rates and minimized frustration and confusion.

Having identified goals, determined prerequisite knowledge and skills, and selected and sequenced examples and problems, the teacher is ready to put these planning steps into action.

*I*mplementing Direct Instruction Lessons

Implementing direct instruction lessons occurs in four phases. They are illustrated in Table 8.4 and discussed in the sections that follow.

Table 8.4 **Phases in Direct Instruction Lessons**

Step	Description	Example
Introduction	A lesson overview is provided and an attempt is made to motivate students.	Sean presented the problem with Jana and Patti wanting to buy a CD and had the students explain why it was important.
Presentation	The concept or skill is explained and illustrated.	Al defined indirect object and explained its relationship to verbs and direct objects.
Guided practice	Students practice with the concept or skill under the guidance of the teacher.	Sean had his students demonstrate the solutions to problems while he monitored their progress.
Independent practice	Students practice on their own.	Al gave his students Spanish sentences in which their job was to identify the indirect object.

Phase 1: Introduction

The introduction phase in a direct instruction lesson performs several functions. First, it draws students into the activity; without student attention your best instructional efforts are wasted. In addition the introduction provides an overview of the content to follow, allowing students to see where the lesson is going, and how it relates to content already learned. The introduction also provides opportunities for the teacher to motivate students, to explain how the new content will be beneficial to them in the future. Let's examine each of these functions.

Focus Focus *is the process teachers use to attract and maintain students' attention during a learning activity.* It is important to draw students into any lesson and to focus their attention on the learning task. However, research suggests that teachers often neglect this important function (Brophy, 2004).

Sean used his soda can problem as a concrete form of focus. It provided a meaningful context for the lesson and an umbrella for the skill that the students were learning. Al used a Spanish sentence and a definition on the board to provide focus.

As another example, let's look at a science teacher introducing the skill of controlling variables. He begins by referring students back to a concrete experience they had the previous day.

> "We talked yesterday about experiments and how experiments help us learn about cause-and-effect relationships. We talked about manipulating or changing something, like in our gerbil food experiment. Today, we're going to talk about how to control variables to make our experiment more precise. Let's talk about the experiment we did yesterday."

Similarly, an art teacher who has been working on one-point perspective and is making the transition to two-point describes similarities and differences between drawing the two types of pictures. In each of these lessons, the teacher linked new material to old, ensuring that the new skill is integrated with familiar ones that students already understand.

Motivation A second element in the introductory phase of direct instruction addresses motivation. Research indicates that positive teacher expectations and clear learning goals contribute to student achievement (Brophy, 2004). Teachers can address both of these variables by clearly communicating what the skill is and why it's important and that all students can learn it if they work and persevere.

To illustrate, let's look at Sean's lesson again. He presented a concrete problem, in which Jana and Patti were saving soda cans to get a free CD and that Jana had saved 15 cans and Patti 12.

Sean:	Now, why do you think it's important to know how many Jana and Patti have together?
Devon:	So, they can know how much they get, like . . . so they can get their CD.
Sean:	Sure. If they know how many they have, they'll know how close they are to getting their CD. If they don't, they're stuck. That's why it's important.

This simple step took little time or effort, and it increased the likelihood that the problem would be meaningful and that students would think it important.

As effective teachers introduce direct instruction lessons, they attempt to connect the new topic to content that students already know. But these efforts are made more difficult by the diversity in background knowledge that exists in most classrooms, as we'll see in the Exploring Diversity section.

Phase 2: Presentation

In the second phase the teacher explains and demonstrates the skill or defines the concept. This part of the lesson is both the most crucial to skills instruction and the most difficult to implement.

Teachers have two goals during this phase. First, we want students to understand the concept or skill; second, we want them to understand how it relates to other ideas.

Earlier, we saw how strongly Sean emphasized understanding in his lesson. He developed the presentation phase with questioning, encouraging student involvement throughout the phase.

To again illustrate this emphasis on involvement and understanding, let's examine the portion of the dialogue in which Sean was helping students see the difference between the 2 in 12 and the 2 in 27.

Sean:	So let's look again. There is an important difference between this 2 (pointing to the 2 in 27) and this 2 (pointing to the 2 in the 12). What is this difference? . . . Katrina?
Katrina:	That 2 . . . is two groups of 10, and that one is just 2 by itself.
Sean:	Yes, that's good thinking, Katrina. Good work, everyone. . . . Show me this 2 (pointing to the 2 in 27, and seeing the students hold two sticks with the beans glued on them).
Sean:	Good, and show me this 2 (pointing to the 2 in the 12, and seeing the students hold up two beans).

It is difficult to overemphasize the importance of this interactive type of questioning and involvement for student learning. Without it, direct instruction becomes a teacher monologue, leaving students bored and disinterested.

Let's look at another example in which Tanya Davis, a middle school English teacher, wants her students to understand the proper use of semicolons.

Tanya: Class, today we're going to continue our discussion of different kinds of punctuation. Who remembers the different kinds of punctuation we've learned about so far? . . . Shelly?

Shelley: Commas and periods.

Tanya: Good, and who can tell us why we use punctuation in our writing? . . . Jon?

Jon: To help the reader understand what we're trying to say.

Tanya: Fine. In today's lesson, we are moving on to semicolons. After today's lesson you'll be able to use semicolons to punctuate your sentences. Semicolons are a hybrid between commas and periods. They tell the reader, "There is a pause here–pause a little longer than a comma but not as long as a period." Because they're a hybrid, they look like this (Tanya writes ';' on the board). One use of a semicolon is between two independent clauses that are not joined by "and," "but," or "or." They're useful for adding variety to our writing; they're an alternative to using conjunctions. For example, look at this sentence (which Tanya displays, "The teacher was concerned about the quiz scores; he planned a special review session." on the overhead). What are the two independent clauses here? Celeena?

Celeena: "The teacher was concerned about the test scores," and "he planned a special review session."

Tanya: Good. Notice how the ideas in the two clauses are related. That's why we don't use a period. Note, too, that the sentence could also be written this way (Tanya then displays "The teacher was concerned about the quiz scores, so he planned a special review session." on the overhead).

Tanya: In this case, we wouldn't need a semicolon. Let's take another sentence and see how a semicolon would work here (displaying "We had to wait in line for hours but the rock concert was well worth the wait."). What are the two independent clauses? . . . Gustavo?

Gustavo: "We had to wait in line for hours," and "the rock concert was worth the wait."

Tanya: Good. . . . So, how would I write this using a semicolon? . . . Biela?

Biela: "We had to wait in line for hours" semicolon and then "The rock concert was worth the wait."

Three aspects of Tanya's presentation are important:

- She described and explained the skill (using semicolons in writing).

- She provided clear examples of when and how the skill is used, by giving concrete examples of using semicolons in sentences.

- She used questioning to involve students throughout the presentation and to monitor comprehension.

We saw earlier in the chapter that effective teachers model behaviors they want their students to imitate; **think-alouds** *are forms of modeling in which teachers describe their thinking while working with examples.* When teachers use think-alouds, they want their students to understand and imitate their thought processes as they work with content. Both Sean and Tanya used think alouds in the presentation phase of their lessons.

Extra care and effort in the presentation phase, as we saw in both Sean's and Tanya's lessons, pay off in the next phase. Researchers have found that effective teachers provide many examples, give additional explanations when needed, check for student understanding, and involve their students throughout. In contrast less effective teachers often spend little time in this phase, instead moving too quickly to student practice (Eggen & Kauchak, 2010; Good & Brophy, 2008). Consequently, students are less successful, and the teacher has to slow down or back up to help individual students correct problems and misconceptions. In extreme cases unsuccessful students become frustrated and quit, and management and motivation problems develop.

Phase 3: Guided Practice

When the teacher believes that the class has a basic understanding of the skill or concept, students are ready for guided practice. In this phase the teacher supplies additional examples or problems and provides students only enough scaffolding or support to ensure that they can make progress on their own. As learners move through the zone of proximal development during this phase, they gradually accept more and more of the responsibility for explaining the concept or demonstrating the skill.

Guided practice occurred in Al's lesson when he asked students to identify the indirect object in sentences. Sean involved his students in the guided practice phase when he gave them the problem of adding 23 and 12 and watched carefully to be sure they were able to demonstrate the solution with the beans and sticks. As their understanding increased, Sean could stop having them use the beans and sticks and use only the numerals—but his emphasis at this point was to ensure that they truly understood the skill rather than simply memorize the procedure.

Student answers and success rates are barometers of learning progress in this phase. As the phase begins, some uncertainty will exist; when it ends, learners should be 80 to 90 percent successful. Choosing appropriate examples, sequencing them from simple to complex, and eliciting correct answers and reasons as students practice all influence success rates learners experience as they proceed through the zone of proximal development, the psychological place where students can benefit from teacher guidance and assistance. Student responses during this phase also provide access to student thinking, thus providing an opportunity to correct or "debug" common errors (Bruning et al., 2004). Let's see how this works with Sean and his students.

Sean's students have progressed to the point that they are now practicing subtraction with which regrouping is required. This is a more demanding skill than just simple subtracting, so the likelihood of misunderstanding and errors is present.

Let's see how Sean handles misunderstanding during the guided practice phase.

"Let's try one more," Sean directs. "Jacinta, Mario, Kevin, and Susan come up to the board and try this one." The rest of you work it at your seat and see if they get the right answer.

He then writes the following on the board:

$$46$$
$$-8$$

As he watches the students at the board, he notices that all have done the problem correctly except Kevin, who is standing and staring at the board. He walks over to Kevin, puts his hand on Kevin's shoulder, and says, "Jacinta, can you explain what you did?"

". . ."

"What did you do first, Jacinta?"

"I tried to subtract 8 from 6."

"And what happened?"

"I couldn't."

"Why not?"

"Because 8 is bigger than 6."

"So then what did you do?"

"I borrowed."

"Did everyone hear that?" Sean asks, turning to the class. "Jacinta tried to subtract 8 from 6 but she couldn't. So she had to borrow. Show us how you did that, Jacinta."

"Well, I went to the 4 and crossed it out and made it a 3."

"Now, what was this 4?" Sean probes, pointing to the 4.

". . ."

"Was it four 10s, or was it four 1s?"

". . . Four 10s."

"How do you know?"

". . . It's here" (pointing to the 4 to indicate that it is in the 10s column).

"So when you crossed out the 4 and made it a 3, what were you doing?"

"Borrowing! Uh . . . I was borrowing 10 ones from the 40 and making it 30."

"Excellent, Jacinta. And where did that 10 go? Kevin do you know?"

"Did we add it to the 6?"

"Good thinking, Kevin. Now can you subtract the 8 from 16?"

"8?"

"Good, write it down. And how much is left in the 10s column?"

"3, . . . I . . . I mean 30."

"Write that down, too. So what is the correct answer, Kevin?"

"38."

"Good work, Kevin. Now let's try another one to be sure."

Several aspects of this process are significant. First, as he did throughout the lesson, Sean emphasized understanding rather than merely performing the skill. Second, he helped Kevin—and the rest of the class—understand the process by questioning them, rather than explaining the process to them. When students struggle to understand concepts and skills, our tendency is to try and solve the problem by explaining, but, unfortunately, verbal explanations alone often do little to increase understanding. Instead, he used questioning to encourage Jacinta to show her thinking—a form of think-aloud. The questioning skills Sean demonstrated are critical to developing understanding in direct instruction lessons.

Phase 4: Independent Practice

Earlier we said that one goal of direct instruction is to develop automaticity. This is a major goal of the independent practice phase. Practice during this phase typically occurs in two steps. In the first, students work with the concept or skill in class, so the teacher can monitor learning and provide extra help if needed. In the second, students practice with the new content as an out-of-class, homework assignment.

An important transition occurs here. In previous stages student interactions were with the teacher, and the purpose of instruction was to help them understand the concept or skill. Now students primarily focus on the problems and examples, and the purpose of practice is to develop mastery and automaticity.

Effective Independent Practice   Research has identified several factors that improve the quality of independent practice (Good & Brophy, 2008):

- Independent practice should be directly related to the content covered earlier in the lesson. This seems self-evident, but, surprisingly, seatwork and homework are often unrelated to previous content. Seatwork and homework do not teach; they reinforce earlier learning!

- Independent practice should always be preceded by careful presentation and guided practice to ensure understanding.

- Monitor students as they work alone. This helps teachers assess learning and allows them to provide additional scaffolding if necessary.

- Use "response-to-need" questions and success rates as measures of the effectiveness for independent practice.

Response-to-need means that students are raising their hands because they need help and they are "responding to the need." Although some teacher assistance should be expected, if too many students are raising their hands, or if the required explanations take too long (30 seconds or more), independent practice is not accomplishing its goal. If this happens, the teacher should move confused students back to the guided practice or even the presentation phase before continuing. No rule exists to tell the teacher exactly how many response-to-need questions are too many, so professional judgment is required.

Problem situations are often quite apparent. We have observed classes in which the introduction and presentation phases were brief and somewhat cursory, guided practice was omitted entirely, and the teacher proceeded directly to independent practice. Students obviously had little idea of what they were supposed to do, so hands were up all over the room, and the teacher was running herself ragged trying to keep up with individual problems. Unconsciously, the teacher had—in effect—individualized instruction; each student had the concept or skill explained to him or her individually. This is not only inefficient in terms of learning but also enormously demanding on the teacher. Predictably, classroom management problems also develop because students are unable to do the seatwork exercises, so they become frustrated and go off task.

As with guided practice, success rates during independent practice also help gauge its effectiveness. Students should be about 90 percent successful in their seatwork to maximize learning.

Homework   Homework should be a logical extension of seatwork done in class and can be an effective strategy for increasing the amount of time and energy students spend on a topic. Research on the effects of homework indicates that it can increase learning—if carefully planned and aligned with instruction (Marzano & Pickering, 2007).

For homework to be effective, it should be a logical extension of classroom work, and success rates need to be similar or even higher than those students experience during their seatwork. This is because there often isn't someone to help students if confusion occurs. To provide focus and prevent confusion assignments should be written on the board rather than given orally.

Homework assignments should be kept relatively short; no assignment should take an elementary student longer than 20 minutes to complete. You may disagree with this figure, but many homework assignments are excessive. If the presentation and guided practice phases are properly executed, students should be able to complete their assignments quickly and effectively. When this happens, performance improves and motivation increases.

In addition to amount, the frequency of homework is important; for example, 10 problems every night is more effective than 50 once a week. Students should expect homework as one of their classroom routines, and it should be collected, scored, and returned. Alternatives for grading homework are discussed in Chapter 13 when we examine assessment.

To view a video clip of a teacher using direct instruction in a high school chemistry class, go to the Book Specific Resources tab in MyEducationLab, select your text, select Video Examples under Chapter 8, and then click on *Direct Instruction in High School Chemistry*.

Exploring Diversity

Direct Instruction with Culturally and Linguistically Diverse Students

Although research has shown direct instruction to be effective with students in general, additional research indicates that direct instruction is especially effective with students from diverse backgrounds (Gersten, Taylor, & Graves, 1999). This explicit approach to teaching concepts and skills provides culturally and linguistically diverse students with additional structure, which facilitates learning. In addition the interactive nature of the model provides opportunities for teachers to link new ideas to students' diverse content backgrounds and to continually assess learning progress. Let's see how.

Structure is important for all students. It organizes ideas and procedures, making them understandable and predictable. Structure is especially important to culturally and linguistically diverse students because school can be chaotic and confusing for them (Peregoy & Boyle, 2008). Additional research in basic skills areas, such as reading and math, suggests that a structured approach, such as direct instruction, facilitates learning in these areas (Gersten et al., 1999).

A second reason that direct instruction is effective with students from diverse backgrounds is that it provides opportunities for academically focused interaction between you and your students. These interactions are important because they help cross cultural and linguistic boundaries. Problems and examples make sense to teachers, which is why they're chosen. However, these same problems and examples may not be meaningful to students. Interactions within direct instruction provide opportunities to clarify examples and elicit culturally relevant examples from students.

Direct instruction can also be effective with English language learning (ELL) students and in sheltered English instruction. In these classes teachers have the dual goals of teaching content while building upon students' developing English skills. Experts in the area (Peregoy & Boyle, 2008) recommend incorporating the following effective ELL instructional elements into your lessons:

- Specific targeting of key concepts or skills
- Activation of students' prior knowledge
- Extensive use of demonstrations and modeling
- Emphasis on students' active involvement
- Opportunities for extensive practice

Each of these recommendations, when integrated into direct instruction, makes this strategy optimally suited for linguistically diverse students.

Technology and Teaching

Capitalizing on Technology in Direct Instruction

To be effective, direct instruction needs to include opportunities to practice the skills students are learning. But extended practice takes time, and teachers often struggle to provide sufficient opportunities for students to develop skill levels needed to develop automaticity with basic skills. Technology provides one solution to this problem.

Drill and Practice

Students often use work sheets and flash cards to practice basic skills, such as word recognition and phonetic analysis in reading, and addition and multiplication facts in math. Educators wondered, "Could computers be used to provide an improved form of practice?" This question led to the development of **drill-and-practice programs**, *software designed to provide extensive practice with feedback* (Lever-Duffy, McDonald, & Mizell, 2003).

Because students can use drill-and-practice programs on their own, teachers don't have to be directly involved. However, they don't substitute for teachers' expertise, and developers of these programs assume that students have had previous instruction related to the facts or concepts. For example, when students first learn about multiplication, effective teachers help them understand that 3×4 means 3 sets of 4 items, or 4 sets of 3 items, and they present several concrete examples to illustrate the concept of *multiplication*. After this initial instruction teachers have students use drill-and-practice programs to help students practice until the skill becomes automatic—that is, until they know the facts without having to think about them.

The best drill-and-practice programs are adaptive, matching the demands of the task to a student's ability. For example, in a program designed to improve knowledge of multiplication facts, an adaptive program begins by pretesting to determine which multiplication facts students already know. The program then strategically presents problems to ensure high success rates. When students fail to answer or answer incorrectly, the program prompts by providing the answer and then retests that fact. The program introduces more difficult problems only when students have reached a certain skill level. Because the ultimate goal is for students to be able to recall math facts automatically, the program shortens the amount of time given to answer as students become more proficient. This also increases motivation by challenging students to become quicker in their responses.

What are the benefits of drill-and-practice programs? First, they provide practice with effective feedback, informing students immediately of what they've mastered and where they need more work. Second, they are often motivating for students turned off by paper-and-pencil exercises (Gee, 2005), and third, they save teachers' time, because they don't have to present information and score students' responses.

Researchers caution, however, that more time on computers does not necessarily equal more learning (Roblyer & Doering, 2010). More important are the quality of the learning experiences and the extent to which they are linked to the teacher's goals.

Tutorials

Tutorials provide a second way for teachers to use technology to teach basic skills. A **tutorial** *is a computerized software program that delivers an entire integrated instructional sequence similar to a teacher's instruction on the topic.* Let's see how Lisa Hoover, a first-grade teacher uses a tutorial to teach basic skills.

Lisa has created a number of learning centers in her classroom where her students work independently. Students can earn "classroom money" for good behavior and finishing assignments and can use the money to purchase prizes from the class store. Students who work in the store as clerks must first complete several of the math units, with the last one focusing on giving change. Lisa's students have widely varying backgrounds, and as a result, she has students who want to take the giving-change unit at different times. In the past they often had to wait or she had to drop some other activity to teach them the rules for calculating and counting change.

To accommodate their differences in background, she has them work with a computerized tutorial that helps them acquire these skills. The tutorial includes pictures of various coins and presents a number of scenarios that provide students with practice in giving change. Now students can complete the unit anytime they have access to one of the computers in the classroom. In addition Lisa designs the tutorial so that it will give students a number of problems and ongoing help until they master the information.

Tutorials include specific learning objectives, multiple pathways to them, and quizzes with feedback geared to the objectives. If a teacher's goal is for students to be able to add positive and negative numbers, the tutorial will pretest students and then present instruction with frequent assessment and feedback. When a student answers 2.8 to the problem, $-2.3 + 0.5 = ?$, for instance, the program responds with, "Think about the sign of the numbers and try again." Then, if the student tries again and answers -1.8, the program responds, "Well done, [student's name]. You understand the idea. Now, try this problem." As students' skills improve, they are given increasingly complex problems.

Tutorials can replicate each of the phases of direct instruction, and they have the added advantage of providing the students with ongoing personalized feedback about their progress. The best tutorials include motivational features such as timed tests that provide challenge and lead to automaticity, as well as charts that illustrate increasing skill development.

Tutorials can be linear, but the best are branched and adapt to learners' responses (Roblyer & Doering, 2010). For example, when a student responds incorrectly to a multiple-choice item, the program explains why that choice isn't correct and repeats the initial instruction, explains the idea in a different way, or directs the learner back to previous instruction.

Effective tutorials are flexible, adaptive, and efficient. Lisa's lesson was available anytime; students didn't have to wait until she had free time to teach them. Also, it provided each student with the right amount of practice to master the content, and her students found the pictures and video clips more motivating than traditional work sheets.

Tutorials exist in a variety of skill areas. For example, *General Physics* (MCH Multimedia, 2009) is a comprehensive multimedia high school and non-calculus college physics tutorial that includes simulations, visual demonstrations, movies, animations, sound effects, and voice comments help to emphasize key concepts. It also includes exercises and quizzes with feedback to provide help with a variety of physics topics, including vectors, kinematics, Newton's laws, and electromagnetic theory.

Programs that teach word-processing skills are some of the most popular applications of tutorials. They include instruction on printing, saving, spell checking, and formatting text with different fonts, sizes, and styles (Roblyer & Doering, 2010). The best include motivational features such as timed tests that provide challenge and lead to automaticity, as well as charts that illustrate the progression of skill mastery.

Tutorials have been criticized for focusing too much on memorized information instead of challenging students to think and apply understanding (Newby, Stepich, Lehman, & Russell, 2006; Roblyer & Doering, 2010). Although this doesn't have to be the case, finding high-quality tutorial software and effective hypermedia materials is a challenge facing teachers who want to integrate tutorials into their classrooms.

Finally, we want to emphasize that no tutorial, regardless of quality, can replace the skills expert teachers demonstrate with their students. Tutorials support effective instruction; they do not replace it.

The Role of Assessment in Direct Instruction

If you are to assist students in learning during direct instruction, you need to monitor their developing thinking (Safer & Fleischman, 2005). As you listen to students describe their developing understanding, you can assess the extent to which students are constructing valid ideas. This is a form of **informal assessment**, which is the *process of using students' comments and answers during learning activities to assess their understanding.*

Student responses are essential in gauging learning progress. To maximize learning two aspects of questioning are important. First, be sure to elicit responses from as many students as possible. This ensures that *all* students understand the concept or skill, not just ones who volunteer. One way to do this is to call on non-volunteers as well as volunteers. Other ways of assessing understanding are to ask for a simple show of hands or an unobtrusive thumbs-up or thumbs-down on the chest indicating whether students got the problem right or correctly categorized the example. Another way to check understanding is to have students work several problems and check the work by switching papers.

In this process, queries such as "Are there any questions?" or "Do you understand?" are generally not helpful. The students who don't understand typically nod along with the ones who do, afraid or embarrassed to admit that they don't understand an idea. If there are questions, the students who have them usually won't admit it. (Think back on your own experience; no one wants to admit that he or she doesn't understand something—everyone assumes he or she is the only one who is confused.)

Questions that actually ask students to demonstrate that they understand new content avoid this problem. Systematic and continuous formative assessment during direct instruction lessons provides teachers with a powerful tool to deal with background differences that students bring to the classroom.

A second important aspect of questioning during guided practice is to gauge the quality of student answers. Correct, quick, and firm answers indicate that students understand the concept or skill, and general, simple praise, such as "Good answer" is effective. This maintains a brisk lesson pace allowing additional examples or problems. Correct but hesitant answers suggest that students are not confident about the new content, and you can respond with appropriate supports such as interspersed explanations and encouraging feedback (e.g., "Yes, the apostrophe in this case indicates a contraction, not a possessive. We see there is no possession suggested in the sentence.")

Incorrect but careless answers also need to be differentiated from more serious problems. If the teacher thinks the student understands the process but got the answer wrong because of a rushed answer (e.g., a computational error), she can simply correct the error and move on. If, however, the mistake appears to indicate a misunderstanding of the concept or skill, additional explanation and questioning can help correct the misconception. If a number of students are making errors, the material may need to be retaught.

The Motivational Benefits of Effective Feedback

As students wrestle with the new concept or skill, effective teachers provide informative feedback. The quality of this feedback influences student motivation in two ways (Brophy, 2004). First, information assists learning, allowing students to understand the new content more efficiently. Seeing their own learning progress is motivating. Second, the content and tone of the feedback influence students' perceptions of their developing ability as learners.

Effective feedback has four essential characteristics:

- It is immediate.
- It is specific.
- It provides corrective information for the learner.
- It has a positive emotional tone. (Eggen & Kauchak, 2010)

As students try out the new concept or skill, the teacher assists by pinpointing errors, suggesting correct alternatives, and doing this in a positive and supportive manner.

A more subtle motivational aspect of feedback focuses on the implicit messages it gives about student competence and effort (Schunk et al., 2008). As students struggle to master new content, teacher comments about effort help reinforce the idea that effort results in achievement. Comments such as "This is a tough idea but hang in there" and "I know your hard work will pay off" help focus students' attention on the critical link between effort and learning. These comments are especially useful for low-ability students and students with learning problems (Brophy, 2004).

However, as with all strategies, professional sensitivity and judgment are essential. If teachers praise profusely when effort is minimal, for example, students tend to discredit the feedback and their own efforts and abilities as learners (Brophy, 2004).

Informal assessments are valuable but incomplete and potentially misleading because they don't provide insights into the learning progress of *all* students. This leads us to the need for **formal assessment**, *which is the process of systematically gathering information about understanding from all learners.* This can be done through quizzes, assignments, and homework, which provide learning samples from all students. When done well, formal assessments allow teachers to look into students' heads and provides students with practice and feedback about learning progress.

Summary

Direct Instruction in the Classroom

Although a great deal of emphasis has been placed on learner-centered instruction, some goals are better met with teacher-centered approaches such as direct instruction. When learners study well-defined content that all are expected to master or when students will have difficulty acquiring content on their own, direct instruction can be effective.

Direct instruction is a strategy used to teach skills and concepts. Skills are forms of learning that have a specific set of operations, can be illustrated with large numbers of examples, and are developed through practice. Concepts are categories that are illustrated through positive and negative examples.

Concepts form an important part of the curriculum. When we teach concepts, we want students to understand (1) the concept's essential characteristics, (2) how these relate to positive and negative examples, and (3) the relationship of the concept to other ideas. This last function is accomplished by linking the concept to superordinate, coordinate, and subordinate concepts.

Planning for Direct Instruction

Planning for direct instruction lessons begins with the formation of a specific learning objective that guides our actions during instruction. A second planning task involves determining prerequisite knowledge that will serve as the foundation for new knowledge. A final planning task is finding or constructing examples or problems to illustrate the content being taught. These also need to be sequenced to ensure high success rates.

Implementing Direct Instruction Lessons

Direct instruction lessons begin with an introduction, which is followed by the teacher presenting and modeling or explaining the concept or skill. Students next practice the new content, first under the supervision of the teacher and then on their own. The goal in direct instruction lessons is to develop the new content to the point of automaticity, so that it transfers to a variety of contexts.

The Role of Assessment in Direct Instruction

Assessment is an essential part of direct instruction, providing both teachers and students with feedback about learning progress. Informal assessment through interactive questioning allows teachers to continually monitor learning progress throughout the lesson. Formal assessment systematically gathers information from all students and provides a final check on learning progress.

*I*mportant Concepts

Automaticity (p. 258)   Non-example (p. 253)
Characteristics (p. 253)   Observational learning (p. 250)
Concept definition (p. 256)   Scaffolding (p. 251)
Concepts (p. 252)   Skills (p. 251)
Coordinate concept (p. 255)   Subordinate concept (p. 255)
Examples (p. 253)   Superordinate concept (p. 255)
Focus (p. 262)   Task analysis (p. 260)
Formal assessment (p. 272)   Think-alouds (p. 264)
Informal assessment (p. 271)   Transfer (p. 259)
Model (p. 254)   Tutorial (p. 270)
Modeling (p. 250)

*P*reparing for Your Licensure Exam

As you've studied this chapter, you've seen how direct instruction provides an effective way to teach concepts and skills. As you read the following case study, look for different ways this teacher used the different phases of direct instruction to promote learning in her classroom.

The Power of Classroom Practice
www.myeducationlab.com

After reading this case, go to the Book Specific Resources tab in MyEducationLab, select your text, select *Preparing for Your Licensure Exam* under Chapter 8 to complete the questions that accompany the case and receive feedback on your responses.

Margaret Fontini looks over the year-long plans she has laid out for her sixth-grade language arts curriculum and discovers notes from her previous teaching year:

Students have trouble with summarization. Don't know where to start.

"I remember that unit. It was like pulling teeth. I just didn't know how to get the idea across. I've got to do better this time," she mumbles to herself as she opens several language arts teacher editions on her bookshelf. On Monday Margaret begins her language arts class by saying, "Okay, class please put your math away. If you haven't finished your problems, be sure to take them home and have them ready for class tomorrow."

After pausing for a few moments while students put their math books away, Margaret continues, "Today in language arts we're going to learn a new skill that will help us with our writing. It's called summarization. It will help you learn in language arts, and it should be helpful in other content areas as well. I'd like everyone to look up here on the overhead. I've got a definition for you."

A GOOD SUMMARY RESTATES THE MAIN IDEA OF THE PASSAGE, DELETES UNIMPORTANT AND REDUNDANT INFORMATION, AND, SOMETIMES, INVOLVES SUPERORDINATION.

After pausing for a few moments to allow her students to read the definition, Margaret continues on.

"Let's see what a good summary looks like. I'd like you to read this passage and then I'm going to show you two summaries. Your job is to see if you can tell me which is the better summary for the paragraph. Here we go."

In the desert there are no clouds to stop the sun's burning rays. So the sun heats up the earth. As a result, it gets very hot, the temperature easily reaching 120 degrees. And rainfall is slight in the desert. Most deserts get less than 10 inches of rain per year. Years may pass between showers. Sometimes 5 or 10 years may go by without a drop of rain falling on the desert.

"Has everyone had a chance to read the paragraph? Now, let's look at two possible summaries that I've created. Look up on the overhead and tell me which is better."

1. The desert is a hot and dry place.
2. The sun in the desert is merciless.

"Who has an idea? Which do you think is better? Tanya?"

"I think number 1 is better. It . . ."

"Good Tanya, I agree with you. Number 1 is definitely better. Let's try another one. Again, read the paragraph and then I'll give you two possibilities to choose from."

The heat doesn't bother the seeds from plants, and they can do without water for an extended period. After a rain the seeds sprout and flowers bloom. Then the desert is covered with many brightly colored flowers. The desert is a beautiful place when there are red, yellow, orange, and blue flowers everywhere. But soon the ground begins to dry up. As the ground dries, the flowers produce new seeds and then die. These new seeds fall to the ground and wait for the next rainfall. When it rains, they grow, blossom, leave new seeds, and then die.

"Has everyone had a chance to read this and think about a summary? Okay then, which of these do you think is the better summary? Look up here on the overhead."

1. Desert flowers bloom only after a rain.
2. Seeds are perfectly suited to the desert.

"Ricardo, do you have an answer?"

"I think number 2 is better because the paragraph is more about seeds than flowers."

"Good, Ricardo. Does everyone agree? Any questions? If not, I have several more paragraphs about the desert that I'd like you to summarize on your own and we'll compare our answers tomorrow."

With that she hands out a piece of paper that has four paragraphs on it.

"Remember class, you're supposed to write a summary for each of these paragraphs. Get busy, and I'll be around to help."

As students start on their assignment, Margaret circulates around the room. As she does this a number of hands go up, asking for help. As she works with each student, she notices that they are all having trouble knowing where to start.

"Hmm, I guess I better do more work on getting started writing a summary. I'll do that first thing in class tomorrow."

Questions for Analysis

Let's examine Margaret's lesson now based on the information in this chapter. In your analysis consider the following questions. In each case, be specific and take information directly from the case study in doing your analysis.

1. How effective was the introduction phase of the lesson? How could Margaret's introduction be improved?

2. How effective was the presentation phase of the lesson? How could it be improved?

3. How effective was the guided-practice phase of the lesson? Explain, making direct reference to the case study in your assessment.

4. Analyze Margaret's examples during teacher-directed practice, using the concept of *scaffolding*.

5. Analyze the quality of the independent practice phase of the lesson. How could the independent practice phase of the lesson be improved?

 *D*iscussion Questions

1. How do the following factors influence the importance of skills in the curriculum?
   a. Grade level
   b. Subject matter
   c. Ability level of students (i.e., high versus low)

2. Some researchers in the area of concept learning have suggested that the optimal number of positive/negative examples to be used in teaching a concept is three. What factors might influence this number?

3. What advantages are there in asking students to generate their own examples and non-examples of concepts? What disadvantages might exist?

4. Why is automaticity important to the following skills:
   a. Learning to print in first grade
   b. Learning to play a musical instrument
   c. Learning a foreign language

5. Teachers often have to make professional compromises: You've just begun a direct instruction lesson and find out that because of a changed school schedule, you have only half as much time as you had planned. How will you adjust your teaching with respect to the four phases of the direct instruction model? Why?
   a. Introduction
   b. Explanation
   c. Guided practice
   d. Independent practice

6. How would you teach for transfer in the following lessons?
   a. Teaching the concept of *verb* to fourth-grade students
   b. Teaching punctuation skills to middle school students
   c. Teaching percentage word problems to high school basic math students

7. What is the optimal amount of daily homework for the students you'll be teaching? How does this figure differ for different grade levels? Why?

Portfolio Activities

1. *Skills and State and District Standards.* Analyze the state standards in your area or level and answer the following questions:
   a. What skills are identified?
   b. What suggestions or recommendations are given about how they should be taught?
   c. How are the skills sequenced?
   d. How is skill acquisition measured?

   How helpful will standards such as these be for you as a teacher when you plan?

2. *Textbooks and Skills.* Examine a text in your area and answer the following questions:
   a. How much of the text is devoted to skills?
   b. How are the skills sequenced?
   c. What provision is there for practice and feedback?
   d. How does the text deal with long-term retention and transfer? How would you need to supplement this text to maximize skill learning in your classroom?

3. *Concept Learning: The Students' Perspective.* Identify a concept that you believe is important. Interview several students, ideally some who are high and low in ability, asking them to explain the concept in terms of the following:
   a. Essential characteristics
   b. Examples
   c. Links to other concepts

   What do students' responses tell you about their understanding of the concept? What implications do their responses have for you as a teacher?

4. *Homework.* Interview a teacher or student and ask the following questions:
   a. How often is homework given?
   b. Is there any pattern to homework assignments (e.g., end-of-week or end-of-unit reviews)?
   c. Is homework graded and returned?
   d. How does it count toward the final grade in the course?
   e. How effective is it in promoting learning?

   How could homework be improved to increase learning in the classroom?

5. *Direct Instruction: Concept Teaching.* Observe a teacher teaching a concept (or teach one yourself, and either audio- or videotape yourself) and critique the lesson in terms of the following criteria:
   a. Characteristics clearly defined
   b. Examples and non-examples linked to characteristics
   c. Superordinate concept familiar to students
   d. Coordinate concept clearly differentiated from the target concept

   How could the lesson be improved?

6. *Interactive Skills Teaching.* Observe a teacher teaching a skill (or teach one yourself and either audio- or videotape yourself) and analyze the lesson in terms of
   a. Introduction
   b. Explanation

    c. Teacher-directed practice

    d. Independent practice

How could the lesson be improved to increase student learning?

7. *Direct Instruction: Trying It Out.* Plan for, teach, and tape a skills lesson using direct instruction. Listen to or watch your tape and address the following questions:

    a. Was your introduction clear? Did it include the following:

        1. What the skill or concept was

        2. How it can be applied

        3. Why it is useful

        4. When it should be used

    b. Did you state a goal or objective for the lesson?

    c. Did you relate the concept or skill to material previously covered?

    d. Did you think aloud while modeling the skill or explaining the concept?

    e. What did student success rates during the following activities suggest about your pace:

        1. Teacher-directed practice

        2. Independent practice

    f. How did the amount of teacher talk vary throughout the lesson?

    g. What percentage of the class understands the concept or can perform the skill at an acceptable level? How do you know? Define what this level is and explain why this level is acceptable.

What would you do differently next time?

To check your comprehension of the content covered in Chapter 8, go to the Book Specific Resources in MyEducationLab, select your text, and complete the Study Plan quiz. In addition to receiving feedback on your answers, a study plan will be generated from the quiz that will direct you to access Review, Practice, and Enrichment materials to enhance your understanding of chapter content.

Lecture Discussions: Interactive Instruction to Promote Learning

Chapter Outline	Learning Objectives
	When you've completed your study of this chapter, you should be able to
Organized bodies of knowledge: Integrated content	1. Explain how organized bodies of knowledge are different from other forms of content in the curriculum.
The limitations of lectures	2. Describe the strengths and weaknesses of teacher lectures.

Lecture discussions: Alternatives to standard lectures
■ The effectiveness of lecture discussions
■ Planning for lecture discussions
  Technology and Teaching:
    Using technology to structure and organize content
■ Implementing lecture discussion lessons
  Exploring Diversity:
    Differences in background knowledge
	3. Explain how lecture discussion lessons can be planned and implemented.

Assessing learning in lecture discussions	4. Describe the role of assessment in lecture discussion lessons.

In Chapter 8 you saw how direct instruction can be used to teach concepts and skills. But sometimes we need to give students the "big picture," explaining how separate ideas are connected. We call this kind of content *organized bodies of knowledge,* and direct instruction isn't designed for this. This leads us to lecture discussions, an instructional strategy that uses social interaction to actively involve students as they learn organized bodies of knowledge.

Lecture discussions are designed as alternatives to traditional lectures. When we see the term *lecture,* we usually think of teacher monologues that are both boring and ineffective. However, this doesn't have to be the case. When combined with frequent periods of teacher-led questioning, lectures can be adapted into effective teaching strategies. As you read the following case study, think about the kind of content the teacher wants her students to understand and the different ways she attempts to involve them in her lesson.

Emma Houston is an American government teacher who is immersed in a unit on the Constitution, including topics such as the electoral college, the three branches of government, and the role and function of each branch. She is now planning a lesson on the constitutional compromise that led to our present Senate and House of Representatives.

As Emma plans her lesson, she outlines the topic in her notebook, sketching the information shown in Figure 9.1.

She inputs the information into a PowerPoint transparency and heads for her first-period class.

As the bell rings, Emma begins, "Okay everyone, let's review what we've been discussing so far in this unit." She then reviews the different branches of the government and the characteristics of each.

Figure 9.1

Representation of Constitutional Compromise

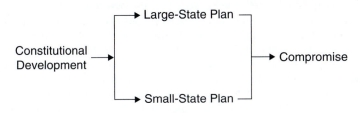

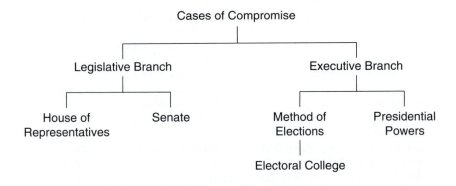

After completing her review she continues by saying, "Listen everyone. . . . To continue our work on the Constitution, I'd like to pose a problem to you. Mrs. Shah [another teacher in the school] has a special project she wants done, and she wants the smartest kid she can find to do it. Manolo wants the job and thinks he is qualified. He's a good writer and gets good grades on his essays. However, Jo also wants the job, and she thinks she is better qualified than Manolo. She's a whiz in math. What is Mrs. Shah going to do?"

"What are they supposed to do in the project?" Katy wonders.

"Well, a variety of things," Emma responds. "Mrs. Shah will have them doing things that involve math and some that involve writing."

"Boy, it's hard to tell," Ramon adds. "How would you know?"

"Maybe take them both," Sue suggests. "Could she do that?"

"That's an excellent idea, Sue. Why not compromise and take them both? Think about that everyone."

She pauses a moment and then continues, "The situation we're going to discuss today is sort of an analogy to Mrs. Shah's problem. The makers of our country's Constitution were in a dilemma when it came to making a decision about how to elect our leaders. The compromises that had to be made are what we're going to discuss today. As we study this compromise, keep Mrs. Shah's problem in mind."

Emma then strides across the front of the room and continues, "I know I've said it before, but it's so important I'll have to repeat it again. The Constitution was a series of compromises between people like you and me. Just as Mrs. Shah could compromise and perhaps take both Manolo and Jo, the people who developed the Constitution had very different views of where this new country was heading. To arrive at something they could all agree on, they had to compromise.

"The forms of the compromise are diagrammed on the transparency you see," Emma says, displaying the information in Figure 9.1 on the overhead.

She continues, "The nature of this compromise process came out very clearly in the part of the Constitution having to do with the way we elect the members of Congress. Originally, when our forefathers were writing the Constitution, there was a lot of disagreement about how votes in the legislature should be allocated. Small states like Rhode Island wanted each state to have the same number of votes. Delaware wanted that too. On the other hand, big states like New York and Pennsylvania wanted the votes to be determined by the number of people in the state. . . . Each idea seemed fair to the states that proposed them. The small states wanted votes allocated by state; the large states wanted the votes to be distributed on the basis of population. Both of the ideas seemed fair, and neither side wanted to give in."

"So, as a compromise, they created a legislature with two bodies. The House of Representatives was based on population, and today we have 435 representatives. The most populous states, of course, have many more representatives than smaller ones. By contrast, the Senate has two members from each state. So, now we have 50 states times 2, which equals 100 senators. . . . See how this is similar to Mrs. Shah's problem. She compromised by selecting both Manolo and Jo, and our country's leaders compromised by using features of both the small state and large state plan."

"Now, let's analyze this process of compromise. How were the states supporting the two proposals different? . . . Miguel?"

". . . New York was a large state, and Rhode Island was a very small state."

"Yes, good, Miguel," Emma smiles. "And what does that mean? . . . Jamie?"

". . . Well, it was bigger," Jamie responds hesitantly.

"Bigger land area or bigger population?" Emma continues.

". . . Both, I think," Jamie continues, "But probably the bigger population was more important."

"Yes, good, Jamie. Now why would the large states think the way they did, and also why would the small states think the way they did? What do you think? . . . Simao?"

". . . It would relate to power," Simao answers. "If the representation was made on the basis of population, the large states would be more powerful than the small states."

"On the other hand, what would happen if representation were completely equal among the states?" Emma continues. ". . . Toni?"

". . . It would sort of throw the balance in the favor of the smaller states. It would mean a state like Wyoming with very little population could maybe stop a proposal from a big state like California."

"So as part of the process of compromise what part of the legislature is based on population? . . . Camille?

"The . . . the House of Representatives?"

"Excellent, Camille. The total number of representatives is 435. The number of representatives from each state is determined by population. That would make populous states happy. And what part of the compromise made the smaller states happy? . . . Kareem?"

"The Senate?"

"Why, Kareem?"

"Because every state gets two, no matter how big or small they are."

"Excellent thinking everyone!" Emma comments enthusiastically.

Although Emma's lesson was teacher directed, it was much more than simply lecturing to students as they sat passively and listened. She emphasized student understanding and encouraged students learn the new content by actively involving them during the lesson. She chose a lecture discussion strategy because of the content she was teaching and the learning objectives she wanted her students to achieve. Let's look at this content in more detail.

Organized Bodies of Knowledge: Integrated Content

To help us understand the type of content Emma taught, let's contrast it with José Alvarez's lesson in Chapter 6 and Al Lombana's in Chapter 8. José wanted his students to understand two related principles: *Heat makes materials expand* and *heat makes molecules move faster.* Al taught the concept of *indirect object.* Each was a specific form of content, and these specific topics were the focus of their lessons. Unlike José's or Al's, Emma's lesson involved combinations of these specific forms of content. It focused on the general topic of political compromise, and within it were concepts such as *Congress, House of Representatives,* and *Senate*, as well as facts, such as the number of representatives and senators in each house of Congress, relative sizes of states, and the way representatives and senators are apportioned to each state. More significantly the lesson didn't focus on any of these elements specifically; rather, it was aimed at understanding the relationships among all these parts. Emma was teaching an **organized body of knowledge**, *which is a combination of facts, concepts, generalizations, principles, and rules, integrated with one another.*

As another example a high school English teacher is comparing novels by twentieth-century American writers. The unit deals with the relationships among a number of facts and concepts such as *plot, setting,* and *character* and generalizations such as "Writers' life experiences are reflected in their writing." It doesn't focus on any of the elements separately.

Organized bodies of knowledge are an important part of the school curriculum. For example, geography students study the topography, climate, culture, and politics of one country and compare them to the same elements in other countries. In a study of immigration in the late nineteenth and early twentieth centuries, American history students examine reasons different groups of immigrants came to the United States, the difficulties they encountered, and the ways they were assimilated into our culture. Chemistry students study the elements in the periodic table and the relationships among them. These all involve organized bodies of knowledge.

One specialized subset of organized bodies of knowledge are **theories**, *which have precisely described relationships among the concepts and generalizations in it*. In science we have the theory of evolution, molecular theory, and theories about the origins of the universe. In the social sciences we have learning theories such as behaviorism and constructivism, sociological theories such as Durkheim's theory of suicide, and economic theories such as supply-side economics. Each of these can be taught using a lecture discussion instructional strategy.

The Limitations of Lectures

A **lecture** *is a form of instruction in which students receive information delivered in a verbal and (presumably) organized way by teachers.* The prevalence of the lecture as a teaching method is paradoxical. Although it is the most criticized of all teaching methods, it continues to be the most commonly used (Cuban, 1984). The popularity of lectures can be traced to three factors (Eggen & Kauchak, 2010):

- Lectures are easy to plan; the planning process is reduced to organizing the content, with less attention devoted to teaching strategy or student motivation.

- Lectures are flexible; they can be applied to virtually all content areas.

- Lectures are simple to implement and require less energy from teachers. Simply "telling" students helps teachers maintain control. So classroom management usually isn't an issue. Guiding students with questioning is much more demanding because of the "thinking on their feet" that it requires. Most teachers can learn to deliver acceptable lectures; guiding student learning through teacher questioning is more challenging.

Lectures can be effective for helping students acquire information not readily accessible in other ways; they can be used to provide information that would take students hours to find on their own. Emma's topic is an example. Finding and organizing all the historical information that led to the organization of our country's legislative branch, as it appears today, would be difficult for her students.

In spite of their popularity, lectures are ineffective for many, if not most, students. They put learners in passive roles by encouraging them to merely listen and absorb information. Student involvement is essential for classroom learning, and research on young (Berk, 2010) and poorly motivated students (Brophy, 2004) helps us understand why. If we observe a class of young children, we'll often notice that they'll sit quietly for the first few minutes of a teacher explanation but soon start to fidget and look around. If the monologue continues, they not only tune out, but start talking and poking one another, seeking some type of activity.

Lectures have similar negative effects on older students, who are usually less disruptive, but still unable to learn passively. Because they've learned that fidgeting and talking can get them into trouble, some prop their heads on their hands and attempt to appear interested. Others give up completely and work on homework for other classes, read, or put their heads down on their desks. Unfortunately, some teachers continue lecturing despite these clear signs that few are listening or learning.

A second reason for lectures' ineffectiveness is that they can, and often do, overload students' capacity to remember information. The component of our memory system that consciously organizes information in an effort to make it meaningful is limited (Feldon, 2007), and the amount of information presented in lectures commonly exceeds its capacity. This helps us understand a common lament from teachers: "I explained it so carefully; it's as if they didn't hear a word I said." It is more likely that the students did hear the words but couldn't process the information quickly enough, so much of it was lost.

A third problem with lectures is that they don't allow teachers to assess whether students are learning. During interactive lessons, students' responses to teachers' questions provide information about learning progress. If understanding is inaccurate or incomplete, teachers can adapt their instruction by providing additional examples and asking more questions to remedy the problem. Because communication is one way in lectures, teachers have no way of making these assessments and adapting their instruction.

The ineffectiveness of lecture is well documented by research. In seven comparisons of lecture to discussion, discussion was superior in all seven studies on measures of retention and higher-order thinking. In addition, discussion was superior in seven of nine studies in terms of student attitude and motivation (McKeachie & Kulik, 1975).

Lecture discussion is designed to overcome these deficiencies by combining brief presentations of content with discussions that actively involve learners. We turn to it now.

Lecture Discussions: Alternatives to Standard Lectures

Lecture discussion *is a teaching strategy that combines short periods of teacher presentation with extensive teacher-student interaction.* This strategy combines the positive aspects of lecture—flexibility and economy of effort—with the benefits of interactive teaching. It is an instructional hybrid, effectively designed to help students understand organized bodies of knowledge. Emma Houston used lecture discussion to teach her students about political compromise. Let's see why it's effective.

The Effectiveness of Lecture Discussions

The effectiveness of lecture discussions is grounded in the research on how we process information and learn (Bruning et al., 2004; Schunk, 2004). Our memory is composed of three interrelated parts:

- **Sensory memory** is *the part of our memory system that briefly holds information from the environment until it can be processed into working memory.* As the term suggests, information enters this memory store through our senses, most commonly sight and hearing, but also taste, touch, and smell.

- **Working memory** is *the part of our memory where we select and organize information in an effort to make it meaningful.* Working memory is where conscious thinking takes place and where students put different ideas together into coherent organized bodies of knowledge. This is also the place where students connect new information with what they already have stored in long-term memory.

- **Long-term memory** is *our permanent information store,* where we keep information until we retrieve it for further use or processing. Its capacity is large, and if information stored in it is well organized, the information is enduring and accessible for later retrieval and for combining with new information during lecture discussions.

These parts are outlined in Figure 9.2, and their role in lecture discussions is discussed in the paragraphs that follow.

In Figure 9.2 we see that as stimuli from the environment enter our consciousness, we select those stimuli that attract our attention and organize the information in working memory as we construct meaning from the experience. During the process of constructing understanding we retrieve information from long-term memory and integrate the new information with the information we retrieve. The better organized our information is in long-term memory, the more effective that integration will be.

Let's see how these processes worked in Emma's lesson. She began by presenting Mrs. Shah's problem. This was intended to attract students' attention and provide a focal point for the lesson. Then, she presented information to students in a brief lecture. Keeping the amount of information presented very brief is important for maintaining attention and avoiding overloading students' working memories. She also helped students organize the information in their working memories by providing an outline on her overhead.

Figure 9.2

Integrating New Knowledge with Prior Understanding

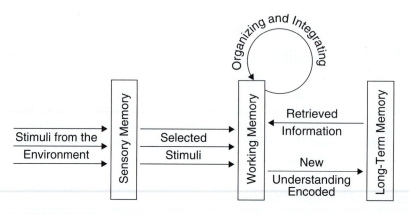

After checking to ensure that students' comprehension of the material she presented was accurate, Emma presented additional information, again asking questions to check for understanding and helping students integrate the new information with what they already knew. This process continues until lessons come to closure.

What and how students retain new information is dependent upon their prior knowledge (Bruning et al., 2004). We see this illustrated in both the real world and in school. A person who has read extensively about a topic has a learning advantage over those with less background knowledge. In this regard "he more you know, the more capacity you have for knowing" works since you have more hooks on which to hang new knowledge.

In summary lecture discussions work because they encourage students to connect new information with what they already know and then organize it for storage in long-term memory. When these connections are made and information is stored in long-term memory in an organized way, we have a successful lecture discussion lesson. Having examined why lecture discussions work, let's turn now to planning for these lessons.

Planning for Lecture Discussions

Planning for lecture discussion lessons involves four steps, outlined in Figure 9.3 and discussed in the sections that follow.

Identifying Topics   The first step in planning for a lecture discussion is to identify an organized body of knowledge. To illustrate this process, let's look at several lessons that involve teaching an organized body of knowledge:

- Kathy Johnson, a middle school socials studies teacher, wants her students to understand differences between the Northern and Southern colonies. Understanding this is important because these differences would later lead to the Civil War.

- Sherry Southerland, an elementary science teacher wants her students to understand how all mammals were similar and different from other kinds of animals.

Figure 9.3

Planning for Lecture Discussions

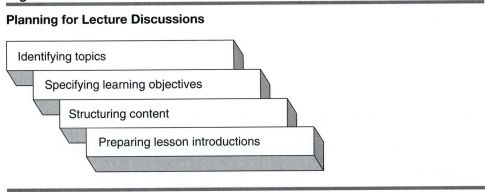

- Identifying topics
- Specifying learning objectives
- Structuring content
- Preparing lesson introductions

■ Dan Kaiser wants his students to understand how ancient Greece and the Age of Pericles influenced the Roman Empire, as well as our lives today.

In reviewing these lessons we see that Kathy wanted her students to identify specific information about the climate, geography, and economies of the Northern and Southern colonies, relationships between these characteristics, and how they ultimately influenced the Civil War. Sherry wanted her students to understand similarities among all mammals, as well as how they were different from other animals. Dan wanted his students to know information about ancient Greece, information about the culture of Greece, and how this culture ultimately influences us today.

Although the teachers' content areas and grade levels varied, all wanted their students to understand an organized body of knowledge. Identifying a topic as an organized body of knowledge is the first step in planning for a lecture discussion lesson.

Specifying Learning Objectives Having determined that the topic you're teaching is an organized body of knowledge, your second planning step is to identify learning objectives. As with teaching other forms of content, a clear and precise learning objective is essential. Emma's objective was clear; she wanted her students to understand the historical framework that led to our present-day Senate and House of Representatives. The point of the lesson was clear throughout, and this is the result of her clear thinking about learning objectives.

Structuring Content The thinking Emma did in planning her lecture discussion was similar to other types of lessons. In each the teacher first considers the topic and then specifies a clear learning objective. Emma chose lecture discussion as the strategy to help her students reach her learning objective because the type of content she was teaching was different—an organized body of knowledge.

The third planning step for lecture discussions is different from other types of lessons, however, and slightly more complex. Although finding good examples of concepts can be demanding, the task is well defined. The same is true when teaching skills; the teacher needs to provide lots of problems students can use to develop that skill. When teaching an organized body of knowledge, organizing and representing the content are more challenging, requiring thoughtful decision making. The following questions are helpful:

- How does this topic relate to previous ones?
- What prerequisite ideas do students need to know?
- How can I organize the information so important ideas are interrelated?
- How should I present the organized information to students?

Answers to these questions help you make decisions about how to structure and represent the topic for your students.

Bodies of knowledge can be organized and represented in several different ways:

- Matrices
- Networks
- Conceptual hierarchies
- Schematic diagrams
- Outlines

Each of these organizes the content and provides a form of sensory focus for students. The essential feature of each is the illustration of conceptual relationships among ideas (Eggen & Kauchak, 2010).

Matrices.   **Matrices** *are two-dimensional tables that illustrate similarities and differences in major ideas.* These can be simple tables for elementary students or detailed charts for older learners. Kathy Johnson used a matrix to represent her topic in her lesson on Northern and Southern colonies, and Sherry Southerland used an abbreviated matrix to illustrate characteristics of mammals and how they were different from other animals.

Figure 9.4 contains another example of a simple matrix in elementary science focusing on similarities and differences in fruits and vegetables. A teacher could present this matrix with all the information filled in or develop it with input from students.

Networks.   **Networks** *are simple diagrams that link related ideas*, and they have proven effective in helping students learn from textbooks and teacher presentations (Novak, 1998). Networks, when shared on a doc cam or whiteboard, can help students see the interrelationship

Figure 9.4

Matrix Comparing Fruits and Vegetables

	Examples	Description	Edible Portion
Fruits			
Vegetables			

Figure 9.5

Network for Parts of a Novel

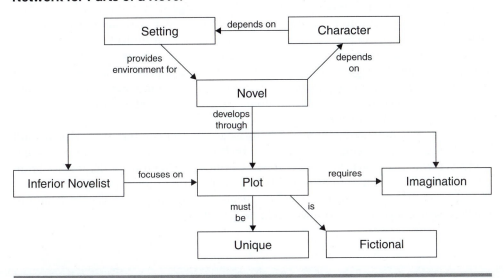

of ideas when a body of knowledge is being taught. A network that illustrates relationships among the parts of a novel is outlined in Figure 9.5.

Conceptual Hierarchies.   **Conceptual hierarchies** are *special types of networks that connect superordinate and subordinate ideas to each other.* In Figure 9.6 we see that nouns and pronouns are subsets of naming words, and adjectives and adverbs are subsets of modifying words. Hierarchies spatially illustrate these superordinate-subordinate relationships. Emma represented cases of compromise in a conceptual hierarchy in her lesson (see Figure 9.1).

Schematic Diagrams.   **Schematic diagrams** are *visual representations of the flow of physical materials or thought processes through a system.* The most common examples of schematic diagrams exist in science to represent topics such as electric circuits. The

Figure 9.6

Conceptual Hierarchy for Parts of Speech

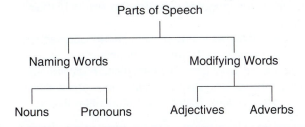

schematic visually represents the flow of electricity through the circuit. Schematics can also be used to represent groups' or individuals' thinking. For example, Emma used a simple schematic to represent the thinking of our country's leaders as they arrived at our present-day Congress. Constitutional development led to both a large-state and a small-state plan, which further evolved into the compromise that exists today. The combination of her hierarchy and schematic effectively represented the topic for her students.

Other forms of organization, such as outlines and models, exist and can also be used to structure content. We begin each chapter with an outline that provides an overview of the content. And, the model in Figure 9.2 helps us visualize the components of our memory system. Models, such as the model of an atom, are commonly used in science to represent topic that we can't observe directly.

Each way of organizing bodies of knowledge represents topics both visually and spatially. Spatially representing ideas within a body of knowledge helps both teachers and students (Winitzky, Kauchak, & Kelly, 1994). During planning it helps the teacher break large amounts of content into manageable parts. During the lesson it provides both focus and a form of conceptual organization for students. During study and review students can use these spatial organizers to connect and integrate ideas.

Technology and Teaching

Using Technology to Structure and Organize Content

Our goal in lecture discussions is for students to come away with a comprehensive and organized understanding of the lesson topic. Organizational aids provide an economical way to represent topics, and technology gives teachers an effective way to present these to students.

Teachers have always used organizational aids in their classrooms, writing outlines and drawing diagrams on chalkboards. Technology provides teachers with more flexible and adaptive ways to do this. For example, a PowerPoint outline of a lecture discussion can be prepared beforehand, making your job easier during the lesson. The outline can then be displayed in its entirety at the beginning of the lesson and returned to with highlighting as the topic is developed. It can also be returned to the next day as the previous day's lesson is reviewed.

In addition to traditional outlines, charting and graphing software make presenting these alternate organizational aids simpler and easier (Roblyer & Doering, 2010). Matrices, such as the one in Figure 9.4, can be presented in outline form to introduce a lesson, with the teacher filling in each cell as the lesson progresses. This not only helps students organize the lesson in their minds, but also provides structure for the teacher.

Technology also makes concept mapping easier and allows you to present information sequentially and in small bits to prevent students from being overwhelmed by large amounts of information (Roblyer & Doering, 2010). A number of software programs exist (e.g., *Inspiration* and *Kidspiration*), and these can also be used by students to organize their thinking during presentations and writing assignments. When teachers use these to structure their lessons, they provide students with concrete examples of organizational strategies that students can model in their own learning endeavors.

To view a video clip of a teacher using organizational aids to communicate the structure of the content, go to the Book Specific Resources tab in MyEducationLab, select your text, select Video Examples under Chapter 9, and then click on *Teaching Organized Bodies of Knowledge: Organizing Content.*

Preparing Lesson Introductions   When we begin lessons or make transitions from one lesson to another, we often incorrectly assume that students are able to quickly focus on the topic at hand. In one study of elementary classrooms, researchers found that only 5 percent of teachers made an explicit effort to introduce lessons in a way that would draw students into them, and as a result, learning suffered (Anderson et al., 1985).

To draw students into a lesson, teachers apply the idea of **focus**, *the process teachers use to attract and maintain attention in learning activities.* Focus provides something tangible and interesting to attend to and alerts students that a transition is taking place.

Although focus is important in all lessons, it is particularly important in lecture discussions because the learning activity begins with the teacher presenting important information. If students have not been drawn into the lesson, they'll miss some of the information, and the remainder of the less will be less meaningful.

Preparing lesson introductions that provide focus for students can be accomplished in several ways:

- **Demonstrations.**   A science teacher used a boiling pot of water and food coloring to illustrate the movement of molecules.

- **Problems.**   A math teacher used the problem of two friends wanting to save soda cans to buy a CD as an introduction to his lesson on adding and subtracting decimals.

- **Overviews.**   A social studies teacher described the condition of the U.S. economy in the 1930s before her lesson on the Great Depression.

In each of these the lesson introduction attracted students' attention and provided a conceptual framework for the rest of the lesson.

An alternate effective way to focus attention and introduce a lecture discussion is through an advance organizer. **Advance organizers** *are verbal or written statements at the beginning of a lesson that preview and structure new material and link it to the students' existing understanding.* Our goal as teachers should be to help learners encode information in organized, meaningful ways. Information logically organized in long-term memory results in

- Increased initial learning

- Better memory and retention

- Improved transfer to new contexts (Mayer, 2002; Ormrod, 2008; Schunk, 2004)

Effective advance organizers provide this organizational structure and exist in a variety of forms. One is a simple overview, such as the following:

Yesterday we talked about the nomadic nature of the Native Americans who lived on the plains. We saw that they were hunters, and their lives were built around following herds of large animals—particularly the buffalo. Today we're going to see how the

Spanish exploration of the new world changed Native Americans' way of life. We'll see how the horse revolutionized the way they lived, their economic base, the way they made war, their values, and even their relationships with their families. Keep these ideas in mind as we go through the lesson.

Advance organizers can also combine visual representations and verbal descriptions. For example, Emma introduced her lesson with her network and hierarchy together with the problem of how Mrs. Shah was trying to select a student for a special project.

Mrs. Shah's problem was an analogy for the problem of large-state and small-state representation in Congress. An **analogy** *describes a comparison between two ideas that are similar in some, but not all, respects.* Additional examples of analogies as advance organizers include the following:

- A tree is a city of cells in which each type of cell has a job to do and depends on the jobs of other cells.

- Birds are reptiles with feathers; except for flight, their bodies work primarily the same way.

- Outer space is the last frontier. The same dangers and hardships faced by the pioneers are encountered by the astronauts.

- Red blood cells are our bodies' oxygen railroad.

In each example, a familiar frame of reference is used to frame and explain new and unfamiliar content. Analogies provide cognitive hooks for new material; the more familiar the old material and the closer the fit of the analogy, the more learning is facilitated. Regardless of the form of the advance organizer, it is intended to provide focus and a conceptual framework for the content to follow.

Having identified the topic, specified learning objectives, structured the content, and prepared a lesson introduction, you are now ready to begin teaching the lesson.

Implementing Lecture Discussion Lessons

When we implement lecture discussions in our classrooms, our goal is to have students understand and remember the connections in the content. Effective lecture discussions are implemented in five steps, which are outlined in Table 9.1 and discussed in the sections that follow.

Table 9.1 Steps in Lecture Discussion Lessons

Step	Description	Example
Introduction	Provide focus for the lesson	Mrs. Shah's problem in Velda's lesson.
Presentation	Present students with background information	Velda provided historical information about the House of Representatives and Senate.
Comprehension monitoring	Assess the extent to which students understand the information that has been presented	Velda asked Miguel to explain the different positions of large and small states.
Integration	Link information in different presentations to each other	Velda asked the students to relate power to the compromises they were discussing.
Closure	The lesson is summarized and ideas are tied together	Refer students back to the advance organizer and make summary statements about the lesson.

Introduction   Lecture discussions begin with a review to activate learners' prior knowledge and some form of lesson overview to attract attention and provide a conceptual framework for the lessons. Lesson beginnings are important because you will be presenting new information, and you want students to be attentive and involved from the beginning.

One common mistake is to present the advance organizer or other form of lesson introduction at the beginning and then ignore it as the lesson develops. If our goal is to have students understand relationships among ideas, these relationships should be emphasized throughout the lesson. Periodically referring to the advance organizer, problem, or demonstration throughout the lesson helps students mentally organize and encode the content. As she introduced her lesson, Emma presented the advance organizer and said, "The compromises that had to be made are what we're going to discuss today. As we study this compromise, keep Mrs. Shah's problem in mind." Then, later in the lesson she said, "So, as a compromise, they created a legislature with two bodies. The House of Representatives was based on population, and today we have 435 representatives. . . . By contrast, the Senate has two members from each state. So, now we have 50 states times 2, which equals 100 senators. . . . See how this is similar to Mrs. Shah's problem. She compromised by selecting both Manolo and Jo, and our country's leaders compromised by using features of both the small-state and large-state plan."

Exploring Diversity

Differences in Background Knowledge

Diversity comes in many forms. One of the most powerful forms of student diversity affecting student learning occurs in the background knowledge that students bring to our classrooms (Bruning et al., 2004; Carnine et al., 2006). This previous knowledge not only influences initial learning during a lesson, but also affects how well students retain information and transfer it to new situations (Mayer, 2008). A major way effective teachers deal with differences in background knowledge is through continual and systematic formative assessment.

Formative assessment involves gathering information about student learning progress during instruction to provide students with feedback and aid the teacher in adjusting instruction (Stiggins, 2007). The timing of formative assessment is crucial; it needs to be continual and systematic, providing both teacher and students with constant feedback about learning progress (Popham, 2005). If learning isn't occurring, instruction needs to be modified to address the learning problem.

Formative assessment is especially important in lecture discussions because the strategy is sequential, with student success at each stage laying the foundation for the next. For example, if students don't understand the basic concepts being revisited during the introduction, they are likely to encounter difficulties during the presentation phase, in which teachers introduce new ideas based upon previously learned ones. In a similar way if students don't understand these new ideas, they'll encounter difficulties when they are connected later in the lesson.

Effective teachers use several diagnostic tools during lecture discussions to provide them with feedback about their students' readiness for subsequent learning. The first is sometimes a pretest that assesses students' background knowledge in the content area being introduced.

A short paper-and-pencil pretest provides the teacher with a quick and efficient snapshot of the entire class's readiness for learning the new material. Then during instruction effective teachers continually monitor learning progress through interactive questioning that focuses on problems and examples. The problems and examples provide a concrete frame of reference for all students and allow the teacher to probe for learning problems and glitches. During comprehension monitoring and integration effective teachers ask all students to demonstrate their developing understanding by interacting with the new content. Information gathered during these phases allows the teacher to determine which ideas were understood and retained.

Presentation

Once the topic is introduced, the teacher presents information in small segments, each similar to a mini-lecture. In her initial presentation Emma described the conflict between large and small states, setting the stage for the importance of compromise. The purpose of this short presentation was to provide an information base for the discussion that followed.

Comprehension Monitoring

After presenting information, the teacher next moves to **comprehension monitoring**, *which is the process of questioning students to assess their understanding of the material.* To illustrate comprehension monitoring let's return to Emma's lesson:

Emma: Now, let's analyze this process of compromise. How were the states supporting the two proposals different? . . . Miguel?

Miguel: . . . New York was a large state, and Rhode Island was a very small state.

Emma: Yes, good, Miguel. And what does that mean? . . . Jamie?

Jamie: . . . Well, it was bigger.

Emma: Bigger land area or bigger population or what?

Jamie: . . . Both, I think. But probably the bigger population was more important.

Comprehension monitoring serves two functions. First, it makes the lesson interactive, involving and drawing students into the activity. When they know they will be questioned about material, they are more likely to pay attention during the presentation, and they're reinforced for doing so.

This illustrates the importance of expectations. If teachers expect all students to listen, learn, and participate and hold them accountable through questioning, they are more likely to remain involved with the lesson. However, if teachers talk for extended periods, or ask questions that are answered by only a few, the rest of the students are less likely to pay attention and may tune out.

A second function of comprehension monitoring is feedback for both you and your students. The quality of student responses helps you determine the extent to which they understand the material, and you can then adjust the presentation accordingly. If students don't appear to understand the information you've presented to this point, you'll need to adjust, perhaps presenting it in a slightly revised way to make it easier to understand.

Questions also provide students with feedback, and encourage meaningful learning. Students' ability to answer your questions helps you gauge the extent to which they understand the content, and it also increases that understanding through active participation and listening to the ideas of others.

Integration

In the fourth step of a lecture discussion lesson, you encourage **integration**, which is *the process of exploring relationships in the information, relating information in one presentation to another, and consolidating new information with previous understandings.*

Integration is a natural extension of comprehension monitoring. The difference between the two lies in the type of questions you ask. During integration students are asked to establish cause-and-effect relationships, make predictions, and hypothesize. The exact type of question depends on the content being taught; the essential characteristic is that your questions encourage students to search for links with other ideas in the lesson.

Content integration is supported by research and makes intuitive sense (Eggen & Kauchak, 2010). When ideas in a lesson are interrelated, deeper understanding results. Links established through questioning help ensure that the new content is being learned as an interconnected body of knowledge.

To illustrate, let's look again at Emma's lesson:

Emma: Yes, good, Jamie. Now why would the large states think the way they did, and also why would the small states think the way they did? What do you think? . . . Simao?

Simao: . . . It would relate to power. If the representation was made on the basis of population, the large states would be much more powerful than the small states.

Emma: On the other hand, what would happen if representation were completely equal among the states? Toni?

Toni: . . . It would sort of throw the balance in the favor of the smaller states. It would mean a state like Wyoming with very little population could maybe stop a proposal from a very populated state like California.

In this short exchange we see that Simao offered a cause-and-effect relationship between the population of states and power, and Toni hypothesized another relationship based on equal representation. Understanding these perspectives was essential to understanding the need for compromise, which was the focus of this part of the lesson. Combining integration with comprehension monitoring results in a thorough understanding of the relationships in an organized body of knowledge.

Lecture Discussion Cycles: The Building Blocks of Lessons

What you saw illustrated in the previous sections was one **lecture discussion cycle,** which is *a recurrent sequence of presenting information, monitoring comprehension, and integration,* and these cycles form the core of lecture discussion lessons. After one cycle is completed, a second occurs, then a third, and so on until the lesson is complete. Each cycle includes a brief teacher presentation, followed by comprehension monitoring and integration.

Integration is the essential link between lecture discussion cycles. With each cycle, integration is broader and deeper as the information in one cycle is integrated with content from earlier ones.

Lecture discussion cycles are effective from a learning perspective because information is presented in small chunks, and students are actively involved in the comprehension monitoring and integration phases.

These cycles also allow you to break instruction into manageable parts, both during planning and in the lesson itself. This process helps you divide potentially overwhelming large bodies of knowledge into parts that are teachable and learnable.

Linking Lecture Discussion Cycles

Each lecture discussion cycle takes only a short period of time, and by linking several of these cycles together, you can consolidate the ideas in an organized body of knowledge into an effective lesson.

This process is outlined in Figure 9.7. Let's see how it occurs in Emma's lesson.

"Now that we understand how compromise produced the present form of our Congress, let's turn to the electoral college and see how the process of compromise shaped the way we elect our president. Note that on the overhead we just talked about the legislative branch," Emma says pointing at the left side of the hierarchy on the overhead (see Figure 9.1).

"Now we're turning to the presidential or executive branch. This is Article 2 of the Constitution. Let's see how our president is elected and how compromise shaped the process. Every four years, sometime in December, 535 people in the Electoral College get together and cast their votes for the next president of the United States. When people vote for the resident in the November elections, they are actually voting for the members of the Electoral College and not directly for the president.

Figure 9.7

Lecture Discussion Cycles in the Total Lesson

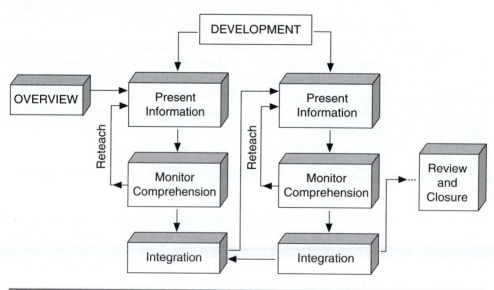

"Let's think about this one. Why are there 535 members? Where did it come from? Where have we seen that number before? . . . Sherry?"

". . . Well, . . . we just learned that there are 435 members of the House and 100 members of the Senate. It must be the two combined?" she says with a question in her voice.

"Good, Sherry. And how are the members of the Senate distributed between the states? . . . Leroy?"

". . . Two each."

"Okay, two per state times 50 states is 100. And what about the House? . . . Who remembers? . . . Terry?"

". . . They're . . . based on population I think, . . . yeah, population. The states with the most people like California and New York have the most, while those with not very many, . . . like North Dakota, have only a couple or so."

"Good complete answer," Emma smiles at Terry. "So, we see that there are 535 members, which are the combined numbers of the House and Senate. Using this information now, how is the election of the president another example of compromise? . . . Ajat?"

"Well . . . there were two views as to how the president should be elected. The small states wanted each state to have equal representation, while the big states wanted it done on the basis of population. Using both was a form of compromise."

"Now, let's ask a big question that pulls this information together. Why was compromise necessary in designing the Electoral College? What difference does it make? . . . Eduardo?"

". . . The president is a big . . . powerful person who influences the country. If we had a president who liked the big states, the little ones would be upset. . . . And it could go the other way too. If they elected a guy who only helped the little states, the others, the big ones, would be upset. So they had to have a . . . system that they all could live with."

"Good description, Eduardo. That's an excellent analysis. Now, let's examine a third compromise dealing with why the president isn't elected directly, instead being chosen by an Electoral College. To do that, we need to know about a fellow by the name of Rousseau and his idea of an enlightened aristocracy."

Let's stop here and examine how this second cycle was structured and how Emma connected the two. In the presentation step of the second cycle she referred her students to the outline and talked about the electoral college. Her outline, together with her statement "Note that on the overhead we just talked about the legislative branch. . . . Now we're turning to the presidential or executive branch" provided a link between the first cycle and the second. Transition signals such as these help students understand and construct connections between related ideas.

In the comprehension-monitoring step of the second cycle, Emma checked to see if students remembered and understood the information about the structure of the legislature. She did this by asking:

"Where have we seen that number before?"

and

"Where did it come from?"

Having determined that students understood the link between the number in the electoral college and the structure of the two branches of the legislature, she then began to explore the implications of this connection by asking:

"Why is that number significant?"
"How is this another example of compromise?"

and

"Why was compromise necessary in designing the electoral college?"
"What difference does it make?"

Her questions linked the electoral college, which was discussed in the second cycle, both to the number of representatives and senators–discussed in the first cycle–and to the concept of compromise, which was the theme of the lesson. Once these links are made, the next cycle is ready to begin with the presentation of additional new material. As you use questions such as these, students develop the inclination to look for these relationships on their own. This is a step toward self-regulated learning.

The lines between comprehension monitoring and integration and one cycle with another are often blurred. It isn't critical to identify precisely where one ends and the other begins. However, understanding the difference between comprehension monitoring and integration is important, because we want learners to do more than summarize, paraphrase, and identify similarities and differences; we also want them to explain, identify causes and effects, and consider hypothetical relationships. All this is part of developing a deep understanding of the topics they're studying.

Why Do Lecture Discussion Cycles Work?

Evidence supports the effectiveness of lecture discussion cycles. Research indicates that the amount learned from a lecture decreases as the length of the presentation increases (Gage & Berliner, 1998). Over time student attention wanes and the amount students learn decreases. These results were obtained with college students, so we can safely predict the effects to be even greater with younger learners.

Further, we know that attention increases when a question is asked and decreases when a student is called on (Lemke, 1982). Student attention also improves during demonstrations, debates, and student-initiated questions, providing strong support for the idea of active student involvement.

Further support for the lecture discussion cycle comes from research on reading. This research indicates that questions interspersed in text material increase comprehension, and this increase is largely due to increased reader attention (Reynolds & Shirey, 1988). We've all had the experience of "drifting off" when reading. Questions attract attention and help the reader focus on important material. Teacher questions during the comprehension monitoring and integration steps of lecture discussions have the same effect.

How long is too long for presenting information without asking a question? As with most questions about effective instruction, the answer depends on the situation, but an approximation is about five minutes. Shorter periods are necessary with younger, less academically talented, or poorly motivated students and with complex or abstract content. Student nonverbal behaviors provide clues about inattention, and student performance during the comprehension-monitoring step can give you additional data.

Closure

Closure, or bringing a lesson together at the end, is a characteristic of all good teaching, and it is particularly important in lecture discussion lessons. Because the process of linking one cycle to earlier ones is continuous, large and complex amounts of information are presented, and it's easy for students to lose track of the lesson's direction and the overall structure of the ideas. Effective closure helps tie ideas together and prevent potential confusion.

One effective way to conclude a lesson is to refer students back to the organizational scheme introduced at the beginning of the lesson. Visual representations, such as hierarchies or matrices, provide a quick summary of the ideas presented. Emma, for example, brought her lesson to closure by referring students back to the overhead that began the lesson. The visual, combined with summary statements by students, provide an efficient and visual way of helping students remember the lesson's content.

Assessing Learning in Lecture Discussions

Assessment is an integral component of all teaching and learning and is also essential in lecture discussion lessons. Formal assessment of students' understanding is accomplished in the same way when using lecture discussions as assessment in general. However, because of the comprehension monitoring and integration steps in the strategy, teachers can use assessment during the lesson to monitor student learning. Because students are continually integrating new information with prior knowledge and describing understanding in their own words, teachers have access to their developing understanding through their responses. As a result, teachers can adapt their instruction during the lesson to meet students' learning needs.

These informal assessments can easily be converted into formal ones. For instance, Emma asked the following questions during the lesson:

"Now, why would the large states think the way they did, and also, why would the small states think the way they did?"

and

"Why was compromise necessary in designing the electoral college? What difference does it make?

She called on students to answer the questions in both cases. Instead, she could easily make the assessments formal by simply writing the questions on the board and having all students respond to them in writing. Doing this has three advantages:

- It gathers the same information from everyone, so it gives her more accurate information about the extent to which *all* students understand the topic.

- It requires that all students are involved. Although question-and-answer sessions involve students, some of them still drift off when they aren't directly answering or likely to be called on.

- It is easy to administer; she can create the questions on the spot and, if desired, could even have students exchange papers to grade them.

In addition, she could also share some of the best responses verbally or by putting them on the doc camera to provide feedback for the rest of the students. If this pattern of using integration as a means of assessing students and providing detailed feedback becomes a pattern, students' thinking and achievement can increase markedly.

Summary

Organized Bodies of Knowledge: Integrated Content

Organized bodies of knowledge are interrelated connections of facts, concepts, and other abstractions. A significant portion of the school curriculum focuses on these forms of content. Theories, which describe precise relationships among concepts, are a specialized subset of organized bodies of knowledge.

The Limitations of Lectures

When lecturing, teachers present information to students in an organized way. Lectures are flexible and easy to plan and implement. They can be effective for helping students acquire information not readily accessible in other ways, but they place learners in passive roles, can easily overload students' memories, and don't allow teachers to monitor learning progress.

Lecture Discussions: An Alternative to Standard Lectures

Lecture discussions combine the flexibility and simplicity of lectures with the benefits of interactive teaching and are effective for teaching organized bodies of knowledge.

Effective lecture discussions begin with an introduction followed by the teacher presenting information in a mini-lecture. Comprehension monitoring and integration follow the presentation.

Lecture discussion lessons are developed when one cycle of presenting information, monitoring comprehension, and integration is linked to earlier cycles. With each succeeding cycle the process of integration becomes broader and deeper.

Assessing Learning in Lecture Discussions

The comprehension monitoring and integration steps of lecture discussions can be effective for informally assessing students' understanding of the topics they're studying. The assessment can be made formal by having students respond in writing to questions, instead of responding to them verbally. It gathers the same information from everyone, requires that all students are involved, is easy to administer and score, and effectively provides each student with detailed feedback.

Important Concepts

Preparing for Your Licensure Exam

At the beginning of the chapter you saw how Emma Houston used lecture discussion to help her students understand an organized body of knowledge. Look now at another teacher attempting to use the same strategy. Read the case study and answer the questions that follow.

The Power of Classroom Practice
www.myeducationlab.com

After reading this case, go to the Book Specific Resources tab in MyEducationLab, select your text, select *Preparing for Your Licensure Exam* under Chapter 9 to complete the questions that accompany the case and receive feedback on your responses.

Steve Grant, a ninth-grade earth science teacher is working with his students in a unit on the solar system. As he began the unit, he took a globe down from the shelf and a transparency illustrating the sun and the planets in relative size to one another from his file cabinet.

He directed his students to read the chapter, and he spent the first day of the unit identifying the parts of the solar system and the names of the planets. He listed the planets on the board in order of their distance from the sun and pointed out that Mercury, Venus, Earth, and Mars were quite small and close to the sun, so they were called the inner planets, and that Saturn, Jupiter, Uranus, and Neptune were called the outer planets. He also told students that Venus was called the Earth's twin because its size was about the same as the Earth's, but that no one could live on Venus because it was too hot. He then showed students a PowerPoint identifying the inner and outer planets on it.

The second day Steve begins class by saying, "All right everyone, what have we learned about the solar system so far?"

"Sun and planets," Wendy volunteers.

"It has our sun and the different planets," Steve affirms. "Who can name the planets? . . . Anyone. Go ahead, David."

". . . Mercury," David began, ". . . Venus, Earth, . . . Mars, . . . Saturn . . ."

"That's good, David, but you missed one. Someone help him out."

"Jupiter," Traci put in.

"Good Traci," Steve smiles. "Remember when we listed the names of the planets on the board, and I said that we needed to know all of them in order. Look back in your notes if you're not sure.

"Jupiter and then Saturn," Steve continues. "Now, what's next?"

"Uranus," several of the students respond in unison.

"Good, and next?"

"Neptune," the class answers.

"Excellent! And what else is part of our solar system?"

"Asteroids," Paula adds.

"Yes! Very good! There is an asteroid belt between Mars and Jupiter. Some scientists think that it is the remains of a giant planet.

"The asteroids are like a bunch of small planets," he continues on. "They vary in size from about what a small moon would be to like even as small as pieces of gravel. They think that perhaps the planet got too close to another planet and maybe even collided. The asteroids are what remain. They are in orbit around the sun, just like the rest of the planets are.

"What else is part of our solar system?"

". . ."

". . . No one? Well, have any of you heard of Halley's Comet? . . . Good, I see several of you nodding. Okay, Halley's Comet is probably the most famous of all the comets, but it is just one of them. . . . Comets go around the sun just as the planets do. oblong orbits."

"Mr. Grant?" Natasha calls out, raising her hand.

"Yes, Natasha."

"Are the comets in between the planets, like the asteroids are?"

"Well, not exactly. They have different kinds of orbits."

"Now today, we want to talk some more about Pluto, once considered the outer-most planet. We know that it is the smallest and the farthest away from the sun. Many believe that its origin is different from the other planets. Now, the reason they think so is that its orbital plane is different from that of the other planets."

"By that I mean the plane that all the planets revolve around the sun in," Steve continues. "Everyone, take a look on page 284 of your books. It shows the orbital planes of the planets.

"Now, Pluto's orbital plane is different," he repeats, "so they think it was different. Like maybe it was captured from out in space and became a part of the solar system that way.

"So remember, everyone, and this should be in your notes. Pluto's origin is different from the other planets.

"Yes, Jack," Steve nods, acknowledging Jack's raised hand.

"What's the orbit got to do with the way the planets were made?"

"Very good question Jack," Steve responds, smiling. "What's the orbit got to do with the planets? Let's take a look."

Steve then displays a transparency showing "globs" of gas being thrown off from the sun. All of globs are on the same plane.

"What does this transparency show us? . . . Jack?"

". . . Globs being thrown off from the sun."

"That's right. You see, scientists think that the planets were once part of the sun, and the sun sort of 'threw' them off," Steve waves in a throwing motion. "Then they gradually cooled off, solidified, and became the planets. So, they were all originally made out of what?"

". . ."

"What is the sun made out of?"

"Gases," the class responds.

"What did he say about orbits?" Benjie whispers to Janet as he looks up from writing his notes. "I didn't get it."

"I'm not sure. He said the planets came off the sun, I think."

"How?"

"I don't know. Just came off I guess."

"Yes. Good. So, what were the planets to start with?" Steve went on.

"Gases."

"Yes. Excellent. So, the planets cooled down from the gases and formed the planets as we know them now."

"Any other questions? . . . Okay. . . . Benjie, do you have a question?" Steve ask, seeing a confused look on Benjie's face. . . . Okay? . . . Good," he gestures as Benjie nodded no.

"So, let's review what we've covered, so far. What do we know about Pluto?"

"It's far from the sun," Nancy volunteers.

"Good, Nancy. What else?"

"Small," Shelley added.

"Okay. And what else?"

"It was made different."

"Yes! Excellent, Shelley. That's what we are looking for. Pluto's origin is different form the other planets."

"Now as a homework assignment, I want you to use your books and fill out the following chart. . . . Here, I have made some outlines for you," and he then hands students the chart that appeared as follows:

	Mercury	Venus	Earth	Mars	Jupiter	Saturn	Uranus	Neptune	Pluto
Distance from sun									
Period of rotation									
Orbital plane									
Length of year									
Equatorial distance									
Density compared to earth									

"Are there any questions?" Steve then asks. . . ."Okay, good. Go ahead and get started, and you'll have a good jump on this before the end of the period. Just raise your hand if you need any help, and I'll come around."

Questions for Analysis

Let's examine Steve's lesson now based on the information in this chapter. In your analysis consider the following questions. In each case, be specific and take information directly from the case study in doing your analysis.

1. In planning for lecture discussions we emphasized that a clear learning objective is important. Based on the lesson, how clear was Steve's thinking about his learning objective?

2. How effectively did Steve structure the content of his unit? Provide evidence from the case study to support your assessment.

3. Assess Steve's lesson introduction. Describe what he might have done to improve it.

4. How effectively did Steve complete the comprehension-monitoring step of a lecture discussion lesson? Provide evidence from the case study to support your assessment.

5. How effectively did Steve promote integration in his lesson? Describe specifically what he might have done to help his students better integrate their understanding of the solar system.

6. In all likelihood, Steve's class is composed of learners from diverse backgrounds. How effective was the lesson for these students?

Discussion Questions

1. Identify several topics you believe can be effectively taught using lecture discussions. Identify other areas in which you believe the strategy would be inappropriate. How are the two areas different?

2. How might lecture discussions be adapted for working with students in the lower elementary grades? What specific things would teachers have to do to make them effective?

3. How might they be adapted for working with students who are not native English speakers? In what stage of the strategy would teachers have to make the most modifications?

4. How is the importance of teaching organized bodies of knowledge influenced by timing? That is, is this type of content more important at the beginning or end of a course or unit?

5. How do the following factors influence the optimal length of one lecture discussion cycle?
    a. Age of students
    b. Difficulty or complexity of material
    c. The students' prior knowledge
    d. Student motivation
    e. The teacher's presentation skills

Portfolio Activities

1. *Organized Bodies of Knowledge: Textbooks.* Examine a chapter in a textbook in your teaching area that deals with an organized body of knowledge. Analyze it in terms of the following (providing specific examples, if possible):
    a. Introduction/overview. How is the content introduced? Does the introduction provide an overview of the content to follow?
    b. Organizational structure. What aids, such as diagrams, outlines, or hierarchies, illustrate the organization of the content?
    c. Comprehension checks. Are there questions inserted in the text to check comprehension?
    d. Integrative links. Do questions or exercises encourage students to link ideas from one section to another?
    e. Summary

2. *Organized Bodies of Knowledge: Organizational Aids.* Take the content in the previous exercise and organize it using one (or more) of the following organizational aids:
    a. Outline
    b. Matrix
    c. Network
    d. Schematic diagram
    e. Conceptual hierarchy

What other way(s) would there be to organize this content? What are the advantages and disadvantages of each?

3. *Interactive Teaching: Organization.* Tape or videotape a lecture or lecture discussion. Take notes from the presentation. Organize the content in terms of one (or more) of the organizational aids discussed in this chapter. How could you use this type of organizational aid in your teaching?

4. *Lecture Discussion: Patterns of Interaction.* Observe a teacher (or professor) using a lecture discussion format. Try to determine beforehand that the lesson will not be entirely lecture. Analyze the lesson in terms of

    a. The length of each lecture discussion cycle (i.e., how long does the teacher talk before asking a question).
    b. What kinds of questions did the teacher ask? (Jot these questions down in order, with times attached to them. Later determine whether these were comprehension monitoring or integrative.) What could the instructor have done to make the lesson more effective?

5. *Lecture Discussion: Applying It in Your Classroom.* Plan, teach, and tape a lesson using the lecture discussion format. Analyze the taped lesson in terms of the following variables:

    a. Introduction/overview
    b. Organizational aids
    c. Average length of one lecture-recitation cycle
    d. Comprehension checks in each cycle
    e. Integrative links in each cycle
    f. Summary

In hindsight, what could you have done differently to make the lesson more effective?

To check your comprehension of the content covered in Chapter 9, go to the Book Specific Resources in MyEducationLab, select your text, and complete the Study Plan quiz. In addition to receiving feedback on your answers, a study plan will be generated from the quiz that will direct you to access Review, Practice, and Enrichment materials to enhance your understanding of chapter content.

10

Guided Discovery

Chapter Outline	Learning Objectives
	When you've completed your study of this chapter, you should be able to
Understanding guided discovery ■ Guided discovery and constructivism ■ Guided discovery and student motivation ■ Misconceptions about guided discovery	1. Describe how guided discovery can promote learning in classrooms.

Planning for guided discovery lessons
■ Identifying topics
■ Specifying learning objectives
■ Selecting examples and non-examples
■ Types of examples
  Technology and Teaching:
    Using databases in guided discovery lessons
■ Planning for social interaction
■ Planning for assessment
	2. Describe the planning process for preparing guided discovery lessons.

Conducting guided discovery lessons
■ Review and introduction
■ The open-ended phase
■ The convergent phase
■ Closure
■ Application
■ Using guided discovery with different-aged learners
  Exploring Diversity:
    Using guided discovery with cultural minorities
	3. Explain how guided discovery lessons are implemented.

Assessing learning in guided discovery lessons ■ Using assessment to increase learning	4. Describe how to assess learning during guided discovery lessons.

Effective teachers have a repertoire of teaching strategies at their command. For some types of learning teacher-centered approaches are more effective, and for others learner-centered approaches are better. Expert teachers are skilled with both. Earlier you learned about direct instruction, a teacher-centered approach to teaching concepts and skills.

In this chapter we turn to guided discovery, a learner-centered strategy that actively involves students in constructing understanding. As you read the following case study involving a teacher helping her students understand conduction, think about the different ways she facilitates learning through the demonstrations she uses and the questions she asks.

Lucy Steiner, a sixth-grade teacher with 28 students in her class, has been working on a unit on heat. Her students have been involved in activities on heat convection and radiation, and now she wants them to understand conduction. The students have also studied matter; the particles that make up matter; and the characteristics of solids, liquids, and gases.

On Sunday evening Lucy, planning for the week's science activities, thinks to herself, "I'll do this one tomorrow, . . . and also the wire and wax activity–that will give them one more way to think about conduction. . . . Yeah, let's see if I have everything." She then glances over to a shelf where she has a coffee maker with a glass coffee pot sitting on it. She gets up and looked in a drawer for a long spoon, a piece of heavy copper wire, some wax, and an alcohol burner. Seeing the materials there, she returns to her planning.

On Monday Lucy begins her science lesson, "Now, . . . let's look at what we have here," bringing out the coffee maker, pot, and spoon, as shown in the following drawing.

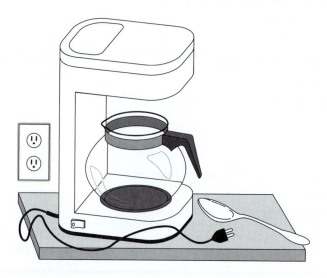

"Let's see what we have here. Who wants to feel the coffee pot and the spoon," Lucy asks. "C'mon up, Sarafina," she gestures to Sarafina, who is sitting near the front of the room.

"How do they feel?"

"Smooth."

"Okay, . . . how else do they feel?"

". . . Cold."

"Okay, good. . . . Sarafina says that the spoon and coffee pot feel smooth and cold," Lucy reports to the rest of the class. "Now, I'm going to pour some water in the coffee pot and put the spoon in it."

She pours the coffee pot about a third full, puts the spoon in it, and plugs it in, so it appears as follows:

"Now," Lucy continues, "let's review for a few minutes. . . . We've been talking about heat and energy. What is one way that heat is transferred, Bharat?"

". . . Radiation?"

"Yes, good, Bharat," Lucy smiles. Who can give us an example? . . . Bev?"

". . . Well . . . like when you hold your hand over a hot burner on a stove, your hand gets warm."

"Good, Bev, . . . and explain why that's an example of radiation, . . . Dominique?"

". . . Your hand gets warm, but . . . t's up above the burner, and . . . there's nothing between your hand, . . . well, there's air between the burner and your hand, but it wouldn't matter. . . . Anyway, your hand gets warm because the waves go up and heat it."

"Yes, excellent explanation," Lucy comments. "How about another example? Jim?"

". . . When we stand out in the sun, it warms us up."

"And what else do we know about radiation, Lakasha? . . . Think about what Dominique said."

". . . It goes even if there's no air . . . Like from the sun to the earth."

"Good, Lakasha," Lucy smiles. "Can you add a little more to that? What do we mean when we say 'no air'?"

". . . Like . . . a vacuum?" Lakasha responds hesitantly.

"And what's that have to do with what Dominique said?"

" . . . She said there was no air, . . . no, . . . she said it wouldn't matter if there was no air."

"Yes, good, both of you.

" . . . It travels in waves," Ramon interjects, keying on what Dominique had said.

"Yes, Ramon, good. . . . Now remember everyone, radiation is a form of heat energy that travels in waves, and it doesn't need any matter to travel through. We can't see the waves, but they move, such as going from the burner to our hand. We know the energy waves move because our hand gets warm."

Lucy then guides students through a similar process in a review of convection, emphasizing that convection requires matter, such as gases and liquids, and the particles of the gas or liquid actually move from one place to another, such as a convection current in the ocean, and the movement of the air in a convection oven.

"Now, let's look at this again," Lucy directs, pointing to the coffee pot. Now, carefully come up and touch the top of the spoon," she directs Sarafina, who came up earlier.

"It's hot," Sarafina reports quickly.

"It's hot!" Lucy repeats. "Now, . . . that brings up a question. The spoon was cold before, and now it's hot. . . . hmm? Now, I want you to be very good observers and thinkers, and I want you to work with your partner and try to explain why the spoon got hot. . . . But, before we start, what do we know for sure?"

". . . The coffee pot did it," Jeremy suggests, referring to the coffee pot and spoon.

"Sure, we know that heating up the coffee pot is important. . . . But, we want to think about exactly how it did it. . . . And, what are you going to keep in mind as you work on our problem?

". . ."

"What have we been discussing?"

". . . Stuff about heat," Leeman volunteers.

"What about heat?"

". . . Radiation and convection," Jessica adds.

"Yes, very good, . . . Keep radiation and convection in mind when you work on your explanation. . . . Now, go ahead."

The students, who were seated next to their partner, slide their desks together and start talking. The room quickly became a buzz of voices, as students worked. Lucy moves among them, sometimes listening to their comments and stopping from time to time to make a comment or suggestion. Several students get up and look more closely at the coffee maker and spoon, and with warnings from Lucy about being careful with the hot pot, hold their hands near the system, feel the end of the spoon, and talk briefly to each other.

After about five minutes Lucy announces, "All right everyone, I think you've been doing some good thinking, so let's share some of our ideas. . . . Which group wants to start?"

"We think it's radiation," Jason volunteers. "The waves go up the spoon and make it hot, . . . like our hand over the burner."

"Go ahead, Sonja," Lucy encourages, seeing her shaking her head.

". . . No, I don't think so," Sonja said uncertainly.

"Why not?" Jason wonders.

"Radiation doesn't need something to travel through, . . . like we said before. . . . When we put our hand over the burner, there wasn't anything there."

"There was air there."

"Yeah, but radiation can go through air. It can't go through something hard, . . . like a spoon."

"Jason asks a good question," Lucy comments. "How do we know that radiation can't go through solids, or at least doesn't go through them very well?"

". . ."

"Suppose you're out in the hot sun, and you move into the shade. . . . How do you feel?"

". . . Cooler," Kathy offers after a few seconds.

"Why do you suppose?"

"The tree . . . or whatever blocked the sun."

"What's your reaction to that?" Lucy turns to Jason.

"I . . . guess so. . . . Yes, that's true."

The class discusses the possibility of radiation making the spoon hot for a couple more minutes, finally concluding that it probably wasn't radiation.

They then turn to a discussion of convection and conclude that although convection could have heated the water in the pot, it couldn't have heated the spoon, since the particles in the spoon couldn't move from one place to another.

Lucy then displays the following drawing on the overhead.

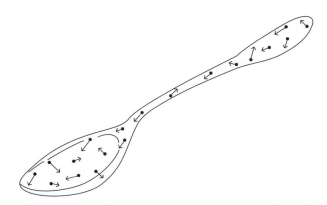

"Let's take a look at this drawing," Lucy directs. "What do you notice about it?"

". . . There's a bunch of little dots with arrows on them in the spoon," Simone offered.

"They represent the molecules in the spoon." Lucy explains. "Remember how we used the dots and arrows to help us visualize the movement of air molecules? . . . But, there's an important difference here. . . . What is it?"

". . ."

"What is an important difference between gases and solids?"

". . . Air molecules move around, but solids don't," Toni responds, seeing Lucy motion to her.

Lucy then guides students into noticing that the spoon was in contact with the pot and reminds them about their study of radiation and convection that the hotter a molecule is the faster and harder it moves.

"Now, what does all this have to do with the spoon?" Lucy asks. "Let's see if another example will help. I'd like everyone to look at this," Lucy continues, as she takes out a piece of wire with three pieces of wax stuck on it.

"We're going to heat the wire with this burner," she continues, placing the burner under one end of the wire, so it appeared as follows:

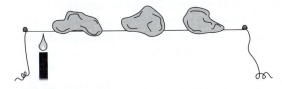

"What do you think will happen?" Lucy continues. Some of her students predict the wire will get hot; others say the wax will melt. Lucy prompts them by asking, "If the wax melts, which will melt first?" From students quizzical looks she can tell they are thinking.

"Well, let's see. Watch carefully," she continues, lighting the burner and putting it under one end of the wire. As the wire heats, the piece of wax closest to the flame starts to droop, then fall. The other two follow in order.

"What happened?" Lucy continues.

After students discuss the fact that the hot wax globs fell in sequence, Lucy encourages them to compare this demonstration with the spoon one.

She then introduces the term *conduction* and through her prompting helps students conclude that conduction has the following characteristics:

1. It is a form of energy transfer.
2. It occurs when rapidly moving molecules bump other molecules, so the other molecules also move faster.

She closes the lesson by asking students, as their homework assignment, to predict and explain what would happen if they replaced a piece of wood or a butter knife for the piece of wire.

Let's think about Lucy's lesson in the context of effective teaching. She first reviewed radiation and convection and then provided focus by displaying her coffee maker and spoon and asking students to explain why the top of the spoon got hot. This attracted students' attention and provided a framework for the rest of the lesson.

Lucy was well organized. She first showed the coffee maker and spoon and then turned to her review while they heated, which allowed her to maximize her instructional time. She communicated clearly throughout the lesson, stayed focused on the topic, used clear language, and emphasized important points with repetition.

One of the most important aspects of her instruction was the way she represented her topic. The students saw a concrete demonstration—the coffee maker and spoon, a model that helped them visualize the molecules moving in the spoon, and the demonstration with the wire and wax.

Her students were highly involved throughout the lesson, both as they worked with their partners and in the whole-class discussion. She asked many questions, distributed them to a variety of students, and prompted when necessary. She applied both the effective teaching research and strategies for involving students throughout her lesson.

 ## Understanding Guided Discovery

Guided discovery is an instructional strategy in which teachers specify learning objectives, arrange information so that clearly defined patterns can be found, and guide students to the objectives (Clark & Mayer, 2003; Moreno, 2004). For example, first, Lucy's topic was specific and clearly defined. She wanted her students to understand the concept of *conduction*. Second, instead of defining *conduction* and then explaining and illustrating it, as she would in a more teacher-centered approach, she presented carefully chosen examples—her demonstration with the coffee pot and spoon, her model showing the vibration of particles in the spoon, and her demonstration with the melting wax on the wire—and third, she used questioning to guide students as they constructed an understanding of the concept. These aspects of Lucy's lesson illustrate the essential characteristics of guided discovery.

Guided discovery is often contrasted with "pure" or unstructured discovery, whereby learners identify patterns and relationships without help from a teacher. Research indicates that unstructured discovery is less effective than guided approaches because time isn't used efficiently. Without help, students often become lost and frustrated, and this confusion can lead to misconceptions (Clark & Mayer, 2003; Mayer, 2008). As a result unstructured discovery is rarely seen in today's classrooms, except in student projects and investigations.

Over the past 25 years, a rapidly expanding literature has changed our views of the ways that students learn and develop, and this understanding has moved the focus in teaching away from teachers as simply providers of information and toward a greater focus on students constructing their own knowledge and understanding (Bransford et al., 2000; Marzano, 2007). This doesn't imply that teachers are less important in promoting student learning, however. In fact, their roles are even more important than they were once believed to be.

Let's see why this is the case. It is now widely believed that learners create their own understanding of the topics they study (Mayer, 2008), and the term used to describe this process of creating understanding is **constructivism**, *which is a view of learning suggesting that learners use their own experiences to create understanding that make sense to them, rather than having understanding delivered to them in already organized forms* (Eggen & Kauchak, 2010). Let's look at this view of learning in more detail.

Guided Discovery and Constructivism

Although different constructivists disagree on some aspects of the knowledge-construction process, most agree on the characteristics listed in Figure 10.1 (Eggen & Kauchak, 2010). Let's take a look at them.

Learners Construct Understanding   The basic principle of constructivism is that learners construct (create), rather than record, their understanding. Lucy facilitated this process through her demonstrations that allowed her students to construct the concept of *conduction.* Lucy played an essential role in the construction process through the questions she asked. She could have simply explained the concept, and this is what teachers commonly do. But these verbal explanations often do little to help ideas "make sense," and learners frequently develop understandings that are incomplete and inaccurate.

Lucy demonstrated a great deal of expertise as she guided students to an understanding of conduction. We examine how she did this in more detail later in the chapter.

Figure 10.1

Characteristics of Constructivism

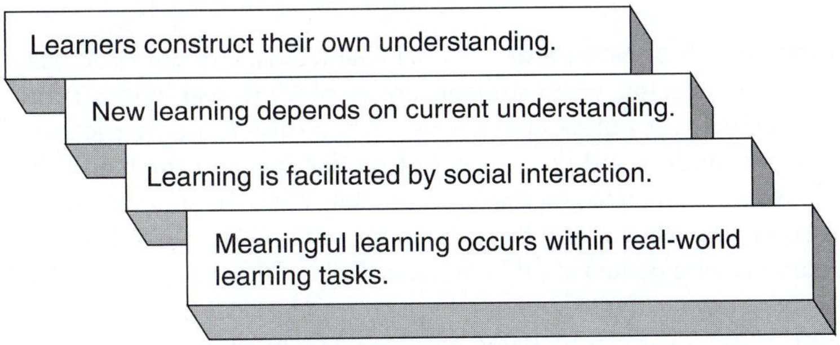

Learners construct their own understanding.

New learning depends on current understanding.

Learning is facilitated by social interaction.

Meaningful learning occurs within real-world learning tasks.

New Learning Depends on Current Understanding   A second characteristic of constructivism suggests that all new learning depends upon previous learning. The importance of learners' prior knowledge is both intuitively sensible and well documented by research (Bruning et al., 2004). Constructivists see all new learning interpreted in the immediate context of students' current understanding.

This aspect of constructivism is important for several reasons. First, it helps explain why some students learn faster than others; they have more prior knowledge. It also explains why reviews are effective at the beginning of lessons; they help activate students' existing knowledge. It also explains why teacher questioning is essential; it helps teachers assess students' prior knowledge, allowing them to connect new information to what students already know.

We see the importance of background knowledge illustrated in Lucy's lesson. Jason interpreted the heating of the spoon in the context of his understanding of radiation; he didn't simply add new understanding to old. His understanding of radiation influenced his interpretation of the heating of the spoon, and a different original understanding would have resulted in a different interpretation. During the lesson, Lucy's students, with her guidance, gradually developed a more mature understanding of heat transfer, based on their previous understandings. This is the foundation of knowledge construction.

Social Interaction Promotes Learning   Lucy's lesson also illustrates the central role of social interaction in constructivist views of learning. Social interaction in a constructivist context refers to content-focused discussions of the topic students are studying (Leinhardt & Steele, 2005). Teachers who base their instruction on constructivist views of learning encourage students to verbalize their thinking and refine their ideas by comparing them with others.

Social interaction was an important component of Lucy's lesson, both as students worked in their groups and when the class as a whole discussed the results. For example, when students worked in their groups, Jason and his partner concluded that radiation heated the spoon, and he retained this idea until it no longer made sense to him. His understanding changed as a result of interacting with other students.

Lucy played an essential role in facilitating the social interaction so that it resulted in student learning. She offered the example of moving into the shade from the hot sun, and she asked Jason what his reaction was to Kathy's comment about the tree blocking the sun. She provided enough guidance and support to help her students make progress, but not so much that she reduced their active role in the knowledge construction process. This is a sophisticated form of instruction requiring a great deal of teacher expertise.

Real-World Tasks Promote Understanding   A final characteristic of constructivism suggests that learning is most effective when students are involved in real-world (sometimes called *authentic*) activities. Let's think about Lucy's lesson once more. Her learning objective was for students to understand the concept of *conduction*, and she helped her students reach the objective with concrete objects—a coffee maker and the spoon—and the real-world problem of explaining why the handle of the spoon got hot. She also asked them to explain why the wax on the wire melted at different rates. Each of these examples helped relate the abstract concept of *conduction* to students' lives.

With some thought, many ideas can be made more realistic by embedding them in real-world tasks, as we see in Table 10.1.

Table 10.1 Real-World Tasks in Various Content Areas

Content Area	Example
Math	Students go to a supermarket as a source of comparison-shopping problems.
English	Students write persuasive essays for a school or class newspaper.
Algebra	Students write algebraic equations to help them make precise solutions composed of solids (chemicals) and liquids.
Geometry	Students solve for the dimensions of buildings, using similar triangles.
Biology	Students explain why some members of the class have attached earlobes, whereas others' earlobes are detached.
Geography	Students explain why some cities, such as San Francisco, Chicago, Seattle, and New York, are large and economically important, whereas Minot, North Dakota, and Oxford, Mississippi, remain relatively small.
History	Students examine the origins of their hometowns and relate them to the history of the region, state, and country at the time.
Art	Students create an original piece of art.
Technology	Students use technology to design or solve work problems.

Guided Discovery and Student Motivation

The ability to promote student motivation is one of the major strengths of guided discovery. To illustrate how guided discovery promotes learner motivation, let's look again at several features of Lucy's lesson:

- Students were faced with a question—what caused the spoon to get hot—that served as a focus for the lesson.
- Students were active throughout the lesson, both in their groups and in the whole-class discussion.
- Students developed understandings that made sense to them and applied in their everyday worlds.

Each of these factors contributes to motivation. First, building lessons around problems and questions stimulates curiosity, a major source of intrinsic motivation (Schunk et al., 2008). Second, the active involvement of students in guided discovery lessons increases students' interest in the activity, contributing to motivation (Schraw & Lehman, 2001). Finally, developing understanding that is practical and makes sense increases students' sense of **self-efficacy**, *their belief in their capability to accomplish tasks and understand the world* (Schunk et al., 2008). The combination of these factors makes guided discovery one of the most effective teaching strategies for increasing student motivation.

Misconceptions About Guided Discovery

Even though guided discovery has been widely researched and discussed, misconceptions about it remain (Eggen, 2001):

- Since guided discovery learning activities are student centered, clear learning objectives and careful preparation are less important than with traditional instruction.

- If learners are involved in social interaction, learning automatically takes place.
- Since teachers are not lecturing and explaining when using guided discovery, their roles are less important than when using traditional instruction.

Let's examine these misconceptions. First, clear learning objectives are even more important when planning guided discovery lessons, because they provide you with a framework that guides both your choice of content representations and the kinds of questions you ask (Eggen, 2001). As students build on their current understanding, you may modify your objectives, but clear objectives are essential starting points.

Second, because students are constructing knowledge as the lesson progresses, you need to carefully monitor the learning process. If students head down "blind alleys" or develop misunderstandings about the topic, you'll need to intervene and redirect the discussion. Lucy, for example, carefully monitored both the group work and the whole-class discussion, intervening when she thought it was necessary to keep her students' developing understanding on track. Let's see how she did this by examining some of the dialogue that occurred after Jason and his partner concluded that radiation caused the handle of the spoon to get hot.

Lucy: Jason asks a good question. How do we know that radiation can't go through solids, or at least doesn't go through them very well?

"..."

Lucy: Suppose you're out in the hot sun, and you move into the shade. . . . How do you feel?

Kathy: Cooler.

Lucy: Why do you suppose?

Kathy: The tree . . . or whatever, blocked the sun.

Lucy: What's your reaction to that?

Jason: I . . . guess so. . . . Yes, that's true.

Lucy's question, "Suppose you're out in the hot sun, and you move into the shade. How do you feel?" led to Kathy's conclusion, "The tree . . . or whatever, blocked the sun," and was essential to untracking an inaccurate and unfruitful conclusion. Without this intervention Jason would have continued to believe that the handle of the spoon was heated by radiation, and he would have constructed an inaccurate understanding of the concept.

The professional judgment required to know when and how extensively to intervene is very sophisticated. Insufficient guidance leaves students with incomplete or inaccurate understandings; too much intervention puts them in passive roles, which decreases motivation as well as learning.

From this discussion we can see that teachers' roles are both more important and more challenging when using guided discovery as a teaching strategy. Guiding students into genuine understanding is a sophisticated process; there are no rules that tell us when to intervene or how extensive the intervention should be. Teachers must make these decisions on their own based on their knowledge of the content and their past experiences with students.

Keeping these misconceptions in mind, let's turn now to planning for guided discovery learning activities.

Planning for Guided Discovery Lessons

Planning for guided discovery lessons involves five steps, which are outlined in Figure 10.2 and discussed in the sections that follow.

Identifying Topics

Most of teachers' planning efforts begin with a topic or content area. This not only makes the planning process more concrete and manageable, it also helps address standards, which are frequently topic or content focused. Lucy began her planning by identifying the concept of *conduction* as the focal point of her lesson.

Specifying Learning Objectives

Having identified the topic, we need to then decide what we want students to know about it. Effective teachers have clear and precise learning objectives in mind and teach directly toward them (Bransford et al., 2000). For example, Lucy wanted her students to understand that

- Conduction is a form of heat transfer.
- Conduction occurs when molecules move and directly interact with one another.

Beginning teachers often specify their objectives in writing, and although veterans tend to not write them down, they are no less clear about what they want their students to understand or be able to do.

Clear learning objectives—whether or not they're specifically stated in writing—are essential because they provide a framework for a teacher's thinking in both planning and implementing a lesson. During planning they guide teachers as they select examples. If objectives aren't clear, teachers don't know what they're trying to illustrate, and the likelihood of selecting the best possible examples is reduced. Clear and precise objectives also makes questioning much easier during lessons. When teachers know exactly what they want their students to understand, questioning that guides students to the objectives is more focused and strategic.

Figure 10.2

Planning for Guided Discovery Lessons

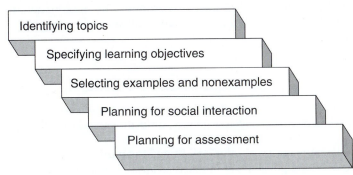

Identifying topics
Specifying learning objectives
Selecting examples and nonexamples
Planning for social interaction
Planning for assessment

Selecting Examples and Non-examples

One of the most important factors in promoting learning is the way you represent the topics you teach. This is true for teaching at all levels and in all content areas. Now, using constructivist views of learning as a framework for guided discovery lessons, we can see why content representations are so important.

First, in the natural world, people have a great many specific experiences, and these are what they use to construct their understanding of how the world works. As young children play together, for example, they gradually construct understandings of socially acceptable and socially unacceptable behavior based on their encounters with and responses of their peers. The same processes are at work in much of what both children and adults learn. Effective teachers facilitate this learning process by creating or finding examples that illustrate the topics they're teaching. In essence, the examples are experiences teachers bring into the classroom that learners use to construct their understanding of the topic.

Let's see how Lucy incorporated these ideas in her planning. Her representations of the concept of *conduction* included

- The coffee maker and spoon—a concrete example

- The model of the molecular motion in the spoon—a way of helping students visualize conduction

- The burner, wire, and wax, which combined the concrete representation with the models and further illustrated conduction

- Her assignment involving the wood and metal knife

Each was intended to illustrate the concept of *conduction* in a slightly different way from the others.

As learners construct understanding, each case or example adds different perspectives that others may have missed. For instance, the coffee maker and spoon will be meaningful to some students, whereas Lucy's model will be more meaningful to others. The same is true for the wire with the wax pieces and the homework assignment.

Non-examples are also important when teaching closely related concepts. For instance, Lucy reviewed the concepts of *radiation* and *convection* and holding their hands over a hot stove and getting warm when standing in the sun—both examples of *radiation*—served as non-examples for *conduction*.

Effective content representations have one essential characteristic—*the information learners' need to understand the topic exists in the representations*, and we see this characteristic illustrated in Lucy's examples. Regardless of their backgrounds, the combination of examples Lucy used contained sufficient information to allow all students to acquire a meaningful understanding of *conduction*.

Types of Examples

Effective teachers use a variety of different kinds of examples to illustrate ideas. These include concrete materials, pictures, models, vignettes, simulations, and role-playing.

Concrete Materials Concrete materials are the "real thing," the most effective type of example that should be used whenever possible. For instance, an ideal example of the concept of *arthropod* (an animal phylum that includes insects; spiders; and crustaceans, such as lobsters, crabs, and shrimp) would be a live lobster (which could be purchased from a seafood store). Children can feel its hard shell and can see its jointed legs and three body parts. All the information students need to understand the concept is observable in the example.

[[[MEL here with DeVonne teaching arthropod]]]

To view a video clip of two teachers' attempts to provide concrete examples for their students, go to the Book Specific Resources tab in MyEducationLab, select your text, select Video Examples under Chapter 10, and then click on *Representing Concepts: Using Concrete Examples.*

Demonstrations and hands-on activities are other forms of concrete examples. For instance, when students connect two wires to a battery and make a bulb light up, they are seeing a real complete circuit.

Pictures   When concrete materials are unavailable, pictures are an acceptable compromise. For instance, because we can't bring young and mature mountains into the classroom, and we probably can't take students to where we can observe them directly, pictures or slides of the Rocky Mountains and Appalachian Mountains are effective ways of illustrating these concepts. The key is to come as close as possible to reality. Detailed, colored photographs are better than black-and-white pictures, which in turn are better than outline drawings.

Models   Some content, particularly in science, is impossible to observe directly. In these cases **models**, which are *representations that allow us to visualize what we can't observe directly*, are effective. For instance, suppose that you want your students to understand that heat increases the speed of molecules. Since we can't see molecules, a demonstration, combined with the models illustrated in Figure 10.3, would be high-quality examples. Placing one balloon in a beaker of ice, another in a beaker of water at room temperature, and a third in hot water would be an effective demonstration, and the longer arrows in the model representing the heated balloon would help students visualize the idea that the molecules in this balloon are moving faster than those in the other two balloons.

Vignettes   **Vignettes** are *short case studies that illustrate concepts*. For example, the following vignettes illustrate the concept of *internal conflict*:

Alyssa's dream had come true. Antonio, a boy she had wanted to date for some time, had asked her to go to the movies. However, as she thought about her homework assignments for that night, she remembered the term paper that was due on Friday. She had been putting off work on the paper until the last moment, and now she didn't know what to do.

Johnny knew if he cheated off Bill's paper, he'd do well on the test, but he also knew that he would feel guilty and dissatisfied.

Although Lupe hated to leave her hometown friends and family, and even her room, which she had lived in since a child, she wanted to go to college in Boston, 500 miles away.

Figure 10.3

Beakers with inflated balloons and models of balloons at different temperatures

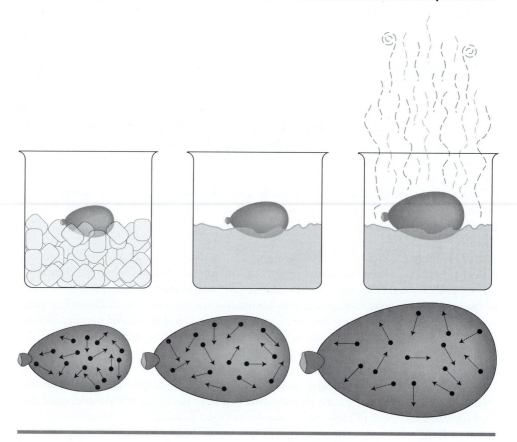

In each of the examples the character is faced with two choices, both of which have positive and negative consequences, illustrating the concept of *internal conflict*. The concept is difficult to describe in the abstract, and a definition such as "to come into collision, clash, or be at variance within oneself" would do little to clarify it for school-age learners. The vignettes, however, clearly illustrate the concept's characteristics. Vignettes and longer case studies are commonly used to illustrate abstract concepts in content areas such as history, government, literature, and psychology when concrete materials, pictures, and models aren't effective. Because of their effectiveness we make extensive use of vignettes and case studies in this text.

Simulation and Role-Play As with vignettes and case studies, simulation and role-play can also be used when concepts are hard to illustrate in any other way. Both involve placing students in real-life situations. For instance, students hear a great deal about the concept of *discrimination*, but most have had little experience with it. A simulation in which some members of the class are discriminated against because of eye or hair color or some other arbitrary characteristic provides a powerful illustration of an important concept. Social studies teachers also use simulations to illustrate our court system, the ways bills become laws, and the drudgery of assembly-line jobs.

To view a video clip of a teacher using examples to illustrate the concept of *arthropod*, go to the Book Specific Resources tab in MyEducationLab, select your text, select Video Examples under Chapter 10, and then click on *Guided Discovery: Studying Arthropods in Fifth Grade.*

Technology and Teaching

Using Databases in Guided Discovery Lessons

Technology can also be used to represent topics that are hard to illustrate otherwise and can play a valuable role in guided discovery lessons. Let's look at an example.

Jan Harrison's high school social studies class is in the middle of a unit on factors influencing economic growth in countries. Students in the class had divided up into groups of two or three and were doing in-depth research on a specific country. They brought their results back to the class for discussion, trying to identify factors that contributed to economic growth. As students shared their information with one another, a lively debate ensued.

"I think it's population density. In the country we're studying, El Salvador, there are 671 people per square mile and the average income is only $700 per person," Hay-Won asserted.

"I'm not so sure," Simon replied. "We've got data from the old USSR and the population density was only 33 people per square mile and their per capita income was only $3,000 per person. But their defense budget was 17 percent of their total GNP.

"Good points, Hay-Won and Simon. Cassie, did you want to add something?" Jan interjects to acknowledge Cassie, who had been waving her hand.

"We found that literacy rate has a lot to do with it. We're studying India and it has a literacy rate of 36 percent and its average income per person is only $300."

"Also interesting data, Cassie. Class, what are we going to do with all this information we have? How can we organize it systematically so we can make sense of all these data?"

After considerable discussion the students decide that they need to organize the information in some way so they could make cross-country comparisons. The class struggles for a while with key elements and finally decides that each group would provide the following information:

- Size of country
- Population
- Density
- Gross national product (GNP)
- Defense budget
- Average personal income
- Literacy rate

When they bring this information back to class, they struggle with how to organize it so that it makes sense.

Table 10.2 Using a Database to Investigate Economic Growth

Name and Size of Country	Pop.	Density	GNP	Defense	Literacy	Average Income
El Salvador						
India						
USSR						

Source: Adapted from Jonassen, 2000.

Further discussion results in the following table that Jan helps them place into the database outlined in Table 10.2.

A **database** *is a computerized record-keeping system that organizes large amounts of information* (Roblyer & Doering, 2010). In developing a database, students learn to organize information, and the analysis of the data gives them practice with critical thinking skills. For instance, Jan's students refined their vocabulary, conducted research, verified the accuracy of data, noted similarities and differences among data, and explored relationships. Once the database is organized, the information in it can be analyzed, as it would be with any other guided discovery lesson.

Lucy, in her unit on different types of energy transfer, might have used the following database to help her students see relationships in their data.

	Examples	Explanation for Heat Transfer	Movement of Molecules
Radiation			
Convection			
Conduction			

The advantage of using a database in her lesson is that all the information and experiences students had encountered over a number of days would be organized and displayed in a single file. The database makes the relationships in the data more apparent, making the information more accessible and meaningful.

As with designing any learning activity, teacher decision making is required at a number of points when using databases. Some questions that need to be answered include the following:

- How much direction should the teacher provide?
- When and how should the basic idea of a database be introduced?
- Who should have responsibility for organizing and constructing the outline of the database?
- Who should take responsibility for analyzing the information in the database?

These decisions are a matter of professional judgment. Greater teacher direction provides faster lesson pace, but students' "learning to learn" on their own is reduced. Decreased teacher intervention gives students a greater chance to learn on their own, but lack of direction can cause frustration and boredom. A good source for helping you learn to incorporate databases into your instruction is Roblyer and Doering (2010).

Planning for Social Interaction

Interaction between teacher and students and students with one another is an essential component of guided discovery lessons. This interaction is essential for three reasons. First, constructing understanding is ultimately an individual process, and because of background differences and cultural factors and perceptions, individuals' constructions will vary. The only way teachers can determine the extent to which students are correctly interpreting the representations they use is to discuss them. We want individual learners' constructions to eventually converge toward the correct one.

Second, discussion provides feedback to both teachers and students. It helps learners understand the extent to which their new constructions are valid, and it provides them with additional information that helps them continue to construct and reconstruct their understanding. Discussion also provides teachers with information that allows them to assess the extent to which students are progressing toward their learning goals.

Third, interaction actively involves students in the knowledge construction process and is motivating. Students like to share ideas with one another; whether in small groups or in whole-class discussion, this interaction results in increased involvement and motivation.

Planning for interaction is essential, and this is why clear learning objectives and high-quality examples are so important. Without them, the lesson lacks focus, and pseudo learning or "anything goes" construction of understanding can result.

Planning for social interaction involves more than "putting the students into groups." Effective social interaction isn't that simple; if group work isn't carefully planned, it can result in confusion and wasted time. Effective group work requires specifying learning tasks clearly, teaching students how to work together effectively, and careful monitoring by the teacher.

In whole-group activities, social interaction is facilitated by teacher questioning. The questioning skills we discussed in Chapter 6 are essential. Without these, discussions tend to revert to mini-lectures, and the benefits of social interaction are lost.

The quality of the representations teachers use also influences student interaction. Effective representations provide students with the information they can use to construct understanding, so they give students focal points for discussing and exchanging ideas. This is why real-world examples are so important. If the examples are ineffective, virtually no amount of teacher guidance will result in meaningful discussions.

Planning for Assessment

An essential part of planning for guided discovery lessons is planning for assessment. Teachers need to consider alternate ways to gather information from students about their learning progress. One way is informal assessments that gather information continually through interactive instructional dialogue (Leinhardt & Steele, 2005). A second way that teachers can gather data about learning progress utilizes data and examples the teacher provides. Rather than answer questions about abstract and isolated problems, teachers can ask students to demonstrate their understanding in real-world contexts. Lucy's students, for example, were asked to predict what would happen if they used a piece of wood or a butter knife instead of a wire for the demonstration with the burner and wax. In addition to assessing students' ability to apply the information they've learned, she gathered information about students' thinking in the process.

In summary when teachers plan for guided discovery lessons, they identify learning objectives, organize and sequence learning activities, and assess learning, just as they would when using a more teacher-centered approach such as direct instruction. Planning for guided discovery activities, however, requires more care in the way content is represented, as well as conscious planning for social interaction.

Conducting Guided Discovery Lessons

You have identified your topic, carefully specified your objectives, and selected or created your examples. You're now ready to begin the lesson. Implementing guided discovery lessons combines five interrelated phases, which are outlined in Figure 10.4 and discussed in the sections that follow.

PEARSON
The Power of Classroom Practice
www.myeducationlab.com

To view a video clip of a teacher using guided discovery to teach haiku poetry, go to the Book Specific Resources tab in MyEducationLab, select your text, select Video

Examples under Chapter 10, and then click on *Guided Discovery in an Elementary Classroom.*

Review and Introduction

As with effective instruction in general, guided discovery lessons begin with a review and then an introduction to the topic. This can be as simple as a statement such as, "Today, I'm going to show you some examples. I want you to be good observers and try to see what kind of pattern exists in them," or it can begin with a demonstration, problem, or display of information. Lucy began her lesson by reviewing the concepts of *radiation* and *convection* and then displaying the coffee maker and spoon. Because students weren't sure what they were going to do with the materials, Lucy capitalized on the motivating effects of curiosity, discussed earlier in the chapter.

Figure 10.4

Implementing Guided Discovery Lessons

- Review and introduction
- The open-ended phase
- The convergent phase
- Closure
- Application

The Open-Ended Phase

The open-ended phase is designed to promote student involvement and ensure their success as the lesson develops. Teachers can start this phase in several ways, but the most common is to present one or more examples and ask students to describe or compare them. Let's see how Lucy conducted this phase:

Lucy:	Now, . . . let's look at what we have here (displaying the coffee maker and spoon). Let's feel the coffee pot and the spoon. C'mon up, Sarafina. . . . How do they feel?
Sarafina:	Smooth.
Lucy:	Okay, . . . how else do they feel?
Sarafina:	Cold.
Lucy:	Okay, good. . . . Sarafina says that the spoon and coffee pot feel smooth and cold.

Lucy simply asked Sarafina to describe what she felt as she touched the coffee maker and spoon. She could have expanded this phase and asked other students to describe what they saw when they observed the materials. The amount of time spent in this phase depends on your professional judgment. If students seem eager to offer a number of descriptions of the example or demonstration, you may choose to involve more students; if they appear as if they are ready to move on, you can move to the next phase.

Open-ended questioning is the primary tool during this phase. **Open-ended questions** *are those for which a variety of answers are acceptable*, and they are effective for involving students and promoting interaction. The ability to capitalize on open-ended questioning to involve students is one of the strengths of guided discovery.

The Convergent Phase

Although open-ended questioning is an effective tool for involving students, you also have a content goal you want students to reach. You strategically move toward this goal in the convergent phase.

Lucy began the convergent phase by putting her students into groups and asking them to explain why the spoon got hot, which was followed by the discussion that led to the conclusion that it couldn't be radiation or convection.

Lucy:	Let's take a look at this drawing (displaying the drawing of the spoon with the dots and arrows). What do you notice about it?
Simone:	There's a bunch of little dots with arrows on them in the spoon.
Lucy:	They represent the molecules in the spoon. . . . Remember how we used the dots and arrows to help us visualize the movement of air molecules? But, there's an important difference here. . . . What is it?
	. . .
Lucy:	What is an important difference between gases and solids?
Dennis:	Solids are heavy and gases aren't.
Lucy:	Okay, and what else? . . . What about the way they move?
Toni:	Air molecules move around, but solids don't.

This questioning sequence was designed to establish that the molecules of solids move, but they don't move from place to place. This is an important characteristic of *conduction*, and establishing these ideas was important in helping students reach the learning objective. Lucy then used her demonstration with the heated wire and pieces of wax to illustrate conduction with other solid materials. All this was part of the convergent phase.

Two aspects of this process are important. First, Lucy didn't *tell* the students about the molecules of solids and the effect of heat on them; she illustrated the idea with her drawing and her demonstration with the wire and wax, and then she guided the students with her questioning as they constructed their understanding.

Second, although the students were constructing their understanding, Lucy was strongly involved in guiding their thinking. Her role in the process is critical. She was able to effectively guide students because her learning objective was clear, the social interaction focused on the learning objective, and she knew where she wanted the lesson to go.

Closure

Closure occurs when the topic is summarized or the concept defined. Lucy brought her lesson to closure when she introduced the term *conduction* and guided students to conclude that it (1) is a form of energy transfer and (2) occurs when rapidly moving molecules bump other molecules, so the other molecules also move faster.

Application

Although being able to state a definition of the idea being taught reflects understanding at one level, to make the topic meaningful and ensure transfer, students need to be able to apply it outside the classroom. Lucy completed the application phase when she gave students the assignment of comparing how a butter knife and piece of wood would react after being heated. This application involved common, real-world examples familiar to students. Real-world examples promote meaningful understanding and encourage students to broaden this understanding to other areas.

Using Guided Discovery with Different-Aged Learners

The basic structure of guided discovery lessons is the same for learners at all developmental levels. However, adaptations are necessary when using the strategy with students at different developmental levels.

Guided Discovery Lessons with Young Children   In general the younger the students or the less experience they have with a topic, the greater the need for concrete, high-quality examples. High-quality examples are the ideal for everyone; with young children and learners lacking experience, they are essential.

Lessons will be probably be shorter with young children than they typically are with older students, and you may adapt your questioning to allow for additional factors, such as more group response, than is typically the case with older students.

If effectively illustrated, however, even young children can understand concepts that are somewhat abstract. Let's look at an example.

Sonia Martinez wants her first graders to understand properties of matter. She brings a transparent plastic drink cup and a package of cotton balls, "fills" the drink cup with the cotton balls, and holds it up for the children.

"What do you notice?" Sonia asks.

The children make a series of observations, and Sonia then asks, "Is the cup full of cotton?"

"Yes!" the children shout in unison.

"What does that mean?"

With some prompting, the children conclude that all the space in the cup is taken up.

"Now, watch what I do," Sonia directs, as she pushes her hand down into the cup, squishing the cotton in the cup.

"Now, what do you notice? . . . Sancha?"

"The cotton is squished down."

"Yes," Sonia smiles. "So, is all the space in the cup taken up."

"No!" the children respond.

"How about the amount of cotton. . . . Do we have more cotton, or less cotton, or is it the same amount?"

"You have . . . less," Tanya answers hesitantly.

"Did I take any cotton balls out of the cup?"

". . . No," Tanya responds.

"So, do I have less cotton?"

"I . . . guess . . . not."

"So, we have the same about of cotton but the amount of space it takes up is less. We say that the cotton is more *dense*. So, when we squish something down, what do we call it?"

"More dense!" several of the children respond together.

"Good," Sonia smiles. "You are all very good thinkers."

Sonia's clever example was the key to the success of her lesson. The children could *see* that the amount of cotton did not change, and they could *see* that the cotton took up less space when she compressed it. A concept such as *density* is commonly believed to be too developmentally advanced for first graders, but Sonia was able to illustrate it concretely enough to allow students to understand it.

Guided Discovery Lessons with Older Students   When using guided discovery with older students, a few minor adaptations are often necessary. For example, older students have a long history of being asked questions that are specific and require one right answer. So they are likely to initially be somewhat reluctant to respond during the open-ended phase, wondering, "What are you looking for?" Some might even ask that question, to which you can respond, "I'm not looking for anything in particular. I want to know what you observe." Once they realize that you truly mean what you say, they gradually get used to the process. Older students are, however, typically less inclined to make a large number of responses during the open-ended phase, so you will probably move to the convergent phase more quickly than you would with younger children.

As with young children, older students will often struggle to put their understanding into words during closure, so prompting them and helping with specific wording will be necessary, even for mature and advanced students.

Even though older students will often bring more prior knowledge to the lesson than do younger students, high-quality examples continue to be essential. At least some of the students will lack the prior knowledge needed to develop a deep understanding of the topic without the use of high-quality examples. As with younger students, you help "level the playing field" with the quality of the examples you provide.

The Power of Classroom Practice
www.myeducationlab.com

To view a video clip illustrating how development influences first graders' thinking, go to the Book Specific Resources tab in MyEducationLab, select your text, select Video Examples under Chapter 10, and then click on *Using High-Quality Examples: Studying Properties of Air in First Grade.*

Exploring Diversity

Using Guided Discovery with Cultural Minorities

Many students who are members of cultural minorities feel unwelcome in school, and they don't have a sense of relatedness to their classmates or teacher (Goldstein, 2004; Gollnick & Chinn, 2009). In addition, members of cultural minorities sometimes have difficulty with the fast-paced, question-and-answer patterns of typical classrooms, and they may interpret direct questions as threatening rather than attempts by teachers to promote learning (Howard, 2001).

Guided discovery, particularly the open-ended phase, can be very effective as a tool for addressing these issues. Open-ended questions are effective for promoting equitable distribution in the classroom, and when minority students see that they're being called on as frequently as other students in the class, and they're able to answer successfully, their sense of relatedness increases. In addition, minority students are often more comfortable responding to open-ended questions than they are with direct questions requiring a single, correct answer. Using open-ended questions as a tool for promoting involvement and making students feel welcome increases the likelihood that they will be more motivated and willing to participate during the lesson.

Being able to respond successfully can also help students feel competent, a feeling that all people need. Helping students feel as if they are welcome and connected to their peers and teacher and helping them feel competent can do a great deal to increase the motivation of members of cultural minorities. Guided discovery can be particularly effective for meeting these goals.

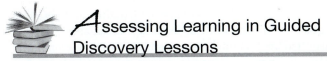

Assessing Learning in Guided Discovery Lessons

Because students are constructing understanding during guided discovery lessons, ongoing assessment is essential. Much of the informal assessment occurs during the convergent phase. Students' answers to Lucy's questions gave her continual indicators of their understanding, which allowed her to intervene when necessary, as she did when Jason tried to use radiation as an explanation for the spoon getting hot.

Ongoing assessment helps teachers make four decisions during guided discovery learning activities:

- When to intervene to guide the lesson in the direction of the learning objective
- How extensively to intervene
- When to provide additional examples or other representations of the topic
- When and how to bring the lesson to closure

We saw all four of these decisions illustrated in Lucy's lesson. With practice, you'll become increasingly skilled at steering guided discovery lessons toward your learning goal. As you develop professionally, keep one essential question in mind as you interact with your students: "What is the learning objective?" This question will help you maintain a focus for the lesson, it will guide your questioning, and it will help you decide whether your lesson should be modified.

Using Assessment to Increase Learning

Teachers sometimes think that assessment is used primarily for assigning grades. It is more important, however, that it be a tool for promoting learning and motivation (Stiggins & Chappuis, 2006). To accomplish this two factors are required. First, the assessment items or tasks must measure more than knowledge and recall of information; second, detailed feedback and discussion of the items are essential. Time spent in providing feedback can be an effective learning tool because students' interest in their performance is high. Because of this interest, explanations and discussions of quiz items often result in more learning than occurs in the initial learning activity, when the students have less at stake.

As part of her assessment, Lucy assigned students the task of deciding what would happen if they substituted a piece of wood or a butter knife for the wire. She then had students share their answers and analyze them. As they discussed the answers, Lucy asked them to provide evidence for their conclusions, further reinforcing the essential characteristics of conduction that were the goal of her lesson.

This process had three positive features:

- It promoted a deep understanding of the topic by providing students with feedback about their thinking.
- It promoted critical thinking; requiring students to present evidence to support their conclusions is the essence of critical thinking.
- It was simple and took little teacher effort; all Lucy had to do was call on students to share their answers. It took no advance preparation.

This last point is important. Teachers' work is extremely demanding, and anything they can do to reduce their workload—without sacrificing learning—is valuable.

Guided discovery is a sophisticated instructional strategy, and you won't be completely successful at it immediately. Most teachers can learn to deliver passable lectures, but becoming competent with guided discovery takes practice and effort. However, if you persevere and practice, your expertise will continually increase; when you do become an expert, you will find that guiding students to understanding they previously didn't possess is one of the most satisfying experiences you can have as a teacher.

Summary

Understanding Guided Discovery

Guided discovery is an instructional strategy designed to teach concepts and other abstractions. When using the strategy, teachers specify learning objectives, present students with information, and guide them to the objectives through questioning.

Guided discovery is grounded in constructivism, a view of learning suggesting that learners develop their own understanding of the topics they study rather than receiving understanding in an already organized form. New learning develops in the context of current understanding and is facilitated by social interaction as learners work with real-world tasks, problems, and questions.

A major positive aspect of guided discovery lessons is their motivational benefits for students. They begin with a problem to solve, which stimulates student curiosity. They also actively involve students through questioning, which is also motivating to students. Finally, because they help students make sense of the world, they contribute to a sense of self-efficacy, students' beliefs that they can understand and change the world.

Planning for Guided Discovery Lessons

Planning for guided discovery lessons begins with identifying a topic and then proceeds with specifying clear and precise learning objectives, selecting examples and non-examples, planning for social interaction, and making decisions about assessment.

Conducting Guided Discovery Lessons

Guided discovery lessons begin with a review of previous related topics and an introduction to the focus of the lesson. It continues with the open-ended phase, in which students observe and describe the examples they encounter; the convergent phase, in which the teacher guides students toward the learning objective; closure, when the topic is summarized; and application, when new understanding is applied in a real-world setting.

Assessing Learning in Guided Discovery Lessons

Because students are constructing their own understanding of the topics they're studying, ongoing assessment is essential when conducting guided discovery lessons. Much of the informal assessment of students' understanding is conducted during the convergent phase, because at this point students are articulating their understanding. If this understanding is invalid, teachers need to intervene.

Important Concepts

Constructivism (p. 313)
Database (p. 322)
Guided discovery (p. 312)
Models (p. 319)

Open-ended questions (p. 325)
Self-efficacy (p. 315)
Vignette (p. 319)

Preparing for Your Licensure Exam

At the beginning of the chapter you saw how Lucy Steiner planned and conducted a lesson using guided discovery. As you read the following case study, evaluate whether the teacher is effectively implementing guided discovery in her teaching.

myeducationlab
The Power of Classroom Practice
www.myeducationlab.com

After reading this case, go to the Book Specific Resources tab in MyEducationLab, select your text, select *Preparing for Your Licensure Exam* under Chapter 10 to complete the questions that accompany the case and receive feedback on your responses.

Jenny Newhall has her fifth-grade students involved in a unit on different kinds of poetry, and for this lesson she wants her students to understand haiku.

She begins the class by saying, "We've been studying different kinds of poetry for several days now, and today I want us to look at another form. . . . Look up here at what I've displayed on the overhead."

Deep in a windless
wood, not one leaf dares to move . . .
Something is afraid.

Into a forest
I called . . . The voice in reply
was no voice I knew.

I called to the wind
"Who's there?". . . Whoever it was
still knocks at my gate.

"What do these three examples have in common? I want you to work with your partner for a few minutes and write down as many things as you can that these three excerpts have in common. When you're finished, we'll discuss them."

"Do we turn our papers in?" Omar asks.

"Yes," Jenny smiled. "Remember, we said that you always turn your papers in, unless I tell you otherwise. . . . Okay, . . . go ahead. You have four minutes."

The students, who were seated next to their partners, turn together, and a buzz of voices soon rises in the room. As students work, Jenny moves up and down the aisles glancing at what students had written and making periodic comments, suggestions, and reminders about what they were supposed to do.

At the end of the four minutes, Jenny announces, "Okay everyone, turn back this way. . . . Good. Now, . . . let's go ahead and see what we've come up with. . . . Tell us one thing you have written down, . . . Go ahead, Latisha."

". . . Three lines in each one."

"Good, . . . Dale?"

"The middle line is longer than the top one and the bottom one."

"Toni?"

". . . There's three little periods in each one."

"What are those little periods called?" Jenny asks, "and what do they mean? . . . Anyone?"

". . ."

"No one? . . . Okay, I'll tell you. . . . They're called 'ellipses' and they're used to indicate that something is left out of the line. . . . See, you learned something new," she smiles. "Now, . . . back to what we're doing. What else? . . . Nita?"

"Everybody already took ours."

"Oh, no," Jenny prompts. "Look a little more carefully. What are each of the examples about? . . . I mean what kind of a theme do they have?"

"They're like . . . I'm not sure what you mean."

"Well, what's the first one about?"

". . . The woods?"

"Yes, each of the excerpts is about nature," Jenny comments. "Good, Nita.

"Now, if you look," she continues, "you'll see that they're also each expressing some form of emotion, . . . like in the first one it says that something is afraid. . . . The emotion may be unstated, but it's there, nevertheless."

"So, let's go on. . . . What else do you see in the examples? . . . Anyone?"

". . ."

"How many syllables in the first line of each poem? . . . Look carefully. . . . How many?"

". . . There's five in the first and second one, . . . and . . . six in the third one," Jamie replies after studying the examples for several seconds.

"Not quite," Jenny smiles. "Actually, there are five in the third one as well. Maybe you thought 'called' has two syllables, but it's really just one. . . . Now, . . . if you look at the third line, you'll see that it also has five syllables in it. . . . Everyone take a good look . . . Do you all see? . . . Very good. . . . Okay, let's take a look at the second line of each. How many syllables there? . . . Look carefully."

". . . I think . . . seven," Noreen offers hesitantly.

"Excellent, Noreen! . . . Indeed it is seven. . . . So we have a pattern in the examples. . . . Go ahead and summarize it for us. . . . Somebody want to volunteer?"

". . . I will," Tony waves, ". . . they have five syllables in the first line, . . . and . . . in the third line, and . . . seven in the middle line."

"Good, and can someone add to that . . . what are they about?"

". . . Nature," Juan notes.

"All right, and one more part. . . . Someone?"

". . . They tell about . . . some . . . emotional something," Donna adds, "But I don't really get that. . . . I don't see it."

"It is a little hard to see," Jenny acknowledges. "It's sort of unstated, but if you look carefully, you can kind of see that it's there."

Jenny then continues, "Now, what I want you to do is get together again and compose a poem similar to the ones we've been studying. . . . Then, we'll share them. . . . Okay? . . . Go ahead."

Questions for Analysis

Let's examine Jenny's lesson now based on the information in this chapter. In your analysis consider the following questions. In each case, be specific and take information directly from the case study in doing your analysis.

1. The chapter focused on guided discovery, which is instruction based on constructivist views of learning. How effectively did Jenny apply the characteristics of constructivism in her lesson? What could she have done to apply constructivist views of learning better in her lesson?

2. Examples are essential when using guided discovery. How effective were Jenny's examples? Refer specifically to her examples in making your response.

3. Questioning is essential in guided discovery lessons. How effective was Jenny's questioning? If you believe it could have been more effective, identify specific instances in the case study where it could have been improved.

4. Assess the effectiveness of Jenny's convergent, closure, and application phases in her lesson. Cite evidence from the case study to support your assessment.

5. As in many classes Jenny's students were from diverse backgrounds. How effectively did her lesson accommodate the background diversity of her students? Again, be specific in your response.

Discussion Questions

1. Think about your present beliefs about good teaching. Where did they come from? What kinds of experiences did you use to form those beliefs? What kinds of experiences are you finding most valuable in your teacher education program in terms of learning to teach? What do your answers to these questions tell you about constructivism as it applies to learning to teach?

2. Identify several topics you believe could be effectively taught using guided discovery. Identify several others for which you believe guided discovery would not be effective. Explain the essential difference or differences in the two sets of topics.

3. Are all kinds of social interaction equally valuable? What factors influence the effectiveness of social interaction as a learning tool in guided discovery lessons?

4. What types of real-world tasks do you encounter in your teacher education programs? How does their authenticity influence their effectiveness in promoting growth?

5. Should all learning tasks be real world? Why or why not? What obstacles do teachers face in attempting to incorporate real-world tasks in their teaching?

6. What can teachers do to make the following teaching activities more nearly grounded in constructivist learning theory?

    a. lectures
    b. learning from text
    c. labs
    d. drill and practice?

7. As technology becomes increasingly important in schools, will guided discovery be a more or less important teaching strategy? Explain your answer.

8. What effect will the current emphasis on standards, accountability, and testing have on the use of guided discovery in the classroom? Explain your answer, using information from the chapter.

*P*ortfolio Activities

1. *Guided Discovery in the Classroom.* Observe an interactive lesson in which a teacher is teaching a concept, generalization, principle, or academic rule. To what extent does the lesson incorporate these components of constructivist views of learning?

    a. Learners construct their own understanding.
    b. New learning depends on current understanding.
    c. Learning is facilitated by social interaction.
    d. Real-world tasks promote learning.

What could the teacher have done to make the lesson more closely based on constructivist views of learning?

2. *Learning: The Students' Perspective.* Interview several students individually after observing a lesson. Ask the following questions:

    a. What did they learn (ask them to explain in their own words)?
    b. How is this idea or skill related to other ones?
    c. Why is it important?

What do their responses tell you about what students take away from a lesson?

3. *Social Interaction.* Observe a class for at least an hour. Note the number of opportunities students have to talk with one another. Are these opportunities structured or unstructured? Are they sanctioned by the teacher? Then interview the teacher. Some questions to ask include the following:

    a. How important is student interaction for learning?
    b. How does it promote learning?
    c. What strategies does the teacher use to structure or encourage social interaction?
    d. What problems are encountered when using social interaction as a learning tool?

How do you plan to use social interaction to promote learning in your classroom?

4. *Real-World Tasks.* Examine a teacher's edition of a text in a content area that you are going to teach. How adequately does the text translate abstract ideas into real-world

tasks? How does the content area influence the kinds of tasks used? How could the teacher supplement the text to link the content area more closely to the real world?

5. *Guided Discovery: Planning.* Plan a lesson using the guidelines found in this chapter.

    a. How did you accommodate or include
- Student construction of understanding
- Student background knowledge
- Social interaction
- Authentic or real-world learning tasks?

    b. How does the planning process differ from planning a different kind of lesson?

    c. What was the most difficult aspect of planning? The easiest? Why?

6. *Guided Discovery: Implementation.* Teach the lesson that you planned for in Exercise 5.

    a. How did your role as a teacher change as compared to other types of lessons? Was it easier or harder?

    b. How did students respond to the lesson?

    c. What were the strengths and weaknesses of the lesson?

    d. What would you do differently next time?

To check your comprehension of the content covered in Chapter 10, go to the Book Specific Resources in MyEducationLab, select your text, and complete the Study Plan quiz. In addition to receiving feedback on your answers, a study plan will be generated from the quiz that will direct you to access Review, Practice, and Enrichment materials to enhance your understanding of chapter content.

11

Problem-Based Instruction

Chapter Outline	Learning Objectives
	When you've completed your study of this chapter, you should be able to
Problem-based learning: An overview ■ Problem-based learning: Why does it work?	1. Describe characteristics of problem-based instruction.
Project-based learning ■ Essential components ■ Implementing project-based instruction in the classroom ■ Assessment and project-based learning ■ Research on project-based instruction	2. Plan and implement project-based instruction.

Problem solving
■ Well-defined and ill-defined problems
■ A problem-solving model
■ Helping learners become better problem solvers
   Technology and Teaching:
     Using technology as a tool to teach problem solving
	3. Plan and implement strategies to help students learn to solve problems.

Inquiry strategies ■ Identifying a question ■ Forming hypotheses ■ Gathering data ■ Assessing hypotheses ■ Generalizing ■ Analyzing the inquiry process	4. Develop learning activities to promote inquiry strategies in learners.

Critical thinking
■ Knowledge of content
■ Basic processes
■ Metacognition: Awareness and control of cognitive processes
■ Attitudes and dispositions
■ Teaching critical thinking in the classroom
   Exploring Diversity:
     Problem-based instruction with developmentally different learners
	5. Plan and implement strategies to teach critical thinking skills.

In this chapter we examine problem-based instruction, a collection of teaching strategies that includes project-based instruction, problem solving, inquiry, and the teaching of critical thinking skills. To introduce you to the topic of problem-based instruction, let's look in on a teacher using this strategy in his classroom.

Students at Bayview Middle School, on the banks of Chesapeake Bay, are actively involved in a debate about farm fertilizers, pesticides, and water pollution. Brad Evers, their social studies teacher, has been working with the other members of his teaching team to prepare students for this debate. Sonya Woodside, the science teacher, has been focusing on the chemical and biological aspects of pollution. Ted Barret, their English teacher, has been helping students use the Internet to gather information and write reports. Kim Starrow, the math teacher, has been focusing on graphing skills to help students integrate graphs into their presentations.

Kasha, a member of the Environmental Group, rises to speak. "Our group is in favor of House Bill 370. It prohibits farmers from using fertilizers and pesticides within 300 feet of any stream flowing into the bay."

"We strongly disagree," replies Jacob, a member of the Farmer's Coalition. "This bill is unfair. It will put many farmers out of business and is unnecessary. Besides, fertilizer helps things grow. What evidence is there that fertilizer hurts anything?"

"But what about us? We make our living off of the fish and oysters in the bay. Shouldn't our jobs be protected as well?" Jared counters as the moderator gives him the floor.

The debate continues with each group given opportunities to present its perspective, using charts, graphs, and printed materials (adapted from Slavin, Madden, Dolan, & Wasik, 1994, pp. 3–4).

Problem-Based Learning: An Overview

Problem-based instruction *is a collection of integrative teaching strategies that use problems as the focal point, teaching problem-solving skills while developing self-directed learning* (Evenson & Hmelo, 2000). Problem-based instruction has the following characteristics (Gijbels, Dochy, Bossche, & Segers, 2005; Lam, 2004):

- Lessons begin with a problem or question, and solving the problem or answering the question becomes the focus of the lesson.

- Students are actively involved in learning while investigating the problem, designing strategies, and finding solutions.

- The teacher's role in problem-based instruction is primarily facilitative, guiding students' efforts through questioning and other forms of instructional scaffolding.

Teachers use problem-based instruction to accomplish multiple goals, including helping students to (1) learn to systematically investigate questions and problems, (2) develop self-regulation and self-directed learning abilities, (3) learn to interact with other students in productive ways, and (4) learn content. These goals were evident in Brad Evers's classroom. Students learned about pollution in the Chesapeake Bay while also developing their own abilities to conduct investigations into meaningful problems.

As the name implies, problem-based instruction begins with a question or problem. In Brad Evers's class the problem involved the effects of pollution on the Chesapeake Bay. Later in the chapter you'll read about one classroom whose students attempt to find the area of an irregularly shaped room and another whose students try to determine whether brand-name or generic aspirins are better. These problems provide the focal point for students' investigations.

The primary goals for problem-based learning activities are the development of problem-solving abilities and self-directed learning; learning content is less prominent

(Gijbels et al., 2005). If learning content is a primary goal, alternate strategies, such as direct instruction, lecture discussion, or guided discovery, are probably more effective in terms of time and energy. However, some evidence indicates that content learned during problem-based lessons is retained longer and transfers better than content learned when other strategies are used (Duffy & Cunningham, 1996; Sternberg, 1998).

But what is self-directed learning and how do problem-based strategies contribute to its development? **Self-directed learning** *occurs when students are aware of and take control of their learning progress.* Self-directed learning is a form of metacognition, which involves knowing what we need to know, knowing what we know, knowing what we don't know, and devising strategies to bridge these gaps (Azevedo & Cromley, 2004).

During problem-based instruction, students first assess what they know about the problem they are facing. On the basis of this assessment, students decide what additional information they need and develop plans to address these deficiencies. As they gather new information, they use this information to solve the problem they're encountering. If the information is sufficient and their goal met, the problem is solved. If not, students reformulate new learning strategies.

The teacher assists in the process by asking facilitative questions, such as

What do you already know?

What additional information do you need?

Where can you find this information?

Questions such as these encourage students to think about the process they are going through, which helps them develop as self-directed learners. Unlike some of the more content-oriented strategies that you've read about, in problem-based instruction the teacher's role is more facilitator and guide rather than information organizer and disseminator.

This chapter describes three different kinds of problem-based instructional strategies: project-based learning, problem solving, and inquiry (see Figure 11.1). Project-based learning presents students with a problem and involves them in the long-term study of some topic. These lessons typically pull from a number of different content areas, and this integrated approach was illustrated in Brad's lesson at the beginning of the chapter. Problem-solving strategies, by contrast, are usually shorter and use a problem as the focus of a lesson to develop content, skills, and self-regulation. In inquiry, the third kind of problem-based learning, students attempt to answer questions about how the world works through active investigations. Before we examine what each of these specific forms of problem-based learning looks like in classrooms, let's see why they work.

Figure 11.1

Variations of Problem-Based Strategies

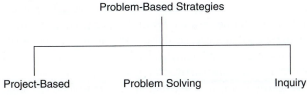

Problem-Based Learning: Why Does It Work?

Problem-based learning is grounded in the philosophy of John Dewey, who advocated the use of experiential learning in classrooms, and constructivist views of learning, which emphasize the central role of students' search for meaning. Let's look at these ideas in more detail.

Philosophical Underpinnings   John Dewey (1859–1952), probably the most influential educational philosopher in America, believed that children are socially active learners who learn by exploring their environments (Dewey, 1916). He believed schools should take advantage of children's natural curiosity by bringing the outside world into the classroom, making it the focus for study.

In studying the world students should be active inquirers. Dewey proposed that this inquiry should be guided by the scientific method, which has the following characteristics:

- Learners are involved in authentic experiences that genuinely interest them.
- Learners examine problems that stimulate thinking and focus their efforts.
- As they solve problems, learners acquire information.
- Learners form tentative solutions that may solve the problem.
- Learners test the solutions by applying them to the problem. Applications help learners validate their knowledge.

We saw elements of these characteristics in Brad's classroom. Knowing that his students would be interested in the bay that they lived on, he designed a problem-based unit that allowed them to explore a problem that affected their lives and the lives of their parents. Dewey believed that the knowledge students learn shouldn't be some inert information found in books or delivered in lectures. Instead, knowledge becomes useful and alive when it is applied to the solution of real-life problems. Dewey's work continues to be influential in areas such as project-based learning, thematic units, and interdisciplinary teaching (Jacobsen, 2003).

Constructivist Frameworks   As we've seen earlier in the text, constructivists believe that student learning is most effective when students actively construct knowledge, connecting it to what they already know. Problem-based learning encourages active knowledge construction by placing students in the middle of active learning situations. Students learn by actively trying to solve problems, such as investigating the effects of pollutants on our waterways.

One particular kind of constructivism, called *sociocultural learning theory*, stresses the importance of social interactions in learning. Based upon the work of the Russian psychologist Lev Vygotsky (1978, 1986), sociocultural theory emphasizes that learning is inherently social and embedded within social and cultural settings. As learners within problem-based lessons interact with one another, they not only learn from one another, but also create new knowledge for themselves.

From a sociocultural perspective, forming a community of learners is crucial. Teachers need to help students learn how to learn from one another. From this perspective the social interaction and group problem-solving skills that are learned are as important as other goals such as learning content and developing higher-level analytical skills. Active listening, turn taking, building upon the ideas of others, and constructive disagreement, interaction skills that are so important in cooperative learning, are also essential in problem-based learning.

Because of the value of social interaction in problem-based learning, all of the strategies described in this chapter are framed as group activities. However, many of these could be assigned as individual projects. For example, individual students could be asked to work on the Chesapeake Bay pollution problem and present their results individually. However, in organizing problem-based learning in this way, teachers miss valuable opportunities to take advantage of social learning.

In the next section we analyze project-based instruction, one of the most widely used problem-based learning teaching strategies.

 # Project-Based Learning

Project-based learning, a comprehensive approach to classroom teaching and learning, involves *"engaging students in projects: relatively long-term, problem-focused, and meaningful units of instruction that integrate concepts from a number of disciplines or fields of study"* (Brophy, 2004, p. 237). During project-based learning,

> Students pursue solutions to authentic problems by asking and refining questions, debating ideas, making predictions, designing plans or experiments, collecting and analyzing data, drawing conclusions, communicating their ideas and findings to others, asking new questions, and creating products. (Good & Brophy, 2003, p. 234)

Essential Components

Project-based learning utilizes the following components:

- An authentic question or problem organizes and drives the activities.
- Collaboration provides opportunities for students to learn to work together toward a common goal.
- Activities include information gathering from a variety of sources, which may involve interdisciplinary connections.
- Answers or solutions to the problem or question lead to a series of products that result in a final presentation project in a form that can be shared with others and critiqued (e.g., debate, report, videotape, presentation).

Let's analyze these characteristics using Brad's classroom as an example.

Authentic Question or Problem   Project-based learning begins with a question or problem that is real to students and that can serve as the focal point for student investigations. An effective problem

- Fulfills a specific educational purpose; it relates to important learning outcomes and connects to a teacher's goals
- Presents an open-ended task to accomplish
- Compels interest by challenging students
- Connects student learning to real-world experience (Gagnon & Collay, 2001)

The question or problem could be a social issue, a topic encountered in the regular curriculum, or one that interests students. Brad used the topic of pollution in the Chesapeake Bay to focus his students' studies. The topic was authentic or real to them because they live along the bay and could relate their studies to their own lives and the lives of their parents, many of whom are farmers and fishermen.

In addition to being authentic, the problems should also be open ended and ill defined, posing a sense of mystery or puzzlement. This is important for several reasons. Ill-defined problems offer challenges to students, providing them with opportunities to wrestle with, understand, and frame the learning task ahead of them. This challenge is similar to one students encounter when they write a more traditional term paper and can be the most educationally rewarding part of the process. In addition, an open-ended problem is motivating, providing students with both challenge and choice (Brophy, 2004).

Additional examples of topics that could serve as focal points for project-based learning are found in Table 11.1.

Each of these questions or problems could serve as the focus of a long-term investigation by students.

Collaboration with Other Students   As students work together on their projects, they develop valuable group interaction skills. They learn to form group goals collaboratively, listen to others' ideas, express their own ideas, and compromise as conflicts occur. These are valuable skills in school as well as in real life.

Collaboration also has cognitive benefits as well (Eggen & Kauchak, 2010). The process of organizing ideas and putting them into words is a challenging task that promotes learning, as anyone who has had to write about something knows. In addition listening to others' ideas and understanding them and incorporating them with our own not only contributes to our own thinking, but also helps create new ideas.

Information Gathering   Project-based learning activities involve students in a variety of information gathering activities:

- Searching printed sources for relevant information
- Using the Internet
- Interviewing people
- Gathering specimens (e.g., plants and animals)

Table 11.1   Project-Based Questions or Problems

Content Area	Question or Problem
High school social studies	What factors influence voter turnout in an election?
High school health	How healthy are the lunches that students eat at our school?
Elementary science	What kinds of plants and animals inhabit a nearby pond?
Middle school history	What is the history of the town or city in which we live?
Middle school social studies	Where do last names come from and what do they mean?
Elementary science/social studies	What are the advantages and disadvantages of different pets?

In Brad's classroom students used books and magazines such as *National Geographic*, as well as the Internet to obtain basic information about the bay and the problems of pollution. They also interviewed a number of people, including farmers and fishermen, as well as public officials, such as water quality officials and wildlife conservation officers. They also collected and analyzed water samples from different sites along the bay.

Often the process of information gathering requires crossing discipline or content boundaries. Note that although all of the original questions in Table 11.1 were embedded in a particular content area or areas, they could potentially lead to interdisciplinary investigations. For example, the high school health project focusing on nutrition could incorporate science topics to frame the question, social studies to investigate issues of sampling, math to report results, and writing to present conclusions. In a similar way the elementary project on pets could involve a broad array of skills such as interviewing, using math to report findings, and reading and writing in the language arts curriculum. Project-based learning often serves as the focal point for interdisciplinary units that connect multiple content areas.

Products The products of project-based learning are an important learning component and need to be shared with others. The creation of a product encourages students to integrate their new learning into some form of cohesive and coherent report. This is a demanding task that fosters learning. Producing a product also brings closure to the project, which carries with it motivational benefits (Schunk et al., 2008). Feedback from others also permits learners to reflect on and extend their emerging knowledge and to revise their products if necessary.

Products can take a number of forms. The most obvious is some type of written report that can be shared with others. Here are some alternatives:

- A multimedia presentation with an audience in mind
- A letter to a politician or newspaper
- A drama or short story
- A debate

Students should view the products they create as not only a worthwhile summary of their efforts, but also as a functional, informing, or persuasive presentation to a specific audience.

Brad's students reported their findings in several ways. To encourage them to consider multiple perspectives on the problem, he assigned them to teams that focused on different aspects of the problem. Prior to the debate each team presented its findings to the whole class using different forms of technology, including videotapes, audiotapes, and PowerPoint. Students then used this information during the debate in which they assumed different roles and perspectives.

Implementing Project-Based Instruction in the Classroom

Project-based learning is complex, from both a teacher's and student's perspectives. For teachers, it requires a number of different roles, starting with planning and ending with assessment. It also requires students to assume different roles, and teachers need to assist students as they learn how to perform these new roles. In this section we describe how teachers can make project-based instruction work in their classrooms, starting with the process of planning.

Planning   All good teaching starts with a goal, which then guides teachers' subsequent instructional efforts. Brad Evers had several goals. He wanted students to learn about pollution and how it affected the area in which they lived. He also wanted students to learn to work together cooperatively on projects and develop their abilities to direct their own learning in the future. These multiple goals are typical in project-based learning.

A second planning task is to identify a topic for study and then frame the topic in terms of a problem for students to investigate. Topics for project-based learning can come from several sources. The most obvious is the assigned curriculum. Although teachers are expected to teach a number of "assigned" topics driven by standards, all it takes is a little creativity to transform these into the focal point of projects. For example, a unit on the Crusades can be converted into active investigations by students into the human efforts that went into the Crusades, including reports on recruitment efforts, songs, and battle strategies. In a similar way a social studies lesson on local political structures or a science lesson on pollution can be converted into project-based instruction on the politics of pollution and the Chesapeake Bay, as Brad did.

Another teacher planning task during project-based learning is to organize resources, both in print and media formats. This task has been made much simpler with the advent of the Internet, but teachers still need to plan for access to computers, the availability of relevant websites, as well as more mundane things such as printing.

Implementing   The first step in implementing project-based learning in the classroom is to orient students to the problem. Let's see how Brad did this in his classroom.

> "Class, I've got some pictures I'd like to show you. They're from a book called, *Then and Now: A Historical Look at Chesapeake Bay*. What do you notice about the first one? Seth?"
>
> "That's Sassafras Creek. I can tell from the old pier that's still there. But there weren't any condos there then."
>
> "Good, Seth. What else do you notice, class?"
>
> Brad continues, sharing with his class both old and modern pictures of the bay, helping them see the changes that have occurred over time to the physical appearance of the bay. Then he shares with them some figures on the number of oysters and fish that were harvested over the years and asks students to explain the decline. During the discussion, he asks if any of the students boat or fish in the bay and asks them to share their experiences. He asks them to go home that evening and ask their parents about their early memories of Chesapeake Bay and how it has changed over time.

An effective problem has several essential characteristics. First, it must be real or meaningful to students. In addition, it must be understandable and afford a starting point for students' investigative efforts. Finally, it must be complex and open ended to provide students with multiple options for their investigations.

After orienting students to the problem, teachers need to organize students into study teams. One of the easiest, but not necessarily the best, way to do this is by student choice. However, the concerns raised in Chapter 7 about this method of composing cooperative learning groups also apply here; groups may not be balanced in terms of ability, ethnicity, or gender. Working with friends or in homogeneous groups often prevents students from learning about others and how to work with students who are different from them.

After students are organized into study teams, teachers need to structure the teams' efforts by establishing timelines, both for intermediate goals and final projects. Timelines provide concrete due dates for different groups to meet and help with student accountability. Teachers can also assist with these timelines by meeting with the different groups on a periodic basis to facilitate each group's progress.

Major tasks each group will need to struggle with are data collection and analysis. For example, the students in Brad's class chose to interview a number of different people connected to the bay. Before they did this, they needed to construct an interview protocol to structure their interviews. They also needed to decide whether the interviews should be audio- or video-recorded or notes taken. Brad helped in the process by asking groups to think ahead and consider what their final reports or products would look like.

The final products that result from project-based learning can and should take multiple forms. Students should take the audience into consideration when planning their reports and should be encouraged to employ a variety of media formats. Even if one of the products is a traditional paper, students should be encouraged to consider ways to make the information in it accessible and interesting. This not only develops perspective taking, a valuable social skill (Berk, 2010), but also employs multiple learning tasks, a major way of addressing student diversity (Tomlinson, 2005). In addition, creating a consumer-oriented exhibit or report is a valuable skill in later life.

One way to think of these final learning products is in terms of exhibits. **Exhibits** *are presentations of student work that document learning.* Characteristics of effective exhibits include the following (Gagnon & Collay, 2001):

- Students produce the exhibit to document their accomplishment of a task.
- Students present their exhibit publicly and explain their thinking.
- Students respond to questions from their teacher or peers.
- Teachers help students understand the learning that has occurred.
- Teachers use the exhibit to determine what learning has taken place.
- Teachers align student explanations and thinking with requirements of state or national standards.

Exhibits provide a public forum where members of the learning community come together to discuss the learning that has taken place during the project-based assignment.

Assessment and Project-Based Learning

Assessment should be an integral part of project-based learning and occurs in three phases. Before project-based instruction occurs, teachers should ascertain, either formally through a written pre-assessment or informally through questions, what students know about the topic. Research suggests that a foundational knowledge base is essential for all forms of problem-based learning, including project-based learning (Gijbels et al., 2005). If the teacher finds that students know little about the topic being investigated, more teacher-centered, information-oriented lessons could be used to establish an information base. This assessment data can also provide valuable information for organizing groups as well as gathering resources.

Assessment can also provide valuable information during project-based lessons. Checklists and rating scales can provide students with valuable feedback about their learning as well as the progress of their project. A rubric such as the one in Figure 11.2 can help students assess their own planning progress as well as provide the teacher with a concrete format to use in conferences with students about their progress and accomplishments.

Figure 11.2

Rubric for Assessing Project-Based Learning

Project Goals	No Evidence		Partial Evidence		Clear Evidence
1. Topic clearly defined	1	2	3	4	5
2. Information-gathering procedures detailed	1	2	3	4	5
3. Data analysis procedures described	1	2	3	4	5
4. Final product planned	1	2	3	4	5

Assessment can also provide valuable information to students about their final project and how effective they were in presenting it to other students. Rubrics similar to the one in Figure 11.2 can be developed, shared with students, and used during presentations to provide feedback about strengths and weaknesses.

To help develop self-direction in their learning, students should be involved in the assessment process from the beginning (Stiggins, 2008). To do this, teachers should

- Inform students at the planning stage what is expected when their projects are completed.

- Use ongoing student conferences to discuss progress and provide feedback.

- Involve students in providing feedback to one another.

- Encourage student self-evaluations of their learning progress.

In assessing project-based learning teachers should focus not only on the products produced but also the growth and changes that are occurring in students.

Research on Project-Based Learning

Research on project-based learning is encouraging, suggesting that it is an effective vehicle to teach basic learning skills at the same time as content (Capon & Kuhn, 2004; Gijbels et al., 2005). Project-based learning also has motivational benefits (Brophy, 2004). In addition there is some evidence that this form of learning can help develop self-directed learning in students.

Project-based learning is an effective vehicle for teaching basic learning skills because these skills are an integral part of students' projects. In addition to developing reading and writing skills project-based learning can also teach a number of valuable learning strategies, including teaching students to

- Prioritize learning objectives
- Identify areas of knowledge deficit
- Search for information broadly
- Integrate information effectively
- Present ideas clearly (Blumberg, 1998)

Because students are actively immersed in these processes in the pursuit of their projects, they can see why they're useful and appreciate their value.

Motivation and Project-Based Instruction   Research also suggests that project-based learning is motivating (Gijbels et al., 2005). Motivational aspects of project-based work include

- Authentic problems that are challenging
- Choice in deciding what and how to do it
- Varied and novel tasks
- Collaboration with peers
- Closure in the form of a final product (Brophy, 2004; Good & Brophy, 2008)

In one study of high school English projects, students identified choice as a significant factor in their learning (Davis, 1998).

Choice is important because it provides opportunities for students to develop self-directed learning skills. Rather than sitting passively listening to a teacher presentation, students involved in projects are constantly asking themselves questions:

- Why am I doing this?
- What are my goals and objectives?
- What do I know and need to find out?
- How can I present my findings to an audience?

Teachers can facilitate the development of self-directed learning by providing feedback to students as they progress through their projects.

However, research on problem-based learning in medicine raises some cautionary flags (Albanese & Mitchell, 1993). Although medical students using problem-based learning became better thinkers and more adept at clinical problem solving, they also scored lower on basic science examinations and viewed themselves as less prepared in terms of basic science knowledge. Other research suggests that although problem-based learning is effective at teaching problem-solving skills, it may not be as effective from a time and energy perspective for teaching content (Dochy, Segers, Van den Bossche, & Gijbels, 2003; Gijbels, Dochy, Van den Bossche, & Segers, 2005).

The message from this research is clear and reinforces a major theme of this text. There is no *one* best way to teach. Each strategy or approach has both strengths and weaknesses. Teachers need to have a clear vision of the overall goals in their curriculum and use different approaches to teach strategically. If your goal is basic content acquisition, other strategies such as lecture discussion and direct instruction may be more appropriate. If, instead, teachers want to develop students' self-directed learning and thinking skills, problem-based learning may be valuable.

This concludes our discussion of project-based learning. In the next section we discuss problem solving, a second form of problem-based learning.

*P*roblem Solving

- You're a sixth-grade middle school teacher, and many of your students come to class without their books, pencils, and other materials.
- Graduation is looming in a year or two and you still haven't firmly decided on a major. Elementary or secondary education, and if secondary, which content area and if elementary, which grade level?

■ You're involved in a close personal relationship with someone, and you're wondering if that person is the one you should marry.

What do these examples have in common? Although different in their orientation, each is a problem. A **problem** *exists when you're in a state different from a desired state, and there's some uncertainty about reaching the desired state* (Bruning et al., 2004). To solve a problem we must figure out how to move from the state we're in to the desired state. **Problem-solving strategies** *use problems as the focus of lessons that develop content, skills, and self-regulation.* Let's see what problem solving looks like in the classroom.

Laura Hunter, a fifth-grade teacher at Bennion Elementary, is trying to teach her students about area by involving them in a problem-solving lesson. The students have been introduced to the concepts *perimeter* and *area* but are still struggling with them.

Laura begins by posing the following problem: "The principal is planning to re-carpet the classroom and needs to know how much carpeting to order." The complexity of the problem is increased by the fact that the room is irregularly shaped and that the linoleum part of the room, which lies along the perimeter of the room under the computers, will not be carpeted.

To help students in their problem solving Laura displays an overhead with the five-step problem-solving model shown in Figure 11.3. Breaking students into groups of four she has each group identify what the problem is. After reporting back to the whole class, each group then is responsible for measuring a different part of the room with rulers, yardsticks, and tape measures. Each group reports back to the group that is coordinating measurements and constructing a diagram of the whole room.

Laura then asks each group to select a strategy to find the carpeted area of the room. As the different groups work on this, two strategies emerge. One is to find the

Figure 11.3

Problem-Solving Model

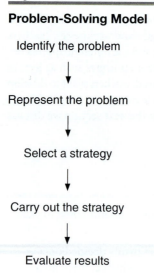

Identify the problem

↓

Represent the problem

↓

Select a strategy

↓

Carry out the strategy

↓

Evaluate results

total area of the room and subtract the linoleum or non-carpeted parts of the room. The other is to compute the area of a rectangle within the carpeted area and then add on additional, irregularly shaped carpeted sections. As students discuss their strategies, they use the diagram they generated and hand-held computers to find the area.

After selecting and implementing their strategies different groups report back to the whole class. The class discusses not only the different problem-solving strategies, but also interpersonal problems within the groups.

In evaluating their results, the students find that the answers generated by the groups differ, and they discuss why. Laura asks for suggestions about ways to make the answers more accurate, and students suggest starting with the same measurements and using the same strategies.

How is this an example of problem solving? The state Laura's students were in was not knowing how much carpet was needed for the room, and the desired state was determining that amount. Her instruction at one level was aimed at helping them figure out how to move to the desired state, that is, get the right answer. At another, more important, level, it was designed to help students become better problem solvers. In the examples at the beginning of this section the desired states are the students bringing their materials, deciding on a major, and finding a marriage partner. From these examples we see that problem solving is actually much broader than the way it is typically presented in schools.

Adopting a more general view of problem solving helps us see that problems and how to solve them are very real parts of our everyday lives. Our hope is that the problem-solving strategies that students learn in schools will transfer over into other dimensions of their lives. We examine these strategies later in this section when we discuss a general problem-solving model.

Well-Defined and Ill-Defined Problems

All too often students are given problems for which the solution method is quite clear (Bransford et al., 2000). This in unfortunate, as it robs students of the opportunity to wrestle with problems that are more like the ones we encounter in real life. Problem-solving experts commonly distinguish well-defined from ill-defined problems (Bruning et al., 2004). A **well-defined problem** *has only one correct solution and a prescribed method for finding it exists*, whereas an **ill-defined problem** *has more than one solution and no generally agreed-upon strategy for reaching it.* Getting our students to bring their materials, deciding upon a major, and finding a marriage partner are all ill-defined problems. For example, in terms of the last problem, we want to find someone who will make us happy in a marriage, but we're often not sure what that means, and even if we did know, how to find someone like that is uncertain.

The distinction between well-defined and ill-defined problems often depends on the learners themselves (Davidson & Sternberg, 2003). As an example, let's look again at Laura's lesson. Finding the amount of carpeting necessary appears to be well defined, and for someone knowledgeable in math, it is; simply determine the total area of the floor, and subtract the area covered by linoleum. Only one answer exists, and the solution is straightforward. For Laura's students, however, the problem was ill defined. Their understanding of the goal wasn't clear, some of them were uncertain about the difference between area and perimeter (as an interview after the lesson revealed), and they used a variety of strategies to reach the goal.

There are several advantages to using ill-defined problems in the classroom. The first is that they are more similar to problems learners encounter in the real world, so they provide practice in dealing with realistic, everyday problems. Because they are more open ended, they can also be more motivating, encouraging students to be more creative in their solutions.

A Problem-Solving Model

Over the past 50 years, experts have tried to develop approaches to problem solving that can be applied in a variety of situations. One result of these efforts is a five-step problem-solving model, which was illustrated in Figure 11.3 and is discussed next (Bransford & Stein, 1984).

Identifying the Problem   On the surface it appears that identifying the problem should be simple. However, particularly with ill-defined problems, and with novice problem solvers, identifying the problem is one of the most demanding aspects of problem solving (Alexander, 2006).

Let's look at a classroom example:

Question: There are 26 sheep and 10 goats on a ship. How old is the captain?

Amazingly, in one study, 75 percent of the second graders who were asked this question answered 36 (Prawat, 1989)! Obviously, they had difficulty understanding what the problem was asking.

Obstacles to effectively identifying problems include

- Lack of experience with the process

- Lack of domain-specific knowledge

- The tendency to rush toward a solution before the problem has been clearly defined

- The tendency to think convergently (Alexander, 2006; Bruning et al., 2004)

Let's see how these obstacles operate in a problem involving classroom teaching.

Jennifer Waites, a second-year teacher, is having classroom management problems. Her students are inattentive and disruptive, and in spite of clearly stated rules and an effort to enforce them consistently, the behaviors persist.

"I'm not sure what to do," Jennifer confides to her friend Linda, an eight-year veteran. "I know that I'm supposed to be consistent, and I'm trying. I told them that I mean business, and I've written several referrals during the past week, but it isn't helping that much. I guess I'll just have to get tougher, but I hate coming down on them all the time. I've thought and thought about it, and that's all I can come up with."

"I'm not sure," Linda responds, "but maybe you ought to try something a little different."

"I don't know what you mean."

"Maybe try working up a few really nifty activities, even if it takes some extra work. If the kids like them, maybe they'll behave better. . . . Whenever my kids are acting up, the first thing I ask myself is if I'm doing a good job of teaching. I mean, that isn't always the case, but it's often a factor in their behavior."

"Gee, I guess I never actually thought about approaching it that way. I admit that most of what I do is sort of lead discussions about what they've read or were supposed to read in the book."

A week later Jennifer reports that she has been working very hard, but that her students are behaving much better.

Jennifer encountered two related obstacles when she tried to solve her "management" problem. The first was lack of experience in thinking about teaching problems; the second was a lack of domain-specific knowledge about management and motivation. She also thought convergently, rushing to the conclusion that her students' lack of attention was due to something in the students rather than something that she was responsible for. Fortunately for Jennifer, her experienced friend Linda was able to help her redefine the problem in a more productive manner.

Even though she was working with a somewhat well-defined problem, Laura attempted to give her students practice in problem solving by beginning with the general problem of carpeting. She did this by asking students in small groups to think about the problem. Let's see how she did this.

After the students work together for several minutes, Laura has each of the groups report its results to the class.

"Fred, what did your team decide you were supposed to do?" Laura begins.

"Measure the area."

"Okay. Grant, can you give me some more details?"

"We decided we should measure the perimeter around and about 2 feet from the computers and the linoleum and measure all around."

"I'm writing 'remember the linoleum,' so you remember to go through that process," Laura notes, writing on the overhead.

"Okay, have we identified all the parts of the problem?...Paige, do you want to add anything?"

"Ahh . . . we could make a drawing of the outside of the room. Like on the graph paper like we did yesterday. Write the measurements on the side," Paige continues.

"Okay, outside measurements," Laura repeats as she writes down what Paige says.

"Okay, who else? . . . Jamison?"

"We decided we had to get the perimeter before we could get the area. Everything else is the same."

"Okay," Laura comments, "so now we know what the problem is."

After further discussion Laura's students concluded that this was an area problem, allowing them to connect it to what they had been studying previously. In the real world the process of identifying the problem can be the most important factor leading to a workable solution.

Representing the Problem   After the problem has been identified, the next step for students is to represent it in a meaningful way. This can be as simple as merely thinking about the problem, to as complex as using drawings, graphs, or tables to represent the problem. The limited amount of information we can hold in our working memory is one obstacle that all problem solvers face. Writing information down on paper helps reduce the amount we must remember as we focus on other aspects of the problem. Concrete examples and drawings are particularly helpful, because they help us rethink the problem and perhaps use analogies as a strategy.

Laura helped her students represent the problem when she encouraged students to measure the room and construct a diagram of it that they could use in their subsequent problem-solving efforts. This helped them focus on important aspects of the problem such as the size and shape of the linoleum, while ignoring other irrelevant aspects of the room, such as the windows and chairs.

Selecting a Strategy   Having identified and represented the problem, a strategy for solving needs to be selected (Alexander, 2006). In solving more well-defined problems, an **algorithm** or *a specified set of steps for solving problems* can be applied. When we solve algebraic equations, multiply whole numbers, or add fractions with unlike denominators, we are using algorithms. One algorithm that Laura's students used was "length times width equals area." However, her students had to modify this by adapting it to the irregularly shaped room they were working with.

Implementing the Strategy   Implementing the strategy is the fourth step in the process. Successful implementation depends on how clearly the problem has been defined and represented. If learners have trouble implementing a strategy, they need to go back to the earlier steps.

Evaluating the Results   Evaluating results, the final step in problem solving, is often challenging for learners (Alexander, 2006). We've all heard teachers complain that their students, particularly when solving math problems, all too often write down answers whether or not they make sense. For example,

> One boy, quite a good student, was working on the problem "If you have six jugs, and you want to put two thirds of a pint of lemonade into each jug, how much lemonade will you need?" His answer was 18 pints. I [Holt] said, "How much in each jug?" "Two thirds of a pint." I said, "Is that more or less than a pint?" "Less." I said, "How many jugs are there?" "Six." I said, "But that doesn't make any sense." He shrugged his shoulders and said, "Well, that's the way the system worked out." (Holt, 1964, p. 18)

Getting an answer, regardless of whether or not it makes sense, is typically students' goal. Young children, in particular, have trouble at this stage, wanting to rush through, find an answer, and get on to the next problem to finish the assignment.

When students learn to evaluate their results, their problem-solving abilities greatly improve. Teachers can help in this process, particularly in math, by having students estimate answers before they begin. Estimates require thought, and when answers and estimates are far apart, questions are raised. The habit of estimating is an important one that teachers should try to help students develop.

To view a video clip of a teacher using problem solving to teach about bar graphs, go to the Book Specific Resources tab in MyEducationLab, select your text, select Video Examples under Chapter 11, and then click on *Increasing Student Motivation: Personalizing Content.*

Helping Learners Become Better Problem Solvers

Within the framework of this general problem-solving model, what specifically can teachers do to help learners become better problem solvers? Concrete suggestions are included in Figure 11.4 and discussed in the sections that follow.

Figure 11.4

Helping Learners Become Better Problem Solvers

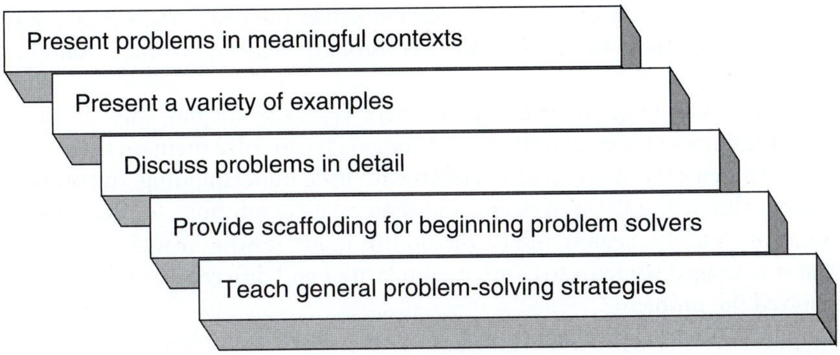

- Present problems in meaningful contexts
- Present a variety of examples
- Discuss problems in detail
- Provide scaffolding for beginning problem solvers
- Teach general problem-solving strategies

Present Problems in Meaningful Contexts   In looking at Laura's lesson again, we see she attempted to set the stage for area problems involving irregularly shaped figures by beginning with a carpeting problem involving her own classroom. Placing problems in concrete contexts such as this improves students' problem-solving ability by helping them see how problems relate to their own personal experience and background knowledge.

Present a Variety of Examples   We saw in other chapters how critical examples are for learning concepts and other abstractions, and it is true for problem solving as well. A major way of acquiring experience in problem solving is to solve a wide variety of examples embedded in meaningful contexts. To develop expertise, Laura's students need to solve a variety of additional area problems.

Discuss Problems in Detail   One of the most common weaknesses in problem solving, particularly in math and science, is that *students don't get enough practice in talking about the problems they are attempting to solve.* Wrestling with problem-related ideas and trying to put them into words are absolutely critical if students are to become better problem solvers (Applebee et al., 2003). We all have difficulty in expressing our thoughts and ideas; this ability, as with most others, improves with practice.

   In our earlier discussion of constructivism we saw that social interaction contributes to understanding. In the case of problem solving having students discuss problems in detail during problem-solving activities increases their understanding of the problem (Alexander, 2006). Laura utilized this research by having students work in groups as they progressed through each of the problem-solving steps. Giving students a chance to dialogue, being patient as they struggle to express themselves, and holding back the tendency to provide more support than necessary all contribute to students' developing understanding.

Provide Scaffolding for Beginning Problem Solvers   Scaffolding provides instructional support, and expert teachers provide only enough to help their students progress and keep their students on track (Puntambekar & Hübscher, 2005). With respect to problem solving, scaffolding is the support teachers provide as beginners attempt to solve specific problems.

Scaffolding is often misinterpreted, however, to suggest that teachers explain a solution while learners watch passively and then attempt it on their own, much as skills have been taught in the past. Effective scaffolding provides only enough support so that learners make progress *on their own.* A painter's scaffold supports the painter, but the painter does the painting; the teacher provides support, but the learner solves the problem. A major way that teachers help students learn to problem solve is through analyzing worked examples (Renkl & Atkinson, 2003).

In typical problem-solving instruction, teachers typically display one or more problems, model solutions to them, and then have students try to solve them on their own. Students tend to memorize the steps involved, often with little understanding. In contrast, analyzing problems, discussing them in detail, and then relating solutions to them makes the entire process much more meaningful. Laura did this in her lesson through interactive questioning that encouraged students to compare similarities and differences in the various ways students solved the problem.

Research supports teaching problem solving through worked examples; students using worked examples required less assistance from the teacher, developed more accurate solutions, and required less instructional time than students involved in traditional instruction (Renkl & Atkinson, 2003). They even outperformed students receiving individualized instruction. In addition using worked examples increases transfer and provides an understanding of the broader principles involved in the problem.

The combination of worked examples *with discussion*, as Laura did in her lesson, is optimal for learning. Worked examples provide representations; the discussion makes the representations and the solution meaningful for students (Atkinson et al., 2000).

Teach General Problem-Solving Strategies   When we teach students to problem solve, we not only want them to learn how to solve the specific problems we're focusing on, we also want them to become better problem solvers in general. Emphasis on broader problem-solving strategies can increase problem-solving abilities by helping students understand the logic and utility of the processes they are using.

Heuristics *are general, widely applicable problem-solving strategies* that students can use in a variety of situations (Bruning et al., 2004; Chronicle, MacGregor, & Ormerod, 2004). Some common heuristics are outlined in Table 11.2.

The heuristics in Table 11.2 are valuable in a variety of problem-solving situations. Since experience is one of the most important factors in acquiring problem-solving expertise, trial

Table 11.2 **Heuristics Used for Problem Solving**

Heuristic	Description
Trial and error	Often used with unfamiliar problems, it amounts to picking a solution and seeing how it works. It can be valuable for giving learners experience with new problems.
Means-ends analysis	Effective for ill-defined problems, it involves breaking the problem into subgoals and working successively on each.
Working backward	Effective in cases where parameters are known, such as what time a class or meeting starts and how far away you are.
Drawing analogies	An attempt to attack unfamiliar problems, it compares them to familiar ones that have already been solved (Mayer, 1992).

and error, although inefficient, is valuable for beginning problem solvers. Since ambiguous desired states are characteristic of ill-defined problems, means-ends analysis helps people determine what the problem actually is. Working backward can also be effective for well-defined problems that lack algorithms. If you know that you can spend $450 a month for rent, for example, working backward can help you make decisions about amenities and whether or not you'll need to look for a roommate. Finally, drawing analogies can be helpful for learners with experience in related problems. Teachers can teach these strategies through modeling and think-alouds, much as they do with other cognitive skills.

Teachers can help students think in terms of general strategies by teaching the strategy and reminding students of the steps in the process. Laura did this by displaying the problem-solving model in an overhead and referring to it continuously during her lesson. The goal in teaching general problem-solving strategies is to help students develop the inclination to clearly identify problems, check to see if the strategies they choose will solve it, try to represent it visually, and evaluate their results.

Teachers can also help students develop these inclinations through questioning. For example, as students attempt to solve problems, the teacher can ask the following questions to help students develop an awareness of the process:

What exactly are you doing?
  (Can you describe it precisely?)
Why are you doing it?
  (How does it fit into the solution?)
How does it help you?
  (What will you do with the outcome when you obtain it?)

To view a video clip of a teacher using problem solving in an elementary classroom, go to the Book Specific Resources tab in MyEducationLab, select your text, select Video Examples under Chapter 11, and then click on *Problem-Based Learning: Finding Area in Elementary Math.*

This completes our discussion of problem solving. In the next section we extend our discussion of problem-based learning as we discuss inquiry-based instruction.

Inquiry Strategies

Inquiry strategies, *another form of problem-based instruction, actively involve students in learning activities designed to answer questions about how the world operates* (Victor & Kellough, 2004). The term *inquiry* may not seem to relate to our everyday lives, but it does. It is, in fact, very much a part of our lives. The questions of how much high-cholesterol food is too much and how much exercise is required to provide aerobic benefit are inquiry problems. The conclusion that second-hand smoke is potentially harmful is the result of an

Technology and Teaching

Using Technology as a Tool to Teach Problem Solving

One of the dilemmas teachers encounter when we try to teach our students how to problem solve is the difficulty of constructing realistic, complex problems for students to wrestle with. All too often when students encounter word problems in math, for example, the goal is clear, only those numbers needed to solve are included, and even the type of computation needed to solve the problem is suggested by the problem's placement in a particular chapter (Cognition & Technology Group at Vanderbilt, 1997). Unfortunately, these aren't the kind of problems most people encounter in their everyday lives. Real-life problems are messier, more complicated, with a number of viable routes providing alternate solutions. Technology provides one way to teach students how to solve these kinds of complex, realistic problems. For example,

> Jasper has just purchased a new boat and is planning to drive it home. The boat consumes 5 gallons of fuel per hour and travels at 8 mph. The gas tank holds 12 gallons of gas. The boat is currently located at mile marker 156. Jasper's home dock is at mile marker 132. There are two gas stations on the way home. One is at mile marker 140.3 and the other is at mile marker 133. They charge $1.10 and $1.25 per gallon, respectively. They don't take credit cards. Jasper started the day with $20. He bought 5 gallons of gas at $1.25 per gallon (not including a discount of 4 cents per gallon for paying cash) and paid $8.25 for repairs to his boat. It's 2:35. Sundown is at 7:52. Can Jasper make it home before sunset without running out of fuel? (Williams, Bareiss, & Reiser, 1996, p. 2)

This problem is part of a videodisc-based series called *The Adventures of Jasper Woodbury* designed to promote problem solving, reasoning, and effective communication. Each segment begins with a 15- or 20-minute adventure or story. The fuel problem described is actually a condensed version; the actual problem contains much more detail, including both relevant and irrelevant data that students must sift through. At the end of each story the character or characters are faced with a challenge or issue that serves as the problem.

The problem is purposefully left open ended to provide opportunities for students to define, represent, and solve complex, real-life problems. Each problem in the series has a number of viable solutions, each with both pros and cons. Students are encouraged to work in groups discussing and comparing their individual problem-solving strategies with other students. Each problem is designed to be solved in three or four days or more. The fact that the video is contained in a hypermedia computer program allows students to return to problem segments to extract data or reaffirm facts.

The creators of the Jasper series call this problem-based approach to instruction **anchored instruction**, *a form of teaching in which problems are embedded in real world contexts.* The *anchor* is the rich, interesting problem situation that provides a focus or reason for setting goals, planning, and using mathematical tools to solve problems. The goal of anchored instruction is to develop knowledge that is useful and flexible and that can be used to solve other problems.

Research on the series has been positive. Middle school students using the Jasper series did as well as controls on basic math concepts but performed better on math verbal problems, were better at planning for problem solving and generating subgoals, and had more positive attitudes toward math (Cognition & Technology Group at Vanderbilt, 1992). One teacher commented:

> The kids would go home so excited and [the parents would say] "I've got to find out about this Jasper. It is all my kid talks about."

and

> "If you have any way of getting to my kids in high school, you'll find that they remember those four Jasper episodes. They may not remember anything else we did that year but they'll remember . . . those episodes because it did hit them and make an impact on them this year." (Cognition & Technology Group at Vanderbilt, 1992, p. 307)

More recent development efforts in this series attempt to make the problem-solving process more open ended by involving students in design problems. For example, in one problem called *Blueprint for Success* students apply geometry concepts in the design of a playground (Williams et al., 1996). Within the physical and financial parameters established by the video, students measure lines and angles, do proportional reasoning, and create and read scale drawings.

inquiry investigation, and the now common ban on smoking in public places is an outcome of this result.

Many other examples exist. Congressional investigations; probes into alleged wrongdoing; and attempts to explain catastrophes, such as bridge failures and airline crashes, are all inquiry problems. The research studies cited throughout this text are all based on inquiry problems, which have attempted to answer questions such as "Why do students in one kind of classroom learn more than those in another?"

Inquiry also occurs on a more personal level. An owner checking her auto's gas mileage when she uses 85 octane gasoline compared to burning 91 octane is conducting an inquiry investigation.

Involving students in inquiry is an effective way to teach content, increase motivation, and help students develop their analytical thinking skills. Let's see how this can happen in the classroom.

Carlos Sanchez, a high school health teacher, is involved in a unit on drugs and drug use with his health students. In the process they've discussed how drugs influence the nervous system, the dangers of addictive drugs, and the possible overuse of prescription drugs and have turned to over-the-counter medications.

"My dad takes two aspirin every night before he goes to bed," Jacinta offers during the discussion. "Do you think that's bad for him?"

"What kind of aspirin?" Jamie wondered out loud.

". . . I dunno, . . . I guess, . . . Bayer. . . . Actually, yes, he makes jokes that Bayer is the best."

"Mr. Sanchez, is Bayer really the best?" asked Jacinta.

"That's an interesting idea," Carlos interjects. "Do we know if Bayer really is better? . . . Of course, the advertisers would have us believe that it's the only one that's any good, and way more Bayer is sold than any other brand."

"My mom takes the cheapest stuff she can find," Luanne shrugs. "We went to the drug store to get a prescription, and the guy, . . . the prescription guy, said they're all alike."

"Really interesting!" Carlos smiles. "Let's see what we can find out about aspirin. . . . Let's think about it for a few minutes. How could we get a handle on whether Bayer really is better than another one, like maybe Norwich? . . . Go ahead and turn to the person next to you, take three minutes, and see if you can come up with some ways of answering that question. We'll brainstorm for a few minutes, and we'll go from there."

After students talk among themselves for the brief period, Carlos calls them together, and they begin to share their ideas.

"Go ahead, someone," Carlos encourages.

". . . We thought we could check the stuff in them, . . . you know, look at the bottle to see if they have the same stuff in them, . . . if one has more stuff, maybe it's better," Nina offers.

"Good idea," Carlos nods smiling. "Who else? . . . Go ahead, Tamara."

". . . We could also check to see which one dissolved faster, . . . cause they talk about how fast they're supposed to work, . . . like if one dissolved faster than another one, maybe it works faster, . . . so . . . maybe it's better."

"Also very good thinking," Carlos smiles, pleased with the responses.

"We could see which one made the pain go away faster," Jack adds.

"That's also a good thought, Jack," Carlos responds. "We'll have to keep that one in mind to see how we might get at that information."

". . . Maybe we could ask some people, . . . You know like Luanne said her drug person, . . . the pharmacist said they're all alike. Maybe we should ask a bunch of people and see what they say."

"That's excellent," Carlos shakes his head and smiles. "That's really excellent thinking. . . . These are all good hypotheses—or best guesses about how to answer our questions. Let's go to work on them."

They decide, with some guidance from Carlos, that they won't try to answer the question about which made the pain go away faster until they have gathered some information about the other questions.

With some additional guidance, the students organize themselves into teams, and the teams set out to gather information. They agree that they will bring in at least three different brands of aspirin and check the ingredients, conduct experiments to see which brand dissolves faster, and interview their parents and pharmacists to gather their opinions.

Since this is Wednesday, the students agreed that they will have their interviews completed by the following Monday. They'll gather their samples of aspirin by Friday and collect the rest of their data then.

Let's stop here and consider what Carlos did with his class. First, we see that his learning activity was a form of problem solving. The students were in a state (not knowing which aspirin was better) different from a desired state (knowing), and they had to devise a solution to move from the present to the desired state. We also see that they were dealing with an ill-defined problem, since the notion of "better" is somewhat ambiguous.

The learning activity differed from typical problem solving, however, in that the solution to the problem involved gathering information, which would be used to answer a specific question. The specificity of the question and the extent to which data gathering procedures are closely linked to the question distinguish inquiry from looser, more unstructured project-based learning. This attempt to answer a question through specific data gathering procedures is the essence of an inquiry investigation. **Inquiry** *is a process that gathers facts and observations and uses them to answer specific questions.* Inquiry is particularly valuable for giving students practice in defining informational questions, gathering data to solve those questions, and developing their abilities to analyze and evaluate data.

Figure 11.5

Steps in the Inquiry Process

Identifying a question

Forming hypotheses

Gathering data

Assessing hypotheses

Generalizing

Analyzing the inquiry process

The basic steps in the inquiry process are outlined in Figure 11.5 and discussed in the sections that follow.

To view a video clip of a teacher using inquiry in a middle school classroom, go to the Book Specific Resources tab in MyEducationLab, select your text, select Video Examples under Chapter 11, and then click on *Problem-Based Learning: Designing Experiments.*

Identifying a Question

The inquiry process begins when students ask or identify a question. The question for Carlos's students was determining which kind of aspirin is the best, or determining if Bayer is really better than other brands.

In many cases involving inquiry problems, an **operational definition**, which is *a description of the term used for the purpose of the investigation*, is required. Carlos's students, for example, were operationally defining "better" as "dissolves faster," "has more effective ingredients," and "endorsed by more people."

Operational definitions are also very much a part of our lives. For example, 0.08 percent blood alcohol level has been operationally defined in many states as the safe driving maximum. Borderline high blood pressure is operationally defined as 140 (systolic) over 90 (diastolic). Technically, death is operationally defined as absence of brain wave activity. If it were absolute, or cut and dried, controversies about the removal of life support systems wouldn't exist. One of the benefits of inquiry activities is providing students with experience in wrestling with operational definitions and how they work in our everyday lives.

Table 11.3 Inquiry Problems in Different Content Areas	
Content Area	**Possible Question**
English/language arts	What factors influence the content of authors' works?
Science	How is plant growth affected by sunlight, water, or type of soil?
Social studies	What are the primary causes of wars and conflicts?
Building technology	What type of building material is best for different structures?
Health	What combination of exercises is most effective for developing cardiovascular fitness?

For the teacher, the first step in planning for inquiry activities involves framing the content you would normally teach in ways that allow students to gather and analyze data. Some examples of possible inquiry questions are offered in Table 11.3.

Forming Hypotheses

Once a question has been posed and analyzed, the class is ready to try to answer or address it. In framing the question in ways that information can be gathered to answer it, students are involved in the process of hypothesizing. A **hypothesis** *is a tentative solution to a problem that can be confirmed with facts or observations*. Although Carlos's students didn't formally state hypotheses, they offered implicit ones to their question with comments such as ". . . We thought we could check the stuff in them, . . . you know, look at the bottle to see if they have the same stuff in them, . . . if one has more stuff, maybe it's better," and ". . . like if one dissolved faster than another one, maybe it works faster, . . . so . . . maybe it's better." They were tacitly hypothesizing that aspirin with more ingredients is better, as is aspirin that dissolves faster. Carlos moved the process forward by introducing the term *hypothesis* and defining it as a "best guess about how to answer our questions."

Gathering Data

Gathering data follows directly from the hypotheses generated. Although seemingly straightforward, it requires guidance and direction from the teacher. To see how this works, let's return to Carlos's class and focus on one of the groups.

The students bring their aspirin samples to class on Friday and begin their work in groups. First, they write down the ingredients for each brand, and then they try to measure how fast the samples dissolve.

"How are we going to do this?" Andrea wonders out loud to David and Lenita.

". . . How about we drop them at the same time into the water, and watch them?" David suggests.

". . . Good idea," Lenita confirms.

The students then pour some water from the tap into two plastic drink cups and drop a Bayer in one and a Norwich in the second one.

"Sheesh, its hard to tell when it's dissolved," David notes after a few minutes.

Carlos, who has been watching the students' progress, stops by the group and says, "Let's think about this for a minute. Look in the cups. What do you notice there?"

". . . The . . . aspirins are . . . dissolved," Lenita says tentatively.

"Okay, and what else?"

"It was hard to tell," Andrea adds.

"All right. . . . Anything else?"

" . . ."

"Look at the amount of water."

"Ahh," Lenita nods with realization. "They're different."

"Dumb," David shrugs.

"Not at all," Carlos counters. "This is why we're doing this activity. See what you're learning from it? What do you notice about the aspirin in these two glasses, Lenita?"

"It looks like the aspirin in the glass with more water dissolved faster."

"Good, so what are two possible explanations for what happened? Andrea, give me one."

"This kind of aspirin (pointing to the one glass) dissolves faster."

"What's another one, David?"

"Hmm, . . . or more water makes aspirin dissolve faster?"

"Now, what might you do?"

"Do it again and keep the amount of water the same," Andrea replies after some thought.

"Good," Carlos encourages. "And, as long as we're at it, . . . what might you do about the fact that it's hard to tell when the aspirins are dissolved?" With some additional prompting, the students conclude that they will conduct several trials and can average the times to get the most accurate reading possible.

Carlos continues to move from group to group, and finally as the period nears a close, he directs, "Turn in all your results to me on Monday *just before school*, and I'll have them on the board when our class begins . . . . Don't forget, *just before school on Monday.*"

From this episode, we see that teacher monitoring and appropriate intervention are important in inquiry activities. Carlos watched students as they worked, and he waited to intervene until they had considered the process and conducted a trial on their own. Had he intervened sooner, the opportunity and responsibility of doing their own thinking would have been taken away from them. In doing this he demonstrated the essence of effective scaffolding.

As students acquire experience—with the teacher providing appropriate support—much can be learned about gathering accurate information. One group, for example, learned about controlling variables, conducting several trials to increase reliability, and averaging to summarize the information. Perhaps even more important than the actual results of the investigation, Carlos's students learned a great deal about the methods scientists use to gather and verify information. Experts believe that experiencing these logical challenges are among the most important goals in classrooms (Perkins, 2001).

Assessing Hypotheses

When students assess hypotheses, they compare their results to the hypotheses they formed earlier. To examine this phase of inquiry, let's return to Carlos's work with his students as he begins his class on Monday.

After completing his routines, Carlos moves to the front of the room and says, "Now, everyone, we've had a lot of fun with this activity, but now we're at what is really the most important part of the whole process. . . . Just getting the information is one thing, but figuring out what it means is another. We're going to really learn a lot here today, so I want you to all be alert and think carefully about what we're doing."

He then turns to the board where the ingredients for each brand were written, tables of dissolving times are displayed, and people's opinions are tallied.

"Let's see what we think all this means," Carlos directs. "What do you notice about the results?"

"... The ingredients are the same," Joanne observes.

"Not quite," Jeff counters. "Well, I guess they're almost the same."

"For the most part," Joanne confirms.

"What do the rest of you think?" Carlos queries. Students discuss the ingredients for a few more minutes, conclude that essential ingredients are virtually the same, and decide that they can't conclude that one was better than another on the basis of the ingredients.

They then turn to the dissolving rates.

"Norwich dissolves faster than Bayer," Leroy offers.

"Not always," Kevin interjects.

"Its average is lower."

"True."

Again the class discusses the results. In the process, Dana wonders, "Because it dissolves faster, does that make it better?"

"Good point," Carlos smiles.

"... Yeh, but they advertise that it helps you fast. It has to dissolve to do that ... doesn't it? ... Sure it does. ... a whole aspirin can't go into your blood stream," Monica offers.

To chuckles from the class, Carlos wonders, "What do you think of Monica's argument?"

After a couple more minutes of discussion, Brad concludes with finality, "... It doesn't make sense to me, that dissolving slower ... is better, since they tell us that ... fast is good."

The class then turns to the opinion poll they gathered, discussing the results in much the same way as they did with the ingredients and dissolving times, and in the process they tentatively conclude that all aspirin are essentially the same.

"Now, we've tentatively concluded that all aspirin seem to be about the same," Carlos says, changing the direction of the discussion. "What does that suggest to us about other products, or does it suggest anything to us? What about McDonald's, Wendy's, and Burger King? Are they all the same? How about toothpaste, ... different brands of orange juice, milk, ... or even cars? Are there any conclusions that we can draw?"

The students offer a number of comments and, with Carlos's guidance, conclude that before they can make any sweeping conclusions they have to know some things, such as, are all the ingredients the same in different brands of toothpaste, for example, and are different cars equipped similarly. They also agree to consider the opinion of "experts," such as *Consumers' Report.*

"Before our time is all gone, I'd like us to think a little about what we did and why. How did we get started on this problem? Who remembers? Antonio?"

"Jacinta asked if Bayer was really the best."

"Good memory, Antonio. That's correct. Our inquiry started with a question. Then we had some tentative ideas or guesses. Who remembers what we call these tentative ideas? Shanda?"

"Hypotheses?"

"Fine, Shanda. Hypotheses are our best guesses about how the world works. And why was it important to use the same amount of water when we were trying to discover which kind of aspirin dissolved the quickest?"

Just then the bell rings and Carlos dismisses his class with a smile and, "Let's stop here and continue this discussion tomorrow. Good work, class. See you tomorrow."

The process of assessing hypotheses is arguably the most valuable part of inquiry lessons and, as we saw in our earlier discussion of problem solving, social interaction and discussion are critical at this point. From their discussion Carlos's students experienced several important aspects of the process, including

- Using evidence, versus opinions, feelings, beliefs, or intuition, as a basis for forming conclusions.

- Examining issues of reliability. For example, to what extent were the methods they used to measure dissolving rates reliable?

- Considering the appropriateness of people's opinions—and particularly the opinions of experts—in making conclusions about hypotheses.

- Developing tolerance for problems, questions, and issues that are somewhat ambiguous.

These are important "life skills," and arguably, they may contribute more to learners' educations than the content they learn.

Generalizing

That next step in an inquiry activity involves considering the generalizability of the results. Carlos initiated this discussion when he asked, "What does that suggest to us about other products, or does it suggest anything to us? What about McDonald's, Wendy's, and Burger King? Are they all the same? . . . Are there any conclusions that we can draw?"

In addition to assessing the results themselves, analyzing conclusions to see if they can generalize to other situations is an important higher-order thinking skill. Critical thinking, which we'll consider in the next section, is one of the most important outcomes of inquiry activities.

Analyzing the Inquiry Process

In the final stage of inquiry, the teacher asks students to analyze and reflect upon the inquiry process. Carlos Sanchez initiated this stage when he said, "Before our time is all gone, I'd like us to think a little about what we did and why." In response to this request, students identified how inquiry began and how hypotheses guided the inquiry process. By talking about inquiry processes in the context of lessons, teachers make abstract ideas become real and help students see how inquiry plays out in real life (Sandoval & Millwood, 2005).

 ## Critical Thinking

A common thread running through all of the problem-based teaching strategies in this chapter is that they provide opportunities to develop students' critical thinking abilities. To succeed in each of these learning activities students need to critically analyze information and ideas to solve problems or answer questions.

But what does *critical thinking* mean, and why is it important? Although definitions vary, **critical thinking** can be described as *the ability to make and assess conclusions based on evidence* (Bruning et al., 2004; Perkins, 2001). Three factors have contributed to interest in critical thinking:

- **Learners' lack of deep understanding of the topics they study.** Many students are unable to give evidence of a more than superficial understanding of concepts and are unable to apply the knowledge they have acquired to real-world problems. This lack of deep understanding of the ideas students are learning is tied to superficial teaching methods that fail to engage students in thinking deeply and critically about the topics they're studying.

- **Increased need for thinking in our modern world.** In the ever-expanding technological and information-oriented world, future jobs will require sophisticated learning skills, and the ability to adapt to rapid change (Jonassen, 2000). Critical thinking skills will be required of the workforce as a whole rather than of a select few.

- **Concerns of business leaders.** Many members of the business world believe that the graduates of our schools cannot use critical thinking skills to speak and write effectively, use math, or learn on the job.

But, what are the components of critical thinking and how can teachers teach this important dimension of learning? Let's turn now to the components associated with critical thinking, which are illustrated in Figure 11.6 and discussed in the sections that follow.

Figure 11.6

Components of Critical Thinking

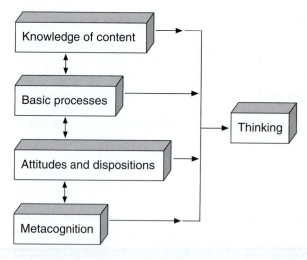

Knowledge of Content

Background knowledge is an essential component of critical thinking (Bruning et al., 2004). To think, we must think about something; that something is the content—often described as domain-specific knowledge—we're studying. The importance of domain-specific knowledge to thinking is essential. To think critically in any domain one must know something about it and, generally, the more one knows the better. This suggests that teachers should plan for students to acquire background knowledge as they teach critical thinking skills.

Basic Processes

Basic processes *are the tools or building blocks of thinking* (Eggen & Kauchak, 2010). Although experts disagree on specific details, most include the processes in Table 11.4.

The students in the case studies in this chapter used these processes continually. For instance, during his lesson Carlos Sanchez said, "How could we get a handle on whether Bayer really is better than another one?" Later, he had his students compare the different aspirins and look for patterns. Then he asked them to think further when he asked, ". . . so what are two possible explanations for what happened?"

Similar examples can be found in many of the lessons you've studied in this text. For example, in Chapter 5 Kathy Johnson had her students compare and contrast the Northern and Southern colonies and suggest cause-and-effect relationships between the geography and economies of the two regions. In Chapter 6 José Alvarez had his students observe, compare, generalize, and develop cause-and-effect relationships as they studied heat, expansion, and the motion of molecules. The basic processes of critical thinking are essential components of effective instruction in all areas.

Table 11.4 **Basic Processes in Thinking**

Action	Processes
Observing	Recalling Recognizing
Finding patterns and generalizing	Comparing and contrasting Classifying Identifying relevant and irrelevant information
Forming conclusions based on patterns	Inferring Predicting Hypothesizing Identifying causes and effects
Assessing conclusions based on evidence	Supporting conclusions with facts or observations Checking consistency Identifying bias, stereotypes, clichés, and propaganda Identifying unstated assumptions Recognizing overgeneralizations and undergeneralizations Confirming conclusions with facts

Metacognition: Awareness and Control of Cognitive Processes

Metacognition *refers to learners' understanding and control of their cognitive processes.* In the case of critical thinking this means that students are aware of the basic processes they're using and are exercising control over them (Schunk, 2004). As an example, let's look at the end of Carlos's inquiry lesson. He made a conscious attempt to encourage students to think about the process of inquiry. Laura Hunter did the same in her problem-solving lesson. As awareness of these processes increases, the disposition to use them increases as well. This leads to the development of self-directed learning, an important goal of problem-based instruction.

Attitudes and Dispositions

Research on the teaching of thinking places increasing emphasis on the part that attitudes and dispositions play in the process (Bruning et al., 2004). The disposition to look for evidence before "jumping to conclusions" is one example. Others include respecting other students' opinions, whether or not we agree with them and maintaining a desire to learn and a tendency to reflect before acting. Each of these attitudes influences students' inclinations to use thinking strategies.

Ultimately, our goal in teaching critical thinking is for learners to develop these dispositions. We want students to be skeptical, for example, about rumors and gossip; in learning activities we want them to ask themselves, "What is this a part of?" "What does this relate to?" and "How do we know?" If learners can acquire these dispositions, they will have taken a giant step toward self-regulated learning.

Teaching Critical Thinking in the Classroom

Critical thinking skills are most effectively taught when

- They are embedded in content that students are learning. This not only gives students something to think about, but also demonstrates how thinking skills are useful in learning.

- Teachers explicitly teach and model them. This provides students with a concrete example to follow.

- The utility and value of them are discussed. This helps students understand when and why they should use them in the future.

- Students are given multiple opportunities to practice them in a number of situations. (Bruning et al., 2004; Perkins, 2001)

We saw examples of these guidelines in Carlos Sanchez's inquiry instruction. He embedded critical thinking skills into his lesson, taught about them during his lesson, explained why they were important, and provided multiple opportunities for students to practice them. In a similar way these guidelines could be found in the other problem-based lessons. This opportunity to teach critical thinking along with content is one reason that problem-based learning strategies are so valuable in the classroom.

Exploring Diversity

Problem-Based Instruction with Developmentally Different Learners

Although problem-based learning works with learners of all ages, a number of developmental differences exist. The following sections outline some suggestions for responding to these differences.

Working with Elementary Students

Young children tend to *center* on the most perceptually obvious aspects of objects and events, and they tend to be quite literal in their thinking, which can lead to false starts and misconceptions. For instance, they tend to equate size with age, meaning someone who is bigger is always older, and, in social studies they may think that lines of latitude and longitude actually exist on the earth.

As a result, explanations presented in the abstract are almost useless. When working with young children, high-quality examples to illustrate problems are even more important than with older learners. In addition, interactive classroom instruction during problem solving allows teachers to both investigate the ideas students currently hold and assist them as they problem solve.

Working with Middle School Students

Middle school students overcome much of the tendency to interpret events literally but often, in the process of problem solving, they fail to recognize relationships among objects and events. For instance, instead of recognizing that rectangles and squares are subsets of parallelograms, they see the figures as belonging to different categories, which leads to problems in their investigative efforts.

To accommodate these tendencies cognitive apprenticeships that include opportunities to think and talk about new ideas are effective, not only during the problem solving itself, but also during the debriefing. For instance, teachers should carefully scaffold students' efforts during group work, and students' *verbalization* of their understanding during small-group work is essential for maximizing learning.

Middle school students are also developing interaction skills, such as perspective taking and social problem solving. This allows teachers to use cooperative learning and other small-group strategies to integrate social interaction into their instruction. Experts caution, however, that teachers should carefully structure and monitor these activities so that learning is maximized (Blatchford et al., 2006; Ding, Li, Piccolo, & Kulm, 2007).

Working with High School Students

High school students' experiences can provide them with a rich store of prior knowledge that increases their ability to solve problems. However, misconceptions in their background knowledge, particularly when working with symbols and abstract ideas, can cause difficulties during problem solving. For instance, in simplifying the expression $2 + 5 \times 3 - 6$, they often get 15 ($2 + 5 = 7$; $7 \times 3 = 21$; $21 - 6 = 15$) instead of the correct answer: 11 ($5 \times 3 = 15$; $15 + 2 = 17$; $17 - 6 = 11$).

As students move to more advanced classes in high school, such as physics, chemistry, and calculus, high levels of active involvement and social interaction become even more important. And, it is in these classes that teachers tend to become more like college instructors, for whom lecture is the most common instructional strategy.

High school students are also able to participate in and benefit from classroom discussions, which provide opportunities to compare and develop their thinking based on the ideas of others (Hadjioannou, 2007). As with all forms of instruction, teachers need to structure and monitor discussions closely to ensure that they are aligned with learning goals.

Summary

Problem-Based Learning: An Overview

Problem-based learning is a family of teaching strategies that use a problem or question as a focal point for student learning. They are designed to help students become self-directed learners as well as teach critical thinking skills and content. They are based on the philosophical foundations of John Dewey, as well as the psychological underpinnings of constructivism.

Project-Based Learning

Project-based learning is an open-ended form of problem-based learning that allows students to investigate a question that is meaningful to them. Following the introduction of a question or problem, students work in groups to gather information to address the issue. The product of their efforts is some type of exhibit that serves as the focal point for a class discussion of the issues raised and content learned.

Problem Solving

Problems involve situations in which an individual attempts to move from one state of knowledge to another. Well-defined problems have clear goals and paths for reaching them, whereas ill-defined problems have vague goals without clear paths for solving them.

Teachers help learners become better problem solvers by presenting problems in meaningful contexts, discussing problems in detail, providing learners with practice defining problems, and scaffolding beginning problem solvers. Analyzing worked examples is one effective form of scaffolding.

Inquiry Strategies

Inquiry strategies give learners practice in defining problems, hypothesizing solutions, gathering data, and assessing hypotheses based on the data. Teachers can help students develop inquiry skills through multiple opportunities to practice them and by discussing the process afterward.

Critical Thinking

Critical thinking involves thorough background knowledge, the application of basic processes, and awareness of the processes being used. Perhaps most important critical thinking involves the development of attitudes and dispositions, such as remaining open minded, basing conclusions on evidence, and maintaining a healthy skepticism.

Important Concepts

Algorithm (p. 352)

Anchored instruction (p. 356)

Basic processes (p. 365)

Critical thinking (p. 364)

Exhibit (p. 345)

Heuristics (p. 354)

Hypothesis (p. 360)

Ill-defined problem (p. 349)

Inquiry (p. 358)

Inquiry strategies (p. 355)

Metacognition (p. 366)

Operational definition (p. 359)

Problem (p. 348)

Problem-based instruction (p. 338)

Problem solving strategies (p. 348)

Project-based learning (p. 341)

Self-directed learning (p. 339)

Well-defined problem (p. 349)

Preparing for Your Licensure Exam

As you've studied this chapter, you've seen how teachers can design and implement instruction to increase learners' problem-solving abilities and promote their higher-order and critical thinking skills. Read the following case study and consider how effectively the teacher implemented the ideas discussed in this chapter.

myeducationlab
PEARSON
The Power of Classroom Practice
www.myeducationlab.com

After reading this case, go to the Book Specific Resources tab in MyEducationLab, select your text, select *Preparing for Your Licensure Exam* under Chapter 11 to complete the questions that accompany the case and receive feedback on your responses.

Patty Kramer, a second-year sixth-grade math teacher, was reading her notes as she planned for the following week's instruction. She keeps a journal in which she writes comments about units and lessons and refers to them when she plans to teach the topics the next time.

She reacts with a nod when she reads, "Can't find areas—don't know how to begin," in a note referring to a section on finding the area of irregularly shaped plane figures. She smiles when she remembers how frustrated she had been when she taught this section the previous year.

Reflecting on her experience, Patty decides, "I'm going to make it real for them this year. We're going to solve some real problems instead of that stuff in the book, something that they can relate to."

After considering a series of possibilities, she thinks, "Why not use the school grounds? They have an irregular shape."

The more she thought about the idea the better she liked it. Finally, she decides, "I'll give it a try. It can't be any worse than last year. All we need to do is measure the grounds and take it from there. I bet they'll like it."

After completing her beginning-of-class routines on Monday, she begins by saying, "I just read an article that says that the cost of educating people like all of you is skyrocketing. What are some of the things that contribute to that cost do you think?"

After thinking a few seconds, Jerome offers, "We have a nice school. I suppose schools are one thing."

"No question about it," Patty nods. "The school itself, and the land it sits on all cost a lot of money."

"How much?" Eddy wonders.

"The school cost about $5 million, but I don't know about the land. That's a really good question. How might we find it out?"

In the course of discussing the question Segundo, whose father is a surveyor, offers, "Don't we have to know how much land we have before we can do anything else? Then, once we know how many acres we have, all we have to find out is how much an acre is worth, and we can figure it out."

The class agrees that Segundo's plan is a good one, and students begin discussing ways to find out how many acres make up the campus.

"What's an acre?" Pamela wonders out loud.

"Good question," Patty smiles. She then draws the following rectangles on the board.

Football field	48,000 sq.ft.

Acre	43,560 sq. ft.

"As it turns out," Patty explains, "an acre is 43,560 square ft.—a little smaller than a football field, which is 48,000 square ft. This measure developed historically in England and we then adopted it here. It's what we use to describe the size of farms and ranches. Now, I drew a rectangle on the board, but obviously, any shape that has this area is an acre."

During their continuing discussion of the problem students decide that they need to measure the school grounds and to do that they could "pace" off the lengths.

In response to the objection that pacing the lengths would be inaccurate, the class—with Patty's guidance—suggests that they get several measurements and average them to get a more accurate figure.

Patty then breaks the class into teams of three. She tells them that the first thing they would do the next day would be to measure the grounds and that they would continue after they had gotten their measurements.

The students take most of Tuesday's class period to gather their measurements. Some teams decide to pace the grounds twice to check on their own consistency.

As the groups return to the room and report their dimensions, Patty reviews with students the process for averaging. Once the averages for the dimensions are computed the information appears on the white board as follows:

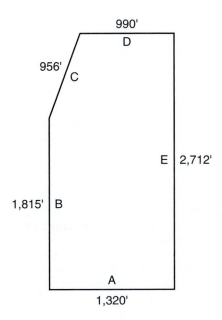

Patty labels each of the legs with a letter for easy reference, and she then begins, "Now, what do we need to do? . . . Kara?"

". . . Find the area, I guess."

"Yes, good. That's what we decided. Now, keep that in mind. We'll begin there tomorrow."

On Wednesday Patty reviews what they had covered and then continues, "Now, how are we going to find the area?"

"The shape is funny," Eddie comments.

"Yes it is," Patty smiles. "Is there anything that we can do about that?"

After some discussion, and again with Patty's guidance, the class decides to draw lines through the figure, so they would have familiar figures to deal with. The figure then appeared as follows:

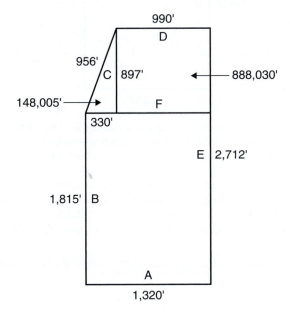

"So, what do we have now?" Patty asks. "Tony?"

". . . A triangle and two rectangles."

"Sure. So how can we find the area, then? . . . Jo?"

". . . Find the area of each and add them up?"

"Great. Let's do it! . . . What do we need to do first?"

"We need to know how to find the area of a rectangle and a triangle," Sandra volunteers

Patty then reviews the formulas for finding the areas of each, and she continues, "Now, what are the dimensions of the triangle? . . . Salvado?"

". . . It's 956 ft."

"That isn't what we need, is it?" Kathy wonders. "We need the other two sides, don't we?"

"How do we know that?" Patty asks.

The class wasn't sure, so Patty demonstrates finding the area of a triangle by comparing it to a rectangle, so the students could see they need the height of the triangle instead of the length of the sides.

The students then conclude that they could get the dimensions of the base and height by subtracting 990 from 1,320, and 1,815 from 2,712, respectively.

They then calculate the areas of the triangle and the two rectangles. Their results appear as follows:

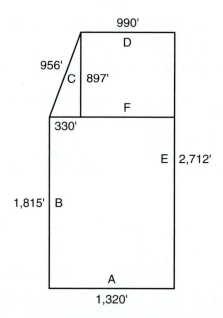

They find the total area by adding the areas of the three figures, and after a short discussion they conclude that they needed to divide the area by 43,560 to get the number of acres. They find that the campus was a little less than 79 acres.

"Gee, 79 football fields. That's a lot," Greg comments.

Patty smiles, nods, and then continues on, "Now, when we found the area of a plane figure, our school grounds, which didn't have a regular shape, what did we do as a strategy? . . . Craig?"

". . . We broke the figure down into a triangle and two rectangles and added up the areas."

"So, what do we do when we have to find the area of an irregularly shaped figure? Can anyone summarize what we've done?"

". . . When we have figures that are shaped funny, we try to break them down into familiar figures and add up the areas."

"Exactly. So, our task wasn't so hard after all. Now," she continues on, "what if the school grounds had been shaped like this instead," and she draws the following figure on the chalkboard.

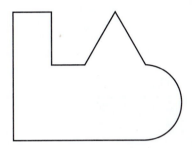

"Now, let's figure out how we can get the area of this figure and what information we need. How might we attack this problem?"

". . . Maybe we could compare it to the school grounds. We already did that," Jeanne offers.

"Good thinking," Patty smiles. "How is this figure similar to or different from the school grounds?"

". . . There's a circular part there," Anya volunteers pointing to the figure.

"Good observation, Anya," Patty nods, smiling. "So, what does that suggest that we do?"

". . . We have to know about the area of a circle, I guess."

"Yes, exactly. And how else do they compare?"

". . . They're the same," Karen notes.

"Go ahead. Explain what you mean, Karen."

". . . The other parts are like the school grounds—a big rectangle, a small rectangle, and a triangle. That's what we did before," Karen explains.

They then review the strategy they plan to use, and Patty directs them to begin finding the areas.

The next morning they review the formula for finding the area of a circle, and then Danetta comments, "I got stuck. We know the lengths [referring to the lengths of the sides of the triangular portion], but we need the height."

"It's the same as that," Jennifer says, pointing to the length of the small rectangle.

"That's really excellent thinking, Jennifer!" Patty waves energetically. "You compared the rectangular and triangular part of the figure and got the height from it. You're all doing a super job. Great!"

She thinks to herself, "This is sure working a lot better than last year."

The class continues, and with Patty's guidance students realize that they had the circumference—actually half the circumference—of the circle instead of the radius, so they review the formula for finding the circumference and get a value for the radius from it.

They finally calculate the area, and Patty then says, "You've all done a super job. Now, for homework, I'm going to give you a couple more areas to calculate. So, what are you going to do first? Rashad?"

". . . We'll look at the problem and decide what the best way to solve it is."

"Exactly, Rashad. You'll first decide on a strategy. Some of your strategies might be different, and that's perfectly okay. The important part is that you have a plan of attack before you leap into the problem. For example, what did we do when we had our new problem?"

". . . We compared it to the school grounds," Josifa observes.

"Exactly! Good, Josifa."

The class discusses several additional possibilities, and Patty then directs, "Okay. Get started. Come back with your answers tomorrow. Be sure you're able to explain to the class how you attacked the problem."

She then gives the class the following figures with the dimensions included, and the class works on the problems until the end of the period. As they work, Patty circulates among them, offering brief suggestions.

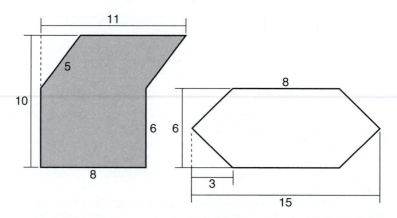

"Is it okay to do this?" Bettina whispers to Patty as Patty leans over her desk. "This is a parallelogram, and I know how to find the area of it, so I thought I'd take a shortcut."

"Absolutely," Patty smiles and whispers back. "Now tell me how you would find the area the other way."

Bettina explains how she could break the parallelogram into a rectangle and two triangles, and Patty nods. As she circulates around the room, Patty sees that Jamey had broken the figure into a rectangle and a parallelogram but had multiplied 11 and 5 to find the area of the parallelogram. He then multiplied the 8 and 6 to get the area of the rectangle and found a total area of 103 square ft. She stops and asks, "Jamey, could you explain how you got that answer?"

"I broke the figure into two parts and then added the areas of each," Jamey responds.

"What did you do here?" Patty asks, pointing to the parallelogram.

"Took 11 times 5," Jamey responds.

"Take another look," Patty suggests.

". . . Looks okay to me. I got the answer to the problem."

"Come on back here," Patty smiles, motioning to a table at the back of the room. "Let's look at the problem again."

She and Jamey go to the back of the room, where Patty, drawing figures and diagrams, guides Jamey through the problem, and she then gives him another one to solve as she watches.

Questions for Analysis

Let's examine Patty's lesson now based on the information in this chapter. In your analysis consider the following questions. In each case be specific and take information directly from the case study in doing your analysis.

1. Was Patty's lesson an example of *problem-based learning, project-based learning,* or both? Explain.
2. How effectively did Patty teach problem solving in her lesson? Identify both strengths and weaknesses in her lesson.
3. How effectively did Patty promote critical thinking in her lesson? Cite specific information from the case study in completing your assessment.
4. As with most classes, there was considerable developmental diversity in Patty's classroom. How effectively did her lesson accommodate developmental differences in her students? Explain.

*D*iscussion Questions

1. What are the major advantages and disadvantages of problem-based learning from a teacher perspective? From a student perspective?

2. Which form of problem-based instruction—project-based learning, problem solving, or inquiry—is most valuable for the content area of the teaching level at which you'll find yourself? Why?

3. Why do most of the problem-solving experiences learners have in schools involve well-defined rather than ill-defined problems? What might teachers do to provide more experiences with ill-defined problems for learners?

4. Inquiry is infrequently used in schools. Why is this so? What could be done to increase the amount of inquiry conducted?

5. Can critical thinking be effectively taught in all content areas? Grade levels? Can critical thinking be taught as effectively with all types of content? If not, for what types— concepts, generalizations, principles, or organized bodies of knowledge—is the teaching of critical thinking most appropriate? What types of content are most appropriate for inquiry lessons?

6. Some critics see the current emphasis on thinking skills as a fad. Others view the development of thinking skills as antagonistic to content acquisition. How would you respond to these critics?

7. Most teachers agree that teaching thinking skills is important. Since this is the case, why is teaching thinking so rarely done? List several reasons. What might be done to overcome these obstacles?

*P*ortfolio Activities

1. *Project-Based Learning.* Design and teach a unit based on project-based learning (or observe one taught by someone else). Analyze the unit afterward using the following questions:

   a. Did the introductory question or problem serve as an effective focal point for students' investigative efforts?
   b. Were the teacher's grouping strategies effective?

    c. Did the teacher effectively use timelines to structure students' efforts?

    d. Did the teacher effectively monitor students?

    e. Did the learning exhibits reflect student learning?

    f. Did the teacher effectively use student exhibits as focal points for student learning?

    g. What suggestion do you have to improve the process?

2. *Problem Solving.* Plan and teach a problem-solving lesson (or observe one taught by someone else). Analyze the lesson afterward using the following questions:

    a. Was the problem well defined or ill defined? Why?

    b. How did the lesson encourage students to define the problem?

    c. How did students represent the problem?

    d. What type of strategies did students use to solve the problem? What heuristics were used?

    e. Were students encouraged to evaluate the results of their problem-solving efforts?

    f. What did the teacher do to help students become better problem solvers? What more could have been done?

3. *Inquiry.* Plan and teach an inquiry lesson (or observe one taught by someone else). Analyze and evaluate the lesson using the following questions:

    a. Was the question or problem well defined?

    b. Did students form a number of hypotheses?

    c. What kinds of data were gathered?

    d. How successful were students in assessing their hypotheses?

    e. Were students encouraged to generalize beyond their immediate problem?

    f. How could the lesson have been improved?

4. *Thinking Skills in the Curriculum.* Interview a teacher. Ask how much emphasis is placed on teaching thinking in class. In the process, ask what is meant by *thinking skills.* Ask for a specific example of how approaches to thinking are taught to students. How could you integrate thinking skills into your curriculum?

5. *Teaching Thinking Skills.* Observe a class in which the teacher is focusing on some type of thinking skill. Use the following simple classification system for the questions the teacher asks:

    a. Factual/recall question.

    b. Question that calls for a comparison, such as "How are these similar (alike, the same, different, etc.)?"

    c. Question that calls for an explanation, such as "Why?"

    d. Question that calls for documentation, such as "How do you know?"

    e. Question that calls for a hypotheses, such as "What would happen if?"

Tally the number of questions that the teacher asks in each of the categories. Add additional categories if needed.

    a. How often are these questions asked?

    b. How do students respond to these questions?

    c. What could the teacher have done to better promote the development of thinking skills during the lesson?

    d. How will you use questions to develop thinking skills in your classroom?

6. *Teaching Thinking Skills: Trying It Out.* Plan and teach a thinking skills–oriented lesson.

    a. How did your planning differ from that for other lessons?

    b. What information did you provide students to think about?

    c. How did students respond to your questions asking them to use thinking skills?

    d. What evidence do you have that students actually developed their thinking skills?

    e. How could the lesson be improved?

To check your comprehension of the content covered in Chapter 11, go to the Book Specific Resources in MyEducationLab, select your text, and complete the Study Plan quiz. In addition to receiving feedback on your answers, a study plan will be generated from the quiz that will direct you to access Review, Practice, and Enrichment materials to enhance your understanding of chapter content.

12

Differentiating Instruction

Chapter Outline	Learning Objectives
	When you've completed your study of this chapter, you should be able to
Understanding differentiated instruction ■ Principles of differentiation ■ What do teachers differentiate?	1. Define differentiation and describe how it can be used to help all students learn.
Planning for differentiated instruction ■ Pre-assessment: The beginning point for all differentiation ■ Flexible time requirements ■ Adapting instructional materials ■ Offering different learning activities ■ Varying learning objectives **Technology and Teaching:** Technology as a tool for differentiating instruction	2. Explain how teachers plan for differentiation in their classrooms.
Instructional strategies to differentiate instruction ■ Grouping ■ Strategy instruction ■ Peer tutoring and cooperative learning	3. Describe how different teaching strategies can be used to accommodate student differences.
The challenge of assessment in diverse classrooms ■ Strategies for differentiating assessment ■ Grading	4. Describe different ways that assessment can be adapted to make them more valid and reliable.

Student diversity is a fact of life in today's classrooms. Effective teachers respond to this diversity by varying their instruction to meet the learning needs of all students. In this chapter we examine different ways that teachers differentiate instruction to better meet the needs of all students in their classrooms.

Differentiation targets three groups of students: those who struggle to succeed in regular classrooms, those who are bored with the existing classroom menu, and those who fail to flourish because they need something different. Anyone who has taught knows that classrooms contain students from each of these groups.

Understanding Differentiated Instruction

Melanie Parker is an intern in Mrs. Jenkins's urban fiftth-grade math class. Like the city, the class is diverse, ranging from students who don't speak English as their native language to children of professors who work at the university in the center of the city. In addition to cultural diversity the students also vary in ability and background experience, something Melanie quickly realizes after she's spent some time with the class.

Melanie sits in the back of the room on her first day and watches Mrs. Jenkins teach a lesson on dividing fractions. As she looks at Mrs. Jenkin's plan book she notices the following standard at the top of the page:

Mathematics, Grade 5

b2 Number operation and quantitative reasoning

The student uses fractions in problem-solving situations (Texas Education Agency 2008b).

The first part of the lesson goes as anticipated, with Mrs. Jenkins first handing back a short exercise the students had completed on multiplying fractions, which was the previous day's lesson. From students' comments, Melanie realizes that the their understanding varies dramatically.

Mrs. Jenkins carefully illustrates and models the process for dividing fractions and then gives the students a problem to solve. She discusses the solution with students and then repeats the process with two additional problems. Then she breaks students into groups to work on problems similar to the ones they discussed in the whole group. Most of the groups work quite well, but Mrs. Jenkins has to work with a few others to help them get started. Based on their test scores on a pretest she had given, Mrs. Jenkins takes four of the students aside to work with them on prerequisite ideas, such as numerator, denominator, multiplying fractions, and the process of inverting a fraction. While she works with the four students, she asks Melanie to help with the other small groups, and Melanie ends up taking several students aside to essentially reteach the topic Mrs. Jenkins just covered.

"What's going on here?" Melanie thinks. "She taught this stuff so carefully. Why didn't they learn it?"

Many teachers face this question after a lesson. Indeed, why didn't they learn it? This question relates to several others:

- What can you do when many of your students struggle to learn basic concepts?

- How can you adjust your instruction to meet the needs of all students?

- Don't all of our students need to learn the same things, and learn them the same way?

Here's what one expert has to say about that last question.

In life, kids can choose from a variety of clothing to fit their differing sizes, styles, and preferences. We understand without explanation, that this makes them more comfortable and gives expression to their developing personalities. In school, modifying, or differentiating instruction for students of different readiness and interests is also more comfortable, engaging, and inviting. One-size-fits all instruction will inevitably sag or pinch—exactly as single-size clothing would—students who differ in need, even if they are chronologically the same age. (Tomlinson, 2005, pp. vi-vii)

The idea of differentiating instruction is grounded in the assumption that not all students learn the same way, and effective teachers adapt their instruction to meet the learning needs of all their students.

Principles of Differentiation

What does a differentiated classroom look like? Instruction in differentiated classrooms is

- **Proactive.** Differentiation is incorporated into initial planning.
- **Student centered.** Differentiation is based upon student needs and interests.
- **Assessment based.** Differentiation is based upon information about students and what they need.
- **A blend.** Differentiation is a mixture of whole-class, group, and individual instruction, designed to meet all students' needs. (Tomlinson, 2005)

Let's examine these principles a bit further. First, effective teachers understand the learning diversity in their classrooms and respond by addressing these differences in their initial planning. Mrs. Jenkins, for example, didn't wait for learning problems to surface; instead, she anticipated students' learning needs and responded accordingly with individual and small-group help. She was proactive.

Differentiation is also student centered, which means that your strategies are based upon student needs and interests. In differentiated classrooms teachers take the extra step to learn about their students and adjust their instruction accordingly. As Melanie talked with Mrs. Jenkins after the class, she asked her about the different groups that were struggling to understand fractions themselves, let alone the process of dividing them. Mrs. Jenkins explained that many of these students were also struggling with language, and school in general.

Assessment, a third component of differentiation, provides teachers with crucial information about what students know and can do and what they'll need to proceed onto the next level. Pre-assessment provides information before instruction, continual and ongoing assessment during instruction allows teachers to gauge the effectiveness of their teaching during lessons, and assessment afterward helps teachers identify those students who need additional help and those who can move on to new learning challenges. On the basis of her pretest Mrs. Jenkins was able to identify students who would need extra help with the concept.

Melanie also asked Mrs. Jenkins about the groups she was assigned to work with. Initially Melanie thought the students were randomly assigned to these groups, but as she worked with them, she soon realized that each group had faster and slower learners, and that more able students were providing much-needed assistance to their struggling peers. Mrs. Jenkins shared her grade book with Melanie, which contained a number of scores from homework assignments, quizzes, and classroom exercises. She used these scores to both assign students to groups and keep track of where everyone was in her class. Mrs. Jenkins's class was assessment based.

Finally, Mrs. Jenkins used a blend of whole-group, small-group, and work with individual students as part of the process of differentiation, because she realized that no one form of instruction meets all learning needs. When understanding a topic, such as dividing fractions, is essential for everyone, you should use whole-class instruction, as Mrs. Jenkins did. When students need to interact with others to practice skills and gain different perspectives on ideas, teachers often use small groups. And when only a few students need additional help, working with them individually or in small groups is effective. We saw this flexibility in Mrs. Jenkins's class. She used whole-class, small-group, and even individual work with students to help maximize the amount they learned.

Differentiation doesn't mean that teachers attempt to individualize instruction for each student, however (Tomlinson, 2005). This was tried more than 40 years ago, without success. Attempting to design individual lessons for 30 students is exhausting for teachers and chaotic for the classroom. Instead, effective differentiation means that the teacher is flexible, with a continual eye on students' learning progress, as was the case in Mrs. Jenkins's classroom. When students need individual attention, the teacher provides it, but only after considering other more time- and energy-efficient ways to handle learning problems. For example, peer tutoring, which we describe later in the chapter, provides a way to help struggling students without requiring the immediate attention of the teacher. Differentiation needs to be workable for both students and teachers.

What Do Teachers Differentiate?

Teachers differentiate their instruction in three ways: (1) content, (2) instructional methods, and (3) the student products they use to determine learning progress. Sometimes these products are traditional assessments such as quizzes and tests; at other times they are projects that students work on individually or in groups. Let's examine each of these elements of differentiation.

Content is the most frequent starting point for teacher planning, and state-mandated standards and high-stakes tests make the process of selecting content essential. If teachers are to be held accountable for the way students perform on tests, then students need to know the content on that test.

However, there are instances in the school curriculum when the specific content isn't essential, and when everyone doesn't have to read the same book or report on the same topic. We know from research on motivation that choice enhances student motivation, so providing options to students, when possible, taps into this (Pintrich, Schunk, & Meese, 2008). A healthy professional exercise for all teachers is to examine objectives and standards closely to decide if each really targets content that is essential for all students.

Instructional strategy is a second way in which instruction can be differentiated. Rejecting a one-size-fits-all approach to teaching, differentiation provides various options for students to learn essential content. **Universal design**, *is a concept from special education that attempts to create learning environments in which individuals with a wide range of learning abilities and styles can succeed in the classroom* (Cohen & Spenciner, 2009; Mastroprieri & Scruggs, 2010). Sometimes this means varying learning materials such as reading texts or instructional approaches, and it can also include using various forms of technology to help students learn, as we'll see later in the chapter.

Using student products to assess learning progress is a third way instruction can be differentiated. Often these products will consist of traditional paper-and-pencil measures, such as homework, quizzes, and tests. Other times the products can be projects or reports that allow students to explore topics that interest them individually and that also document their learning progress. For example, an elementary social studies unit on the states required all students to take a quiz on basic facts about the states and then allowed them to choose a particular state and do a report or project.

With this overview as a foundation let's see how teachers plan for differentiation.

Planning for Differentiated Instruction

Melanie Parker is continuing her work in Mrs. Jenkins's sixth-grade classroom and, as part of her student teaching experience, has been given responsibility for planning and implementing a unit on decimals. With Mrs. Jenkins's help, she constructs a quiz that she'll give before the unit to see where students are in terms of their existing knowledge of place value and decimals. Mindful of her experience earlier with the lesson on fractions, she realizes she has to plan for the range of student abilities and needs in Mrs. Jenkins's class. She doesn't know where to begin.

Planning performs several crucial roles for teachers; it helps them organize instruction and also provides emotional security in terms of knowing what to do and how to proceed. The process of planning also provides opportunities for teachers to accommodate diversity. In the first part of this section we examine the role of pre-assessments in differentiating instruction. Then we turn to planning strategies that keep objectives constant for all students and vary either the time or resources available to students. Next we examine strategies that provide different learning options for students. Finally we examine ways that technology can be used to help differentiate instruction.

Pre-Assessment: The Beginning Point for All Differentiation

Imagine walking into a classroom and being asked to teach a lesson to students you have never worked with before. The first question you would want to ask is "What do they already know?" We can't teach effectively if we don't know what our students know and need. Finding this out through various forms of assessment is even more important when we differentiate our instruction.

Assessment for differentiation takes place at several points in the school year. It starts at the beginning of the year with global measures of student strengths and weaknesses, as well as background interests and information about learners as individuals. Beginning-of-year assessments not only provide teachers with valuable information for planning, but also communicate to students that you care about them as individuals.

Pre-assessment continues throughout the school year, when effective teachers continually gather information before every unit they teach. These pre-assessments are more specific than earlier, beginning-of-the-year ones designed to provide teachers with a global snapshot of students' strengths and weaknesses. Unit level pre-assessments, by contrast, target individual concepts and ideas that students will need to succeed in the unit. Sometimes these assessments tell us that students aren't ready to begin studying a topic without additional help; other times they identify students who already have mastered a good deal of what you'll be teaching and who will need alternate learning activities for challenge and growth. Mrs. Jenkins used pre-assessment before her lesson on dividing fractions and Melanie did the same before her unit on decimals. In general, the more specific the pre-assessment and the closer it is to actual instruction, the more valuable it will be for differentiating instruction.

After checking standards, effective teachers form learning objectives and use these objectives to target key concepts for pre-assessment. They'll use these same objectives to frame their instruction, and they'll also use these objectives to construct assessment items to measure the effectiveness of their instruction.

Pre-assessing can take many forms, varying from traditional paper-and-pencil pretests to homework and classroom exercises. It can also include the continual classroom observations that teachers use on a daily basis to gauge learning progress. The bottom line is this—the better you know your students, the better you will be able to differentiate instruction to help them learn.

Pre-assessment tells you where students are and what they need. But what options do you have to accommodate the differences uncovered by pre-assessment? Figure 12.1 provides an overview of these options, which are described in the following sections.

Flexible Time Requirements

When students in Melanie's class finished their math assignments, they put them in their folders and went to the back of the room to find a math game. Many of these were on the three computers located in one corner of her room. Some of the other games had dice, others had playing cards, and still others used flash cards. All were designed to reinforce the math skills on which the students were working. In addition they gave struggling students more time to work on their math, while also providing faster students with challenge and enrichment.

Time is a constant in all classrooms; teachers have only so much time to teach their students, so time must be allocated strategically. But learners differ in the amount of time needed to master a topic; research indicates that the amount of time needed to master a content area may vary from two to four times as much for slower students (Good & Brophy, 2008). When the amount of time available for learning is the same for all students, the gap between faster and slower students can grow wider and wider (Bloom, 1981). One way to accommodate these differences in learning ability is to provide extra time for slower students.

The most common way that teachers accommodate differences in learning rates is by giving a common assignment and providing extra time for students who need it. For this strategy to work the classroom needs enrichment activities available to students who

Figure 12.1

Differentiation Options During Planning

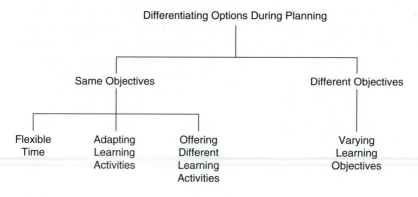

Table 12.1 Enrichment Options for Faster Students

Enrichment Option	Description
Free reading	A shelf of books or magazines, (e.g., *Ranger Rick, National Geographic World*) are kept in the back of the room for students to use.
Games	A part of the room is sectioned off for students to play academic games on the floor.
Computers	A menu of computer software games and simulations provides student choice.
Learning centers	Learning materials with objectives, directions, and learning activities guide students.
Individual research projects	Students choose long-term projects to investigate; teachers assist by helping to gather individual books and other resources.
Peer tutoring	Structured learning activities help students assist each other.

complete their assignments quickly. Mrs. Jenkins did this by making computers and math games available when students completed their assignments early. Alternate enrichment options are described in Table 12.1.

These enrichment options perform several functions. First, they give struggling students extra time to work on important concepts. Struggling students need extra time to practice applying the idea in straightforward ways. Enrichment activities also provide challenge and choice for faster students, who can become bored when they have to wait for other students to complete their work. These activities allow students to stretch and bend the idea to see how it interacts with and relates to other ideas. Enrichment activities provide the teacher with opportunities to work with struggling students either individually or in small groups.

In addition to flexible time requirements embedded in whole-group instruction two other instructional formats—mastery learning and team assisted individualization—keep objectives constant but vary the time and resources available to students.

Mastery Learning   **Mastery learning** *is a system of instruction that allows students to progress at their own rate through a unit of study* (Tanner & Tanner, 2007). Objectives specify the essential learning outcomes for the unit, and frequent formative quizzes provide feedback about learning progress. When students pass the quizzes, they are allowed to continue; when they don't pass, they are moved into alternate learning activities. Summative final exams are used to document mastery of the content. Individual differences are accommodated by allowing students extra time to master objectives and by providing corrective instruction to remedy learning problems.

Research on mastery learning is generally positive, especially when the criterion measure is specific to the content covered, and these gains are especially positive for low achievers (Verdinelli & Gentile, 2003). However, a major obstacle to implementing mastery learning is logistical; finding the extra time to work with students who need it can be a difficult balancing act when large numbers of students are working at different points in the curriculum (Good & Brophy, 2008). Team assisted individualization addresses this problem.

Team Assisted Individualization   **Team assisted individualization** *is a hybrid of mastery learning and cooperative learning that uses students as tutors in small groups* (Alexander, 2006). In it students work on individualized learning materials in mixed-ability learning teams. The learning materials are designed to give students structure for their learning efforts; the teams provide structure and support through teammates helping with and checking assignments. In addition team rewards provide motivational incentives for team members. Within this structure the teacher provides direct instruction to small groups of students who are working on the same topic or skill. This teacher-led direct instruction provides quality instruction to all students; the cooperative learning teams provide support and assistance for students needing individual help.

Research on this instructional strategy has yielded positive results (Slavin, 1995). In six studies involving elementary math, students in team assisted individualization gained significantly more in computational skills than students in traditional programs.

So far we've looked at strategies that keep objectives constant for students and examined ways that teachers accommodate different learning rates. In the following sections we look at ways that teachers differentiate objectives as well as learning materials and activities.

Adapting Instructional Materials

Before Melanie taught her first lesson on the unit on decimals, she examined students' textbooks to see how they could be used to supplement her instruction. She found that the text did a decent job of explaining some concepts, such as place value, but wasn't as good with others. Before she assigned the chapter, she outlined it and shared the outline with students during her introduction to the unit.

During the unit she also passed out a sheet with definitions of key concepts and supplemented her instruction with exercises that targeted decimals and fractions, decimals as parts of a whole, and basic math operations using decimals. Both the definitions and exercises contained multiple examples of students using decimals in their everyday lives.

As Melanie worked with the textbook, she wondered if it was "over the heads" of her ELL students. As she looked around for other resources, she found several fourth-grade textbooks that introduced place value and decimals in a simpler, more straightforward fashion. Melanie gave these to her ELL students, who found that the explanations of place value in the fourth-grade texts used simpler vocabulary and were easier to understand. Before she passed these supplementary texts out, she highlighted key passages to help her ELL students navigate through the chapter.

Effective teachers also plan for differentiating instruction by adapting instructional materials to make the content clearer (Vaughn & Bos, 2009). This approach to differentiation keeps objectives the same for all students, as with flexible time requirements, but provides additional help by altering the learning resources available to students. One way to do this is to use alternate texts and highlight essential information. Outlines and concept maps can also be used to help students see the big picture and how individual concepts are related to each other. Study guides and supplementary questions encourage students to read actively and focus on important ideas and concepts.

Melanie did this when she outlined the chapter and shared this with students and also when she passed out a sheet of key chapter concepts defined and related to their own experiences with decimals. Doing this not only augmented the content in the text, it also increased motivation to learn the new content by showing students how decimals could be useful to them in their everyday lives.

Extracting information from texts often involves note taking, and struggling students frequently have problems knowing what information is important and how to organize

Figure 12.2

A Note-Taking Format

Key Concept	Text Notes	Class Notes

their notes. A simple note-taking format for helping students navigate through text can be found in Figure 12.2. The first column identifies key concepts that students should learn; the second column provides a space for students to write notes from their texts that target these important concepts. Finally, the third column provides an opportunity to augment the text with class notes. The combination of all three columns organizes class content and provides structure for students' study efforts. Initially teachers can provide these note-taking guides to aid students; later, after practice and feedback from you, students can be given responsibility for identifying these themselves.

As you examine the learning materials available to your students, ask yourself several questions:

- How well do existing materials present and explain important ideas?
- Do existing texts organize content in meaningful ways and make this organization clear and meaningful to students?
- What can I do to augment existing materials to make them more effective?

Adapting existing learning materials is an important first step in effectively differentiating instruction.

Offering Different Learning Activities

Camille Robertson circulates around the room as her eighth graders discuss their science projects. Each group was responsible for investigating a science topic and reporting on it to the rest of the class. Some were doing written reports, others were growing seeds under different kinds of light, and still others were experimenting with batteries and light bulbs.

The way students prefer to learn varies; some are good listeners and profit from teacher presentations, whereas others prefer to read or discuss an idea with their peers. One way to differentiate instruction to address these preferences is to use a variety of teaching strategies during whole-class instruction (Tomlinson, 2005). Another way to differentiate is to provide a number of learning options, while keeping learning objectives the same. Camille did this by allowing her students to choose from a variety of activities to satisfy her science investigation requirement.

To capitalize on students' strengths, students need choices in the learning tasks they work on so that all members of the class can participate and succeed (Tomlinson, 2003, 2005).

For example, in one social studies project that focused on the Crusades, students had a number of learning options:

> [D]ifferent groups of students study castle floor plans and pictures of ruins, listen to recordings of Crusade songs, analyze the text of a speech by Pope Urban, and examine half-human pictures of infidels in the Crusaders' Handbook. To grasp the deeper concepts of how historians learn, students spend several days on this project so they can experience each of the media in turn: text, music, and spatial-visual material. (Cohen, 1991, p. 5)

In addition students were provided with options about how they could demonstrate what they learned.

> Each group presented products which required a variety of creative intellectual abilities. Students created their own version of a Crusader castle and showed how it could be defended, wrote a song about current events that echoes the purpose of the music of the Crusades, and performed a skit illustrating how the Crusader Handbook was used to recruit naive villagers. As students presented these products, the teacher stimulated a general discussion on the different sources used by historians. (Cohen, 1991, p. 5)

Multi-ability classrooms such as this one allow all students to contribute to the group. As opposed to narrow, convergent tasks that have only one right answer, **multi-ability tasks**

- *Are open ended, involving general answers or several ways to solve problems*
- *Provide opportunities for different students to make various kinds of contributions*
- *Use a variety of skills and call on a wide variety of knowledge*
- *Incorporate reading, writing, constructing, and designing skills*
- *Incorporate the use of multimedia* (Tomlinson, 2003, 2005)

Multi-ability classrooms promote learning for all students by providing alternate ways for students to learn and succeed.

As another example of differentiation through choice let's consider a sixth-grade language arts teacher who uses different learning activities in a unit on the novel *Tuck Everlasting* (Tomlinson, 2005). Everyone in the class read the same novel. The teacher's goal for the unit was for all students to understand the novel, but how they interacted with it and reported their reading progress differed from student to student. Students who were struggling with the novel were placed in pairs to discuss questions the teacher had prepared to clarify the plot and get them started on their journal entries. Another group of students quickly worked either independently or in groups (student choice) to answer the same questions and then wrote their own suggestions for additional questions to be discussed by the whole class. A third group galloped through the text and were given several options, including writing an alternative ending for the text or an interview with the author or one of the main characters. The teacher's general goal for the unit was to have all of her students read, understand, and enjoy the novel; the options she provided gave students different ways to learn the content.

Other examples of accommodating different learning preferences by providing students with options and choice include typing notes from good note takers and sharing them with others, placing chapters on cassettes and making these available in listening centers, and allowing students to choose how they will demonstrate their knowledge of a topic, as we saw in the social studies and language arts examples. When teachers provide students with a menu of options, they need to clearly communicate how these different products will be graded and scored. This provides structure to the learning activities and helps ensure that learning objectives are reached.

Some of the most effective alternate learning activities are those that provide corrective instruction and are specifically designed to help students correct earlier problems. For example, a first-grade teacher who has discovered that several of her students are having problems with letter-sound correspondence might design a learning center with a tape recorder and interactive materials to remedy the problem. The center specifically targets the problem content area while providing success experiences for students. Providing learning options makes sense both instructionally and motivationally.

Varying Learning Objectives

> Every Friday Carlos Torres gave his students half an hour to confer with him and work on their term papers. He wanted each of his high school English students to read one author in depth, and this semester-long project provided students with an opportunity to learn more about an author and read more of his or her works.

An alternate way to differentiate instruction is to offer students choices in the learning objectives they pursue (Tomlinson, 2005). Some learning objectives are foundational; all students need to learn how to read and do basic math computations, for example. However, other topics are interesting to individual students or good to know but not essential for all students. These topics provide opportunities for teachers to provide choices to students about the learning objectives they'll pursue.

Special projects, term papers, and individual experiments all offer students the opportunity to choose topics that interest them personally. Personalization is an important factor in motivation, and student choice is one way to capitalize on personalization (Stipek, 2002). Carlos accommodated student interest by designing his course so that 70 percent of the grade was based on core content whereas the other 30 percent was based on projects. This allowed him to cover essential English content while still providing opportunities for student choice.

Technology and Teaching

Technology as a Tool for Differentiating Instruction

Technology offers another way to differentiate instruction. In the past 20 years the growth of technology has greatly expanded the instructional tools available to teachers as they attempt to meet the learning needs of all their students. Computers, videodiscs, integrated learning systems, video recorders, and DVDs provide teachers with more effective ways to present information and provide practice and feedback. In this section we focus on two uses of computers as alternate instructional tools that allow teachers to differentiate instruction. The first uses computers to provide students with alternate or additional sources of information; the second uses computers to provide additional instructional support during skill learning.

Computers as Alternate Instructional Resources

Classroom computers provide valuable links to alternate sources of information that students can use to learn core material, as well supplement the information found in texts. The Internet provides quick and easy access to a wealth of information for projects and reports, and encyclopedias on CD-ROM can be used when Internet connections are a problem.

The Internet also provides a wealth of materials that teachers can use to illustrate ideas and provide supplementary instruction. For example, The National Library of Visual Manipulatives (http://nvlm.usu.edu/en/nav/vlibrary.html) allows both teachers and students to access a variety of math manipulatives through the Internet. To supplement her instruction on fractions, Mrs. Jenkins used the site to provide pictures and concrete illustration of

- Fractions as parts of a whole
- Wholes divided into different equivalent fractions
- Operations such as addition and subtraction with fractions

Seeing and being able to manipulate objects on the Internet provided her struggling students with an alternative way to learn the content.

Computers as Adaptive Reinforcement Tools

Computers have also proven to be a valuable resource in providing practice and reinforcement for students who need extra help. Computers' strength lies in their ability to provide differentiated instruction, speeding up when students have mastered basic facts and slowing down when error rates indicate learning problems. You learned about drill-and-practice programs when we discussed direct instruction in Chapter 8. There we emphasized drill-and-practice programs' ability to provide immediate and focused practice and feedback. Effective drill-and-practice programs also differentiate by varying the speed of presentation and adapting the corrective feedback to the needs of learners.

In addition to adaptive drill-and-practice programs, tutorials can also be used to introduce new information using text, graphics, and exercises with feedback. Adaptive computer tutorials not only present new information, but also provide informative feedback that is specific to learner needs (Lever-Duffy et al., 2003).

A tutorial on high school accounting, for example, might first explain the formula "annual depreciation = cost/ expected life" and then ask, "If an electric pasta machine costs $400 and is expected to last four years, what is the annual depreciation?" In response to the answer "$100," the computer would say, "Good," and go on to the next problem or concept. A student who typed $400 might be told, "Sorry, but you're probably not ready to work for H & R Block. $400 is the cost. To find annual depreciation, divide this figure by the expected life (four years). Please type the correct answer."

In providing new information, computer tutorials can be adaptive without being redundant, matching new content to students' learning needs. So, for example, if students already understood depreciation, the computer would move them to the next concept. This allows faster students to move ahead while providing additional help for students who need it.

Like differentiated lessons in general the most effective tutorials pretest students at the beginning to identify strengths and weaknesses. Using this information teachers can then use the tutorial to remediate background weaknesses or accelerate students past information they already know. Effective tutorials also provide teachers with detailed information about an individual student's learning progress so the teacher can adapt instruction accordingly.

Carnegie Learning's *Cognitive Tutor* is one example of a tutorial that is adaptive (Carnegie Learning, 2010).

A series of programs pretest students and then combine instruction with frequent assessment and feedback through math problems of increasing complexity. For example, when the student responds 2.8 to the problem, $-2.3 + 0.5 = ?$, the program responds, "Think about the sign of the numbers." Challenge is provided with a "Skillometer," a bar graph that increases with learning progress and decreases when students ask for hints.

Tutorials can fulfill several needs, including initial instruction, additional support for a student whose understanding isn't fully developed, advanced study for higher achievers, or alternatives to teacher-led instruction. The best are branched, adapting to learners' responses and learning needs (Roblyer & Doering, 2010). When a student responds incorrectly to a multiple-choice item, the program explains why that choice isn't correct and repeats instruction. Effective tutorials are carefully sequenced so that new concepts and skills are systematically developed and grounded in existing understanding.

By combining a rich instructional menu with opportunities to experiment with new learning in a supportive, nonthreatening way, computers provide an effective way to differentiate instruction for students who either require more help or need additional stimulation.

*I*nstructional Strategies to Differentiate Instruction

You will encounter a range of learning abilities in your classroom, as well as cultural and learning style differences. In responding to this diversity a teacher has several major instructional options:

1. **Group students according to their ability.** This allows teachers to teach to a particular ability level but carries with it other problems.

2. **Provide strategy instruction for slower students.** Strategy instruction increases students' ability to learn by teaching them more efficient ways of performing academic tasks.

3. **Use peer tutoring and cooperative learning.** Students can be a valuable teaching resource, and using students capitalizes on the benefits that social interaction in learning can provide.

Let's examine each of these options more closely.

Grouping

Melanie Parker is ready to begin her unit on decimals during her student teaching internship. She considers her students' pre-assessment math quiz. The scores are bimodal; half of her class understands fractions and place value and half are still struggling. If she continues with her planned review lessons, half the class will be bored; if she goes ahead without review, the other half will be lost. What to do?

The next day she begins her math class by explaining that some students are ready for decimals and some need some more work before they begin. She gathers the students who still need work on place value around her in one corner of the room and gives them a sheet with review problems on it. She tells them that they would get back together as soon as she introduced decimals to the other group. As she works with the decimal group, she keeps one eye on them and the other on the group working on place value. Some hands go up, but she has to tell them to wait a few minutes until she is done with the other group. It wasn't an easy juggling act, but she didn't know what her alternatives were.

Grouping is a common instructional response to student diversity, especially at the elementary level, and it can take several forms (Good & Brophy, 2008). **Between-class ability grouping**, for example, *divides all 75 third graders into three groups: one high, one medium, and one low. Grouping across grade levels,* also called the **Joplin Plan**, mixes, for example, third-, fourth-, and fifth-grade students of similar reading ability in the same reading class. These students would then return to their own classrooms for other subjects. **Within-class grouping** *breaks students in an individual class into different groups for specific subjects.* Melanie Parker did this in her math class.

In middle, junior high, and high schools ability grouping goes further, with high-ability students studying advanced and college preparatory courses and lower-ability students receiving vocational or work-related instruction. In some schools students are grouped only in certain areas, such as English or math. In others the grouping exists across all content areas, a practice called **tracking**, which *places students in a series of different classes or curricula on the basis of ability and career goals.* Some form of tracking exists in most middle, junior high, and high schools (Oakes, 2008).

Why is ability grouping so popular? Advocates claim that it increases learning because it allows teachers to adjust methods, materials, and instructional pace to better meet students' needs (Chorzempa & Graham, 2006). Because lesson components and assessments are similar for students in a particular group, instruction is also easier for the teacher, they argue.

However, research has uncovered several serious problems with both ability grouping and tracking:

- Homogeneously grouped low-ability students achieve less than heterogeneously grouped students of similar ability. Often this problem results from inferior instruction in lower-level classes (Burris, Heubert, & Levin, 2006; Chorzempa & Graham, 2006)

- Within-class grouping creates logistical problems for teachers, because different lessons and assignments are required, and monitoring students in different tasks is difficult (Good & Brophy, 2008). We saw this in Melanie's classroom.

- Improper placements occur, and placement tends to become permanent. Cultural minorities are underrepresented in high-ability classes and overrepresented in those with lower-ability students (O'Conner & Fernandez, 2006).

- Low-ability groups are stigmatized, and the self-esteem and motivation of students in these groups decrease (Oakes, 2008).

In addition rates of absenteeism, delinquency, truancy, and dropping out of school are much higher for students in low-ability groups than for students in general (Slavin, 2009). Tracking also often results in racial or cultural segregation of students, which impedes social development and the ability to form friendships across cultural groups (Oakes & Wells, 2002).

Sometimes, however, as Melanie concluded, groups are necessary. This often occurs in subjects that are hierarchically organized such as reading and math, for which later skills build on prerequisite ones. When grouping is used, experts recommend the following precautions (Good & Brophy, 2008):

- Use grouping only when necessary; avoid grouping in subjects that are not hierarchical (e.g., music, art, science, social studies).

- Assess frequently, keep groups flexible, and reassign students when their learning progress warrants it.

- Make sure that the quality of instruction to low-ability students is comparable to that provided for high-ability students.

- Constantly be aware of the potential negative consequences of grouping.

It is likely that you'll experience some form of ability grouping when you start teaching, either with your cooperating teacher or the other teachers you'll work with. Although teachers generally prefer to work with high-ability groups, you will likely work with students placed in low-ability groups at some point in your career. Teachers can avoid many of the problems associated with ability grouping and tracking by having appropriately high expectations for all students and working with them in heterogeneous groups whenever possible. Instructional adaptations will be needed, however, to ensure the success of students of varying abilities. Some effective adaptive strategies include the following:

- Challenge students in all of your groups and use instructional strategies that actively engage all students.

- Provide additional instructional support for those who need it. This support might include adapting learning materials or supplementing them with additional resources.

- Give students extra time to complete assignments.

- Combine both whole-class and small-group instruction. Small-group work provides variety and can help students learn from one another.

You will continually need to adapt instruction to meet your students' needs, and these adaptations are even more important when you differentiate instruction.

Strategy Instruction

A second way to differentiate instruction is to provide strategy instruction to struggling students. Research indicates that a major difference between high- and low-ability students is their knowledge and use of learning strategies (Turnbull, Turnbull, & Wehmeyer, 2010). In addition to richer content backgrounds high-ability students use this knowledge more efficiently in learning new information than do their lower-ability peers. For example, consider the thinking of a high-ability elementary student faced with the task of learning a list of 10 spelling words for a quiz.

> Okay . . . 10 words for the quiz on Friday. That shouldn't be too hard. I have two days to learn them.
>
> Let's see. These are all about airports. Which of these do I already know—airplane, taxi, apron, and jet? No problem. Hmm. . . . Some of these aren't so easy like causeway and tarmac. I don't even know what a "tarmac" is. I'll look it up . . . Oh, that makes sense. It's the runway. I'd better spend more time on these words. I'll cover them up and try to write them down and then check 'em. Tonight, I can get Mom to give me a quiz and then I'll know which ones to study extra tomorrow.

This student's actions were strategic in several ways. She assessed the task and adapted her studying to match it; she spent more time and effort on the words she didn't know; and she monitored her progress through quiz-like exercises. Low-ability students, by contrast, passively approach the task, reading the list with little thought to what they know or ways of improving (Gersten & Baker, 2001). They spend time on words they already know and make little effort to test themselves in order to receive feedback to direct their future efforts.

Some examples of strategies in different areas are found in Table 12.2.

In each of these content areas efforts to teach learning strategies to our students are productive, resulting in more efficient learning as well as increased achievement (Turnbull et al., 2010).

Effective strategy instruction includes talking about the strategy, modeling it while thinking out loud, and providing opportunities for practice. For example, if you were trying to teach the spelling strategy, you could have all students take a pretest and talk about the importance of the differences between words they know and don't know. Then you might suggest different ways of practicing, such as self-quizzes, peer quizzes, and flash cards. Finally, you could do long-term follow-up by reminding students from time to time to use these strategies when they're learning.

Table 12.2 Learning Strategies in Different Content Areas

Strategy Area	Examples
General memorization	Selectively rehearsing important information, categorizing, grouping, imaging
All content areas	Note taking, outlining, selectively underlining, self-quizzing
Reading	Summarizing, outlining, underlining
Math	Identifying givens in word problems, selectively rehearsing math facts
Writing	Outlining, considering the audience, illustrating ideas with facts, making coherent transitions

Peer Tutoring and Cooperative Learning

A final way to deal with learning diversity and to differentiate instruction in your classroom is to use students themselves to help one another. Peer tutoring places students in one-to-one pairs and supplies them with structured learning materials for practice and feedback (Vaughn, Bos, Candace, & Schumm, 2006). Cooperative learning strategies place students of differing abilities in groups and uses social interaction to promote learning (Johnson & Johnson, 2006). The research on both of these practices is positive. We discussed cooperative learning in greater detail in Chapter 7 and provide a detailed discussion of peer tutoring below.

Peer Tutoring: Students as Resources   Effective teachers use all available resources, one of which is the students themselves. In this section we describe how to differentiate instruction by using students as peer tutors to enhance the learning of content, while at the same time developing interpersonal and social skills.

Jim Corbin, a resource teacher for students with exceptionalities, and Maria Sandoval, a first-grade teacher, are talking in the teacher's lounge over lunch. Both are encountering problems in the area of reading.

"I just don't have enough time to spend with my slower students," Maria comments. "I know what they need . . . quality time in small groups where I can give them individual help and encouragement—but I've got 27 students in that class, and when I spend extra time with them, I feel guilty about slighting the others."

"I know how you feel," Jim replies, and after hesitating briefly he continues. "Numbers aren't my problem; it's motivation. I'm working with fourth and fifth graders who are really discouraged. They just don't think they can do it."

As Jim and Maria talk, they wonder if there is any way that they can help each other. They've both heard of peer tutoring but have never heard of resource students acting as tutors for regular students. They both have their doubts but agree to give it a try.

For the next week Jim prepares his students, teaching them to explain and demonstrate the reading skills they are teaching, and showing them how to provide helpful praise and feedback. Maria helps by pulling together reading materials that provide a concrete agenda for the tutoring sessions.

The next Monday Jim brings his nine resource students down to pick up the first graders. When they return to the resource room, Jim circulates around the room, monitoring each pair's progress. As Jim anticipated, some tutors do better than others, but all groups seem to work reasonably well. Jim can tell it is working for his students by the way they enter his classroom and get ready for the tutoring sessions. Before, they dragged themselves in, and it was like pulling teeth to get them to work. Now, they arrive on time and appear eager to work. He wonders how it is working for Maria's students.

Why Peer Tutoring Works   **Peer tutoring,** as the term implies, *involves students teaching students.* Peer tutoring offers two specific benefits. First, because the sessions are one to one, instruction is individualized, which is effective for all teaching situations and especially for skill learning. Second, peer tutoring can be motivational, for both the tutor and the one being helped. Helping someone learn is intrinsically motivating for the tutors, and the satisfaction that comes with increased understanding motivates those being helped (Brophy, 2004).

The idea of students helping students is not new. The ancient Greeks and Romans used tutors, and in nineteenth-century England, where pupil-teacher ratios of 400 or 500 to one often existed, teachers coped by first teaching older monitors who then worked with younger students. Teachers in America's one-room schoolhouses dealt with the vast differences in grades 1 through 8 by having older or more capable students help others.

Two primary peer tutoring arrangements exist. **Cross-age tutoring**, such as the English system and the one Jim and Maria used, employs *older students to help younger ones*. Cross-age tutoring benefits from the more mature tutor's knowledge and skills but is harder to manage logistically, because of difficulties with scheduling and coordination. **Same-age peer tutoring**, *which employs students from the same grade level as tutors*, addresses this problem and can be used in any heterogeneous class where students are at different levels of learning.

As we saw in the introductory episode, peer tutoring has also been successfully used with students with exceptionalities (Fuchs, Fuchs, & Thompson, 2001). When using peer tutoring with students with exceptionalities, experts recommend that teachers make a special effort to model procedures and explain how they will contribute to learning (Vaughn et al., 2006). Also, research suggests that peer tutoring is effective not only for teaching content and skills, but also for fostering social interaction and improved attitudes toward those with exceptionalities (Saddler & Graham, 2005).

A Basic Peer Tutoring Model   Peer tutoring is most commonly used to supplement typical teacher-led instruction. We call this the basic tutoring model and examine it in this section.

The strategy has two phases: planning and implementation, each involving four steps, which are summarized in Table 12.3 and discussed in the sections that follow.

Planning for Peer Tutoring.   The first step in planning for peer tutoring is to identify a topic for which peer tutoring can be effective. Peer tutoring can be used with any topic that includes convergent information with clear right and wrong answers. For example, math skills such as two-digit by one-digit multiplication, language arts concepts such as identifying adjectives or proper nouns, finding the longitude and latitude of various locations in social studies, and a variety of grammar and spelling rules can all be taught using peer tutoring. Organized bodies of knowledge and thinking skills, with their complexity and divergence, are less applicable to peer-tutoring activities.

After the identification of a topic, your next task is to prepare instructional materials that students can use when they work with each other. Convergent topics allow the teacher to construct specific practice and feedback exercises that provide structure for the tutoring sessions. Tutors then focus on the problems and exercises in the materials. Maria Sandoval

Table 12.3 **Steps in Planning and Implementing Peer Tutoring**

Planning	Implementing
1. Identify a topic.	1. Group presentation.
2. Prepare instructional materials.	2. Break into peer-tutoring groups.
3. Assign students to pairs.	3. Monitor progress.
4. Train students to be effective tutors.	4. Evaluate tutoring pairs.

did this when she pulled learning materials together for Jim Corbin's students. These materials provide valuable practice and feedback for content taught during initial whole-group activities.

The next planning step is to assign students to pairs. One peer tutoring arrangement is to pair a high with a low achiever and let the more advanced student do all the tutoring. **Reciprocal tutoring,** a different option, *pairs students of comparable ability, with students taking turns being the tutor.* In this arrangement students usually slide into a pattern whereby they simply work together, rather than have one formally designed as tutor for a period of time and then switching.

The next task is to train students to be effective tutors. Like teachers, effective tutors are made, not born. Preparing both the tutors and the students being tutored is important for the effectiveness of the process (Alexander, 2006; Chi, Siler, & Jeong, 2004). Untrained tutors sometimes imitate the worst from their teachers, including punitiveness and a lack of helpful feedback. Effective training components should include

- **Explaining objectives.** At the beginning of a session, the tutor should provide focus by explaining the major skill or concept to be learned. The teacher assists by putting this at the top of the tutoring worksheet.

- **Staying on task.** When an extraneous subject comes up, have tutors remind their partners of the objective and call their attention to the number of examples, pages, or steps left to do.

- **Emotional support.** Encourage tutors to make supportive comments for incorrect answers, such as "Not quite. Let's look at it again. What is the first thing you did?"

- **Praise and other positive feedback.** Discuss the importance of positive feedback and provide examples of different forms of praise (e.g., "Good answer!" "Great, you're really getting this."). If possible, have the tutor link the praise to specific behaviors ("Good, you remembered to carry the three to the hundreds column."). At the end of the lesson have the tutor state what was learned and relate this to the session objective.

- **Encouraging verbalization.** Instruct the tutor to encourage thinking out loud, both for himself or herself and his or her partner. This makes the cognitive operations being taught observable, providing a model for the partner and feedback for the tutor.

Implementing Peer Tutoring Activities.   The first step in implementing peer tutoring sessions is a group presentation that introduces and teaches the content in the same way that you normally would. This stage is important because it lays the conceptual foundation for the tutoring that will follow by providing common understandings and vocabulary.

After the group presentation break students into peer tutoring groups, giving them the worksheets you designed to reinforce the content you've just presented. As you do this, clearly specify the amount of time they have for the tutoring session, and write this on the board as a reminder. Also, clearly state your expectations for what they are to do and hand in when the session is completed.

As the groups work, you need to carefully monitor their progress. Circulate around the room to answer questions and ensure that the tutoring is proceeding smoothly. To the extent possible, answer only procedural questions, and answer content questions only when the tutor is unable to do so. This places responsibility for learning on the peer teams. Check the exercise sheets at the end of the session for any error patterns that might suggest areas for reteaching.

After the groups have worked together, you'll need to evaluate the effectiveness of existing tutoring pairs. If a tutoring pair is not functioning, rearrange the students. One of the motivational advantages of peer tutoring is the fact that students are exposed to different teaching styles and personalities; to take advantage of this reconstitute the tutoring pairs periodically.

Peer tutoring works because it places students in an active learning role and individualizes instruction. One of its advantages is that it can be easily combined with large-group instruction. As such, it provides individualized practice and feedback, and an effective way to differentiate instruction.

The Challenge of Assessment in Diverse Classrooms

As we've seen in this chapter, differentiation in the classroom means that teachers make a conscious effort to adjust their instruction to meet the needs of all students. This is true of assessment as well. If teachers hope to gain an accurate picture of what students know and are able to do, we have to adapt our assessment procedures. We may have students, for example, who aren't familiar with the standard assessment practices of schools, such as multiple-choice or true-false formats. They may not understand the purposes of assessment, may lack test-taking strategies, and may also have difficulties understanding assessment items because of problems with the English language.

Strategies for Differentiating Assessment

Teachers can respond to differences in students' assessment backgrounds in several ways (Popham, 2002):

- Provide practice with test taking
- Teach test-taking strategies
- Use clear language in items
- Make provisions for nonnative English speakers

Provide Practice with Test Taking   For students who are unfamiliar with test-taking routines, providing practice with the different item formats that appear on classroom and standardized tests can be particularly effective. In addition clearly communicating the importance of assessment is essential, because some students may not understand how assessment influences learning, grades, and even promotion to the next grade. Teaching specific test-taking strategies can be helpful in these cases.

Teach Test-Taking Strategies   Teaching test-taking strategies helps students improve their performance through awareness and understanding of test-taking demands. Some specific strategies include

- Efficient use of time during tests
- Carefully reading directions
- Adapting to different testing formats

For instruction in strategy use to be most effective, teachers need to remind students about test-taking strategies as tests and quizzes are discussed. For example, in multiple-choice items, one or two of the choices will often directly contradict the stem and can therefore be eliminated. Reducing the choices to a plausible two is an effective strategy. When faced with essay items, preparing a brief outline is a simple strategy that can be used to increase the logic and organization of the response. Reminding students of these strategies and illustrating them can significantly improve learners' performance, particularly with young, low-ability, and minority students who have limited test-taking experience (Popham, 2002).

Use Clear Language in Items   With students from diverse cultural backgrounds, language that is confusing or unfamiliar to them is always a possible problem. For example, students may have difficulty with items that take certain knowledge for granted, such as familiarity with American sports such as baseball, common forms of transportation, historical figures, or music and other elements of U.S. culture.

This problem has no easy solution, but being aware of and sensitive to the possibilities of unfamiliar content are beginning points. Also, encourage students to ask questions during tests, and students should have opportunities to discuss the items on tests when they are handed back.

Make Provisions for Nonnative English Speakers   What if the next exam you take for one of your classes was written in Spanish? For most of us, this would be very difficult, and many of our students encounter a similar difficulty in our classrooms when tests are given in a nonnative language (Abedi et al., 2004). As with other potential forms of bias in testing, easy solutions don't exist. However, some possibilities for accommodating nonnative English speakers follow:

- Provide extra time to take the test. Allow students to take the test before or after school, using a translation dictionary.
- Translate the test into students' native languages until their English proficiency improves.
- If one is available, use an interpreter during tests.

Each of these suggestions is designed to ensure, to the extent possible, that our assessments reflect actual achievement and not learners' familiarity with common background knowledge or vocabulary. These accommodations increase the validity of our assessment procedures and also provide the teacher with more accurate information about learning progress.

Grading

In previous sections we discussed the benefits of differentiating instruction and talked about different ways to differentiate our assessment procedures to both aid struggling students and gain a more accurate picture of what these students know and are able to do. But what about grading?

Here is the dilemma—grades perform both a communication and motivational function and these roles often conflict. Grades play a crucial role in communicating learning progress to both students and their parents. The single most widely used mechanism that you'll have for letting students know how well they're doing in your class is the letter grade you give them. Although many districts supplement this letter grade in lower elementary grades with additional descriptions of learning progress (e.g., "Can print letters," "Can orally count to 10"), these supplementary descriptions typically fade out by the middle elementary grades and are nonexistent at the middle and high school levels, replaced by a single grade. All too often this single grade becomes a symbol of frustration for many students who can't compete successfully in our classrooms.

Most of you who have made it this far in your academic careers haven't experienced what it is like to struggle and fail repeatedly in academic subjects. Or if you have struggled, your efforts were usually limited to a single subject or area. Unfortunately, a significant portion of our students struggle to keep up with their peers in all content areas, and their grades show it. The dilemma is how to motivate these students within a system that requires you to accurately assess the learning progress they have made with a single grade. There are no easy solutions to this dilemma, but we'll explore the pros and cons of several options in the following section.

Teachers often consider a number of factors, in addition to achievement, when deciding on students' grades. These include student aptitude and ability, effort, and attitudes and compliance. However, experts advise against doing this because it sends mixed messages about what students actually learned and can do (Stiggins, 2008). In addition to confusing our message about achievement, letter grades that include other factors are not only hard to quantify (e.g., Mary *really* tried this term, but Johnny didn't) but also difficult to explain to parents (e.g., I gave your child an A because he's not very talented but tried really hard). The letter grade that you give students should accurately reflect their achievements in your classroom.

So teachers wanting to differentiate in their classrooms are stuck between a rock and a hard place when it comes to grading, and experts agree that there is no one "right way" to proceed when using report cards and letter grades with differentiated instruction (Mastroprieri & Scruggs, 2010).

However, guidelines exist to assist you as you wrestle with the problem (Stiggins, 2008; Tomlinson, 2005):

- **Thoroughly research and understand existing grading policies.** Your classroom is embedded within both a school and district, and you need to understand how your grading system fits within the larger context. Carefully examine the report card you'll be using; talk to other, more experienced teachers; and if still confused, talk to your principal about the district's expectations for your grading practices.

- **Align your grades with your learning objectives.** And be ready to explain both of these to students and parents. The first part of this explanation should occur continuously in your classroom as you introduce lessons and assessments. Students should know what you expect them to learn and how you'll assess them. Standards, when shared with students, can be valuable here. Also be ready to explain your classroom instruction to parents when you meet with them to discuss the grades their child received.

- **Consider criterion-referenced grading.** We discuss this topic in greater detail in Chapter 13, but for now we want to briefly contrast criterion- versus norm-referenced grading. Norm-referenced grading involves grading on the curve, which ultimately results in winners and losers because some students learn more and faster than others. Grading on the curve creates a stacked deck, with which slower students are destined to lose.

Criterion-referenced grading systems identify essential knowledge and skills, and evaluate students on their mastery of that content. In addition to minimizing between-student competition, criterion-referenced grading also presents a clearer picture of what students have actually accomplished.

- **Supplement letter grades with detailed descriptions of learning progress.** You might be limited to a single grade on a report card, but you can also augment this with a supplementary sheet that describes knowledge and skills mastered, content that is still being worked on, and future learning objectives. Although this takes additional effort, both parents and students benefit from knowing about the specifics of learning progress.

- **Consult with special educators when working with students with exceptionalities.** These students pose special grading challenges because of modifications to instruction and assessment that are often written into individualized education plans (IEPs). Fortunately, you are not alone in this process, and you can utilize the expertise of special educators who have wrestled with these issues before.

Differentiated grading is a thorny topic with no clear answers. As you work to differentiate the instruction in your classrooms, grading becomes a complex issue that affects both you and your students. We hope the information in this section will provide you with the professional knowledge to adapt your assessment procedures to meet the learning needs of all your students.

Summary

Understanding Differentiated Instruction

Differentiated instruction is proactive, student centered, and assessment-based and blends whole-group instruction with both group and individual teaching. Teachers differentiate in three major ways: by varying the content they present to students, by adapting instructional methods, and by designing assessment procedures that meet the needs of all students.

Planning for Differentiating Instruction

Teachers can help accommodate the diversity in their students by differentiating instruction. Instruction can be differentiated by varying the time available for learning, the materials and resources provided, learning activities, or objectives. Technology can also be a valuable tool for differentiation, with adaptive tutorials providing practice and feedback that is geared to each student's individual needs.

Instructional Strategies to Differentiate Instruction

Grouping is a common strategy used to differentiate instruction in classrooms. Advocates claim that it allows teachers to customize instruction to the learning needs of a particular group of students. Critics counter that it often results in lowered expectations, subpar instruction for lower-ability groups, and lowered achievement. Teachers are cautioned to be flexible in their grouping practices and to continually monitor their instruction for high expectations and quality instruction.

Strategy instruction is a second way to differentiate instruction. Frequently lower-ability students fail to use effective learning strategies when they study. Effective teachers help students learn these strategies through systematic instruction that explains the skill, models it in practice, and provides comprehensive practice and feedback.

Peer tutoring provides another way to differentiate instruction. Cross-age tutoring uses older students to help younger ones; same-age peer tutoring uses students in the same class to help each other. Structure is essential for effective peer tutoring; student work sheets provide a focused instructional agenda for both tutor and tutees.

The Challenge of Assessment in Diverse Classrooms

Assessment presents a major instructional challenge for teachers wanting to differentiate their instruction. Student diversity makes it more difficult for teachers to obtain an accurate picture of student learning progress. Teachers can accommodate learner diversity by providing practice with test-taking skills, being sensitive to language and content that might be confusing to learners from different cultures, discussing test items after students have responded to them, and making special provisions for nonnative English speakers in administering and scoring tests.

Grading in differentiated classrooms presents another challenge to teachers. The primary function of grading is communication, but this function often conflicts with motivating students. In their efforts to differentiate their grading practices teachers need to be aware of school and district policies and align their grades with their learning objectives.

$\mathcal{I}$mportant Concepts

Between-class ability grouping (p. 392)

Cross-age tutoring (p. 396)

Joplin plan (p. 392)

Mastery learning (p. 385)

Multi-ability tasks (p. 388)

Peer tutoring (p. 395)

Reciprocal tutoring (p. 397)

Same-age peer tutoring (p. 396)

Team assisted individualization (p. 385)

Tracking (p. 392)

Universal design (p. 382)

Within-class grouping (p. 392)

$\mathcal{P}$reparing for Your Licensure Exam

In this chapter you read about different ways that teachers differentiate instruction in their classrooms. Read the following case study, and answer the questions that follow.

After reading this case, go to the Book Specific Resources tab in MyEducationLab, select your text, select *Preparing for Your Licensure Exam* under Chapter 12 to complete the questions that accompany the case and receive feedback on your responses.

Kari Statler sits, taking notes, alongside the seven other new teachers hired at John F. Kennedy Middle School, a large urban school serving a diverse and often at-risk student population. The assistant principal is going over statewide procedures for testing students in the different content areas. In addition she describes how this school is adapting the curriculum to align with state standards. The meeting concludes with a discussion of the new parental involvement program, which asks students to accompany their parents to parent-teacher conferences in order to explain their grades on report cards and sometimes translate for their parents.

Back in her room Kari looks at the stack of books on her desk. "Whew, this is going to be a busy year," she thinks to herself. "All I keep hearing is tests, tests, tests. First the district, then the state, and maybe even a new one by the English department. Hmm, I had all these great ideas about teaching creative writing to students, but now it looks like all they want me to teach is grammar and punctuation. I can't do just that. My kids deserve more than that. They'll learn punctuation and grammar, but they'll also learn to write—and maybe even to enjoy it. I know they can do both, and that's my goal for the year—everyone writing clearly, with correct punctuation and grammar—and liking it besides!" A smile crosses her face.

The first week is a whirlwind of students, bells, and forms to fill out. By the second week, Kari has settled into an instructional routine. Every day begins with a short assignment to assess the content discussed the day before. Students grade their own papers, and Kari stresses the need for student honesty and responsibility. When the grading is complete, Kari asks for a show of hands to see how well everyone did. She also collects the papers so she can analyze them for any individual or group patterns or trends and so that she can adjust her instruction if necessary.

Before she begins her unit on writing, she administers a major pretest on basics of writing, such as sentence and paragraph structure, as well as grammar and punctuation. She has decided during her planning that the skills on the pretest are ones that all her students need to learn. However, she also wants to provide her students with choices in terms of the topics they write about and the writing projects they work on in groups.

When she scores the pretest, she finds an enormous range in students' knowledge of writing basics and mechanics. Some can write and punctuate grammatically correct paragraphs, whereas others are struggling to put words together in coherent sentences. This is discouraging.

Over the weekend Kari regroups and thinks about different ways she can accommodate differences in her students' background knowledge. She decides some need a crash mini-course in writing mechanics, but others are ready to begin the original unit she planned. To keep them all together in the unit she plans to give her advanced students alternate activities they can work on while she works with her struggling students. These involve reading different short stories that they select from a book of readings and working together with another student to write a report on the stories.

On Monday she gathers the struggling students together at the front of the room and uses direct instruction to teach basic rules of grammar and punctuation. Students struggle, but Kari sticks with it, and after two weeks she believes the whole class is ready to focus on writing.

To begin her unit on writing, she passes out two paragraphs, one clearly written and the other not. She asks students to pair up and analyze the two, looking for similarities and differences. She strategically pairs weaker with stronger students to take advantage of stronger students' greater background knowledge. In the whole-class discussion that follows Kari uses interactive questioning to establish the need for a topic sentence, supporting sentences that relate to the topic, and a summarizing sentence that pulls together all the related ideas in the paragraph.

Next, Kari has each student write a paragraph on his or her favorite subject in school. Students write these on clear transparencies, which Kari collects and displays anonymously for the class to evaluate. "So far, so good," Kari thinks as she circulates among her working students.

Questions for Analysis

1. How did Kari attempt to differentiate her instruction during planning? What else might she have done during this process?

2. What did Kari do to differentiate her instruction? What other strategies might she have tried to differentiate her instruction?

3. Which of the three major instructional strategies for differentiating instruction—grouping, strategy instruction, and peer tutoring—did Kari employ?

4. Focus on the lesson Kari taught to begin her unit on writing. How did she differentiate instruction in that lesson? What else could she have done to differentiate her instruction?

Discussion Questions

1. Of the methods described for differentiating instruction, which are the most teacher labor intensive? Least teacher labor intensive? What implications does this have for your teaching?

2. How are tutorial programs different from regular instructional programs? What obstacles do you anticipate in using technology as an individualization tool? What could you do to eliminate or minimize these obstacles?

3. Of the three major instructional strategies listed to accommodate diversity—grouping, strategy instruction, and peer tutoring—which have the most positive long-term potential for students? Least positive potential? Why?

4. How would you respond to parents who raise concerns about their son or daughter being involved in peer tutoring, either as a tutor or student?

5. What are major advantages and disadvantages of grading on the curve? For using criterion-referenced grading?

6. Is differentiation easier or harder in self-contained elementary classrooms versus middle or high school classes in which teachers meet with students for a period each day? Why?

Portfolio Activities

1. *Planning for Differentiation: Teacher Perspectives.* Interview a teacher to investigate how the teacher plans for differentiation. Ask the following questions:

   a. How much diversity exists in the class, and what dimensions of diversity have the largest impact on teaching and learning?

   b. When the teacher plans, how does he or she take these differences into account?

   c. How does the teacher use assessment to adjust or adapt her planning?

   d. Of the different strategies for accommodating learning differences, which are the easiest to implement? Hardest to implement?

2. *Differentiating Strategies: Teacher Perspectives.* Interview a teacher to investigate the teacher's use of the following strategies to deal with differences in learning ability: (a) grouping, (b) strategy instruction, (c) peer tutoring, and (d) cooperative learning. Ask these questions:

   a. Are individual differences in learning ability or learning style a challenge for the teacher? Why or how?

   b. Does the teacher use any of the strategies mentioned in this book? Which ones work and why? Have any been tried that didn't work? Why didn't they work?

   c. Does the teacher employ any other strategies for differentiating instruction?

   How do you plan to differentiate instruction in your own classroom?

3. *Differentiating Instruction: Technology.* Observe a teacher for several class periods and then arrange to interview him or her about the use of technology to differentiate instruction. Ask the following questions:

   a. What kinds of technology are available in this classroom?

   b. Which forms of technology are most useful for instruction in general?

   c. Which forms of technology are most useful for differentiating instruction?

   d. What are the major obstacles to your using technology to differentiate instruction?

   e. If you could purchase one kind of technology to help you differentiate instruction in your classroom, what would it be, and how would you use it?

4. *Peer Tutoring.* Identify a classroom that is using peer tutoring. Observe a peer-tutoring session and analyze it in terms of the following dimensions:

   a. Goals

   b. Instructional materials

   c. Type of peer tutoring (e.g., cross-age or reciprocal)

   d. Training (you will have to interview the teacher for this)

   e. Teacher monitoring

   f. Teacher's evaluation of the process (a short interview will be needed)

   g. What suggestions do you have for making peer tutoring more effective?

5. *Differentiating Assessments.* Interview a teacher about how he or she differentiates assessment procedures. Ask the following questions:
   a. How important is it to differentiate procedures during assessment?
   b. What strategies do they use during assessment to differentiate their assessments?
   c. What are the major obstacles to doing more to differentiate assessment procedures?

6. *Grading.* Interview a teacher about the topic of differentiated grading. Ask the following questions:
   a. What are the school or district policies about differentiating grades?
   b. Does the teacher differentiate grades in his or her classroom? If so, how? If not, why?
   c. What are the major obstacles to differentiating grading practices in his or her classroom?
   d. What advice does he or she have for you in terms of differentiating grading practices?

To check your comprehension of the content covered in Chapter 12, go to the Book Specific Resources in MyEducationLab, select your text, and complete the Study Plan quiz. In addition to receiving feedback on your answers, a study plan will be generated from the quiz that will direct you to access Review, Practice, and Enrichment materials to enhance your understanding of chapter content.

Assessing Learning

Chapter Outline	Learning Objectives
	When you've completed your study of this chapter, you should be able to
Classroom assessment	1. Describe the functions performed by assessment and the characteristics of an effective assessment system.
■ Formal and informal assessment	
■ Functions of an assessment system	
■ Characteristics of effective assessment	
■ Teachers' assessment patterns	
Using assessment to promote learning	2. Explain how effective teachers prepare students for, administer, and analyze assessment results.
■ Preparing students	
■ Administering tests	
■ Examining results	
■ Research on classroom testing: Implications for teachers	
Exploring Diversity:	
Effective assessment with learners from diverse backgrounds	
Alternative assessment	3. Describe how alternative assessment can be used in classrooms.
■ Performance assessment	
■ Portfolio assessment	
Designing an assessment system	4. Design an effective assessment system for your classroom.
■ Standards, accountability, and assessment	
■ Grades and grading	
■ Communication	
Technology and Teaching:	
Using technology in assessment	

Effective teaching involves careful planning, classroom management, and the use of different instructional strategies to help students learn. However, one important question remains unanswered: "How do we know if students are actually learning in our classrooms?" In this chapter we attempt to answer that question by examining traditional and alternative assessment, teachers' assessment practices, grading, homework, and communication with parents, all of which make up the topic of classroom assessment. As you read the following case studies, look for ways the teachers used assessment to promote learning in their classrooms.

Steve Vockel's fourth graders are working on applying rules for adding *-ing* to words. After putting several words on the board, Steve circulates among the students, making periodic comments.

"Check this one again, Nancy," he says when he sees that she has written *jumpping* on her paper. Later he comments at lunch, "My kids just can't seem to get the rule straight. Either they forget about the long vowel so they double the consonant on a word like *blow* or they forget about two consonants at the end of a word like *jump* and double the *p*. I don't know what to do about it. If I spend more time on it, we won't get other material covered."

Terry Graham gives her high school chemistry class a one- or two-problem quiz every other day. As she scores students' answers to a problem in which the mass of an element in grams is converted to moles and number of atoms, she thinks, "I need to do some more of these." "They can convert moles to grams, but they can't go the other way."

Marianne Generette's middle school math students are passing their pre-algebra homework in to her. They had exchanged papers, scored the homework, and gone over problems causing difficulty.

"How many got all the problems right?" she asks the class.

"Good!" she responds to the show of hands. "You get this stuff. Remember that we have a test on this whole chapter on Friday, but for now we're going to move on to subtraction of integers."

In each of these classrooms the teacher was gathering information about his or her students' achievement and progress. A seatwork assignment for Steve, a quiz for Terry, and homework in Marianne's case provided information to make instructional decisions, such as moving to a new topic in Marianne's class. Periodically, even the conscientious gathering of data results in uncertainty, which was Steve's problem. He was caught in the dilemma of concluding that his students didn't understand the rule, but at the same time feeling the need to move on.

 ## Classroom Assessment

Classroom assessment *includes all the processes involved in making decisions about students' learning progress* (Nitko, 2004; McMillan, 2007), and it's the focus of this chapter.

Assessment includes a range of processes including observing students as they work, listening to their answers in discussions, and examining the results of teacher-made and standardized tests. It also includes alternative assessments, which directly measure student performance through real-life tasks, such as having fourth graders write a letter, observing science students complete a lab activity, or seeing technology students design and use a spreadsheet. It involves decisions as well, such as assigning grades or choosing to reteach a difficult topic. *A teacher's* **assessment system** *includes all of these elements and is designed to gather information about students' learning progress.*

myeducationlab
The Power of Classroom Practice
www.myeducationlab.com

To view a video clip of a teacher using assessment in her decision making, go to the Book Specific Resources tab in MyEducationLab, select your text, select Video Examples under Chapter 13, and then click on *Using Assessment in Decision Making*.

Formal and Informal Assessment

Teachers gather information continually when they listen to students' answers, notice uncertain looks on their faces, and see that some aren't paying attention. These are **informal assessments**, *which are information gathered in incidental ways* (Black, Harrison, Lee, Marshall, & William, 2004). **Formal assessment**, in comparison, *is the process of gathering information in a systematic way*, such as constructing and giving tests, quizzes, and homework to determine how much students have learned.

Both forms of assessment are important to teachers because they provide different kinds of information. Decisions about grading and reporting should be based on formal assessments, but many of the decisions teachers make on an everyday basis are based on informal assessments. Deciding to call on an inattentive student, for example, is based on observing the student's behavior—an informal measurement.

Functions of an Assessment System

Before we deal with the specifics of assessment, we need to understand the different functions that an assessment system performs. These can be divided into two broad categories—instructional and institutional.

We assess students to promote learning, which is its most important instructional function (Stiggins, 2008). The relationship between learning and assessment is clear and consistent. Students learn more in classes in which assessment is a regular part of classroom routines, particularly when assessments are frequent and provide feedback to learners (Brookhart, 2002; Shepard, 2001).

The reasons for this link are easy to understand. Practice and feedback are essential components of effective teaching, and assignments, quizzes, tests, and alternative assessments give students opportunities to demonstrate and receive feedback about their understanding. This feedback is helpful both to them and to other interested parties, such as their teachers, parents, and school and district administrators.

For teachers, assessments provide information about the effectiveness of their instruction. If students are not learning, you need to do something differently; if they are, you can move forward, building on this knowledge base.

Assessment results also provide valuable information for parents, allowing them to make decisions about homework, television, and a host of other school-related issues. Research confirms what we intuitively know—a supportive home environment including a commitment to homework and restriction of television contributes to learning (Berk, 2010).

In addition to instructional functions, assessment also fulfills institutional needs. Schools and districts need to know how their students perform on standards-based assessments. This is especially important in this era of standards and accountability, which requires both schools and teachers to document what students have learned. Assessment information also allows schools and school districts to adapt instructional practices to make them more effective.

Characteristics of Effective Assessment

Effective assessment in the real world of classroom teaching has three essential features: it must be *valid*, *reliable*, and *practical*. To be useful, while remaining professionally sound, teachers' assessments must possess all three features.

Validity   **Validity** *is the degree to which the assessment measures what it is supposed to measure.* It describes the logical link between the information you gather and the decisions you make from that information (Miller, Linn, & Gronlund, 2009).

One way of thinking about validity is to ask, "Is the assessment consistent with the specific goals being assessed?" The opposite is surprisingly common. We have all had teachers who taught one thing and then tested something else. This not only upsets students but also makes the test invalid.

Another way of thinking of validity is in terms of **instructional alignment** (Bransford et al., 2000; Anderson & Krathwohl, 2001) *which means that instruction is congruent with the teacher's goals and tests are congruent with both.* In the case studies at the beginning of the chapter Steve's assignment would be aligned if one of his language arts goals was for students to learn how to add *-ing* endings to words. In a similar way the quizzes and assignments of the other two teachers would be aligned if they matched their goals and instruction. When a logical match exists between measurement procedures and what was intended and taught, we have both alignment and validity.

Two factors detract from validity. In attempts to simplify their work, teachers tend to assess students on the basis of characteristics that are easily measured, such as their behavior and the number of assignments they complete rather than the quality of the work, the difficulty of the assignment, or the appropriate weight of one assignment compared to another (Stiggins, 2008). Teachers also tend to fix on initial impressions of students, which may be based on inaccurate information, and then use additional information to corroborate their initial impressions (Good & Brophy, 2008). When this happens, validity suffers.

One way to guard against these tendencies is to design and implement a systematic assessment system, which leads us to the concept *reliability.*

Reliability   We are teaching a concept and we ask students to give examples to apply the concept to a new situation. A volunteer raises her hand and provides an excellent example. We ask another student and get the same result. We do it once more, and again the student provides a very good example. We then conclude that the entire class understands the concept. However, we have heard from only three students, and further, they were volunteers. We have little idea about the class's overall understanding and particularly that of less able or more reluctant responders. Our conclusion easily could be invalid, because it was based on unreliable information.

Reliability *describes the extent to which measurements are consistent* (Miller et al., 2009). Because we didn't get information from all students, consistency was impossible, so the results were unreliable. Unreliable measurements cannot be valid even if the measurements are consistent with the teacher's goals. A bathroom scale that gives a different reading each time we step on it (assuming our weight doesn't change) would be an example of an unreliable instrument.

How common is the tendency to use unreliable assessments in teachers' decision making? Research indicates that it is more common than we would expect (Stiggins, 2008). As teachers make the routine decisions necessary to keep a class or lesson moving, they tend to gather group data; that is, they tend to rely on the responses and nonverbal behavior of a subset of the class for feedback as the basis for deciding to repeat instruction or to move on to the next topic. A systematic attempt to gather assessment data from *all* students, and not just volunteers, makes the process more reliable and valid.

Practicality   In addition to being valid and reliable an assessment system also needs to be practical. Assessment is one component of effective teaching, but it cannot take so much time and energy that other components are compromised. Experts estimate that teachers spend one-fourth to one-third of their professional time on assessment (Stiggins, 2004). Elementary teachers are responsible for reading, math, science, social studies, spelling, language arts, and sometimes art, music, and physical education. Middle, junior high, and secondary teachers typically have five sections of 25 to 35 students a day, often with two or more preparations. Teachers are busy people and can't use assessment procedures that aren't practical and efficient.

The assessments that the teachers in our introductory case studies used were economical. Steve quickly wrote the words on the board and easily scored the responses. Terry took only minutes to prepare her chemistry problem, and Marianne had the students score their own papers. In each case the assessment took little valuable instructional time and required minimal teacher time and energy.

Teachers' Assessment Patterns

How do effective assessment practices vary from grade level to grade level? These variations are important because they influence learning and motivation as well as cognitive development (Black et al., 2004). Teachers of elementary students typically

- Rely more heavily on performance assessments, whereby teachers gather and evaluate samples of students' work, such as pieces of students' writing or solutions to problems.

- Depend heavily on commercially prepared and published tests, which help them simplify the demands on their time.

- Include affective goals, such as "Works and plays well with others." Typical kindergarten progress reports, for example, will have a third or more of the categories devoted to personal or social growth (Guskey, 2002).

In the upper grades and high school, assessment patterns change:

- Teachers rely less on published tests, choosing instead to prepare their own.

- Teachers depend more heavily on tests than on performance measures for their assessments.

- Objective tests, such as multiple choice and fill-in-the-blanks, become more popular than subjective measures, such as essay tests.

- Emphasis on grades for cognitive performance increases, with correspondingly less emphasis given to affective goals.

Let's examine these patterns in more detail.

The lower elementary grades are characterized by considerable agreement about essential content and skills. Commercially prepared tests are useful because a high degree of consensus about the curriculum exists. Later, the curriculum becomes more differentiated and idiosyncratic. One history teacher's approach and emphasis will be different from another's, for example, so commercially prepared tests no longer meet each teacher's needs. As a result teachers tend to customize the assessment process by preparing their own tests.

The press for simplification and time-efficient assessments exists for all teachers; they use assessment items that are easy and quick to score. Analysis of teacher-made tests (Stiggins, 2008) found the following:

1. Essay questions were used infrequently.

2. The most frequently used item format was short answer, such as

Which two planets in our solar system have orbits that overlap?

What is the primary climate region in Spain?

3. Matching items were the next most commonly used by teachers.

4. Most test items measured *knowledge* of facts, terms, rules, or principles, with few items measuring students' ability to apply this knowledge.

5. Once items are constructed, teachers tend to reuse them without analysis and revision.

There are two primary reasons for these patterns. The first is the need for efficiency and simplicity, and the second is teachers' lack of knowledge about effective assessment procedures and feelings of inadequacy about their assessment capabilities (Kahn, 2000; Stiggins, 2008).

With these factors in mind, the research findings are not surprising. Teachers write recall questions because they are the easiest to write and score. When the efforts of constructing and scoring items are combined, the easiest formats to use are short answer and matching. Essay questions, although easy to construct, are extremely difficult to score, and teachers are notoriously inconsistent in comparing one student's essay to another's (Stiggins, 2008). Evidence indicates that factors such as grammar, punctuation, and even penmanship can influence essay scoring (Airasian & Russell, 2008; Haladyna & Ryan, 2001).

In contrast, multiple-choice items are easy to score, but good ones are difficult to construct; true-false questions, appearing easy to prepare on the surface, are actually very demanding if prepared well. This, in combination with the widespread criticism of the format (i.e., the ease of guessing), explains why true-false questions are not widely used.

In addition to greater use of teacher-made tests, in the upper grades there is also greater emphasis on grades and accountability (Airasian & Russell, 2008; Stiggins, 2008). Often at the lower levels, formal grades (e.g., A, B, C) are replaced with descriptive statements (e.g., "Can print all the letters of the alphabet clearly," or "Can count from one to ten orally"). Later, more emphasis is placed on the accountability and comparison aspects of grading.

Assessment differences also exist across subject-matter areas. Teachers in science and social studies tend to use more objective assessments, whereas those in the language arts—including reading, writing, and speaking—make greater use of performance assessments. It is easier to make up objective items in more convergent areas, whereas skill areas lend themselves more to performance assessments.

Having examined teachers' assessment patterns, we turn now to ways that you can use both traditional and alternative assessments to promote learning. We begin with traditional assessments.

Using Assessment to Promote Learning

In this section we look at ways teachers can make testing more effective by preparing their students for tests, administering them, and analyzing the results. These strategies apply to any item format and content area, and most grade levels. To begin, let's look at a seventh-grade social studies teacher preparing his class for a unit test. His goals for the unit were for students to understand the concept *culture*, to apply it to various groups in Central America and Mexico, and to know basic facts about these countries.

Andy Robinson is finishing his unit on Mexico and Central America.

"Okay, everyone," Andy begins, "listen carefully, now. We're finishing our study of Central America and its cultural traditions, and we're having a test tomorrow."

"Oh, Mr. Robinson, do we have to?" Sheila groans in mock protest.

"How else will you know how much you've learned?" Andy smiles back at Sheila. "Just think. We have it tomorrow, I'll give it back to you on Friday, and I'll even give you the weekend off."

"ALL RIGHT!" the class shouts.

Andy holds up his hand to settle them down and continues, "Now, let's think about the test. First, let's talk about the individual items you'll encounter on the test; then, I'll give you an overview of the whole test. I'm going to ask you to think extra hard with some of the questions, but you've all been working hard, and I know you'll do well. Every time you've had a tough test, you've tried harder and done better."

He continues, "We've been comparing cultures, and I want you to get more practice in making those comparisons, plus I want you to keep working on writing clearly. Take a look at this," Andy says, displaying the following paragraphs on the overhead projector:

Read the description, and identify (in the example) the characteristics of culture that were discussed in class.

Jorge (pronounced HOR-hay) is a small Mexican boy who is growing up on a farm in the mountains outside Mexico City. He rises early and goes to the corner in his home that serves as a chapel for his morning prayers. He then breakfasts on a large meal of beans and corn tortillas made from the products of the family farm. His mother always asks him if the Virgin Mary gave him her blessings, and Jorge always says "yes" with a smile. Jorge walks to school a mile down the dusty road. He leaves as his father goes out to cultivate the corn that is the primary source of income for the family. Jorge's mother then milks the goats and turns the rich cream into delicious butter and cheese.

In the early afternoon, Jorge returns from school and talks with his family in their dialect, which is Spanish with some influence from the Mayans. As the day cools, Jorge often plays soccer with boys in the nearby village while his father strums his guitar and his mother hums the rhythmic Latin melodies they all love. They go to bed shortly after sunset to prepare for the next day.

"Read the example carefully, take out a piece of paper, and answer the question that is given in the directions," Andy continues after waiting for a few moments.

After about 10 minutes, Andy begins, "Someone tell me what they wrote as a response."

"It says in the example that they eat beans and tortillas, and we discussed the food a group eats as part of their culture," Karim responds.

"Yes, good, Karim," Andy praises. "Notice, everyone, that Karim didn't just say 'food,' but instead, identified the specific foods they eat in the example. This indicates that he is relating the information in the example to what we discussed in class."

The class continues, with students identifying religion, type of work, and recreation in Jorge's family as additional examples of culture.

"They're in good shape," Andy thinks as he listens to their analysis. He continues, "That's all very good. Now, on the test tomorrow, you're going to have to do something like this. Remember, when you write your responses, you're going to have to relate the example to ideas we have discussed in class, just as we did with Jorge and his family."

He continues, "You're also going to need to know different countries' climates, natural resources, and physical features, as well as be able to locate them on a map and identify their capitals. For example, what country is this?" he asks, pointing to an outline map of Nicaragua. "Miguel?"

"Nicaragua!" Miguel responds instantly.

"Give us another example," the class requests.

"Okay," Andy smiles and displays the following on the overhead:

We are about 17 degrees north of the equator and are about in the middle of this country. We are in the most populous country in Central America. Most of the people here are of Indian or mixed European and Indian descent. This description best fits:

a. Belize
b. Guatemala
c. Honduras
d. Mexico

"What is the answer? Marinda?" Andy asks.

"It's Guatemala," Marinda says nervously after some hesitation.

"Yes, excellent, Marinda!" Andy encourages, knowing that Marinda appears to be genuinely nervous in anticipating tests and frequently misses them, the following day producing a note saying she has been sick. "Now, tell us why it's Guatemala," Andy continues. "Sue?"

"First, 17 degrees only goes through sort of the middle of Guatemala and Belize," Sue responds.

"Also, Guatemala is the most populous country in Central America, and most of the people are of Indian descent," Martina adds.

"Now, I'd like to share with you an outline that I used in preparing the test. It should give you a clear picture of how to spend your study time." With that, he displays Figure 13.1 on an overhead.

Figure 13.1

Test Content Matrix

	TYPE OF ITEM
Facts about Countries:	Fill-in-the-blank
Capitals	Multiple choice
Climate	25 questions $\times$ 1 = 25 points
Natural Resources	
Physical Features	
Cultures of Countries	Short answer
	3 questions $\times$ 5 = 15 points
Cultures of Countries	Essay
	10 points

"Will the essay question be like the one we practiced on, Mr. Robinson?" asks Antonio.

"Good question. Yes, the same format, but I'll give you different information to work with," Andy answers, concluding his review.

Let's look now at what Andy did and relate this to what we know about effective assessment practices.

Preparing Students

As he prepared his students for the test, Andy did three things that helped his students achieve at their best: (1) he established positive expectations in his students as they prepared for the test, (2) he specified precisely what the test would cover, and (3) he gave them a chance to practice the kinds of skills they would be expected to demonstrate when they took the actual test. These factors work in combination to make our assessments both valid and reliable. Let's look at each now.

Positive teacher attitudes and expectations about a test are important both for motivation and performance (Schunk et al., 2008). Andy established high expectations when he said, "I know you'll do well. Every time you've had a tough test, you've tried harder and done better." Research examining two decades of studies on the relationship between expectations and performance concluded that teacher expectations can positively influence student test performance (Good & Brophy, 2008).

Specifying test content provides both information and security to students by outlining a structured set of content and skills to be mastered. Further, it can help reduce test anxiety. Andy specified skills students would have to demonstrate when he said he wanted them to practice making comparisons, and he provided structure when he said they would "need to know different countries' climate, natural resources, and physical features."

In addition he shared *an overview of the test, including major content to be covered and the types of items to be expected*. This outline, called a **table of specifications**, serves two functions. First, it helps teachers systematically plan their tests. A cross grid with content on one axis and item type or level (e.g., high versus low or knowledge versus application) on the other ensures that the test accurately reflects the teacher's goals and instruction. Aligning the test with instruction increases validity.

Just describing what students need to know may not provide sufficient guidance for some students (particularly those in middle school or younger), so Andy did not stop at that point. In addition he illustrated his overview with sample exercises that paralleled those students would experience on the test. He offered a practice essay item and also provided practice with a multiple-choice format. Ensuring that students understand a particular format is important. When students take a test, two things are always being measured—their understanding of the content on the test *and* their ability to respond to the format being used. If the second task interferes with the first, the validity of the test is reduced.

Practice with anticipated assessment formats can increase students' test-taking skills, which in turn can reduce the impact of the format on students' performance. These positive effects are especially powerful with young and minority children.

Reducing Test Anxiety   *Test anxiety is a relatively stable, unpleasant reaction to testing situations that lowers performance.* Experts suggest that test anxiety consists of two components (Schunk et al., 2008). The *emotional component* can include increased pulse rate, dry mouth, feelings of fright, and even "going blank." Its *cognitive or worry* *component* involves thoughts about failure, concerns about parents being upset, or being embarrassed by a low score. As they're taking a test, test-anxious students tend to be preoccupied with test difficulty, which interferes with their ability to focus on individual items.

Test anxiety increases when

- High pressure to succeed exists.
- Time limits are imposed.
- Tests contain unfamiliar items or formats.
- Learners perceive the content or test as difficult.

Unannounced tests and "pop" quizzes have an especially adverse effect on test anxiety.

Teachers can help reduce test anxiety, particularly with respect to the worry component, by doing the following (Schunk et al., 2008):

- Avoid comparing students to one another, such as announcing test scores and grades.
- Use criterion-referenced noncompetitive measures. (We discuss criterion referencing later in the chapter.)
- Increase the frequency of quizzes and tests.
- Teach students test-taking skills.
- Discuss test content and procedures prior to testing.
- Give clear directions and be sure students understand the test.
- Provide students with enough time to take tests.

Administering Tests

To illustrate effective test administration procedures, let's again join Andy and his students.

Andy surveys his classroom before his students arrive, and even though his room is quite crowded, he moves the desks as far apart as possible and has them ready when students walk in. He opens a window and then changes his mind, reacting to the noise of a lawn mower outside.

As the students pour into the room, he directs them to their seats, asking for their attention. When they are all looking at him, he instructs them to clear everything off their desks, as he passes out the tests.

"Tear the last sheet off the back of the test and write your name on it. Do that right now. Now, as you take the test, put all your answers on this sheet. When you're finished, turn the test over, and I'll come around and pick it up. Then, begin the assignment written on the board. It's due on Tuesday. If anyone gets too warm as you're working, raise your hand, and I'll turn on the fan," he continues, referring to the large floor fan at the front of the room.

"Work carefully on the test, now," he says with a smile. "You're all well prepared, and I know you will do your best. You have the whole period, so you should have plenty of time."

Andy stands in the front corner of the room, scanning the class as his students work. As he watches, he notices Marinda periodically looking out the window for several seconds at a time. Finally, he goes over to her desk, looks at her paper, and whispers as he touches her shoulder, "It looks like you're moving along okay. Try and concentrate on the test a little harder now, and you'll do fine."

> Suddenly, the intercom breaks into the silence. "Mr. Robinson," the voice says, "Mrs. Brown [the principal] needs to see you for a moment. Could you come down to the office?"
>
> "I'll come down at the end of the period," Andy replies to the box. "I'm in the middle of a test right now."
>
> "Thank you," the voice responds, as the intercom goes silent.
>
> As students finish their papers, Andy moves to their desks, picking up the tests, and stacking them on a table in front of the room. Students then begin the assignment Andy referred to just before they began taking the test.

Now, let's look at how Andy handled the administration of the test. He got to the room early and arranged the seating in advance to ensure adequate distance between desks, and he arranged the overall physical environment to minimize distractions, such as the lawn mower outside. Distractions can affect test performance, especially for younger and low-ability students. Teachers administering standardized tests often deal with this problem by hanging a sign on the closed door.

Andy waited until he had everyone's attention and then gave specific directions for taking the test, collecting the papers, and doing an assignment after finishing. As students progressed with the test, Andy carefully monitored their behavior. When he noticed that Marinda seemed distracted, he went to her, offered encouragement, and urged her to increase her concentration.

As the test progressed, he stayed in the room and refused to go to the main office until after students were finished. Unfortunately, cheating is part of classroom reality, and some students will cheat if the opportunity presents itself. However, external factors, such as the teacher's leaving the room and the emotional climate of the class, contribute more to student cheating than the inherent characteristics of the students themselves (Finn & Frone, 2004).

Examining Results

To see how Andy Robinson used the results of his test to promote learning, let's return to his class once more.

> Friday morning, students file into the room and ask as they enter, "Do you have our tests finished yet?"
>
> "You know, I do," Andy responds. "I was up half the night scoring them."
>
> "How did we do?"
>
> "Mostly well, but there were a few problems, and I want to go over them this morning, so when you have another test it won't happen again," he replies, quickly handing the students back their tests.
>
> "What does this mean that you wrote on my paper, 'You identified *recreation* as a part of culture, but you didn't say what it was in the example'?" Sondra asks from the back of the room.
>
> "Remember on Wednesday we said that you needed to identify both the characteristic and an example of it from the description, like soccer and music from the example with Jorge that we analyzed," Andy responds. "Antonio swam, dived, and fished, and you needed to say that in your essay. We'll discuss the essay question in a bit, but let's start from the beginning of the test."
>
> "A number of you had trouble with item 15," he continues. "Many of you took choice c. What is the correct answer? . . . Ann?"

Andy then discusses several of the items that gave students problems, in each case describing what is wrong with the incorrect choices. When he discusses the essay question in detail, he finishes by saying, "I have placed two exceptionally good essay responses on the board for everyone to examine. We'll discuss these tomorrow. I will be here after school today and tomorrow morning before class. If you have any other questions, come and see me either time."

With that, he gathers up the tests, putting his original copy with notes for revising several of the items in a special file folder, and begins his lesson for the day.

Let's see how Andy's actions both promoted learning and made his job easier. First, he scored and returned the test the following day; second, he discussed the test; and finally, he made positive comments about students' performance. All of these actions have positive effects on achievement.

Students need to receive feedback on their work, whether it is a test, quiz, or homework, and this feedback should occur as soon as possible. In discussing the test, Andy carefully reviewed the items students had most commonly missed, providing corrective feedback in each case. In discussing objective items, incorrect answers, if missed by a large number of students, should be explained (Miller et al., 2008). Correct items can be skipped over unless the information is important for later study. This uses class time efficiently.

For the essay questions, Andy provided specific feedback in the cases of incorrect or incomplete answers. In addition, he displayed examples of excellent responses (with the students' names removed) for students to read. Finally, Andy made positive comments about the general performance of the class on the test.

Research on Classroom Testing: Implications for Teachers

Research on effective testing has several implications for teachers:

1. Test thoroughly and often. Be certain that adequate information is gathered about *each student.* When used properly, paper-and-pencil tests provide an important source of information for teachers.

2. Be certain that instruction and testing are aligned; the topics and content emphasized in class should be the same ones emphasized on the test.

3. During instruction and review sessions, give students a chance to practice with the kinds of items they will encounter on the test.

4. After you give a test, hand it back to students as soon as possible, carefully review commonly missed items, and then collect the copies again. This saves teacher time and energy. Teachers don't have time to continually create new test items; the learning derived from review of the test comes primarily from the discussion and not from the students' having the tests available for further review.

5. File a copy of the test, write notes on the copy, and revise the items that may have been misleading.

6. Choose an objective format, such as multiple choice, for outcomes that can be effectively measured with these items. Use essay items when you want to measure students' ability to organize and present information or make and defend an argument. Keep essay items relatively short and describe clearly what the essay should contain (Stiggins, 2008).

7. Establish positive expectations for students as they anticipate the test. Tests need to be constructed so that students have an opportunity to demonstrate what they've learned. The key is to establish positive expectations and then manage to have the students meet them, which, in turn, reinforces similar expectations for subsequent tests (Brophy, 2004).

This concludes our discussion of the effective use of traditional assessments. In the next section we examine alternative assessments, which can provide teachers with different types of assessment information.

Exploring Diversity

Effective Assessment with Learners from Diverse Backgrounds

As you've seen in earlier chapters, learner diversity influences teaching and learning in a number of ways. The process of assessment is one of the most important.

The current reform movement, with its emphasis on standards, has heightened awareness of the challenges of educating students from diverse backgrounds. The problem is particularly acute in urban settings, where diversity is the most pronounced (Armour-Thomas, 2004).

Student diversity influences classroom assessment in three ways. First, learners from diverse backgrounds may lack experience with general testing procedures, different test formats, and test-taking strategies. Second, they may not fully understand that assessments promote learning and instead view them as punitive. Third, because most assessments are strongly language based, language may be an obstacle (Garcia, 2005).

The following recommendations respond to these issues (Popham, 2005):

■ Attempt to create a learning-focused classroom environment, emphasizing learning over performance. Emphasize that assessments promote learning and provide feedback and are used to measure learning progress.

■ Deemphasize grades, and keep all assessment results private. Establish a rule that students may not share their scores and grades with one another. (This is difficult to enforce, but it is a symbolic gesture and an attempt to protect students who want to succeed but face peer pressure not to.)

■ Increase the number of assessments, and provide detailed and corrective feedback for all items. Encourage students to ask questions about test items, and when they answer incorrectly, ask them to explain their answers. Emphasize that mistakes are part of learning, and present students with evidence of their learning progress.

■ Drop one or two quizzes a marking period for purposes of grading. This practice reduces test anxiety and communicates to students that you are "on their side" and want them to succeed. It also contributes to a positive classroom climate.

■ Make provisions for nonnative English speakers by allowing extra time and providing extra help with language aspects of your assessments.

Of these suggestions, feedback and discussion are the most important. Although important in all classrooms, they are essential for effective assessment with learners from diverse backgrounds. Students' explanations for their answers often reveal misconceptions, which you can then address. Feedback from students can also help you identify content bias in your questions (Popham, 2005). For example, some students may have limited experiences with electric appliances such as an iron or vacuum cleaner, summertime activities such as camping and hiking, musical instruments such as a banjo, or transportation such as cable cars (Cheng, 1987). If assessment items require knowledge or experiences with these items, you are measuring both the intended topic and students' general knowledge, which detracts from validity. The only way you can identify these potential sources of bias is to discuss assessment items afterward. Then you can revise and more carefully word your assessments to help eliminate bias.

The likelihood of content bias is greater if you have nonnative English speakers in your classes. Suggestions for supporting these students include the following (Abedi et al., 2004):

- Provide extra time to take tests.
- Allow a translation glossary or dictionary to be used during the test.
- Read directions aloud. (It is even better if you can read the students the directions in their native languages.)
- Allow them to take the test at a different time, and read it to them, clarifying misunderstandings when possible.

The primary function of assessment in general, and with learners from diverse backgrounds in particular, is to provide evidence of increasing competence. Teacher sensitivity to potential obstacles to accurate assessments communicates teacher support for all students' learning.

Alternative Assessment

Although traditional assessment formats remain popular, they are being increasingly criticized for the following reasons:

- Traditional testing focuses on knowledge and recall of information.
- Traditional tests provide little insight into the way learners are thinking.
- Traditional tests don't assess students' ability to apply their understanding to real-world problems. (French, 2003)

In response to these criticisms, **alternative assessments** that *directly measure student performance through "real-life" tasks* are being emphasized (Frey & Schmitt, 2005; Popham, 2005).

Examples of alternative assessments include

- Writing an editorial for the school newspaper
- Compiling a portfolio of writing samples produced over the year with student evaluations of their strengths and weaknesses
- Designing and constructing a study desk in a woodworking class
- Writing and illustrating a book for young readers

In addition to products, such as the editorial, the desk, or the book, teachers also want to examine learners' thinking as they use alternative assessments.

Let's look at the two most widely used forms of alternative assessments, *performance assessments* and *portfolios.*

Performance Assessment

A middle school science teacher notices that her students have difficulty designing and conducting simple science experiments such as determining which brand of aspirin dissolves faster.

A health teacher reads in a professional journal that the biggest problem people have in applying first aid is not the mechanics per se, but knowing how to apply these mechanics in real-life situations. In an attempt to address this problem, the teacher has a periodic unannounced "catastrophe" day. Students entering the classroom encounter a catastrophe victim with an unspecified injury. In each case they had to first diagnose the problem and then apply first aid interventions.

These teachers are using performance assessments to gather information about their students' thinking. **Performance assessments** *ask students to demonstrate their knowledge and skill by carrying out an activity or producing a product* (Airasian & Russell, 2008). What can you do to make your performance assessments both valid and reliable? The answer to this question is found during the planning of performance assessments.

Designing Performance Assessments   Experts identify four steps in designing performance assessments (Miller et al., 2009): (1) specifying desired outcomes, (2) selecting the focus of evaluation, (3) structuring the evaluation setting, and (4) designing evaluation procedures.

Specifying Desired Outcomes.   The first step in designing any assessment is to develop a clear idea of what you're trying to measure. A clear description of the skill or process helps students understand what is required and assists the teacher in designing appropriate instruction. An example in the area of speech is outlined in Figure 13.2.

Figure 13.2

Performance Outcomes in Speech

Oral Presentation
_____ 1. Stands naturally.
_____ 2. Maintains eye contact.
_____ 3. Uses gestures effectively.
_____ 4. Uses clear language.
_____ 5. Has adequate volume.
_____ 6. Speaks at an appropriate rate.
_____ 7. Topics are well organized.
_____ 8. Maintains interest of the group.

(Adapted from Linn & Gronlund, 2000)

Selecting the Focus of Evaluation.   Having specified performance outcomes, you next decide whether the assessment will focus on processes or products. Processes are often the initial focus, with a shift to products after procedures are mastered (Miller et al., 2009). Examples of both processes and products as components of performance assessments are found in Table 13.1.

Structuring the Evaluation Setting.   The value of performance assessments lies in their link to realistic tasks; ultimately, teachers want students to apply the skill in the real world. Time, expense, and safety may prevent realistic measurement procedures, however, and intermediate steps might be necessary.

For example, in driver education the goal is to produce safe drivers. However, putting students in heavy traffic to assess how well they function behind the wheel is both unrealistic and dangerous. Alternate assessment options that vary the amount or degree of realism exist. For example, at the low realism/high safety end of the continuum students can respond to written cases or use a simulator. At the high realism/low safety end of the performance continuum they can actually drive, first starting in parking lots and quiet roads, and ultimately in rush hour city traffic.

Designing Evaluation Procedures.   The final step in creating performance assessments is to design evaluation criteria. Reliability, or consistency, in grading across different performances is a primary concern. Well-defined criteria in the form of scoring rubrics, similar to those used with essay items, increase both reliability and validity (Stiggins, 2008). Clearly written criteria provide models of excellence and performance targets for students. Effective criteria have four elements:

1. One or more dimensions that serve as a basis for assessing student performance

2. A description of each dimension

3. A scale of values on which each dimension is rated

4. Definitions of each value on the scale

Let's look now at three alternate ways to evaluate learner performance: (1) systematic observation, (2) checklists, and (3) rating scales.

Table 13.1   **Processes and Products as Components of Performance**

Content Area	Product	Process
Math	Correct answer	Problem-solving steps leading to the correct solution
Music	Performance of a work on an instrument	Correct fingering and breathing that produces the performance
English composition	Essay, term paper, or composition	Preparation of drafts and thought processes that produce the product
Word processing	Letter or copy of final draft	Proper stroking and techniques for presenting the paper
Science	Explanation for the outcomes of a demonstration	Thought processes involved in preparing the explanation

Figure 13.3

Checklist for Assessing Inquiry

_____ **1.** Stated problem
_____ **2.** Stated hypotheses
_____ **3.** Identified controlled variables
_____ **4.** Identified independent and dependent variables
_____ **5.** Makes three measurements of dependent variables
_____ **6.** Organizes data in a chart or table
_____ **7.** Assesses hypotheses in written form

Systematic Observation   **Systematic observations** *involve describing learners' performances based on preset criteria.* For example, a science teacher attempting to teach her students inquiry skills might identify the following criteria:

1. Specified the problem

2. Stated hypotheses

3. Identified variables

4. Gathered, organized, and displayed data

5. Used data to assess the hypotheses

The teacher's notes as she observed students designing experiments would then be based on the criteria, increasing their reliability and providing feedback for students.

Checklists   **Checklists** *are written descriptions of dimensions that must be present in an acceptable performance* and extend systematic observation. When checklists are used, students' performances are simply "checked off" rather than described in notes. For example, the science teacher wanting to assess learners' inquiry abilities might prepare a checklist such as the one that appears in Figure 13.3. (Notes could be added if desired, which would then combine elements of both checklists and systematic observations.)

Checklists are useful when behaviors either do or don't exist, such as "Identified controlled variables." In cases such as "Assesses hypotheses in written form," the results aren't just present or absent; some hypotheses will be better than others. This leads us to rating scales.

Rating Scales   **Rating scales** *are written descriptions of dimensions and scales of values on which each dimension is rated.* They allow a better assessment of quality than is possible with checklists. A sample rating scale, based on the checklist in Figure 13.3, is illustrated in Figure 13.4.

Although labor intensive to construct, rubrics should be created for each of the dimensions (Stiggins, 2005). For example, definitions of values, such as the following, might be used to evaluate whether the problem was stated clearly:

Rating = 5
Problem is clear and complete. Students understand both the content and the importance of the problem. It provides a basis for hypothesizing solutions.

Figure 13.4

Rating Scale for Assessing Inquiry

Rate each item. A rating of 5 is excellent, and a rating of 1 is poor.

5 4 3 2 1   **1.** States problem clearly.

5 4 3 2 1   **2.** States hypotheses clearly.

5 4 3 2 1   **3.** Controls variables effectively.

5 4 3 2 1   **4.** Uses effective data-gathering techniques.

5 4 3 2 1   **5.** Presents data effectively.

5 4 3 2 1   **6.** Draws appropriate conclusions.

Rating = 4
Problem is reasonably clear. It is appropriate, but more significant problems exist with respect to the topic. A clear basis for hypothesizing solutions is provided.

Rating = 3
The problem is stated somewhat ambiguously. The basis for hypothesizing solutions isn't clear.

Rating = 2
The statement isn't in the form of a problem. Understanding of the problem and its significance isn't indicated in the statement.

Rating = 1
No problem stated.

Definitions for each of the other dimensions in the rating scale would be similar to those just listed, providing acceptable levels of reliability for both student performance and products.

Portfolio Assessment

The use of portfolios, another form of alternative assessment, has the additional advantage of involving students in the design, collection, and evaluation of learning products. **Portfolios** are *purposeful collections of student work that are reviewed against preset criteria* (Popham, 2005; Stiggins, 2008). Because they are cumulative, connected, and collected over a period of time, they can provide a "motion picture" of learning progress versus the snapshots provided by disconnected tests and quizzes. The physical portfolio or collection of students' products, such as essays, journal entries, artwork, and videotapes, is not the assessment per se; the portfolio assessment also includes the students' and teacher's judgments of learning progress based on these products.

Two features distinguish portfolios from other forms of assessment. First, portfolios collect work samples over time, reflecting developmental changes; second, they involve students in design, collection, and evaluation. The following are some examples of portfolio assessments:

■ Pieces of art produced throughout the grading period or year

■ Samples of math papers including computation and problem solving

- Drafts of different kinds of essays in language arts
- Drawings and written explanations for the results observed in demonstrations and hands-on activities in science

Portfolios should reflect learning progress. For example, different essays could indicate changes that occurred during a grading period, semester, or entire course. These samples can then be used in parent-teacher conferences and as feedback for the students themselves.

When using portfolios we need to involve students in deciding what will be included and how it will be evaluated. By involving students in these decisions, teachers help students become aware of options in assessing their own growth, which is another way of increasing learner self-regulation.

One lower elementary school student had this to say about the learning progress reflected in a yearlong portfolio:

> Today I looked at my stories in my writing folder. I read some of my writing since September. I noticed that I've improved some stuff. Now I edit my stories and revise. Now I use periods, quotation marks. Sometimes my stories are longer. I used to misspell words and now I look in a dictionary or ask a friend and now I write exciting and scary stories and now I have very good endings. Now I use capitals. I used to leave out words and write short simple stories. (Paulson, Paulson, & Meyers, 1991, p. 63)

Through the processes of self-analysis and evaluation students become more aware of their own growth as learners.

Designing an Assessment System

In addition to traditional tests and quizzes and alternative assessments, an effective assessment system also includes grading and reporting and communicating with students, parents, and school officials. We examine the design of the total assessment system in this section.

Where to start? There are so many decisions to make, such as the number of tests and quizzes, the kinds of assignments, the weight of each, and grading, that it is hard to know where to begin.

One way to begin is to analyze your teaching situation. What information are you expected to provide, and when is it due? Looking at a report card is a reasonable beginning point. In analyzing a report card the following questions have immediate consequences for your assessment decisions:

- What areas are evaluated?
- How is student performance described (e.g., letter grade, percentage, or descriptive statement)?
- How frequently do grades need to be given?
- How are affective dimensions such as cooperation and following rules reported?
- How are tardiness and absences reported?

These may seem mundane, but we have encountered first-year teachers who were only weeks away from their first report cards and conferences with parents when they realized they were expected to give grades in penmanship and citizenship, and they had to scurry to gather the necessary information! Talking to other teachers can help clarify existing practices and avoid pitfalls, and your principal can be valuable in explaining the school's and district's expectations. When you're done designing your assessment system, you should be able to confidently defend it to a parent or administrator.

Once you understand what is expected of you, and knowing that your assessments should be valid, reliable, frequent, and efficient, you can begin designing your own system. Routines are helpful in structuring your assessment system. The following represents one routine in elementary math:

Monday:	Review last week's work; introduce new concepts
Tuesday:	Develop concepts and skills in class
Wednesday:	Clear up misunderstandings and use homework to encourage retention and transfer
Thursday:	Reinforce understanding; review for quiz
Friday:	Quiz

Teachers who use a system such as this report that students like the structure the routine provided. They know what to expect and what is expected of them.

Standards, Accountability, and Assessment

Standards and accountability will be major factors influencing the design of your assessment system. The primary way standards will affect your teaching is through the process of accountability. **Accountability** *is a process of making learning objectives explicit and holding both teachers and students responsible for attaining these.* It means that your students will be required to demonstrate that they understand the topics they study, and you will be held responsible for ensuring that your students meet certain standards.

This is where assessment enters the picture. States use assessment to hold students (and their teachers) accountable for meeting prescribed learning standards. In some cases, the assessments are **high-stakes tests**, *standardized assessments that states and districts use to determine whether students will advance from one grade to another, graduate from high school, or have access to specific fields of study.* For example, if graduating from high school depends on students' performance on the test, the stakes are high, which is why the tests are described this way. If you recently graduated from high school, you might have taken one of these tests yourself. When you teach, you will be on the other side of the fence; you will then be responsible for preparing your students to pass these assessments.

As with standards, state tests have different labels, such as the *Texas Assessment of Knowledge and Skills (TAKS)* (Texas Education Agency, 2008c), the *Florida Comprehensive Assessment Test* (Florida Department of Education, 2008), the *California Standards Test* (California State Board of Education, 2008b), or the *Illinois Standards Achievement Test* (Illinois State Board of Education, 2008b).

States also vary in the way they administer the tests. For example, the *TAKS* is given at every year in grades 3 through 10 in reading and math; science is given in grades 5, 8, and 10; and social studies is given in grades 8 and 10. On the other hand the *Florida*

Comprehensive Assessment Test, which also tests all students in grades 3 through 10 in reading and math, administers the science portion to students in grades 5, 8, and 11, and social studies is not measured on the exam. When you begin teaching, you need to become fully aware of the testing schedule for your state, as you and your students will be held accountable for their performance on the tests.

To help teachers align their instruction with state standards, sample test items that parallel the items on the standardized assessments or older versions of the tests themselves are usually available. Both are linked to specific standards. These sample items and older versions of the tests are useful in two ways. First, you need to interpret the meaning of the standards, and sample items help you with this process. Second, the sample items help guide you as you prepare your students for the tests. The following are sample items that measure the extent to which students have reached standards.

For example, one fourth-grade math standard from the state of Texas states,

(4.2) Number, operation, and quantitative reasoning. The student describes and compares fractional parts of whole objects or sets of objects
    The student is expected to:
    (A) use concrete objects and pictorial models to generate equivalent fractions.

A sample test item from the *TAKS* designed to measure the extent to which students have reached the standard looks like this (Texas Education Agency, 2008c):

The model is shaded to represent a fraction.

Which model below shows an equivalent fraction?

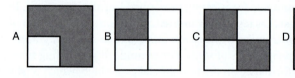

Now let's look again at the middle school science standard from the state of Illinois with a corresponding assessment item from the *Illinois Standards Achievement Test* linked to the standard (Illinois State Board of Education, 2008c).

Illinois Science Assessment Framework
    Standard 12F—Astronomy (Grade 7)
    12.7.91 Understanding that objects in the solar system is for the most part in regular and predictable motion. Know that those motions explain such phenomena as the day, the year, the phases of the moon, and eclipses.

12.7.91

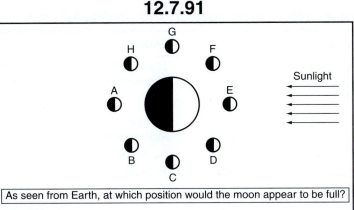

As seen from Earth, at which position would the moon appear to be full?

A Position A
B Position B
C Position C
D Position D

These sample standards and items are similar in two ways. First, the items measure more than students' ability to remember factual information, which is typical of many, if not most, standards. Each of the sample items goes beyond factual knowledge and measures students' understanding of conceptual knowledge. This means that when you align your instruction with standards, you need to teach students to do more than simply memorize information, and you should also develop assessments that do more than measure their knowledge of facts.

Second, the items on state assessment tests are typically written in a multiple-choice format, which both increases their reliability and makes them easier to score. The fact that these items are multiple choice has an important implication for you; you'll need to be sure your students are comfortable with this format. This suggests that some of the teacher-made assessments you create should be in the same format as the examples here. This is a demanding process, but one that will help you prepare your students for their assessments and increase the likelihood that their test scores reflect what they actually know. In addition these standards-aligned items should be an integral part of your grading system, a topic we take up in the next section.

Grades and Grading

An essential part of assessment involves decisions about grading (Guskey, 2002). You already know the form that these will take on report cards; your job now is to translate your assignments, quizzes, tests, and alternative assessments into a comprehensive system. Two major ways of doing this are summarized in Table 13.2.

A point system is straightforward; the importance of each assignment and quiz is reflected in the points allocated. Then these are added up and grades are given. Weighted scores are slightly more complex. As an illustration let's see how one system, using Steve Vockel's spelling exercises on the board illustration, might work. He gave them 10 words to spell and then scored students' papers. Then he gave another short exercise of five items and a third of eight items. In scoring these items, teachers typically convert the raw scores to a percentage. A student who got 8 of 10 correct in the first case would have a score of 80 written in the grade book; 2 of 5 in the

Table 13.2 Weighted Scores and Point Grading Systems	
Point System	**Weighted Scores**
Every graded assignment or quiz is given a point value. These are then added up to provide a total score.	Every assignment is given a letter grade and all grades are then weighted.

Point System			Weighted Scores	
Example:			*Example:*	
Assignments (20 × 10 pts.)		200	Assignments (20)	25%
Quizzes (8 × 25 pts.)		200	Quizzes (8)	25%
Tests (4 × 100 pts.)		400	Tests (4)	50%
Total possible points =		800	Total =	100%

Grade Range
  A 750–800
  B 700–750
  C 650–700
  D 600–650

second case would be a score of 40; and 7 of 8 in the third case would be a score of 88. Teachers then typically find an average to arrive at the final score on which the student's grade is based. In this case the student's average would be a 69, which in most grading systems is a D. However, in reality, the student responded to a total of 23 items, 17 of which he answered correctly. His actual percentage is 74—five points higher and a C in most grading systems. The problem with the system we just illustrated is that each of the exercises is given the same weight, even though the number of items is markedly different—10, 5, and 8, respectively.

If this system seems flawed, why is it so common? Two reasons. First, it is simple, and as we have noted repeatedly, the need to simplify is powerful. Second, both students and parents tend to prefer the percentage system because it is simpler and easier to understand as well. We have talked to teachers who have used the raw scores, converting to a percentage only at the end of a marking period and later went back to the percentage system throughout because of confusion and comments from students.

Norm- and Criterion-Referenced Evaluations   In assigning grades within either system, you have two options. One, called **criterion referenced**, *uses preestablished percentages or number totals for grades* (e.g., 90–100, A; 80–90, B; 70–80, C; etc.). The advantage of this approach is that it communicates grading standards clearly and is noncompetitive; students compete only against the criteria (Stiggins, 2008). The disadvantage is that it is often difficult to know where to set the grading criteria, especially the first time you teach a course, so you may end up giving too many or too few high grades. The second problem is fairly easy to fix; you can lower the criteria and students won't complain. The other situation is more problematic as you don't want to be changing criteria or grades after the fact. Students will howl.

The alternative, called **norm referenced**, *compares each student's performance to that of the other students in the class.* Grading "on the curve" is an example. Most experts favor criterion referencing because it deemphasizes competition and focuses on content mastery, and it is also the most common system in place in classrooms.

Homework   Another major grading decision is how to handle homework. Research indicates that homework can have a positive impact on learning (Marzano, 2007), but it provides little guidance about how to integrate it into your assessment system.

A major issue here is accountability. Students should feel responsible for doing homework and should understand that homework is crucial to learning. They also need to be rewarded for conscientious efforts. Implementing a system that doesn't bury you under mounds of paperwork is the problem. Here are some possible options:

1. Assign homework, grade it yourself, and record the scores. This is the best option for promoting learning, but it is demanding and time consuming. This option can be viable if you have an aide or a parent volunteer who can help with some of the routine work.

2. Assign homework, select samples from the assignment, have the students turn in those samples, and record the score on those problems. This is a compromise. The teacher scores the homework, but the amount graded is reduced. Students sometimes resent having done all the homework and getting credit for only part of it.

3. Have students grade their own papers in class, and score all the homework as a group. This saves teacher time and gives students immediate feedback. However, it takes class time, is subject to cheating, and doesn't work for written work and projects involving higher-level outcomes.

4. Assign homework, give the students credit for having done the homework whether or not it is correct, and then use class time to cover material students found difficult. This option has the advantage of allowing students to correct their own mistakes. However, students often don't try as hard when homework isn't actually scored.

5. Assign homework, collect it at random intervals, and score and mark it. This option reduces the teacher's workload, but the homework must be collected regularly or students tend to stop doing it.

6. Do not grade homework, but give frequent short quizzes based on the material covered in the homework. This can be effective with older and higher-achieving students, who understand the links between homework and achievement. It is ineffective with low achievers and poorly motivated students.

Which system should you adopt? We recommend that you talk to other teachers and experiment to find out what works best for you with the students you have and the specific teaching situation you are in.

Communication

Communication is an integral part of an effective assessment system (Guskey, 2002; Stiggins, 2008). At the beginning of the school year you need to explain to students what is expected of them and share this information with parents. As information is gathered throughout the school year, it needs to be shared with both students and parents so both know how students are doing. Ways of doing this are the focus of this section.

We have seen throughout this text how expectations influence learning. For positive expectations to increase learning both students and parents must know what your expectations are—this is why communication is critical in an effective assessment system. Further, researchers have documented the importance of the home-school partnership, and effective communication with parents is a critical dimension of this partnership (Epstein, 2001; Olsen & Fuller, 2003). Effective teachers use a variety of ways to communicate their expectations to parents and students.

Written Communication   In the primary grades, communication may be more directly with parents than with students. As children get older, our communication efforts should target both. The letter in Figure 13.5 is used each year by a fifth-grade teacher to communicate expectations.
This letter is clear and concise, communicates positive expectations, and sets the tone for a productive school year.

At the junior high and high school levels, parents and students often are interested in the content of the course and how student work will be graded. One algebra teacher sent the document shown in Figure 13.6 home at the beginning of the school year.

Note how the algebra teacher's letter described (1) the content of the course, (2) instructional activities, and (3) grading procedures and student requirements. These were addressed in a positive, businesslike manner and set the stage for a productive school year. We recommend a document like this at the beginning of your school year. It is straightforward and informative and communicates not only positive expectations but also organization and competence.

Open House   Most school systems have a scheduled open house at a specified date early in the school year. Parents are invited to attend, and at the middle and high school levels they move through an abbreviated schedule of a typical day's activities. Teachers describe their policies and expectations and invite input from parents. The written expectations teachers have are often distributed in these sessions.

The image you project as a teacher is critical at this time. Because the open house is often the only time you will see a parent during the year, the impression you make will be lasting. Proper dress, careful use of language and grammar, clear and neatly written communications, and a warm and pleasant but professional manner are all important in creating a good impression.

Parent-Teacher Conferences   An additional opportunity to communicate expectations, grading policies, and student progress is through conferences during which parents and teachers meet face to face. Some teachers have experimented with inviting students to these conferences and have noted the benefits of students' being informed of and rewarded for their efforts in class. Suggestions for conducting successful parent-teacher conferences follow (Olsen & Fuller, 2003):

1. Organize and prepare before the meeting. The files and records of each of your students should be readily available during the meeting.

2. Begin with a positive statement (e.g., "Mary is such a lively, energetic second grader"—despite the fact that she is about to drive you crazy). This puts the parent at ease and sets the stage for later comments.

3. Be factual in your statements and use supporting documentation. At the elementary level this might consist of samples of the student's work; at the secondary level it should include scores and averages on assignments and tests.

4. Listen carefully to parents' questions and concerns. This shows you care, and it provides you with information about the student.

Figure 13.5

Letter to Parents

Dear Parents and Students,

I am looking forward to an exciting year in fifth grade, and I hope you are too! In order for us to work together most effectively, some guidelines are necessary. They are listed below. Please read through the information carefully and sign at the bottom of the page. Thank you for your cooperation and help in making this year the best one ever for your youngster.

Sincerely,
Mrs. Kathy Mease

Survival Guidelines

1. Follow directions the first time they are given.
2. Be in class, seated, and quiet when the bell rings.
3. Bring covered textbooks, notebook and/or folder, paper, pen, and pencils to class daily.
4. Raise your hand for permission to speak or to leave your seat.
5. Keep hands, feet, and objects to yourself.

Homework Guidelines

1. Motto—I will always TRY, and I will NEVER give up!
2. I will complete all assignments. If the assignment is not finished or is not ready when called for, a zero will be given.
3. Head your paper properly—directions were given in class. Use pen/pencil—no red, orange, or pink ink. If you have questions, see Mrs. Mease.
4. Whenever you are absent, it is your responsibility to come in early in the morning (7:30–8:00) and make arrangements for makeup work. Class time will not be used for this activity. Tests are always assigned three to five days in advance—if you are absent the day before the test, you should come prepared to take the test because you will be expected to take it.
5. No extra credit work will be given. If you do all the required work and study for the tests, there should be no need for extra credit.
6. A packet of papers is sent home with the children each Tuesday. Please look them over carefully. If you have any questions or comments, please feel free to call Lone Trail Elementary School (272–8160). I will return your call promptly.

Again, my best wishes for a terrific year.

_____ Student _____ Parent

5. To end the session, summarize the discussion and end on an optimistic note (e.g., "Jim *can* learn math, and if we both encourage him on his homework, I'm sure we'll see a difference next report card").

Phone Conferences, Emails, and Texting   One of the most effective forms of communication is a simple phone call. It is effective for one important reason—it communicates that

Figure 13.6

Course Expectations in Algebra

Course Expectations

I. Course Title: Algebra I

II. Course Description: This course explores basic algebraic concepts and applications, including a complete review of the number system. The main emphasis of the course is on solving linear and quadratic equations.

III. Course Objectives

    A. To understand the basic terms and symbols used in the study of algebra.

    B. To perform the basic operations with signed numbers.

    C. To solve simple linear equations and inequalities with one unknown.

    D. To understand the graphical properties of linear equations.

    E. To perform basic operations with polynomials.

    F. To solve quadratic equations using factoring.

    G. To perform fundamental operations with algebraic fractions.

    H. To solve quadratic equations using the quadratic formula.

    I. To apply equation-solving techniques to story problems.

IV. Learning Activities

    A. Daily assignments

    B. Teacher demonstration

    C. Class discussion

    D. Note taking and writing projects

    E. Peer tutoring

    F. Reviews

    G. Student demonstration

V. Grading Procedure: Grades will be based on test performance, notebooks, daily assignments, and quizzes. Grades will be weighted as follows:

    Tests—40%   Quizzes—40%   Daily assignments—20%

    Final grades will be determined on the following scale:

    93–100% A   65–72% D

    85–92%   B   0–64%   F

    73–84%   C

VI. Materials

    A. Text: *Holt Algebra One,* Holt, Rinehart & Winston Publishers, 1996.

    B. Calculator: It is recommended that each student obtain a scientific calculator.

    C. Paper, pencil, and pen.

    D. Learning log.

VII. Student Expectations

    A. Students must come prepared to class each day with their book, notebook, pencil and paper, and assignments.

    B. School policy states that four unexcused absences will result in failure. Makeup tests must be taken within three days of return from absence. Makeup assignments must be turned in on the second day of return from absence. No makeup quizzes will be given. The low quiz in each grading period will be dropped.

C. To facilitate roll taking and grading, students are expected to sit in the seats assigned to them.

D. Cheating will not be tolerated. Anyone guilty of cheating will receive a zero on the test.

E. Courtesy and respect are expected to be shown at all times. This includes not eating during class, listening to the lecture, and staying on task. Stereos and headsets are to be left in students' lockers.

I have read this document and understand the grading procedures and classroom rules. Please feel free to call the school at any time if you have questions or concerns (936–1148).

_____ Student _____Parent

---

you care enough about a student to spend your personal time discussing problems or concerns about that individual in a one-to-one conference with a parent or caregiver. For this reason a negative or defensive reaction by parents is rare, and the outcomes of these conversations are almost always productive. Even better, a periodic phone call to tell about improved work or behavior can pay big dividends. Parents are rarely called when their child does something *good*, so a call with positive feedback can be very effective in promoting a positive home-school partnership.

The Internet provides an additional way to communicate with parents and has the added advantage of being able to contact parents flexibly in terms of time. Teachers find it useful when their schedules and parents' don't mesh. You need to be careful, though, that parents have convenient access to the Internet; many low-SES parents do not.

Communication: Report Cards   We have all had experience with report cards. Although their form varies, report cards at a given level generally communicate similar information. An excerpt from a report sent to the parents of kindergarten children is shown in Figure 13.7.

Notice that this report (1) includes affective and personal growth goals; (2) is based primarily on performance measures; and (3) uses an *O, S, I, N* scale versus an *A, B, C, D* scale for reporting. On a form like this, there also would be space for some short written comments.

Compare this kindergarten report to one used in the intermediate grades (Figure 13.8).

We can see from this example that affective goals such as social behaviors and attitudes are still evaluated at the junior high level, but a separate scale is used. In addition information is provided in basic skills areas in terms of absolute achievement, progress made during the quarter, and effort. This provides information to both students and their parents about self-regulated learning, a major goal of middle school education.

As students progress into high school, teachers place less emphasis on affective considerations, and grades are often quantified in terms of percentages (see Figure 13.9). This latter point has strong implications for the kind of grading system the teacher designs, a point we made earlier.

Interim Progress Reports   Report cards are commonly sent home every nine weeks. Schools also typically report progress at midterm as well. In some cases students get interim progress reports only when they are experiencing difficulty; in others all students receive them. The purpose of the report is to provide feedback to both students and parents regarding progress, and they can be especially helpful if problems develop. Your school will have a form and a standard procedure for completing interim progress reports.

Figure 13.7

Kindergarten Progress Report

KINDERGARTEN PROGRESS REPORT

2005-2006

MARKING KEY

O – Outstanding
S – Satisfactory
I – Improvement Shown
N – Needs Improvement
Ø – Not Evaluated

Name: _____

Teacher: _____

School: _____

Attendance	1	2	3	4	Total
Days Present					
Days Absent					
Days Tardy					

SOCIAL DEVELOPMENT AND WORK HABITS	1	2	3	4
Works and plays well with others				
Is kind and courteous				
Listens attentively				
Uses socially acceptable language				
Respects rules				
Accepts correction graciously				
Respects rights of others				

LANGUAGE READINESS	1	2	3	4
Recognizes colors: R O GR Y BL P BR BK WH				
Reads color words: R O GR Y BL P BR BK WH				
Identifies and uses opposites				
Knows rhyming sounds				
Know directions (up, down, left, right)				

MATHEMATICS	1	2	3	4
Recognizes shapes ◯△▢⬭◇				
Counts objects 1, 2, 3, 4, 5, 6, 7, 8, 9, 10, 11, 12, 13, 14, 15, 16, 17, 18, 19, 20				
Correctly writes 0, 1, 2, 3, 4, 5, 6, 7, 8, 9, 10				
Recognizes 0, 1, 2, 3, 4, 5, 6, 7, 8, 9, 10, 11, 12, 13, 14, 15, 16, 17, 18, 19, 20				
Counts to _____				

MOTOR SKILLS	1	2	3	4
Demonstrates large-muscle control (hop, skip, jump, throw, catch, run, balance)				
Demonstrates fine-motor control:				
Forms letters and numbers correctly				
Holds pencil and crayon correctly				
Traces over lines				
Can cut out geometric shapes				

436

Figure 13.8

Intermediate Grade Report Card

STUDENT ID _____

BEHAVIOR AND ATTITUDES	Report Period			
	1	2	3	4
1. Accepts responsibility				
2. Follows directions				
3. Completes assignments on time				
4. Shows judgment in use and care of materials				
5. Displays creativity				
6. Is courteous and considerate of others				
7. Uses time well				
8. Works well in groups				
9. Abides by school rules				

BEHAVIOR AND ATTITUDES

These behaviors are important to success in school. These factors reflect attitude toward school, self, and others. They have a direct bearing on the progress being made in the basic skills.

E – Excellent

S – Satisfactory

NI – Needs Improvement

ACHIEVEMENT, PROGRESS, AND EFFORT	1			2			3			4		
	Achievement	Progress	Effort	Achievement	Progress	Effort	Achievement	Progress	Effort	Achievement	Progress	Effort
Reading												
Language Arts												
Handwriting												
Spelling												
Mathematics												
Health												
Science												
Social Studies												
Art* — Satisfactory Performance												
Art* — Needs Improvement												
Music* — Satisfactory Performance												
Music* — Needs Improvement												
Phys. Ed.* — Satisfactory Performance												
Phys. Ed.* — Needs Improvement												

* Letter grades are not given in these subject areas because of the difficulty of precise measurement of acquired skills.

Figure 13.9

High School Report Form

• REPORT CARD •

NAME		SCHOOL	STUDENT NUMBER	HOME ROOM	SCHOOL YEAR
ADDRESS		CITY		ZIP CODE	TELEPHONE

PERIOD FROM-THRU	COURSE NAME	WGT	TEACHER NAME	TEA NO.	1ST GRD	1ST C	1ST ABS	2ND GRD	2ND C	2ND ABS	1ST SEM EXAM	2ND SEM AVG	3RD GRD	3RD C	3RD ABS	4TH GRD	4TH C	4TH ABS	2ND SEM EXAM	2ND SEM AVG	YR AVG	CREDIT EARNED
1	M/J LIFE SCI ADV			082	93A	0	0	90B	0	1		92B	90B	0	3	93A	0	2		92B	92B	
2	M/J BAND 4			129	97A	0	0	**A	0	2		99A	97A	0	3	95A	0	3		96A	97A	
3	ALGEBRA			029	96A	0	0	93A	0	1		95A	91BS		3	91BS		2		91B	93A	
4	POL. SCIENCE			053	92BS		1	91B	0	1		92B	93AS		2	94AS		2		94A	93A	
5	AM. LITERATURE			004	93AS		1	90B	0	1		92B	89BS		2	93AS		2		91B	91B	
6	M/J PHYS ED 2			101	96AS		0	97AS		1		97A	97AS		1	94AS		2		96A	96A	

PROMOTED

Technology and Teaching:

Using Technology in Assessment

Because of its ability to store large amounts of data and process it quickly, technology is proving to be especially valuable in classroom assessment. Technology, and particularly computers, can serve three important and time-saving assessment functions (Roblyer & Doering, 2010):

- Planning and constructing tests
- Analyzing test data, especially data gathered from objective tests
- Maintaining student records

One theme of this chapter has been the value of frequent classroom assessment. Computers provide an efficient way to store these data, analyze them, and present them to students in an understandable way. These functions are summarized in Table 13.3 and discussed in the paragraphs that follow.

Planning and Constructing Tests

Constructing effective test items can be a difficult and time-consuming task for teachers. The word-processing capabilities of computers provide teachers with an effective tool for writing and revising individual items; once items are written, computers are useful for assembling them into a complete test. Initially, items focus on specific content or topics. Later, they can be grouped into similar item types and sequenced from easiest to hardest. This sequence helps reduce test anxiety by providing easy entry into a test.

A number of commercially prepared software programs can assist in this process (e.g., Create a Test, Exam Builder, Test Writer, Test IT! Deluxe, Quick Quiz, and Test Generator). These programs have the following capabilities:

- Develop a test file or item bank of multiple-choice, true-false, matching, and short-answer items that can be stored in the system. Within a file items can be organized by topic, chapter, objective, or difficulty.

Table 13.3 Assessment Functions Performed by Computers

Function	Examples
Planning and construction	Preparing objectives
	Writing and storing items
	Creating tests Printing tests
Scoring and interpreting tests	Scoring tests
	Summarizing results
	Analyzing items
Maintaining student records	Developing a class summary
	Recording results
	Preparing grade reports
	Developing student profiles
	Reporting results to students

- Select items from the created file bank randomly, selectively, or by categories to generate multiple versions of a test.
- Modify items and integrate these into the total test.
- Produce student-ready copies and an answer key.

Analyzing Test Data

Once administered tests need to be scored and analyzed. A high school teacher with 5 sections of 30 students and a 40-item exam faces a logistical challenge—$5 \times 30 \times 40 = 6,000$ individual items! Scoring and analyzing test data, converting scores to grades, and recording the grades can be enormously time consuming.

Most schools now have computers that can machine-score or scan teacher-made tests. To use this time-saving feature, test items need to be placed in formats that can be transferred to machine-scored answer sheets (i.e., multiple choice, true-false, matching).

There are also a number of software programs available to machine-score tests (e.g., Test Scorer, Quickscore, and Test Analysis), and their average cost is around $200. These programs can

- Score objective tests and provide descriptive statistics such as test mean, median and mode, range, and standard deviation.
- Generate a list of items showing difficulty level, the percentage of students who selected each response, the percentage of students who didn't respond to an item, and the correlation of each item with the total test.
- Sort student responses by score, grade/age, or gender.

A sample printout for a 15-item multiple-choice quiz given to a class of 35 students appears in Table 13.4. The printout identifies the item number, the number of students who selected each choice, the correct answer, the statistical average for the quiz (mean), a measure of the spread of scores (standard deviation), and the middle score (median).

The quiz was first machine-scored, and the software program provided an immediate printout of the descriptive statistics and distribution of student responses. The distribution of responses is particularly useful in analyzing the quality of the items and possible student misconceptions.

Table 13.4 Computer Analysis of Test Results

ITEM	1	2	3	4	5	6	7	8	9	10	11	12	13	14	15
A	34	0	0	0	0	30	1	0	4	0	0	0	8	1	1
B	0	0	0	1	7	4	0	0	8	19	13	1	0	0	6
C	1	2	30	27	3	1	11	34	4	11	21	16	10	28	3
D	0	33	5	7	5	0	13	1	17	2	0	18	17	6	17
E	0	0	0	0	20	0	10	0	2	3	0	0	0	0	7
Blank Responses	0	0	0	0	0	0	0	0	0	0	1	0	0	0	1
Correct Answer	A	D	C	C	E	A	C	C	D	C	C	D	D	C	C

Total number of students processed: 35

Statistical analysis
  Mean: 09.22
  Standard deviation: 2.084
  Median: 09.00

Although many teachers use a criterion-referenced rather than a norm-referenced system for assigning their own grades, the descriptive statistics included with the analysis give an indication of the quiz's difficulty and class performance as a whole. For instance, a mean of 9.22 on a 15-item quiz suggests that the quiz was difficult for students, so some questions might exist about (1) the students' understanding of the content, (2) the difficulty of the items, 3) the quality of some of the items, or all three. This type of analysis, together with teacher reflection and revision of test items, can improve the overall effectiveness of your assessment system.

Maintaining Student Records

An effective assessment system gathers comprehensive information about student performance frequently. To be useful to you this information needs to be stored so that it is easily accessible. In addition students need to know where they stand in the course to make the best use of their time and resources. Computers provide an efficient way of storing, analyzing, and reporting student assessments.

One teacher commented:

I keep my grades in an electronic gradebook. By entering my grades into an electronic gradebook as I grade papers, I always know how my students are progressing and exactly where my students stand in relation to each other. It does take a little time to enter the grades, but it makes my job easier during reporting periods. All I have to do is open my disk and record my students' grades on the grade sheet. (Morrison & Lowther, 2002, p. 348)

For teachers with some background in technology, general spreadsheet programs can be converted into individualized grade sheets (Forcier & Descy, 2005). Commercial software is available, and most of the programs designed to analyze individual test score data also have the following capabilities:

- Begin a new class file for each class or subject. These can be stored by name and/or student identification number.
- Average grades, create new grades, change old ones, add extra credit.
- Compute descriptive statistics such as the mean, median, mode, and standard deviation for any test or set of scores.
- Translate numerical or raw scores into letter grades.
- Record the type of activity and the point value for each activity.
- Average grades on a quarterly, semester, and/or yearly basis.

The amount of time and energy saved and the increased decision-making capability make computers an invaluable asset in the assessment process.

This brings us to the end of this chapter and to the end of the text. We hope the information you have read and studied has been useful and practical. As we have seen, research has much to offer the classroom teacher, but only the teacher can translate this research into practice. Professional judgment is a critical element in all the decisions teachers make. This should not be a matter of concern, for it is one of the characteristics that makes teaching a challenging profession. With sincere effort, you will make an important contribution to education—the most rewarding of professions. We hope this text contributes to your efforts.

Summary

Classroom Assessment

Classroom assessment includes the information teachers gather and the decisions they make about learning progress.

Assessment performs both instructional and institutional functions. Effective assessment increases learning and provides information for students, teachers, parents, and school and district administrators.

Assessments are valid when they are consistent with goals and learning activities. They should also be reliable, which means they're consistent, and they should be practical, which means they're efficient and usable.

Using Assessment to Promote Learning

Effective assessment practices include establishing positive expectations, preparing students for tests, specifying what will be on the test, and giving students a chance to practice with the content and format.

During testing, effective teachers create a comfortable environment, carefully monitor students, and provide specific directions for taking the test and spending time when they have finished the test.

Effective teachers also score and return tests promptly, discuss frequently missed items, and make supportive comments about students' performance.

Assessment should be an ongoing part of instruction. Teachers should take great care in preparing items, they should test thoroughly and often, and defective items should be revised.

Alternative Assessment

Alternative assessments ask students to perform in realistic ways similar to performances required in the world outside the classroom. Systematic observation, checklists, and rating scales can all be used to provide assessments that have acceptable levels of reliability.

Portfolios—collections of students' work that are evaluated—provide an additional form of alternative assessment. Portfolios have the additional advantage of allowing students input into the selection and evaluation of materials included in the portfolio.

Designing an Assessment System

An effective assessment system includes tests, quizzes, homework, and other sources of information about student progress. Talking to school leaders and other teachers can help in designing your system.

Communication needs to be an integral part of an effective assessment system. Positive and concrete expectations set the stage for future learning, and this information should be shared with both students and parents. Effective communication includes open houses, parent-teacher conferences, report cards, and interim progress reports. One of the most effective is the simple practice of phoning parents. This communicates commitment to students as individuals and a teacher's willingness to spend personal time to help students.

Important Concepts

Accountability (p. 427)

Alternative assessments (p. 421)

Assessment system (p. 409)

Checklists (p. 424)

Classroom assessment (p. 409)

Criterion referenced (p. 430)

Formal assessment (p. 410)

High-stakes test (p. 427)

Informal assessment (p. 410)

Instructional alignment (p. 411)

Norm referenced (p. 430)

Performance assessment (p. 422)

Portfolios (p. 425)

Rating scales (p. 424)

Reliability (p. 411)

Systematic observation (p. 424)

Table of specifications (p. 416)

Test anxiety (p. 416)

Validity (p. 411)

Preparing for Your Licensure Exam

As you've studied this chapter, you've seen how effective teachers design and implement assessments that gather accurate information and increase learning. Read the following case study now and consider how effectively the teacher implemented the ideas discussed in the chapter.

After reading this case, go to the Book Specific Resources tab in MyEducationLab, select your text, select *Preparing for Your Licensure Exam* under Chapter 13 to complete the questions that accompany the case and receive feedback on your responses.

Darren Wilson, an English teacher at Greenland Pines Middle School, teaches three sections of standard English and two sections of advanced English. We look in now as he begins a unit on singular and plural possessives with one of his standard English classes.

The tardy bell rings at 8:50 as Darren begins, "All right, listen, everyone. . . . We've had some practice in making nouns plural, . . . and today, we're going to begin studying possessives . . . both singular and plural. Everybody turn to page 239 in your text. . . . We see at the top of the page that we're dealing with possessives. . . . Possessives are very important in our writing. We want to be able to write well, and this is one of the places where people often get confused. . . . So, when we're finished with our study here, you'll all be able to use possessives correctly in your writing."

He then writes the following on the board:

> Add an apostrophe 's' to singular nouns or plural nouns that don't end in 's'.
> Add an apostrophe after the 's' if the plural noun doesn't end in 's'.
> If a singular or plural pronoun is possessive, do not add an apostrophe.

"Let's review briefly," Darren continues. "Who can spell the plural form of 'city' for me?"

"C I T I E S," Horace volunteers.

"Okay, good, . . . So, what would be the possessive form of the word?"

". . . Apostrophe after the 's'," Marvella offers.

"Yes," Darren smiles. "Good, now what is the plural form of child? . . . Juanita?"

". . . Children."

"All right, make it possessive," Darren probes.

". . . Ahh, s apostrophe . . . no, . . . apostrophe s . . . yeh, it doesn't end in 's'."

"Good thinking," Darren comments with a smile. He then presents and has students discuss two more examples, and as they finish, he says, "Now, let's talk about homework. Look at these sentences on the overhead."

He then shows an overhead with 10 sentences containing the following four:

1. Did you get the card that belonged to Esteban?
2. The plots of the stories were quite interesting.
3. Joe owns a new car; the car is red.
4. The breeze blew the hats of the women off.

"Now," Darren continues. "Rewrite the sentences in their possessive form, correctly using apostrophes. . . . That's your homework for tomorrow. . . . If you jump on it, you should be finished by the end of the period."

On Tuesday Darren first goes over the exercises the students completed for homework and then reviews some additional examples for which they have to create plural forms of nouns, make them possessive, and properly punctuate possessive pronouns.

Near the end of class Darren announces, "Class, tomorrow we're going to have a test on all of this stuff; singular nouns, plural nouns, pronouns, . . . the whole works. You have your notes, so study hard . . . Are there any questions? . . . Okay, good. I expect you all to do well. I'll see you tomorrow."

On Wednesday morning students file into class, and as the bell rings, Darren picks up the tests and, amid some groans and murmurs, asks, "Everybody ready?"

The test is composed of two parts. The first includes 15 sentences that have to be rewritten as the students have done with the homework exercises. They involve combinations of singular nouns, plural nouns, and pronouns that have to be punctuated properly. The second part of the test directs students to write a paragraph that includes at least one example of each rule for forming possessives.

"Just a reminder," Darren interjects before the students start working. "For the second part of the test . . . remember that the paragraph has to make sense. It can't just be a bunch of sentences on the paper."

The students go to work, and Darren watches, periodically walking up and down the aisles. Seeing that the period is half over, and some of the students are only starting on their paragraphs, he announces, "You have 20 minutes left. Watch your time and work quickly. You need to finish by the end of the period."

He continues monitoring, again reminding them to work quickly when 10 minutes are left and again when 5 minutes are left.

Trang, Niksha, Nevella, and Rudy hastily finish the last few words of their paragraphs just as the bell rings. Nevella turns in her paper as Darren's third-period students are filing in the room.

"Here," Darren says. "This pass will get you into Mrs. Jeffrey's class if you're late. . . . How did you do?"

"Okay, I think," Nevella says over her shoulder as she scurries out of the room, "except for the last part. It was hard. I couldn't get started."

"I'll look at it," Darren replies. "Get moving now."

On Thursday and Friday Darren moves on to punctuating different kinds of clauses and phrases. He scores the tests over the weekend and returns the papers on Monday. As he hands them back, he says, "Here are your papers. You did fine on the sentences, but your paragraphs need a lot of work. Why did you have so much trouble with them, when we had so much practice?"

"It was hard, Mr. Wilson."

"Not enough time."

"I hate to write."

Darren listens patiently and then says, "Be sure you write your scores in your notebooks. . . . Okay. . . . You have them all written down? . . . Are there any questions?"

"Number 8," Enrique asks.

"Okay, let's look at 8," and he explains the item, finishing by saying, "Any others?"

A sprinkling of questions is heard around the room, and Darren responds, "We don't have time to go over all of them. I'll discuss three more."

He then responds to three students who seemed most urgent in waving their hands. He then collects their tests and moves on to the topic for the day.

Questions for Analysis

Let's examine Darren's lesson now based on the information in this chapter. In your analysis consider the following questions. In each case be specific and take information directly from the case study in doing your analysis.

1. Alternative assessment was discussed in the chapter. How effective was Darren's alternative assessment?

2. How well was Darren's instruction aligned? Explain specifically what he could have done to increase instructional alignment.

3. Preparing students for tests, administering tests, and analyzing results were discussed in the section on effective testing. How effectively did Darren conduct each of these? If you believe one or more of the parts could have been conducted more effectively, describe specifically what he might have done.

4. Accommodating background diversity in learners is a theme of this text. How effectively did Darren's assessment accommodate the diversity in his students?

5. Identify the primary strengths and the primary weaknesses in Darren's teaching and assessment. Be specific in your analysis.

 # Discussion Questions

1. What advantages are there to establishing measurement routines? Are there any disadvantages to these routines?

2. Some have suggested that grades act as motivators. Do they work that way for you? What about the students you will teach? For what kinds of students will grades be the most motivating? The least motivating? How does age and grade level affect grades as motivators?

3. How does your specific teaching focus (e.g., subject matter or grade level) influence the kind of assessment instruments you will use?

4. Identify advantages and disadvantages of the following ways to assess student performance. How does the concept of validity affect the selection of one compared to the other?

    a. essay
    b. short answer
    c. multiple choice
    d. true/false
    e. performance assessment

5. Consider each of the options for collecting, scoring, and using homework that we presented in this chapter. What advantages and disadvantages does each have in addition to those we listed? How does the type of student (e.g., younger versus older, high ability versus low ability) influence the effectiveness of any option? What other options for handling homework exist?

6. What kind of grading system, norm- or criterion-referenced, do you prefer? Why? Do you think your opinion is similar to that of the students you will be teaching?

 *P*ortfolio Activities

1. *Assessment System.* Analyze the assessment system for the course in which you are using this book. Comment on the following dimensions:

    a. type of evaluation instruments used (e.g., objective versus performance assessment)
    b. validity
    c. frequency
    d. course expectations
    e. norm- or criterion-referenced grading

How do each of these influence motivation and learning?

2. *Report Cards.* Examine a report card and answer the following:

    a. How are grades reported?
    b. How often are report cards given?
    c. In addition to content areas such as social studies and science, what other areas (e.g., citizenship) are evaluated?

What challenges does the report card present to you as a teacher?

3. *Evaluation Policy.* Is there a document summarizing your district's or school's evaluation policy? If so, examine it and answer the following questions:

    a. Is there a statement of philosophy? If so, summarize the major points.
    b. How are parents involved in the process?
    c. What are each teacher's individual responsibilities?
    d. How do D's and F's influence promotion?

    e. What is the relationship of grades to extracurricular activities?

    f. How are unexcused absences and tardiness treated?

What challenges will you encounter integrating these policies into your classroom assessment system?

4. *Test Administration.* Observe a teacher administering a test or quiz. How did the teacher deal with the following issues:

    a. expectations

    b. directions

    c. feedback

    d. grades

    e. makeups

What suggestion do you have to make this process more effective?

5. *Homework.* Interview a teacher to see how the following aspects of homework are handled:

    a. correcting

    b. grades

    c. late or missing

    d. makeups for absences

How do you plan to implement homework in your classroom?

6. *Record Keeping.* Interview a teacher at your grade level or in your subject matter area and find out what his or her record-keeping responsibilities are in terms of the following:

    a. individual attendance records

    b. tardiness

    c. report cards

    d. cumulative folders

What suggestions does the teacher have for making the process more efficient? How will you handle these tasks in your classroom?

To check your comprehension of the content covered in Chapter 13, go to the Book Specific Resources in MyEducationLab, select your text, and complete the Study Plan quiz. In addition to receiving feedback on your answers, a study plan will be generated from the quiz that will direct you to access Review, Practice, and Enrichment materials to enhance your understanding of chapter content.

References

Abedi, J., Hofstetter, C., & Lord, C. (2004). Assessment accommodations for English language learners: Implications for policy-based empirical research. *Review of Educational Research, 74*(1), 1–28.

Airasian, P., & Russell, M. (2008). *Classroom assessment* (6th ed.) New York: McGraw-Hill.

Albanese, M., & Mitchell, S. (1993). Problem-based learning: A review of literature on its outcomes and implementation issues. *Academic Medicine, 68*, 52–81.

Alberto, P., & Troutman, A. (2009). *Applied behavior analysis for teachers* (8th ed.). Upper Saddle River, NJ: Prentice Hall.

Alder, N. (2002). Interpretations of the meaning of care: Creating caring relationship in urban middle school classrooms. *Urban Education, 37*(2), 241–266.

Alexander, P. (2006). *Psychology in learning and instruction.* Columbus, OH: Merrill/Prentice Hall.

Allen, T. (2004). No school left unscathed. *Phi Delta Kappan, 85*(5), 396–397.

American Association for the Advancement of Science (AAAS). (1993). *Benchmarks for science literacy.* Washington, DC: Author.

Anderson, L., & Krathwohl, D. (Eds.). (2001). *A taxonomy for learning, teaching, and assessing: A revision of Bloom's taxonomy of educational objectives.* New York: Addison Wesley Longman.

Anderson, P., & Summerfield, J. (2004). Why is urban education different from suburban and rural education? In S. R. Steinberg & J. L. Kincheloe (Eds.), *19 urban questions: Teaching in the city* (pp. 29–39). New York: Peter Lang.

Anderson, R., Hiebert, E., Scott, J., & Wilkinson, I. (1985). *Becoming a nation of readers.* Washington, DC: National Institute of Education.

Ansell, S., & Park, J. (2003). Tracking tech trends. *Education Week, 22*(35), 43–49.

Applebee, A., Langer, J., Nystrand, M., & Gamoran, A. (2003). Discussion-based approaches to developing understanding: Classroom instruction and student performance in middle and high school English. *American Educational Research Journal, 40*(3), 685–730.

Archer, J. (2003). Increasing the odds. *Education Week, 22*(17), 52–56.

Armour-Thomas, E. (2004). What is the nature of evaluation and assessment in an urban context? In S. Steinberg & J. Kincheloe (Eds.), *19 urban questions: Teaching in the city* (pp. 109–118). New York: Peter Lang.

Aspy, C., Oman, R., Vesely, S., McLeroy, K., Harris-Wyatt, V., Rodine, S., & Marshall, L. (2004). Adolescent violence: The protective effects of youth assets. *Journal of Counseling and Development, 82*(3), 268–276.

Atkinson, R., Derry, S., Renkl, A., & Wortham, D. (2000). Learning from examples: Instructional principles from the worked examples research. *Review of Educational Research, 70*(2), 181–214.

Azevedo, R., & Cromley, J. (2004). Does training on self-regulated learning facilitate students' learning with hypermedia? *Journal of Educational Psychology, 96*(3), 523–535.

Babad, E., Bernieri, F., & Rosenthal, R. (1991). Students as judges of teachers' verbal and nonverbal behavior. *American Educational Research Journal, 28*(1), 211–234.

Baker, D. (2006, July 3). For Navajo, science and tradition intertwine. *Salt Lake Tribune,* pp. D1, D5.

Bandura, A. (1986). *Social foundations of thought and action: A social cognitive theory.* Upper Saddle River, NJ: Prentice Hall.

Bandura, A. (1993). Perceived self-efficacy in cognitive development and functioning. *Educational Psychologist, 28*(2), 117–148.

Bandura, A. (2001). *Social cognitive theory. Annual Review of Psychology.* Palo Alto, CA: Annual Review.

Banks, J. (2008). *An introduction to multicultural education* (4th ed.). Boston: Allyn & Bacon.

Barr, R. (2001). Research on the teaching of reading. In J. Richardson (Ed.), *Handbook of research on teaching* (4th ed., pp. 390–415). Washington, DC: American Educational Research Association.

Barr, R., & Parrett, W. (2001). *Hope fulfilled for at-risk and violent youth* (2nd ed.). Boston: Allyn & Bacon.

Barton, A., Drake, C., Perez, J., St. Louis, K., & George, M. (2004). Ecologies of parental engagement in urban education. *Educational Researcher, 33*(4), 3–12.

Barton, P. (2004). Why does the gap persist? *Educational Leadership, 62*(3), 9–13.

Baumrind, D. (1991). The influence of parenting style on adolescent competence and substance use. *Journal of Early Adolecence, 11*, 56–95.

Berk, L. (2008*). Infants & children* (6th ed.). Boston: Allyn & Bacon.

Berk, L. (2010). *Development through the lifespan* (5th ed.). Boston: Allyn & Bacon.

Berliner, D. (1994). Expertise: The wonder of exemplary performances. In J. Mangieri & C. Collins (Eds.), *Creating powerful thinking in teachers and students* (pp. 161–186). Fort Worth, TX: Harcourt Brace.

Berliner, D. (2000). A personal response to those who bash education. *Journal of Teacher Education, 51*, 358–371.

Bielenberg, B., & Fillmore, L. W. (2004/2005). The English they need for the test. *Educational Leadership, 62*(4), 45–49.

Bitter, G., & Legacy, J. (2008). *Using technology in the classroom* (7th ed.). Boston: Allyn & Bacon.

Black, P., Harrison, C., Lee, C., Marshall, B., & Wiliam, D. (2004). Working inside the black box: Assessment for learning in the classroom. *Phi Delta Kappan, 86*(1), 9–21.

Blair, J. (2000). AFT urges new tests, expanded training for teachers. *Education Week, 19*(32), 11.

Blair, J. (2003). Skirting tradition. *Education Week, 22*(17), 35–38.

Blatchford, P., Baines, E., Rubie-Davies, C., Bassett, P., & Chowne, A. (2006). The effect of a new approach to group work on pupil–pupil and teacher–pupil interactions. *Journal of Educational Psychology, 98*(4), 750–765.

Bloom, B. (1981). *All our children learning.* New York: McGraw-Hill.

Bloom, B., Englehart, M., Furst, E., Hill, W., & Krathwohl, O. (1956). *Taxonomy of educational objectives: The classification of educational goals: Handbook 1. The cognitive domain.* White Plains, NY: Longman.

Blumberg, P. (1998, April). *Evaluating the evidence that problem-based learners are self-directed learners: A review of the literature.* Paper presented at the annual meeting of the American Educational Research Association, San Diego.

Blumenfeld, P., Hicks, L., & Krajcik, J. (1996). Teaching educational psychology through instructional planning. *Educational Psychologist, 31*(1), 51–61.

Bohn, A. P. (2003). Familiar voices: Using ebonics communication techniques in the primary classroom. *Urban Education, 38*(6), 688–707.

Bohn, C., Roehrig, A., & Pressley, M. (2004). The first days of school in the classrooms of two more effective and four less effective primary-grades teachers. *Elementary School Journal, 104*(4), 269–288.

Borg, W., & Ascione, F. (1982). Classroom management in elementary mainstreaming classrooms. *Journal of Educational Psychology, 74*, 85–95.

Borko, H., & Putnam, R. (1996). Learning to teach. In D. Berliner & R. Calfee (Eds.), *Handbook of educational psychology* (pp. 673–708). New York: Macmillan.

Borman, G. D., & Overman, L. R. (2004). Academic resilience in mathematics among poor and minority students. *Elementary School Journal, 104*(3), 177–196.

Bos, C., & Vaughn, S. (2006). *Strategies for teaching students with learning and behavior problems* (6th ed.). Boston: Allyn & Bacon.

Bradsher, M., & Hagan, L. (1995). The kids network: Student-scientists pool resources. *Educational Leadership, 53*(2), 38–43.

Bransford, J., Brown, A., & Cocking, R. (Eds.). (2000). *How people learn: Brain, mind, experience, and school.* Washington, DC: National Academy Press.

Bransford, J., Darling-Hammond, L., & LePage, P. (2005). Introduction. In L. Darling-Hammond & J. Bransford (Eds.), *Preparing teachers for a changing world: What teachers should learn and be able to do* (pp. 1–39). San Francisco: JosseyBass/Wiley.

Bransford, J., & Stein, B. (1984). *The IDEAL problem solver.* New York: Freeman.

Brookhart, S. (2002). What will teachers know about assessment and how will that improve instruction? In R. Kissitz & W. Shafer (Eds.), *Assessment in educational reform: Both means and ends.* Boston: Allyn & Bacon.

Brophy, J. (1996). *Teaching problem students.* New York: Guilford Press.

Brophy, J. (2004). *Motivating students to learn* (2nd ed.). Boston: McGraw-Hill.

Brown, D. (1991). *The effects of state-mandated testing on elementary classroom instruction.* Unpublished doctoral dissertation. Knoxville: University of Tennessee-Knoxville.

Brown, D. (2004). Urban teachers' professed classroom management strategies: Reflections of culturally responsive teaching. *Urban Education, 39*(3), 266–289.

Brown, D. (2006). It's the curriculum, stupid: There's something wrong with it. *Phi Delta Kappan, 87*(10), 777–783.

Brown, K., Anfara, V., & Roney, K. (2004). Student achievement in high performing, suburban middle schools and low performing, urban middle schools: Plausible explanations for the differences. *Education and Urban Society, 36*(4), 428–456.

Brown, R., & Evans, W. (2002). Extracurricular activity and ethnicity: Creating greater school connections among diverse student populations. *Urban Education, 37*(1), 41–58.

Brown-Chidsey, R. (2007). No more "Waiting to fail." *Educational Leadership, 65*(2), 40–46.

Bruning, R., Schraw, G., Norby, M., & Ronning, R. (2004). *Cognitive psychology and instruction* (4th ed.). Upper Saddle River, NJ: Prentice Hall.

Buck, G., Kostin, I., & Morgan, R. (2002). *Examining the relationship of content to gender-based performance difference in advanced placement exams* (Research Report No. 2002–12). New York: College Board.

Bullock, A., & Hawk, P. (2001). *Developing a teaching portfolio: A guide for preservice and practicing teachers.* Upper Saddle River, NJ: Merrill/Prentice Hall.

Burbules, N., & Bruce, B. (2001). Theory and research on teaching as dialogue. In V. Richardson (Ed.), *Handbook of research on teaching* (4th ed., pp. 1102–1121). Washington, DC: America Educational Research Association.

Burris, C., Heubert, J., & Levin, H. (2006). Accelerating mathematics achievement using heterogeneous grouping. *American Educational Research Journal, 43*(1), 105–136.

Bushaw, W., & Gallup, A. (2008). The 40th annual Phi Delta Kappa/Gallup poll of the public's attitudes toward the public schools. *Phi Delta Kappan, 90*, 9–20.

Byrnes, J. P. (2003). Factors predictive of mathematics achievement in White, Black, and Hispanic 12th graders. *Journal of Educational Psychology, 95*, 316–326.

California Department of Education. (2010). *English-language arts content standards for California public schools.* Retrieved March 30, 2010, from http://www.cde.ca.gov/be/st/ss/documents/elacontentstnds.pdf.

California State Board of Education. (2008). *Content standards.* Retrieved November 1, 2008, from http://www.cde.ca.gov/be/st/ss/.

Capon, N., & Kuhn, D. (2004). What's so good about problem-based learning? *Cognition and Instruction, 22*(1), 61–79.

Carnegie Learning. (2010). *Cognitive tutor® software demonstrations.* Retrieved March 2010 from http://mathrelief.carnegielearning.com/demoproblem.cfm.

Carnine, D., Silbert, J., Kame'enui, E., Tarver, S., & Jongjohann, K. (2006). *Teaching struggling and at-risk readers: A direct instruction approach.* Upper Saddle River, NJ: Merrill/Pearson.

Carter, K. (1986). Test-wiseness for teachers and students. *Educational Measurement: Issues and Practice, 5*(6), 20–23.

Cavanaugh, S. (2010). Resurgent debate, familiar themes. *Education Week, 29*(17), 5–11.

Cazden, C. (1986). Classroom discourse. In M. Wittrock (Ed.), *Handbook of research on teaching* (3rd ed., pp. 432–464). New York: Macmillan.

Cazden, C. (2001). *Classroom discourse* (2nd ed.). Portsmouth, NH: Heinemann.

Certo, J., Cauley, K., & Chafen, C. (2002, April). *Students' perspectives on their high school experience.* Paper presented at the annual meeting of the American Educational Research Association, New Orleans.

Charles, C., & Senter, G. (2008). *Building classroom discipline* (9th ed.). Boston: Pearson/Allyn & Bacon.

Charner-Laird, M., Watson, D., Szczesuil, S., Kirkpatrick C., & Gordon, P. (2004, April). *Navigating the "Culture Gap": New teachers experience the urban context.* Paper presented at the annual meeting of the American Educational Research Association, San Diego.

Cheng, L. (1987). *Assessing Asian language performance.* Rockville, MD: Aspen.

Chi, M., Siler, S., & Jeong, H. (2004). Can tutors monitor students' understanding accurately? *Cognition and Instruction, 22*(3), 363–387.

Chorzempa, B., & Graham, S. (2006). Primary-grade teachers' use of within-class ability grouping in reading. *Journal of Educational Psychology, 98*(3), 529–541.

Christenson, S., & Havsy, L. (2004). Family-school-peer relationships: Significance for social, emotional, and academic learning. In J. Zins, R. Weissberg, M. Wang, & H. Walberg (Eds.), *Building academic success on social and emotional learning* (pp. 59–75). New York: Teachers College Press.

Chronicle, E., MacGregor, J., & Ormerod, T. (2004). What makes an insight problem? The roles of heuristics, goal conception, and solution recoding in knowledge-lean problems. *Journal of Experimental Psychology: Learning, Memory, and Cognition, 30*(1), 14–27.

Clark, R., & Mayer, R. (2003). E-learning & the science of instruction. San Francisco: Jossey-Bass/Pfieffer.

Cognition and Technology Group at Vanderbilt. (1992). The Jasper Series as an example of anchored instruction: Theory, program description, and assessment data. *Educational Psychologist, 27*(3), 291–315.

Cognition and Technology Group at Vanderbilt. (1997). *The Jasper Project: Lessons in curriculum, instruction, assessment, and professional development.* Mahwah, NJ: Erlbaum.

Cohen, E. (1991). Strategies for creating a multiability classroom. *Cooperative Learning, 12*(1), 4–7.

Cohen, J. (2006). Social, emotional, ethical, and academic education: Creating a climate for learning, participation in democracy, and well-being. *Harvard Educational Review, 76*(2), 201–237.

Cohen, L., & Spenciner, L. (2009). *Teaching students with mild and moderate disabilities* (2nd ed.). Upper Saddle River, NJ: Merrill.

Coll, C., Bearer, E., & Lerner, R. (Eds.). (2004). *Nature and nurture: The complex interplay of genetic and environmental influences on human behavior and development.* Mahwah, NJ: Erlbaum.

Common Core State Standards Initiative. (2010). Current status of common standards inititative. Retrieved April 2, 2010, from www.corestandards.org.

Cook, B. (2004). Inclusive teachers' attitudes toward their students with disabilities: A replication and extension. *Elementary School Journal, 104*(4), 307–320.

Corporation for Public Broadcasting (2003). *Connected to the future: A report on children's Internet use from the Corporation for Public Broadcasting.* Retrieved February, 23, 2004 from http://www.cpb.org/Ed/ resources/connected.

Council of Chief State School Officers (2010). *Proposed INTASC revisions.* Retrieved 12/6/2010 from http://www.ccsso.org /Resources/Programs/Interstate_Teacher_Assessment_ Consortium_(InTASC).html).

Cross, T. (2005). *The social and emotional lives of gifted kids: Understanding and guiding their development.* Austin, TX: Prufrock Press.

Cuban, L. (1984). *How teachers taught: Constancy and change in American classrooms: 1890–1980.* White Plains, NY: Longman.

Cuban, L. (2005). *Growing instructional technology in U.S. classrooms.* Salt Lake City: University of Utah, 2005 J. George Jones & Velma Rife Jones Lecture.

Dangel, H., & Wang, C. (2008). Student response systems in higher education: Moving beyond linear teaching and surface learning. *Journal of Education Technology Development and Exchange, 1*(1), 93–104.

Darling-Hammond, L. (2000). Teacher quality and student achievement: A review of state policy evidence. *Educational Policy Analysis Archive, 8,* 1–48. Retrieved January 28, 2005, from http://eppa. asu.edu/ eppa/v8n1/.

Darling-Hammond, L., & Bransford, J. (Eds.). (2005). *Preparing teachers for a changing world.* San Francisco, CA: John Wiley & Sons.

Davidson, J., & Sternberg, R. (Eds.). (2003). *The psychology of problem solving.* Cambridge, England: Cambridge University Press.

Davis, G. (2003). Identifying creative students, teaching for creative growth. In N. Colangelo & G. Davis (Eds.), *Handbook of gifted education* (3rd ed., pp. 311–324). Boston: Allyn & Bacon.

Davis, G., & Rimm, S. (2004). *Education of the gifted and talented* (5th ed.). Boston: Allyn & Bacon.

Davis, H. (1998). *Project-based learning.* Salt Lake City: University of Utah, Department of Educational Studies. Delisle, J. (1984). *Gifted children speak out.* New York: Walker.

Delpit, L. (1995). *Other people's children: Cultural conflict in the classroom.* New York: The New Press.

Denig, S. J. (2003, April). *A proposed relationship between multiple intelligences and learning styles.* Paper presented at the annual meeting of the American Educational Research Association, Chicago.

Devlin-Scherer, R., Burroughs, G., Daly, J., & McCarten, W. (2007). The value of the teacher work sample for improving instruction and program. *Action in Teacher Education, 29*(1), 51–60.

Dewey, J. (1916). *Democracy and education.* New York: Macmillan.

Dillon, J. (1987). *Questioning and discussion: A multidisciplinary study.* Norwood, NJ: Ablex.

Ding, M., Li, X., Piccolo, D., & Kulm, G. (2007). Teacher interventions in cooperative-learning mathematics classes. *Journal of Educational Research, 100*(3), 162–176.

Dochy, F., Segers, M., Van den Bossche, P., & Gijbels, D. (2003). Effects of problem-based learning: A meta-analysis. *Learning and Instruction, 13,* 533–568.

Donovan, M. S., & Bransford, J. D. (2005). *How students learn history, mathematics, and science in the classroom.* Washington, DC: National Academies Press.

Downey, J. (2003, April). *Listening to students: Perspectives of educational resilience from children who face adversity.* Paper presented at the annual meeting of the American Educational Research Association, Chicago.

Doyle, W. (1986). Classroom organization and management. In M. Wittrock (Ed.), *Handbook of research on teaching* (3rd ed., pp. 392–431). New York: Macmillan.

Duffy, T., & Cunningham, D. (1996). Constructivism: Implications for the design and delivery of instruction. In D. Jonassen (Ed.), *Handbook of research for educational communications and technology* (pp. 170–195). New York: Macmillan.

Dunkin, M., & Biddle, B. (1974). *The study of teaching.* New York: Holt, Rinehart & Winston.

Dunn, R., & Dunn, K. (1978). *Teaching students through their individual learning styles.* Reston, VA: Reston Publishing.

Dunn, R., & Dunn, K. (1987). Dispelling outmoded beliefs about student learning. *Educational Leadership, 44*(6), 55–62.

Dykstra, D. (1996). Teaching introductory physics to college students. In C. Fosnot (Ed.), *Constructivism: Theory, perspective & practice* (pp. 182–204). New York: Teachers College Press.

Echevarria, J., & Graves, A. (2007). *Sheltered content instruction* (3rd ed.). Boston: Allyn & Bacon.

Ediger, M. (2004). The psychology of lesson plans and unit development. *Reading Improvement, 41*(4), 197–207.

Educational Testing Service. (2008). *The Praxis Series*^{TM}*: Principles of Learning and Teaching: Grades 7–12 (0524).* Retrieved July 15, 2008 from http://www.ets. org/Media/Tests/PRAXIS/pdf/0524.pdf.

Eggen, P. (1998, April). *A comparison of inner-city middle school teachers' classroom practices and their expressed beliefs about learning and effective instruction.* Paper presented at the annual meeting of the American Educational Research Association, San Diego.

Eggen, P. (2001, April). *Constructivism and the architecture of cognition: Implications for instruction.* Paper presented at the annual meeting of the American Educational Research Association, Seattle.

Eggen, P., & Austin, C. (2004, April). *A longitudinal study of teachers' and educational leaders' conceptions of classroom interaction.* Paper presented at the annual meeting of the American Educational Research Association, San Diego.

Eggen, P., & Kauchak, D. (2007). *Educational psychology: Windows on classrooms* (7th ed.). Upper Saddle River, NJ: Prentice Hall.

Eggen, P., & Kauchak, D. (2010). *Educational psychology: Windows on classrooms* (8th ed.). Upper Saddle River, NJ: Prentice Hall.

Emmer, E., Evertson, C., & Worsham, M. (2009). *Classroom management for secondary teachers* (8th ed.). Boston: Allyn & Bacon.

Epstein, J. (2001, April). *School, family, and community partnerships: Preparing educators and improving schools.* Paper presented at the annual meeting of the American Educational Research Association, Seattle.

Evans, C., Kirby, U., & Fabrigar, L. (2003). Approaches to learning, need for cognition, and strategic flexibility among university students. *The British Journal of Educational Psychology, 73,* 507–528.

Evenson, D., & Hmelo, C. (Eds.). (2000). *Problem-based learning: A research perspective on learning interactions.* Mahwah, NJ: Lawrence Erlbaum.

Evertson, C. (1980, April). *Differences in instructional activities in high- and low-achieving junior high classes.* Paper presented at the annual meeting of the American Educational Research Association, Boston.

Evertson, C., & Weinstein, C. (2006). Classroom management as a field of inquiry. In C. M. Evertson & C. S. Weinstein (Eds.), *Handbook of classroom management: Research, practice, and contemporary issues* (pp. 3–15). Mahwah, NJ: Erlbaum.

Evertson, C., Emmer, E., & Worsham, M. (2009). *Classroom management for elementary teachers* (8th ed.). Boston: Allyn & Bacon.

Farkas, R. (2003). Effects of traditional versus learning-styles instructional methods on middle school students. *Journal of Educational Research, 97*(1), 42–51.

Fast, J. (2008). *Ceremonial violence: A psychological explanation of school shootings.* New York: Overlook Press.

Feldman, A., & Matjasko, J. (2005). The role of school-based extracurricular activities in adolescent development: A comprehensive review and future directions. *Review of Educational Research, 75*(2), 159–210.

Feldon, D. (2007). Cognitive load and classroom teaching: The double-edged sword of automaticity. *Educational Psychologist, 42,* 123–137.

Fies, C., & Marshall, J. (2006). Classroom response systems: A review of the literature. *Journal of Science Education and Technology, 15*(1), 101–109.

Fine, L. (2001). Studies examine racial disparities in special education. *Education Week, 19*(26), 6.

Fine, L. (2002). Writing takes a digital turn for special-needs students. *Education Week, 21*(20), 8.

Finn, C., & Petrilli, M. (2009). Stimulating a race to the top. *Education Week, 28*(24), 31.

Finn, K., & Frone, M. (2004). Academic performance and cheating: Moderating role of school identification and self-efficacy. *Journal of Educational Research, 97*(3), 115–122.

Fischer, L., Schimmel, D., & Stellman, L. (2006). *Teachers and the law* (7th ed.). New York: Longman.

Florida Department of Education. (2008). *Florida Comprehensive Assessment Test.* Retrieved November 1, 2008, from http://fcat.fldoe.org/fcatsmpl.asp.

Florida Department of Education. (2009). *Sunshine state standards.* Retrieved November 1, 2010, from http://etc. usf.edu/flstandards13/sss/index.html.

Forcier, R., & Descy, D. (2005). *The computer as an educational tool: Productivity and problem solving* (4th ed.). Upper Saddle River, NJ: Merrill/Prentice Hall.

French, D. (2003). A new vision of authentic assessment to overcome the flaws in high-stakes testing. *Middle School Journal, 35*(1), 14–23.

Frey, B., & Schmitt, V. (2005, April). *Teachers' classroom assessment practices.* Paper presented at the annual meeting of the American Educational Research Association, Montreal, Canada.

Friedman, I. A. (2006). Classroom management and teacher stress and burnout. In C. M. Evertson & C. S. Weinstein (Eds.), *Handbook of classroom management: Research, practice, and contemporary issues* (pp. 925–944). Mahwah, NJ: Erlbaum.

Fuchs, D., Fuchs, L., & Thompson, A. (2001). Peer-assisted learning strategies in reading: Extensions for kindergarten, first grade, and high school. *Remedial and Special Education, 22*, 15–21.

Gage, N., & Berliner, D. (1998). *Educational psychology* (6th ed.). Boston: Houghton-Mifflin.

Gagnon, G., & Collay, M. (2001). *Designing for learning.* Thousand Oaks, CA: Corwin.

Gall, M. (1987). Discussion methods. In M. Dunkin (Ed.), *International encyclopedia of teaching & teacher education* (pp. 232–236). Elmsford, NY: Pergamon Press.

Garcia, D. (2004). Exploring connections between the construct of teacher efficacy and family involvement practices: Implications for urban teacher preparation. *Urban Education, 39*(3), 290–315.

Garcia, E. (2005, April). *A test in English is a test of English: Assessment's new role in educational equity.* Paper presented at the annual meeting of the American Educational Research Association, Montreal, Canada.

Gardner, H., & Moran, S. (2006). The science of multiple intelligences theory: A response to Lynn Waterhouse. *Educational Psychology, 41*(4), 227–232.

Garza, E., Reyes, P., & Trueba, E. T. (2004). *Resiliency and success: Migrant children in the United States.* Boulder, CO: Paradigm Publishers.

Gay, G. (2005). Politics of multicultural teacher education. *Journal of Teacher Education, 56*(3), 221–228.

Gee, J. (2005). *Learning by design: Games as learning machines.* Retrieved April 23, 2006, from http://labweb.education. wisc.edu/room130/papers.htm.

Gersten, R., & Baker, S. (2001). Teaching expressive writing to students with learning disabilities: A meta-analysis. *Elementary School Journal, 101*(3), 251–272.

Gersten, R., Taylor, R., & Graves, A. (1999). Direct instruction and diversity. In R. Stevens (Ed.), *Teaching in American schools* (pp. 81–106). Upper Saddle River, NJ: Merrill/Prentice Hall.

Gettinger, M., & Kohler, K. M. (2006). Process–outcome approaches to classroom management and effective teaching. In C. M. Evertson & C. S. Weinstein (Eds.), *Handbook of classroom management: Research, practice, and contemporary issues* (pp. 73–95). Mahwah, NJ: Erlbaum.

Gewertz, C. (2010). Proposed standards go public. *Education Week, 29*(25), 1, 14–15.

Gijbels, D., Dochy, F., Van den Bossche, P., & Segers, M. (2005). Effects of problem-based learning: A meta-analysis from the angle of assessment. *Review of Educational Research, 75*(1), 27–61.

Gill, M., Achton, P., & Algina, J. (2003). Authoritative schools: A test of a model to resolve the school effectiveness debate. *Contemporary Educational Psychology, 29*, 389–409.

Glasser, W. (1969). *Schools without failure.* New York: Harper & Row.

Glasser, W. (1977). Ten steps in good discipline. *Today's Education, 66*, 61–63.

Goldstein, R. (2004). Who are our urban students and what makes them so different? In S. R. Steinberg & J. L. Kincheloe (Eds.), *19 urban questions: Teaching in the city* (pp. 41–51). New York: Peter Lang.

Gollnick, D., & Chinn, P. (2009). *Multicultural education in a pluralistic society* (8th ed.). Upper Saddle River, NJ: Merrill/Prentice Hall.

Good T., Grouws, D., & Ebmeier, J. (1983). *Active mathematics teaching.* New York: Longman.

Good, T., & Brophy, J. (2003). *Looking in classrooms* (9th ed.). New York: Longman.

Good, T., & Brophy, J. (2008). *Looking in classrooms* (10th ed.). Boston: Allyn & Bacon.

Gootman, E., & Gebelof, R. (2008, June 19). Poor students lose ground in city's gifted programs. *New York Times*, A25.

Gordon, T. (1974). *Teacher effectiveness training.* New York: Wyden.

Gray, T., & Fleischman, S. (2004/2005). Successful strategies for English language learners. *Educational Leadership, 62*(4), 84–85.

Gregory, A., & Weinstein, R. (2004, April*). Toward narrowing the discipline gap: Cooperation or defiance in the high school classroom.* Paper presented at the annual meeting of the American Educational Research Association, San Diego.

Gronke, A. (2009). Plugged-in parents. *Edutopia, 5*(1), 16.

Gronlund, N. (2004). *How to write and use instructional objectives* (7th ed.). Upper Saddle River, NJ: Merrill/Prentice Hall.

Guskey, T. (2002, April). *Perspectives on grading and reporting: Differences among teachers, students, and parents.* Paper presented at the annual meeting of the American Educational Research Association, New Orleans.

Hadjioannou, X. (2007). Bringing the background to the foreground: What do classroom environments that support authentic discussions look like? *American Educational Research Journal, 44*(2), 370–399.

Haladyna, T., & Ryan, J. (2001, April). *The influence of rater severity on whether a student passes or fails a performance assessment.* Paper presented at the annual meeting of the American Educational Research Association, Seattle.

Hallahan, D., & Kauffman, J. (2009). *Exceptional children* (11th ed.). Needham Heights, MA: Allyn & Bacon.

Hardman, M., Drew, C., & Egan, W. (2008). *Human exceptionality* (9th ed.). Needham Heights, MA: Allyn & Bacon.

Hardy, L. (2002). A new federal role. *American School Board Journal, 189*(9), 20–24.

Harry, B. (1992). An ethnographic study of cross-cultural communication with Puerto Rican American families in the special education system. *American Educational Research Journal, 29*(3), 471B488.

Hasselbring, T., & Bausch, M. (2005/2006). Assistive technologies for reading. *Educational Leadership, 63*(4), 72–75.

Heath, S. B. (1989). Oral and literate traditions among Black Americans living in poverty. *American Psychologist, 44*, 367–373.

Hecht, E. (2006). There is no really good definition of mass. *Physics Teacher, 44*(1), 40–45.

Henricsson, L., & Rydell, A. M. (2004). Elementary school children with behavior problems: Teacher-child relations and self-perception. A prospective study. *Merrill-Palmer Quarterly, 50*, 111–138.

Heward, W. (2009). *Exceptional children* (9th ed.). Upper Saddle River, NJ: Merrill/Pearson.

Hogan, T., Rabinowitz, M., & Craven, J. (2003). Representation in teaching: Inference from research on expert and novice teachers. *Educational Psychologist, 38*, 235–247.

Honawar, V. (2009). Teacher gap: Training gets a boost. *Education Week, 28*(17), 28–29.

Hong, S., & Ho, H. (2005). Direct and indirect longitudinal effects of parental involvement on student achievement: Second-order latent growth modeling across ethnic groups. *Journal of Educational Psychology, 97*(1), 32–42.

Hopkins, J. (2006). All students being equal. *Technology & Learning, 26*(10), 26–28.

Horn, R. (2003, April). *Utilizing Vygotsky to promote critical constructivism in the age of standardization.* Paper presented at the annual meeting of the American Educational Research Association, Chicago.

Howard, T. (2001). Powerful pedagogy for African American students: A case of four teachers. *Urban Education, 36*(2), 179–202.

Ilg, T., & Massucci, J. (2003). Comprehensive urban high schools: Are there better options for poor and minority children? *Education and Urban Society, 36*(1), 63–78.

Illinois State Board of Education. (2008a). *Illinois Science Assessment Framework Standard 12F—Astronomy (Grade 7).* Retrieved November 1, 2010, from http://www.champaignschools.org/index2.php?header=./science/&file=MSCurriculum/astronomy.

Illinois State Board of Education. (2008b). *Student assessment.* Retrieved November 1, 2008, from http:// www.isbe.state.il.us/assessment/ISAT.htm.

Illinois State Board of Education. (2008c). *2008 Science ISAT: Grades 4 and 7,* p. 45. Retrieved November 27, 2008, from http://www.isbe.state.il.us/assessment/pdfs/ 2008/Science_ISAT.pdf.

Interstate New Teacher Assessment and Support Consortium (INTASC). (1993). *Model standards for beginning teacher licensing and development: A resource for state dialogues.* Washington, DC: Council of Chief State School Officers.

International Reading Association & National Council of Teachers of English. (2008). *Standards for the English language arts.* Retrieved November 9, 2008, from http://www.ncte.org/library/files/Store/Books/Sample/StandardsDoc.pdf.

Jackson, P. (1968). *Life in classrooms.* New York: Holt, Rinehart & Winston.

Jacobsen, D. (2003). *Philosophy in classroom teaching: Bridging the gap* (2nd ed.). Upper Saddle River, NJ: Prentice Hall.

Jennings, J. (2002). Knocking on your door. *American School Board Journal, 189*(9), 25–27.

Jensen, A. (1998). *The g factor: The science of mental ability.* Westport, CT: Prager/Greenwood.

Johnson, D., & Johnson, F. (2006). *Joining together* (9th ed.). Boston: Allyn & Bacon.

Jonassen, D. (2000). *Computers as mindtools for schools* (2nd ed.). Columbus, OH: Merrill.

Jones, S. (2005, February 14). More discipline? *Teachers College Record* (ID Number 11746). Accessed March 29, 2005, from http://www.tcrecord.org.

Jones, V., & Jones, L. (2010). *Comprehensive classroom management: Creating communities of support and solving problems* (9th ed.). Boston: Allyn & Bacon.

Julyan, C. (1989). National Geographic kids network: Real science in the elementary classroom. *Classroom Computer Learning, 10*(2), 30–41.

Kagan, S. (1999). *Cooperative learning* (13th ed.). San Juan Capistrano, CA: Resources for Teachers.

Kahn, E. (2000). A case study of assessment in a grade 10 English course. *Journal of Educational Research, 93*(5), 276–286.

Kaplan, D., Liu, X., & Kaplan, H. (2001). Influence of parents' self-feelings and expectations on children's academic performance. *Journal of Educational Research, 94*(6), 360–365.

Karten, T. (2005). *Inclusion strategies that work: Research-based methods for the classroom.* Thousand Oaks, CA: Corwin Press.

Kerman, S. (1979). Teacher expectations and student achievement. *Phi Delta Kappan, 60,* 70–72.

Kilbane, C., & Millman, N. (2003). *What every teacher should know about creating digital teaching portfolios.* Columbus, OH: Merrill.

Kincheloe, J. (2004). Why a book on urban education? In S. Steinberg & J. Kincheloe (Eds.), *19 urban questions: Teaching in the city* (pp. 1–27). New York: Peter Lang.

Kleiman, C. (2001, October 30). *Internet helps parents keep an eye on kids* [Electronic version]. *Chicago Tribune.* Retrieved May 17, 2005, from http://www. chicagotribune.co.

Kober, N. (2006). *A public education primer: Basic (and sometimes surprising) facts about the U.S. education system.* Washington, DC: Center on Education Policy.

Kounin, J. (1970). *Discipline and group management in classrooms.* New York: Holt, Rinehart & Winston.

Kounin, J., & Sherman, L. (1979). School environments as behavior settings. *Theory into Practice, 18,* 145–151.

Krathwohl, D., Bloom, B., & Masia, B. (1964). *Taxonomy of educational objectives: The classification of educational goals: Handbook 2. Affective domain.* New York: McKay.

Kratzig, G., & Arbuthnott, K. (2006). Perceptual learning style and learning proficiency: A test of the hypothesis. *Journal of Educational Psychology, 98*(1), 238–246.

Kroesbergen, E., van Luit, E., & Maas, C. (2004). Effectiveness of explicit and constructivist mathematics instruction for low-achieving students in the Netherlands. *Elementary School Journal, 104,* 233–251.

Kuhn, D. (2007). Is direct instruction the right answer to the right question? *Educational Psychologist, 42,* 109–113.

Labov, W. (1972). *Language in the inner city: Studies in the "Black" English vernacular.* Philadelphia: University of Pennsylvania Press.

Lam, D. (2004). Problem-based learning: An integration of theory and field. *Journal of Social Work Education, 40*(3), 371–389.

Lee, F. (2007, September 25). Return to a showdown at Little Rock. *New York Times,* B1, B6.

Lee, V., & Burkam, D. (2002). *Inequality at the starting gate: Social background differences in achievement as children begin school.* Washington, DC: Economic Policy Institute.

Lee, V., & Burkam, D. (2003). Dropping out of high school: The role of school organization and structure. *American Educational Research Journal, 40*(2), 353–393.

Leinhardt, G., & Steele, M. (2005). Seeing the complexity of standing to the side: Instructional dialogues. *Cognition and Instruction, 23*(1), 87–163.

Lemke, J. (1982, April). *Classroom communication of science* (Final report to NSF/RISE). Washington, DC: National Science

Foundation. (ERIC Document Reproduction Service No. ED 222 346)

Leonard, J. (2008). *Culturally specific pedagogy in the mathematics classroom: Strategies for teachers of diverse students.* New York: Routledge.

Leos, K. (2004, April). *No Child Left Behind.* Paper presented at the annual conference of the National Association for Bilingual Education, Albuquerque.

Lever-Duffy, J., McDonald, J., & Mizell, A. (2003). *Teaching and learning with technology.* Boston: Allyn & Bacon.

Lewis, J., DeCamp-Fritson, S., Ramage, J., McFarland, M., & Archwamety, T. (2007). Selecting for ethnically diverse children who may be gifted using Raven's Standard Progressive matrices and Naglieri Nonverbal Abilities test. *Multicultural Education, 15*(1), 38–43.

Linn, R., & Gronlund, N. (2000). *Measurement and assessment in teaching* (8th ed.). Upper Saddle River, NJ: Merrill/Prentice Hall.

Lose, M. (2008). Using response to intervention to support struggling learners. *Principal, 87*(3), 20–23.

Lovelace, M. (2005). Meta-analysis of experimental research based on the Dunn and Dunn Model. *Journal of Educational Research, 98*(3), 176–183.

Luckasson, R., Borthwick-Duffy, S., Buntinx, W. H. E., Coulter, D. L., Craig, E. M., Reeve, A., Schalock, R. L., Snell, M. E., Spitalnik, D. M., Spreat, S., & Tassé, M. J. (Eds.). (2002). *Mental retardation: Definition, classification, and systems of supports* (10th ed.). Washington, DC: American Association on Mental Retardation.

Macionis, J. (2009). *Society: The basics* (9th ed.). Upper Saddle River, NJ: Prentice Hall.

Mager, R. (1962). *Preparing instructional objectives.* Palo Alto, CA: Fearon.

Mager, R. (1998). *Preparing instructional objectives: A critical tool in the development of effective instruction* (3rd ed.). Atlanta, GA: Center for Effective Performance.

Marshak, D. (2003). No child left behind: A foolish race into the past. *Phi Delta Kappan, 85*(3), 229–231.

Marzano, R. (2003). *What works in schools.* Alexandria, VA: Association for Supervision and Curriculum Development.

Marzano, R. (2007). *Classroom assessment and grading that work.* Alexandria VA: Association for Supervision and Curriculum Development.

Marzano, R., & Marzano, J. (2003). The key to classroom management. *Educational Leadership, 61*(1), 6–13.

Marzano, R., & Pickering, D. (2007). Errors and allegations about research on homework. *Phi Delta Kappan, 88,* 507–513.

Mastroprieri, M., & Scruggs, R. (2010). *The inclusive classroom* (4th ed.). Upper Saddle River, NJ: Merrill.

Mathis, W. (2003). No child left behind: Costs and benefits. *Phi Delta Kappan, 84*(9), 679–697.

Maughan, A., & Ciccetti, D. (2002). Impact of child maltreatment and interadult violence on children's emotion regulation abilities and socioemotional adjustment. *Child Development, 73,* 1525–1542.

Mayer, R. (2002). *The promise of educational psychology: Volume II. Teaching for meaningful learning.* Upper Saddle River, NJ: Prentice Hall.

Mayer, R. (2008). *Learning and instruction* (2nd ed.). Upper Saddle River, NJ: Pearson.

McCarthy, J. (1991, April). *Classroom environments which facilitate innovative strategies for teaching and learning.* Paper presented at the annual meeting of the American Educational Research Association, Chicago.

McCombs, J. (2005, March). *Progress in implementing standards, assessment for highly qualified teacher provisions of NCLB: Initial finding from California, Georgia, and Pennsylvania.*

McKeachie, W., & Kulik, J. (1975). Effective college teaching. In F. Kerlinger (Ed.), *Review of research in education* (Vol. 3). Washington, DC: American Educational Research Association.

McMillan, J. (2007). *Classroom assessment: Principles and practices for effective standards-based instruction* (4th ed.). Boston: Allyn & Bacon.

McNeil, M. (2010). Duncan carving deep mark on policy. *Education Week, 29*(18), 1, 18.

Medley, D. (1979). The effectiveness of teachers. In P. Peterson & H. Walbert (Eds.), *Research on teaching: Concepts, findings, and interpretations* (pp. 11–27). Berkeley, CA: McCutchan.

Meece, J. L., & Kurtz-Costes, B. (2001). Introduction: The schooling of ethnic minority children and youth. *Educational Psychologist, 36,* 1–7.

Meter, P., & Stevens, R. (2000). The role of theory in the study of peer collaboration. *Journal of Experimental Education, 69*(1), 113–127.

Miller, M., Linn, R., & Gronlund, N. (2009). *Measurement and assessment in teaching* (10th ed.). Upper Saddle River, NJ: Merrill/Pearson.

Moreno, R. (2004). Decreasing cognitive load for novice students: Effects of explanatory versus corrective feedback in discovery-based multimedia. *Instructional Science, 32,* 99–113.

Morrison, G., & Lowther, D. (2002). *Integrating computer technology into the classroom* (2nd ed.). Upper Saddle River, NJ: Merrill/Prentice Hall.

Morrison, G., Ross, S., & Kemp, J. (2004). *Designing effective instruction* (4th ed.). Hoboken, NJ: John Wiley & Sons.

Murnane, R., & Tyler, J. (2000). The increasing role of the GED in American education. *Education Week, 19(34),* 64, 48.

Murray, F. (1986, May). *Necessity: The developmental component in reasoning.* Paper presented at the sixteenth annual meeting of the Jean Piaget Society, Philadelphia.

National Center for Education Statistics (2005). *Digest of education statistics, 2005.* Retrieved November 23, 2008, from http://www.nces.ed.gov/programs/digest/d05/tables/dt05_053.asp.

National Commission on Excellence in Education. (1983). *A nation at risk: The imperative for educational reform.* Washington, DC: Government Printing Office.

National Council of Teachers of Mathematics. (1991). *Professional standards for teaching mathematics.* Reston, VA: Author.

National Council of Teachers of Mathematics. (2000). *Principles and standards for school mathematics.* Reston, VA: Author.

National Council of Teachers of Mathematics. (2008). *Math standards.* Retrieved November 8, 2008, from http://www.nctm.org/standards/.

Neuman, S., & Celano, D. (2001). Access to print in low-income and middle-income communities: An ecological study of our neighborhoods. *Reading Research Quarterly, 36*(1), 8–26.

Newby, T., Stepich, D., Lehman, J., & Russell, J. (2006). *Instructional technology and teaching and learning* (3rd ed.). Upper Saddle River, NJ: Merrill/Prentice Hall.

Nieto, S. (2004). *Affirming diversity* (4th ed.). New York: Longman.

Nikitina, S. (2006). Three strategies for interdisciplinary teaching: Contextualizing, conceptualizing, and problem-centering. *Journal of Curriculum Studies, 38*(3), 251–271.

Nitko, A. (2004). *Educational assessment of students* (4th ed.). Upper Saddle River, NJ: Pearson.

Noblit, G., Rogers, D., & McCadden, B. (1995). In the meantime: The possibilities of caring. *Phi Delta Kappan, 76,* 680–685.

Noddings, N. (2001). The caring teacher. In V. Richardson (Ed.), *Handbook of research on teaching* (4th ed., pp. 99–105). Washington, DC: American Educational Research Association.

Noddings, N. (2003). *Happiness and education.* Cambridge, England: Cambridge University Press.

Noguera, P. (2003a). *City schools and the American dream: Reclaiming the promise of public education.* New York: Teachers College Press.

Noguera, P. (2003b). The trouble with black boys: The role and influence of environmental and cultural factors on the academic performance of African American males. *Urban Education, 38*(4), 431–459.

Novak, J. (1998). *Learning, creating, and using knowledge: Concept maps as facilitative tools in schools and corporations.* Mahwah, NJ: Erlbaum.

Oakes, J. (2008). Keeping track: Structuring equality and inequality in an era of accountability. *Teachers College Record, 110*(3), 700–712.

Oakes, J., & Saunders, M. (2004). Education's most basic tools: Access to textbooks and instructional materials in California's public schools. *Teachers College Record, 106*(10), 1967–1988.

Oakes, J., & Wells, A. (2002). Detracking for high student achievement. In L. Abbeduto (Ed.), *Taking sides: Clashing views and controversial issues in educational psychology* (2nd ed., pp. 26–30). Guilford, CT: McGraw-Hill Duskin.

O'Conner, C., & Fernandez, S. (2006). Race, class, and disproportionality: Reevaluating the relationship between poverty and special education placement. *Educational Researcher, 35*(6), 6–11.

Olsen, G., & Fuller, M. (2003). *Home-school relations: Working successfully with parents and families* (2nd ed.). Boston: Allyn & Bacon.

Olson, J., & Clough, M. (2004). What questions do you have? In defense of general questions: A response to Croom. Retrieved August 20, 2004, from http://www. tcrecord.org/content.asp? content ID=11366.

Ormrod, J. (2008). *Human learning* (5th ed.) Upper Saddle River, NJ: Merrill/Prentice Hall.

Orr, A. (2003). Black-white differences in achievement: The importance of wealth. *Sociology of Education, 76,* 281–304.

Osterman, K. (2000). Students' need for belonging in the school community. *Review of Educational Research, 70,* 323–367.

Padilla, A. (2006). Second language learning: Issues in research and teaching. In P. Alexander & P. Winne (Eds.), *Handbook of educational psychology* (2nd ed., pp. 571–592). Mahwah, NJ: Erlbaum.

Parish, J., Parish, T., & Batt, S. (2001, April). *Academic achievement and school climate—interventions that work.* Paper presented at the annual meeting of the American Educational Research Association, Seattle.

Patton, C., & Roschelle, J. (2008). Why the best math curriculum won't be a textbook. *Education Week, 27*(36), 24–25, 32.

Paulson, F., Paulson, P., & Meyers, C. (1991). What makes a portfolio a portfolio? *Educational Leadership, 48*(5), 63.

Peregoy, S., & Boyle, O. (2008). *Reading, writing, and learning in ESL* (5th ed.). New York: Longman.

Perkins, D. (2001). Wisdom in the wild. *Educational Psychologist, 36,* 265–268.

Perkins-Gough, D. (2004). A two-tiered education system. *Educational Leadership, 62*(3), 87–88.

Perry, N., Turner, J., & Meyer, D. (2006). Classrooms as contexts for motivating learning. In P. Alexander & P. Winne (Eds.), *Handbook of educational psychology* (2nd ed., pp. 327–348). Mahwah, NJ: Erlbaum.

Philips, S. (1972). Participant structures and communicative competence: Warm Springs children in community and classroom. In C. Cazden, V. John, & D. Hymes (Eds.), *Functions of language in the classroom* (pp. 370–394). New York: Teachers College Press.

Piaget, J. (1952). *Origins of intelligence in children.* New York: International Universities Press.

Piaget, J. (1959). *Language and thought of the child* (M. Grabain, Trans.). New York: Humanities Press.

Piaget, J. (1970). *The science of education and the psychology of the child.* New York: Orion Press.

Popham, W. (2002). *Classroom assessment: What teachers need to know* (3rd ed.). Boston: Allyn & Bacon.

Popham, W. (2005). *Classroom assessment: What teachers need to know* (4th ed.). Boston: Allyn & Bacon/Pearson.

Prawat, R. (1989). Promoting access to knowledge, strategy, and disposition in students: A research synthesis. *Review of Educational Research, 59,* 1–41.

Public Agenda. (2004). *Teaching interrupted.* Retrieved June 12, 2004, from http://www.publicagenda.org.

Puntambekar, S., & Hübscher, R. (2005). Tools for scaffolding students in a complex learning environment: What have we gained and what have we missed? *Educational Psychologist, 40*(1), 1–12.

Putnam, R., & Borko, H. (2000). What do new views of knowledge and thinking have to say about research on teacher learning? *Educational Researcher, 29*(1), 4–15.

Quinlan, T. (2004). Speech recognition technology and students with writing difficulties: Improving fluency. *Journal of Educational Psychology, 96*(2), 337–346.

Raskauskas, J., & Stoltz, A. (2007). Involvement in traditional and electronic bullying among adolescents. *Developmental Psychology, 43*(3), 564–575.

Ream, R. K. (2003). Counterfeit social capital and Mexican-American underachievement. *Educational Evaluation and Policy Analysis, 25*(3), 237–262.

Renkl, A., & Atkinson, R. K. (2003). Structuring the transition from example study to problem solving in cognitive skills acquisition: A cognitive load perspective. *Educational Psychologist, 38,* 15–22.

Reynolds, R., & Shirey, L. (1988). The role of attention in studying and learning. In C. Weinstein, E. Goetz, & P. Alexander (Eds.),

Learning and study strategies (pp. 77–110). New York: Academic Press.

Reys, B., Reys, R., & Chávez, O. (2004). Why mathematics textbooks matter. *Educational Leadership, 62*(5), 61–66.

Richardson, V. (Ed.). (2001). *Handbook of research on teaching* (4th ed.). Washington, DC: American Educational Research Association.

Rigor, rewards, quality: Obama's education aims. (2009). *Education Week, 28*(25), Rimm-Kaufman, S., La Paro, K., Downer, J., & Pianta, R. (2005). The contribution of classroom setting and quality of instruction to children's behavior in kindergarten classrooms. *Elementary School Journal, 105*(4), 377–394.

Rist, R. (1973). *The urban school: A factory for failure.* Cambridge, MA: Massachusetts Institute of Technology Press.

Roberts, S. (2007, November 17). In name count, Garcias are catching up to Joneses. *New York Times.* Accessed November 17, 2007, from http://www.nytimes.com/ 2007/22/17/us/ 17surnames.html?th&emc=th.

Roblyer, M., & Doering, A. (2010). *Integrating educational technology into teaching* (5th ed.). Upper Saddle River, NJ: Merrill/ Prentice Hall.

Rose, L., & Gallup, A. (2000). The 32nd annual Phi Delta Kappa/Gallup Poll of the public's attitudes toward the public schools. *Phi Delta Kappan, 82,* 41–58.

Rosenshine, B. (1979). Content, time, and direct instruction. In P. Peterson & H. Walberg (Eds.), *Research on teaching: Concepts, findings, and implications* (pp. 28–56). Berkeley, CA: McCutchan.

Rosenshine, B. (1980). How time is spent in elementary classrooms. In C. Denham & A. Lieberman (Eds.), *Time to learn.* Washington, DC: National Institute of Education.

Rosenshine, B., & Stevens, R. (1986). Teaching functions. In M. Wittrock (Ed.), *Handbook of research on teaching* (3rd ed., pp. 376–391). New York: Macmillan.

Rowe, M. (1986). Wait-time: Slowing down may be a way of speeding up. *Journal of Teacher Education, 37*(1), 43–50.

Rubinson, F. (2004). Urban dropouts: Why so many and what can be done? In S. R. Steinberg & J. L. Kincheloe (Eds.), *19 urban questions: Teaching in the city* (pp. 53–67). New York: Peter Lang.

Saddler, B., & Graham, S. (2005). The effects of peer-assisted sentence-combining instruction on the writing performance of more and less skilled young writers. *Journal of Education Psychology, 97*(1), 43–54.

Safer, N., & Fleischman, S. (2005). How student progress monitoring improves instruction. *Educational Leadership, 62*(5), 81–83.

Salvia, J., & Ysseldyke, J. (2004). *Assessment in special and remedial education* (9th ed.). Boston: Houghton Mifflin.

Samuels, C. (2008). "Response to intervention" sparks interest, questions. *Education Week, 27*(20), 1, 13.

Samuels, C. (2009). "What works" guide gives RTI thumbs up on reading. *Education Week, 28*(23), 7.

Sandoval, W. A., & Millwood, K. A. (2005). The quality of students' use of evidence in written scientific explanations. *Cognition and Instruction, 23*(1), 23–55.

Sattler, J. M. (2001). *Assessment of children: Cognitive applications* (4th ed.). San Diego, CA: Jerome M. Sattler, Inc.

Schiever, S., & Maker, C. J. (2003). New directions in enrichment and acceleration. In N. Colangelo & G. Davis (Eds.),

Handbook of gifted education (3rd ed., pp. 163–173). Boston: Allyn & Bacon.

Schraw, G., & Lehman, S. (2001). Situational interest: A review of the literature and directions for future research. *Educational Psychology Review, 13*(1), 23–52.

Schunk, D. (2004). *Learning theories* (4th ed.). Columbus, OH: Merrill.

Schunk, D., Pintrich, P., & Meece, J. (2008). *Motivation in education: Theory, research, and applications* (3rd ed.). Upper Saddle River, NJ: Merrill/Pearson.

Senftleber, R., & Eggen, P. (1999, April). *A comparison of achievement in science content and process skills in a three year integrated versus traditional middle school science program.* Paper presented at the Annual Meeting of the American Educational Research Association, Montreal, Canada.

Shepard, L. (2001). The role of classroom assessment in teaching and learning. In V. Richardson (Ed.), *Handbook of research on learning* (4th ed., pp. 1066–1101). Washington, DC: American Educational Research Association.

Shields, P., & Shaver, D. (1990, April). The *mismatch between the school and home cultures of academically at-risk students.* Paper presented at the annual meeting of the American Educational Research Association, Boston.

Short, D., & Echevarria, J. (2004/2005). Teacher skills to support English language learners. *Educational Leadership, 62*(4), 8–13.

Shuell, T. (1996). Teaching and learning in a classroom context. In D. Berliner & R. Calfee (Eds.), *Handbook of educational psychology* (pp. 726–764). New York: Simon & Schuster.

Shulman, L. (1986). Those who understand: Knowledge growth in teaching. *Educational Researcher, 15*(2), 4–14.

Shulman, L. (1987). Knowledge and teaching: Foundations of the new reform. *Harvard Educational Review, 57,* 1–22.

Siegel, M. (2002, April). *Models of teacher learning: A study of case analyses by preservice teachers.* Paper presented at the annual meeting of the American Educational Research Association, New Orleans.

Silver-Pacuilla, H., & Fleischman, S. (2006). Technology to help struggling students. *Educational Leadership, 63*(5), 84–85.

Slavin, R. (1985). Team-assisted individualization: A cooperative learning solution for adaptive instruction in mathematics. In M. Wang & H. Walberg (Eds.), *Adapting instruction to individual differences.* Berkeley, CA: McCutchan.

Slavin, R. (1987). Ability grouping and student achievement in elementary schools: A best-evidence synthesis. *Review of Educational Research, 57,* 293–336.

Slavin, R. (1995). *Cooperative learning* (2nd ed.). Needham Heights, MA: Allyn & Bacon.

Slavin, R. (2009). *Educational psychology* (9th ed.). Boston: Allyn & Bacon.

Slavin, R., Madden, N., Dolan, L., & Wasik, B. (1994). Roots and wings: Inspiring academic excellence. *Educational Leadership, 52,* 10–14.

Smith, J., & Land, M. (1981). Low-inference verbal behaviors related to teacher clarity. *Journal of Classroom Interaction, 17,* 37–41.

Smith, L., & Cotten, M. (1980). Effect of lesson vagueness and discontinuity on student achievement and attitude. *Journal of Educational Psychology, 72,* 670–675.

Smith, T., Polloway, E., Patton, J., & Dowdy, C. (2004). *Teaching students with special needs in inclusive settings* (4th ed.). Boston: Allyn & Bacon.

So, W., & Watkins, D. (2005). From beginning teacher education to professional teaching: A study of the thinking of Hong Kong primary science teachers. *Teaching and Teacher Education, 21*(5), 525–541.

Stahl, R., DeMasi, K., Gehrke, R., Guy, C., & Scown, J. (2005, April). *Perceptions, conceptions and misconceptions of wait time and wait time behaviors among pre-service and in-service teachers.* Paper presented at the annual meeting of the American Educational Research Association, Montreal, Canada.

Starnes, B. (2006). What we don't know *can* hurt them: White teachers, Indian children. *Phi Delta Kappan, 87*(5), 384–392.

Sternberg, R. (1998). Principles of teaching for successful intelligence. *Educational Psychologist, 33*(2/3), 65–72.

Sternberg, R. J. (2003). *Wisdom, intelligence, and creativity synthesized.* Cambridge, England: Cambridge University Press.

Sternberg, R. (2004). Culture and intelligence. *American Psychologist, 59,* 325–338.

Stevens, R., Wineburg, S., Herrenkohl, L., & Bell, P. (2005). Comparative understanding of school subjects: Past, present, and future. *Review of Educational Research, 75*(2), 125–157.

Stiggins, R. (2004). New assessment beliefs for a new school mission. *Phi Delta Kappan, 86*(1), 22–27.

Stiggins, R. (2005). *Student-centered classroom assessment* (4th ed.). Upper Saddle River, NJ: Merrill/Prentice Hall.

Stiggins, R. (2007). Assessment through the student's eyes. *Educational Leadership, 64*(8), 22–26.

Stiggins, R. (2008). *Student-involved assessment for learning* (5th ed.). Upper Saddle River, NJ: Merrill/Pearson.

Stiggins, R., & Chappuis, J. (2006). What a difference a word makes: Assessment FOR learning rather than assessment OF learning helps students succeed. *Journal of Staff Development, 27,* 10–14.

Stipek, D. (2002). *Motivation to learn: Integrating theory and practice* (4th ed.). Boston: Allyn & Bacon.

Swanson, C. (2008). Grading the states. *Education Week, 27*(18), 36–38.

Tanner, D., & Tanner, L. (2007). *Curriculum development: Theory into Practice* (4th ed.). Upper Saddle River, NJ: Pearson.

Texas Education Agency. (2008a). *Texas Essential Knowledge and Skills.* Retrieved November 1, 2010, from http://www.tea.state.tx.us/teks/.

Texas Education Agency. (2008b). *Chapter 111. Texas Essential Knowledge and Skills for Mathematics: Subchapter A. Elementary.* Retrieved November 2008, from http://www.tea.state.tx.us/rules/tac/chapter111/ch111a.html.

Texas Education Agency. (2008c). Texas Assessment of Knowledge and Skills (TAKS)—Spring 2006. Retrieved November 17, 2008, from http://scotthochberg.com/files/taas/math4.pdf.

Thirunarayanan, M. O. (2004). The "significantly worse" phenomenon: A study of student achievement in different content areas by school location. *Education and Urban Society, 36*(4), 467–481.

Tomlinson, C. (2003). *Fulfilling the promise of the differentiated classroom: Strategies and tools for responsive teaching.* Alexandria, VA: Association for Supervision and Curriculum Development.

Tomlinson, C. (2005). *How to differentiate instruction in mixed-ability classrooms* (2nd ed.). Alexandria, VA: Association for Supervision and Curriculum Development.

Tong, F., Lara-Alecio, R., Irby, B., Mathes, P., & Kwok, O. (2008). Accelerating early academic oral English development in transitional bilingual and structured English immersion programs. *American Educational Research Journal, 45*(4), 1011–1044.

Turiel, E. (2006). The development of morality. In N. Eisenberg (Vol. Ed.), *Handbook of child psychology: Vol. 3. Social, emotional, and personality development* (6th ed., pp. 789–857). Hoboken, NJ: John Wiley & Sons.

Turnbull, A., Turnbull, R., & Wehmeyer, M. (2010). *Exceptional lives: Special education in today's schools* (6th ed.). Upper Saddle River, NJ: Merrill/Pearson.

Tyler, R. (1950). *Basic principles of curriculum and instruction.* Chicago, IL: University of Chicago Press.

U.S. Census Bureau. (2003). *Statistical abstract of the United States* (123rd ed.). Washington, DC: U.S. Government Printing Office.

U.S. Census Bureau. (2004). *The foreign-born population in the United States: 2003.* Washington, DC: U.S. Government Printing Office.

U.S. Census Bureau. (2005). *Income, poverty, and health insurance coverage in the United States, 2004.* Washington, DC: U.S. Government Printing Office.

U.S. Department of Education, Office of Special Education Programs. (2002). *Twenty-fourth annual report to Congress on the implementation of the Individuals with Disabilities Education Act.* Washington, DC: Author.

U.S. Department of Education. (2000). *Digest of education statistics, 1999.* Washington, DC: National Center for Educational Statistics.

U.S. Department of Education. (2004). *Twenty-sixth annual report to Congress on the implementation of the Individuals with Disabilities Education Act.* Washington, DC: U.S. Government Printing Office.

U.S. Department of Education. (2005). *The condition of education in 2005 in brief.* Washington DC: National Center for Education Statistics.

U.S. English. (2008). Status of English-only movement. Accessed March 23, 2008, from http://www.us-english.org.

Valencia, R., & Suzuki, L. (2001). *Intelligence testing and minority students.* Thousand Oaks, CA: Sage.

Van Merriënboer, J., Kirschner, P., & Kester, L. (2003). Taking the load off a learner's mind: Instructional design for complex learning. *Educational Psychologist, 38*(1), 5–13.

Vaughn, S., & Bos, C. (2009). *Strategies for teaching students with learning and behavior problems* (7th ed.). Boston: Allyn & Bacon.

Vaughn, S., Bos, C., Candace, S., & Schumm, J. (2006). *Teaching exceptional, diverse, and at-risk students in the general education classroom* (3rd ed.). Boston: Allyn & Bacon.

Verdinelli, S., & Gentile, J. R. (2003). Changes in teaching philosophies among in-service teachers after experiencing mastery learning. *Action in Teacher Education, 25*(2), 56–66.

Victor, E., & Kellough, R. (2004). *Science K-8: An integrated approach* (10th ed.). Upper Saddle River, NJ: Pearson.

Villegas, A., & Lucas, T. (2002). *Educating culturally responsive teachers.* Albany, NY: State University Press.

Vygotsky, L. (1978). *Mind in society: The development of higher psychological processes* (M. Cole, V. John-Steiner, S. Scribner, & E. Souberman, Eds. and Trans.). Cambridge, MA: Harvard University Press.

Vygotsky, L. (1986). *Thought and language.* Cambridge, MA: MIT Press.

Waxman, H., Huang, S., Anderson, L., & Weinstein, T. (1997). Classroom process differences in inner-city elementary schools. *Journal of Educational Research, 91*(1), 49–59.

Wayne, A., & Youngs, P. (2003). Teacher characteristics and student achievement gains: A review. *Review of Educational Research, 73,* 89–122.

Weiner, L. (2002, April). *Why is classroom management so vexing to urban teachers? New directions in theory and research about classroom management in urban schools.* Paper presented at the annual meeting of the American Educational Research Association, New Orleans.

Weinert, F., & Helmke, A. (1995). Learning from wise mother nature or big brother instructor: The wrong choice as seen from an educational perspective. *Educational Psychologist, 30*(3), 135–142.

Weinstein, C., & Mignano, A., Jr. (2007). *Elementary classroom management: Lessons from research and practice* (4th ed.). New York: McGraw-Hill.

Weiss, I., & Pasley, J. (2004). What is high-quality instruction? *Educational Leadership, 61*(5), 24–28.

Wenner, G. (2003). Comparing poor, minority elementary students' interest and background in science with that of their white, affluent peers. *Urban Education, 38*(2), 153–172.

Wiggins, G., & McTighe, J. (2006). *Understanding by design* (2nd ed.). Upper Saddle River, NJ: Pearson.

Wiles, J., & Bondi, J. (2007). *Curriculum development: A guide to practice* (7th ed.). Upper Saddle River, NJ: Pearson.

Williams, S., Bareiss, R., & Reiser, B. (1996, April). *ASK Jasper: A multimedia publishing and performance support environment for design.* Paper presented at the annual meeting of the American Educational Research Association, New York.

Wilson, B., & Corbett, H. (2001). *Listening to urban kids: School reform and the teachers they want.* Albany, NY: State University of New York Press.

Wilson, S., Shulman, L., & Richert, A. (1987). 150 different ways of knowing: Representations of knowledge in teaching. In J. Calderhead (Ed.), *Exploring teacher thinking* (pp. 104–124). London, England: Cassel.

Wilson, S., & Youngs, S. (2005). Research on accountability processes in teacher education. In M. Cochran-Smith & K. Zeichner (Eds.), *Studying teacher education: The report of the AREA panel on research and teacher education* (pp. 591–644). Mahwah, NJ: Lawrence Erlbaum.

Winitzky, N. (1998). Multicultural and mainstreamed classrooms. In R. Arends, *Learning to teach* (4th ed., pp. 132–170). New York: McGraw-Hill.

Winitzky, N., Kauchak, D., & Kelly, M. (1994). Measuring teachers' structural knowledge. *Teaching and Teacher Education, 10*(2), 125–139.

Wood, K. (2005). *Interdisciplinary instruction* (3rd ed.). Upper Saddle River, NJ: Pearson.

Woolfolk-Hoy, A., Davis, H., & Pape, S. (2006). Teacher knowledge and beliefs. In P. Alexander & P. Winne (Eds.), *Handbook of educational psychology* (2nd ed., pp. 715–737). Mahwah, NJ: Erlbaum.

Yeh, Y. (2006). The interactive effects of personal traits and guided practices on preservice teachers' changes in personal teaching efficacy. *British Journal of Educational Technology, 37,* 513–526.

Zahorik, J. (1996). Elementary & secondary teachers' beliefs in their effectiveness: Research on a school improvement hypothesis. *Teachers College Record, 97*(2), 227–251.

Zehr, M. (2009). NYC test sizes up ELLs with little formal schooling. *Education Week, 28*(23), 13.

Zwiers, J. (2004/2005). The third language of academic English. *Educational Leadership, 62*(4), 60–63.

Zwiers, J. (2007). *Building academic language: Essential practice for content classrooms.* San Francisco: Jossey-Bass.

Name Index

Subject Index